AN EXEGETICAL SUMMARY OF
MARK 1–8

AN EXEGETICAL SUMMARY OF
MARK 1–8

Richard C. Blight

SIL International®
Dallas, Texas

© 2012 by SIL International®

ISBN: 978-1-55671-299-9
Library of Congress Control Number: 2012935155
Printed in the United States of America

All Rights Reserved

No part of this publication may be reproduced, stored in a retrieval system, or transmitted in any form or by any means—electronic, mechanical, photocopy, recording, or otherwise—without the express permission of SIL International®, with the exception of brief excerpts in journal articles or reviews.

Copies of this and other publications
of SIL International® may be obtained from

SIL International Publications
7500 West Camp Wisdom Road
Dallas, TX 75236-5699, USA

Voice: 972-708-7404
Fax: 972-708-7363
publications_intl@sil.org
www.ethnologue.com/bookstore.asp

PREFACE

Exegesis is concerned with the interpretation of a text. Exegesis of the New Testament involves determining the meaning of the Greek text. Translators must be especially careful and thorough in their exegesis of the New Testament in order to accurately communicate its message in the vocabulary, grammar, and literary devices of another language. Questions occurring to translators as they study the Greek text are answered by summarizing how scholars have interpreted the text. This is information that should be considered by translators as they make their own exegetical decisions regarding the message they will communicate in their translations.

The Semi-Literal Translation

As a basis for discussion, a semi-literal translation of the Greek text is given so that the reasons for different interpretations can best be seen. When one Greek word is translated into English by several words, these words are joined by hyphens. There are a few times when clarity requires that a string of words joined by hyphens have a separate word, such as "not" (μή), inserted in their midst. In this case, the separate word is surrounded by spaces between the hyphens. When alternate translations of a Greek word are given, these are separated by slashes.

The Text

Variations in the Greek text are noted under the heading TEXT. The base text for the summary is the text of the fourth revised edition of *The Greek New Testament,* published by the United Bible Societies, which has the same text as the twenty-sixth edition of the *Novum Testamentum Graece* (Nestle-Aland). The versions that follow different variations are listed without evaluating their choices.

The Lexicon

The meaning of a key word in context is the first question to be answered. Words marked with a raised letter in the semi-literal translation are treated separately under the heading LEXICON. First, the lexicon form of the Greek word is given. Within the parentheses following the Greek word is the location number where, in the author's judgment, this word is defined in the *Greek-English Lexicon of the New Testament Based on Semantic Domains* (Louw and Nida 1988). When a semantic domain includes a translation of the particular verse being treated, **LN** in bold type indicates that specific translation. If the specific reference for the verse is listed in *A Greek-English Lexicon of the New Testament and Other Early Christian Literature* (Bauer, Arndt, Gingrich, and Danker 1979), the outline location and page number is given. Then English equivalents of the Greek word are given to show how it is translated by commentators who offer their own translations of the whole text and, after a semicolon, all the versions in the list of abbreviations for translations. When reference is made to "all versions," it refers to only the versions in the list of translations. Sometimes further comments are made about the meaning of the word or the significance of a verb's tense, voice, or mood.

The Questions

Under the heading QUESTION, a question is asked that comes from examining the Greek text under consideration. Typical questions concern the identity of an implied actor or object of an event word, the antecedent of a pronominal reference, the connection indicated by a relational word, the meaning of a genitive construction, the meaning of figurative language, the function of a rhetorical question, the identification of an ambiguity, and the presence of implied information that is needed to understand the passage correctly. Background information is also considered for a proper understanding of a passage. Although not all implied information and background information is made explicit in a translation, it is important to consider it so that the translation will not be stated in such a way that prevents a reader from arriving at the proper interpretation. The question is answered with a summary of what commentators have said. If there are contrasting differences of opinion, the different interpretations are numbered and the commentaries that support each are listed. Differences that are not treated by many of the commentaries often are not numbered, but are introduced with a contrastive 'Or' at the beginning of the sentence. No attempt has been made to select which interpretation is best.

In listing support for various statements of interpretation, the author is often faced with the difficult task of matching the different terminologies used in commentaries with the terminology he has adopted. Sometimes he can only infer the position of a commentary from incidental remarks. This book, then, includes the author's interpretation of the views taken in the various commentaries. General statements are followed by specific statements, which indicate the author's understanding of the pertinent relationships, actors, events, and objects implied by that interpretation.

The Use of This Book

This book does not replace the commentaries that it summarizes. Commentaries contain much more information about the meaning of words and passages. They often contain arguments for the interpretations that are taken and they may have important discussions about the discourse features of the text. In addition, they have information about the historical, geographical, and cultural setting. Translators will want to refer to at least four commentaries as they exegete a passage. However, since no one commentary contains all the answers translators need, this book will be a valuable supplement. It makes more sources of exegetical help available than most translators have access to. Even if they had all the books available, few would have the time to search through all of them for the answers.

When many commentaries are studied, it soon becomes apparent that they frequently disagree in their interpretations. That is the reason why so many answers in this book are divided into two or more interpretations. The reader's initial reaction may be that all of these different interpretations complicate exegesis rather than help it. However, before translating a passage, a translator needs to know exactly where there is a problem of interpretation and what the exegetical options are.

Acknowledgements

I am grateful for the help I received in preparing this book for publication. Dr. J. Harold Greenlee researched the variant readings of the Greek text and helped with the text notes. My son, Thomas C. Blight, read this book for its literary style and made many helpful suggestions. Matthew E. Carlton was preparing the second edition of his own *Translator's Reference Translation of the Gospel of Mark* when he agreed to edit this book. He was able to provide many useful comments concerning its contents. He also performed the final automated consistency check of the text.

ABBREVIATIONS

COMMENTARIES AND REFERENCE BOOKS
An asterisk (*) indicates a book that translators may find especially helpful as they study the text of Mark.

AB1	Mann, C. S. *Mark.* The Anchor Bible. New York: Doubleday, 1986.
AB2	Marcus, Joel. *Mark 1–8.* The Anchor Bible. New York: Doubleday, 1999.
AB2	Marcus, Joel. *Mark 8-16.* The Anchor Yale Bible. New Haven: Yale University Press, 2009.
BAGD	Bauer, Walter. *A Greek-English Lexicon of the New Testament and Other Early Christian Literature.* Translated and revised from the 5th ed., 1958 by W. F. Arndt and F. W. Gingrich; 2d edition, revised and augmented by F. W. Gingrich and F. W. Danker. Chicago: University of Chicago Press, 1979.
BECNT*	Stein, Robert H. *Mark.* Baker Exegetical Commentary on the New Testament. Grand Rapids: Baker, 2008.
BNTC	Hooker, Morna D. *The Gospel According to Saint Mark.* Black's New Testament Commentary. Peabody, Mass.: Hendrickson, 1991.
CBC	Bock, Darrell L. *The Gospel of Mark.* Cornerstone Biblical Commentary, Vol. 11. Carol Stream, Illinois: Tyndale, 2005.
CGTC	Cranfield, C. E. B. *The Gospel According to St. Mark.* The Cambridge Greek Testament Commentary. Cambridge: Cambridge University Press, 1959.
EBC*	Wessel, Walter W. "Mark," in *The Expositor's Bible Commentary*, vol. 8. Grand Rapids: Zondervan, 1984.
EGT	Bruce, Alexander Balmain. *The Synoptic Gospels.* Expositor's Greek Testament, vol. 1. 1910. Reprint. Grand Rapids: Eerdmans, 1980.
Gnd	Gundry, Robert H. *Mark.* Grand Rapids: Eerdmans, 1993.
Hb	Hiebert, D. Edmond. *The Gospel of Mark.* Revised edition. Greenville, South Carolina: Bob Jones University Press, 1994.
ICC	Gould, Ezra P. *The Gospel According to St. Mark.* The International Critical Commentary. Edinburgh: T & T Clark, 1896.
LN	Louw, Johannes P., and Eugene A. Nida. *Greek–English Lexicon of the New Testament Based on Semantic Domains.* New York: United Bible Societies, 1988.
Lns	Lenski, R. C. H. *The Interpretation of St. Mark's Gospel.* Minneapolis, Minn.: Augsburg, 1946.

My	Meyer, Heinrich August Wilhelm. *Critical and Exegetical Handbook to the Gospels of Mark and Luke.* Translated from the fifth edition by Robert Wallas and revised by William Dickson. New York: Funk and Wagnalls, 1884.
NAC	Brooks, James A. *Mark.* The New American Commentary. Nashville, Tenn.: Broadman, 1991.
NCBC	Anderson, Hugh. *The Gospel of Mark.* The New Century Bible Commentary. Grand Rapids: Eerdmans, 1976.
NICNT	Lane, William L. *The Gospel of Mark.* The New International Commentary on the New Testament. Grand Rapids: Eerdmans, 1974.
NIGTC*	France, R. T. *The Gospel of Mark.* The New International Greek Testament Commentary. Grand Rapids: Eerdmans, 2002.
NTC	Hendriksen, William. *The Gospel of Mark.* New Testament Commentary. Grand Rapids: Baker,
PNTC	Edwards, James R. *The Gospel According to Mark.* The Pillar New Testament Commentary. Grand Rapids: Eerdmans, 2002.
Sw	Swete, Henry Barclay. *The Gospel According to St. Mark.* Reprinted from 3rd edition, 1909. Grand Rapids: Eerdmans, 1956.
Tay	Taylor, Vincent. *The Gospel According to St. Mark.* Second edition. New York: St. Martin's Press, 1966.
TH*	Bratcher, Robert G., and Eugene A. Nida. *A Translator's Handbook on the Gospel of Mark.* London: United Bible Societies, 1961.
TRT*	Carlton, Matthew E. *The Gospel of Mark.* Translator's Reference Translation. Dallas, Texas: SIL International, 2001.
WBC	Guelich, Robert A. *Mark 1–8:26.* Word Biblical Commentary. Dallas, Texas: Word, 1989.
WBC	Evans, Craig A. *Mark 8:27–16:20.* Word Biblical Commentary. Nashville, Tenn.: Nelson, 2001.

GREEK TEXT AND TRANSLATIONS

GNT	The Greek New Testament. Edited by B. Aland, K. Aland, J. Karavidopoulos, C. Martini, and B. Metzger. Fourth ed. London, New York: United Bible Societies, 1993.
CEV	The Holy Bible, Contemporary English Version. New York: American Bible Society, 1995.
ESV and ESVfn	ESV Study Bible, English Standard Version. Wheaton, Ill.: Crossway Bibles, 2008.
GW	God's Word. Grand Rapids: World Publishing, 1995.
KJV	The Holy Bible. Authorized (or King James) Version. 1611.

NASB	New American Standard Bible. La Habra, Calif.: Lockman Foundation, 1995.
NCV	New Century Version. Dallas: Word Publishing, 1991.
NET and NETfn	The NET Bible, New English Translation. Version 6r,715, Biblical Studies Press, 2006.
NIV and NIVfn	NIV Study Bible, New International Version. Grand Rapids: Zondervan, 1995.
NLT and NLTfn	NLT Study Bible, New Living Translation. Second edition. Carol Stream, Ill.: Tyndale House, 2008.
NRSV	The Holy Bible: New Revised Standard Version. New York: Oxford University Press, 1989.
REB	The Revised English Bible. Oxford: Oxford University Press and Cambridge University Press, 1989.
TEV	Good News Bible, Today's English Version. Second edition. New York: American Bible Society, 1992.

GRAMMATICAL TERMS

act.	active	mid.	middle
fut.	future	opt.	optative
impera.	imperative	pass.	passive
imperf.	imperfect	perf.	perfect
indic.	indicative	pres.	present
infin.	infinitive	subj.	subjunctive

EXEGETICAL SUMMARY OF MARK 1–8

DISCOURSE UNIT—1:1–15 [CBC]. The topic is the prologue on the beginning of the Gospel.

DISCOURSE UNIT—1:1–13 [Hb, NICNT, PNTC; NLT, REB]. The topic is the prologue [EBC], the prologue to the gospel [NICNT], the beginning of the Good News [NLT], the gospel appears in person [PNTC], the coming of the Servant [Hb], John the Baptist and Jesus [REB].

DISCOURSE UNIT—1:1–8 [CBC, EBC, NICNT; CEV, ESV, GW, NASB, NCV, NET, NIV, NLT, TEV]. The topic is the Good News about Jesus, the herald in the wilderness [NICNT], preparing the way [EBC], John the Baptist prepares the way [CBC; ESV, GW, NIV, NLT], John prepares for Jesus [NCV], the ministry of John the Baptist [NET], the preaching of John the Baptist [CEV, NASB, TEV].

DISCOURSE UNIT—1:1 [Hb, NIGTC]. The topic is the heading [NIGTC], the title of the book [Hb].

1:1 Beginning^a of-the gospel^b of-Jesus Christ Son of-God.^c

TEXT—Manuscripts reading Χριστοῦ υἱοῦ θεοῦ 'Christ Son of God' are given a C rating by GNT to indicate that choosing it over a variant text was difficult. A variant reading is Χριστοῦ υἱοῦ τοῦ κυρίου 'Christ Son of the Lord'. Another variant reading is Χριστοῦ 'Christ' and it is followed by AB2.

LEXICON—a. ἀρχή (LN 68.1) (BAGD 1.b. p. 111): 'beginning' [BAGD, LN, Lns, NTC], 'the beginning' [AB1, AB2, BECNT, BNTC, WBC; ESV, KJV, NASB, NET, NIV, NRSV, REB], 'this is the beginning' [GW, NCV]. This word is moved to verse 2: 'It began' [CEV]. This noun denotes the initiation of an action, process, or state of being [LN].

b. εὐαγγέλιον (LN 33.217) (BAGD 1.b., 3. p. 318): 'gospel' [BAGD, BECNT, LN, Lns, NTC, WBC; ESV, KJV, NASB, NET, NIV, REB], 'good news' [AB2, BAGD, BNTC, LN; CEV, NRSV], 'Good News' [GW, NCV, NLT, TEV], 'proclamation' [AB1]. This noun denotes the content of the good news, and in the NT the good news is about Jesus Christ [LN]. The noun means 'good news' or 'gospel' [BAGD] and by the time Mark wrote this book, the word *gospel* had become a technical term referring to the announcement of the Christian good news [EBC], the preaching about Jesus Christ and God's saving power accomplished through him for all who believe [NETfn]. It wasn't until much later that the church began to refer to the four books that dealt with the life and teaching of Jesus as the 'Gospels' [BAGD (3.)].

c. υἱὸς τοῦ θεοῦ 'Son of God' [LN 12.15]: This is a title applied to Jesus. It is parallel in semantic structure to phrases consisting of υἱός 'son' followed by the genitive of class or kind. It means one who has the essential characteristics and nature of God [LN]. This title appears at 1:1; 3:11; 15:39.

QUESTION—What is the function of this verse?

This verse appears to function as a title [EBC, NETfn], but it is not clear whether it is intended to refer to the entire book or only to the section about the ministry of John the Baptist [EBC]. The verse is like a title in that it does not contain a verb and it ends with a period. It is not clear how the initial word of the verse ἀρχή 'beginning' fits in with the rest of the verse.

1. Verse 1 functions as the title for the entire book of Mark [AB2, Hb, Lns, NCBC, NETfn, PNTC, Tay; probably CEV, NLT, TEV]. The verse stands apart from the first discourse section of the book that begins with verse 2 [EGT]. The presence of the noun ἀρχή 'beginning' is explained in various ways.

   1.1 The entire book of Mark is about *the beginning stages* of the gospel [AB2, Hb, Lns, NCBC, Tay]: *The beginning of the gospel of Jesus Christ, the Son of God.* This implies that there would be more to tell about the gospel after the book of Mark has been written. What follows after this beginning account of the gospel would take place after the resurrection of Jesus when his disciples were sent out to preach the good news [AB2, Hb].

   1.2 The word 'beginning' is an allusion to the word 'beginning' in the first verse of Genesis [NETfn, PNTC]. God was bringing about a 'new beginning' with this good news about the coming of Christ [NETfn].

   1.3 Although some versions include verse 1 under a section heading that includes 1:1–8, the first verse is stated as though it is the title for the whole book and the word 'beginning' is moved so as to begin a separate sentence that continues on into the next verse: '¹This is the Good News about Jesus the Messiah, the Son of God. It began ²just as the prophet Isaiah had written…' [NLT], '¹This is the good news about Jesus Christ, the Son of God. ²It began just as the prophet Isaiah had written…' [TEV; similarly CEV].

2. Verse 1 functions as a title for the first section of the book [AB1, BECNT, BNTC, CGTC, ICC, My, NICNT, Sw; ESV, KJV, NCV; probably GW, NASB, NIV, NRSV, REB which supply their own section heading for the unit that includes verse 1]: *The beginning (event) of the gospel of Jesus Christ, the Son of God.* 'Beginning' refers to the temporal beginning of the appearance of the gospel [BECNT]. There are different views of the extent of this first discourse unit.

   2.1 The gospel begins with 1:2–8, which tells how the prophetic passages in 1:2–3 find their fulfillment in the ministry of John the Baptist [BECNT, BNTC, ESVfn; ICC, My; ESV, GW, NASB, NCV, NET, NIV, NRSV]. The actual beginning of the gospel is the good news that God's promises in the OT would be fulfilled in Jesus Christ [ESVfn].

2.2 The gospel begins with 1:2–13, which tells how the prophetic passages in 1:2–3 find their fulfillment in the ministry of John the Baptist and in the coming of Jesus into the wilderness [CGTC, NICNT; REB].

2.3 The gospel begins with 1:2–15, a discourse unit that covers the preaching of John the baptizer and the preaching of Jesus when he appeared in Galilee [AB1].

3. Instead of functioning as a title, verse 1 simply begins a sentence that continues into verse 2 [LN (68.1), NTC]. The most natural meaning for verse 1 seems to be: 'The good news about Jesus Christ, the Son of God, began with John the Baptist. It was John who, as predicted, prepared the way for Christ's coming' [NTC]. The word 'beginning' is closely related to what immediately follows in verse 2: 'The good news about Jesus Christ the Son of God began as the prophet Isaiah had written…' [LN (68.1)].

QUESTION—How are the nouns related in the genitive construction τοῦ εὐαγγελίου Ἰησοῦ Χριστοῦ 'the gospel of Jesus Christ'?

1. The name 'Jesus Christ' is an objective genitive [BECNT, BNTC, CBC, EBC, EGT, Gnd, Hb, ICC, LN (68.1), Lns, My, NICNT, NIGTC, NTC, Sw, Tay, TH, WBC; CEV, GW, NCV, NIV, NLT, TEV]: the gospel *about Jesus Christ.* This book is about the person and deeds of Jesus Christ [BECNT].

2. Mark intended that this ambiguous genitive construction would indicate that the gospel is about Jesus Christ and also that the gospel was proclaimed by Jesus Christ [AB2, CGTC, ESVfn, NCBC, NETfn]: *the gospel about Jesus Christ that he proclaimed.* It is possible that an interplay between the two concepts is intended and mean that the gospel Jesus proclaims is in fact the gospel about himself [NETfn]. This is the gospel that was proclaimed by Jesus, and in a secondary sense it is the gospel about Jesus [CGTC, ESVfn].

QUESTION—How is the word Χριστοῦ 'Christ' used here?

The Greek word Χριστοῦ 'Christ' and the Hebrew word for 'Messiah' both mean 'anointed' [Hb; NET]. In the OT, the kings, priests, and prophets were anointed with oil to signify that their authority was from God. Long after King David's death, the oppressed Jews were longing for the coming of a descendant of David who would rule over Israel as the promised Messiah [NLTfn].

1. The word 'Christ' is a title that emphasizes Jesus' role as God's promised Messiah [AB1, AB2, CBC, CGTC, Gnd, My, NAC, NCBC, NIGTC, NTC, PNTC, WBC; NLT]: *Jesus the Messiah.* There are seven occurrences of the word Χριστοῦ 'Christ' in Mark (1:1; 8:29; 9:41; 12:35; 13:21; 14:61; 15:32) and every occurrence clearly has the sense of being a title that refers to the Jewish Messiah [NIGTC]. All references except 1:1 and 9:41 include a definite article, *'the* Christ'. The lack of a definite article with 'Christ' in this verse is probably because it is in the genitive case [AB2].

2. 'Christ' is used in this verse as part of Jesus' personal name [BECNT, BNTC, EGT, Hb, ICC, Lns, TH; CEV, TEV]: *Jesus Christ*. The combination 'Jesus Christ' was being used by Christians as a personal name for Jesus by the time Mark wrote this book and that is the meaning Mark intended for just this first verse. All the other occurrences of the word Χριστοῦ 'Christ' in Mark stand alone and each context indicates that it is then functioning as the title 'Messiah' [BECNT]. This verse is the only place in Mark where the word Χριστοῦ is translated by CEV and TEV as 'Christ' instead of the title 'Messiah'. In this verse the absence of an article with the name 'Christ' indicates that it is used as a personal name [Hb, ICC].

QUESTION—What is meant by the title υἱοῦ θεοῦ 'Son of God'?

This refers to the unique relationship Jesus had with God [NAC, NLTfn], and it has the full New Testament Trinitarian sense of that title [Hb, NTC]. 'Son of God' would be a mysterious term to many of the readers of this book, but they would come to understand it better as they read about all that Jesus does and says throughout the book [CBC, NICNT]. Although there is no article with 'Son' in the Greek text, it is definite and refers not to '*a* Son of God', but to '*the* Son of God' [NTC]. The phrase is translated 'the Son of God' [BECNT, BNTC, NTC; all versions], 'Son of God' [AB1, WBC], 'God's Son' [Lns].

DISCOURSE UNIT—1:2–13 [NIGTC]. The topic is the prologue: setting the scene by introducing the characters or actors in the drama.

DISCOURSE UNIT—1:2–8 [Hb]. The topic is the ministry of John the Baptist.

1:2 Just-as[a] it-has-been-written in[b] Isaiah the prophet,[c]

TEXT—Manuscripts reading ἐν τῷ Ἠσαΐᾳ τῷ προφήτῃ 'in Isaiah the prophet' are given an A rating by GNT to indicate it was regarded to be certain. A variant reading is ἐν τοῖς προφήταις 'in the prophets' and it is followed by KJV. One old Latin manuscript evidently reads ἐν Ἠσαΐᾳ καὶ ἐν τοῖς προφήταις 'in Isaiah and in the prophets'.

LEXICON—a. καθώς (LN 64.16): 'just as' [AB1, LN; CEV, NLT], 'even as' [Lns], 'as' [AB2, BECNT, BNTC, NTC, WBC; ESV, KJV, NASB, NCV, NET, NRSV, TEV], not explicit [GW, REB]. The corresponding relationship of this conjunction is supplied at the beginning of verse 4: 'And so' [NIV]. This conjunction indicates a similarity in events and states, and may imply that something is in accordance with something else [LN].

b. ἐν (LN 83.13, 90.6): 'in' [LN (83.13, 90.6); KJV], 'by' [LN (90.6)]. The phrase 'it has been written in Isaiah the prophet' [AB2, Lns] is also translated 'it was written in Isaiah the prophet' [AB1], 'it is written in Isaiah the prophet' [BNTC, NTC; ESV, NASB, NET, NIV], 'it is written in the prophet Isaiah' [NRSV], 'in the prophet Isaiah it stands written' [REB], 'it is written in the book of Isaiah the prophet' [BECNT], '(as) the prophet Isaiah had written' [NLT, TEV], '(as) written by the prophet

Isaiah' [WBC], 'the prophet Isaiah wrote' [GW, NCV], 'God had said in the book written by Isaiah the prophet' [CEV]. This preposition indicates a position, such as a part of a document being 'in' something [LN (83.13)], or it identifies the agent of the action [LN (90.6)].

c. προφήτης (LN 53.79) (BAGD 1. p. 723) 'prophet' [BAGD, LN; all translations], 'inspired preacher' [LN]. This noun denotes one who proclaims inspired utterances on behalf of God [LN]. It denotes someone who proclaims and interprets the divine revelation [BAGD]. This word occurs at 1:2; 6:4, 15; 8:28; 11:32.

QUESTION—What relationship is indicated by the conjunction καθώς 'just as'?

1. It is connected with 1:1 to indicate how the gospel account began [AB2, BECNT, BNTC, Gnd, LN (68.1), NAC, NCBC, NIGTC, WBC; CEV, NCV, NLT, TEV]: *the gospel began just as it has been written in Isaiah the prophet*. This agrees with all the other occasions of the use of καθώς 'just as' in Mark where the 'just as' clause depends on the clause preceding it [BECNT, Gnd, WBC]. This connection is supported by the fact that '*your* face' and 'the way of *you*' refer back to Jesus Christ in 1:1 [BECNT].

2. It is connected with 1:4 to indicate how the two OT passages in 1:2–3 relate to the ministry of John the Baptist [AB2, BNTC, EGT, GNT, Hb, LN, Lns, NTC, TH; ESV, NIV, NRSV, TEV]: *Just as it has been written in Isaiah the prophet..., so came John baptizing in the wilderness*. The quotes are parenthetical explanations of what was written, so the thought is 'just as it is written...John the Baptizer appeared' [TH]. The following verses 1:4–8 speak of the messenger, the wilderness, and the Lord that are mentioned in the OT passages [NIVfn].

3. It is connected only to the quotation in 1:2–3 [Sw; KJV, NASB, NET; probably GW, REB which omit the conjunction]: *Just as it has been written in Isaiah the prophet are the words, "Look, I am sending my messenger before your face..."*

QUESTION—What is meant by the following quotation being 'written *in* Isaiah the prophet'?

This means that the quoted words are written '*in the roll* of Isaiah the prophet' [TH]. The words were written *by* Isaiah [WBC; NLT, TEV]. The words quoted in 1:2–3 are what God said in the book written *by* Isaiah the prophet [CEV].

QUESTION—Where does the quotation in verse 2 appear in Scripture?

The introduction to the quotation appears to say that Isaiah the prophet is being quoted in verses 2 and 3. However, all the commentaries agree that only the quotation in verse 3 is from Isaiah. The quotation in verse 2 is either from Malachi 3:1 alone, or it combines a quotation from Exodus 23:20 with a quotation from Malachi 3:1. Mark was following the Jewish practice of naming just the most prominent prophet of the sources being quoted [BECNT, ESVfn, Gnd, NLTfn, PNTC]. Mark mentions Isaiah's name because he intended to comment about the part in Isaiah that concerns John's appearance and his activity in the wilderness [CBC, ESVfn]. The combined quotations are attributed to Isaiah because the better-known Isaiah passage about the messenger appearing in the wilderness links the two OT passages to the coming of John the Baptist in the wilderness in verse 4 [Hb, Lns, NIGTC].

"Look,[a] I-am-sending[b] my messenger before your face,[c] who will-prepare[d] the way[e] of-you;

TEXT—Manuscripts reading τὴν ὁδόν σου 'the way of you' are followed by GNT, which does not mention any variant reading. A variant reading is τὴν ὁδόν σου ἔμπροθέν σου 'the way of you before you' and it is followed by KJV.

LEXICON—a. ἰδού (LN 91.13): 'look' [AB2, BNTC, LN; NET, NLT], 'behold' [BECNT, NTC; ESV, KJV, NASB], 'lo' [Lns], 'see' [NRSV], 'listen' [LN], 'pay attention' [AB1, LN], 'take note' [WBC], not explicit [CEV, GW, NCV, NIV, REB, TEV]. This particle is used to draw attention to something [LN]. Here it draws attention to the important announcement that is to be made [Hb, TH]. It is used to stress the need for paying close attention to God's promise, and should not be translated as a command to view some object [TH].

b. pres. act. indic. of ἀποστέλλω (LN 15.66) (BAGD 1.b.β. p. 98): 'to send' [AB1, AB2, BAGD, BNTC, LN, NTC, WBC; all versions except NCV, NIV], 'to commission' [Lns]. Since this is a prophecy, some translate the present tense as future: 'I will/shall send my messenger' [BECNT; NCV, NIV]. The present tense indicates that the sending of the messenger is imminent [Hb]. This verb means to cause someone to depart for some particular purpose [LN]. It includes the idea of a commission that gives authority and responsibility to the messenger [TH].

c. πρόσωπον (LN 85.26) (BAGD 1.c.ζ. p. 721): 'face' [BAGD], 'presence' [LN]. The phrase πρὸ προσώπου σου 'before your face' [AB1, AB2, Lns, NTC; ESV, KJV] is also translated 'before you' [BECNT, WBC], 'ahead of you' [BNTC; all versions except CEV, ESV, KJV], not explicit [CEV]. This noun is being used as a figurative extension of the word 'face' to denote the personal presence of an individual at a particular place [BAGD, LN]. To be sent 'before someone's face' simply means to be sent 'before some person' [BAGD].

d. fut. act. indic. of κατασκευάζω (LN 77.6) (BAGD p. 418): 'to prepare, to make ready' [BAGD, LN]. See the following lexical item for translations of this word. This verb means to cause someone to be thoroughly prepared [LN]. This preparation is used in a mental or spiritual sense of getting people ready for something that will happen [BAGD].

e. ὁδός (LN 1.99) (BAGD 1.a. p. 554): 'way, road, highway' [BAGD, LN], 'street' [LN]. The clause ὃς κατασκευάσει τὴν ὁδόν σου 'who will prepare the way of you' is translated 'who/he will prepare your way'

[BECNT, WBC; ESV, NASB, NCV, NET, NIV, NLT, NRSV, REB; similarly AB1, Lns, NTC; KJV], 'who will set your way in order' [AB2]. Some translations indicate that this relative clause expresses the purpose for sending the messenger: 'to prepare the way for you' [GW], 'to prepare your way' [BNTC], 'to get the way ready for you' [CEV], 'to open the way for you' [TEV]. This noun is a general term for a thoroughfare, either within a population center or between two such centers [LN]. The picture of 'preparing the road' goes beyond the idea of building or repairing a road. It means making all the arrangements needed to properly welcome a king or a victorious conqueror [TH].

QUESTION—What Scripture passages are quoted in verse 2?

1. The entire quotation in verse 2 is from Malachi 3:1 [EGT, ESVfn, Hb, ICC, Lns, My, NAC, NIVfn, NLTfn, NTC, Sw, TH, TRT]. The text of Malachi 3:1 reads, 'Behold I send my messenger, and he will prepare the way before me' [ESV].

2. The quotation in verse 2 is a conflation of a passage from Exodus 23:20 ('Behold, I send an angel before you' [ESV]) and a passage from Malachi 3:1 ('and he will prepare the way before me' [ESV]) [AB1, AB2, BECNT, BNTC, CBC, CGTC, EBC, Gnd, NCBC, NETfn, NICNT, NIGTC, PNTC, Tay, WBC]. The first part of the quotation in this verse, 'Look I am sending my messenger before your face', appears to be drawn directly from Exodus 23:20 since the Greek Septuagint translation of Exodus 23:20 and the text in Mark agree word for word and the Greek word ἄγγελόν can mean either 'angel' or 'messenger' [AB1, AB2, BNTC, CGTC, NICNT, Tay]. Instead of 'Look, I send my messenger' in Malachi 3:1, Mark has used the wording of the Greek Septuagint translation of Exodus 23:20 'Look I am sending my messenger *before your face*'. Although '*your* face' refers to the people of Israel in the Exodus passage, Mark uses 'you' in his messianic interpretation of the passage to refer to Jesus [AB2, BECNT, BNTC, CGTC, Gnd, Hb, ICC, NICNT, NIGTC, Tay, WBC].

QUESTION—Who is speaking in the quotation 'I am sending my messenger'?

God, the LORD, is the speaker [BECNT, Hb, TH, TRT; CEV, TEV]. A prophet speaks on behalf of God, so here Isaiah is writing what God said [TRT]. God was speaking through the prophet [AB2]. This is made explicit in some translations: 'It began just as God said in the book written by Isaiah the prophet' [CEV], 'as the prophet Isaiah had written, "God said, I will send my messenger..."' [TEV].

QUESTION—Who is the messenger, and how will he prepare the way?

According to Malachi 4:5, the messenger is Elijah the prophet, whom the NT identifies as John the Baptist because John came 'in the spirit and power' of Elijah (Matt. 11:10–14; 17:11–12; Lk. 1:17) [BNTC, NAC; NET]. In Mark, verse 4 indicates that the prophesied messenger is John the baptizer [BECNT]. 'Preparing the way' is a metaphor alluding to the custom of repairing the road to a city as a way of honoring an important person who will be traveling over that road when coming to visit the city [TRT]. This gives a picture of a king sending a representative ahead of him to make sure that the roads have been put in good condition for his coming [Hb]. It does not literally mean that the messenger will work on a road, but that the messenger will prepare the people for the Lord's coming [TRT]. It refers to John's advance work of removing hindrances in the hearts of the people so that they will be ready to receive the Messiah [Hb, NTC, WBC]. John prepared the way by his preaching [AB2].

QUESTION—Why did Mark change Malachi 3:1 from 'he will prepare the way before *me*' to 'he will prepare the way of *you*'?

Mark used 'you' in his messianic interpretation of the passage to speak of the Lord Jesus [AB2, EBC, Hb, ICC, NICNT, NIGTC, WBC]. Mark has changed 'the way of *me* (the LORD)' to 'the way of *you* (the Lord Jesus)' [Gnd], so that God's promise to the people of Israel is now addressed to Jesus himself [AB2, BECNT, Hb, Lns]. In Malachi 3:1 the messenger precedes the Lord, and in Malachi 4:5–6 Elijah precedes the Day of the Lord. Therefore in Mark the words 'before you' refers to the Lord who is identified in verses 1–15 as Jesus the Messiah, the Son of God [WBC]. The way was to be made ready for 'the Lord', and it turns out that the one who comes after John is both the Lord and the Messiah (8:29), and the rest of the account shows that Jesus, the Messiah, is also a member of the Godhead [ESVfn]. When God promised that he himself would come to the people, it turns out that he would come in the person of the Messiah. This Messiah is the Lord, who is also God. This is possible because of the distinction between these two divine persons of the triune God [Lns].

1:3 A -voice^a shouting^b in the wilderness,^c

LEXICON—a. φωνή (LN 33.103) (BAGD 2.e. p. 871): 'voice' [BAGD, LN; all translations except CEV, TEV], 'someone' [CEV, TEV]. This noun denotes the human voice used as an instrument of communication [LN].
  b. pres. act. participle of βοάω (LN 33.81) (BAGD 2. p. 144): 'to shout' [BAGD, LN], 'to cry out' [LN]. The phrase 'a voice shouting' is translated 'the voice of one/someone shouting' [AB2; NET], 'he is a voice shouting' [NLT], 'someone is shouting' [CEV, TEV], 'a voice crying' [BNTC], 'a voice cries/cries-out' [GW, REB], 'a/the voice of one crying/crying-out' [WBC; ESV, KJV, NASB, NRSV], 'a voice calling' [AB1], 'a/the voice of one calling/calling-out' [BECNT; NIV; similarly NCV]. This verb means to cry or shout with an unusually loud volume [LN]. It implies that a solemn proclamation is being made [BAGD].
  c. ἔρημος (LN 1.86) (BAGD 2. p. 309): 'wilderness' [AB2, BAGD, BECNT, BNTC, LN, NTC, WBC; ESV, KJV, NASB, NET, NLT, NRSV, REB], 'desert' [AB1, BAGD, LN; CEV, GW, NCV, NIV, TEV], 'lonely place' [BAGD, LN]. This adjectival noun denotes a largely uninhabited region that usually has but little vegetation [LN]. This word also occurs at 1:4, 12.

QUESTION—What passage is being quoted in this verse?

This passage is from Isaiah 40:3, and the Hebrew text says: 'A voice cries: "In the wilderness prepare the way of the LORD; make straight in the desert a highway for our God"' [ESV]. The point in the Isaiah passage is that the preparation for God starts in the wilderness [CBC]. Mark has quoted from the Greek Septuagint translation in which the wilderness can be connected more naturally with the location of the herald instead of the location where the road was to be prepared [Hb, ICC, Sw; all versions]. Either connection is appropriate because the location of the one who is shouting and the location of the road to be prepared were both in the wilderness [Hb, Lns, NTC]. One commentary has connected 'in the wilderness' with the following clause: 'in the desert make ready the Lord's road' to agree with the Hebrew text of Isaiah [AB1].

QUESTION—What is meant by 'a voice' shouting?

The verb refers to the loud voice of someone shouting to get the attention of others in order to gain an effective hearing of his message [Hb]. That person would have to shout in order to be heard by the crowds who came out into the wilderness to hear him [TRT]. Mark is applying the Isaiah passage to John's role as a herald who was proclaiming a baptism of repentance in preparation for the coming of the one who was greater than he [WBC].

'Prepare^a the way^b of-(the) Lord,^c make straight^d his paths,^e'"

LEXICON—a. aorist act. impera. of ἑτοιμάζω (LN 77.3) (BAGD 1. p. 316): 'to prepare, to make ready' [LN], 'to put in readiness' [BAGD]. The clause 'prepare the way of the Lord' [AB2, BECNT, BNTC, WBC; ESV, NRSV; similarly KJV] is also translated 'prepare the way for the Lord' [GW, NCV, NET, NIV, REB], 'make ready the way of the Lord' [NTC; NASB], 'make ready the Lord's road' [AB1], 'get the road ready for the Lord' [CEV, TEV], 'prepare the way for the LORD's coming' [NLT]. This verb means to cause something to be ready [LN].

b. ὁδός (LN 1.99) (BAGD 1.a. p. 554): 'way' [AB2, BAGD, BECNT, BNTC, LN, NTC, WBC; all versions except CEV, TEV], 'road' [AB1, BAGD, LN; CEV, TEV], 'highway' [BAGD, LN], 'street' [LN]. This noun is a general term for a thoroughfare, either within a population center or between two such centers [LN].

c. κύριον (LN 12.9) (BAGD 2.c.α. p. 459): 'Lord' [AB1, AB2, BAGD, BECNT, BNTC, LN, NTC, WBC; all versions except NLT], 'LORD' [NLT], 'Ruler, One who commands' [LN]. This noun is a title for both God and Christ, and refers to the one who exercises supernatural authority over mankind [LN]. This title is used as a designation of God, and it is also used in reference to Jesus [BAGD].

c. εὐθύς (LN 79.88) (BAGD 1. p. 321): 'straight' [BAGD, LN], 'direct' [LN]. The clause εὐθείας ποιεῖτε τὰς τρίβους αὐτοῦ 'make straight his paths' [BECNT, WBC] is also translated 'make his paths straight' [AB2, BNTC; ESV, GW, KJV, NASB, NET, NRSV], 'make straight paths for him' [NIV], 'make a straight path for him' [CEV], 'make the road straight for him' [NCV], 'make the paths he travels on straight' [LN], 'make for him a straight way to travel' [AB1], 'make a straight path for him to travel' [TEV], 'clear a straight path for him' [REB], 'clear the road for him' [NLT]. This adjective describes something as being straight in contrast to something that is crooked [LN].

d. τρίβος (LN 1.100) (BAGD p. 826): 'path' [AB2, BAGD, LN, NTC; all versions except NCV, NLT], 'beaten path' [BAGD, LN], 'road' [NCV, NLT]. This noun denotes a well-worn path or thoroughfare [LN]. It refers to a beaten track [Tay].

QUESTION—What is the relationship of the nouns in the genitive construction 'the way of the Lord'?

Instead of preparing the way *of* the Lord', some translate this *'for* the Lord' [CEV, GW, NCV, NET, NIV, REB, TEV], or more specifically, 'for the Lord's coming' [NLT]. This means to prepare the road over which the Lord will come [TH].

QUESTION—Who is the 'Lord'?

The passage in the Hebrew text is 'prepare the way of *Yahweh*, make straight in the desert a highway for *our God'*. Reverent Jews regarded God's name 'Yahweh' to be too sacred to be uttered, so they avoided saying 'Yahweh' out loud by substituting the word *adonai* 'Lord'. The Greek Septuagint commonly translates God's holy name *Yahweh* as κύριος 'Lord'. Most English translations follow the same practice, and in order to distinguish God's name from other uses of the word 'lord' they print his name in small capital letters, 'LORD'. Mark interprets the Lord's coming in the OT prophecies as the coming of the Lord Jesus Christ, the Son of God [BECNT]. Mark intended that 'the Lord' would refer to Jesus, who was commonly called by that title [Gnd, Hb, ICC, NAC]. So instead of ending with the Septuagint translation 'the paths of our God', Mark has substituted 'his paths' in order to refer back to the Lord Jesus [BECNT, Hb, NIGTC, TH, WBC]. John is the herald of not simply the Messiah, but of God himself, who appeared in the person of Jesus of Nazareth [PNTC]. The path was to be prepared for 'the Lord', and the one who comes after John the Baptist is both the Messiah and a member of the Godhead [ESVfn].

1:4 appeared[a] John the (one) baptizing[b] in the wilderness[c] and proclaiming[d]

TEXT—Manuscripts reading Ἰωάννης ὁ βαπτίζων ἐν τῇ ἐρήμῳ καὶ κηρύσσων 'John the one baptizing in the wilderness and proclaiming' are given a C rating by GNT to indicate that choosing it over a variant text was difficult. A variant reading is Ἰωάννης βαπτίζων ἐν τῇ ἐρήμῳ καὶ κηρύσσων 'John, baptizing in the wilderness and proclaiming' and it is followed by KJV. Other variant readings are Ἰωάννης ὁ βαπτίζων ἐν τῇ ἐρήμῳ κηρύσσων 'John the one baptizing in the wilderness proclaiming' and Ἰωάννης ἐν τῇ ἐρήμῳ βαπτίζων καὶ κηρύσσων 'John in the wilderness baptizing and proclaiming'.

LEXICON—a. aorist mid. (deponent = act.) indic. of γίνομαι (LN 85.7) (BAGD II.5. p. 160): 'to appear' [AB1, AB2, BAGD, BNTC, LN, WBC; ESV, NASB, NRSV, REB, TEV], 'to show up' [CEV], 'to come' [BECNT, Lns, NTC; NIV], 'to be (in a place)' [LN; GW, NLT], not explicit [KJV, NCV, NET]. This verb means to come to be in a place [LN].

b. pres. act. participle of βαπτίζω (LN 53.41) (BAGD 2.a. p. 131): 'to baptize' [BAGD, LN]. John is identified as the one who baptized: 'John the baptizer' [NET, NRSV], 'John the Baptizer' [BNTC, WBC; GW], 'John the Baptist' [CEV, NASB, NLT, REB], 'John, the one who baptized' [AB1]. John is the subject of the verb 'baptizing': 'John was baptizing people' [NCV], 'John came, baptizing' [BECNT, NTC; NIV; similarly Lns], 'John appeared, baptizing' [AB2; ESV], 'John appeared in the desert, baptizing' [TEV], 'John did baptize' [KJV]. This verb means to use water in a religious ceremony that is designed to symbolize purification and initiation on the basis of repentance [LN].

c. ἔρημος (LN 1.86) (BAGD 2. p. 309): 'wilderness, desert, lonely place' [BAGD, LN]. This adjectival noun denotes a largely uninhabited region, and usually the region has little vegetation [LN]. This is the same word that is used in 1:3.

d. pres. act. participle of κηρύσσω (LN 33.256) (BAGD 2.b.β. p. 431): 'to proclaim' [AB1, AB2, BAGD, BNTC, NTC, WBC; ESV, NRSV, REB], 'to herald' [Lns], 'to preach' [BAGD, BECNT, LN; KJV, NASB, NCV, NET, NIV, NLT], 'to tell (everyone/people)' [CEV, GW, TEV]. This verb means to publicly announce religious truths and principles while urging acceptance and compliance [LN]. This means to publicly proclaim a message as a herald does [Hb]. It means to announce in a loud voice [CGTC].

QUESTION—How is this verse connected with 1:4?

Some provide the connecting conjunction 'so' [AB1, NTC; CEV], 'so it was that' [BNTC], or they close 1:4 with a comma [CGTC, GNT; ESV, NRSV]: *Just as it has been written in Isaiah the prophet, "...," so John appeared in the wilderness*. Its connection to 1:2–3 is shown by beginning 1:4 with 'This messenger was John the Baptist' [NLT]. This verse is tied to 1:3 by the emphasis on the identical phrase 'in the wilderness' [CBC, NCBC, NICNT, Sw]. The 'voice' in the wilderness is now identified to be the voice of John the Baptist [AB1, PNTC]. John was preaching in the wilderness and his task was to prepare the way of the Lord [NTC, PNTC]. This is the historical fulfillment of the prophecy quoted in 1:3 [BNTC, EGT, Lns, WBC]. In Isaiah 40:3, the 'Lord' refers to the Lord God of Israel. In applying the prophecy to the announcement made by John the Baptist, it shows that the promised 'Lord' is Christ, the Son of God [NLTfn, NTC, PNTC]. There are a number of match-ups between 1:2–3 and 1:4: God sends his messenger and

John appears with a message; the messenger was shouting his message in the wilderness and John was proclaiming his message in the wilderness; the messenger told the people to prepare the way of the Lord and John preached the baptism of repentance for the forgiveness of sins [Gnd].

QUESTION—How is the syntax to be interpreted in this clause?

1. 'Baptizing' identifies John [AB1, BNTC, CGTC, EGT, Hb, ICC, NCBC, NIGTC; CEV, GW, NASB, NET, NLT, NRSV, REB]: *John the Baptizer was proclaiming*. Mark uses this same title 'John the Baptizer' in 6:24 ('the head of John the baptizer') and then follows it with the equivalent, but more familiar, title 'John the Baptist' in 6:25 ('the head of John the Baptist') [BNTC, NIGTC]. This title refers to the characteristic activity of John [Hb]. While Matthew and Luke consistently use the noun form ὁ βαπτιστής 'the Baptist', Mark prefers the substantive participle ὁ βαπτίζων 'the one who baptizes', or 'the baptizer' [NETfn]. A few of the translations of this verse use the more familiar title 'John the Baptist' [CEV, NASB, NLT, REB].
2. 'Baptizing' is an activity of John parallel with 'proclaiming' [AB2, BECNT, Lns, My, NTC, PNTC; ESV, KJV, NCV, NIV, TEV]: *John was baptizing and proclaiming*.

QUESTION—What is meant by the verb ἐγένετο 'appeared' in the phrase 'John appeared'?

John appeared on the stage of history [Gnd, Hb, ICC]. This indicates the beginning of a new narrative [BECNT]. It introduces a new scene and actor in the story [NIGTC]. The verb 'appeared' reports the historical fact that in due time John came as God said he would [Lns]. The promised messenger appeared in the wilderness where God would once again act to deliver the people [WBC].

QUESTION—Where was this wilderness setting?

The precise location of John's baptizing is uncertain [PNTC]. John carried out his ministry in the wilderness of Judea (Matt. 3:1), which was probably the rugged area west of the Dead Sea [EBC, Hb, NLTfn, TH]. The mention of the Jordan River in 1:5 indicates that this wilderness of uncultivated and uninhabited country was somewhere in the area between the Lake of Galilee and the Dead Sea [NIGTC, PNTC]. It was probably located just south of the Lake of Galilee [PNTC]. Since crowds from Jerusalem and Judea were coming to hear John, it was probably located in the lower Jordan valley [NICNT, NIGTC].

a-baptism of-repentance[a] for[b] (the) forgiveness[f] of-sins.

LEXICON—a. μετάνοια (LN 41.52) (BAGD p. 512): 'repentance' [BAGD, LN], 'a change of one's mind' [BAGD]. The phrase βάπτισμα μετανοίας εἰς ἄφεσιν ἁμαρτιῶν 'a baptism of repentance for the forgiveness of sins' [AB1, BECNT, BNTC; ESV, GW, NASB, NET, NIV, NRSV] is also translated 'a repentance-baptism for the forgiveness of sins' [WBC], 'the baptism of repentance for the remission of sins' [KJV; similarly Lns],

'a baptism of conversion for the forgiveness of sins' [NTC], 'a baptism of repentance leading to the forgiveness of sins' [AB2], 'a baptism in token of repentance, for the forgiveness of sins' [REB], 'a baptism of changed hearts and lives for the forgiveness of sins' [NCV] '(preached that) people should be baptized to show that they had repented of their sins and turned to God to be forgiven' [NLT]. Some quote the words that John preached: 'Turn back to God and be baptized! Then your sins will be forgiven' [CEV], 'Turn away from your sins and be baptized, and God will forgive your sins' [TEV]. This noun denotes a change in one's way of life as the result of a complete change of thought and attitude with regard to sin and righteousness [LN]. It refers to a deep change of mind and a changed attitude toward sin that results in a change of conduct [Hb].
   b. εἰς (LN 89.48, 89.57) (BAGD 4.f. p. 229): 'for' [AB1, BECNT, BNTC, Lns, WBC; all versions except CEV, NLT, TEV], 'for the purpose of, in order to' [LN (89.57)], 'with the result that, so that as a result' [LN (89.48)], 'then' [CEV], 'and' [TEV]. The phrase 'for the forgiveness (of sins)' is translated 'to be forgiven' [NLT]. This preposition indicates result [LN (89.48)], or intent [LN (89.57)].
   c. ἄφεσις (LN 40.8) (BAGD 2. p. 125): 'forgiveness' [BAGD, LN]. See the preceding lexical item *a.* for translations of this word. This noun denotes the removal of the guilt resulting from wrongdoing [LN]. It is the cancellation of the guilt of sin [BAGD]. The person's guilt is cancelled without demanding the deserved punishment [Hb].
QUESTION—What is meant by the genitive construction βάπτισμα μετανοίας 'a baptism of repentance'?
   The word μετανοίας 'of-repentance' is a descriptive genitive that refers to a *repentance-type* of baptism [BECNT]. It was a baptism characterized by repentance [Hb]. Some translate the phrase 'a baptism of repentance' as 'a repentance-baptism' [BECNT, EBC, NIVfn, WBC]. 'Repentance-baptism' suggests that John's call to repentance and the act of baptism were integrally related in his ministry [WBC]. In semantic terms, the nouns in the genitive construction βάπτισμα μετανοίας '*baptism* of *repentance*' are both *event* words and the connection between the event of baptizing and the event of repenting must be determined. The outward act of baptism was a sign and pledge of an inward act of repentance [AB1, ESVfn, ICC, NIGTC, WBC]. The baptism was preceded by repentance [EBC, NIVfn]. The baptism was administered to only those who were repentant [AB1, BECNT, Hb, Lns]. This repentance-baptism required a person's repentance and gave expression to it [WBC]. Baptism was the most distinctive feature of John the Baptist's ministry, but the focus of his preaching was not on baptism itself, but on repentance in view of God's coming judgment [NIGTC]. In the next verse, the verb 'were being baptized' precedes the participial phrase 'confessing their sins' to indicate that people were baptized as they confessed their sins. It can be assumed that the people would not have come to John to be baptized unless they had already repented of their sins [AB2].

QUESTION—How is the added phrase εἰς ἄφεσιν ἁμαρτιῶν 'for the forgiveness of sins' to be understood in connection with the genitive construction βάπτισμα μετανοίας 'a baptism of repentance'?

The preposition εἰς 'for' indicates either result or purpose as determined by the context [TH]. Mark's wording, 'a baptism of repentance for the forgiveness of sins', could be interpreted to mean that forgiveness of sins is an automatic result of accepting John's baptism, but the intervening words 'of repentance' makes that a doubtful interpretation [NIGTC]. The syntax does not allow any definite conclusion as to precisely how the event-nouns 'baptism', 'repentance', and 'forgiveness' relate to one another [AB2, NICNT, NIGTC].

1. The preposition εἰς 'for' indicates the purpose for repenting of their sins [NLT]: John 'preached that people should be baptized to show that they had repented of their sins and turned to God to be forgiven' [NLT].
2. The preposition εἰς 'for' indicates the result of repenting of one's sins [EBC, ESVfn, ICC, NIVfn]. God's direct response to true repentance is forgiveness, and baptism indicated that repentance has already occurred [EBC]. Baptism was not the means by which a person's sins were forgiven, it was a ceremony that indicated the person had truly repented [ESVfn]. Repentance is the real cause for forgiveness while baptism is the outward act by which this inward change finds formal expression [ICC].
3. The preposition εἰς 'for' indicates the result of being baptized by John after having repented of one's sins [BECNT, CGTC, Hb, Lns, My, NCBC, PNTC, Sw, Tay; CEV, TEV]. 'Turn back to God and be baptized! Then your sins will be forgiven.' [CEV; similarly TEV]. Submitting to John's repentance-baptism as an outward testimony of personal repentance was the condition for receiving God's forgiveness [Hb]. In association with repentance the experience of John's baptism resulted in the forgiveness of sins [BECNT]. Remission of sins is the result of the baptism of repentance, and every such baptism bestowed remission upon the person baptized [Lns]. Baptism in such a state of moral reform accomplished the forgiveness of sins [PNTC]. Baptism gives expression to the act of repentance and thereby becomes an effective action leading to the remission of sins [Tay]. Probably John thought baptism had some real effectiveness towards forgiveness [CGTC].
4. John's purpose in proclaiming a 'repentance-baptism' was that people would receive the forgiveness of their sins. John called for repentance and offered a confirming baptism as the necessary prerequisite for the later forgiveness of sins that would accompany faith in the 'Greater One' when he came [WBC]. The aim of this baptism was that men should receive forgiveness of sins from the Messiah when he appeared [My].

QUESTION—How were the people baptized?

The meaning of the word βαπτίζω 'baptize' in BAGD is 'dip, immerse, plunge, sink, drench, overwhelm'. The phrases ἐν τῷ Ἰορδάνῃ ποταμῷ '*in the Jordan River*' (1:5) and ἀναβαίνων ἐκ τοῦ ὕδατος '*coming up out of* the water' (1:10) taken together suggest that the mode of John's baptism was immersion. However, there is no concrete evidence for John's method of baptizing people, and it may be that he did not always use the same method [NIGTC]. Although most commentaries do not discuss the mode of baptism, some think that the baptism was by immersion [BECNT, NAC, NCBC], and others do not [Lns].

QUESTION—What is meant by 'repentance'?

The Greek noun μετάνοια 'repentance' literally means 'a change of mind' [BECNT, BNTC, ICC, NAC, NCBC, PNTC, Tay]. It is more than regretting or grieving over one's sins. It is a profound change of mind that changes one's attitude toward sin [Hb]. It implies a deliberate turning or conversion to God [BNTC, PNTC]. In the light of both the OT and NT, it is not just a change of inward disposition, but a complete change of one's life [NAC, NCBC], and a return to God [NAC]. It is an act of heart, will, and mind in which there is a deliberate turning from sin to God [TH].

1:5 And[a] were-going-out[b] to him all the Judean region[c] and all the Jerusalemites, and they-were-being-baptized[d] by him in the Jordan river confessing[e] their sins.

LEXICON—a. καί (LN 89.87): 'and' [BECNT, BNTC, LN, Lns, NTC; ESV, KJV, NASB, NRSV, REB], 'and then' [LN], not explicit [AB2, WBC; CEV, GW, NCV, NET, NIV, TEV]. This conjunction indicates a sequence of closely related events [LN].

b. imperf. mid./pass. (deponent = act.) indic. of ἐκπορεύομαι (LN 15.40) (BAGD 1.c. p. 244): 'to go out' [BAGD, BECNT, LN, Lns, NTC, WBC; ESV, KJV, NASB, NCV, NET, NIV, NRSV, TEV], 'to go' [CEV, GW], 'to depart out of' [LN], 'to travel out to' [AB2]. The phrase 'were going out to him' is translated 'flocked to him' [BNTC; REB], 'went out to see and hear John' [NLT]. This verb means to move out of an enclosed or well-defined area [LN]. The imperfect tense pictures a constant procession of people going out to John from all parts of Judea [AB1, EBC, Hb, Lns, Sw, TH, WBC].

c. χώρα (LN **11.64**) (BAGD 1.b. p. 889): 'region' [BAGD, **LN**], 'district' [BAGD, BNTC], 'country' [Lns; ESV, NASB], 'countryside' [BECNT; NIV], 'land' [NTC; KJV], 'area' [WBC]. The phrase πᾶσα ἡ Ἰουδαία χώρα 'all the Judean region' is translated 'all of Judea' [NLT], 'all Judea' [GW]. By metonymy, the location 'region' stands for its inhabitants [BAGD, Hb, LN, NTC], and some translations make this clear: 'everyone living in the region of Judea' [**LN**], 'everyone from the region of Judea' [AB1], 'from Judea (and Jerusalem) crowds of people' [CEV], 'people from the whole Judean countryside' [NET, NRSV], 'everyone from the countryside of Judea' [REB], 'all of the people from the region of Judea' [AB2], 'all the people from Judea (and Jerusalem)' [NCV], 'many people from the province of Judea' [TEV]. In this context, the noun denotes the inhabitants of a region [LN].

d. imperf. pass. indic. of βαπτίζω (LN 53.41) (BAGD 2.a. p. 131): 'to be baptized' [AB2, BAGD, BECNT, BNTC, LN, Lns, NTC, WBC; ESV, KJV, NASB, NCV, NIV, NRSV, REB]. This passive verb is also translated actively: 'he baptized them' [CEV, GW, NLT, TEV], 'he was baptizing them' [NET]. This verb means to employ water in a religious ceremony designed to symbolize purification and initiation on the basis of repentance [LN]. The imperfect tense indicates the continuity of the action and indicates that John was baptizing them one by one as they came to him [Hb, TH].

e. pres. mid. participle of ἐξομολογέομαι, ἐξομολογέω (LN 33.275) (BAGD 2.a. p. 277): 'to confess, to admit' [BAGD, LN]. The phrase 'confessing their sins' [BECNT, BNTC, Lns, NTC, WBC; ESV, KJV, NASB, NIV, NRSV, REB] is also translated 'as they confessed their sins' [GW, NET], 'when they confessed their sins' [NLT], 'they confessed their sins (and were baptized)' [NCV; similarly TEV], 'they told how sorry they were for their sins' [CEV]. This verb means to acknowledge a fact publicly, often in reference to previous bad behavior [LN]. The repentant persons acknowledged their sin and renounced their sinful ways [WBC].

QUESTION—What is the function of the frequent use of καί 'and' to begin sentences and paragraphs throughout this book?

In the Hebrew text of the OT, the word *vav* is commonly used to carry the narrative along. Mark was influenced by his familiarity with the Hebrew text and used καί 'and' as the equivalent of *vav* as he was writing narratives in Greek. In contemporary English style it is not acceptable to begin every sentence with 'and', so many English translations leave 'and' untranslated, or they render it as 'now', 'so', 'then', or 'but' depending upon the context [NETfn].

QUESTION—Since the city of Jerusalem is located in the region of Judea, why is it mentioned separately?

Jerusalem was the capital city of Judea and had the largest population of all the Judean cities. While 'all the Judean region' points out the wide area from which people came, mentioning 'all the Jerusalemites' separately emphasizes the large number of people going out to hear John [Gnd]. This is translated 'all of Judea, including all the people of Jerusalem' [NLT], 'everyone flocked to him from the countryside of Judea and the city of Jerusalem' [REB].

QUESTION—How could *all* of the people of Judea and Jerusalem go out to hear John and be baptized by him?

The word 'all' is to be taken rhetorically [Hb, ICC, NCBC, TH] since the Jewish leaders did not believe that John was a prophet, and many of the people must have turned away from the severity of his message [ICC]. Mark uses hyperbole to emphasize the huge numbers of people who did go and were baptized [AB2, BNTC, EBC, Gnd, My, NAC, NIGTC, NIVfn, NTC, Tay, TH, TRT, WBC]. This is translated 'many people from the province of Judea and the city of Jerusalem' [TEV].

QUESTION—When did the people confess their sins?
The present participle indicates that people were confessing their sins at the time of their baptism [Lns]. They publicly acknowledged their sins when they were baptized [EBC, Hb]. Their submission to baptism was itself a confession of their sinfulness [CGTC, NCBC], and it is possible that a spoken confession preceded the actual baptism [CGTC]. The confession could have taken place before or during the baptism [Tay]. John first preached repentance, then those who were moved to repentance confessed their sins and John baptized them [Lns]. This does not mean that they gave full colorful details of all the sins they had ever committed [Hb]. The people confessed their sins to God with a loud voice that was heard by John [TH].

1:6 **And John was clothed (in) hairs[a] of-a-camel and a-belt[b] of-leather around his waist, and (was) eating locusts[c] and wild[d] honey.**

TEXT—Manuscripts reading τρίχας 'hairs' are given an A rating by GNT to indicate it was regarded to be certain. A variant reading is δέρριν 'skin'.

LEXICON—a. θρίξ (LN 8.12) (BAGD p. 364): 'hair' [BAGD, LN]. The phrase ἦν ἐνδεδυμένος τρίχας καμήλου 'was clothed in hairs of a camel' is translated 'was clothed with camel's hair' [BECNT, Lns; ESV, NASB, NRSV], 'wore clothes/clothing made from/of camel's hair' [CEV, NCV, NIV, TEV], 'was dressed in camel's hair' [BNTC], 'was dressed in clothes made from camel's hair' [GW, KJV; similarly AB1], 'wore a garment made of camel's hair' [NET; similarly AB2, NTC, WBC], 'his clothes were woven from coarse camel hair' [NLT], 'was dressed in a rough coat of camel's hair' [REB]. This noun denotes the hair of either a person or an animal [LN]. Here it is the hair of an animal, and to be dressed 'in camel's hair' is somewhat like the expression to be dressed 'in wool' [BAGD].

b. ζώνη (LN 6.178) (BAGD p. 341): 'belt' [AB2, BAGD, BECNT, BNTC, LN, NTC, WBC; all versions except CEV, KJV], 'strap' [CEV], 'a band of hide' [AB1], 'girdle' [BAGD, LN, Lns; KJV]. This noun denotes a band of leather or cloth worn around the waist outside of one's clothing [LN]. A belt was needed to keep the loose robe in place [Hb].

c. ἀκρίς (LN **4.47**) (BAGD p. 33): 'locust' [AB1, BECNT, BNTC, LN, Lns, NTC, WBC; all versions except CEV], 'grasshopper' [AB2, **LN**; CEV]. This noun denotes an insect of the family *Acrididae*. In Europe, the term 'locust' is used for the many varieties of these insects while the term 'grasshopper' is used for the smaller sized varieties. In North America, however, all of these insects are generally called 'grasshoppers' and the term 'locust' refers to cicadas of the family *Cicadadae* [LN].

d. ἄγριος (LN 20.6) (BAGD 1. p. 13): 'wild' [BAGD, LN], 'found in the open field' [BAGD]. The phrase μέλι ἄγριον is translated 'wild honey' [all translations]. This adjective refers to being wild [LN]. It pertains to honey from wild bees [BAGD].

QUESTION—How was John dressed and what did this signify?

John was dressed in 'camel hair', not camel's skin with hair on it, and this means that he wore a coarse robe that was woven from the hair of a camel [CGTC, EBC, Hb, ICC, Lns, PNTC, Sw, TH, TRT, WBC]. This was the kind of rough hairy garment worn by the poor and the ascetic [Hb, Lns, NTC, TH]. It was a long and loose robe [Lns, NTC, TH]. Most men wore belts in order to keep their robes from flapping apart and also to enable them to tuck up their garment when they wanted to walk rapidly [Lns, NTC]. Unlike modern belts with buckles, this was a waistband that would allow money or other things to be contained in it [TH]. It was a wide strip of leather worn around one's waist and abdomen [EBC, WBC]. Belts were often made of soft materials and richly adorned as a sign of wealth, but John simply used a piece of untanned leather that corresponded with his coarse coat [Hb, ICC]. John's clothing was the same kind that Elijah wore when he was described in 2 Kings 1:8, 'He wore a garment of hair, with a belt of leather about his waist' [ESV]. John's very appearance would remind people of the prophet Elijah who was expected to return as the forerunner of the Messiah (Malachi 4:5–6) [AB1, BECNT, BNTC, EBC, Hb, Lns, NAC, NCBC, NETfn, NICNT, NIGTC, NIVfn, NLTfn, PNTC, Tay, TRT]. Mark, however, does not specifically identify John as Elijah until 9:12–13 [Gnd, NCBC, NICNT, NIGTC]. Others think there is little reason to consider it to be a direct allusion to Elijah since this was the common garb of a wilderness nomad and corresponded to the prophetic dress described in Zech. 13:4 [NTC, WBC].

QUESTION—Why did John eat locusts and wild honey?

This was the kind of food found in the wilderness, so it was the customary food of those who lived in the wilderness and had to eat off the land [BNTC, Hb, ICC, Lns, NCBC, NETfn, NICNT, NIGTC, NLTfn, Tay]. It had a high vitamin content and was a common part of the local diet [AB1, PNTC]. Locusts were one of the foods allowed by the Law in Leviticus 11:22, and they were eaten roasted or boiled [NIGTC]. John's diet was nutritious, even though it was simple and monotonous [NIGTC]. This was not all that John ate [BECNT, BNTC, NTC], but it is the food that Mark wanted to emphasize to make the point that John's ministry was in the wilderness [BECNT, NTC].

QUESTION—What is meant by μέλι ἄγριον 'wild honey'?

1. Wild honey is honey made by wild bees [AB1, EBC, Hb, Lns, Sw, TH, TRT]. Wild bees produced their honey in hollow trees or rocky recesses in the wilderness [Hb].
2. It is uncertain whether this refers to honey produced by wild bees or to the sweet sap of certain trees [CGTC, ICC, Tay].

1:7 And he-was-proclaiming,[a] saying, "The-one more-powerful[b] than-I is-coming[c] after me,

LEXICON—a. imperf. act. indic. of κηρύσσω (LN 33.256) (BAGD 2.b.β. p. 431): 'to proclaim' [BAGD], 'to preach' [BAGD, LN]. The phrase 'he was proclaiming, saying' is translated 'he proclaimed' [WBC; NET, NRSV, REB], 'he proclaimed this message' [AB2], 'this was the message he proclaimed' [BNTC], 'in his proclamation, he said' [AB1], 'he heralded, saying' [Lns], 'he announced' [GW; similarly NLT], 'he announced to the people' [TEV], 'he was preaching, saying' [BECNT, NTC], 'he was preaching, and saying' [NASB], 'he preached, saying' [ESV, KJV], 'this is what John preached to the people' [NCV], 'John told the people' [CEV], 'this was his message' [NIV]. This verb means to publicly announce religious truths and principles while urging acceptance and compliance [LN]. 'Proclaiming' best fits the text since what follows is a specific announcement [ICC]. The imperfect tense indicates that such preaching was John's habitual activity [EGT, ICC, TH, TRT]. This word also occurs at 1:4.

b. ἰσχυρός (LN 87.44) (BAGD 1.a. p. 383): 'powerful' [BAGD, LN], 'strong, mighty' [BAGD], 'great' [LN]. The phrase 'the one more-powerful than I' is translated 'the one who is more powerful than I' [NRSV; similarly CEV, GW, NET, NIV], 'one more powerful than I am' [NET; similarly CEV, NIV], 'the one stronger than I/me' [AB2, BECNT, Lns], 'one/he who is mightier than I' [BNTC, NTC; ESV], 'one mightier than I am' [REB; similarly KJV, NASB], 'the one greater than I' [WBC], 'someone who is greater than I am' [NLT; similarly AB1; NCV], 'the man who is much greater than I am' [TEV]. This adjective refers to the high status of a person [LN]. This adjective is used to describe the physical strength or the mental and spiritual power of human beings [BAGD].

c. pres. mid./pass. (deponent = act.) indic. of ἔρχομαι (LN 15.81) (BAGD I.1.a.η. p. 311): 'to come' [BAGD, LN], 'to come before the public, to appear, to make an appearance' [BAGD]. The phrase ἔρχεται ὀπίσω μου 'is coming after me' [AB1, AB2, BECNT, Lns; NCV, NET, NRSV] is also translated 'comes after me' [WBC; GW; similarly ESV, KJV], 'who will come after me' [TEV], 'after me comes' [BNTC, NTC; ESV, REB; similarly NASB], 'after me will come' [NIV], 'is going to come' [CEV], 'is coming soon' [NLT]. This verb means to move toward or up to a reference point [LN]. It is a futuristic present tense [BECNT; CEV, NIV, TEV]. The present tense often has a future meaning, but here there is an emphasis on an immediate coming [TH].

QUESTION—In what way was the coming one more powerful than John?

The use of the article in the phrase '*the* one more powerful' indicates that the coming one is superior to John in some way [Hb, NIGTC, NTC]. The coming one was outstanding, distinctive, and unique [Hb]. The coming one was greater than John [AB1, Lns, WBC; NCV, NLT, TEV]. He had greater authority than John [TH], greater majesty [NTC], greater dignity [Gnd, NICNT]. John baptized with water, but Jesus is mightier because he will baptize with the Holy Spirit (1:8) [Hb, ICC, NTC]. Jesus was stronger than John because he could perform exorcisms and other miracles [AB2]. The following chapters will illustrate how Jesus manifested his superior power in his ministry [BNTC, Gnd].

QUESTION—What is meant by the one coming ὀπίσω 'after' John?

This indicates a temporal sequence [BECNT, Gnd, Lns, WBC]. John was born before Jesus was born, and John began his public ministry before Jesus began his ministry [NTC]. The phrase 'coming after me' has a sense of immediacy [AB1, Hb, Lns, NCBC, Tay, TH]. The Messiah's approach was imminent [CGTC].

of-whose-(strap) I-am- not -worthy[a] bending-down[b] to-untie the strap of- the sandals[c] of-him.

LEXICON—a. ἱκανός (LN 75.2) (BAGD 2. p. 374): 'worthy, fit, appropriate, competent' [BAGD], 'qualified' [BAGD, LN], 'adequate' [LN]. The phrase 'I am not worthy' [BECNT, BNTC, WBC; ESV, GW, KJV, NET, NIV, NRSV, REB] is also translated 'I am not even worthy' [NLT], 'I am not worthy so much as to' [AB2], 'I am not fit' [Lns, NTC; NASB], 'I am not good enough even to' [CEV, NCV, TEV]. This adjective describes someone as being adequate for doing something [LN].
  b. aorist act. participle of κύπτω (LN **17.29**) (BAGD p. 458): 'to bend down' [BAGD, **LN**, NTC; GW, NET, TEV], 'to kneel down' [NCV], 'to stoop' [Lns], 'to stoop down' [AB2, BECNT, BNTC, LN; CEV, ESV, KJV, NASB, NIV, NRSV, REB], 'to stoop down like a slave' [NLT], 'to bow' [WBC]. This verb means to bend over into a stooping position [LN].
  c. ὑπόδημα (LN **6.182**) (BAGD p. 844.): 'sandal' [AB2, BAGD, BECNT, BNTC, **LN**, Lns, NTC, WBC; all versions except KJV], 'shoe' [LN; KJV]. This noun denotes any type of footwear, but usually refers to a sandal rather than a shoe [LN]. This denotes a sandal that consists of a leather sole fastened to the foot by means of a leather strap [BAGD].

QUESTION—Who is the referent of the pronominal adjective οὗ 'of whose' strap?

This refers to the sandal straps of the one who is mightier than John [CGTC, Lns, NTC, Tay, TH]. The relative οὗ 'of whose' and the final pronoun αὐτοῦ 'of him' are both in the genitive case, and both refer to 'the strap of the sandals' [TH], so αὐτοῦ 'of him' is redundant [CGTC]. This type of construction is probably influenced by Hebrew grammar [CGTC, Tay, TH], but it is not necessary to use both words to say 'the strap of *his* sandals' in English [TH].

QUESTION—What is meant by John's statement that he was not worthy to untie the strap of the coming one's sandal?

This is a metaphor that emphasizes the contrast between John and the coming one [NTC]. It refers to a slave-master relationship, and one of the most menial tasks required of a slave was to untie and remove his master's dusty sandals [BNTC, Lns, NCBC, NIGTC, WBC], and then take the sandals away to clean them [Lns, NTC]. This was considered an extremely demeaning task [BECNT]. Even Hebrew slaves were exempt from such a lowly task [BECNT, CBC, CGTC, NICNT, WBC]. This indicates that John did not feel himself to be worthy enough to perform even the most menial service of a slave of such a mighty one [Hb, NTC]. John regards himself as less than a slave compared to that coming one [CBC, TRT].

QUESTION—What is the function of adding the detail about 'stooping down' when talking about untying the sandal strap?

Instead of being a superfluous addition, this highlights the menial character of the act of untying someone's sandals [AB2, Hb, ICC].

1:8 **I baptized/baptize you with/by-water[a] but he will-baptize you with/by (the) Holy[b] Spirit.[c]"**

TEXT—Manuscripts reading ὕδατι '(with) water' are given an A rating by GNT to indicate it was regarded to be certain. A variant reading is ἐν ὕδατι 'in water' and it is followed by KJV. Another variant reading transposes the clause ἐγὼ ἐβάπτισα ὑμᾶς ἐν ὕδατι 'I have baptized you in water' to follow λέγων 'saying' in 1:7.

LEXICON—a. ὕδωρ (LN 2.7) (BAGD 1. p. 833): 'water' [BAGD, LN]. The word ὕδατι 'water' in the dative case and the phrase ἐν πνεύματι ἁγίῳ 'with/by the Holy Spirit' are translated 'with water…with the Holy Spirit' [AB1, BECNT, Lns, NTC, WBC; all versions], 'with water…in the Holy Spirit' [AB2], 'in water…in the Holy Spirit' [BNTC].

b. ἅγιος (LN 88.24): 'holy' [LN], 'Holy' [all translations], 'pure, divine' [LN]. This adjective describes someone as being holy in the sense of having superior moral qualities and having certain essentially divine qualities in contrast to what is human [LN].

c. πνεῦμα (LN 12.18). 'Spirit' [LN; all translations]. The noun 'spirit' denotes a supernatural non-material being, and 'Holy Spirit' is the title for the third person of the Trinity [LN]. A spirit is a living being who has its own personality without having a physical body. It does not imply that the spirit was once someone who had died [TRT].

QUESTION—What is indicated by the use of the aorist tense of the verb in ἐγὼ ἐβάπτισα ὑμᾶς 'I baptized/baptize you'?

1. The aorist tense indicates that John was speaking to people whom he had just baptized [Hb, NIGTC]: *I baptized you*.
2. The aorist tense indicates that John considered his ministry to be fulfilled in the light of the coming ministry of the Messiah [BECNT, BNTC, Sw]: *I baptized you*. John's ministry was part of the age of the old covenant, but the Coming One was bringing in the kingdom of God with the gift of the Spirit [BECNT].
3. This refers to an act still going on [AB1, CGTC, Tay, TH, WBC; CEV, NCV, NET, NIV, NLT, TEV]: *I baptize you*. This is a gnomic aorist that focuses on the action without specifying the time when it happens, so in English this is best translated with the present tense 'I baptize' [TH]. It reflects the Semitic perfect tense that has a present meaning [CGTC, Tay, WBC].

QUESTION—What is being contrasted by the conjunction δέ 'but'?

The personal pronouns ἐγώ 'I' beginning the first clause, and αὐτός 'he', beginning the second clause emphasize the contrast between John and the Coming One [BECNT, CGTC, EBC, Gnd, Hb, Lns, Tay, TH, WBC]: *I, on my part, baptized you with water, but he, on his part, will baptize you with the Holy Spirit.* The emphatic contrast between the two men focuses on the kinds of baptism each administered [EBC, Hb, Lns, NIGTC, NTC, Tay, WBC]. It implies that the physical outward water baptism is a preliminary rite of less significance than the spiritual and internal Spirit baptism [EBC, NIGTC].

QUESTION—What relationship is indicated by the use of the dative case for the noun ὕδατι 'water' which is contrasted with the prepositional phrase ἐν πνεύματι ἁγίῳ 'with/by the Holy Spirit'?

1. The use of the dative case and the preposition indicate the different elements used to perform baptism [AB1, BECNT, EBC, Gnd, ICC, Lns, NIGTC, NTC, PNTC, Sw, TH, WBC]: *I baptize by means of water, but he will baptize by means of the Holy Spirit*. This indicates the means by which the baptism is performed, but it is ambiguous as to whether or not the water baptism was by immersion [PNTC]. This relationship could be considered as either instrumental or manner [Sw].

2. The dative case and the preposition are locative and focus on the element into which the baptized person is placed [BNTC]: *I baptize in water, but he will baptize in the Holy Spirit.*

3. The dative case and the preposition mean 'in connection with'. The liquid 'water' and the person 'Holy Spirit' cannot be used in the same sense of means or element. Since both must have the same relationship in the comparison, the broader relationship 'in connection with' should be used [Lns].

QUESTION—What is meant by 'he will baptize you *with/in* the Holy Spirit'?

While a literal baptism *with water* is a natural connection, it is not easy to use a comparison in which the Spirit is like water used for baptism. So perhaps the wider idea of being *overwhelmed* by the Spirit could be used without picturing a literal immersion *into* the Holy Spirit [NICNT]. Water cleanses a person outwardly, but the Holy Spirit cleanses a person inwardly [ICC]. It is through the ministry and death of Jesus that people would be cleansed from sin by the Holy Spirit [WBC]. This refers to the bestowal of the gift of the Holy Spirit that all Christians would receive at the start of the new age promised by the prophets [BECNT, WBC]. It will be the fulfillment of the prophesy about the pouring out of the Spirit promised in the OT at Isaiah 44:3 [BNTC, ESVfn], and also Isaiah 32:15; Ezek. 11:18–19; Joel 2:28 [ESVfn]. Jesus will cause the Spirit *to come upon* his disciples with power (Acts 1:8), *to be poured out on* them (Acts 2:17, 33,) and *to fall on* them (Acts 10:44, 11:15) [Hb, NTC]. In a special sense this happened on the day of Pentecost at the beginning of this new age [EBC, Hb, NTC].

DISCOURSE UNIT—1:9–15 [CBC]. The topic is the baptism and temptation of Jesus.

DISCOURSE UNIT—1:9–13 [NASB, NCV, NET, NIV, TEV]. The topic is the baptism of Jesus [EBC; NASB], Jesus is baptized [NCV], the baptism and temptation of Jesus [NET, NIV, TEV].

DISCOURSE UNIT—1:9–11 [Hb; CEV, ESV, GW, NLT, NRSV]. The topic is the baptism of Jesus [Hb; CEV, ESV, NLT, NRSV], John baptizes Jesus [GW], the Lord in the wilderness [NICNT].

1:9 And it-happened[a] in those days Jesus came from Nazareth of Galilee and was-baptized in[b] the Jordan by John. 1:10 And immediately[c] coming-up out-of[d] the water

LEXICON—a. aorist mid. (deponent = act.) indic. of γίνομαι (LN 91.5) (BAGD I.3.f. p. 159): 'to happen' [BAGD, LN], 'to take place' [BAGD]. The phrase καὶ ἐγένετο ἐν ἐκείναις ταῖς ἡμέραις 'and it happened in those days' is translated 'now it happened in those days that' [NTC], 'and it came to pass in those days' [AB2, BECNT, Lns; KJV], 'now in those days' [NET], 'in those days' [WBC; ESV, NASB, NRSV], 'one day' [NLT], 'not long afterward' [TEV], 'about that time' [CEV], 'at that time' [GW, NCV, NIV], 'at this time it happened that' [AB1], 'it was at this time that' [BNTC; REB]. This verb functions to mark new information, either concerning participants in an episode or concerning the episode itself. It normally occurs in the formulas ἐγένετο δέ 'there was' or καὶ ἐγένετο 'and it happened that', but it is often left untranslated [LN]. This phrase indicates the progress of a narrative and is usually omitted in translations [BAGD]. It is one of the frequent connecting links in Mark's Gospel [EBC]. It introduces a new unit [BECNT], or a new actor in the story [NIGTC]. The phrase indicates that this episode is distinct and more significant from what was mentioned in the preceding verses [Hb].
b. εἰς (LN 90.6) (BAGD I.d.γ. p. 228): 'in' [BAGD; all translations], 'inside, within' [LN]. This preposition indicates a position defined as being within certain limits [LN].
c. εὐθύς (LN 67.53) (BAGD p. 321): 'immediately' [AB2, BAGD, BECNT, LN, Lns, NTC; ESV, NASB, NCV], 'at once' [BAGD], 'at that moment' [WBC], 'at the moment when' [AB1], 'as soon as' [CEV, TEV], 'right away' [LN], 'straight away' [BNTC; KJV], 'then' [BAGD, LN], 'just as' [NET, NRSV], not explicit [GW, NIV, NLT, REB]. This adverb indicates a point of time immediately subsequent to a previous point of time but the actual interval of time can differ appreciably depending upon the nature of the events and the manner in which the sequence is presented by the writer [LN].
d. ἐκ (LN 84.4): 'out of' [LN]. The phrase ἀναβαίνων ἐκ τοῦ ὕδατος 'coming up out of the water' [KJV, NASB] is also translated 'was coming up out of the water' [AB1, AB2; NCV, NET, NIV; similarly NRSV,

REB], 'came up out of the water' [ESV, NLT, TEV; similarly BNTC, WBC], 'came out of the water' [BECNT; CEV, GW], 'was stepping out of the water' [NTC], 'while going out of the water' [Lns]. This preposition indicates extension from an area or space, usually implying a removal out of a delimited area [LN].

QUESTION—What does 'those days' refer to?

These were the days during the time of John's baptizing ministry [EGT, Hb, ICC, NAC, NTC, Sw, Tay]. They were the days during the ministry of Jesus [BECNT]. The phrase links the following narrative with the preceding one to indicate that Jesus is the fulfillment of the expectation aroused by John [BNTC]. The phrase 'in those days' is a Semitic idiom that indicates a temporal sequence that can be translated 'then' [TH].

QUESTION—How was Jesus connected with the village of Nazareth?

It is implied that Jesus had been residing in Nazareth, a small town in lower Galilee [EGT, Hb, ICC, NLTfn]. It was his hometown [NAC, NCBC]. He had been living in Nazareth with his mother and other members of the household until he had reached the age of thirty [EBC, Lns]. Because Nazareth was a small village of less than five hundred residents, the designation 'Nazareth *of Galilee*' helps the readers know the location of this insignificant village [BECNT, EGT].

QUESTION—Why did Jesus come to be baptized by John?

Jesus regarded his baptism to be the proper way to begin his ministry. It was not because he himself had sins to acknowledge. When he was baptized, he joined himself with sinners as their representative in order to redeem them [CGTC, Hb]. Part of God's plan and purpose for Jesus was the complete identification of Jesus with sinful mankind at the very outset of his ministry [EBC]. Jesus was baptized in the role of a lowly penitent receiving the sign of repentance on behalf of the people of God [NIGTC]. Jesus, the sinless Son of God, chose to put himself by the side of all the sinful people for whom this sacrament was ordained, thus signifying that he was now ready to take upon himself the guilt of all these sinners [Lns]. The baptism of Jesus signified that Jesus was going to take upon himself the guilt of the sins of all those for whom he would die. So after the baptism, John told his disciples, 'Look, the Lamb of God who is taking away the sin of the world' (John 1:29) [NTC].

QUESTION—Do the prepositions in the phrases ἐβαπτίσθη εἰς τὸν Ἰορδάνην 'was baptized εἰς *'into'* the Jordan' and ἀναβαίνων ἐκ τοῦ ὕδατος 'coming up εἰς *'out of'* the water' indicate the mode of baptism?

The prepositions εἰς 'into' and ἐκ 'out of' may point to immersion [ICC]. In Classical Greek, the word εἰς meant 'into'. However, in the Koiné Greek of the NT, the line between εἰς and ἐν 'in' had become blurred [AB2]. In the NT, the preposition εἰς is practically the equivalent of the preposition ἐν 'in' [BAGD, CGTC, Lns, Sw, Tay]. There is no difference between 'baptized ἐν' in verse 5 and 'baptized εἰς' in verse 9 [TH]. Both phrases are translated 'baptized in' [all translations].

1. Jesus was baptized into the Jordan by immersion [Hb, NAC, Sw, WBC]. The statement is literally '*into* the Jordan' and the verb 'baptize' basically means 'to dip' or 'to immerse'. Taken together, they support baptism by immersion [Hb]. The passive verb ἐβαπτίσθη 'was baptized' and the genitive of direct agency ὑπὸ Ἰωάννου '*by* John' imply that Jesus was immersed in the Jordan River by John [WBC]. The use of a permanent river suggests the need for a large quantity of water. The verb βαπτίζω 'baptize' is defined in BAGD as 'dip, immerse, plunge, sink, drench, and overwhelm'. So the prepositions ἐν/εἰς in the phrase 'baptize *in* the Jordan River' and the phrase ἀναβαίνων ἐκ '*coming up out of* the water' suggest immersion. However we do not have any firm evidence about John's method and it remains a matter of debate [NIGTC].
2. The mode of baptism is not indicated. Perhaps Jesus stepped *into* the water so that the water covered his feet and John poured or sprinkled water on his head. However, we have been given no details concerning the mode of baptism [NTC]. Different modes of baptism are seen in early Christian paintings, but none show baptism by immersion. If the mode of baptism had been a vital thing for us to know, the Holy Spirit would have indicated it to us with sufficient clearness, but he has done nothing of the kind [Lns].

QUESTION—What is the function of the word εὐθύς 'immediately' in verse 10?

This word occurs 11 times in the first chapter and 37 times in the whole book of Mark. It usually introduces a new incident or a new phase in an episode [NIGTC]. This word often appears at the beginning of an account where it functions as little more than a conjunction without a strong temporal meaning and can be translated 'and then'. When it occurs in the middle of an account, the temporal reference is more significant [BECNT]. In the Greek Septuagint translation of the OT, καὶ εὐθύς 'and immediately' translates the common Hebrew formula 'and behold' [AB2].

1. 'Immediately' begins the sentence as an introduction to a new phase of the episode [BNTC, NAC, NCBC, NIGTC; probably GW, NIV, NLT, REB which do not translate the word]: *and then coming up out of the water he saw the heavens being opened and the Spirit descending.* The frequent use of 'immediately' suggests that the ministry of Jesus had a steady forward movement toward the cross [NCBC]. It is used to heighten the dramatic tension [NAC].
2. 'Immediately' functions as an adverb modifying the verb εἶδεν 'he saw'. It is translated or explained to indicate that it clearly has a temporal meaning [AB2, CBC, CGTC, EGT, Gnd, Hb, Lns, NICNT, NTC, WBC; CEV, NCV, NET, NRSV, TEV]: *and immediately/at once/as soon/just as he was coming up out of the water, he saw the heavens being opened and the Spirit descending.* He immediately saw the following vision and heard the words from heaven [Gnd]. Some translations reposition the word 'immediately' so that it follows the participial phrase 'coming up out of

the water' and directly connects it with 'he saw' [AB2; ESV]: *and coming up out of the water, immediately he saw* the heavens being opened and the Spirit descending. The very moment Jesus started to step out of the water, he saw the heavens suddenly opened wide and the Spirit descending on him [NTC].

QUESTION—What is meant by ἀναβαίνων ἐκ τοῦ ὕδατος 'coming up out of the water'?

Jesus was coming up *from beneath* the water [NAC]. Jesus was coming up *out of the river* he had entered to be baptized [Sw] and was just starting to step out of the water [NTC]. The baptism had been completed and Jesus was walking out of the water onto the riverbank [Lns].

he-saw the heavens[a] being-split-open[b] and the Spirit as[c] a-dove descending to/on/into[d] him.

TEXT—Manuscripts reading εἰς αὐτόν 'towards/on/into him' are followed by GNT, which does not mention any variant reading. A variant reading is ἐπ' αὐτόν 'upon him' and it is followed by KJV.

LEXICON—a. οὐρανός (LN 1.5, 1.11) (BAGD 2.a. p. 594): 'heaven' [BAGD, LN (1.11)], 'sky' [LN (1.5)]. The plural form τοὺς οὐρανοὺς 'the heavens' [AB2, BECNT, BNTC, Lns, NTC, WBC; ESV, KJV, NASB, NET, NLT, NRSV, REB] is also translated 'heaven' [AB1; GW, NCV, NIV, TEV], 'the sky' [CEV]. This noun denotes the supernatural dwelling place of God and other heavenly beings, and there seems to be no semantic distinction in NT literature between the singular and plural forms of the word [LN (1.11)], or it denotes the space above the earth, which includes the sun, moon, and stars in a vault arching high over the earth from horizon to horizon [LN (1.5)]. It is the dwelling place of God [BAGD]. Both the plural and singular forms of the noun refer to 'heaven' where God lives, or the 'sky' where the sun, moon, and stars are located [TRT]. The same plural noun is used to indicate the location of God's voice in the next verse.

b. pres. pass. participle of σχίζω (LN **19.27**) (BAGD 1.b. p. 797): 'to be split' [BAGD, **LN**], 'to be torn' [LN], 'to be torn apart, to be divided, to be separated' [BAGD]. The phrase σχιζομένους τοὺς οὐρανοὺς 'the heavens being split open' is translated 'the heavens split open' [NTC], 'the heavens splitting apart' [NET, NLT], 'heaven split open' [GW], 'the heaven split' [WBC], 'the heavens/heaven being torn part' [AB1, BECNT; ESV; similarly NRSV], 'the heavens being ripped apart' [AB2], 'the heavens being rent asunder' [Lns], 'heaven being torn open' [NIV], 'the heavens breaking/break open' [BNTC; REB], 'heaven opening' [TEV], 'heaven open' [NCV], 'the heavens opening' [NASB], 'the heavens opened' [KJV], 'the sky split open' [**LN**], '(he saw) the sky open' [CEV]. This verb means to split or to tear an object into at least two parts, and the adverb 'suddenly' may provide some of the implications of the splitting involved in this verb [LN]. This present participle indicates that this action was in progress [ICC, TH].

c. ὡς (LN 64.12): 'as, like' [LN]. The phrase τὸ πνεῦμα ὡς περιστερὰν καταβαῖνον εἰς αὐτόν 'the Spirit as/like a dove descending to/on/into him' is translated 'the Spirit like a dove descending to him' [AB1], 'the Spirit like a dove coming down to him' [WBC], 'the Spirit coming down to him as a dove' [GW], 'the Spirit as a dove coming down on him' [Lns], 'the Spirit like a dove descending on/upon him' [NTC; KJV, NASB], 'the Spirit descending on him like a dove' [ESV, NET, NIV; similarly NRSV], 'the Spirit coming down on him like a dove' [BNTC; TEV], 'the Holy Spirit descending on him like a dove' [NLT], 'the Spirit, like a dove, descending upon him' [AB2, BECNT], 'the Spirit descend on him, like a dove' [REB], 'the Holy Spirit coming down to him like a dove' [CEV], 'the Holy Spirit came down on him like a dove' [NCV]. This conjunction indicates a relationship between events or states [LN].

d. εἰς (LN 83.43, 84.16, 84.22) (BAGD 1. p. 228): 'to' [AB1, BAGD, LN (84.16), WBC; CEV, ESV, GW], 'toward' [BAGD, LN (84.16)], 'in the direction of' [LN (84.16)], 'on' [BNTC, LN (83.47), Lns, NTC; ESV, NCV, NET, NLT, NRSV, REB, TEV], 'upon' [AB2, BECNT; KJV, NASB], 'into' [BAGD, LN (84.22)]. This preposition indicates an extension toward a special goal [LN (84.16)], or a position on the surface of an area [LN (83.43)], or an extension toward a goal that is inside an area [LN (84.22)].

QUESTION—Did Jesus see a physical event or a vision?

1. Jesus saw something physically coming toward him [Hb, Lns, NTC, Tay]. What Jesus saw was visible, and John could also see it [Hb]. Jesus saw something resembling a dove descending directly toward him, and this was also seen by John and others [NTC].
2. Jesus saw a vision in his mind [AB1, CGTC, Gnd, ICC, NAC, NCBC, NIGTC, Sw, WBC]. 'Seeing' in relation to heaven often indicates a visionary experience [WBC]. The text tells only what Jesus saw and thus supports the visionary character of the seeing [Gnd]. The bystanders apparently did not see any visible phenomenon [AB1, CBC]. Since this was a vision, the true identity of Jesus was concealed from any people that were there [AB1, CBC, NAC]. The vision was primarily for Jesus. In John 1:32, John the Baptist says that he saw the Spirit descending from heaven like a dove, so John was permitted to share the vision with Jesus [Sw].

QUESTION—What is meant by the heavens σχιζομένους 'being split open'?

The passive voice 'being split open' indicates that God made an opening in the sky [Hb, TRT] to signal a new era of communication between heaven and earth [Hb]. The use of the verb σχιζομένους 'being split' here and in 15:38, where the curtain in the temple was split in two from top to bottom, signifies that these are eschatological events, not a means for the Spirit to descend from heaven [BECNT]. This signified a cosmic event and echoes

Isaiah 64:1, 'Oh that you would rend the heavens and come down' [EBC]. Only God could perform such an act of power as splitting the heavens [Gnd]. The heavens were split open to enable the Spirit to descend like a dove [WBC]. We are not told what the splitting of the heavens looked like, but the Spirit came down out of that opening [Lns]. The words τοὺς οὐρανούς 'the heavens' can mean either the place where God abides or the sky. In either case, God's voice came from heaven [TH].

QUESTION—What is meant by the Spirit descending εἰς 'to/on/into' Jesus?

1. The Spirit descended *to* Jesus [AB1, Tay, WBC; CEV, ESV, GW]: *the Spirit descended from heaven to where Jesus was*. Although Matthew and Luke have ἐπ' αὐτόν 'upon him', Mark has εἰς αὐτόν 'to him'. It is more difficult to account for Mark's wording and therefore it is more likely to be the original reading [AB1, Tay]. It also has the strongest manuscript attestation [Tay]. Mark's report of the Spirit coming *to* Jesus does not speak of any endowment of the Spirit given to Jesus [AB1, Tay]. Jesus is not constrained by an internal impulse but by an external power [Tay].

2. The Spirit descended *upon* Jesus [AB2, BECNT, BNTC, CGTC, Gnd, Lns, NIGTC, NTC, TRT; all versions except CEV, ESV, GW]: *the Spirit descended from heaven and landed upon Jesus*. The general usage of the preposition εἰς 'into' is not decisive in this verse because of the apparent absurdity of an imagery of Jesus seeing a bird descending 'into' himself, so it is best to take the preposition in its wider sense as being roughly equivalent to ἐπί 'upon' [NIGTC]. In Koiné Greek, εἰς plus an accusative object can be equivalent to ἐπί 'upon' that object [AB2]. Jesus saw something resembling a dove descending lower and lower and coming directly toward him. John and probably the others who were there saw the dove settle on the head of Christ [NTC]. The dove could have landed on his head or on his shoulder [TRT].

3. The Spirit descended *into* Jesus [BAGD, EGT, Hb, PNTC, TH]: *the Spirit descended from heaven and entered into Jesus*. This meaning is supported by BAGD at καταβαίνω (1.b. p. 408) where the phrase καταβαῖνον εἰς in this verse is translated 'come down and enter into him' [BAGD]. If Mark had intended to say that the Spirit descended *upon* Jesus, he would have used the preposition ἐπί 'upon' as the parallel passages in Matt. 3:10 and Luke 3:22 have it. Instead of coming *upon* Jesus as in the manner the Spirit of God came 'upon' OT leaders, the Spirit descended to enter into Jesus in order to fill and lead him. From that time on, Jesus acted with the authority and power of God [TH]. This does not imply that the Holy Spirit had not already been present in the life of Jesus before his baptism [Hb]. It was at this time the Spirit entered Jesus to empower him for his messianic ministry [Hb, PNTC]. The Spirit entered into Jesus to take up his abode [EGT].

QUESTION—How did the Spirit descend ὡς περιστεράν 'as a dove'?

1. 'As a dove' is an adjectival phrase and describes the Spirit as looking like a dove [AB2, BECNT, CGTC, Gnd, Hb, Lns, NETfn, NIGTC, NTC, Tay,

TH, WBC]: *Jesus saw the Spirit descending in the form of a dove.* Jesus could hardly have seen an invisible Spirit coming down as a dove comes down, so most commentators take the phrase to be adjectival [WBC]. Since Jesus saw the Spirit descending, he must have seen a bodily form descending [AB2, NIGTC, WBC]. Luke certainly refers to a bodily form when he wrote 'and the Spirit descended in bodily form like a dove' (Luke 3:22) [TH]. The Spirit is by nature invisible like the Father, yet in the OT God was able to appear to people whenever he wished [Lns].

2. 'As a dove' is an adverbial phrase and describes the manner in which the Spirit was descending [CBC; probably AB2, BNTC; CEV, ESV, NCV, NET, NIV, NLT, NRSV, TEV which seem to take this as an adverb modifying 'descending']: *Jesus saw the Spirit descending like a dove descends.* It doesn't mean that the Spirit looked like a dove, but that the Spirit approached Jesus as a dove would [CBC].

QUESTION—Is there any symbolism in the mention of a dove?

There was no symbolism connected with a dove during that period of history [NIGTC, WBC]. Probably a dove was selected because it was the most common bird [NIGTC]. The importance of the event is the fact of the Spirit's coming [WBC]. The mention of a descending dove is metaphorical [Tay], but there is no clear clue for interpreting this comparison with a dove [BECNT, Tay]. The appearance of the dove symbolizes purity [NIVfn, NTC], and guilelessness [NIVfn]. The dove appeared because it was the preeminent bird of sacrifice for the Jews [Hb].

1:11 **And a-voice^a came from the heavens, "You are the Son of-me, the beloved,^{b} with you I-was-well-pleased.^{c}"**

TEXT—Manuscripts reading ἐγένετο ἐκ τῶν οὐρανῶν 'came from the heavens' are given a B rating by GNT to indicate it was regarded to be almost certain. Variant readings are ἐκ τῶν οὐρανῶν ἠκούσθη 'was heard from the heavens' and ἐκ τῶν οὐρανῶν 'from the heavens'.

LEXICON—a. φωνή (LN 33.103) (BAGD 2.d. p. 871): 'voice' [BAGD, LN]. The phrase 'a voice came from the heavens' is translated 'a voice came from heaven' [AB1, BNTC, NTC, WBC; ESV, NCV, NET, NIV, NRSV, REB, TEV], 'a voice came out of the heavens' [AB2; NASB, Lns], 'a voice came out of heaven' [BECNT], 'there came a voice from heaven, saying' [KJV], 'a voice from heaven said' [CEV, GW, NLT]. This noun denotes the human voice as an instrument of communication [LN].

b. ἀγαπητός (LN 25.45, 58.53) (BAGD 1. p. 6): 'beloved' [BAGD, LN (25.45)], 'the object of one's affection, one who is loved, dear' [LN (25.45)], 'only beloved' [BAGD], 'only, only dear' [LN (58.53)]. The phrase 'the son of me, the beloved (Son)' is translated 'you are my Son, the beloved one' [WBC], 'you are my Son, the Beloved' [AB1, Lns, NTC; NRSV], 'you are my Son, whom I love' [GW, NCV, NIV], 'you are my beloved son' [AB2, BECNT, BNTC], 'you are my beloved Son' [ESV, KJV, NASB, REB], 'you are my dearly loved Son' [NLT], 'you are my own dear Son' [CEV, TEV], 'you are my one dear Son' [NET]. This adjectival noun denotes one who is loved [LN (25.45)], and the phrase 'the beloved' indicates that this one is particularly loved and cherished as the only one of his class [LN (58.53)]. This adjectival noun denotes one who is beloved, yet the context here strongly suggests the meaning 'only beloved' [BAGD]. The article of this separate phrase 'the beloved one' makes it emphatic [BECNT, Gnd, Hb, NTC].

    c. aorist act. indic. of εὐδοκέω (LN 25.87) (BAGD 2.a. p. 319): 'to be well pleased, to take delight in' [BAGD], 'to be pleased with, to take pleasure in' [LN]. The phrase 'with you I was well pleased' [Lns] is also translated 'in you I am well pleased' [NASB; similarly NTC; KJV], 'with you I am well pleased' [BECNT, BNTC; ESV, NIV, NRSV], 'I am very pleased with you' [WBC; NCV], 'I am pleased with you' [CEV, GW, TEV], 'in you I have taken delight' [AB2], 'in you I take delight' [REB], 'in you I take great delight' [NET], 'you bring me great joy' [NLT], 'on you my favor rests' [AB1]. This verb means to be pleased with someone [LN].

QUESTION—Whose voice was heard from heaven and who heard it?

The voice was God's voice [AB2, BECNT, BNTC, CBC, Gnd, NCBC, NICNT, NIGTC, NTC, TH, WBC]. The Jewish practice of using the word 'heaven' in order to avoid saying the name 'God' indicates that God himself spoke [NAC]. From what the voice from heaven said, it is clear that the speaker was God, the Father [Hb, Lns, NIGTC, NTC]. Here it says that God was speaking to his Son, but the context does not indicate that anyone else heard the words [Hb]. In John 1:34, John the Baptist told the people that Jesus was the Son of God, which implies that John also heard this declaration from heaven [Hb, Lns].

QUESTION—What is meant by the statement, 'You are my Son'?

The present tense indicates the eternal and essential relationship that Jesus has with the Father [BECNT, BNTC, CGTC, Hb, NICNT, NIGTC, NTC, Tay]. The present tense of σὺ εἶ 'you are' states an abiding reality, and it does not mean 'you have become my Son' as though God was establishing a new relationship [BECNT, CGTC, Hb, NICNT, NIGTC]. 'Son' is used in the highest sense of the unique relationship Jesus had with God, the Father [BNTC, NICNT]. Jesus is the second person of the Godhead [Lns] who fully shares the divine essence [NTC]. Some connect these words with the OT use of the title 'son' [AB2, CBC, ICC, NAC, NCBC, PNTC, TH]. It reflects the statement in Psalm 2:7, 'you are my son, today I have begotten you' [AB2, NAC, NIGTC, PNTC, TH], which refers to the coronation of a king of Israel [NAC, NCBC]. The voice from heaven addressed Jesus in terms that echo the role of receiving the conquering Messiah, but this does not suggest an adoption ceremony in which Jesus became God's Son at that time. The voice declared what Jesus is, not what he has become [NCBC, NIGTC]. Jesus was the true King of the new people of God's people, the new Israel, later called the church [NAC].

QUESTION—What is meant by the phrase ὁ ἀγαπητός 'the beloved'?
Since the phrase 'the beloved' stands separate, there is equal emphasis on the two statements that Jesus is the Son of God and that he is the beloved Son [Hb, NTC]. The phrase 'the beloved' suggests the uniqueness of Jesus' being the only one of this class [AB1, BAGD, BNTC, CBC, Hb, NIGTC, Sw, WBC; NET]. The word carries some of the theological weight of μονογενής 'only' [CBC, TH], and contrasts the only Son of God with people such as the prophets who may think of God as 'Father' in a lesser sense [NIGTC]. The grammar allows for two interpretations [TH]: 'the beloved' may modify 'the Son' and be translated 'my beloved Son' (So AB2, BECNT, BNTC; CEV, ESV, KJV, GW, NASB, NCV, NET, NIV, NLT, REB, TEV), or it may stand alone as a title, 'my Son, the Beloved' (So AB1, Lns, NTC; NRSV). This does not imply that there is another son who is not beloved [TRT].

QUESTION—What is the significance of the aorist tense of the verb εὐδόκησα 'I *was* well pleased'?
1. This is a timeless aorist that is best translated with the present tense [AB1, AB2, BECNT, CGTC, Gnd, Hb, NTC, Tay, TH; all versions]: *I am well pleased*. This verb indicates that the Father has always been pleased with the Son and still was [Hb].
2. The aorist tense indicates the historical process by which God came to take pleasure in Jesus during his earthly life, 'I have come to take pleasure in you'. This is in accord with Luke 2:59 where it says that Jesus grew in favor 'with God and man' [ICC, Sw]. This also includes the Father's satisfaction with the Son during his preexistent life [Sw].
3. This is the simple historical aorist that refers to God's *past pleasure in choosing* Jesus for the performance of a particular function in history [EBC, Lns, NICNT]: *I was well pleased to choose you*. When applied in reference to persons, the verb εὐδοκέω is equivalent to the verbs ἐκλέγομαι 'to select or choose' and αἱρετίζω 'to choose' and means 'to select or choose for oneself'. This refers back to the time in heaven when God chose his Son for the work of redemption and the Son accepted that work. Now the Son stood there at the Jordan ready to begin this work and the Father is announcing his pleasure in having made that prior choice [Lns]. This implies that the Father was pleased to choose the Son in the past to perform the task upon which he is about to enter [NICNT].

DISCOURSE UNIT—1:12–13 [NICNT; CEV, ESV, GW, NLT]. The topic is Jesus and Satan [CEV], the temptation in the wilderness [NICNT], the temptation of Jesus [EBC; ESV, NLT], the temptation by Satan [Hb], Satan tempts Jesus [GW].

1:12 And immediately[a] the Spirit leads/drives- him -out[b] into the wilderness.[c]

LEXICON—a. εὐθύς (LN 67.53) (BAGD p. 321): 'immediately' [AB1, AB2, BAGD, BECNT, LN, Lns, NTC, WBC; ESV, KJV, NASB, NET, NRSV], 'at once' [BAGD; GW, NIV, REB, TEV], 'right away' [LN; CEV],

'straight away' [BNTC], 'then' [BAGD, LN; NCV, NLT]. This adverb indicates a point of time immediately subsequent to a previous point of time but the actual interval of time can differ appreciably depending upon the nature of the events and the manner in which the sequence is presented by the writer [LN]. This word also occurs at 1:10.
- b. pres. act. indic. of ἐκβάλλω (LN 15.44, **15.174**) (BAGD 2. p. 237): 'to lead out, to send out' [BAGD, LN (15.44)], 'to drive out, to send away' [LN (15.174)]. The phrase 'the Spirit leads him out' is translated 'the Spirit led him out' [**LN**], 'the Spirit brought him' [GW], 'the Spirit sent him out' [NTC; NIV], 'the Spirit sent Jesus' [NCV], 'the Spirit made him go' [TEV], 'God's Spirit made Jesus go' [CEV], 'the Spirit drove him' [AB1; NET; similarly WBC; KJV], 'the Spirit drove him out' [BNTC; ESV, NRSV, REB], 'the Spirit drives him' [BECNT], 'the Spirit drives him forth' [Lns], 'the Spirit compelled Jesus to go' [NLT], 'the Spirit impelled him to go out' [NASB], 'the Spirit cast him out' [AB2]. This verb means to lead or bring out of a structure or area [LN (15.174)], or to cause to go out, often implying the use of force [LN (15.44)]. In this verse the verb ἐκβάλλω 'to drive out' is used without the connotation of force and means 'to lead out' [BAGD].
- c. ἔρημος (LN 1.86) (BAGD 2. p. 309): 'wilderness' [AB2, BAGD, BECNT, BNTC, LN, WBC; ESV, KJV, NASB, NET, NLT, NRSV, REB], 'desert' [AB1, BAGD, LN; CEV, GW, NCV, NIV, TEV], 'lonely place' [BAGD, LN]. This adjectival noun denotes a largely uninhabited region, usually a place with little vegetation [LN]. This word also occurs at 1:3, 4.

QUESTION—What is the function of the word εὐθύς 'immediately'?

The function of 'immediately' cannot be known for certain because of Mark's excessive use of this adverb, but it is reasonable to assume that this closely follows what happened in the preceding verse [CGTC, NTC]. 'And immediately' indicates a new scene, but since the action is initiated by the same Spirit who had just come upon Jesus, it is clear that the two events are closely tied together [NIGTC]. The Spirit had just come upon Jesus at his baptism and at once the Spirit leads Jesus to the wilderness [EBC, Hb, NICNT, PNTC]. At once Jesus is thrust into the fray to pursue the ministry to which he is ordained and for which he is endowed [PNTC].

QUESTION—What is the significance of the present tense of the verb ἐκβάλλε 'leads out'?

This is the first occurrence of the historic present tense in this book [AB1, BECNT, EGT, Hb, Tay, TH]. It is a characteristic feature of Mark's style [BECNT, Hb, Tay], and occurs 159 times in this book [NIGTC]. Mark uses the present tense to indicate transitions in the story [AB2, EGT]. It depicts the action as taking place before the reader's eyes [Hb]. The sense of this historic present tense is that of past tense [AB1, AB2, BNTC, NTC, WBC; all versions except KJV].

QUESTION—What is meant by the Spirit 'leading out' Jesus into the wilderness?
1. This verb often means 'to drive out', but here it does not have that connotation of force [BAGD] and so the verb is translated 'to lead out' [LN], 'to send out' [NTC; NCV, NIV], 'to bring out' [GW].
2. Mark uses this verb eleven times in relation to the expulsion of demons, and in the context of the vigorous word 'immediately', it appears to mean something stronger than 'sent out', perhaps 'forced out' or 'drove out' [EBC]. This verb is translated 'to drive out' [AB1, BECNT, Lns, WBC; ESV, KJV, NET, NRSV, REB], 'to compel' [NASB, NLT], 'to make (him) go' [CEV, TEV], 'to cast out' [AB2]. This is a strong verb that literally means to 'throw out, to force out', and it includes the idea of compulsion. Mark uses the verb in 1:34 and 39 to tell about Jesus casting out demons, but here the verb means that the Holy Spirit *impelled* Jesus to go out into the wilderness by filling him with an inner urge to go [NTC]. Some translate this strong verb as 'drove' and take it to mean that the Spirit took control of Jesus [WBC] and compelled him to go into the wilderness [ICC, WBC]. The force involved was a strong urge [Lns], a strong impulse [Hb], a psychological compulsion [EGT, TH]. This does not mean that Jesus was forced out into the wilderness against his will [EGT, Hb, Lns, NAC, NTC, Sw, TH] and it is not surprising that this same event in Matt. 4:1 and Luke 4:1 uses the verb ἀνήχθη 'led' [BECNT]. This verb emphasizes the seriousness of the coming conflict that will occur in the wilderness [NIGTC].

QUESTION—Where was the ἔρημος 'wilderness'?
The location of this part of the wilderness is not known [Hb, NIGTC]. John and Jesus were already in a wilderness [BECNT]. Probably it was the same wilderness where John appeared in 1:4 [NAC, WBC]. Leaving the general area of the wilderness where the baptism took place, Jesus went to a more isolated part where there were wild beasts [ICC, TRT]. But since Jesus was now *entering* the wilderness, it probably was a different wilderness than the one in which the Jordan River was located [BNTC, Lns]. A wilderness was especially associated with evil powers [CGTC, NCBC, Tay].

1:13 **And he-was in the wilderness forty days being-tempted/tested**[a] **by Satan,**

LEXICON—a. pres. pass. participle of πειράζω (LN 27.46, **88.308**) (BAGD 2.d. p. 640): 'to be tempted' [BAGD, LN (88.308)], 'to be tested, to be examined, to be put to the test' [LN (27.46)]. The participial phrase 'being tempted/tested by Satan' is translated 'being tempted by Satan' [BECNT, BNTC, Lns, NTC; ESV, NASB, NIV, TEV], 'tempted by Satan' [WBC; NCV, NRSV, REB], 'tempted of Satan' [KJV], 'enduring temptations from Satan' [NET], 'Satan tried to make him sin' [**LN**], 'where he was tempted by Satan' [AB1; GW, NLT], 'being tested by Satan' [AB2] 'while Satan tested him' [CEV]. This verb means to try to get someone to sin [LN (88.308)], or to try to learn the nature or character of someone by submitting him to a thorough and extensive testing [LN (27.46)]. This word occurs at 1:13; 8:11;10:2; 12:15.

QUESTION—Does the verb πειραζόμενος mean that Jesus was 'tempted' or 'tested' by Satan?

1. The verb means that Satan tried to *tempt* Jesus to sin [AB1, BECNT, BNTC, CBC, CGTC, Hb, ICC, Lns, NICNT, NTC, TRT, WBC]. The verb can mean 'tested' as God tested Abraham (Heb. 10:127), but since this is an action of Satan, it means that Satan tried hard to entice Jesus to sin [BNTC, Lns, NTC]. The Holy Spirit led Jesus into the wilderness to test him, not to try to get him to sin. It was Satan who tried to tempt Jesus to sin [TRT]. The Spirit thrust Jesus into the wilderness to be confronted with Satan and Satan's temptations [NICNT]. His battle with Satan in the wilderness is the key to understanding the authority Jesus had over evil spirits. Jesus is the stronger one who has confronted the prince of demons and is able to plunder his house (3:22–27) [BNTC].

2. The verb means that Satan *tested* Jesus [AB2, NAC, NCBC, NIGTC; CEV]. This was a trial of strength [NCBC]. The verb should be taken in the positive light of testing since this was initiated by the Holy Spirit even though the immediate agent was Satan [NIGTC].

QUESTION—What is the significance of the present passive participle form of the verb πειραζόμενος 'being tempted/tested', and how long did it last?

The present tense indicates that Jesus was tempted during the entire period of forty days [CBC, EGT, ESVfn, Gnd, Hb, ICC, Lns, My, NCBC, Sw, TH, WBC]: *Jesus was being tempted by Satan during those forty days.* Jesus was tempted during the entire period, and the three temptations described in Matt. 4:2 and Luke 4:3 came at the end of that period [Hb, ICC, Lns] when he was exhausted and weak [Hb]. The continual temptations during those days caused Jesus to forget about food, but it is not necessary to assume that Jesus did not sleep during that period [Lns]. The fact that Satan continued to tempt Jesus through the whole forty days implies that Satan failed in every attempt [CBC]. Satan did not cease from tempting Jesus throughout his ministry, but it was this particular confrontation with Satan in the wilderness that is emphasized [NICNT]. Jesus' entire ministry was one continuous encounter with Satan [EBC].

and he-was among[a] the wild-beasts,[b] and the angels were-ministering[c] to-him.

LEXICON—a. μετά (LN 83.9) (BAGD A.1. p. 508): 'among' [AB1, BAGD, BNTC, LN, NTC; NLT, REB], 'with' [AB2, BECNT, LN, Lns, WBC; all versions except NLT, REB, TEV]. The clause 'and he was among the wild beasts' is translated 'wild animals were there also' [TEV]. This preposition indicates a position within an area determined by other objects and located among these objects [LN].

b. θηρίον (LN **4.3**) (BAGD 1.a.β. p. 361): 'wild beast' [AB1, BECNT, BNTC, NTC; KJV, NASB, NRSV, REB], 'wild animal' [AB2, **LN**, Lns, WBC; CEV, ESV, GW, NCV, NET, NIV, NLT, TEV], 'animal' [LN]. This noun denotes any living creature other than a human being [LN]. It refers to animals that have four legs [BAGD].

c. imperf. act. indic. of διακονέω (LN 35.37) (BAGD 2. p. 184): 'to minister to' [BECNT, Lns; ESV, KJV, NASB], 'to take care of' [LN; CEV, GW, NLT], 'to wait on' [WBC; NRSV], 'to attend' [NIV], 'to render service to' [NTC], 'to serve' [BAGD]. The clause 'and the angels were ministering to him' is translated 'and angels were ministering to his needs' [NET], 'and angels attended to his needs' [REB], 'and angels looked after him' [BNTC], 'but angels came and helped him' [AB1; TEV], 'and the angels came and took care of him' [NCV]. This verb means to take care of someone by rendering humble service [LN].

QUESTION—Why are the wild beasts mentioned, and what kind of beasts were they?

The wild animals are mentioned to indicate the character of the wilderness [BECNT, EGT, ICC, NICNT, NLTfn] and accentuate its wildness [CGTC, Gnd, TH]. The presence of wild beasts indicates that Jesus was far from human habitation [EGT, Hb]. It implies his utter loneliness [Hb, NTC] and peril [NTC]. The wild beasts could be hyenas [NTC, TH], jackals [ICC, NLTfn, NTC, TH], wolves [NLTfn], leopards [ICC, NLTfn, TRT], bears [ICC, NLTfn], wild boars [ICC], panthers [NTC], lions [NTC, TRT], foxes and gazelles [TH]. The presence of the wild beasts adds an element of terror to the location [Hb], as these ferocious animals prowled about and endangered Jesus [Lns]. These animals were dangerous and hostile [BECNT, BNTC, CBC, Hb, ICC, Lns, My, NAC, NICNT, NIGTC, PNTC, TH]. This mention of wild beasts heightens the fierceness of Jesus' entire temptation experience [EBC]. There are a few who think that being μετά 'among' the wild beasts means that Jesus was peacefully living among the wild animals [AB1, WBC] as though paradise had been restored [AB1].

QUESTION—When did the angels minister to Jesus, and what did they do?

1. The angels were ministering to Jesus throughout the forty days [CBC, Gnd, Hb, ICC, My, NCBC, NICNT, PNTC, Sw, TH, WBC]. The imperfect tense indicates that the angels ministered to Jesus on repeated occasions during the entire time [CBC, Hb, TH]. The angels might have protected Jesus from the wild animals [ICC, My, NIGTC, NIVfn]. They might have ministered to him by giving him spiritual assurances of God's presence [Hb, Sw]. They cared for his physical needs [Sw, TH], especially by providing food [TH].

2. The angels were ministering to Jesus at the end of the forty days [BECNT, CGTC, Lns, NTC, Tay]. We learn from Matthew 4:11 that when the devil left, the angels came and ministered to Jesus, probably as a reward because of his obedience [NTC]. Jesus fasted throughout the forty days, but after the temptation by Satan God sent his angels to provide for the

Son's needs, including bodily nourishment [NTC]. The angels came to serve food to Jesus [BECNT, Lns].

DISCOURSE UNIT—1:14–13:37 [Hb]. The topic is the ministry of the Servant.

DISCOURSE UNIT—1:14–8:21 [NIGTC]. The topic is act one: Galilee.

DISCOURSE UNIT—1:14–5:43 [NLT]. The topic is the question, 'Who is this Jesus?'

DISCOURSE UNIT—1:14–3:35 [REB]. The topic is proclaiming the kingdom.

DISCOURSE UNIT—1:14–3:34 [Hb]. The topic is the ministry in Galilee.

DISCOURSE UNIT—1:14–3:6 [EBC, NICNT]. The topic is the initial phase of the Galilean ministry [NICNT], the early Galilean ministry [EBC].

DISCOURSE UNIT—1:14–45 [PNTC]. The topic is the beginnings of the Galilean ministry.

DISCOURSE UNIT—1:14–28 [NASB]. The topic is Jesus preaching in Galilee.

DISCOURSE UNIT—1:14–20 [EBC; GW, NCV, NET, NIV, NLT, TEV]. The topic is the introduction to Jesus' ministry [NLT], preaching in Galilee and the call of the disciples [NET], the calling of the first disciples [EBC; GW, NIV], Jesus chooses some followers [NCV], Jesus calls four fishermen [TEV].

DISCOURSE UNIT—1:14–15 [Hb, NICNT, NIGTC; CEV, ESV, NASB, NLT]. The topic is the introduction: the entrance into Galilee [NICNT], Jesus begins his work [CEV], Jesus begins his ministry [ESV], the beginning of the Galilean ministry [NASB], the essential message of Jesus [NIGTC], a summary of Jesus' message [NLT], the summary of the preaching [Hb].

1:14 Now[a] after John was-handed-over[b] Jesus came to Galilee proclaiming[c] the gospel[d] of-God,

TEXT—Manuscripts reading εὐαγγέλιον 'gospel' are given an A rating by GNT to indicate it was regarded to be certain. A variant reading is εὐαγγέλιον τῆς βασιλείας 'gospel of the kingdom' and it is followed by KJV.

LEXICON—a. δέ (LN 89.87, 89.93) (BAGD p. 171): This conjunction can mark a sequence of closely related events ('and, and then') [LN (89.87)], or an additive relation that is not coordinate ('and, and also, also, in addition, even') [LN (89.93)]. It can emphasize a contrast ('but'), mark a simple transition ('now, then'), or mark a resumption of an interrupted discourse ('and also, but also') [BAGD]. Here it is translated 'now' [BECNT, Lns, NTC; ESV, KJV, NASB, NET, NRSV], 'later on' [NLT], 'but' [AB2], not explicit [AB1, BNTC, WBC; CEV, GW, NCV, NIV, REB, TEV].

b. aorist pass. infin. of παραδίδωμι (LN 37.111) (BAGD 1.b. p. 614): 'to be handed over' [AB2, BAGD, LN, WBC], 'to be delivered up' [Lns], 'to be turned over to' [BAGD, LN], 'to be arrested' [AB1, BECNT; CEV, ESV, NLT, NRSV, REB], 'to be taken into custody' [NTC; NASB], 'to be imprisoned' [NET], 'to be put in prison' [GW, KJV, NCV, NIV, TEV]. This verb means to deliver a person into the control of someone else and it is used in reference to handing over a presumably guilty person to the authorities for punishment [LN]. The verb means 'to be delivered over', and it was used by the police and law courts as a technical term for delivering up a prisoner [BECNT].

c. pres. act. participle of κηρύσσω (LN 33.256) (BAGD 2.b.β. p. 431): 'to proclaim' [AB2, BAGD, BNTC; ESV, NET, NIV, NRSV, REB], 'to preach' [BAGD, BECNT, LN, NTC, WBC; KJV, NASB, NCV, NLT], 'to herald' [AB1, Lns], 'to tell' [CEV, GW]. This verb means to publicly announce religious truths and principles while urging acceptance and compliance [LN]. This word also occurs at 1:4, 7, 38.

d. εὐαγγέλιον (LN 33.217) (BAGD 1.a. p. 318): 'gospel' [LN], 'good news' [BAGD, LN]. The phrase 'the gospel of God' [Lns; ESV, NASB, NET, REB] is also translated 'the good news of God' [AB2; GW, NIV, NRSV], 'the gospel from God' [BECNT, NTC, WBC], 'the Good News from God' [BNTC; NCV, TEV], 'the good news that comes from God' [CEV], 'God's Good News' [NLT], 'the Proclamation of God' [AB1]. This noun denotes the content of the good news [LN]. This word also occurs at 1:1.

QUESTION—What relationship is indicated by δέ 'now'?

The phrase 'now after' indicates a discontinuity with the preceding verses [AB2, BECNT, Gnd]. It marks a shift from the wilderness setting to Galilee [Gnd]. It indicates a turning point in the story [BECNT, Tay].

QUESTION—What is the purpose for beginning this new discourse unit with the subordinate clause 'after John was handed over'?

This subordinate clause is a surprise since nothing has been said to indicate that John the Baptist was going to be arrested [NIGTC]. Mark is showing that the forerunner of Jesus had completed his task and it was only then that Jesus began his Galilean ministry [EBC]. Probably John's arrest was already known to the readers [Hb, ICC], but the details of his arrest, charge, and execution are not given in this book until 6:17–20 [Hb]. John the Baptist was arrested about one and a half years after Jesus had been tempted in the wilderness [TRT]. According to John 3:22–30, the ministries of John and Jesus overlapped [BNTC], and according to John 4:1–3, John the Baptist's imprisonment had something to do with Christ's departure from Judea to go to Galilee [NTC]. Mark tells nothing about any previous work by Jesus in Galilee and Judea because it simply lies outside Mark's subject matter [Sw]. Jesus did not begin his own distinctive ministry until John was removed from the scene, so John's arrest is mentioned to indicate that the time for Jesus to act had come [BNTC, EBC, NICNT].

QUESTION—Who handed over John in the statement παραδοθῆναι Ἰωάννην 'John was handed over'?
1. The expression 'handed over' is legal terminology for delivering up a prisoner without focusing on the human person who does this [AB1, Gnd, Hb, NIGTC, NTC, TH, TRT; CEV, ESV, NLT, NRSV, REB]: *John was arrested.*
2. The passive voice of παραδοθῆναι 'was handed over' is a divine passive, indicating that God handed over John [BECNT, BNTC, NAC, NCBC, PNTC, Tay, WBC]: *God delivered up John.* This passive verb could refer to the human activity involved in John's arrest by Herod's agents, but in the Psalms the divine passive of this same action refers to God delivering his servants up to suffering and death. God's action may be intended here since the following announcement 'the time has been fulfilled' (1:15) refers to the fulfillment of God's plan [AB2]. This emphasizes God's control of the event [BECNT]. The perfect tense indicates that the event has come to pass with lasting significance, and the passive voice indicates that God was at work in bringing it to pass [WBC].

QUESTION—What was Jesus' reason for going to Galilee?
In verse 9 Jesus came from his home in the land of Galilee to be baptized by John in the Jordan River, so now he naturally returns home [Gnd, WBC]. Galilee was the northernmost of the Israel's three provinces, Judea, Samaria, and Galilee [Hb].

QUESTION—How are the nouns connected in the genitive construction 'the gospel of God'?
1. The 'gospel of God' means the gospel *that comes from* God [AB1, BECNT, BNTC, CBC, CGTC, EGT, ICC, Lns, NAC, NCBC, NICNT, PNTC, Sw, Tay, TH, WBC; CEV, NCV, TEV]. God the Father is the author and sender of the gospel [ICC, Sw]. Mark starts out in 1:1 with the genitive construction 'the gospel *of* Jesus Christ', meaning the good news *about* Jesus Christ, so probably God has a different connection with the gospel in the genitive construction 'the gospel *of* God' and here it means 'the good news *that comes from* God' [PNTC]. Jesus was proclaiming God's message of good news [CGTC] about God's kingdom [CBC, ICC] being close at hand [NCBC].
2. This means the gospel *about* God [ESVfn, NICNT, NTC]. The next verse is about the kingdom of God and his decisive action in sending forth his Son at this moment in history [NICNT]. The gospel was about God's free gift of salvation to mankind [NTC]. It was the good news that God's rule over people's hearts and lives was now being established and that people should repent and believe the gospel [ESVfn].

1:15 **and saying, "The time has-been-fulfilled[a] and the kingdom of God has-approached.[b] Repent[c] and believe[d] in the gospel."**

LEXICON—a. perf. pass. indic. of πληρόω (LN 59.33) (BAGD 2. p. 671): 'to be made complete' [LN], 'to be completed, to have reached its end'

[BAGD]. The phrase πεπλήρωται ὁ καιρός 'the time has been fulfilled' [AB2] is also translated 'the time is fulfilled' [BECNT, NTC; ESV, KJV, NASB, NET, NRSV], 'the time has arrived' [REB], 'the time has come' [AB1, BNTC; CEV, GW, NIV], 'the right time has come' [NCV, TEV], 'the appointed time has come to pass' [WBC], 'the time promised by God has come at last' [NLT], 'the season has been fulfilled' [Lns]. This verb means to make something total or complete [LN].
  b. perf. act. indic. of ἐγγίζω (LN 67.21) (BAGD 5.b. p. 213): 'to approach, to come near' [BAGD, LN]. The phrase ἤγγικεν ἡ βασιλεία τοῦ θεοῦ 'the kingdom of God has approached' is translated 'the kingdom of God has come' [BECNT], 'the kingdom of God has come near' [Lns; NRSV], 'the Kingdom of God has come in history' [WBC], 'the kingdom of God is at hand' [BNTC, NTC; ESV, KJV, NASB], 'the kingdom of God is near' [GW, NCV, NET, NIV, NLT, TEV], 'the dominion of God has come near' [AB2], 'God's kingdom will soon be here' [CEV], 'the kingdom of God is upon you' [REB], 'God's Reign is upon you' [AB1]. This verb refers to the occurrence of a point of time close to a subsequent point of time [LN].
  c. pres. act. impera. of μετανοέω (LN 41.52) (BAGD p. 512): 'to repent' [BAGD, LN], 'to change one's way' [LN], 'to change one's mind, to feel remorse, to be converted' [BAGD]. The command 'repent' [AB1, AB2, BECNT, BNTC, WBC; ESV, KJV, NASB, NET, NIV, NRSV, REB] is also translated 'be repenting' [Lns], 'repent of your sins' [NLT], 'turn away from your sins' [TEV], 'turn back to God' [CEV], 'change the way you think and act' [GW], 'change your hearts and lives' [NCV], 'be converted' [NTC]. This verb means to change one's way of life due to a complete change of thought and attitude towards sin and righteousness [LN]. This verb occurs at 1:15; 6:12. See this verb at 6:12, and also the noun form μετάνοια 'repentance' at 1:4.
  d. pres. act. impera. of πιστεύω (LN 31.85) (BAGD 1.a.ε. p. 660): 'to believe' [BAGD, LN; all translations], 'to have faith in, to trust' [LN]. This verb means to believe with complete trust and reliance [LN].
QUESTION—What relationship is indicated by the initial conjunction καί 'and'?
  This adds a summary statement of the 'gospel of God' that Jesus was proclaiming [BECNT, EGT, Gnd, Hb, WBC].
QUESTION—What is meant by πεπλήρωται ὁ καιρός 'the time has been fulfilled'?
  '*The* time' refers to a particular point in time appointed by God [BECNT, BNTC, NAC, NICNT, PNTC, Tay, TH, TRT, WBC]. It was the decisive time for God to act. God was now doing something special with the coming of Jesus [EBC]. Through the coming of Jesus God now begins to act in a new and decisive way to bring his promise of redemption to the point of fulfillment [NICNT]. Jesus is inaugurating the final phase of the kingdom of God with this announcement [PNTC].

QUESTION—What is the kingdom of God?

The word βασιλεία 'kingdom' refers to 'kingship' in the sense of the exercise of royal power [TH]. It focuses on the *reign* of a king, not the territory over which a king rules [BECNT]. It means God's kingship [CGTC, NTC], rule [CBC, Gnd, NTC, Tay], reign [NAC, Tay], dominion [AB1], and sovereignty [AB1, NTC, Tay, TH]. Although the primary meaning of 'kingdom' is the actual rule of a king, it necessarily involves the people or realm over which he rules [Hb]. In Mark, the present kingdom of God is a spiritual kingdom rather than the future earthly one. It is God's kingly reign in the hearts of people [NAC].

QUESTION—What is meant by saying that the kingdom of God 'has approached'?

With the appearance of Jesus [BNTC, CGTC, EBC, Hb, NAC, NICNT, Tay] the kingdom of God had drawn near [BNTC, CGTC, Hb, ICC, Lns, NAC, NCBC, NICNT, NTC, Tay]. God's kingdom has drawn near spatially in Jesus' person and also temporally by ushering in the events of the End Times [EBC]. The kingdom was 'at hand' in the region of Galilee because the ministry of Christ was just beginning there [NTC]. God's kingdom dynamically began in Jesus' person and it would be extended as he gained followers [NLTfn]. The kingdom was now so near that the people who were listening to Jesus could enter it at that very moment [Hb, Lns]. God was establishing his rule over the hearts and lives of people and that is why people must repent and believe in order to enter it [ESVfn].

QUESTION—What is meant by the command to repent?

Repentance is contrition and sorrow for sin [Lns]. It demands a decisive change [PNTC]. A person repents by turning from sin and yielding to God [NLTfn]. A person repents when he turns to God in total surrender upon believing the gospel about God's rule [WBC]. People were to be converted to a new way of life by having a radical change of heart and life [BNTC, NTC].

QUESTION—What is meant by believing in the gospel?

This refers to believing Jesus' message that the kingdom of God was at hand [CGTC, ICC]. The Good News for those who listened to Jesus' preaching was that God's reign had arrived through the coming of the Messiah. For those who would later be reading Mark's written account, the gospel would also included the news of Jesus' death, resurrection, ascension, and promised return (15:1–16:8) [NLTfn]. Believing in the gospel is more than an intellectual belief that the good news is true, it includes a response that consists of both an acceptance and a commitment [Hb, NIGTC, NTC].

DISCOURSE UNIT—1:16–8:26 [CBC]. The topic is Jesus' public ministry.

DISCOURSE UNIT—1:16–1:45 [CBC]. The topic is the calling of the disciples and the beginning of miracles.

DISCOURSE UNIT—1:16-20 [CBC, Hb, NICNT, NIGTC; CEV, ESV, NLT, NRSV]. The topic is the formation of the 'Jesus Circle' [NIGTC], the first disciples [CBC; NLT], Jesus calls the first disciples [ESV, NRSV], the call to four fishermen [Hb], Jesus chooses four fishermen [CEV], the call to become fishers of men [NICNT].

1:16 **And going-along[a] beside the Lake[b] of Galilee he-saw Simon and Andrew the brother of Simon casting[c] into the lake, because they-were fishermen.**

LEXICON—a. pres. act. participle of παράγω (LN 15.15) (BAGD 2.a.α. p. 613): 'to go along' [LN, NTC; GW, NASB, NET], 'to move along' [LN], 'to pass along' [Lns; ESV, NRSV], 'to pass by' [AB2, BAGD, LN, WBC], 'to walk by' [AB1, BNTC; KJV, NCV, REB], 'to walk beside' [NIV], 'to walk along (the shore of)' [BECNT; CEV, NLT, TEV]. This verb means to continue moving along [LN]. In the phrase παράγων παρά 'to go along by', the preposition παρά 'beside' is redundant [WBC]. This word also occurs at 2:14.

b. θάλασσα (LN 1.70) (BAGD 2. p. 350): 'lake' [BAGD, LN; CEV, NCV, TEV], 'sea' [AB1, AB2, BECNT, BNTC, LN, Lns, NTC, WBC; all versions except CEV, NCV, TEV]. This noun denotes a particular body of water that is normally rather large and it refers to both seas and lakes. In the NT, the word θάλασσα is used to refer to the Mediterranean Sea, the Red Sea, and the Lake of Galilee. The use of θάλασσα to refer to a lake reflects Semitic usage in which all bodies of water from oceans to pools could be referred to by this one term. Normal Greek usage would use the word λίμνη to refer to lakes and pools [LN]. Mark follows the local practice of calling this fresh water lake a θάλασσα 'sea', but Luke always uses the more precise term λίμνη 'lake' [CGTC, NIGTC, Tay, WBC]. This noun occurs at 1:16; 2:13; 3:7; 4:1, 39, 41; 5:1, 13, 21; 6:47, 48, 49; 7:31; 9:42; 11:23.

c. pres. act. participle of ἀμφιβάλλω (LN **44.8**) (BAGD p. 47): 'to cast' [BAGD], 'to cast a net' [AB1, AB2, BECNT, BNTC, WBC; CEV, ESV, KJV, NASB, NET, NIV, NRSV], 'to cast a fishnet' [**LN**], 'to throw a net' [Lns; GW, NCV, NLT], 'to throw a casting-net' [NTC], 'to work with casting-nets' [REB], 'to catch fish with a net' [TEV]. This verb means to cast a net in order to catch fish. This kind of net would be a circular net with small weights on its edge and small enough to be thrown by one person [LN]. The verb 'cast' is a technical term for throwing out a circular net, and in this verse Jesus saw them casting their nets into the lake [BAGD].

QUESTION—What relationship is indicated by the use of the participle παράγων 'passing by'?

This is a circumstantial participle meaning '*as* he was going along' [BECNT, BNTC; CEV, GW, KJV, NASB, NET, NIV, NLT, NRSV, TEV], '*while* he was going along' [NTC], or '*when* he was going along' [AB1; NCV, REB].

QUESTION—What is the Lake of Galilee and what was Jesus doing there?

The Lake of Galilee is an inland lake about twelve and a half miles long and seven and a half miles wide [Hb]. This lake is located in the Jordan Rift Valley about 700 feet below sea level where it is supplied by the melting snows on Mount Hermon to its north [BECNT]. Jesus made his base in Galilee at the lakeside town of Capernaum where there was a prosperous fishing industry [NIGTC].

QUESTION—Which of the two brothers was the youngest?

In some languages the words for 'brother' differ according to whether the person is an older brother or a younger brother. The general practice of the Jews was to list the name of the older brother first in a list [TH, TRT]. Simon (Peter) is listed first in Matt. 4:18; 10:2; Mark 1:16; 3:18, but Andrew is listed first in John 1:40, 44. It may be that Simon Peter is listed first in this verse because of his importance and not because of his age, so there is no way to be certain about their relative ages [TRT].

QUESTION—Was this the first time Jesus had ever met Simon and Andrew?

This account focuses attention on Jesus' call to these two fishermen and their immediate response, but it is not necessarily implied that Jesus had not previously met these men [WBC]. Although this verse seems to say that these men responded to the call of a complete stranger [NAC, NIGTC], we learn from John 1:35–42 that they had previously met Jesus when they were disciples of John the Baptist [BECNT, ICC, Lns, NIGTC, NTC, Tay]. Perhaps they had been followers of Jesus for some time and had witnessed his miracles in Galilee (John 3:22) and Jerusalem (John 2:13). Then after Jesus returned to Galilee these men had gone back to Capernaum to resume their fishing [Sw].

QUESTION—What and how were they casting into the lake?

Fishermen used a circular casting net that they either threw out from a boat or cast while wading into the lake [BECNT, NIGTC]. Some think they were in their boat [Lns, Sw], probably casting the net first from one side of the boat, then from the other side [Lns]. Others think the fishermen were wading along the shore [BECNT, PNTC]. The circular nets usually had a diameter of ten to fifteen feet, and the outer edge of a net was weighted so that the net would rapidly sink into the water to imprison the fish beneath it [NICNT].

1:17 And Jesus said to-them, "Come after[a] me and I-will-make[b] you to-become fishermen of-men." **1:18** And immediately leaving the nets they-followed[c] him.

LEXICON—a. ὀπίσω (LN **36.35**) (BAGD 2.a.β. p. 575): 'after' [BAGD, LN]. The command δεῦτε ὀπίσω μου 'come after me' [BECNT, BNTC; CEV, KJV] is also translated 'come on after me' [AB2], 'come with me' [AB1; TEV], 'come, follow me' [NTC, WBC; GW, NCV, NIV, NLT, REB], 'follow after me' [**LN**], 'follow me' [ESV, NASB, NET, NRSV], 'this way, after me' [Lns]. Coming 'after' a person means to accept that person as one's leader [LN].

b. fut. act. indic. of ποιέω (LN 13.9) (BAGD I.1.b.θ. p. 681): 'to make, to cause to be' [BAGD, LN], 'to bring it about' [BAGD]. The clause ποιήσω ὑμᾶς γενέσθαι ἁλιεῖς ἀνθρώπων 'I will make you to become fishermen of men' [KJV] is also translated 'I will make you become fishers of men' [AB2, NTC; ESV, NASB; similarly BECNT, Lns], 'I will/shall make you fishers of men' [BNTC; NIV, REB], 'I will make you fish for people' [NCV, NRSV], 'I will turn you into fishers of people' [NET], 'I will make you fishers who catch men' [AB1], 'I will show you how to fish for people' [NLT], 'I will teach you to catch people' [TEV], 'I will teach you how to catch people instead of fish' [GW], 'I will teach you how to bring in people instead of fish' [CEV]. This verb means to cause some state to exist [LN].

c. aorist act. indic. of ἀκολουθέω (LN **36.31**) (BAGD 3. p. 31): 'to follow' [BAGD, **LN**; all translations except CEV, TEV], 'to go with' [CEV, TEV], 'to be a disciple of' [LN]. This verb means to be a follower or a disciple of someone, and it has the sense of adhering to the teachings or instructions of a leader and promoting his cause [LN]. This is a figurative use of 'follow' and means to follow someone as his disciple [BAGD]. They literally followed Jesus as he traveled and they also followed him in the sense of being his disciples [TH].

QUESTION—What is meant by the command 'Come after me'?

The command is literally 'Hither! After me!' and it emphasizes Jesus' leadership [Gnd]. The use of the word ὀπίσω 'after' indicates that Jesus was calling them to become his disciples [BNTC, NICNT] since a disciple is one who breaks all other ties to follow his master as a servant [NICNT]. It was a summons to apprenticeship. It marked Jesus as a prophet who picks his pupils, not a rabbi who would be adopted by his pupils [NCBC, NIGTC].

QUESTION—What is meant by the phrase ἁλιεῖς ἀνθρώπων 'fishers of men'?

This was a fresh metaphor that compared their new work with their former work of catching fish. Jesus was going to teach them to win men for the Kingdom [BNTC], for the gospel and salvation [Lns]. The brothers' daily occupation of fishing may have suggested this metaphor [CGTC, Lns, Tay, WBC]. Expressed as a simile, it says 'you will *catch* men as if you were *catching* fish' [TH]. Some suggestions for providing a common connection between the two sides of the comparison are 'You are *good at* catching fish, but I will teach you to be *good at* bringing people to faith in me' and 'no longer will *your main work* be to catch fish, instead I will teach you how to teach people to become my followers' [TRT]. The goal of a fisher of men is to gain more disciples as he rescues them from judgment [NIGTC]. The translation of this metaphor should not imply that they would learn how to chase people with fishing nets and hooks in order to catch them for Jesus, or that they would arrest or kill people, or that they would round up people to make them slaves [TRT].

QUESTION—What is the function of the word εὐθύς 'immediately'?

Although the phrase 'and immediately' is usually used in Mark as a simple connective without a temporal dimension, here it has its full temporal meaning to indicate an immediate response [BECNT, CGTC, EBC, Gnd, NCBC, Tay]. Probably they dropped their nets right there in the water as they left their occupation to follow Jesus [BECNT]. At Jesus' command, they stopped practicing their trade without bothering to haul in their nets and went with Jesus [BECNT, Gnd]. This does not imply that they abandoned their property. They must have made arrangements about what would happen to their nets and business [Hb]. They probably kept their possessions, since later on their boat was used in Jesus' ministry (3:9; 4:1; 5:31; 6:32, 45; 8:13) [BECNT, NIGTC].

1:19 And having-gone-on[a] a-little he-saw James the (son) of-Zebedee and John the brother of him and they (were) in the boat preparing[b] the nets, **1:20** and immediately he-called[c] them. And leaving their father Zebedee in the boat with the hired-men[d] they-departed[e] after him.

LEXICON—a. aorist act. participle of προβαίνω (LN 15.16) (BAGD 1. p. 702): 'to go on' [BAGD, LN], 'to move on' [LN]. The participial phrase προβὰς ὀλίγον 'having gone on a little' is translated 'going a little further/farther' [BNTC; NCV, REB], 'going on a little farther' [ESV, NASB, NET], 'going on a little way' [AB2], 'as he went a little farther' [NRSV], 'as Jesus went on a little farther' [GW], 'when he had gone a little farther' [AB1, NTC; NIV], 'when he had gone a little farther thence' [KJV], 'proceeding a little further' [WBC], 'after proceeding a little further' [BECNT], 'he went a little farther on' [**LN**; TEV], 'having walked forward a little' [Lns], 'Jesus walked on' [CEV], 'a little farther up the shore' [NLT]. This verb means to continue to move forward [LN].

b. pres. act. participle of καταρτίζω (LN 75.5) (BAGD 1.a. p. 417): 'to make adequate' [LN], 'to restore to its former condition' [BAGD]. The phrase καταρτίζοντας τὰ δίκτυα 'preparing the/their nets' [AB1, AB2, BECNT; NIV] is also translated 'getting their nets ready' [TEV], 'preparing their nets to go fishing' [GW], 'putting their nets in order' [WBC], 'mending the/their nets' [BNTC, NTC; CEV, ESV, KJV, NASB, NCV, NRSV, REB], 'mending nets' [NET], 'repairing the/their nets' [Lns; NLT]. This verb means to make something completely adequate or sufficient for something [LN]. Nets were put into their proper condition by cleaning, mending, and folding them [BAGD].

c. aorist act. indic. of καλέω (LN 33.312) (BAGD 1.e. p. 399): 'to call, to call to a task' [LN], 'to summon' [BAGD]. The phrase 'he called them' [AB2, BECNT, BNTC, Lns, NTC, WBC; all versions except CEV] is also translated 'he summoned them' [AB1], 'Jesus asked them to come with him' [CEV]. 'Called' has the meaning 'summoned' [Gnd]. This was a legal term for a summons before a court but it had developed into a call to discipleship [BAGD]. This verb means to urgently invite someone to

accept responsibilities for a particular task, and implies having a new relationship with the one who does the calling [LN].
- d. μισθωτός (LN 57.174) (BAGD p. 523): 'hired man' [BAGD, BECNT, BNTC, Lns, NTC; GW, NET, NIV, NLT, NRSV, REB, TEV], 'hired person' [LN], 'hired worker' [LN; CEV, NCV], 'hired servant' [ESV, KJV, NASB], 'hired hand' [AB1, AB2, WBC]. This noun denotes a person who has been hired to perform a particular service or work [LN].
- e. aorist act. indic. of ἀπέρχομαι (LN 15.37) (BAGD 4. p. 84): 'to depart, to go away, to leave' [LN], 'to go after, to follow someone' [BAGD], The phrase 'departed after him' is translated 'went after him' [AB2, BNTC; KJV], 'followed after him' [Lns], 'followed him/Jesus' [BECNT, NTC, WBC; ESV, GW, NCV, NET, NIV, NLT, NRSV, REB], 'went to follow him' [AB2], 'went away to follow him' [NASB], 'went with him/Jesus' [CEV, TEV]. This verb means to move away from a reference point with the emphasis upon the departure [LN].

QUESTION—Which of the brothers was the younger brother?

James is listed first, so John probably was the younger brother [AB2, Hb, ICC, Sw, Tay, TH, TRT].

QUESTION—What is the significance of mentioning James' father, Zebedee?

This distinguishes this James from the two other men named James mentioned in this book: James the son of Alpaeus (3:18) and James the Younger (15:40) [AB2, BECNT, WBC]. Zebedee is mentioned here in order to set the scene for leaving him in the boat in the next verse. The fact that they left their father in the boat indicates the powerful impact Jesus had on them [Gnd].

QUESTION—What kind of a boat were they in?

It would have been a regular fishing boat equipped with sails and oars [Hb]. The boat was probably capable of holding from six to twelve people, but it was small enough to be drawn up on the shore by hand [TH].

QUESTION—What was involved in preparing the nets?

They were preparing the nets for their next occasion to go fishing [AB2, BECNT, CGTC, Hb, NTC, TH]. The verb means 'to put in order' [AB2] and this refers to mending and folding the nets [AB2, BAGD, BECNT, CGTC, Hb].

QUESTION—What is the function of the word εὐθύς 'immediately' in respect to Jesus calling them?

1. The temporal emphasis is in view here [BNTC, EBC, Gnd, ICC, TRT; all versions; probably AB1, AB2, NTC]. Jesus called them without any preliminary act on his part [ICC]. Their response was as immediate as that of the first two disciples [BNTC].
2. This word seems to function with little or no chronological significance [BECNT, Tay; probably WBC which does not translate this word]. It probably means no more than 'and so' or 'now' [Tay].

QUESTION—What is the significance of mentioning the hired men?

The mention of the hired men suggests the size and importance of Zebedee's business [EBC, Lns, WBC]. He had a prosperous fishing business [BNTC, Hb]. It may also indicate that their father was not left entirely alone to run his fishing business [EBC].

DISCOURSE UNIT—1:21–45 [NLT]. The topic is Jesus' healing miracles.

DISCOURSE UNIT—1:21–39 [NIGTC]. The topic is preaching and healing: the general impression during a day in Capernaum.

DISCOURSE UNIT—1:21–34 [Hb]. The topic is the ministry in Capernaum.

DISCOURSE UNIT—1:21–28 [CBC, EBC, NICNT; CEV, ESV, GW, NASB, NCV, NET, NIV, NLT, TEV]. The topic is the excitement in the synagogue [Hb], a man with an evil spirit [CEV, TEV], the man with an unclean spirit [NASB], Jesus heals a man with an unclean spirit [ESV], driving out an evil spirit [EBC], Jesus drives out an evil spirit [NIV], Jesus casts out an evil spirit [CBC; NLT], Jesus forces out an evil spirit [NCV], Jesus forces an evil spirit out of a man [GW], Jesus' authority [NET], a new teaching with authority [NICNT].

1:21 And they-enter into Capernaum. And immediately/then^a on-the Sabbath^b entering into the synagogue^c he-was-teaching. **1:22** And they-were-amazed^d at his teaching, because he-was teaching them as having authority^e and not as the scribes.^f

LEXICON—a. εὐθύς (LN **67.53**) (BAGD p. 321): 'immediately' [AB2, BAGD, BECNT, LN, Lns, NTC; NASB], 'right away' [LN], 'straight away' [BNTC; KJV], 'then' [BAGD, LN, WBC; CEV, GW], not explicit [AB1; ESV, NCV, NET, NIV, NLT, NRSV, REB, TEV]. This adverb indicates a point of time immediately subsequent to a previous point of time but the actual interval of time differs appreciably, depending upon the nature of the events and the manner in which the sequence is presented by the writer [LN]. The meaning 'immediately' is weakened to 'then' in Mark 1:21, 23, 29 [BAGD].

b. σάββατον (LN 67.184) (BAGD 1.b.β. p. 739): 'Sabbath' [BAGD, LN], 'Saturday' [LN]. The plural form τοῖς σάββασιν 'on the Sabbaths' is translated as a single Sabbath day: 'on the Sabbath' [AB1, AB2, BECNT, BNTC, Lns, NTC, WBC; ESV, NASB, REB], 'on the Sabbath day' [KJV, NCV], 'when the Sabbath came' [NET, NIV, NRSV], 'when the Sabbath day came' [NLT], 'the next Sabbath' [CEV], 'on the next Sabbath' [TEV], 'on the next day of worship' [GW]. This noun denotes the seventh or last day of the week, the most important religious day of the week since it was consecrated to the worship of God [LN]. The plural form was often used for a single Sabbath day [AB1, AB2, BAGD, NICNT, Tay, TH]. This word occurs at 1:21; 2:23, 24, 27, 28; 3:2, 4; 6:2; 16:1.

c. συναγωγή (LN 7.20) (BAGD 2.a. p. 783): 'synagogue' [AB1, AB2, BAGD, BECNT, BNTC, LN, Lns, NTC, WBC; all versions except CEV],

MARK 1:21–22

'the Jewish meeting place' [CEV]. This noun denotes an assembly building associated with religious activity. It normally refers to a building where Jewish worship took place and the Law was taught [LN]. The synagogue was built as a place for worship on the Sabbath day, but during the week it served as a schoolhouse and even as a courtroom for trying minor cases [Hb]. This word occurs at 1:21, 23, 29, 39; 3:1; 6:2; 12:39, 13:9.

d. imperf. pass. indic. of ἐκπλήσσομαι, ἐκπλήσσω (LN 25.219) (BAGD 2. p. 244): 'to be amazed' [AB2, BAGD; all versions except ESV, KJV, NRSV], 'to be astonished' [BECNT, BNTC, NTC; ESV, KJV], 'to be astounded' [AB1; NRSV], 'to be greatly astounded' [LN], 'to be overwhelmed' [WBC], 'to be dumbfounded' [Lns]. This verb means to be so amazed that one is practically overwhelmed [LN]. The imperfect tense indicates the listeners were overwhelmed with amazement all through Jesus' teaching [Gnd]. This word occurs at 1:22; 6:2; 7:37; 10:26; 11:18.

e. ἐξουσία (LN 37.35) (BAGD 2. p. 278): 'authority' [BAGD, LN], 'capability, might, power' [BAGD]. The phrase ὡς ἐξουσίαν ἔχων 'as having authority' [BECNT] is also translated 'as one having authority' [Lns, WBC; NASB, NRSV], 'as one who had authority' [AB2, BNTC, NTC; ESV, KJV, NET, NIV], 'like a person who had authority' [NCV], 'as an authority in his own right' [AB1], 'with authority' [CEV, GW], 'with certainty' [**LN**], 'he taught with authority' [TEV], 'he taught with a note of authority' [REB], 'he taught with real authority' [NLT]. This noun denotes the right to control or govern over people [LN]. It refers to doing something with ability and power [BAGD].

f. γραμματεύς (LN 53.94): 'a person learned in the Law, an expert in the Law' [LN]. The phrase 'not as the scribes' [BECNT, Lns, NTC, WBC; ESV, KJV, NASB, NRSV] is also translated 'unlike the/their scribes' [AB1, BNTC; GW, REB], 'not as/like their teachers of the law' [NCV, NIV], 'not like the experts in the law' [NET], 'he wasn't like the teachers of the Law' [TEV], 'not like the teachers of the Law of Moses' [CEV], 'not in the way scribes did' [AB2], 'quite unlike the teachers of religious law' [NLT]. This noun denotes a recognized expert in Jewish law [LN]. Originally the noun 'scribe' referred to a copyist of the law, but in NT times the word had taken on the meaning of a biblical scholar who was an interpreter of the law and an expounder of tradition [TH]. The scribes studied, interpreted, and taught people the Old Testament laws and also the traditions that had developed from those laws [TRT]. This word occurs at 1:22; 2:6, 16; 3:22; 7:1, 5; 8:31; 9:11, 14; 10:33; 11:27; 12:28, 32, 38; 14:1, 43, 53; 15:1, 31.

QUESTION—Who entered Capernaum?

The pronoun 'they' refers to Jesus and the four fishermen he had just called to follow him. All five of them entered the city of Capernaum, which was located on the northwest shore of the Lake of Galilee [AB2, EGT, Gnd, Hb, Lns, NICNT, NIGTC]. Translations identify 'they' as 'Jesus and his disciples' [CEV, TEV], 'Jesus and his followers' [NCV], 'Jesus and his companions' [NLT].

QUESTION—What is the function of the adverb εὐθύς 'immediately/then'?

1. It has a temporal meaning [AB2, BAGD, BNTC, EGT, Gnd, Hb, ICC, Lns, My, Sw, TH, TRT; ESV, KJV, NASB]: *immediately*. The word 'immediately' seems to imply that they arrived in the city on the Sabbath day [EGT]. But since all the brothers were working when Jesus called them, the preceding events along the lakeside would not have happened on the Sabbath day. So the Sabbath in this verse must refer to the next Sabbath after they entered Capernaum [BNTC]. Jesus called the fishermen on Friday and on that day they went to the city. Then on Saturday Jesus *promptly* went to the synagogue [Hb, Lns]. Εὐθύς probably refers to what was done on the *immediately following* Sabbath. Accordingly, one may translate this expression 'and on the next Sabbath he went into the synagogue and taught' [BAGD (p. 321)]. Jesus entered the synagogue on the very next Sabbath after they entered Capernaum [Hb, ICC]. It may be translated 'as soon as it was the Sabbath' or 'scarcely was it the Sabbath' [TH]. Others take the word 'immediately' to modify the verb 'he was teaching' instead of 'he entered' [AB2]. This adverb stresses how quickly Jesus took charge [Gnd].
2. It is a simple transitional connective [AB1, BECNT, BNTC, NCBC, NETfn, Tay, WBC; CEV, ESV, GW, NET; probably NCV, NIV, NLT, NRSV, REB, TEV which do not translate this word]: *then*. This is Mark's typical transitional connective that lacks any chronological meaning [WBC]. It is unlikely that Mark meant that Jesus entered the synagogue immediately at sundown or that the minute he entered he began to teach [BECNT]. This adverb has a weakened, inferential use in this verse and is left untranslated because it does not contribute significantly to the flow of the narrative [NETfn].

QUESTION—Why would Jesus be allowed to teach in the synagogue?

Jesus was not an unknown man who just walked into the synagogue and imposed himself on the congregation. The synagogue leaders allowed qualified individuals to read the Scriptures and teach from them [EBC, Hb, ICC, Lns, NIGTC, Tay]. Synagogue worship consisted of prayers, readings from the Law and the Prophets, and then expositions of the readings. Any man who was competent and wished to do so could contribute an exposition at the invitation of the synagogue leader [BNTC]. Since Jesus had to be invited to teach in the synagogue, it is implied that he had already been active in Capernaum long enough to be known and respected [BECNT, NAC, NIGTC, NLTfn]. It was Jesus' custom to attend the synagogue (Luke 4:16) and probably after the prescribed portion of the law had been read Jesus then indicated that he desired to speak. When he was given permission to do so, he explained the portion just read and applied it to the needs of the people who were there [NTC].

QUESTION—Who are included in the pronoun 'they' of the phrase '*they* were amazed at his teaching'?

The third person plural form of the verb is an impersonal plural that was not meant to specify any particular persons [AB2, BECNT, CGTC, Tay]. It refers to all the people who heard Jesus teach [TEV].

QUESTION—What amazed the people about Jesus' teaching?

The noun διδαχῇ 'teaching' could be taken in the active sense of the act of teaching or in the passive sense of the content of what he taught [CGTC, Gnd, Lns, TH].

1. The people were amazed at the manner in which Jesus taught [BECNT, CGTC, EBC, Gnd, ICC, NAC, NCBC, Sw, Tay, TH; TEV]: *they were amazed at the way he taught.* The following clause gives the reason for their amazement. It was because Jesus was teaching them with authority [CGTC, Gnd, ICC, NAC, Tay]. They were amazed at his teaching ministry as a whole, but his manner of teaching with authority is contrasted with the way the scribes taught [BECNT].
2. The people were amazed at the manner in which Jesus taught them and also at the content of what he taught [AB1, Hb, Lns, NICNT, NIGTC]: *they were amazed at what he taught and the way in which he taught it.* The manner of Jesus' teaching that impressed his hearers cannot be separated from his message that has already been summarized in 1:15 [Lns]. People recognized that Jesus himself was something out of the ordinary and found his teaching to be of a surprising and even shocking nature [NIGTC].

QUESTION—How did the scribes teach?

The scribes' authority came from quoting other scribes [ICC, NLTfn]. Their teaching was based upon tradition [ESVfn, NICNT, Tay]. They relied on secondhand authority and supported their views with long and scholarly quotations from the rabbis as they made minute distinctions concerning Levitical regulations and petty legalistic requirements [Hb].

QUESTION—What is meant by Jesus teaching them ὡς ἐξουσίαν ἔχων 'as having authority'?

In contrast with the scribes who appealed to the authority of others, Jesus taught in a manner that showed that he knew he had the authority to say what he did [Gnd, NAC, NLTfn]. He taught with the authority of a prophet of God [CGTC, NICNT]. Jesus taught with his own divine authority [ESVfn]. He had an inner assurance of knowing eternal truths [Hb, Tay].

1:23 And immediately/then[a] there-was in their synagogue a-man with[b] an-unclean[c] spirit and he-shouted[d]

TEXT—Manuscripts reading εὐθύς 'immediately' are followed by GNT, which does not mention any variant reading. Some manuscripts do not include this word and they are followed by KJV.

LEXICON—a. εὐθύς (LN 67.53) (BAGD p. 321): 'immediately' [AB2, BECNT, LN, Lns], 'suddenly' [WBC; CEV, NLT], 'at once' [BAGD], 'right away' [LN], 'just then' [NTC; NASB, NCV, NET, NIV, TEV]. The weakened sense 'then' [BAGD, LN] is translated 'now' [BNTC; REB], 'at that time' [GW], not explicit [AB1]. This adverb refers to a point of time immediately subsequent to a previous point of time [LN]. The meaning 'immediately' is weakened to 'then' in Mark 1:21, 23, 29 [BAGD].

  b. ἐν (LN 13.8) (BAGD 1.5.d. p. 260): 'with, in' [LN], 'under the impulsion of' [BAGD]. The phrase ἄνθρωπος ἐν πνεύματι ἀκαθάρτι 'a man with an unclean spirit' [AB1, BECNT, BNTC, Lns, NTC, WBC; ESV, KJV, NASB, NET, NRSV] is also translated 'a man with an evil spirit' [TEV], 'a man with an evil spirit in him' [CEV], 'a man who had an evil spirit in him' [NCV], 'a man possessed by an unclean spirit' [REB], 'a man who was possessed by an evil spirit' [NIV, NLT], 'a man who was controlled by an evil spirit' [GW], 'a man in an unclean spirit' [AB2]. This preposition refers to being in some state or condition [LN]. It designates a close personal relationship and the phrase 'to be in a spirit' means to be under the special influence of that spirit, even a demonic spirit [BAGD]. The preposition ἐν has the force of the Hebrew b^e 'having' [TH]. The phrase 'with an unclean spirit' also occurs at 5:2.

  c. ἀκάθαρτος (LN 12.39) (BAGD 2. p. 29): 'unclean' [AB1, AB2, BECNT, BNTC, Lns, NTC, WBC; ESV, KJV, NASB, NET, NRSV, REB], 'evil' [CEV, GW, NCV, NIV, NLT, TEV], 'impure, vicious' [BAGD]. The phrase πνεῦμα ἀκάθαρτον 'unclean spirit' refers to an evil supernatural spirit that is ritually unclean and causes persons to be ritually unclean [LN]. As the moral sense becomes predominate, the ceremonial meaning fades, especially in relation to *evil* spirits in 1:23, 26, 27; 3:11, 30; 5:2, 8, 13; 6:7; 7:25; 9:25 [BAGD].

  d. aorist act. indic. of ἀνακράζω (LN 33.83) (BAGD p. 56): 'to shout, to scream' [LN], 'to cry out' [BAGD, LN]. The phrase ἀνέκραξεν λέγων 'he shouted saying' is translated 'he cried out, saying' [AB2, BNTC, NTC; KJV, NASB], 'he yelled out, saying' [Lns], 'he yelled' [WBC; CEV], 'he cried out' [ESV, NET, NIV, NRSV], 'he shouted' [GW, NCV], 'he began shouting' [NLT], 'he screamed' [AB1; TEV], 'he shrieked out' [BNTC], 'he shrieked at him' [REB]. This verb means to shout or cry out [LN]. It is a strong emotional outcry [BNTC, CGTC, Hb, NCBC, Tay]. In modern English translations it is sufficient to translate the verb combination ἀνέκραξεν λέγων 'he shouted saying' as 'he shouted' [TH].

QUESTION—What is meant by the adverbial phrase '*immediately/then* there was in their synagogue'?

  1. The adverb's temporal meaning 'immediately' is in focus [AB2, BECNT, Gnd, ICC, Lns, NTC, Tay, TH, TRT, WBC; CEV, ESV, NASB, NCV, NET, NIV, NLT, NRSV, TEV]: *immediately* there was in their synagogue a man. This adverb indicates a rapid sequence of events [ICC].

    1.1 The adverb modifies the verb ἦν 'there was', but the wording εὐθὺς ἦν 'immediately there was' [AB2, BECNT, Lns, NTC, Tay, WBC; ESV,

NASB, NCV, NET, NRSV] is not meaningful in English unless the verb 'was' is taken to mean 'appeared' [BECNT, TH], 'came into' [TEV], or 'entered' [CEV]. It probably means 'immediately after Jesus had finished teaching' since Jesus had taught enough to bring about the reaction described in verse 22 [AB2]. A demon-possessed man was not normally allowed inside a synagogue, so probably as soon as the demoniac entered the building where Jesus was teaching he began shouting at Jesus [TRT; CEV; probably NASB, NCV, NET, NRSV, TEV].

1.2 Some translations apparently revise the syntax so that the adverb modifies the verb ἀνέκραξεν 'he shouted' [NIV, NLT]: 'just then a man...cried out' [NIV], 'suddenly, a man...began shouting' [NLT].

2. The adverb εὐθύς functions as a mild connective [BAGD, BECNT, BNTC, Hb, NIGTC; GW, REB]: *now/then* there was in their synagogue a man. This introduces a particular event in the general scene that has been set by the previous two verses [NIGTC]. Some translations seem to take this to mean that demoniac was already in the synagogue, and at this point he started shouting [GW, KJV, REB]. This demoniac was not so violent as to be excluded from society, but the unclean spirit felt a tension in the presence of Jesus that forced out a cry of protest [Hb].

QUESTION—Who is the referent of 'their' in the phrase 'their synagogue'?

The pronoun 'their' refers to the people who were amazed at Jesus' teaching in the previous verse [EGT]. These were the regular attendants at the synagogue and it is implied that the man with an unclean spirit was not one of that number [Hb].

QUESTION—What is meant by ἄνθρωπος ἐν πνεύματι ἀκαθάρτῳ 'a man *with* an unclean spirit'?

The primary meaning of the preposition ἐν is 'in', and here it means that the man's personality had been taken over by the demon, and when the man cried out, Jesus rebuked 'him', the unclean spirit [AB2]. The man was moving *in the sphere of* the unclean spirit's power and was under his control [Hb, Sw]. The preposition literally says that the man was 'in connection with' the demon, and this means that he was joined to this spirit [Lns]., Such a connection is explained in Luke 4:33 where it refers to a man ἔχων 'having' a spirit of an unclean demon [Lns, Tay]. The use of ἐν 'in' is a Semitism that means he *had* an unclean sprit [CGTC]. It means the man was *possessed* by an unclean spirit [AB1, AB2, Hb, ICC, NICNT, NIGTC, NTC]. This demon was a separate being who controlled the behavior of the man [NIGTC]. Some think that demon possession has continued through the ages and happens today. Others make a distinction between demon possession and demon influence and think that demon possession was limited to that period of special spiritual manifestations during the days in which the New Testament church was born [NTC].

QUESTION—What is meant by an *'unclean* spirit'?
>The phrase 'unclean spirit' is practically a synonym of 'demon' since the two terms are used interchangeably in 3:22 and 30, and also in 7:25 and 26, 29, 30 [BECNT, BNTC, EGT, Hb, ICC, NAC]. Perhaps the use of 'unclean spirit' in this verse was meant to contrast 'unclean' with the word 'holy' in the next verse where Jesus is called 'the holy one of God' [BNTC].
>>1. The adjective 'unclean' describes the spirit [Hb, Lns; probably CEV, GW, NCV, NIV, NLT, TEV which translate the words 'unclean spirit' as 'evil spirit']: *a spirit who was unclean.* This spirit's nature had become utterly foul [Lns]. 'Unclean' describes the moral nature of the spirit as being impure and foul [Hb].
>>2. The adjective 'unclean' describes the person who is possessed by the spirit [NCBC, TH]: *a spirit that makes its victim unclean.* The adjective 'unclean' does not refer to the appearance or character of the evil spirit. When such a spirit possessed a man, it was the man who became ceremonially unclean [TH].

QUESTION—Who is the subject of the verb ἀνέκραξεν *'he* shouted' and how does this relate to the use of ἡμῖν 'us' in the next verse?
>The subject is the man who appeared in the synagogue [TH]. The spirit spoke through the man [EBC, My, NICNT, NIVfn, NLTfn] by using the man's lips and voice [BNTC, Lns]. Even though the man spoke the words, the wording originated from the one demon who possessed him. So when he said 'us' in the next verse the demon was speaking on behalf of all demons [AB2, BECNT, BNTC, CGTC, EBC, EGT, Gnd, Hb, ICC, Lns, NLTfn, Sw, Tay, WBC]. The demon spoke for all demons because he realized that what was going to happen to him would happen to all of his fellow demons as well [Hb, NIGTC]. Another view is that since there was only one evil spirit speaking through the man, the singular pronoun 'I' refers to the demon while the pronoun 'us' refers to both the demon and the man [TRT].

1:24 saying, "What^a to-us and to-you, Jesus (the) Nazarene^b? Have-you-come to-destroy^c us? I-know you who you-are, the Holy^d (One) of-God."

TEXT—Manuscripts reading Τί ἡμῖν 'What to us' are followed by GNT, which does not mention any variant reading. A variant reading is Ἔα, τί ἡμῖν 'Ah, what to us' and it is followed by KJV, which translates ἔα 'ah' as 'Let us alone'.

LEXICON—a. The expression Τί ἡμῖν καὶ σοί; 'What to us and to you?' is translated 'What do we have to do with you?' [AB2, Lns; KJV], 'What have you to do with us?' [BECNT; ESV, NRSV], 'What do you want with us?' [AB1, BECNT; CEV, GW, NCV, NIV, REB, TEV], 'What business do we have with each other?' [NASB], 'What do we have in common?' [WBC], 'Why are you interfering with us?' [NLT], 'Why do you bother us?' [NTC], 'Leave us alone!' [NET]. It corresponds to a Hebrew idiom, 'Why do you meddle with me?' [TH].

MARK 1:24 63

b. Ναζαρηνός (LN 93.536) (BAGD p. 532): 'Nazarene' [BAGD, LN], 'inhabitant of Nazareth' [BAGD]. The phrase 'Jesus the Nazarene' [AB2, WBC; NET] is also translated 'Jesus of Nazareth' [AB1, BECNT, BNTC, NTC; all versions except CEV, GW, NET], 'Jesus from Nazareth' [CEV, GW], 'Jesus Nazarene' [Lns]. This adjectival noun denotes a person who lives in Nazareth, or is a native of Nazareth [LN].

c. aorist act. infin. of ἀπόλλυμι (LN 20.31) (BAGD 1.a.α. p. 95): 'to destroy' [BAGD, LN; all translations]. This verb means to destroy or to cause the destruction of persons, objects, or institutions [LN]. Here it refers to eternal destruction [BAGD].

d. ἅγιος (LN 88.24) (BAGD 2.c.β. p. 10): 'holy one' [BAGD, LN]. The phrase ὁ ἅγιος τοῦ θεοῦ 'the Holy One of God' [BECNT, BNTC, Lns, NTC, WBC; ESV, GW, KJV, NASB, NET, NIV, NRSV, REB] is also translated 'the holy one of God' [AB2], 'God's Holy One' [AB1; CEV, NCV], 'the Holy One sent from God' [NLT], 'God's holy messenger' [TEV]. This adjectival noun denotes someone who is holy in the sense of having superior moral qualities and possessing certain essentially divine qualities [LN].

QUESTION—What is meant by the question, 'What to us and to you?'

This is equivalent to saying 'Why do you meddle with us?' [Hb, TH], 'Why are you interfering with us?' [CBC], 'You have no business with us yet!' [NICNT], 'Leave us alone!' [Lns], 'Go away and leave us alone!' [NIGTC], 'We have nothing to do with one another!' or 'Why bother us'? [NETfn]. This clause is an exact rendering of a Hebrew expression used in Judges 11:2 and 1 Kings 17.18 where it means 'Why are you interfering with us?' [BNTC, CGTC, Gnd]. The sense of the question is 'What is it that we have in common which gives you the right to interfere with us?' [ICC].

QUESTION—Are the words 'Have you come to destroy us' a question or a statement?

These words may be punctuated as either a question or a statement [Hb] and there is nothing in the grammar or the context to enable us to decide for sure [EBC, TH].

1. The demon was asking a question [AB2, BNTC, GNT, NTC, Sw, WBC; all versions]: *Have you come to destroy us?*
2. The demon was making a statement [EBC, EGT, Lns, NICNT, Tay]: *You have come to destroy us!* This is a defiant assertion [Tay]. The unclean spirit clearly understood the significance of Jesus' presence [NICNT]. The demons recognized the role of judgment included in the ministry of Jesus [EBC]. With this statement of fact, the demon reproached Jesus for what he intended to do [Lns].

QUESTION—Where did the demon think Jesus had come from?

The question was not "Have you *come from Nazareth* to destroy us?" It was, "Did you *come from heaven* into the world to destroy us?" [NTC]. He realized that Jesus had been sent from God [BECNT].

QUESTION—What is meant by 'destroying' the demons?
Destroying the unclean spirits does not mean to annihilate them. It refers to sending them to their ruin in the abyss where they will be tormented [Hb]. Jesus will send the demons to 'their' place [ICC]. This refers to the demons being hurled into the abyss where Satan is kept [NTC].

QUESTION—Who is the subject of the verb οἶδα 'I know' in the statement 'I know who you are'
The subject is the unclean spirit who recognized the divine character of Jesus [NICNT, NTC, WBC]. This is not a confession of belief [NICNT]. Some think this may have been an attempt to use Jesus' name to gain control over him or to make him harmless [AB2, CGTC, EBC, Gnd, NAC, NCBC, NICNT, NIGTC, PNTC]. But there is no indication that the demon tried to gain control over Jesus. Through supernatural insight and understanding the demon stated that he knew Jesus was the Holy One from God [BECNT].

QUESTION—What is meant by the genitive construction 'the Holy One *of* God'?
Some take it to mean 'the Holy One *sent from* God' [NLT], 'God's holy messenger' [TEV]. Another takes it to mean 'the Holy One who *belongs to* God' [TH]. Others understand it to refer to the special relationship Jesus had with God [NAC]. Jesus, the sinless and pure one, was wholly *consecrated to* God [Hb, ICC, NTC, WBC] and was employed in God's service [ICC]. The way in which the demon addressed Jesus indicates that he was aware that he had come up against a superior spiritual power [NIGTC].

1:25 **And Jesus rebuked[a] him saying, "Be-quiet[b] and come-out[c] of him."**

LEXICON—a. aorist act. indic. of ἐπιτιμάω (LN 33.419) (BAGD 1. p. 303): 'to rebuke' [AB2, BAGD, BECNT, LN, Lns, NTC; ESV, KJV, NASB, NET, NRSV, REB], 'to reprove' [BAGD, BNTC, LN], 'to censure' [BAGD], 'to cut short' [NLT], 'to subdue' [WBC], 'to order' [GW, TEV], 'to command' [AB1; NCV], 'to say sternly' [NIV], 'to tell' [CEV]. For the phrase ἐπετίμησεν λέγων 'rebuked saying' many translations omit the participle 'saying' [AB1; all versions except ESV, KJV, NASB]. This verb means to express strong disapproval of someone [LN].

b. aorist pass. impera. of φιμόω (LN 14.86) (BAGD 2. p. 862): 'to be quiet' [LN, NTC; CEV, NASB, NCV, NIV, NLT, TEV], 'to keep quiet' [GW], 'to be silent' [AB1, BAGD, BECNT, BNTC, Lns, WBC; ESV, NET, NRSV, REB], 'to shut up' [AB2], 'to stop making a sound' [LN], 'to hold one's peace' [KJV]. This verb means to cause someone to cease making a sound [LN]. It has the force of telling the demon to 'shut up' [AB2, Gnd, NIGTC, WBC]. Instead of a harsh 'shut up', it is a firm way of demanding silence, somewhat like 'be silent' or 'keep quiet' [TH; GW].

c. aorist act. impera. of ἐξέρχομαι (LN 15.40) (BAGD 1.a.δ. p. 274): 'to come out' [AB1, AB2, BAGD, BECNT, BNTC, Lns, WBC; all versions], 'to get out' [NTC], 'to go out of, to depart out of, to leave from within' [LN]. This verb means to move out of an enclosed or well defined two or three-dimensional area [LN]. When Jesus commanded the unclean spirit to come out of the man, it became clear that the spirit was a real personality distinct from the man himself [Hb].

QUESTION—Whom did Jesus rebuke and what did he rebuke him about?

Jesus rebuked the unclean spirit that possessed the man and controlled what the man said [CGTC, Gnd, Hb, Sw, Tay, TH]. Jesus had come to confront Satan and strip him of his power, but this purpose would have been compromised if the demon's defiant shouting went unrebuked [NICNT]. The spirit was rebuked because he had no authority to proclaim the identity of Jesus, and had no right to have possession of the man [Sw]. This was a command to desist from an action being performed, so the meanings 'prohibited', 'stopped', 'sternly commanded' are preferable to 'rebuked' [TH].

QUESTION—Why did Jesus silence the demon?

Jesus did not want to be authenticated by such an undesirable witness [Lns, NIGTC, NTC, Sw]. If Jesus had accepted the demon's testimony, people might think that Jesus was in league with Satan [Hb]. Jesus also wanted to avoid a premature popular adulation [NIGTC]. This command demonstrated Jesus' absolute authority over the demon [NICNT].

1:26 And the unclean spirit having-convulsed[a] him and having-shouted[b] with a-loud voice came-out of him.

LEXICON—a. aorist act. participle of σπαράσσω (LN **23.167**) (BAGD p. 760): 'to convulse' [AB2, BAGD, BECNT, BNTC, Lns, WBC; ESV, NRSV], 'to throw into convulsions' [AB1, LN, NTC; GW, NASB, NET, NLT, REB], 'to throw into a fit' [LN], 'to shake' [CEV], 'to shake hard' [TEV], 'to shake violently' [NCV, NIV], 'to tear' [KJV]. This verb means to cause a person to shake violently with convulsions [LN]. It describes a seizure and convulsion [Hb].

b. aorist act. participle of φωνέω (LN 33.77) (BAGD 1.b. p. 870): 'to shout' [LN], 'to cry out' [BAGD, BECNT, LN, WBC; ESV, NASB, NET], 'to cry' [BNTC, Lns; KJV, NRSV], 'to scream' [NLT], 'to call out, to speak loudly' [BAGD, LN], 'to utter a (loud) cry' [AB2], 'to give a (loud) shout' [AB1, AB2; CEV], 'to give a (loud) scream' [TEV], 'to give a (loud) cry' [NCV, REB], 'to give a (loud) shriek' [NTC; GW; similarly NIV]. This verb means to speak with considerable volume or loudness [LN]. It was a loud inarticulate shout [Gnd].

QUESTION—Why did the unclean spirit convulse the man and cause him to shout with a loud voice?

The demon did this in a burst of rage [Hb, Lns]. This last expression of the demon's malice was a violent protest against a command he had to obey [AB2]. This was a desperate attempt to resist Jesus' command [NIGTC]. Even though the demon had to obey the command, he was able to display his malice [AB2, Sw]. Mark includes this act as a visible and audible demonstration that Jesus' command had exorcised the demon [Gnd].

QUESTION—How are the aorist participles 'having convulsed' and 'having shouted' related to the main verb 'came out (of him)'?
1. Both participles describe the actions of the unclean spirit while he was coming out of the man [TH; probably AB2; ESV, NRSV]: *as the unclean spirit was convulsing the man and shouting with a loud voice, he came out of him.* The actions of both aorist participles are simultaneous with the action of the main verb 'came out' [TH].
2. The first participle describes the unclean spirit's action before he came out of the man and the second participle describes what he did as he was coming out of the man [NICNT, NTC, Tay; GW, NIV, REB; probably AB1]: *the unclean spirit convulsed the man and then was shouting with a loud voice as he came out of him.* The unclean spirit convulsed the man, and with a loud shriek left him [NICNT].
3. Both participles describe the actions of the unclean spirit before he came out the man [BECNT, Lns, WBC; KJV, NCV, NLT; probably ICC, TRT; CEV, NASB, NET, TEV]: *the unclean spirit convulsed the man and shouted with a loud voice, and then came out of him.* 'The evil spirit screamed, threw the man into a convulsion, and then came out of him' [NLT].

1:27 And all were-amazed^a so-as to-discuss^b with each-other saying, "What is this? A-new teaching with authority.^c He- even^d -commands the unclean spirits, and they-obey him."

TEXT—Manuscripts reading Τί ἐστιν τοῦτο; διδαχὴ καινὴ κατ' ἐξουσίαν καί 'What is this? A new teaching according to authority; even' are given a B rating by GNT to indicate it was regarded to be almost certain. A variant reading is Τί ἐστιν τοῦτο; Τίς ἡ διδαχὴ ἡ καινὴ αὕτη ὅτι κατ' ἐξουσίαν καί 'What is this? What (is) this new teaching; because with authority even' and it is followed by KJV. Other manuscript variants read Τί ἐστιν τοῦτο; διδαχὴ καινὴ αὕτη ὅτι κατ' ἐξουσίαν 'What is this? A new teaching (is) this; because according to authority', Τίς ἡ διδαχὴ ἡ καινὴ αὕτη ὅτι κατ' ἐξουσίαν καί 'What is this new teaching; because according to authority even', and Τίς ἡ διδαχὴ ἡ καινὴ αὕτη ἡ ἐξουσιαστικὴ αὐτοῦ καὶ ὅτι 'What (is) this new authoritative teaching of him and that'.

LEXICON—a. aorist pass. indic. of θαμβέομαι, θαμβέω (LN **25.209**) (BAGD 2. p. 350): 'to be amazed' [BAGD, BECNT, BNTC, LN, Lns; all versions except CEV, GW, NLT], 'to be astounded' [AB1, BAGD, WBC], 'to be astonished' [**LN**], 'to be startled' [LN], 'to be stunned' [GW], 'to be completely surprised' [CEV], 'to be gripped with amazement' [NLT], 'to be awestruck' [AB2], 'to be dumbfounded' [NTC]. This verb means to experience astonishment as the result of some unusual event [LN]. This verb is virtually synonymous with ἐκπλήσσομαι 'to be amazed' in 1:22 [Gnd, NIGTC, NTC]. This word occurs at 1:27; 10:24, 23.
b. pres. act. infin. of συζητέω (LN **33.157**) (BAGD 1. p. 775): 'to discuss' [BAGD, BECNT, **LN**; NLT], 'to talk with, to speak with, to converse'

[LN], 'to say' [CEV, GW, TEV], 'to ask' [AB1, AB2, BNTC, NTC; NCV, NET, NIV, NRSV, REB], 'to question' [Lns; ESV, KJV], 'to argue' [WBC], 'to debate' [NASB]. This verb means to converse with someone and implies there is a reciprocal response [LN]. It refers to an intense discussion among those present at the synagogue [NIGTC, WBC]. The questioning was done in a positive sense [BECNT].

c. ἐξουσία (LN 37.35) (BAGD 2. p. 278): 'authority' [BAGD, LN], 'authority to rule, right to control' [LN]. Some connect the phrase κατ' ἐξουσίαν 'with authority' with the preceding phrase 'a new teaching': 'a new teaching with authority' [AB2, BECNT, Lns; ESV, NASB, NET], 'a new teaching—and with authority!' [NIV; similarly NRSV], 'a new kind of teaching, spoken with authority' [BNTC], 'this man is teaching something new, and with authority' [NCV], 'some new kind of powerful teaching' [CEV], 'this is a new teaching that has authority behind it' [GW], 'What sort of new teaching is this? It has such authority!' [NLT]. Others connect the phrase 'with authority' with the following verb 'he commands': 'with authority he commands' [KJV], 'this man has authority to give orders' [TEV]. Some translate the phrase 'with authority' as a separate sentence: 'He speaks with authority.' [AB1; REB]. This noun denotes the right to control or govern over someone [LN].

d. καί (LN 89.93) (BAGD II.2. p. 393): 'even' [AB2, BAGD, BECNT, BNTC, LN, Lns; CEV, ESV], 'also, in addition' [LN], not explicit [AB1, WBC; GW, KJV]. This conjunction indicates an additive relation that is not coordinate [LN]. Here it functions as an ascensive adverb 'even' [BAGD, Lns, NIGTC, TH], and marks the climax of their astonishment [Tay].

QUESTION—What relationship is indicated by the conjunction ὥστε 'so as'?

The conjunction ὥστε 'so as' with the infinitive verb 'to discuss' indicates the result of their being amazed [BECNT, EGT, ICC, Tay, TH].

QUESTION—What is meant by the question 'What is this?'?

This is a rhetorical question that expresses the people's amazement [Gnd, Lns, NICNT]. It sets the stage for the following statements that explain why they were amazed [BECNT, WBC]. 'This' refers to the nature of the event that had just taken place [AB2]. They wanted to know the meaning of what was happening [NCV, NLT]. 'This' refers to both the teaching and the expulsion of the unclean spirit that had taken place in the synagogue [EGT, Hb, Lns, NTC]. The following clause beginning with καί 'even' makes it clear that the most remarkable aspect of Jesus' authority was his authority over demons [NIGTC]. Jesus' style of casting out a demon was strikingly different from what they were familiar with [NIGTC].

QUESTION—What is meant by a καινός 'new' teaching?

It was new in respect to its quality [CGTC, Tay]. Both the contents and the method of teaching were different from anything they had heard at the synagogue before [NTC]. The *newness* of Jesus' teaching with an authoritative manner does not refer to the content of his teaching, but to the overwhelming authoritative manner with which he taught. It surpassed anything the audience had ever experienced before [Gnd].

QUESTION—What is the referent of the phrase κατ' ἐξουσίαν 'with authority'?

This phrase can be joined grammatically with either the preceding noun 'teaching' or the following verb 'he commands' [BECNT, BNTC, TH]. The same authority that Jesus displayed in his teaching was shown by his command to the demon [NICNT].

1. The phrase refers backwards to the new teaching [AB2, BECNT, CGTC, EGT, Gnd, ICC, Lns, My, NICNT, Sw; all versions except KJV, REB]: *a new teaching that has authority behind it*. The fact that 'authority' is connected with teaching in 1:22 supports connecting it with teaching in this verse [BECNT, CGTC, Gnd, ICC, Lns, Sw].
2. The phrase refers forward to the action of commanding unclean spirits [Sw, TH; KJV, TEV]: *with authority he commands the unclean spirits*.
3. The phrase is translated so as to refer both backward and forward [AB1, NTC; REB]: 'A new kind of teaching! He speaks with authority. When he gives orders, even the unclean spirits obey' [REB].

QUESTION—After Jesus had commanded the unclean spirit to be quiet and come out of the man in 1:25, why did people talk about τοῖς πνεύμασι 'the spirits'?

The plural noun 'spirits' generalizes what Jesus does, since the people assumed that if Jesus could cast out one demon, then he could cast out other demons as well [Gnd, Hb, Lns, NICNT, NTC].

1:28 **And the news/fame^a of-him immediately went-out everywhere into all the surrounding-region^b of-Galilee.**

LEXICON—a. ἀκοή (LN 33.213) (BAGD 2.a. p. 31): 'news' [BNTC, LN, NTC; CEV, GW, NASB, NCV, NET, NIV, NLT, TEV], 'report' [AB1, BAGD, LN, Lns], 'information' [LN], 'fame' [AB2, BAGD, BECNT; ESV, KJV, NRSV, REB]. This noun denotes the content of the news that is heard [LN].

b. περίχωρος (LN 1.80) (BAGD p. 653): 'surrounding region' [LN, Lns; ESV, GW, NRSV], 'surrounding district' [NASB], 'the region surrounding' [WBC], 'the region around' [BAGD; KJV, NET], 'the region' [AB2, BNTC, NTC; NIV, NLT], 'the province' [TEV], 'the district' [AB1], 'the area' [NCV], 'the countryside' [BECNT], 'the neighborhood' [BAGD], 'throughout (Galilee)' [REB], 'all over (Galilee)' [CEV]. This adjectival noun denotes an area or region around or near some central or focal point [LN].

QUESTION—Does the phrase ἡ ἀκοὴ αὐτοῦ mean 'the *news* about him' or 'the *fame* of him'?

1. The phrase means the 'news' or 'reports' about him [AB1, BNTC, CGTC, EGT, Gnd, Hb, Lns, NICNT, NTC, PNTC, Tay, TH, TRT]: *the news about him spread everywhere.*

2. The phrase means 'his fame' [AB2, BECNT, EBC, NIGTC, Sw, WBC]: *his fame spread everywhere.*

QUESTION—Where did this news or fame of Jesus spread?
1. It spread throughout all the region of Galilee [AB2, BECNT, BNTC, Gnd, Hb, Lns, NIGTC, NTC, PNTC, TRT; NIV, TEV]: *all the surrounding region, namely, the region of Galilee itself.* The genitive phrase τῆς Γαλιλαίας 'of Galilee' explains what is meant by the reference to 'all the surrounding region' [BECNT, NIGTC].
2. It spread throughout all the part of Galilee that surrounded Capernaum [AB1, EBC, ICC, Tay]: *all the surrounding region in that part of Galilee.* It probably refers to all the parts of Galilee in the neighborhood of Capernaum [Tay].
3. It spread throughout all the areas bordering Galilee [My, WBC; probably KJV]: *all the regions that surround Galilee.*

DISCOURSE UNIT—1:29–45 [CBC; NASB]. The topic is that Jesus' work continues in Capernaum and Galilee [CBC], crowds healed [NASB].

DISCOURSE UNIT—1:29–39 [CEV, NCV]. The topic is that Jesus heals many people.

DISCOURSE UNIT—1:29–34 [ESV, GW, NASB, NET, NIV, NLT, TEV]. The topic is that Jesus heals many people [ESV, NIV, NLT, TEV], Jesus heals many at Simon's house [NASB], healings at Simon's house [NET], Jesus cures Simon's mother-in-law and many others [GW].

DISCOURSE UNIT—1:29–31 [EBC, Hb, NICNT]. The topic is the healing of Peter's mother-in-law.

1:29 **And immediately/then[a] having-gone out of-the synagogue they-went into the house of-Simon and Andrew with James and John.** **1:30** **Now the mother-in-law of-Simon was-lying-down[b] having-a-fever,[c] and immediately they-speak to-him concerning her.**

TEXT—In 1:29, manuscripts reading εὐθὺς ἐκ τῆς συναγωγῆς ἐξελθόντες ἦλθον 'immediately having gone out of the synagogue *they* went' are given a C rating by GNT to indicate that choosing it over a variant text was difficult. A variant reading is εὐθὺς ἐκ τῆς συναγωγῆς ἐξελθὼν ἦλθεν 'immediately having gone out of the synagogue *he* went' and it is followed by Sw, Tay; ESV. Another variant reading is ἐξελθὼν δὲ ἐκ τῆς συναγωγῆς ἦλθεν 'and having gone out of the synagogue he went'.

LEXICON—a. εὐθύς (LN 67.53) (BAGD p. 321): 'immediately' [BAGD, LN], 'right away' [LN], 'at once' [BAGD], 'then' [BAGD, LN], not explicit [NLT]. The phrase 'immediately having gone out...they went into' is translated with the adverb 'immediately' modifying the participle 'having gone': 'immediately they/he left...and entered' [NTC; ESV], 'departing immediately...they left for' [WBC]. Others translate with the adverb 'immediately' modifying the main verb 'they went': 'immediately, having come out of..., they went to' [Lns], 'immediately after they came out..., they came into' [NASB], 'immediately having left..., they entered' [BECNT], 'leaving..., they immediately went into' [AB2], 'as soon as they left..., they went to/entered' [NET, NIV, NRSV; similarly CEV, NCV], 'forthwith, when they were come out of..., they entered into' [KJV], 'after they left..., they went directly to' [GW], 'on leaving..., they went straight to' [REB; similarly AB1], 'left...and went straight to' [TEV; similarly BNTC]. This adverb indicates a point of time immediately subsequent to a previous point of time but the actual interval of time differs appreciably, depending upon the nature of the events and the manner in which the sequence is presented by the writer [LN]. The meaning 'immediately' is weakened to 'then' in Mark 1:21, 23, 29 [BAGD].

b. imperf. mid./pass. (deponent = act.) indic. of κατάκειμαι (LN 17.27) (BAGD 1. p. 411): 'to lie down' [BAGD, LN]. See the following lexical item for translations of this word. This verb means 'to lie down' and often implies that there is some degree of incapacity [LN]. The imperfect tense indicates that this was her state when Jesus arrived [ICC].

c. pres. act. participle of πυρέσσω (LN **23.159**) (BAGD p. 730): 'to have a fever' [LN]. The phrase 'was lying down having a fever' is translated 'was lying down with a fever' [BECNT], 'was lying down because she had a fever' [AB2], 'was lying down, sick with a fever' [NET], 'was lying sick with a fever' [NTC; NASB; similarly BNTC], 'lay ill with a fever' [WBC; ESV], 'lay sick of a fever' [KJV], 'was sick in bed with a fever' [NCV, TEV; similarly CEV], 'was sick in bed with a high fever' [NLT], 'was in bed with a fever' [AB1, **LN**; GW, NIV, NRSV, REB], 'was prostrate, suffering from fever' [Lns]. This verb means to be sick with a fever [LN].

QUESTION—What is the function of the adverb εὐθύς 'immediately/then'?
1. The temporal connection 'immediately' is in focus [CGTC, Hb, ICC, Lns, NTC, Sw, WBC; all versions except NLT]. On the Sabbath day it was customary to eat the main meal right after the synagogue service [TRT] and probably Simon's house was not far from the synagogue [AB2, EBC, NICNT]. As soon as the congregation had broken up (1:26), Jesus went to Simon's house (1:29) [CGTC, Hb, ICC, Lns, NTC, Sw, WBC]. The intervening verses 1:27–28 are to be considered parenthetical [Sw].
2. Here εὐθύς means 'then' or 'and next' to indicate that a new section is beginning [BAGD, TH; probably NLT]. It has the meaning 'and then' or 'next' in this kind of context [TH].

QUESTION—Who are the referents of the verb ἦλθον '*they* went' and who owned the house?

The subjects of this plural verb continue to be Jesus and his disciples Simon, Andrew, James, and John [EGT, ICC]. The house belonged to the two brothers, Simon and Andrew [BECNT, EBC, Hb], and their guests were Jesus along μετά 'with' James and John [TH, TRT]. Simon and Andrew were originally from Bethsaida (John 1:44), but perhaps when they learned that Jesus was establishing his headquarters in Capernaum they moved there to be with him [BECNT, Hb]. Likely Simon's home became Jesus' base of operation in Capernaum [NIGTC].

QUESTION—What is known about Simon's mother-in-law and her illness?

It is likely that her husband had previously died and she had come to live with her daughter who was married to Simon [Hb]. Later Simon Peter's wife would accompany him on his preaching tour (1 Cor. 9:5) [CGTC, Hb, NAC, NIGTC, Sw, Tay]. A fever was considered to be an independent disease in those days [NICNT]. The information that the mother-in-law was lying down indicates the seriousness of the fever [BECNT, Gnd]. Luke 4:38 says that she had a high fever [AB1, Tay].

QUESTION—Who spoke to Jesus concerning the woman, and what did they tell him?

The subjects of the plural verb λέγουσιν 'they speak' were Simon and Andrew, and likely the other two disciples [NTC]. They had waited until they returned to the house, but they told Jesus about her just as soon as they entered the house [Sw]. 'They' could refer to other people in the house [TRT]. It is possible λέγουσιν 'they speak' functions as an impersonal plural and just means 'Jesus was told' [BECNT, Tay, TH]. In that case, probably Simon was the one who told him [Tay]. The statement 'they speak to him concerning her' could have been just a natural imparting of information to a guest, but more likely it was done because they had just seen Jesus' power to heal in the synagogue and now they wanted him to heal this woman [NIGTC]. They must have asked Jesus to use his healing power on her [BECNT, Hb, NTC, Tay].

1:31 **And having-approached, he-raised[a] her taking (her) by-the hand. And the fever left[b] her, and she-was-serving[c] them.**

TEXT—Manuscripts reading ἀφῆκεν αὐτὴν ὁ πυρετόν 'the fever left her' are followed by GNT, which does not mention any variant reading. A variant reading is ἀφῆκεν αὐτὴν ὁ πυρετόν εὐθέως 'immediately the fever left her' and it is followed by WBC; KJV. Although most translations do not follow the Greek text that includes the word 'immediately', it is nevertheless implied [TRT].

LEXICON—a. aorist act. indic. of ἐγείρω (LN 17.10) (BAGD 1.a.β. p. 214): 'to raise, to help to rise' [BAGD], 'to cause to stand up' [LN]. The phrase 'he raised her taking her by the hand' is translated 'he raised her up, taking her by the hand' [NASB], 'he raised her up, having grasped hold of her hand' [Lns], 'he raised her up by gently taking her hand' [NET], 'he took her by the hand and lifted her up' [NTC; ESV, KJV, NRSV], 'he grasped her by the hand and raised her up' [AB2; similarly BECNT, BNTC], 'he took her by the hand and helped her up' [AB1; CEV, TEV; similarly GW, NCV, NIV], 'he took her by the hand, and helped her sit up' [NLT], 'he took hold of her hand, and raised her to her feet' [REB], 'seizing her hand,

he raised her' [WBC]. This verb means to cause someone to stand up, possibly implying that the person had some previous incapacity [LN]. Jesus helped her sit up [TH; NLT], or stand up [LN, TRT; REB].
b. aorist act. indic. of ἀφίημι (LN 15.48) (BAGD 3.a. p. 126): 'to leave' [BAGD, LN; all translations except GW], 'to go away' [GW], 'to depart from' [LN]. This verb refers to a separation caused by moving away from someone [LN].
c. imperf. act. indic. of διακονέω (LN **46.13**) (BAGD 2. p. 184): 'to serve' [BAGD, LN], 'to wait upon' [LN]. The clause 'she was serving them' is translated 'she began to serve them' [BECNT, **LN**, WBC; ESV, NET, NRSV; similarly AB2; NCV], 'she ministered unto them' [KJV], 'she waited on them' [AB1, BNTC; NASB], 'she began to wait on them' [NTC; NIV, TEV], 'she attended to their needs' [REB], 'she went on serving them' [Lns], 'she served them a meal' [CEV], 'she prepared a meal for them' [GW, NLT]. This verb means to serve food and drink to those who are eating [LN]. The imperfect tense indicates the beginning of the action [AB2, BECNT, CGTC, LN, NTC, WBC; ESV, NCV, NET, NIV, NRSV, TEV].

QUESTION—What is meant by saying Jesus 'approached'?

It means Jesus went to the woman [AB1, Lns, NTC, PNTC, Sw; CEV, GW, NASB, NIV, TEV], he went to her bedside [NCV, NLT]. It could mean that Jesus entered the room where the sick woman was [Tay, TH].

QUESTION—Why did Jesus take the woman by the hand?

This physical contact served to established rapport with the suffering woman and make it obvious that the healing was an intentional act by Jesus [Hb]. Another view is that the very touch of Jesus' hand conveyed strength to the sick woman [WBC]. The participial phrase 'taking her by the hand' indicates that the woman was cured as Jesus raised her up [EGT, Sw, Tay].

QUESTION—What is meant by saying 'the fever left her'?

Mark almost personifies the fever by saying that it *left* her [Tay]. It is a natural idiom that simply means she was cured of the fever [NIGTC].

QUESTION—What is the significance of adding that the woman served them?

The fact that the woman was now able to serve them shows that she was fully cured [BECNT, BNTC, CBC, Gnd, ICC, Tay, WBC]. She had regained her strength with no lingering weakness that would ordinarily accompany convalescence [BNTC, Hb, Lns, Sw]. Serving the food was the expected role of a mother-in-law in a household [NIGTC], so the woman immediately resumed her usual duties [Sw]. She served them the evening meal [Lns, NICNT]. Her daughter would have helped her serve this meal [Lns]. The food would have already been prepared on the previous day since Jews were forbidden to cook on the Sabbath day [TRT].

DISCOURSE UNIT—1:32–34 [EBC, Hb, NICNT]. The topic is healing many people [EBC], a healing ministry at sundown [Hb], the sick healed at evening [NICNT].

1:32 And evening having-come, when the sun set,[a] they-were-bringing to him all the (ones) having illness[b] and the (ones) being-demon-possessed.[c]
1:33 And the whole city was gathered-together[d] at the door.

LEXICON—a. aorist act. indic. of δύνω (LN **15.113**) (BAGD p. 209): 'to set, to go down' [BAGD, LN], 'to sink' [LN]. The phrase 'when the sun set' [BECNT; similarly Lns; KJV] is also translated 'when the sun had set' [BNTC; GW], 'after the sun had set' [**LN**; NASB, TEV], 'after the sun went down' [NCV], 'after the sun had gone down' [AB2], 'and the sun set' [WBC], 'at sundown' [ESV, NRSV], 'after sunset' [AB1, NTC; CEV, NET, NIV, NLT, REB]. This verb means to move or sink down, and is used to describe the sun sinking below the horizon [LN].

b. κακῶς (LN 23.148) (BAGD 1. p. 398): 'badly' [BAGD, LN]. The idiom κακῶς ἔχοντας 'having badly' means 'to be ill, to be sick' [BAGD, LN]. The phrase 'the ones having illness' is translated 'the ill' [WBC], 'who were ill' [BECNT, BNTC; NASB, REB], 'who were sick' [AB1, AB2; CEV, ESV, GW, NCV, NET, NRSV; similarly NIV, NLT, TEV], 'that were diseased' [KJV], 'that were afflicted' [NTC]. The phrase κακῶς ἔχω 'to have badly' or 'to fare badly' is an idiom meaning to be in a bad condition, that is, 'to be ill' [LN]. This adverb occurs at 1:32, 34; 2:17; 6:55.

c. pres. mid./pass. (deponent = act.) participle of δαιμονίζομαι (LN 12.41) (BAGD p. 169): 'to be demon-possessed' [LN], 'to be possessed by a demon' [BAGD]. The phrase '(the ones) being demon possessed' is translated 'who were demon-possessed' [AB1; NASB, NET; similarly NTC, WBC; NIV, NLT, NRSV], 'who were possessed by demons' [BNTC; REB; similarly BECNT; GW, KJV], 'those possessed with demons' [Lns], 'who had demons' [TEV], 'who had demons in them' [CEV, NCV], 'who were oppressed by demons' [ESV], 'who were afflicted by demons' [AB2]. This verb means to be possessed by a demon [LN]. This word occurs at 1:32; 5:15, 16, 18.

d. perf. pass. participle of ἐπισυνάγομαι (LN **15.124**) (BAGD p. 301): 'to gather' [BAGD, **LN**]. The phrase 'gathered together at the door' [Lns; ESV, KJV] is also translated 'gathered at the door' [AB1, BECNT, NTC, WBC; NASB, NCV, NIV, NLT, REB], 'gathered around the door' [NRSV; similarly BNTC], 'gathered by the door' [NET], 'gathered at his door' [GW], 'gathered around the door of the house' [CEV], 'gathered in front of the house' [TEV]. This verb means to gather or come together at a particular location [LN]. The perfect tense indicates that the crowd of people who brought the sick soon formed a dense mass as they waited for Jesus to help them [Hb].

QUESTION—What is the function of the phrase 'when the sun set' following the words 'and evening having come'?

'Evening' could mean 'late afternoon' since the Jews divided the 'evening' into two time periods with the first beginning at 3 p.m. [Hb, NTC] and the second at 6 p.m. [NTC]. The addition 'when the sun set' makes the point that the Sabbath day had now ended [AB1, BECNT, EBC, EGT, Hb, ICC, Lns, NICNT, NIGTC, NTC], and the first day of the week had begun [BECNT]. Although the pious Jews had seen Jesus cast out the demon at the synagogue and wanted to bring their sick to Jesus for healing, they had to wait until the Sabbath day had ended [TH]. The Jewish day ended when the sun set, so now that the Sabbath day restrictions had ended, the people were free to bring their sick ones to Jesus [AB2, BNTC, CGTC, ICC, NIGTC, Sw, TH, WBC].

QUESTION—Who were bringing all of the sick and demon-possessed people to Jesus?

The third person plural verb ἔφερον 'they were bringing' is an impersonal plural [AB2, BECNT, TH], or indefinite plural [CGTC, Gnd, Hb, Tay]. It refers to the people of the city [TH]. When it says they were bringing *all* of the suffering people, it is a literary exaggeration called hyperbole [BECNT, NIGTC, WBC]. It means that a great number of ill people were brought from all over the city of Capernaum [Lns].

QUESTION—What is significant about the description of the people who were brought to Jesus?

Throughout his book Mark distinguishes between the people who were suffering from various human afflictions and those who were demon-possessed [BNTC, Hb, ICC, Lns, NICNT, NIGTC]. The phrase 'the ones having illnesses' refers to the people who had different kinds of physical sicknesses and diseases, and the people who were demon-possessed are mentioned separately [NICNT, TH]. This separation is also made in the next verse where it says that Jesus *healed* the people having various diseases and *cast out the demons* of the people who were demon possessed [BECNT, Hb, NIGTC].

QUESTION—Where was the door that the people gathered about?

This refers to the door of the house of Simon and Andrew [BECNT, BNTC, CGTC, EGT, Hb, Lns, NICNT, NTC, Tay, WBC], or perhaps Jesus had his own house in Capernaum by now [My]. The word 'door' focuses on the opening through which people passed in and out of the house, not on the wooden door that closed the doorway. Either Jesus was standing in or near the doorway, or people passed through this doorway to get inside where Jesus was healing people [TH].

QUESTION—Was Capernaum a city or a town, and how could the whole city be gathered at the door?

The word πόλις 'city' is used to refer to both the city of Jerusalem (11:19) and the town of Capernaum. Probably Mark called Capernaum a city because it was the town with the most significant settlement in the area [NIGTC]. Translations refer to Capernaum as a city [AB2, BECNT, Lns, WBC; ESV, GW, KJV, NASB, NRSV] or as a town [AB1, BNTC, NTC; CEV, NCV, NET, NIV, NLT, REB, TEV]. The '*whole* city/town' [all versions except TEV], or '*all* the people of the town' [TEV], is a colloquial exaggeration [EGT] in the form of a hyperbole [BECNT, BNTC, NAC, Tay,

TRT, WBC]. The expression is a figure of speech in which the *city* stands for the inhabitants of the city, and where the *whole* city or *all of the inhabitants* of the city is hyperbole to emphasize the large number of people gathered at the house [TH].

1:34 **And he-healed**[a] **many (people) having illnesses with-various diseases**[b] **and he-cast-out**[c] **many demons**[d]

LEXICON—a. aorist act. indic. of θεραπεύω (LN 23.139) (BAGD 2. p. 359): 'to heal' [AB1, AB2, BAGD, BECNT, BNTC, LN, Lns, NTC, WBC; all versions except GW, NRSV], 'to cure' [LN; GW, NRSV]. This verb means to cause someone to recover his health [LN].

   b. νόσος (LN 23.155) (BAGD 1. p 543): 'disease' [BAGD, LN], 'sickness' [LN], 'illness' [BAGD]. The phrase 'many people having illnesses with various diseases' is translated 'many who were ill/sick with various diseases' [BECNT; ESV, GW, NASB, NET, NLT, NRSV; similarly AB2, WBC], 'many that were ill with many kinds of diseases' [Lns], 'many who were sick with all kinds of diseases' [TEV], 'many who suffered from various diseases' [REB; similarly BNTC], 'many who were afflicted with various diseases' [NTC], 'many who had various diseases' [AB1; NIV], 'many who had different kinds of sicknesses' [NCV], 'many that were sick of divers diseases' [KJV], '(he healed) all kinds of terrible diseases' [CEV]. This noun denotes the condition of being diseased [LN]. The primary meaning of this word is 'disease', but it probably refers to all the things mentioned in this book: fever, leprosy, paralysis, withered hand, flow of blood, deafness, and blindness [BECNT, NIGTC].

   c. aorist act. indic. of ἐκβάλλω (LN **53.102**) (BAGD 1. p. 237): 'to cast out' [AB2, BECNT, **LN**, Lns, NTC, WBC; ESV, KJV, NASB, NLT, NRSV], 'to drive out' [AB1, BAGD, BNTC; NET, NIV, REB, TEV], 'to expel' [BAGD], 'to force out' [CEV, GW], 'to make to go out, to exorcise' [LN], 'to force (many demons) to leave people' [NCV]. This verb means to cause a demon to stop possessing or controlling a person [LN]. '*Cast out* many demons' is an idiom that means Jesus ordered many demons to leave people and they left [TRT]. In reference to 'casting' out demons, this verb occurs at 1:34, 39; 3:15, 22, 23; 6:13; 7:26; 9:18, 28, 38; 16:9, 17.

   d. δαιμόνιον (LN 12.37) (BAGD 2. p. 169): 'demon' [AB1, AB2, BAGD, BECNT, BNTC, LN, Lns, NTC, WBC; all versions except KJV], 'devil' [KJV], 'evil spirit' [BAGD, LN]. This noun denotes an evil supernatural being or spirit [LN]. This word occurs at 1:34, 39; 3:15, 22; 6:13; 7:26, 29, 30; 9:38; 16:9, 17.

QUESTION—What is implied by saying that Jesus healed *many* ill people?

Jesus actually healed *all* of the many sick and demon-possessed people who came to him [AB1, AB2, BECNT, BNTC, CGTC, Hb, Lns, NAC, NICNT, NTC, PNTC, Tay, TRT]. It does not imply that there were some who were not healed due to lack of time or ability [Hb, My]. 'Many' emphasizes the large number of people who came for healing [Lns, NICNT, NIGTC]. The use of 'many' is a Semitic idiom that means 'everyone' was healed [AB1, AB2, CGTC, NAC, TRT]. Matthew 8:16 says that Jesus healed *all* of them [Hb, Lns, NTC, TRT].

QUESTION—What were the δαιμόνια 'demons'?

The demons were intelligent beings distinct from the people they possessed. The demons knew things about Jesus that the people whom they possessed did not know [Hb, Lns]. They used the vocal cords of the people they possessed [ICC, NTC]. No distinction is to be drawn between a demon and the 'unclean spirit' that is mentioned in verses 23 and 26 [TH]. In Mark, all ten occurrences of the word 'demon' are in the context of unclean spirits being 'cast out' [BECNT, Gnd, WBC]. The designation 'demoniac' is a short way of referring to 'a man with an unclean spirit' [Gnd].

and he did- not -allow^a the demons to-speak, because they knew^b him.

TEXT—Manuscripts reading ᾔδεισαν αὐτόν 'they knew him' are given an A rating by GNT to indicate it was regarded to be certain. Variant readings are ᾔδεισαν αὐτὸν Χριστὸν εἶναι 'they knew him to be Christ' and ᾔδεισαν τὸν Χριστὸν αὐτὸν εἶναι 'they knew him to be the Christ'.

LEXICON—a. imperf. act. indic. of ἀφίημι (LN 13.140) (BAGD 4. p. 126): 'to allow' [AB1, BAGD, BNTC, LN, NTC, WBC; GW, NCV, NLT], 'to let' [AB2, BAGD, LN, Lns; CEV, NIV, TEV], 'to permit' [BAGD, BECNT; ESV, NASB, NET, NRSV], 'to suffer' [KJV]. This verb means to leave it up to someone to do something [LN].

b. pluperfect act. indic. of οἶδα (LN 28.1) (BAGD 1.a. p. 555): 'to know, to know about' [BAGD, LN], 'to have knowledge of' [LN]. The clause ὅτι ᾔδεισαν αὐτόν 'because they knew him' [AB2, BECNT, Lns, WBC; ESV, KJV, NET, NRSV] is also translated 'because they knew who he was' [AB1, BNTC, NTC; NASB, NCV, NIV, REB, TEV; similarly CEV, NLT], 'after all, they knew who he was' [GW]. This verb means to possess information about someone [LN].

QUESTION—What relationship is indicated by ὅτι 'because'?

This conjunction indicates the reason why Jesus didn't allow the demons to speak [BNTC, CGTC, EGT, ICC, Lns, TH, WBC]. It is implied that if Jesus had not silenced them, they would have shouted out their knowledge as did the demon in 1:24 where he said, 'I know you who you are, the Holy One of God' [BECNT, Lns, NICNT]. The demons knew who Jesus was and what his mission was [TH]. They knew that Jesus was the Holy One of God [BECNT, Lns, WBC], the Son of God [Hb, NTC, WBC], and the Messiah [Hb, ICC, Lns, NTC, TRT]. It was the demons who knew who Jesus was, not the people who were inhabited by the demons [ICC, PNTC].

QUESTION—Why didn't Jesus want the demons to speak about him?

The reason the demons were commanded not to make Jesus known (1:25; 3:11–12) was to keep Jesus from being regarded as a political threat to the Roman Empire. Such commands of silence remained in effect until Jesus entered Jerusalem to proclaim his messiahship by what he said and did [BECNT]. Jesus did not want any testimony about himself to be given grudgingly or in fear. His identity was to be revealed by God in human hearts [Hb]. The demons knew things that Jesus was not ready to have revealed [NIGTC]. In Luke 4:41, it says the demons knew that he was the Messiah, but Jesus would not allow the demons to frustrate his plans because he wanted to first show by his teaching and deeds what kind of Messiah he was before he openly declared himself [EBC, NIVfn].

DISCOURSE UNIT—1:35–45 [Hb]. The topic is the tour of Galilee.

DISCOURSE UNIT—1:35–39 [EBC, Hb, NICNT; ESV, GW, NASB, NET, NIV, NLT, TEV]. The topic is leaving Capernaum [EBC], the decision to leave Capernaum [NICNT], the departure from Capernaum [Hb], Jesus preaches in Galilee [ESV, NLT, TEV], a preaching tour in Galilee [NASB], spreading the good news in Galilee [GW], praying and preaching [NET], Jesus prays in a solitary place [NIV].

1:35 And having-risen very early[a] while-night he-went-out[b] and went-away to an-uninhabited[c] place and there he-was-praying.[d]

LEXICON—a. πρωΐ (LN 67.187) (BAGD p. 724): 'early' [BAGD], 'early in the morning' [BAGD, LN]. The phrase πρωΐ ἔννυχα λίαν 'very early while night' is translated 'very early while it was still dark' [WBC], 'early in the morning, while/when it was still dark' [NTC; ESV, NIV; similarly AB2, BNTC; NASB, NCV, NET], 'in the morning, while it was still very dark' [NRSV], 'the next morning, a long time before sunrise' [AB1], 'in the morning, (rising up) a great while before day' [KJV], 'very early the next morning, long before daylight' [TEV], 'in the morning, long before sunrise' [GW], 'in the morning, still very much in the night' [Lns], 'very early before dawn' [BECNT], 'before daybreak the next morning' [NLT], 'very early the next morning' [CEV, REB]. This adverb refers to the early part of the daylight period [LN].

b. aorist act. indic. of ἐξέρχομαι (LN 15.40) (BAGD 1.a.β. p. 274): 'to go out' [AB1, BAGD, BECNT, LN, Lns, NTC, WBC; ESV, KJV, NET, NLT, NRSV, REB], 'to go outside' [AB2], 'to go' [CEV, GW], 'to depart out of' [BAGD, LN]. The verb 'he went out' is translated 'he left the house' [BNTC; NASB, NCV, NIV], '(he got up and) left the house. He went out of town' [TEV]. This verb means to move out of an enclosed or well-defined area [LN]. This word also occurs at 1:38; 6:1, 10, 34.

c. ἔρημος (LN 1.86) (BAGD 1.a. p. 309): 'empty, desolate' [BAGD], 'lonely place, desert, wilderness' [LN]. The phrase ἔρημον τόπον 'an uninhabited place' [WBC] is also translated 'a lonely place' [AB2, BNTC, Lns, NTC; NCV, TEV], 'a deserted place' [BECNT; NET, NRSV], 'a solitary place' [KJV, NIV], 'an isolated place' [NLT], 'a secluded place' [NASB], 'a remote spot' [REB], 'a desolate place' [ESV], 'a place where he could be alone' [CEV, GW]. This adjective describes a

largely uninhabited region that usually has little vegetation. It contrasts with a population center [LN].
   d. imperf. mid./pass. (deponent = act.) indic. of προσεύχομαι (LN 33.178) (BAGD p. 713): 'to pray' [AB1, AB2, BAGD, BECNT, LN, Lns, NTC, WBC; all versions except NET, REB], 'to speak to God' [LN]. The phrase 'and there he was praying' is translated 'to spend time in prayer' [NET], 'and remained there in prayer' [REB]. This verb means to speak to God, or to make requests of him [LN]. The imperfect tense could mean that he started praying [TH], or spent a prolonged time in prayer [NAC, NETfn]. It tells what Jesus was doing while Simon and the others were looking for him [ICC].

QUESTION—What did Jesus go out of?
   Jesus went out of the house [AB2, BNTC, Gnd, Lns, NTC; NASB, NCV, NIV]. It may have been Simon's house [AB2, Gnd, Lns, NTC], or some other house where he had spent the night [NTC]. Jesus went out of the house and out of the town [Gnd, Sw; TEV] of Capernaum [EGT].

QUESTION—Where was the ἔρημον τόπον 'uninhabited place'?
   The phrase ἔρημον τόπον is literally 'a wilderness place', but the wording and setting distinguishes this from the wilderness in 1:4 where John had been preaching [BECNT, NIGTC, TH]. This was some secluded spot just outside the town of Capernaum [NIGTC, Sw]. The land around Capernaum was cultivated at that time [CGTC, Hb, NICNT, Tay], so the word ἔρημος does not denote a barren and desolate wilderness unless Jesus had gone to one of the ravines in the nearby mountain range [Hb]. It was a place that was uninhabited [BECNT, Hb, WBC], solitary [EGT, Hb, ICC, NIGTC, PNTC, TH, WBC], isolated [TH], lonely and secluded [BNTC, CGTC, Lns, NAC, NIGTC, NTC, Tay]. Jesus went to this out-of-the-way place so he could avoid the crowds [Gnd, WBC] and be undisturbed [Lns].

1:36 And Simon and the (ones) with him searched-for[a] him. **1:37** And they-found him and they say to-him, "All are-looking-for[b] you."
LEXICON—a. aorist act. indic. of καταδιώκω (LN 27.43) (BAGD p. 410): 'to search for' [AB1; ESV, NASB, NET], 'to diligently search for' [BAGD, LN], 'to go in search of' [NTC; REB], 'to look for' [CEV, GW, NIV], 'to go to look for' [NCV], 'to go looking for diligently' [LN], 'to seek for' [LN; KJV], 'to hunt for' [BAGD; NRSV], 'to hunt down' [AB2], 'to go out in search of' [TEV], 'to go out to find' [NLT], 'to pursue' [BECNT, BNTC, WBC], 'to chase after' [Lns], 'to follow after' [KJV]. This verb means to try to learn the location of someone by diligently tracking him down [LN]. This verb is literally 'to pursue, to track down' and implies intentness [TH], determination [Hb, TH], persistence [ICC], diligence [NTC], and desperation [AB2]. Probably the word is no stronger than 'to seek after' or 'to search for' since there is a natural tendency for a word to become weakened in use [CGTC]. They had a sense of urgency to find Jesus because the crowd back at the house was waiting to see Jesus

[WBC]. The verb κατεδίωξεν 'searched for' is singular because in Greek grammar a verb agrees in number with just the first component of its compound subject [BECNT].
   b. pres. act. indic. of ζητέω (LN **27.41**) (BAGD 1.a.α. p. 338): 'to look for' [AB1, AB2, BAGD, BNTC, LN, NTC, WBC; all versions except KJV, NRSV], 'to search for' [NRSV], 'to seek for' [KJV], 'to seek' [BAGD, BECNT, Lns], 'to try to find' [**LN**]. This verb means to try to learn the location of someone, often by going from place to place in the process of searching [LN].
QUESTION—Who were the ones who were with Simon?
   They were Andrew, James, and John, who are mentioned in 1:29 [CGTC, Gnd, ICC, Lns, NICNT, NIGTC, NIVfn, NTC, Tay, TH, TRT, WBC]. There could have been others as well [Lns, TH, TRT], such as Philip and Nathanael (John 1:43–45) [NIVfn]. In the next verse Jesus' words to them 'Let *us* go elsewhere' indicates that these people were the disciples who were traveling with him [Gnd]. These disciples had discovered that Jesus had already left the house when they awoke that morning [Lns, NTC, TH].
QUESTION—What is implied by their words to Jesus, 'All are looking for you'?
   This gives the reason they had been searching for Jesus [Hb, Lns]. They thought Jesus would be pleased to know that everyone was looking for him [EBC]. They implied that Jesus ought to return to Capernaum with them in order to continue his ministry among the crowd of people who wanted him to come back [Hb, ICC, Lns, NICNT, NIGTC, NTC].
QUESTION—Who were πάντες 'all' the people looking for Jesus?
   They were 'all' the people of Capernaum [ICC], which demonstrates his great popularity there [BECNT]. The word 'all' is hyperbole like the words 'all' and 'whole' in 1:32–33 [BECNT, EGT, WBC]. The same crowd of people who had gathered about the door the previous night returned in the morning expecting to find Jesus there [Lns, NICNT, NTC]. They wanted Jesus to remain in their city [Hb, Tay] in order to continue his teaching [Gnd, NIGTC], healing, and exorcism [Gnd, NIGTC, WBC].

1:38 And he-says to-them, "Let-us-go elsewhere[a] to the neighboring towns,[b] in-order-that also there I-may-preach.[c] Because for this I-came.[d]"
LEXICON—a. ἀλλαχοῦ (LN **83.4**) (BAGD p. 39): 'elsewhere' [AB2, BAGD, BECNT, BNTC, LN, Lns, NTC; NET], 'somewhere else' [GW, NASB, NIV], 'in another direction' [WBC], not explicit [CEV, KJV, NCV]. The clause 'let us go elsewhere' [**LN**] is also translated 'let us go on' [ESV, NLT, NRSV], 'let us move on' [AB1; REB], 'we must go on' [TEV]. This adverb describes a location other than the one in the immediate context [LN].
   b. κωμόπολις (LN **1.91**) (BAGD p. 461): 'town' [LN], 'market town' [BAGD, LN]. The phrase εἰς τὰς ἐχομένας κωμοπόλεις 'to the neighboring towns' [AB2, BECNT, WBC; NRSV, REB] is also translated

'into the neighboring villages' [BNTC], 'into the surrounding villages' [NET], 'to the nearby towns' [**LN**; CEV; similarly NASB], 'to the nearby villages' [NIV], 'to the small towns that are nearby' [GW], 'to other towns around here' [NCV], 'to the other villages around here' [TEV], 'into/to the next towns' [NTC; ESV, KJV], 'to the next villages in the neighborhood' [AB1], 'to other towns' [NLT], 'into the adjacent country towns' [Lns]. This noun denotes a town whose legal standing or constitution gave it the status of a κώμη 'village' [BAGD, LN (1.91)].

c. aorist act. subj. of κηρύσσω (LN 33.256) (BAGD 2.b.β. p. 431): 'to preach' [AB2, BAGD, BECNT, BNTC, LN, NTC, WBC; ESV, KJV, NASB, NCV, NET, NIV, NLT, TEV], 'to proclaim' [BAGD], 'to proclaim the/my message' [WBC; NRSV, REB], 'to tell the good news' [CEV], 'to spread the Good News' [GW]. This verb means to publicly announce religious truths and principles while urging acceptance and compliance [LN]. This word also occurs at 1:14.

d. aorist act. indic. of ἐξέρχομαι (LN 15.40) (BAGD 1.a.β. p. 274): 'to go out, to depart out of' [BAGD, LN]. The clause 'because for this I came' is translated 'because that is why I came' [TEV; similarly NLT], 'this/that is why I have come' [CEV, GW, NIV], 'that is the reason I came' [NCV], 'that is why I came out' [ESV], 'for that is what I came out here to do' [NET; similarly BNTC; NRSV, REB], 'for I came out to do that' [WBC], 'for I came out for this purpose' [BECNT], 'for that is what I came for' [NASB], 'that is what I came to do' [AB1], 'because for this purpose I came forth' [NTC], 'for therefore came I forth' [KJV], 'for this I did come forth' [Lns], 'for this is why I have come forward' [AB2]. This verb means to move out of an enclosed or well-defined area [LN]. This word also occurs at 1:35.

QUESTION—What is meant by κωμόπολις 'town'?

In 1:33 Mark referred to the town of Capernaum as a πόλις 'city', probably because it was the town with the most significant settlement in the area. So the use of the compound word κωμό-πολις 'village-city' for the settlements around Capernaum probably indicates that they had a lower status then Capernaum [NIGTC]. They were well populated villages that were not organized as towns [Hb]. They were too big to be called villages, but not important enough to be called cities [AB2, BECNT, ICC]. They were small country towns [AB1, CGTC, Sw], village towns [EGT], or villages [Tay]. These settlements are translated 'towns' [AB2, BECNT, NTC, WBC; CEV, ESV, KJV, NASB, NCV, NLT, NRSV, REB], 'small towns' [GW], 'country towns' [Lns], or 'villages' [AB1, BNTC; NET, NIV, TEV].

QUESTION—What did Jesus come to proclaim?

Jesus came to preach the Good News from God (1:14–15) [BECNT, CBC, PNTC, Sw, WBC]. Jesus proclaimed the gospel of God, a message that included a demand for a decision in regard to God's absolute claim on their lives [NICNT]. Preaching the good news of the kingdom of God was central in his mission, and the accompanying miracles served to authenticate his message [Hb, NTC].

QUESTION—What is meant by Jesus' statement, 'Because for this I came'?

This is ambiguous since it could mean that Jesus came out of Capernaum in order to extend his ministry elsewhere in Galilee or that he had come from God to proclaim God's message over an extended area [NICNT]. In the context of this narrative, it appears that Jesus was referring to his departure from Capernaum, but it is possible that Jesus was referring to the purpose he came into the world, since there is a similar situation in Luke 4:43 where Jesus said 'because for this purpose I was sent' [NICNT, NIGTC, TH].

1. 'I came' refers to coming out of the city of Capernaum where they had stayed the previous night [AB1, BECNT, BNTC, EGT, ICC, My, TH, WBC; probably ESV, NET, NRSV, REB which translate this 'I came out']: *I came out of Capernaum.* Jesus came out of Capernaum in order to preach in the neighboring towns in Galilee [ICC, WBC], or throughout the whole region of Galilee [AB1, NTC]. His coming into the world included much more than remaining in Capernaum [ICC].
2. 'I came' is a veiled reference to the fact that Jesus had come from God to accomplish this preaching mission [CBC, EBC, Hb, ICC, Lns, NAC, NTC, Sw]: *I came forth from the Father to this earth.* Jesus had come from heaven to earth [NTC]. Although Jesus had come out of Capernaum in order to pray, this statement refers to coming forth from God for the purpose of preaching in a larger field than the city of Capernaum [Hb].

1:39 And he-went[a] proclaiming in their synagogues in all[b] Galilee and casting-out the demons.

TEXT—Manuscripts reading ἦλθεν 'he went' are given a B rating by GNT to indicate it was regarded to be almost certain. A variant reading is ἦν 'he was' and it is followed by NIGTC, Sw, Tay; KJV.

LEXICON—a. aorist act. indic. of ἔρχομαι (LN 15.7): 'to go, to come' [LN]. The verb ἦλθεν 'he went' [AB1, BECNT, Lns, WBC; CEV, ESV, GW, NASB, NCV, NET, NRSV, REB] is also translated 'he came' [AB2], 'he traveled' [BNTC, NTC; NIV, NLT, TEV]. This verb means to move from one place to another, either coming or going as the context requires [LN]. 'He went proclaiming' refers to Jesus' habitual activity at this time [NIGTC].

b. ὅλος (LN 63.1): 'all, whole, entire' [LN]. The phrase εἰς ὅλην τὴν Γαλιλαίαν 'in all Galilee' is translated 'through the whole of Galilee' [BNTC; REB], 'throughout the whole of Galilee' [BECNT], 'throughout the whole region of Galilee' [AB2], 'throughout the region of Galilee' [NLT], 'throughout all Galilee' [NTC; ESV, KJV, NASB], 'throughout Galilee' [NIV, NRSV], 'all through Galilee' [AB1], 'all over Galilee' [GW], 'everywhere in Galilee' [CEV, NCV], 'into all of Galilee' [WBC; NET], 'into entire Galilee' [Lns]. This adjective pertains to being whole, complete, or entire [LN].

QUESTION—What relationship is indicated by the beginning conjunction καί 'and'?

This conjunction is translated 'so' [GW, NCV, NET, NIV, NLT, REB, TEV], 'then' [CEV]. In the previous verse Jesus had said, 'Let us go elsewhere in order that there also I may proclaim', and this verse tells how he accomplished that purpose [NTC]. This one verse summarizes Jesus' itinerant ministry throughout Galilee [AB1, BECNT, BNTC, Hb, NAC, NCBC, NTC, Tay, WBC]. It must have required a number of weeks, possibly months [Hb, Sw].

QUESTION—What is meant by the phrase εἰς ὅλην τὴν Γαλιλαίαν 'in all Galilee'?

Jesus went not only to the neighboring towns mentioned in verse 38, but he went on to preach in towns all over Galilee [WBC]. The region of Galilee was about forty miles from its north to south borders and twenty-five miles from its east to west borders [NLTfn]. He surpassed the plan he had announced in 1:38 [AB2, Tay]. It is unlikely that this should be pressed to include every single bit of Galilee [NIGTC]. He went to the major towns that had synagogues [EGT, NICNT, Sw].

QUESTION—What is the significance of mentioning only the miracles of casting out demons that accompanied Jesus' teaching in the synagogues?

In 1:21–28 Jesus had taught in the synagogue in Capernaum and cast out an unclean spirit, so now he is doing the same thing as he went to the synagogues throughout Galilee [BNTC, CBC, Gnd, WBC]. Casting out demons was the most spectacular demonstration of his authority, and must have continued to draw the most attention [Hb, Lns, NIGTC]. The plural noun 'demons' indicates that the number of demon-possessed people was considerable in the land of Galilee [Lns]. Since casting out demons was the most spectacular type of miracle, it probably was selected to represent all of the many kinds of miracles he performed [ICC, Lns]. The next paragraph refers to other types of miracles as he healed people [Hb].

DISCOURSE UNIT—1:40–3:6 [NIGTC]. The topic is the controversial aspects of Jesus' ministry.

DISCOURSE UNIT—1:40–45 [EBC, Hb, NICNT; CEV, ESV, GW, NCV, NET, NIV, NLT, NRSV, TEV]. The topic is a man with leprosy [NIV], healing a leper [EBC], Jesus heals a man [CEV, TEV], Jesus heals a sick man [NCV], Jesus heals a man with leprosy [NLT], the cleansing of a leper [Hb, NICNT; NET], Jesus cleanses a leper [ESV, NRSV], Jesus cures a man with a skin disease [GW].

1:40 And a-leper[a] comes to him, begging[b] him and kneeling and saying to-him, "If you-are-willing[c] you-are-able to-cleanse[d] me."

TEXT—Manuscripts reading καὶ γονυπετῶν 'and kneeling' are given a C rating by GNT to indicate that choosing it over a variant text was difficult. A variant reading is καὶ γονυπετῶν αὐτόν 'and kneeling down to him' and it is followed by WBC; KJV. Another variant reading omits this phrase altogether and it is followed by AB2.

LEXICON—a. λεπρός (LN 23.162) (BAGD p. 472): 'a leper' [AB1, BAGD, BECNT, BNTC, LN, NTC, WBC; ESV, KJV, NASB, NET, NRSV, REB], 'a man with leprosy' [CEV, NIV, NLT], 'a man with a skin disease' [NCV], 'a man with a serious skin disease' [GW], 'one having a dread skin disease' [LN], 'a man suffering from a dreaded skin disease' [TEV], 'a man with scale-disease' [AB2]. This adjectival noun denotes a person who suffers from a dread skin disease [LN].

b. pres. act. participle of παρακαλέω (LN 33.168) (BAGD 3. p. 617): 'to beg' [NTC; CEV, GW, NCV, NIV, NRSV], 'to request' [BAGD, LN], 'to appeal to' [BAGD, LN, WBC], 'to implore' [BAGD; ESV], 'to entreat' [BAGD], 'to beseech' [BECNT; KJV, NASB], 'to plead' [AB2], 'to ask for help' [AB1; NET], 'to beg for help' [CEV, REB, TEV], 'to beg to be healed' [NLT]. This verb means to earnestly ask for something [LN].

c. pres. act. subj. of θέλω (LN 25.1): 'to desire, to want, to wish' [LN]. The phrase ἐὰν θέλῃς 'if you are willing' [AB1, BNTC, Lns; GW, NASB, NET, NIV, NLT] is also translated 'if you will' [NTC; ESV, KJV, NCV], 'if only you will' [REB], 'if you want to' [AB2, BECNT, WBC; TEV], 'if only you wanted to' [CEV], 'if you choose' [NRSV]. This verb means to desire to have or to experience something [LN].

d. aorist act. infin. of καθαρίζω (LN 23.137) (BAGD 1.b.α. p. 387): 'to make someone clean' [BAGD], 'to heal and make ritually pure, to heal and to make ritually acceptable' [LN]. The clause δύνασαί με καθαρίσαι 'you are able to cleanse me' [AB2] is also translated 'you are able to make me clean' [BECNT], 'you can make me clean' [BNTC, WBC; ESV, GW, KJV, NASB, NET, NIV, NRSV, REB, TEV], 'you can cleanse me' [NTC], 'you can heal me and make me clean' [NLT], 'you can heal me' [AB1; NCV], 'you have the power to make me well' [CEV]. This verb means to heal a person of a disease that caused ceremonial uncleanness [LN]. It refers to the healing of diseases that make a person ceremonially unclean, and it is especially used of leprosy [BAGD]. This word occurs at 1:40, 41, 42; 7:19.

QUESTION—How is this verse connected with what precedes it?

This verse lacks any local, temporal, or personal connections with the preceding verse, probably because Mark has added this account to set the stage for the conflict narratives in 2:1–3:6 [NAC, WBC]. It continues the theme of healing by giving an example of Jesus' healing powers that went beyond anything that has been related so far [BNTC]. Probably this was one the miracles of healing performed by Jesus during his tour of Galilee mentioned in the preceding verse [EGT, NTC, PNTC, Sw].

QUESTION—What disease is referred to by the word λέπρα 'leprosy'?

Medical authorities who have examined the descriptions of the Hebrew word in Lev. 13–14 think that the biblical term is a collective noun that designates a wide variety of chronic skin diseases, including the leprosy known as

Hanson's disease [AB1, BECNT, BNTC, CGTC, EBC, NAC, NICNT, NIGTC, PNTC, WBC]. Because of the uncertainty of the exact nature of the disease some translate λεπρός as 'a man with a skin disease' [LN (23.162); NCV, TEV], 'a man with a serious skin disease' [GW], and 'a man suffering from a dreaded skin disease' [TEV]. Most, however, translate it as 'a leper'. This man's condition may well have been the true leprosy of Hanson's disease [Hb, NIGTC, NTC] because the cure of a minor skin disorder would not have accounted for the excitement that this healing caused [Hb]. Some think that this was not Hansen's disease [AB2, Tay], but some variety of a condition in which the skin became scaly [AB2], or in which the skin had bright white spots along with patches of raw flesh and spreading scabs [Tay].

QUESTION—What did the leprous man beg Jesus to do?

He begged Jesus to help him [BNTC; NET, REB, TEV] by healing him [NLT]. The words 'begging him' and 'saying to him' are not consecutive acts. The leper begged for Jesus' help by saying 'If you are willing you are able to cleanse me.' [CEV, GW, NCV, NET, NIV, NLT, TEV]: *he begged him, "If you are willing you are able to cleanse me."*

QUESTION—What is meant by the conditional clause, 'If you are willing'?

Although the leper had seen or heard enough of Jesus' healing ministry to know that Jesus had the power to heal him, he wasn't sure that Jesus would be willing to do so [BECNT, BNTC, CGTC, EBC, EGT, Hb, ICC, Lns, NETfn, NTC, PNTC, Tay, TH, WBC].

QUESTION—Why did the leper ask to be cleansed rather than to be healed?

A person with leprosy was considered to be ceremonially 'unclean', a condition that required him to live outside the city gates in order to avoid contact with other people [ICC]. His request με καθαρίσαι 'cleanse me' does not mean 'pronounce me ceremonially clean' in the sense that ceremonial cleansing would be carried out according to OT Law. The request 'cleanse me' simply means 'heal me' [AB1, BECNT, CGTC, NICNT, Sw, Tay, TH, WBC; CEV, NCV]. Since a leper was considered to be 'unclean' because of his leprosy, his physical cure would naturally be viewed as a cleansing [Hb] A few versions actually translate the request as 'heal me' [AB1; NCV], or 'make me well' [CEV]. However, the translation 'cleanse me' [all translations except AB1; CEV, NCV] seems appropriate since in verse 44 Jesus commands the healed leper to go to a priest to offer a sacrifice and have the priest pronounce him ceremonially clean.

1:41 And **being-moved-with-compassion,**[a] **stretching-out**[b] **his hand he-touched**[c] **(him) and says to-him, "I-am-willing, be-cleansed." 1:42 And immediately the leprosy went-away**[d] **from him, and he-was-cleansed.**[e]

TEXT—In 1:41, manuscripts reading σπλαγχνισθείς 'moved with compassion' are given a B rating by GNT to indicate it was regarded to be almost certain. A variant reading is ὀργισθείς 'moved with anger' and it is followed by AB2, BNTC, CGTC, EBC, NAC, NCBC, NICNT, NIGTC, PNTC, Tay, WBC; REB, mostly because they are following the rule that the reading hardest to explain is likely to be original. Another variant reading omits this word altogether.

TEXT—In 1:42, manuscripts beginning the verse with καί 'and' are followed by GNT, which does not mention any variant reading. A variant reading is καὶ εἰπόντος αὐτοῦ 'and when he spoke' and it is followed by KJV.

LEXICON—a. aorist pass. (deponent = act.) participle of σπλαγχνίζομαι (LN 25.49) (BAGD p. 762): 'to be moved with compassion' [BECNT, Lns; KJV, NASB, NET, NLT], 'to feel compassion for, to have great affection for' [LN], 'to be filled with compassion' [NIV], 'to be moved with pity' [ESV, NRSV], 'to be filled with pity' [TEV], 'to have pity, to feel sympathy' [BAGD]. The participle σπλαγχνισθείς 'being moved with compassion' is also translated 'in compassion' [AB1], 'Jesus felt sorry for him/the man' [CEV, GW, NCV], 'while his heart went out to him' [NTC]. This verb means to experience great affection and compassion for someone [LN]. Some follow the alternative reading ὀργισθείς and translate it 'moved with anger' [BNTC], 'moved to anger' [REB], 'being angered' [WBC], 'becoming incensed' [AB2]. This word occurs at 1:41; 6:34; 8:2; 9:22.

b. aorist act. participle of ἐκτείνω (LN 16.19) (BAGD 1. p. 245): 'to stretch out' [AB2, BECNT, BNTC, LN, Lns, NTC, WBC; ESV, NASB, NET, NRSV, REB], 'to reach out' [AB1, LN; GW, NCV, NIV, NLT, TEV], 'to hold out' [BAGD], 'to extend' [BAGD, LN], 'to put forth' [KJV]. The words ἐκτείνας τὴν χεῖρα αὐτοῦ ἥψατο 'stretching out his hand he touched' is translated 'he put his hand on him' [CEV]. This verb means to cause an object to extend in space [LN]. It is used in relation to healing someone by a touch [BAGD].

c. aorist mid. indic. of ἅπτομαι, ἅπτω (LN 24.73) (BAGD 2.b. p. 103): 'to touch' [BAGD, LN; all translations except CEV], 'to put (his hand) on' [CEV]. This verb means to touch, and implies there is a relatively firm contact [LN].

d. aorist act. indic. of ἀπέρχομαι (LN **13.93**) (BAGD 1.b. p. 84): 'to go away' [BAGD, Lns; GW], 'to depart' [BAGD, BECNT; KJV], 'to leave' [AB1, AB2, BNTC, **LN**, NTC, WBC; ESV, NASB, NCV, NET, NIV, NRSV, REB, TEV], 'to disappear' [CEV, NLT], 'to cease to exist, to pass away, to cease' [LN]. This verb means to go out of existence [LN].

e. aorist pass. indic. of καθαρίζω (LN 23.137) (BAGD 1.b.α. p. 387): 'to be made clean' [BAGD], 'to be healed and made ritually pure, to be healed and made ritually acceptable' [LN]. The word ἐκαθαρίσθη 'he was cleansed' [AB2, Lns, NTC, WBC; KJV, NASB] is also translated 'he was made clean' [BECNT; ESV, NRSV], 'he was clean' [AB1, BNTC; GW, NET, REB, TEV], 'he/the man was healed' [NCV, NLT], 'he was cured' [NIV], 'he was well' [CEV]. This verb means to heal a person of a disease that has caused ceremonial uncleanness [LN]. It refers to the healing of diseases that make a person ceremonially unclean, and it is used especially in relation to leprosy [BAGD]. This word occurs at 1:40, 41, 42; 7:19.

QUESTION—What relationship is indicated by the use of the participle σπλαγχνισθείς 'being moved with compassion'?

The participle indicates the reason for the following action [EBC, Lns, NTC; CEV, NCV]: *because he was moved with compassion*, he touched him and healed him.

QUESTION—If the reading ὀργισθείς 'moved with anger' is followed, why would Jesus be angry?

Jesus was angry at the disease [Tay]. He was indignant over the misery suffered by the leper [PNTC]. Jesus had a righteous indignation at the ravages of sin and disease [NICNT]. Jesus was angry at the physical and social suffering caused by disease [NIGTC]. Jesus had a godly anger against Satan for afflicting this man with leprosy [BNTC, CGTC, EBC, WBC]. Perhaps Jesus was angry because the leper doubted that God desired that he be healed [NAC].

QUESTION—Why would Jesus touch the leper?

Jesus usually touched people as he healed them [AB1, BNTC, NIGTC, Tay, WBC]. This symbolic touch accompanied his words to indicate that the healing was an act of his own will [Hb]. The touch was a sign of a benediction [ICC]. This was the healing touch of Jesus [NTC]. The healing power from Jesus was apparently transmitted by physical contact with the person in need [NTC]. Jesus could have healed the leper by his word alone, but he touched the 'untouchable' leper to express his compassion [CGTC, EBC]. This showed that Jesus was not troubled about becoming ceremonially unclean by touching a leper [BECNT, BNTC, CGTC, NCBC, NIGTC, NIVfn]. Neither was he troubled about being exposed to the disease [BECNT, NIGTC].

QUESTION—What is meant by Jesus' command to the leper, 'be cleansed'?

The aorist passive imperative καθαρίσθητι 'be cleansed' was not given as a priestly pronouncement that would declare the leper to be ceremonially clean. Such an announcement could not be made until the healed leper followed Jesus' instructions about going to a priest and offering sacrifices (1:44). The command 'be cleansed' was a declaration that complete healing would follow immediately [NICNT]. The passive voice 'be cleansed' indicates that the man was the passive recipient of the cleansing [Hb]. Many languages cannot use a passive verb with an imperative, so the nearest equivalent of Jesus' command would be 'I make you well' or 'now you are well' [TH]. The passive voice could be the divine passive and mean that God was the active agent in the cure [AB2].

QUESTION—What is meant when it says 'the leprosy *went away* from him'?

This is an anthropomorphism that means the symptoms of the leprosy could be seen to vanish away when the man was cured [NIGTC]. Anyone who met the man would see that he was healed [NICNT].

1:43 And having-sternly-warned[a] him, immediately he-sent- him -away.[b]

LEXICON—a. aorist mid. (deponent = act.) participle of ἐμβριμάομαι (LN 33.320, 33.421) (BAGD p. 254): 'to sternly warn' [BAGD, BECNT, NTC; NASB, NRSV], 'to strictly warn' [CEV], 'to strongly warn' [NCV], 'to warn' [GW], 'to give a stern warning' [BNTC], 'to sternly charge' [Lns; ESV], 'to straitly charge' [KJV], 'to insist sternly' [LN (33.320)], 'to speak sternly' [TEV], 'to denounce harshly, to scold' [LN (33.421)], 'to growl at' [AB2], 'to silence' [WBC]. The participle 'having sternly warned' is translated 'with a stern warning' [AB1; NLT; similarly REB], 'with a strong warning' [NET, NIV]. This verb means to state something with sternness [LN (33.320)], or to exhibit irritation or even anger when expressing a harsh reproof [LN (33.421)].

b. aorist act. indic. of ἐκβάλλω (LN 15.68): 'to send, to send out, to send forth' [LN]. The phrase ἐξέβαλεν αὐτόν 'he sent him away' [AB1, BECNT, BNTC, NTC, WBC; ESV, GW, KJV, NASB, NET, NIV, NRSV, TEV] is also translated 'he sent him on his way' [CEV, NLT], 'he dismissed him' [REB], 'he told the man to go away' [NCV], 'he rushed him off' [Lns], 'he cast him out' [AB2]. This verb means to send out or away from, presumably for some purpose [LN].

QUESTION—What is meant by the verb ἐμβριμάομαι 'to sternly warn'?

Although the verb normally means to angrily reprove or scold someone, it is hard to find a cause for anger here [BECNT, ICC, NIGTC]. This verb is a strong word without a good English equivalent [AB1]. The word seems to express some degree of displeasure [EBC, Hb, ICC, NAC, NCBC, NICNT, NIGTC, TH]. Perhaps Jesus was exasperated because he foresaw that the man would disobey his instructions [EBC, Hb, NAC, NICNT, NIGTC]. Perhaps Jesus was vexed at the whole situation in which a clamor would be made only about the externals of this healing [ICC, NCBC]. Instead of implying anger, this word refers to a stern and urgent admonition to emphasize the seriousness of the need for secrecy [BECNT, CGTC, Lns, NTC, Sw, Tay, TRT, WBC]. Although Jesus spoke in a loud and harsh tone that showed his agitation, there is nothing to suggest that he was angry with the healed man [Tay]. Jesus 'growled' at the man to stress the forcefulness with which he was telling him what he must do [Gnd]. Jesus' stern order was given so that the man would rush to Jerusalem and have a priest pronounce him clean of leprosy before the story of Jesus' part in the healing became known to the priests there [Lns].

QUESTION—What is meant by the verb ἐκβάλλω 'to send away'?

This is the same verb used when Jesus cast out demons in 1:34, and when the Holy Spirit led Jesus out into the wilderness in 1:12. The verb refers to sending the man away from Jesus' presence and from the people around him [AB1, BECNT, Hb, WBC; all versions]. It means to send him out quickly or forcefully [BECNT]. The verb prefix ἐκ- 'out' indicates that the man was sent out of some location, which could imply that the miracle had taken place in a house or a synagogue [EGT, ICC, NAC, TH].

1:44 And he says to-him, "See[a] (that) you-say nothing[b] to-nobody.[b] But go show[c] yourself to-the priest and offer[d] for your cleansing what Moses commanded, for a-testimony[e] to-them."

LEXICON—a. pres. act. impera. of ὁράω (LN 30.45) (BAGD 2.b. p. 578): 'to see that' [AB2, BECNT, BNTC, WBC; ESV, NASB, NET, NIV, NRSV, REB; similarly KJV], 'to see to it that' [Lns], 'to be sure' [NTC], 'to take care' [AB1, BAGD], 'to take notice of, to consider, to pay attention to, to concern oneself with' [LN], 'to listen' [TEV], 'to be on one's guard' [BAGD], not explicit [CEV, GW, NCV, NLT]. This verb means to take special notice of something [LN]. This imperative reinforces the command [Lns, TH]. It is equivalent to saying 'Beware lest you say anything to someone' [TH].
  b. μηδείς...μηδείς (LN 92.23) (BAGD 2.b.α., 2.b.β. p. 518): The double negative in the phrase μηδενὶ μηδὲν εἴπῃς 'say nothing to nobody' is translated 'say nothing to anyone' [AB1, BNTC, WBC; ESV, NASB, NRSV; similarly Lns], 'say nothing to any man' [KJV], 'do not say anything to anyone' [AB2; NET; similarly NTC], 'don't tell anyone about this' [CEV, GW, NCV, NLT, TEV], 'don't tell this to anyone' [NIV], 'tell no one anything' [BECNT], 'tell nobody' [REB]. This adjectival substantive is a negative reference to an entity, event, or state [LN].
  c. aorist act. impera. of δείκνυμι (LN 28.47) (BAGD 1.a. p. 172): 'to show' [BAGD, LN; all translations except CEV, NLT, TEV], 'to make known' [BAGD, LN], 'to demonstrate' [LN]. The phrase 'go show yourself to the priest' is translated 'go straight to the priest and let him examine you' [TEV; similarly NLT], 'just go and show the priest that you are well' [CEV]. This verb means to make known the character or significance of something by visual, auditory, gestural, or linguistic means [LN].
  d. aorist act. impera. of προσφέρω (LN 57.80) (BAGD 2.a. p. 720): 'to offer' [AB2, BAGD, NTC; ESV, GW, NASB, NIV, NRSV, TEV], 'to present, to bring' [BAGD, LN], 'to make the offering' [AB1, BNTC; REB], 'to make the offerings' [WBC], 'to bring the offering' [NET], 'to bring as an offering' [Lns]. The phrase 'offer for your cleansing what Moses commanded' is translated 'offer the sacrifices that Moses commanded for your cleansing' [NIV], 'bring for your cleansing what things Moses commanded' [BECNT], 'take a gift to the temple as Moses commanded' [CEV], 'offer the gift Moses commanded for people who are made well' [NCV], 'take along the offering required in the law of Moses for those who have been healed of leprosy' [NLT]. This verb means to present something to someone, often involving the actual physical transport of the object in question [LN]. This verb refers to presenting offerings or gifts [BAGD].
  e. μαρτύριον (LN 33.264) (BAGD 1.a. p. 493): 'testimony, witness' [LN], 'that which serves as a testimony or proof' [BAGD]. The phrase εἰς μαρτύριον αὐτοῖς 'for/as a testimony to them' [NTC; KJV, NASB, NET, NIV, NRSV] is also translated 'as a testimony for them' [Lns], 'for

a proof to them' [ESV], 'for a witness to them' [BECNT], 'as a witness to them' [AB2], 'as evidence to them' [BNTC], 'as evidence to them that you are clean' [AB1], 'as proof to people that you are clean' [GW], 'this will show the people what I have done' [NCV], 'this will be a public testimony that you have been cleansed' [NLT], 'that will certify the cure' [REB], 'and everyone will know that you have been healed' [CEV], 'in order to prove to everyone that you are cured' [TEV], 'as evidence against them' [WBC]. This noun denotes the content of what is witnessed or said [LN].

QUESTION—When did Jesus speak these words?

This seems to be an apparent contradiction in the sequence of events since it seems that Jesus is now talking to the man after having warned him and sent him away in the preceding verse. This verse, however, is simply telling what Jesus had said to the man before sending him away [TH]. The sequence is changed in some translations so that the warning clearly pertains to 1:44 [GW, NCV, NET, NIV, NLT, REB]: 'Immediately Jesus sent the man away with a very strong warning. He told him…' [NET].

QUESTION—Why didn't Jesus want the man to tell anyone about his healing?

Jesus wanted to avoid the very situation that developed in the following verse after the man disobeyed this command [ICC, NIGTC, Sw, Tay, TRT, WBC]. The command to be silent was probably meant to last only until the cleansing had taken place [NETfn]. Publicity about the miracle would hinder Jesus' plan to begin his preaching ministry [Tay]. Jesus didn't want to gain the reputation of being just another miracle-worker since this wasn't the essential purpose of his ministry [EBC].

QUESTION—Why was it necessary for the man to show himself to the priest?

Even though the man had been healed of the disease, he remained 'unclean' until the priest pronounced him ceremonially clean [BNTC, Hb]. Only the priest on duty in the temple could pronounce the man to be ceremonially clean [ESVfn, NIGTC, WBC]. The article *the* priest' specifies the priest on duty [Tay], and that priest would be the priest on duty at the temple in Jerusalem [Hb, Lns].

QUESTION—What had Moses commanded to be used as an offering to bring about a leper's cleansing?

The ceremony of cleansing is described in Lev. 14:1–7. It involved the offering of two ceremonially clean birds. The first bird was killed and the second bird was released after being dipped in the blood of the first. The remaining blood would then be sprinkled over the healed man to complete the ritual [NTC].

QUESTION—What is meant by doing this 'for a testimony to them'?

1. This would be a proof to people in general that the man was cleansed [BECNT, CGTC, EBC, EGT, Gnd, NLTfn, TRT, WBC]. The indefinite third person plural 'them' refers to people in general. The cleansing ceremony performed by the priest would prove to everyone that the man had been declared to be ceremonially clean, and thus the miracle of

healing by Jesus would be authenticated [Gnd]. This would be a testimony to the priest and the people of the reality of the cure [EBC].
2. This would be a proof to the priests that the man was cleansed [BNTC, Tay]. Showing himself to the priest would be evidence of his cure, and the plural 'them' indicates that the priest on duty in the temple was representative of all the priests [BNTC].
3. This would be a proof to the priests that Jesus had the power to heal [AB2, Hb, Lns, NTC, Sw], and that Jesus obeyed the Mosaic Law [AB1, AB2, Lns, NTC]. 'Them' refers to the priestly class that was hostile toward Jesus [Hb, Lns]. It would be a messianic sign to the priests [Hb, Sw].
4. The would be a testimony against the priests [CBC, NAC, NICNT, NIGTC, WBC]. If the priests determine that the healing has taken place and accept the sacrifice for the cleansing of the leper, but still refuse to recognize the person and power through whom the healing had come, they will stand condemned by the very evidence they have supplied [NAC, NICNT]. This would also be evidence against those priests who accused Jesus of disregarding the law [WBC].

1:45 But the (one) having-gone-out[a] began to-proclaim[b] freely/many-(things) and to-spread[c] the word,

LEXICON—a. aorist act. participle of ἐξέρχομαι (LN 15:40) (BAGD 1.a.β. p. 274): 'to go out' [AB2, BAGD, LN, Lns, NTC; ESV, KJV, NASB, NET, NIV, NLT, NRSV], 'to go away' [AB1, BAGD; REB, TEV], 'to leave' [GW, NCV], 'to depart' [BECNT, WBC], 'to depart out of, to leave from within' [LN], not explicit [CEV]. This verb means to move out of an enclosed or well-defined two or three-dimensional area [LN]. This verb means to go away from a region or a house [BAGD].

b. present act. infin. of κηρύσσω (LN 33.207) (BAGD 2.a. p. 431): 'to proclaim' [BAGD, LN], 'to tell' [LN], 'to speak of, to mention publicly' [BAGD]. The phrase ἤρξατο κηρύσσειν πολλά means 'began to proclaim *freely*' and it is translated 'began to proclaim it freely' [NASB, NRSV], 'began to talk freely' [GW, NIV], 'began to talk freely about it' [ESV], 'talked about it so much (that)' [CEV; similarly TEV], 'began to publish it much' [KJV], 'began to announce it freely' [BNTC], 'began to announce it publicly' [NET], 'began to herald greatly' [Lns], 'made the whole story public' [REB], 'began to make the news public' [AB1], 'began to publish the matter...so widely' [NTC], 'began to proclaim it all over' [AB2], 'proclaiming to everyone what had happened' [NLT], 'he began to tell everyone that Jesus had healed him' [NCV]. The phrase ἤρξατο κηρύσσειν πολλά means 'began to proclaim *many things*' [BECNT, WBC]. The verb means to announce extensively and publicly [LN]. This verb is used with the same meaning at 1:45; 5:20; 7:36.

c. pres. act. infin. of διαφημίζω (LN 33.214) (BAGD p. 190): 'to spread the news about' [BAGD, LN], 'to spread information about' [LN]. The phrase 'to spread the word' [WBC; NLT, NRSV; similarly BECNT] is also translated 'to spread the news' [ESV; similarly NIV], 'to spread the news everywhere' [TEV], 'to spread the news around' [NASB], 'to spread the news abroad' [AB2], 'spread the story widely' [NET], 'to spread the news far and wide' [BNTC], 'spreading it far and wide' [REB], 'spreading the news around' [NTC], 'spread his story so widely' [GW], 'he spread the news about Jesus' [NCV], 'spread the matter abroad' [Lns], 'to blaze abroad the matter' [KJV], 'told so many people' [CEV], not explicit [AB1]. This verb means to spread information extensively and effectively concerning someone or something [LN]. It means to make known by word of mouth [BAGD].

QUESTION—What was the disobedience indicated by the conjunction δέ 'but' at the beginning of this verse?

All agree that by spreading the news of how Jesus had healed him, the man had disobeyed the command, 'See that you say nothing to no one'. The second part of Jesus' command about going to a priest and offering sacrifices is not treated in the text and there are different views about whether he went to a priest at all, and if he did go, whether he went before or after he began proclaiming the news about Jesus.

1. The man disobeyed Jesus by going out and spreading the news without first going to the priest and offering the sacrifices [BECNT, EBC, ICC, Lns, Sw, WBC; GW, NET; probably NICNT; NASB, NCV, NIV, NRSV, REB, TEV which seem to indicate that this verse refers to what happened immediately after verse 44]. The man's disobedience was the act of spreading the news even after Jesus had commanded him to say nothing [Lns, WBC]. The participle 'going out' indicates that the man began spreading the news as soon as he left Jesus [GW, NET]: 'as the man went out he began to announce it publicly and spread the story widely' [NET]. It is not clear whether or not the man ever did show himself to a priest [AB2, BECNT, NICNT, PNTC]. This is not a story about the leper, but a story about Jesus Christ, the Son of God (1:1), so the information about whether the man went to a priest or not is unimportant [BECNT]. Some assume that the man eventually did carry out Jesus' orders to show himself to a priest [Lns, WBC]. Another thinks that the man probably never did go to a priest to obtain the required social recognition of his cure [EGT].

2. The man obeyed Jesus by showing himself to the priest and offering the required sacrifices so he could be pronounced clean. But then he disobeyed Jesus by going out to spread the news of what Jesus had done for him [NIGTC, TRT]. It is implied that the man first went to the priest and had the priest offer the sacrifices for cleansing since he would have to be pronounced clean by the priest before he could freely go among others to tell them about what Jesus had done [TRT]. The man would have been socially excluded from contact with people until the accomplishment of

his eight-day cleansing ceremony in Jerusalem, so there must have been a time lag between verses 44 and 45 [NIGTC].

QUESTION—What did the leper go out of?

The verb ἐξελθών 'having gone out' has the prefix ἐκ- 'out', which seems to indicate that the man went out of the town or out of a house, and in this context he probably went out of a house [TH].

QUESTION—What is indicated by the accusative adverb/adjective πολύς 'freely/many things'?

1. It indicates the manner in which the man proclaimed the news of his healing [AB2, CGTC, EBC, Gnd, Hb, ICC, Sw, Tay, TH; all versions]: *he proclaimed the news freely*. The man repeatedly gave a lengthy account of what happened [Hb, Sw]. He proclaimed the news everywhere [EBC].
2. It indicates the content of what the man proclaimed [BECNT, NIGTC, WBC]: *he proclaimed many things*. This does not tell what the many things were that he proclaimed, but whatever it was resulted in Jesus' massive popularity [NIGTC].

QUESTION—What was the word that the man spread?

Mark often used the phrase τὸν λόγον 'the word' to mean the sum of the Christian proclamation and that may be the sense here [WBC]. Although spreading 'the word' may mean that the disobedient man's proclamation was recognized as being the good news, it is not necessary to read 'the word' as a technical term for preaching the Christian gospel. [NIGTC]. There is no indication that the healed man was preaching the Good News of the nearness of God's kingdom, so this probably refers to the powerful words Jesus spoke to him, 'I am willing, be cleansed' [Gnd; probably EGT]. The healed man kept telling people about what had happened [EBC, TH]. This 'word' was an account of his healing [EGT, Lns, NIGTC].

so-that no-longer he was-able to-enter into a-city[a] openly,[b]

LEXICON—a. πόλις (LN 1.88) (BAGD 1. p. 685): 'city' [AB2, BAGD, BECNT, BNTC, LN, Lns, WBC; GW, KJV, NASB], 'town' [AB1, LN, NTC; all versions except GW, KJV, NASB]. This noun denotes a population center without specific reference to size [LN]. In English, 'town' better represents the place than 'city' [TH].

b. (LN 28.63) (BAGD p. 853): 'openly' [AB2, BAGD, BECNT, BNTC, LN, Lns, NTC, WBC; CEV, ESV, GW, KJV, NET, NIV, NRSV], 'publicly' [BAGD, LN; NASB, TEV]. The clause 'no longer he was able to enter into a city openly' is translated 'could not enter a town if people saw him' [NCV], 'could no longer show himself in any town' [AB1; REB], 'large crowds soon surrounded Jesus, and he couldn't publicly enter a town anywhere' [NLT]. This adverb describes the manner by which something is easily known by the public [LN].

QUESTION—What relationship is indicated by the conjunction ὥστε 'so that'?

The conjunction indicates the result of the man's disobedience [BECNT, EBC, Hb, NIGTC, WBC].

MARK 1:45 93

QUESTION—Who is the referent of the pronoun αὐτόν 'he'?
The pronoun refers to Jesus [all translations].

QUESTION—What city couldn't Jesus openly enter, and why couldn't he?
So far the only πόλις 'city' mentioned has been Capernaum, and one version translates this as 'enter into the city' [KJV], but here the words 'to enter into *a city*' probably is a general reference to any town in the area instead of a particular city [AB1; NIGTC; NET, REB]. The noun πόλις is translated 'a city' [AB2, BECNT, BNTC, Lns, WBC; NASB], 'any city' [GW], 'a town' [CGTC; CEV, ESV, NCV, NIV, NLT, NRSV, TEV]. Jesus avoided the cities and towns until the excitement died down [Hb]. Because of such publicity, Jesus could no longer enter a city or town without a tumultuous crowd gathering around him [BECNT, Hb, NICNT]. He had to stay away for a while to let the excitement die down [WBC]. The word 'openly' means that he could only enter a town at night or in a manner that did not attract attention. But in general he stayed outside the walls of a city [Sw]. The following conjunction 'but' probably indicates that Jesus did not enter the cities at all during the time he was living in the desolate places [Gnd]. Jesus wasn't in danger himself if he entered a city, but it would endanger the success of his mission [Sw].

but he-was outside^a in desolate places and they-were-coming to him from-every-direction.^b

LEXICON—a. ἔξω (LN 83.20) (BAGD 1.a.α. p. 279): 'outside' [BAGD, LN], 'apart from' [LN]. The clause 'he was outside in desolate places' is translated 'he was out in desolate places' [ESV], 'had to remain out in deserted places' [AB2], 'stayed in remote places' [NET], 'he remained outside in the uninhabited places' [WBC], 'he remained outside in the open country' [AB1], 'he stayed outside in remote places' [REB], 'stayed out in unpopulated areas' [NASB], 'stayed outside in lonely places' [BNTC; NIV], 'he stayed out in lonely places' [TEV], 'was outside in lonely places' [Lns], 'stayed out in the country' [NRSV] 'stayed outside the cities in deserted places' [BECNT], 'he stayed in places where nobody lived' [NCV], 'he stayed in places where he could be alone' [GW], 'he had to stay away from the towns' [CEV], 'he had to stay out in the secluded places' [NLT], 'was without in desert places' [KJV]. This adverb indicates a position not contained within a particular area [LN].

b. πάντοθεν (LN **84.7**) (BAGD p. 608): 'from all directions' [BAGD, BNTC, LN], 'from every quarter' [ESV, KJV, NRSV], 'from all quarters' [REB], 'from everywhere' [AB1, AB2, BECNT, **LN**, Lns, WBC; CEV, GW, NASB, NCV, NET, NIV, NLT, TEV]. This word indicates the extension from a source and involves all possible points [LN].

QUESTION—Why were the people coming to Jesus from every direction?
The conjunction 'and' adds the information that Jesus' work continued in these desolate places, while the imperfect tense 'were coming' indicates that people kept coming to him during this time [Lns]. Jesus' purpose to spread

his message in the synagogues throughout Galilee had been frustrated, but since he wasn't in hiding, he continued to preach to the many people who came to where he was [Hb].

DISCOURSE UNIT—2:1–3:12 [CBC, PNTC]. The topic is trouble with the authorities [PNTC], a controversy leading to rejection [CBC].

DISCOURSE UNIT—2:1–3:6 [EBC, Hb, NICNT; NLT]. The topic is controversy stories [NLT], conflict in Galilee [NICNT], conflicts with the scribes [Hb], conflict with the religious leaders [EBC].

DISCOURSE UNIT—2:1–17 [NCV]. The topic is Jesus heals a paralyzed man.

DISCOURSE UNIT—2:1–13 [NASB]. The topic is the paralytic healed.

DISCOURSE UNIT—2:1–12 [CBC, EBC, Hb, NICNT; CEV, ESV, GW, NET, NIV, NLT, NRSV, TEV]. The topic is the first controversy: Jesus as Son of Man heals a paralytic and forgives sin [CBC], healing a paralytic [EBC], healing and forgiving a paralytic [NET], the paralytic forgiven and healed [Hb], Jesus heals a crippled man [CEV], Jesus heals a paralyzed man [NLT, TEV], Jesus heals a paralytic [ESV, NIV, NRSV], authority to forgive sins [NICNT], Jesus forgives sins [GW].

2:1 And having-entered again into Capernaum after[a] (some) days it-was-heard[b] that he-is in a-house.[c]

LEXICON—a. διά (LN **67.59**) (BAGD A.II.2. p. 180): 'after' [BAGD, LN]. The phrase δι' ἡμερῶν 'after some days' [AB1, BECNT, Lns, WBC; ESV, KJV, NET, NRSV, REB] is also translated 'some days later' [BNTC, NTC], 'a few days later' [**LN**; CEV, NCV, NIV, TEV], 'several days later' [AB2, BAGD; GW, NLT], 'several days afterward' [NASB]. The phrase δὶ ἡμερῶν, literally 'through days', is an idiom that refers to a point of time subsequent to another point of time after an interval of a few days [LN].

b. aorist pass. indic. of ἀκούω (LN 33.212) (BAGD 3.e. p. 32): 'to be heard' [BAGD, LN], 'to be learned' [BAGD]. The verb 'it was heard' [Lns; NASB] is also translated 'it was learned' [WBC], 'it was reported' [BECNT, NTC; ESV, NRSV], 'the report went out' [GW], 'it was noised' [KJV], 'it was rumored' [AB2], 'the news spread' [AB1; NCV, NET, TEV], 'the news spread quickly' [NLT], 'the news went round' [BNTC; REB], 'people heard' [CEV, NIV]. This verb means to receive information about something and normally such information was conveyed by word of mouth [LN]. This is an impersonal verb that means 'it was heard' or 'it was reported' [Lns, Tay].

c. οἶκος (LN **7.2**) (BAGD 1.a.α. p. 560): 'house' [LN]. The phrase 'he is in a house' is translated 'he was in the house' [BNTC, WBC; KJV], 'he was at home' [AB1, AB2, BECNT, **LN**, Lns, NTC; CEV, ESV, NASB, NCV, NET, NRSV, REB, TEV], 'he was home' [GW], 'he had come home' [NIV], 'he was back home' [NLT]. This noun denotes a building consisting of one or more rooms, and normally refers to a dwelling place [LN]. Since the noun 'house' does not have an article and the verb 'is' is in the present tense, it probably means that Jesus 'was at home' [Hb].

QUESTION—What is the phrase 'after some days' connected with?
1. It is connected with the preceding words [AB1, AB2, BECNT, BNTC, CGTC, EBC, Lns, NTC, PNTC, Sw, Tay, TH, TRT, WBC; all versions except CEV]: *and when he entered again into Capernaum after some days.* The words 'after some days' connects chapter 2 with the passage in 1:40–45 about Jesus healing the man with leprosy [BECNT, PNTC]. The length of his first tour is left indefinite [Hb, Sw]. Some think that this covers all the days since Jesus left Capernaum in 1:39 for a tour of Galilee [Hb, Sw, WBC]. This interval may have been weeks [AB1].
2. It is connected with the following words [EGT, Gnd, WBC; CEV]: *he entered Capernaum and after some days it was heard that he was at home.* Jesus had been traveling throughout Galilee and now he returns to Capernaum [EBC]. The phrase suggests a short period of time, too short a time for the preaching tour after his first visit to Capernaum, so this must refer to the days from the time he came back to Capernaum until people learned that he was again at home [EGT, Gnd, WBC; CEV]. In 1:45 it says that Jesus could not enter the city openly, so after he entered Capernaum incognito it wasn't long until people knew about it [Gnd].

QUESTION—What is referred to by the adverb πάλιν 'again'?
The word 'again' looks back to the first time Jesus entered Capernaum in 1:21 [BECNT, EGT, Gnd, Hb, ICC, Sw, Tay].

QUESTION—Whose house was Jesus in?
1. Jesus was in the house of Peter and Andrew [AB2, CGTC, EBC, EGT, Gnd, NAC, NICNT, NIGTC, NIVfn, PNTC, Sw, Tay, TRT, WBC]. This is probably the same house that is mentioned in 1:29 [AB2, NICNT]. It was the base of operations for Jesus during his ministry in Capernaum [AB2].
2. Jesus was in his own home in Capernaum [ESVfn, Lns, TH]. Jesus was 'at home' in his own house [TH]. This is where his mother and other relatives were now living [Lns].

2:2 And many were-gathered-together[a] so-as no-longer[b] to-have-room not-even at[c] the door, and he-was-telling[d] them the word.

LEXICON—a. aorist pass. indic. of συνάγω (LN 15.125) (BAGD 2. p. 782): 'to gather together' [AB1, AB2, LN, Lns, NTC; ESV, KJV, NASB, NCV], 'to gather' [BAGD, BECNT, WBC; GW, NET, NIV], 'to gather around' [NRSV], 'to come together' [BAGD; TEV], 'to assemble' [BAGD], 'to collect' [BNTC]. The phrase 'many gathered together' is translated 'so many of them came to the house' [CEV], 'soon the house where he was staying was so packed with visitors' [NLT], 'such a crowd collected' [REB]. This verb means to come together [LN].

b. μηκέτι (LN 67.130) (BAGD 2. p. 518): 'no longer' [BAGD, LN]. The phrase 'so as no longer to have room' is translated 'so that there was no longer room' [NASB; similarly AB2], 'so that there was no longer any room left' [NTC; similarly BECNT, Lns, WBC; NET], 'that there was no longer room for them' [NRSV], 'that there was no room for them' [REB], 'that there was no room left' [AB1, BNTC; NIV], 'so that there was no more room' [ESV; similarly NLT], 'so that there was no room in the house' [NCV], 'there was no room left' [GW, TEV], 'insomuch that there was no room to receive them' [KJV], 'that there wasn't even standing room' [CEV]. This adverb indicates an extension of time up to a point but not beyond it [LN]. This emphasizes the size of the crowd that gathered due to Jesus' fame and popularity [BECNT, Gnd].

c. πρός (LN 83.24) (BAGD III.7 p. 711): 'at' [AB1, BAGD, LN; CEV, ESV], 'by' [BAGD, LN; NET], 'toward' [Lns], 'near' [BAGD, NTC, WBC; NASB], 'outside' [NCV, NIV, NLT, REB], 'in front of' [AB2, BNTC; GW, NRSV, TEV], 'around' [BECNT], 'about' [KJV]. This preposition indicates a position near another location or object [LN]. The word indicates proximity, either 'outside the door', 'in front of the door', or 'around the door' [NETfn].

d. imperf. act. indic. of λαλέω (LN 33.70) (BAGD 2.b. p. 463): 'to tell' [LN, Lns], 'to speak' [AB1, AB2, BAGD, BECNT, NTC, WBC; GW, NASB, NRSV], 'to teach' [CEV, NCV], 'to preach' [BNTC; ESV, KJV, NET, NIV, NLT, TEV], 'to proclaim' [BAGD; REB]. This verb means to speak or talk [LN]. The imperfect tense indicates that Jesus was speaking to the crowd while the men with the paralytic were approaching the house [Hb, ICC, Sw, TH; CEV].

QUESTION—What is meant by the phrase 'not even at the door'?

This refers to the space around the door, so people were probably standing outside the door in the street [Sw, Tay]. Such a large crowd had gathered that people filled the house and overflowed into the narrow street [BNTC, EBC, ICC, NIGTC, Tay, TH]. 'At the door' refers to the space outside the house, and the 'door' must mean the *doorway* since the door would have been open at the time [TH]. The open doorway was blocked by the crowd, so it was impossible to bring the paralytic into the room where Jesus was teaching the word [Lns].

QUESTION—What is meant by τὸν λόγον 'the word'?

The word is the good news, the gospel [BNTC, EBC, EGT, Gnd, Hb, ICC, My, NCBC, NTC, PNTC, Sw, Tay, TH]. This is translated as 'God's word' [TRT; GW, NLT], 'God's message' [NCV]. This was the message about the nearness of God's kingdom and the necessity for repentance and faith (1:14–15) [NICNT, WBC].

2:3 And they-come bringing[a] to him a-paralytic[b] being-carried[c] by four (men).

LEXICON—a. pres. act. participle of φέρω (LN 15.187) (BAGD 4.b.β. p. 855): 'to bring' [BAGD, BECNT, BNTC, Lns, NTC, WBC; ESV, KJV, NASB, NET, NIV, NRSV], 'to bear, to carry, to take along' [LN], not explicit [CEV, GW, NCV, NLT, TEV]. This active verb is also translated in the passive voice: 'a man was brought' [AB1; REB; similarly AB2]. This verb means to bear or carry something from one place to another [LN]. In this verse the verb means 'bringing' since the next clause uses a different verb 'being carried' to clarify the manner in which the paralytic was brought to Jesus [CGTC, TH].

b. παραλυτικός (LN 15.187) (BAGD p. 620): 'a paralytic' [AB2, BAGD, BECNT, LN, Lns, NTC, WBC; ESV, NASB, NET, NIV], 'a paralyzed man' [BNTC; GW, NCV, NLT, NRSV, TEV; similarly AB1; REB], 'one sick of the palsy' [KJV], 'a lame person' [BAGD], 'a crippled man' [CEV]. This adjectival noun denotes someone who was lame and/or paralyzed [LN]. This man was unable to walk, but it isn't known whether the cause was some type of paralyzing disease or an injury [NICNT, NIGTC]. Some think it was caused by a disease [EGT, NAC, NTC], but another thinks it was caused by an injury [NTC].

c. pres. pass. participle of αἴρω (LN 15.203) (BAGD 2. p. 24): 'to be carried' [AB2, BECNT, LN, Lns, NTC, WBC; ESV, NASB, NET, NIV, NRSV], 'to be carried along' [BAGD], 'to be borne' [KJV]. This passive verb is translated actively with the four men as the subject: 'carrying' [AB1, BNTC; CEV, GW, NCV, TEV; similarly REB], 'carrying on a mat' [NLT]. This verb means to lift up and carry away [LN].

QUESTION—Who are the referents of 'they' in the phrase '*they* come bringing to him the paralytic'?

The verb 'they come' has an indefinite antecedent and it is clear that it could not refer to the crowd of people being taught by Jesus in the preceding verse. Some languages require a more definite subject in their discourse structures [TH]. Instead of 'they came' some English translations supply the implied subject: '*some people* came' [NET, NRSV], '*some men* came' [NIV], '*four people* came' [NCV], '*four men* came' [CEV, GW, NLT, TEV]. One translation avoids the problem of how many people came by using a past passive verb: 'a man was brought' [REB]. Because of the two different verbs 'bringing' and 'carried', this could mean that the total number of people coming with the paralytic was more than four [TH].

1. 'They' refers to a group of people, and four of that group were carrying the paralytic [EGT; NET, NIV, NRSV]: some people were bringing a paralytic to Jesus, and *four of them* were carrying him. This can mean that four men were actually carrying the paralytic and they were accompanied by a group of his friends [EGT]. This is translated 'some people came bringing to him a paralytic, carried by four of them' [NET; similarly NIV, NRSV].

2. 'They' refers to the four men who were carrying the paralytic [AB2, Hb; CEV, GW, NCV, NLT, TEV; probably EBC]: they come bringing to Jesus a paralytic, and *these four men* were carrying him. This verse is translated 'Four men came to him carrying a paralyzed man' [GW; similarly CEV, NCV, NLT].

QUESTION—What was wrong with the paralytic?

Nothing of the nature of the man's affliction is known beyond the fact that he was unable to walk [NICNT, NIVfn]. One side of the paralytic's body had become useless [Lns]. Certain muscles were unable to function due to an injury of the motor areas of the brain or spinal cord [NTC]. For languages that require the translation to distinguish between chronic and acute illnesses, we can assume that this paralysis was of quite some duration [TH].

QUESTION—How did the four men carry the paralytic?

The next verse says that the men were carrying the paralytic on some sort of a pallet [Hb].

2:4 **And not being-able to-bring to-him/him because-of the crowd[a] they-unroofed[b] the roof where he-was, and having-dug-out-an-opening[c] they-lowered the pallet[d] upon (which) the paralytic was-lying.**

TEXT—Manuscripts reading προσενέγκαι 'to bring to' are given a B rating by GNT to indicate it was regarded to be almost certain. A variant reading is προσεγγίσαι 'to come near' and it is followed by AB2, BNTC, Hb, Lns, NTC; KJV, NASB. Another variant reading is προσελθεῖν 'to come to'.

LEXICON—a. ὄχλος (LN **11.1**) (BAGD 1. p. 600): 'crowd' [AB1, AB2, BAGD, BECNT, BNTC, LN, Lns, NTC, WBC; all versions except KJV], 'multitude' [LN], 'throng' [BAGD], 'the press' [KJV]. This noun denotes a casual non-membership group of people fairly large in size that has assembled for some purpose [LN].

b. aorist act. indic. of ἀποστεγάζω (LN **45.11**) (BAGD p. 98): 'to unroof, to remove the roof' [BAGD, LN]. The phrase ἀπεστέγασαν τὴν στέγην 'they unroofed the roof' [AB2, BECNT, WBC] is also translated 'they took off the roof' [**LN**], 'they removed the roof' [ESV, NASB, NET, NRSV], 'they uncovered the roof' [Lns; KJV], 'they opened up the roof' [AB1; NTC], 'they broke through the roof' [BNTC], 'they made a hole in the roof' [TEV], 'they made an opening in the roof' [NIV, REB]. The words 'they unroofed the roof where he was, and having dug out an opening' are translated 'they made a hole in the roof above him' [CEV], 'they dug a hole through the roof above his head' [NLT], 'they made an opening in the roof over the place where Jesus was' [GW], 'they dug a hole in the roof right above where he was speaking' [NCV]. This verb means to take the roof off of a house [LN].

c. aorist act. participle of ἐξορύσσω (LN **19.42**) (BAGD p. 277): 'to dig out' [BAGD], 'to dig out an opening, to break loose, to take out' [LN]. The participle ἐξορύξαντες 'having dug out an opening' [**LN**] is translated 'having dug it up' [Lns], 'having dug a hole' [BECNT;

similarly NCV, NLT], 'when they had dug an opening' [NASB; similarly NTC], 'when they had dug through the roof' [AB1], 'after digging through it' [WBC; NIV; similarly AB2; NRSV], 'when they had made a hole' [BNTC; similarly CEV], 'when they had made an opening' [ESV, TEV; similarly GW], 'when they had broken it up' [KJV], 'when they had broken through' [REB], 'after tearing it out' [NET]. This verb means to break something loose, usually doing this by digging out and opening up an area [LN].

d. κράβαττος (LN **6.107**) (BAGD p. 447): 'pallet' [AB2, BAGD, **LN**, Lns, NTC; NASB], 'mat' [BECNT, BNTC, WBC; CEV, NCV, NIV, NLT, NRSV, TEV], 'cot' [LN; GW], 'stretcher' [AB1, LN; NET], 'mattress' [BAGD], 'bed' [ESV, KJV, REB]. This noun denotes a relatively small and often temporary type of object on which a person could lie or recline [LN]. It was a poor man's bed [BAGD, Hb]. Perhaps it was a straw-filled mattress [NTC]. It was an improvised stretcher [TH]. The pallet was used as a stretcher because it had a wooden frame [AB2]. This word occurs at 2:4, 9, 11, 12; 6:55.

QUESTION—How does the dative case of the pronoun αὐτῷ 'him' function in the phrase προσενέγκαι αὐτῷ 'to bring him'?

1. 'Him' is the direct object of the verb and refers to the paralytic [AB1; BECNT, BNTC; NET, REB]: not able to bring *him* (into the house). This is translated 'they were not able to bring him in' [NET], 'they could not bring him near' [AB1; similarly REB], 'not being able to bring him (the paralytic) (to Jesus)' [BECNT].
2. 'Him' is the indirect object of the verb and refers to Jesus [AB2, Lns, NTC, WBC; all versions except NET, REB]: not able to bring (the paralytic) *to him (Jesus)*.

QUESTION—How could the men with the pallet get up on the roof?

Most houses had outside staircases to their flat roofs, so they could easily reach the roof of the house in which Jesus was teaching [BECNT, CGTC, EBC, EGT, Hb, My, NAC, NCBC, NICNT, NIGTC, Sw, Tay, TH]. This roof was flat [BECNT, Hb, LN (45.11), NAC, NICNT, NIGTC, NLTfn, NTC, TH] so they walked across the roof to a spot just above the room where Jesus was teaching inside the house [Sw, TH].

QUESTION—What is meant by 'they unroofed the roof' by 'digging out' an opening?

They unroofed only a portion of the roof, that is, 'they made a hole in the roof' [LN (45.11); CEV]. The clause 'they unroofed the roof where he was' means that they did this only to the portion of the roof above the spot where Jesus stood inside the crowded house [TH]. Luke 5:17 says that they removed tiles from the roof to make an opening. Since roofs in Israel were normally made of wooden beams covered with mud or clay [EBC, NLTfn], either the roof of this house was different and had tiles or Luke was interpreting this account in a way his Greek readers could understand [NLTfn]. Some assume that the roof did have some form of tiles. Digging out an opening refers to the removal of the tiles and their support [Lns]. They dug through the tiles, laths, and plaster of the roof [EGT]. Probably this roof had stone slabs or plates of burnt clay laid across the beams of the roof and these were covered with a coating of clay. They could have dug away the clay and lifted the tiles away without damaging the rest of the roof [Hb]. A normal roof was built across the house rafters from matting, branches, and twigs that were all covered by earth that had been trodden hard [NCBC, Tay]. Roofs constructed by thatching wooden beams with rush and then daubing them with mud were made sturdy enough so that people could sleep and work on top of them [NIGTC]. The roof was flat, held up by heavy beams over which were laid planks or sticks that were covered with sun-baked clay [LN (45.11)]. In this verse, ἐξορύσσω 'to dig out' probably refers to making an opening in the roof by digging through the clay of which the roof was made and moving aside the debris so that it wouldn't fall on the heads of those inside the house [BAGD (p. 277)].

QUESTION—How did the men lower the mat?

The men probably fastened ropes to the four corners of the mat and lowered the paralytic through the opening they had made in the roof [Hb, NTC, TH].

2:5 And having-seen their faith^a Jesus says to the paralytic, "Child,^b your sins are-forgiven.^c"

TEXT—Manuscripts reading ἀφίενται 'are forgiven' are given a B rating by GNT to indicate it was regarded to be almost certain. A variant reading has the perfect tense ἀφέωνται 'have been forgiven'.

LEXICON—a. πίστις (LN 31.85) (BAGD 2.b.α. p. 663): 'faith, trust' [LN]. The aorist participial phrase ἰδὼν τὴν πίστιν αὐτῶν 'having seen their faith' [Lns] is also translated 'seeing their faith' [AB2, WBC; NASB, NLT], 'upon seeing their faith' [BECNT], 'when Jesus saw their faith' [AB1, BNTC, NTC; ESV, GW, KJV, NET, NIV, NRSV, REB; similarly NCV], 'when Jesus saw how much faith they had' [CEV; similarly TEV]. This noun denotes complete trust and reliance [LN]. Here faith refers to a belief and trust in the Lord's help in regard to physical and spiritual distress [BAGD].

b. τέκνον (LN 9.46) (BAGD 2.a. p. 808): 'child' [BECNT, Lns], 'my child' [AB2, BAGD, LN; NLT], 'son' [NTC, WBC; ESV, KJV, NASB, NET, NIV, NRSV], 'my son' [AB1, BAGD, BNTC; REB, TEV], 'young man' [NCV], 'friend' [GW], 'my friend' [CEV], 'my dear friend, my dear man' [LN]. This noun denotes a person of any age for whom there is a special relationship of endearment and association [LN]. This is an affectionate form of address [AB1, CGTC, Hb, Lns, NAC, Tay]. This term indicates that Jesus was a superior who acted with authority and benevolence [PNTC]. This term would be used by an authoritative person as he addressed someone having less authority [TRT]. 'Child' does not mean that the paralytic was a boy [Hb, NAC, TH, TRT], nor does it mean that he was Jesus' natural son [TRT].

c. pres. pass. indic. of ἀφίημι (LN 40.8) (BAGD 2. p. 126): 'to be forgiven' [LN], 'to be pardoned' [BAGD, LN], 'to be cancelled, to be remitted' [BAGD]. The present passive participle ἀφίενταί 'are forgiven' [AB1, AB2, BECNT, BNTC, NTC, WBC; all versions except KJV] is also translated 'be forgiven thee' [KJV], 'dismissed are thy sins' [Lns]. This verb means to remove the guilt resulting from wrongdoing [LN]. The present tense indicates that his sins were forgiven at that moment [AB1, CGTC, Gnd, Hb, NICNT, NTC, Tay, TH].

QUESTION—What relationship is indicated by the use of the participle ἰδών 'having seen' their faith?

This participle indicates a temporal circumstance [AB1, AB2, BNTC, TH; CEV, ESV, GW, KJV, NCV, NET, NIV, NRSV, REB]: *when he saw their faith*.

QUESTION—To whom does '*their* faith' refer to?
1. 'Their faith' refers to the four men who had lowered the paralytic through the hole to Jesus [EGT, Gnd, NAC, NIGTC, PNTC]. The faith of the four men was apparent from all they had to do to get the paralytic to Jesus [EGT]. The faith exercised by the eagerness of the four men to help the paralytic is in focus [NAC, NIGTC]. After seeing how the four men on the roof above him had demonstrated their faith, Jesus then turned to speak to the paralytic in front of him [Gnd, PNTC].
2. 'Their faith' refers to the four men and the paralytic [BECNT, BNTC, CBC, EBC, Hb, ICC, Lns, NETfn, NIVfn, NLTfn, Tay, TH, TRT; NET]. Jesus saw that the faith of the four men was strong and inventive enough to find an unusual way of placing the sick man before him. The faith of the paralytic should also be included since he wasn't brought to Jesus against his will and must have consented to being lowered through the roof [Lns].

QUESTION—What did these people have faith about?

They were confident that Jesus could help the man [TH, WBC]. They believed that Jesus had the power to heal the paralytic [Hb, Lns, NIGTC, Tay]. The paralyzed man must also have recognized that he needed to come to Jesus to be saved from the burden of his sins [Lns].

QUESTION—In the announcement, 'your sins are forgiven', who has forgiven the paralytic's sins?

The use of the passive verb ἀφίενταί 'are forgiven' makes the statement ambiguous. It either means that Jesus himself has forgiven the paralytic's sins or that Jesus was making a prophetic announcement that God has forgiven the man by using the passive 'are forgiven' to reverently avoid speaking the divine name [CGTC].
1. This means that Jesus has forgiven the man [BECNT, BNTC, EBC, ESVfn, Gnd, Hb, Lns, NIGTC, NLTfn, NTC, PNTC, WBC; probably AB2]: *I forgive your sins*. Jesus was not just stating a fact that the man's sins were forgiven, he was actually assuming the authority to forgive the man [NIGTC]. The people understood the words of Jesus to be a claim to

divine authority [NLTfn]. The whole controversy in this passage is about what Jesus had done in forgiving the paralytic's sins, not whether God has forgiven him [BECNT, Lns]. This view agrees with the following dialogue where Jesus does not correct the scribes' understanding that he was the one who forgave the man's sins [BECNT, NIGTC].

2. This means that God has forgiven the man [NETfn, NICNT; probably AB1, TH]: *God forgives your sins.* Jesus' use of the passive was the customary Jewish way of speaking of God's action while avoiding speaking the divine name [NETfn, NICNT].

QUESTION—How were the paralytic's sins connected with his need to be healed?

We can assume that the paralytic was deeply concerned about his sins even though we are not told that his personal sins caused his illness [NTC]. Probably the man's paralysis brought all of his ordinary sinfulness to mind, and Jesus had seen all this guilt and repentance in the man's heart [Hb, Lns]. Some think that the abrupt reference to forgiveness at this point indicates that Jesus had traced the man's affliction to sin [CGTC, ICC, Tay, WBC]. It is possible that the words '*your* sins' shows that Jesus knew of the particular sins of the man and their relationship to his illness [PNTC].

2:6 **And some of-the scribes**[a] **were-sitting there and reasoning**[b] **in their hearts,**

LEXICON—a. γραμματεύς (LN 53.94): 'scribe' [AB1, AB2, BAGD, BECNT, BNTC, Lns, NTC, WBC; ESV, GW, KJV, NASB, NRSV, REB], 'expert in the Law' [BAGD, LN; NET], 'scholar versed in the law' [BAGD], 'one who is learned in the Law' [LN], 'teacher of the law/Law' [NCV, NIV, TEV], 'teacher of the Law of Moses' [CEV], 'teacher of religious law' [NLT]. This noun denotes a recognized expert in Jewish law as it relates to both canonical and traditional laws and regulations [LN]. The major task of scribes was to copy the sacred text of the OT, and the great amount of time they spent at their work helped qualify them to make judgments about the law [CBC]. They were schooled in the written law of God and its interpretation [NICNT]. They were men of importance in Jewish affairs [Hb]. This word occurs at 1:22; 2:6, 16; 3:22; 7:1, 5; 8:31; 9:11, 14; 10:33; 11:27; 12:28, 32, 38; 14:1, 43, 53; 15:1, 31.

b. pres. mid./pass. participle of διαλογίζομαι (LN 30.10) (BAGD 1. p. 186): 'to reason' [BAGD, BECNT, Lns, NTC, WBC; KJV, NASB], 'to question' [ESV, NRSV], 'to ponder' [AB1, AB2, BAGD], 'to consider' [BAGD], 'to consider carefully, to think out carefully, to reason thoroughly' [LN]. The phrase διαλογιζόμενοι ἐν ταῖς καρδίαις αὐτῶν 'reasoning in their hearts' is translated 'questioning in their minds' [AB1], 'thinking to themselves' [NCV, NIV, REB], 'thought to themselves' [BNTC; NLT, TEV], 'they started wondering' [CEV], 'turning these things over in their minds' [NET], 'they thought' [GW]. This verb means to think or reason with thoroughness and completeness [LN]. It is a Hebrew expression that refers to inward deliberation [Tay].

QUESTION—Why were these scribes among the crowd in the house?

The scribes were concerned about the growing popularity of Jesus and had come to keep a close watch on him [Hb]. Since they were sitting there, they must have arrived early in order to easily hear and see Jesus [EGT]. This first incident involving scribes in this book shows that they were already hostile towards Jesus [BECNT, CGTC, Gnd, Lns, NICNT]. They hoped that they could find Jesus wrong on some theological point [EBC].

QUESTION—What is meant by the phrase 'reasoning in their hearts'?

The scribes were thinking and reflecting on this matter without saying anything out loud [TH]. 'Heart' denotes the inner person, and more specifically, the mind [ICC], the seat of intellectual activity [NAC]. Mark puts their thoughts into words in the next verse [CGTC], but this was all unspoken, even though their thoughts probably showed in their faces [AB1, CGTC, Tay].

2:7 "Why (is) this (one) speaking thus? He-blasphemes.[a] Who is-able to-forgive sins except[b] one, God?"

LEXICON—a. pres. act. indic. of βλασφημέω (LN 33.400) (BAGD 2.b.α. p. 142): 'to blaspheme' [AB1, AB2, BAGD, BECNT, LN, Lns, NTC, WBC; ESV, NASB, NET, NIV], 'to speak blasphemies' [KJV], 'to revile, to defame' [LN]. The phrase 'he blasphemes' is also translated 'it/this is blasphemy' [BNTC; NLT, NRSV, REB, TEV], 'he's dishonoring God' [GW], 'he is speaking as if he were God' [NCV], 'he must think he is God' [CEV]. This verb means to speak against someone in such a way as to harm or injure his reputation. One way in which βλασφημέω 'to blaspheme' and βλασφημία 'blasphemy' were used in regard to 'defaming God' was by claiming some kind of equality with God. Any such statement was regarded as being harmful and injurious to the nature of God [LN].

b. The Greek phrase εἰ μή 'if not' means 'except, but only' [LN (89.31)]. The phrase 'except one, God' [Lns] is also translated 'except One, that is, God' [AB2], 'except God alone' [AB1], 'but God alone' [BECNT, BNTC, NTC; ESV, NASB, NET, NIV, NRSV], 'but God only' [KJV], 'except the One God' [WBC]. The question 'Who is able to forgive sins except one, God?' is translated 'Who but God can forgive sins?' [REB], 'Who besides God can forgive sins?' [GW], 'Only God can forgive sins.' [CEV, NCV, NLT], 'God is the only one who can forgive sins!' [TEV]. The phrase εἰ μή 'except' indicates contrast by designating an exception [LN].

QUESTION—What is implied by the question, 'Why is this one speaking thus?'

This is a rhetorical question that makes an emphatic statement: 'By speaking thus he blasphemes!' [TH; CEV, NCV, NLT]. Speaking of Jesus as οὕτως 'this one', or 'this fellow' showed their contempt for him [BNTC, CGTC, Hb, Lns, My, Tay, TH].

QUESTION—Why would they consider what Jesus said to be blasphemy?

The scribes took Jesus words to mean that he was personally claiming the right to forgive sin, so they accused Jesus of blasphemy because only God has the right to forgive sin [BECNT, BNTC, EBC, Hb, ICC, NIVfn, NTC, PNTC, Sw, Tay, WBC]. Another view is that by using the passive statement 'your sins are forgiven', Jesus was telling the man that God forgave the man's sins. If that were the case, however, the scribes' accusation of blasphemy would be ignoring the possibility of a man speaking on God's behalf [ICC]. The scribes objected to Jesus' assumption that he could even speak for God [NICNT; NET]. Although this could be interpreted in a safely monotheistic sense that God forgave the man's sins, neither the scribes nor Jesus took that option [NIGTC].

QUESTION—What is meant by the scribes' question, 'Who is able to forgive sins except one, God'?

This is a rhetorical question that serves to make an emphatic declaration that only God is able to forgive sins [NIGTC]. Some translate this question as a statement [NIGTC; CEV, NCV, NLT, TEV]: *Only God can forgive sins!* They reasoned that Jesus blasphemed against God by claiming to do something that only God could do [Gnd, Hb, Lns, WBC]. Their mistake was that they considered Jesus to be a mere man in spite of all the evidence that they had received to the contrary [Lns].

2:8 **And immediately having-known in his spirit[a] that thus they-were-reasoning[b] in/among themselves Jesus says to-them, "Why are- you -reasoning these (things) in your hearts[c]?**

LEXICON—a. πνεῦμα (LN 26.9) (BAGD 3.b. p. 675): 'spirit' [BAGD, **LN**], 'spiritual nature, inner being' [LN]. The phrase 'having known in his spirit' is translated 'perceiving in his spirit' [NTC; ESV; similarly BECNT; KJV, NRSV], 'aware in his spirit' [NASB], 'realized in his spirit' [NET; similarly Lns], 'recognizing in his spirit' [AB2], 'knowing in his spirit' [WBC; NIV], 'aware in his own mind' [AB1], 'knew inwardly' [GW], 'Jesus knew' [CEV, NCV, NLT, REB, TEV], 'Jesus realized' [BNTC]. This noun denotes the non-material, psychological faculty that is potentially sensitive and responsive to God [LN]. It denotes the part of the human personality that is the source and seat of insight, feeling, and will [BAGD].

b. pres. mid./pas. (deponent = act.) indic. of διαλογίζομαι (LN 30.10) (BAGD 1. p. 186): 'to reason' [BAGD, BECNT, LN, Lns, NTC, WBC; KJV, NASB], 'to consider' [BAGD], 'to ponder' [AB2, BAGD], 'to question' [ESV], 'to think' [NIV], 'to consider carefully, to think out carefully, to reason thoroughly' [LN]. The phrase 'thus they were reasoning in/among themselves' is translated 'what they were thinking' [AB1, BNTC; CEV, GW, NLT, REB, TEV; similarly NCV], 'they were discussing these questions among themselves' [NRSV], 'they were contemplating such thoughts' [NET]. This verb means to think or reason with thoroughness and completeness [LN].

c. καρδία (LN 26.3) (BAGD 1.b.β. p. 403): 'heart' [AB2, BECNT, LN, Lns, NTC, WBC; ESV, KJV, NASB, NET, NLT, NRSV], 'inner self, mind' [LN]. The question 'Why are you considering these things in your hearts?' is translated 'Why are you thinking such/these things?' [AB1; CEV, NCV, NIV; similarly BNTC; TEV], 'Why do you have these thoughts?' [GW]. This is a figurative extension of the word 'heart' to denote the causative source of a person's psychological life in its various aspects, especially in relation to his thoughts [LN].

QUESTION—What is meant by Jesus 'having known in his spirit'?

Knowing 'in his spirit' means the same as knowing in himself [Tay, TH], in his heart [BECNT], in his mind [NAC]. Jesus knew inwardly and intuitively what was going on in their minds [Hb, ICC, Sw]. In this verse, 'spirit' does not refer to the Holy Spirit [BECNT, Gnd, Hb, Tay; probably ESV, KJV, NASB, NET, NIV, NRSV which do not capitalize 'spirit']. Jesus knew this simply because he was the Son of God, or because God had given him this insight [CBC]. This knowledge was derived from his supernatural power of discernment [NIGTC]. Jesus used his divine attributes when his work required it, so in this case he knew their thoughts because of his omniscience [Lns]. Perhaps this is just the result of his spiritual discernment, not supernatural knowledge [NAC, Tay]. Any person with insight would have been able to know what the scribes were thinking on this occasion [NAC].

QUESTION—Were the scribes reasoning such things silently in their minds or vocally among themselves?

1. They were reasoning these things in their minds [AB2, BECNT, EBC, EGT, Hb, NAC, NCBC, PNTC, Sw, Tay, TH, TRT; all versions except NRSV]. The words ἐν ἑαυτοῖς 'in themselves' could mean that they were talking among themselves, but that is unlikely since in 2:6 their reasoning was in their 'hearts', and here Jesus knew in his spirit what they were reasoning [BECNT].

2. They seem to have also been discussing these things among themselves [NRSV; perhaps WBC which translates this 'among themselves'].

QUESTION—What is implied by the question Jesus asked the scribes?

This was a rhetorical question that functioned as a reprimand [Hb, NTC]. The question means, 'You are wrong to be thinking like that!' [TRT]. They made this false accusation because they had come there to find fault with Jesus [NTC].

2:9 Which is easier,[a] to-say to-the paralytic, 'Your sins are forgiven' or to-say, 'Stand-up[b] and pick-up[c] your mat and walk'[d]?

TEXT—As in 2:5, manuscripts reading ἀφίενται 'are forgiven' are given a B rating by GNT to indicate it was regarded to be almost certain. A variant reading has the perfect tense ἀφέωνται 'have been forgiven'.

106   MARK 2:9

LEXICON—a. εὔκοπος (LN 22.39) (BAGD p. 321): 'easy' [LN]. The comparative sense is translated 'easier' [all translations]. This adjective pertains to that which is easy in the sense of not requiring great effort [LN].
  b. pres. act. impera. of ἐγείρω (LN 17.9) (BAGD 1.b. p. 214): 'to stand up' [AB1, LN; NCV, NET, NIV, NLT, NRSV, REB], 'to get up' [AB2, BECNT, LN, NTC; CEV, GW, NASB, TEV], 'to arise' [Lns, WBC; KJV], 'to rise' [BECNT; ESV]. This verb means to get up from a reclining position [LN].
  c. aorist act. impera. of αἴρω (LN 15.203) (BAGD 1.a. p. 24): 'to pick up' [BAGD, BECNT, WBC; CEV, GW, NASB, NLT, TEV], 'to lift up' [BAGD], 'to take up' [AB2, BAGD, BECNT, Lns; ESV, KJV], 'to take' [AB1; NCV, NET, NIV, NRSV, REB], 'to carry, to remove, to take away' [LN]. This verb means to lift up and carry away [LN].
  d. pres. act. impera. of περιπατέω (LN 15.227) (BAGD 1.c. p. 649): 'to walk' [BAGD, LN; all translations except BECNT; CEV, GW], 'to walk about' [BAGD]. This imperative verb is translated 'go home' [GW], 'go on home' [CEV], 'go to your home' [BECNT]. This verb means to walk along or to walk around [LN].
QUESTION—What would the scribes choose as being easier to say?
  1. The scribes would think that it was easier to say 'Your sins are forgiven!' [AB2, BECNT, BNTC, EBC, EGT, Gnd, Hb, My, NAC, NCBC, NICNT, NIGTC, NLTfn, PNTC, Sw, Tay, TH, WBC]. It was easier for Jesus to announce that the man's sins are forgiven since there was no way to confirm whether or not forgiveness has actually taken place. But if Jesus told the paralytic to stand up and walk, it would immediately be apparent whether or not the man had been healed [BECNT, Tay, TH]. It is the verifiability of the statements that determines which is easier, so when the word of healing is confirmed by observation, then the validity of the easier word of forgiveness is verified [WBC]. Although the scribes would have thought it was easier for Jesus to say that the man's sins were forgiven because it couldn't be verified, the accurate answer is that it was easier to heal than to take on God's role of forgiving sins [AB2, BECNT, BNTC, ESVfn, NAC, NCBC, NIGTC, Sw], or that both words were equally the work of God [EBC, NAC]. The logic behind this question is that if Jesus can perform the visible miracle of healing the paralytic, it would be evidence that he also has the power to do the invisible miracle of forgiving the man's sins [ESVfn, WBC].
  2. The scribes would be uncertain about which would be easier [CBC, CGTC, ICC, Lns, NETfn, NIVfn, NTC]. The question was asked in order to cause them to think about the answer. To declare that the man's sins are forgiven is easier to say since one can't see if it really happened. On the other hand, it is harder to accomplish because Jesus would have to actually possess the authority to forgive sin. [NETfn]. Jesus posed a question that wasn't easy to answer. They should realize that both forgiving sins and healing equally showed the presence of God's reign

and the fulfillment of the OT promises [CGTC]. Neither is easier or harder since both statements require the identical power of God [Lns]. The two statements are just two ways of saying the same thing. Because the disease was the consequence of the man's sin, the cure would be a remission of the penalty [ICC].

QUESTION—Why did Jesus command the man to walk?

Jesus wanted the man to *walk about in front of everyone* in order to prove that he was completely healed [Lns, TH]. Others think that Jesus was simply telling the man to take up his mat and *go on home* [BECNT; CEV, GW].

2:10 But in-order-that[a] you-may-know that the Son of-Man[b] has authority[c] to-forgive sins on earth[d]—" he-says to-the paralytic, **2:11** "I-say to-you, 'Stand-up, pick-up your pallet and go to your house.'"

LEXICON—a. ἵνα (LN 89.59): 'in order that' [BECNT, LN, Lns, NTC, WBC], 'so that' [AB1, AB2, BNTC, LN; NASB, NET, NRSV], 'for the purpose of' [LN], 'that' [ESV, KJV, NIV], not explicit [REB]. Since this dependent purpose clause is not finished with a consequence clause, some translations change it to an independent clause: 'I want you to know that...' [GW], 'I will show you that...' [CEV], 'I will prove to you that...' [NCV, NLT, TEV]. This conjunction indicates the purpose for events and states [LN].

b. υἱὸς τοῦ ἀνθρώπου (LN 9.3) (BAGD 2.e. p. 835): This title is translated 'the Son of Man' [BAGD, LN; all translations except AB1], 'The Man' [AB1]. It is a title with Messianic implications that Jesus used concerning himself [LN]. Jewish thought at the time of Jesus knew of a heavenly being who was looked upon as a 'Son of Man' or 'Man' who exercised Messianic functions such as judging the world [BAGD].

c. ἐξουσία (LN 76.12) (BAGD 3. p. 278): 'authority' [AB1, AB2, BAGD, BECNT, BNTC, LN, Lns, NTC, WBC; all versions except CEV, KJV], 'right' [CEV], 'power' [LN; KJV]. This verb means the power to do something, with or without an added implication of authority [LN].

d. γῆς (LN 1.39): 'earth' [LN; all translations], 'world' [LN]. This noun denotes the surface of the earth as the dwelling place of mankind and is used in contrast with the heavens above it [LN].

QUESTION—What relationship is indicated by δέ 'but'?

This conjunction indicates contrast [AB1, AB2, BECNT, BNTC, Gnd, Lns, NTC, Sw, WBC; ESV, KJV, NASB, NCV, NET, NIV, NRSV, REB]: *but*. It means '*but be the answer what it may*, to convince you that the word of absolution was not uttered without authority, I will confirm it by the word of healing of which you may see the effects' [Sw]. The conjunction contrasts the abstract question in 2:9 about which is easier to say with the concrete demonstration that follows [Gnd].

QUESTION—Who is saying, 'But in order that you may know that the Son of Man has authority to forgive sins on earth'?

    1. These words are a continuation of what Jesus was saying to the scribes [AB2, BECNT, BNTC, CBC, Gnd, Hb, ICC, Lns, NAC, NCBC, NTC, Tay, TH, TRT, WBC; all versions]: *in order that you scribes may know that the Son of Man has authority to forgive sins on earth.* Instead of finishing this purpose clause with words such as 'I will do this', Jesus turned from the scribes and directly addressed the paralytic [NETfn, TH]. Verse 10 progresses like this: Jesus told the scribes, 'But in order that you (plural) may know that the Son of Man has authority to forgive sins on earth, *(at this point Jesus turned from speaking to the scribes to face the paralytic)* I say to you (singular), "Stand up, etc."' Mark inserted the words, 'he says to the paralytic' to account for the shift from second person plural when speaking to the scribes to the second person singular when he addressed the paralytic [Gnd]. The act of healing itself proved that Jesus had authority to forgive sins [BECNT]. To indicate that the purpose clause is left unfinished some end the clause with a dash [BNTC, GNT, TH, WBC; ESV, NASB, NET, NRSV, REB] or ellipsis marks [NIV].

    2. Mark interrupts his story about Jesus to tell his readers to note the significance of the miracle of healing that he will relate in the next verse [CGTC, NICNT]: *in order that you readers may know that the Son of Man has authority to forgive sins on earth.* The fact that Jesus healed the paralytic is a proof to believers that Jesus can and does forgive sinners [CGTC]. Mark is telling his readers, "Know that the Son of Man has authority on earth to forgive sins." After this note to the readers, Mark indicates his return to the story of the incident itself with the words, 'he said to the paralytic' [NICNT].

QUESTION—What is the significance of the title ὁ υἱὸς τοῦ ἀνθρώπου 'the Son of Man'?

In Hebrew, the phrase 'son of man' is an idiom meaning 'human being' or 'person' [NLTfn]. In a number of languages there are serious complications involved with a literal translation of 'Son of Man' since the phrase is likely to be understood in a more or less literal sense of 'son of *a man*' and thus deny the virgin birth [LN (9.3), TH]. The title Jesus used is ambiguous since it could refer to an ordinary human being or to a supernatural being, requiring people to decide for themselves the kind of person he was [Hb, NAC]. As a title, it does not mean 'man' in the generic sense, but *'the Man'*, which could be used as a messianic designation [Tay]. The use of 'the Son of Man' as a title comes from the pictorial description in Dan 7:13–14 where one 'like a son of man' (meaning someone 'like a human being') came with the clouds of the sky to approach the 'Ancient of Days' where he was given eternal ruling authority, honor, and sovereignty over all the nations of the world [EBC, Hb, ICC, Lns, NETfn, NIGTC, NLTfn]. Jesus often referred to himself as 'the Son of Man' because it was not an inflammatory title such as

'Messiah' would have been at this stage of his ministry [NLTfn]. In Mark's account, Jesus gradually reveals the full meaning of the term and when fully understood it refers to his exalted authority [ESVfn]. This title enabled Jesus to reveal who he was to his followers and yet conceal his identity from outsiders [BECNT]. Jesus used the title 'Son of Man' because it was not so commonly recognized as 'Messiah'. If he had used the title 'Messiah', he would have brought on a crisis by forcing people to decide on his claim and probably reject him without getting to really know him [Hb, ICC]. Jesus did not use the title 'Son of Man' in order to distinguish his humanity from his deity as the 'Son of God' [NLTfn]. There are a few who do think that the title is used in the Son's incarnate life to mean the ideal Man and the head of the race [Sw].

QUESTION—How would the scribes know that Jesus had authority to forgive sins on earth?

Jesus connected the two actions so that when the man miraculously walked, it would be visible proof that God had worked through Jesus and it was true that the man's sins were forgiven [NETfn]. Jesus claimed that his authority was not merely to *declare* sins to be forgiven by God, but to actually forgive sins [NIGTC, WBC]. This says that he *has* authority to forgive sins, not that he *has been given* such authority [BECNT].

QUESTION—What do the words 'on earth' qualify?

1. 'On earth' refers to the location of Jesus' authority [AB1, AB2, Gnd, Hb, ICC, NIGTC, Sw, Tay, TH, WBC; all versions]: *the Son of Man has authority here on earth to forgive sins*. Since God has the prerogative to forgive sin in heaven, the claim of Jesus to forgive sin was a claim to be God's representative here on earth [Hb, ICC, Tay]. Another view is that Jesus was emphasizing the fact that what had been considered an exclusive heavenly function was now exercised on earth because of the presence of the Son of Man, who in Dan. 7:13–14 received from God authority over all the earth [NIGTC].
2. 'On earth' identifies the location where the sins were committed [CGTC]: *the Son of Man has authority to forgive sins committed on earth*.

QUESTION—Why is the last part of Jesus' command to the paralytic changed from 'and walk' in 2:9 to 'and go to your house'?

The paralytic had presumably been carried from his home to Jesus. To show the completeness of his healing, Jesus told him to walk back to his home [Gnd]. It implies that the man was a resident of Capernaum [Hb].

2:12 And he-got-up and immediately taking-up the mat he-went-outside in-front-of[a] all, causing all to-be-astonished[b] and to-praise[c] God saying, "This we-have- never –seen."

LEXICON—a. ἔμπροσθεν (LN 83.33) (BAGD 2.c. p. 257): 'in front of, before' [BAGD, LN]. The phrase 'in front of all' is translated 'in front of them all' [AB2; NET], 'in front of everyone' [BNTC, **LN**], 'before them all' [Lns, WBC; ESV, KJV], 'before all of them' [BECNT; NRSV], 'in the

sight of everyone' [NASB], 'in full view of them all' [NTC; NIV, REB; similarly AB1], 'while they all watched' [**LN**; TEV], 'while everyone watched' [CEV, GW], 'while everyone was watching him' [NCV], 'through the stunned onlookers' [NLT]. This preposition refers to a position in front of an object [LN].
    b. pres. mid. infin. of ἐξίστημι (LN 25.220) (BAGD 2.b. p. 276): 'to be astonished' [BAGD, NTC; REB], 'to be amazed' [AB2, BAGD, BECNT, Lns, WBC; all versions except CEV, REB, TEV], 'to be completely amazed' [TEV], 'to be astounded' [AB1, BNTC], 'to be astonished greatly, to be greatly astounded, to be astounded completely' [LN]. The clause 'causing all to be astonished' is translated 'while everyone watched in amazement' [CEV]. This verb means to cause someone to be so astounded and practically overwhelmed [LN]. Literally meaning 'to lose one's mind', it has the weakened sense of being astonished and fearful in the presence of a miraculous event [BAGD]. This word occurs at 2:12; 5:42; 6:51.
    c. pres. act. infin. of δοξάζω (LN 33.357) (BAGD 1. p. 204): 'to praise' [BAGD, LN], 'to glorify' [LN], 'to honor, to magnify' [BAGD]. The phrase 'and to praise God saying' is translated 'and praised God, saying' [BNTC; GW, NIV, TEV], 'and praised God, exclaiming' [NLT], 'and praised God. They said' [NCV; similarly REB], 'They praised God and said' [CEV], 'and praised God' [AB1], 'and glorified God, saying' [AB2, NTC, WBC; ESV, KJV, NET, NRSV], 'and were glorifying God, saying' [BECNT; NASB; similarly Lns]. This verb means to speak of someone as being unusually fine and deserving of honor [LN]. The present tense indicates that they continued praising God [Lns].

QUESTION—Who were 'all' the people who praised God with these words?
    1. With the exception of the critical scribes, 'all' refers to the bystanders in general [BECNT, EGT, Hb, Lns, NAC, NCBC, NIGTC, NTC, Tay, WBC]. No doubt the scribes who had just criticized Jesus are included in the 'all' who were astonished at the healing of the paralytic, but they would not have joined in giving praises to God for what Jesus had done [EGT, NIGTC]. The scornful and critical scribes had not experienced a change of heart and mind so as to join in praising God for the healing performed by Jesus, but the praising by the by-standers was sufficiently general to use of the word 'all' [NTC].
    2. 'All' refers to everyone present [EBC, Gnd, NICNT]. Using 'all' twice seems to be emphasizing the fact that the scribes along with everyone else who had watched the healing were praising God [Gnd]. Even though the scribes were shaken by the miracle and seemed to praise God by saying 'This we have never seen,' it doesn't mean that they thanked God for sending Jesus or even that they acknowledged the relationship between Jesus' words of forgiveness and the healing of the paralytic [NICNT].

QUESTION—What was the οὕτως 'this' that they had never seen?
1. 'This' refers to the physical healing of the paralytic [AB1, BNTC, CGTC, Gnd, Hb, NCBC, Tay, TRT]. It is natural that the people would concentrate on the healing they had seen instead of the invisible forgiveness verified by it [Gnd].
2. The people had witnessed healing before (1:32–34), but now they had just witnessed something new and unprecedented when Jesus declared the forgiveness of sins and demonstrated his right to do so [BNTC, EBC, NIGTC]. The emphasis is on the forgiveness of sins. In forgiving the man's sins Jesus was also declaring the presence of God's kingdom among them [EBC]. Through the miracle they had seen his power to forgive sins [Lns].

DISCOURSE UNIT—2:13–17 [CBC, EBC; CEV, ESV, GW, NET, NIV, NLT, NRSV, TEV]. The topic is the second controversy: Jesus calls Levi and eats with sinners [CBC], Jesus calls Levi [ESV, NRSV, TEV], the calling of Levi [NIV], Jesus chooses Levi [CEV], Jesus chooses Levi (Matthew) to be a disciple [GW], the call of Levi and his feast [Hb], the call of Levi; eating with sinners [NET], eating with sinners [EBC], Jesus calls notorious sinners [NLT].

DISCOURSE UNIT—2:13–14 [NICNT]. The topic is the call of a tax farmer.

2:13 And he-went-out[a] again beside the lake.[b] And all the crowd was-coming to him, and he-was-teaching them.

LEXICON—a. aorist act. indic. of ἐξέρχομαι (LN 15.40): 'to go out' [AB2, BECNT, BNTC, Lns, NTC, WBC; ESV, NASB, NET, NIV, NLT, NRSV, REB], 'to go out of, to depart out of, to leave from within' [LN], 'to go forth' [KJV], 'to go (to)' [CEV, GW, NCV], 'to go (back)' [AB1; TEV]. This verb means to move out of an enclosed or well defined two or three dimensional area [LN].

b. θάλασσα (LN 1.70) (BAGD 2. p. 350): 'lake' [BAGD, LN], 'sea' [LN]. The phrase 'beside the lake' [NIV] is also translated 'beside the sea' [AB2; ESV, NRSV], 'by the sea' [BECNT, WBC; NET], 'by the seaside' [KJV], 'by the seashore' [NASB], 'beside the shore of the lake' [BNTC], 'along the sea' [Lns], 'along the seashore' [NTC], 'to the seashore' [AB1; GW], 'to the lakeshore' [NLT], 'to the lakeside' [REB], 'to the lake' [NCV], 'to the shore of Lake Galilee' [CEV, TEV]. This noun denotes a particular body of water that is normally rather large [LN]. This noun occurs at 1:16; 2:13; 3:7; 4:1, 39, 41; 5:1, 13, 21; 6:47, 48, 49; 7:31; 9:42; 11:23.

QUESTION—How closely are the events of this paragraph connected with the preceding paragraph?

This incident follows the healing of the paralytic quite closely [Gnd, Hb, Lns, Sw, TRT], perhaps as soon as the crowd in the previous paragraph had dispersed [Hb, Sw]. Others think there is no direct narrative link with the preceding incident [EBC, NCBC, NIGTC]. This is the second of five separate incidents about Jesus coming into conflict with the religious leaders [EBC]. Jesus' public teaching before crowds is a recurring theme in the Capernaum events, and this is another occasion when the crowds gathered around him [EGT, NCBC, NIGTC, WBC].

QUESTION—What did Jesus 'go out of' again?

Jesus went out of his own house [Lns]. He went out of the house and out of the city of Capernaum to walk along the shore of the Lake of Galilee [Gnd, Hb, Sw, TH]. Perhaps he went to the lakeshore for its refreshing breezes [Hb, NTC], and for quiet prayer [Hb]. The word 'again' refers to his departure from Capernaum in 1:35, 38, and since he went out of the town to go to the lakeshore, it also refers to 1:16 [Gnd, TRT]. The word 'again' refers back to the scene where Jesus had started his ministry at Capernaum in 1:16 [BECNT, EGT, Hb, ICC, Lns, NIGTC, NTC, TH, TRT].

QUESTION—What is indicated by the use of the imperfect tenses of 'was coming' concerning the crowd and 'was teaching' concerning Jesus?

These imperfects probably indicate the coming and going of groups of people that Jesus successively taught [CGTC, Gnd, Hb, Lns, NICNT, Sw, Tay, TH]. The words 'all the crowd' means 'the whole crowd' or 'all the people' and does not refer to the same crowd mentioned in 2:4 [TH]. Others take it to refer to the same crowd in the preceding paragraph, although it was now growing larger [Sw, TRT].

DISCOURSE UNIT—2:14–22 [NASB]. The topic is the calling of Levi (Matthew).

2:14 And going-along[a] he-saw Levi the (son) of Alphaeus sitting at[b] the tax-office,[c] and he-says to-him "Follow[d] me." And rising-up[e] he-followed him.

TEXT—Manuscripts reading Λευίν 'Levi' are given an A rating by GNT to indicate it was regarded to be certain. A variant reading is Ἰάκωβον 'Jacob'.

LEXICON—a. pres. act. participle of παράγω (LN 15.15) (BAGD 2.a.α. p. 613): 'to go along' [BNTC, LN; NET, REB], 'to move along' [AB2, LN, 'to walk along' [AB1; CEV, NCV, NIV, NLT, NRSV, TEV], 'to pass by' [BAGD, BECNT, Lns, NTC, WBC; ESV, KJV, NASB], 'to leave' [GW]. This verb means to continue to move along [LN]. This word also occurs at 1:16.

b. ἐπί (LN 83.23): 'at' [AB2, BECNT, LN, Lns, WBC; CEV, ESV, KJV, NET, NIV, NLT, NRSV], 'in' [GW, NASB, NCV, TEV], 'by' [LN]. The phrase 'sitting at the tax office' is translated 'at his seat in the custom house' [BNTC; REB], 'at his place in the customs house' [AB1]. This preposition indicates a position that is in the immediate vicinity of an object [LN].

c. τελώνιον (LN 57.183) (BAGD p. 812): 'tax office' [BAGD, LN, Lns; GW], 'tax booth' [AB2; ESV, NASB, NET, NRSV], 'revenue office' [BAGD, LN], 'toll booth' [WBC], 'tax collector's booth' [NCV, NIV, NLT], 'the place for paying taxes' [CEV], 'custom house' [AB1, BNTC; REB], 'custom booth' [BECNT], 'the receipt of custom' [KJV]. The

clause is translated, 'he saw a tax collector, Levi son of Alphaeus, sitting in his office' [TEV]. This noun denotes a place where taxes and revenue were collected from those entering the town to sell produce [LN].
d. pres. act. impera. of ἀκολουθέω (LN 15.156) (BAGD 3. p. 31): 'to follow' [BAGD, LN; all translations except CEV], 'to accompany as a follower, to go along with' [LN]. The imperative 'Follow me' is translated 'Come with me' [CEV]. This verb means to follow or accompany someone who takes the lead in determining the direction and the route of movement [LN]. It means to follow someone as a disciple [BAGD].
e. aorist act. participle of ἀνίσταμαι (LN 15.36) (BAGD 2.d. p. 70): 'to rise' [BAGD; ESV, REB], 'to arise' [WBC; KJV], 'to get up' [AB1, AB2, BNTC; CEV, GW, NASB, NET, NIV, NLT, NRSV, TEV], 'to rise up' [BECNT, Lns], 'to stand up' [NCV], 'to depart, to go away from, to leave' [LN], 'to set out' [BAGD]. This verb means to move away from a reference point, and it may imply getting up and leaving [LN].

QUESTION—What relationship is indicated by the use of the participle παράγων 'going along'?

The participle indicates a temporal circumstance in regard to the main verb 'he saw': *as* he was going along [AB1, BECNT, BNTC, NTC, WBC; all versions except GW, NCV], *while* he was going along [NCV], *when* he was going along [GW].

QUESTION—How did Jesus happen to see Levi as 'he was going along'?

Jesus was going along the lake by the place where Levi sat [My]. Jesus may have been teaching as he walked along the shore of the lake when his teaching was interrupted by this encounter with Levi [EBC]. Or the teaching at the lakeshore had finished, and Jesus was walking along the shore of the lake on his way back to Capernaum [Lns]. The tax office was probably on the roadside [WBC], near the wharf at Capernaum [Hb].

QUESTION—Who was Levi, the son of Alphaeus?

Mark and Luke call this tax collector Levi in their accounts of the incident, while Mathew says that the man sitting at the tax office was named Matthew (Matt. 9:9). Most assume Levi was an alternative name for Matthew, and that this man is the same person who appears under the name Matthew in all the lists of the twelve Apostles [NIGTC]. Levi was his original name, and Jesus may have renamed him Matthew, or else Levi simply changed his name to 'Matthew' (meaning 'a gift of the Lord') to commemorate his call to become a disciple [Hb]. Most people who were named Levi were Levites, the descendants of the biblical Levi [AB2]. Perhaps the noun Λευίν was not his name but simply describes the man as being a Levite [AB1].

QUESTION—Where was Levi 'sitting *at* the tax office' and what is meant by 'taxes'?

The preposition ἐπί 'at' seems to say that Levi was not inside the tax office but sitting near the office [ICC]. However, many translations say that Levi was 'in' the tax office [GW, NASB, NCV, TEV]. Levi did not collect personal taxes on a person's wealth. He collected *custom charges* on produce that was transported to or through Capernaum [TH]. These were the taxes on transported goods [PNTC], which are called usage taxes [CBC], custom duties [EGT, NIGTC], tolls [CBC, CGTC, Gnd, NLTfn, Sw, Tay, WBC], or tariffs [NTC]. Since the customs office was in Capernaum, Levi would have been in the service of Herod Antipas, the ruler of Galilee [BECNT, BNTC, EBC, NICNT, TH]. The Jews considered such tax collectors to be outcasts from society [NICNT].

DISCOURSE UNIT—2:15–17 [NICNT]. The topic is the Messiah eating with sinners.

2:15 And it-happens[a] (that) he-reclined[b] in the house of-him, and many tax-collectors[c] and sinners[d] were-reclining with-Jesus and his disciples;[e]

LEXICON—a. pres. mid./pass. (deponent = act.) indic. of γίνεται (LN 13.107) (BAGD I.3.f. p. 159): 'to happen' [BAGD, LN], 'to occur, to come to be' [LN]. The phrase 'and it happens' is translated 'and it happened that' [WBC; NASB], 'and it comes to pass' [BECNT], 'and it came to pass' [AB2, Lns; KJV], 'later' [CEV, GW, NCV, NLT], 'later on' [AB1; TEV], 'and' [NTC; ESV, NRSV], 'and when' [BNTC], not explicit [NET, NIV, REB]. This verb means 'to happen', and implies that what happens is different from the previous setting [LN]. Although older versions have 'it came to pass', the function of this verb is to indicate progress in a narrative and usually the word is omitted in translation [BAGD].
  b. pres. mid./pass. (deponent = act.) infin. of κατάκειμαι (LN 17.23) (BAGD 3. p. 411): 'to recline' [BAGD, LN], 'to recline at table' [AB2, Lns, NTC; ESV], 'to recline at the table' [NASB], 'to recline for dinner' [BECNT], 'to be at table' [AB1], 'to sit at dinner' [NRSV], 'to dine' [BAGD, LN, WBC], 'to have a meal' [BNTC; NET, REB, TEV], 'to have dinner' [CEV, GW, NCV, NIV], 'to eat, to sit down to eat' [LN], 'to sit at meat' [KJV]. The phrase 'he reclined in the house of him' is translated 'Levi invited Jesus (and his disciples) to his home as dinner guests' [NLT]. This verb means to be in a reclining position as one eats [LN]. It refers to reclining on a dining couch [BAGD].
  c. τελώνης (LN 57.184) (BAGD p. 812): 'tax collector' [AB1, AB2, BAGD, LN, NTC; all versions except KJV], 'tax gatherer' [BNTC], 'toll collector' [BECNT, WBC], 'revenue officer' [BAGD, LN], 'publican' [Lns; KJV]. This noun denotes someone who collects taxes for the government [LN].
  d. ἁμαρτωλός (LN 17.23) (BAGD 2. p. 44): 'sinner' [AB2, BAGD, BECNT, BNTC, LN, Lns, NTC, WBC; ESV, GW, KJV, NASB, NET, NRSV, REB], 'outcast' [LN], 'nonobservant Jew' [AB1]. The phrase 'and sinners' is translated 'and "sinners"' [NCV, NIV], 'and other sinners' [CEV], 'and other outcasts' [TEV], 'and other disreputable sinners' [NLT]. This noun denotes a person who customarily sins. In contexts such as this verse, the noun may refer to persons who were irreligious in the

sense of having no concern for observing the details of the Law and such people were often treated as social outcasts [LN].

e. μαθητής (LN 36.38) (BAGD 2.a. p. 485): 'disciple' [AB1, AB2, BAGD, BECNT, BNTC, LN, Lns, NTC, WBC; all versions except CEV, NCV], 'follower' [LN; CEV, NCV], 'adherent' [BAGD]. This noun denotes a person who is a disciple or follower of someone [LN].

QUESTION—What relationship is indicated by the beginning phrase, Καὶ γίνεται 'And it happens'?

This is a transitional formula [Hb] that indicates progress in the narrative [BAGD], a new development in the story [NIGTC], or an important occurrence [Lns]. It implies that there was a period of time between the call of Levi and the feast given for Jesus and his disciples [Hb]. Some translate this phrase as 'later' [CEV, GW, NCV, NLT], or 'later on' [TEV]. Instead of the usual past tense 'and it *came* to pass' in narratives, this verse uses the present tense 'and it *comes* to pass', suggesting there was only a short interval of time between 2:13–14 and 15–17 [BECNT, Gnd]. This was probably Levi's farewell party since he was leaving home to become one of Jesus' disciples [EBC].

QUESTION—Why were these people reclining to eat?

Although the Jews did not always recline while eating, it was their practice to recline at the table when guests were present for a feast [AB2, BECNT, Hb, NAC, NIGTC, NTC, WBC]. This banquet was arranged by Levi to celebrate his call to discipleship [WBC]. Guests reclined on a couch with their unsandled feet extended toward the outer edge, and they used their right hands for eating while leaning on their left elbows [Hb]. The couches faced a short table on which the food was placed [BECNT]. Couches were large enough to accommodate several persons [Lns]. They may have reclined on pillows or rugs [WBC], mattresses, couches, or divans [NTC]. See lexical item *b.* above for the ways CEV, GW, NCV, NET, NIV, NLT, NRSV, and REB describe the function of reclining at feasts when that practice is unknown to the readers.

QUESTION—Who are the referents of 'he' and 'him' in the clause '*he* reclined in the house of *him*'?

1. Jesus reclined in Levi's house [AB2, BECNT, CGTC, EGT, Gnd, Hb, NICNT, NIGTC, NTC, PNTC, TH, TRT, WBC; CEV, GW, NCV, NET, NIV, NLT, TEV]. The parallel passage in Luke 5:29 says that Levi was the host, so the antecedent of 'him' must be 'Levi' [NTC, WBC]. This was Levi's house and many translations name Jesus as the guest and Levi as the owner of the house [CEV, GW, NCV, NET, NIV, NLT, NRSV, TEV]. Jesus is the immediate antecedent of 'he' [NTC].

2. Levi reclined in his own house [Lns, Tay]. Levi is first described as reclining at a table in his own house since he was the host and had prepared this feast for Jesus and his disciples. If Mark had intended for the pronoun 'he' to refer to Jesus, he would have specified 'Jesus' at that

point instead of only mentioning Jesus and his disciples as being guests [Lns].
3. Jesus reclined in his own house [BNTC, ICC, My]. Probably Mark means that Jesus was the host for this feast since the preceding pronoun 'him' at the end of the preceding verse refers to Jesus [BNTC, My].

QUESTION—Why were tax collectors despised by the Pharisees?

The public distrusted and hated the local custom collectors because these men worked for an unpopular government and usually got a substantial profit from overcharging whenever they could [NIGTC]. The tax collectors collected various kinds of taxes, a prominent tax being the custom tax charged on goods in transit. These tax collectors were universally despised for their dishonesty and their cooperation with the Roman authorities [Hb, WBC]. They were considered to be traitors [EBC].

QUESTION—Who were the ἁμαρτωλοί 'sinners' present at the feast?

These were people who did not carefully observe the Law, especially the dietary laws, in the way the Pharisees did [EBC, Hb, TH]. Probably their sins included moral sin as much as ritual offences [BECNT, Hb, NIGTC].
1. The tax collectors and the sinners were two different classes of people that were despised by the Pharisees [AB2, ESVfn, ICC, NICNT, NTC, PNTC, Sw, WBC; perhaps GW, KJV, NASB, NCV, NET, NIV, NRSV, REB which separate the two classes of people with 'and' without adding 'other']. 'Sinners' was a technical term the Pharisees used for people who showed no interest in the scribal traditions and did not follow their standards [NICNT]. Others think that there would be no point in criticizing Jesus for eating with the 'sinners' who did not live according to the ritual laws of the Pharisees since the Pharisees already included Jesus and his disciples in that same category [NTC, WBC]. So in this criticism, 'sinners' must refer to people of ill-repute who had an immoral lifestyle [PNTC, WBC] or people who blatantly violated God's law [NTC].
2. Tax collectors were also regarded as 'sinners' [BECNT, BNTC, Hb, TRT; CEV, NLT, TEV; probably Lns]. 'Sinners' is a general term that includes the tax collectors [BECNT]. Some translations refer to the second group of people who were not tax collectors as '*other* sinners' [BECNT; CEV, NLT] or 'other outcasts' [TEV].

QUESTION—Who were the disciples at the feast with Jesus?

The reference to Jesus' disciples would at least include the four men whom Jesus had called to follow him in 1:16–20, and the following remark that there were 'many' disciples following Jesus may mean that there were many more than just those four at the feast [BNTC, WBC]. These disciples were the ones who were Jesus' constant companions [NIGTC]. If these disciples were the twelve Apostles [BECNT, CGTC], the following account of the call of the Twelve in 3:13–19 is mentioned for other than chronological considerations [BECNT].

because[a] there-were many and they-were-following him.

LEXICON—a. γάρ (LN 89.23) (BAGD 2. p. 152): 'because' [LN], 'for' [AB2, BAGD, BECNT, BNTC, LN, Lns, NTC; ESV, KJV, NASB, NET, NIV, NRSV, REB], 'you see' [BAGD], not explicit [CEV, GW, NCV, NLT, TEV]. This conjunction indicates the cause or reason between events [LN]. It is an explanatory conjunction [BAGD].

QUESTION—Who were the people who were following Jesus and what relationship is indicated by γάρ 'because'?

1. The many people were the 'many tax collectors and sinners' whom Levi had invited to the feast [AB2, BECNT, EGT, Gnd, Hb, ICC, Lns, NAC, NICNT, NIGTC, NTC, Sw, Tay, TH, TRT; CEV, GW, NLT, REB, TEV; probably NIV]: *there were many tax collectors and sinners reclining with Jesus and his disciples, because there were many of such people who were following Jesus*. The conjunction 'because' indicates the reason for the many tax collectors and sinners being at the dinner with Jesus [Gnd]. Although it might seem strange that there were many tax collectors and sinners at the table with Jesus, many of them now considered Jesus to be their friend and were beginning to follow him [Lns, NTC].
2. The many people were the disciples who accompanied Jesus to the feast [BNTC, CGTC, NICNT]: *Jesus had disciples with him at the feast because there were many disciples who were following him*. This is a parenthetical remark to explain the reference to 'his disciples' since there has been no previous indication that Jesus had so many disciples [CGTC]. Since Mark has mentioned only five disciples of Jesus so far, he must abruptly indicate that Jesus was accompanied by many disciples at this point [Tay].
3. Following a variant reading of the text discussed in the next verse, the phrase 'and they were following him' is moved to the next verse to refer to the scribes of the Pharisees: 'The scribes of the Pharisees also followed him. And when they saw that he was eating with sinners and toll collectors, they began to say to his disciples…' It does not mean that the scribes were disciples of Jesus, it simply explains how the scribes came into this scene [WBC].

2:16 **And the scribes[a] of-the Pharisees having-seen that he-eats with sinners and tax-collectors were-saying to his disciples "(Why) does-he-eat with tax-collectors and sinners?"**

TEXT—Manuscripts reading ἠκολούθουν αὐτῷ. ¹⁶καὶ οἱ γραμματεῖς τῶν Φαρισαίων ἰδόντες 'they were following him. ¹⁶And the scribes of the Pharisees having seen' are given a C rating by GNT to indicate that choosing it over a variant text was difficult. A variant reading is ἠκολούθουν αὐτῷ. ¹⁶καὶ οἱ γραμματεῖς καὶ οἱ Φαρισαίων ἰδόντες 'they were following him. ¹⁶And the scribes and the Pharisees having seen' and it is followed by KJV. Another variant reading is ἠκολούθουν αὐτῷ ¹⁶καὶ γραμματεῖς τῶν

Φαρισαίων. καὶ ἰδόντες 'they were following him ¹⁶also the scribes of the Pharisees. And having seen' and this reading seems to be followed by WBC.

TEXT—Manuscripts reading ἐσθίει 'he eats' are given a B rating by GNT to indicate it was regarded to be almost certain. A variant reading is ἐσθίει καὶ πίνει 'he eats and drinks' and it is followed by KJV, NASB. Other variant readings are ἐσθίετε καὶ πίνετε 'you (plural) eat and drink', ἐσθίει ὁ διδάσκαλος ὑμῶν 'your teacher eats', and ἐσθίει καὶ πίνει ὁ διδάσκαλος ὑμῶν 'your teacher eats and drinks'.

LEXICON—a. γραμματεύς (LN 53.94) (BAGD 2. p. 165): 'scribe' [BAGD], 'one who is learned in the Law' [LN], 'an expert in the Law' [BAGD, LN]. The phrase 'the scribes of the Pharisees' [AB2, BECNT, Lns, WBC; ESV, NASB, NRSV] is also translated 'the scribes who were Pharisees' [NTC; GW], 'the teachers of the law who were Pharisees' [NCV, NIV], 'the teachers of religious law who were Pharisees' [NLT], 'some scribes who were Pharisees' [BNTC; REB], 'some Pharisee-lawyers' [AB1], 'some teachers of the Law, who were Pharisees' [TEV], 'some of the teachers of the Law were Pharisees' [CEV], 'the scribes and Pharisees' [KJV], 'the experts in the law and the Pharisees' [NET]. This noun denotes a recognized expert in Jewish law [LN]. This word occurs at 1:22; 2:6, 16; 3:22; 7:1, 5; 8:31; 9:11, 14; 10:33; 11:27; 12:28, 32, 38; 14:1, 43, 53; 15:1, 31.

QUESTION—How were 'the scribes of the Pharisees' connected with the Pharisees?

These were scribes who belonged to the Pharisee party [CGTC, EBC, Tay, TH; ESV, NASB, NRSV]. This phrase implies that not all Pharisees were professional scribes [NIGTC], and actually only a minority of the Pharisees were scribes [CGTC]. The phrase also implies that not all scribes were Pharisees [AB2, Hb, NICNT, NIVfn; CEV], although most of them were [Hb].

QUESTION—Were the scribes also guests at the dinner?

Probably the scribes did not actually enter the house since they would have felt that they would be contaminated if they did so [Hb]. These scribes waited outside until the guests came out of the house and then they accosted the disciples [Lns, NIGTC, NTC].

QUESTION—What is implied by the scribes' question, 'Why does he eat with tax collectors and sinners?'

This is a rhetorical question implying that such a scandalous action was incomprehensible [Hb]. It was a hostile accusation in the form of a question [AB2, BECNT, Gnd]. The question indicated their outrage at such an unacceptable action [NIGTC]. They thought that association with such a group would cause not only ritual defilement but also moral contamination [AB2, WBC]. They were protesting that Jesus, who claimed to teach and heal by God's authority, was mixing with sinners [BNTC]. This sentence is translated as an accusation instead of a question: 'He eats with the tax collectors and nonobservant Jews!' [AB1].

QUESTION—Why did the scribes direct their question to the disciples instead of Jesus himself?

The scribes did not yet dare to criticize Jesus directly [Gnd, Hb, Lns, NTC, Sw]. Perhaps they were also trying to shake their faith in a Master who was setting such a bad example [Hb]. Since disciples of the Pharisees directly ask Jesus similar questions in 2:18 and 2:23–24, they were probably asking the disciples because they could not get into the house where Jesus was the guest of honor [NIGTC].

2:17 **And having-heard, Jesus says to-them "The (ones) being-healthy^a have no need of-a-physician^b but the (ones) having illness.^c**

LEXICON—a. pres. act. participle of ἰσχύω (LN 23.130) (BAGD 1. p. 383): 'to be healthy' [LN], 'to be in good health' [BAGD]. The phrase 'the ones being healthy' is translated 'people/those who are healthy' [BECNT, LN, NTC; NASB, NET], 'the healthy' [AB1, Lns, WBC; NIV, REB], 'healthy people' [CEV, GW, NCV, NLT], 'people/those who are well' [BNTC; ESV, NRSV, TEV], 'they that are whole' [KJV], 'the strong' [AB2]. This verb refers to a state of being healthy, robust, and vigorous [LN].
  b. ἰατρός (LN 23.141) (BAGD 1. p. 368): 'physician' [AB1, BAGD, BECNT, LN, Lns, WBC; ESV, KJV, NASB, NET, NRSV], 'doctor' [AB2, BNTC, LN, NTC; CEV, GW, NCV, NIV, NLT, REB, TEV], 'healer' [LN]. This noun denotes a person who heals people [LN].
  c. κακῶς (LN 23.148) (BAGD 1. p. 398): 'badly' [BAGD, LN]. The phrase 'the ones having illness' is translated 'those who are ill' [Lns, NTC, WBC], 'those who are sick' [BECNT, BNTC; ESV, GW, KJV, NASB, NET, NRSV, TEV], 'sick people' [CEV, NLT], 'the sick' [AB1, AB2; NCV, NIV, REB]. The phrase κακῶς ἔχω 'to have badly' or 'to fare badly' is an idiom meaning to be ill [LN]. This adverb occurs at 1:32, 34; 2:17; 6:55.

QUESTION—How did Jesus hear what the scribes said?
  1. What the scribes had said to the disciples was reported to Jesus later [AB1; Hb, Lns, NAC, Sw, Tay]. The scribes probably were not present at the meal where Jesus was eating [NAC, Tay].
  2. Jesus overheard what the scribes were saying to his disciples [Gnd, TRT; CEV, NASB, TEV]. Not waiting for his disciple to relay the question on to him, Jesus spoke directly to the scribes [Gnd].

QUESTION—To whom did Jesus speak?

Jesus spoke directly to the scribes who had criticized him [Gnd, Hb, Lns, TH; CEV, NASB]. Jesus answered the scribes who had asked the question [TH]. He directed his statement to the scribes, not to the crowd [Gnd].

I-came not to-call^a righteous^b (people) but sinners.^c"

TEXT—Manuscripts ending this sentence with ἁμαρτωλούς 'sinners' are followed by GNT, which does not mention any variant reading. A variant reading is ἁμαρτωλούς εἰς μετανοίαν 'sinners to repentance' and it is followed by KJV.

LEXICON—a. aorist act. infin. of καλέω (LN 33.307) (BAGD 2. p. 399): 'to call' [AB1, AB2, BAGD, BECNT, LN, Lns, NTC, WBC; all versions except CEV, NCV], 'to summon' [BNTC, LN], 'to invite' [NCV], 'to invite…to be my followers' [CEV]. This verb means to communicate directly or indirectly with someone who is presumably at a distance in order to tell that person to come [LN].
- b. δίκαιος (LN 88.12) (BAGD 1.b. p. 195): 'righteous' [BAGD, LN], 'just' [LN]. The phrase 'righteous people' [AB2; NTC; similarly Lns] is also translated 'the righteous' [BECNT, BNTC, NICNT; ESV, KJV, NASB, NET, NIV, NRSV], 'respectable people' [TEV], 'good people' [CEV, NCV], 'the virtuous' [REB], 'the self-righteous' [AB1], 'those who think they are righteous' [NLT], 'people who think they don't have any flaws' [GW]. This adjective describes someone as being in accordance with what God requires [LN]. In it's religious aspect, the verb refers to keeping God's law and not violating his sovereignty [BAGD].
- c. ἁμαρτωλός (LN 88.295) (BAGD 2. p. 44): 'sinner' [BAGD, LN]. This plural noun is translated 'sinners' [AB1, AB2, BECNT, BNTC, Lns, NTC, WBC; all versions except NLT, TEV], 'those who know they are sinners' [NLT], 'outcasts' [TEV]. This adjectival noun denotes a person who customarily sins [LN].

QUESTION—What is implied by the verb ἦλθον 'I came'?

With the verb 'I came' Jesus was referring to his whole mission and the purpose of his ministry [CGTC, Hb, NAC, NCBC, TH]. He was not just talking about coming to the banquet [TH]. Perhaps it is also indicates that he was conscious of his pre-existence [CGTC].

QUESTION—What did Jesus come to call people to do?

The verb καλέσαι 'to call' means to invite or summon people to something. He is speaking of calling people to repentance [Hb, NAC, NIGTC, Tay, TRT]. In 1:15 Jesus called people to repent and believe in the gospel [NIGTC]. As Savior, he calls people to be saved [EBC, ICC], or calls them to enter the kingdom of God [NAC, NICNT]. Jesus was sent by God to offer forgiveness and a place in the kingdom of God to sinners [BECNT]. He came to invite sinners to be his followers [CEV].

QUESTION—Who were the 'righteous' people?

Jesus now uses the term 'righteous' and 'sinners' in the way the Pharisees did when they made distinctions between righteous people and sinners [ICC, Lns, NICNT, Sw, TH]. These were the terms in current use to describe the two classes of society [EGT]. Jesus used the description 'righteous' as referring to what the scribes thought of themselves, not their actual state before God [EBC, Lns, NICNT, NIVfn, NTC]. In other sections of Mark, it is clear that Jesus did not actually consider the scribes to be righteous [ICC]. Jesus did not come to call people who considered themselves to be righteous but to call outcasts who knew they needed to be made whole [NICNT, NLTfn]. There is irony in his reference to 'righteous' people [AB1, AB2, BECNT, TH], and this is brought out in some translations: 'those who think they are righteous' [NLT], 'people who think they don't have any flaws' [GW]. Some do not consider this to be a case of irony [CGTC, EGT, NIGTC, WBC]. Jesus was not affirming that some people were relatively righteous or even denying that there were some who were so righteous that they do not need to repent. He was simply pointing out that since it is not surprising to find a physician among the sick people, it should not be surprising that Jesus associated with sinners [CGTC]. Both the proverb and the statement Jesus makes about the purpose of his mission concern the priority of those who are in need. In expressing the priority of the sinners Jesus contrasts them with their hypothetical opposites and there is no need to try to identify people who were actually righteous [NIGTC].

QUESTION—Why didn't Jesus include the word 'tax collectors' with the word 'sinners' when he responded to the scribes?

Jesus did this to limit the contrast to one class on each side [Gnd]. 'Tax collectors' is left out in order to maintain the parallelism in the proverb: well/sick and righteous/sinners. The word 'sinners' includes both the tax collectors and the sinners mentioned in verse 16 [BECNT].

QUESTION—What is the point of this illustration?

It points out the priority of people in need [NIGTC]. Jesus used a proverb that was already well-known [AB1, BECNT, BNTC, Gnd, Hb, NICNT, NIGTC, NLTfn, NTC, Sw, Tay] and he compared himself to a doctor and the sinners to sick people [NLTfn]. Jesus' call is to salvation, and in order to be saved there must be a recognition of one's need [EBC].

DISCOURSE UNIT—2:18–22 [CBC, EBC, Hb, NICNT; CEV, ESV, GW, NCV, NET, NIV, NLT, NRSV, TEV]. The topic is the third controversy: Jesus did not practice fasting [CBC], the new situation [NICNT], a question about fasting [EBC, Hb; ESV, NRSV, TEV], a discussion about fasting [NLT], people ask about going without eating [CEV], Jesus is questioned about fasting [GW, NIV], Jesus' followers are criticized [NCV], the superiority of the new [NET].

2:18 **And the disciples of-John and the Pharisees were fasting,[a] and they-come and say to-him, "Why (do) the disciples of-John and the disciples of-the Pharisees fast, but your disciples (do) not fast?"**

TEXT—Manuscripts reading οἱ Φαρισαῖοι 'the Pharisees' in the initial clause are followed by GNT, which does not mention any variant reading. A variant reading is οἱ τῶν Φαρισαίων 'the (disciples) of the Pharisees' and it is followed by KJV.

LEXICON—a. pres. act. participle of νηστεύω (LN 53.65) (BAGD p. 538): 'to fast' [BAGD, LN]. The phrase ἦσαν...νηστεύοντες 'were fasting' [AB1, AB2, BECNT, BNTC, NTC, WBC; ESV, GW, NASB, NET, NIV, NRSV] is also translated 'were engaged in fasting' [Lns], 'on one occasion...were fasting' [TEV], 'when...were fasting' [NLT], 'when... were keeping a fast' [REB], 'used to fast' [KJV], 'often went without eating' [CEV], 'often gave up eating for a certain time' [NCV]. This verb means to go without food for a set time as a religious duty [LN]. It refers to a religious rite that either signified a person's grief or prepared a person for a time of intense prayer [BAGD].

QUESTION—What is indicated by the use of the imperfect tense in the phrase 'were fasting'?

1. The imperfect tense indicates that they were fasting at the time they asked this question [AB1, EGT, Hb, Lns, NTC, Sw, Tay, TH; NLT, REB, TEV; probably ESV, GW, NASB, NET, NIV, NRSV]. The occasion for this particular fast is not known [TH].
2. The imperfect tense refers to their ongoing custom of fasting [NAC; CEV, KJV, NCV]. The imperfect tense can mean that they made a practice of fasting [NAC]. They 'often went without eating' [CEV; similarly NCV], they 'used to fast' [KJV].

QUESTION—Why did the Pharisees fast?

Fasting was commonly practiced in Judaism [BECNT, WBC]. The Law required only the fast of the Day of Atonement (Lev. 16:29), but four other fasts were observed after the Exile [EBC]. Fasting was associated with the death of a loved one, illness, bad times, repentance, and mourning [BECNT]. When combined with prayer, it signified self-denial and humiliation in order to show one's submission to God's will [WBC]. Pharisees routinely fasted twice a week (Luke 18:12) and their fast days were the second and fifth day of the week [BECNT, Hb, NAC, NIGTC, PNTC, Sw, Tay, TH, TRT]. All of the Jews fasted when they were in mourning or when they were specially seeking God's favor [NLTfn].

QUESTION—Why did the disciples of John fast?

The disciples of John would have fasted on the Day of Atonement since it was required of all Jews, so the question was about voluntary acts of fasting [BECNT]. Perhaps they had adopted the Pharisee's practice of fasting to show their mourning over sin [NICNT, NIGTC, NTC]. Fasting would deepen their consciousness of sin and induce repentance [Hb]. They probably fasted in mourning over the imprisonment of John the Baptist [EBC, NTC] and later for his death [Hb, NTC].

QUESTION—Who were the disciples of the Pharisees?

Pharisees as such were not teachers who had disciples, but some of the Pharisees were also scribes who often had disciples whom they taught [EBC, Gnd, NAC, NICNT, NIVfn, NTC, Sw, WBC]. It probably refers to the disciples of the 'scribes of the Pharisees' in 2:16 [NTC]. This might refer to people who were influenced by the ideals and practices of the Pharisees [BECNT, EBC, NAC, NICNT].

QUESTION—Who came and asked the question?

1. Some people came and asked the question [BECNT, CGTC, EGT, Gnd, NIGTC, NTC, PNTC, Tay, TH]. Since the questioners speak of the disciples of John and of the Pharisees in the third person, it appears that the subjects of the verbs 'they come and say' are not the fasting groups themselves [BECNT, Gnd, NIGTC] The impersonal plural means 'people came' [Tay, TH]. They were commoners, not Pharisees [PNTC].

2. The disciples of John and the disciples of the Pharisees came and asked the question [Hb, ICC, Lns, My, NICNT, NTC]. Many who had been John's disciples probably thought that the discipline of fasting they had learned from John should be maintained [NICNT]. Since Matt. 9:14 says that John's disciples asked the question, it is possible that the Pharisees used the perplexity of those disciples to get them bring the question to Jesus [Hb], or at least the Pharisees were present [Lns, NTC].
3. The scribes came and asked the question [AB2, Sw, WBC]. In this context, the logical subjects were the members of 'the Pharisees' who were the scribes who opposed Jesus [WBC].

QUESTION—Was the question rhetorical?
1. This was a real question [Hb, Lns, NIGTC, NTC]. They wanted to know the reason why the disciples of Jesus didn't fast like the disciples of John and the Pharisees [Hb]. John's disciples asked for enlightenment, but the Pharisees asked in order to discredit Jesus [Lns]. Or someone who was not a member of either fasting group was seeking information about the practices of the different groups of disciples [NIGTC].
2. This was a rhetorical question intended to criticize Jesus and his disciples for not fasting [AB2, BECNT, NICNT, PNTC, WBC]. This challenge implied that Jesus and his followers should be following the same custom of fasting [PNTC]. The Pharisees or their scribes confronted Jesus with this question [WBC]. This criticism of Jesus' disciples was really an attack on Jesus [BECNT, BNTC].

2:19 And Jesus said to-them, "The sons of-the wedding-hall[a] are- not[b] -able to-fast while the bridegroom[c] is with them, (are-they)?

LEXICON—a. νυμφῶν (LN 7.34, 11.17) (BAGD 2. p. 545): 'wedding hall' [LN (7.34)], 'bridal chamber' [BAGD]. The phrase οἱ υἱοὶ τοῦ νυμφῶνος 'the sons of the wedding hall' [BECNT] is also translated 'the sons of the bridal hall' [Lns], 'the children of the bridechamber' [KJV], 'the friends of the bridegroom' [BNTC, LN (11.17); CEV, NCV], 'the groomsmen' [WBC], 'the attendants of the bridegroom' [NASB], 'the bridegroom's attendants' [BAGD, NTC], 'the bridegroom's friends' [AB1; REB], 'the guests of the bridegroom' [NIV], 'the guests at a wedding party' [TEV], 'the wedding guests' [AB2, LN; ESV, GW, NET, NLT, NRSV]. The noun νυμφών 'wedding hall' denotes a relatively large room that often served as a place for a wedding [LN (7.34)]. The idiom 'sons of the wedding hall' refers to all the guests at a wedding, or just the friends of the bridegroom who are participating in the wedding festivities [LN (11.17)]. This idiom refers to the group of wedding guests who stood closest to the groom and had an essential part in the wedding ceremony [BAGD].

b. μή (LN 69.3): 'not' [LN, Lns], '(can) not...(can they)?' [WBC; NASB, NET, NRSV; similarly BECNT, WBC], not explicit [AB1, AB2, BNTC, NTC; all versions except NASB, NET, NRSV]. This interrogative particle

indicates a negative proposition [LN]. Questions prefaced with μή 'not' in Greek anticipate a negative answer that can be indicated by adding 'can they?' at the end of the question [NETfn].
  c. νυμφίος (LN 10.56) (BAGD p. 545): 'bridegroom' [AB1, AB2, BAGD, BECNT, BNTC, LN, Lns, NTC, WBC; all versions except GW, NLT], 'groom' [GW, NLT]. This noun denotes a man who is about to be married, or who just got married [LN].

QUESTION—What kind of a question did Jesus ask?

In Greek, the question begins with the negative particle μή 'not' in order to indicate that this question expects a negative answer [CGTC, Hb, Lns, NTC, Sw, Tay, TH]. It is a rhetorical question that emphasizes the fact everyone knows that they wouldn't fast when the bridegroom is with them [CGTC, EGT, Hb, Lns, NTC, Tay, WBC]. Some show the expected answer by translating this as a statement followed by 'can they?' [WBC; NASB, NET, NRSV]: 'While the bridegroom is with them, the attendants of the bridegroom cannot fast, can they?' [NASB]. Some translate this as a question and then supply an answer [NLT, TEV]: 'Do you expect the guests at a wedding party to go without food? Of course not!' [TEV]. One translates this as a statement: 'The friends of the bridegroom do not give up eating while the bridegroom is still with them' [NCV]. One combines the question with the following statement: 'The friends of a bridegroom don't go without eating while he is still with them' [CEV].

QUESTION—Who are οἱ υἱοὶ τοῦ νυμφῶνος 'the sons of the wedding hall'?

The idiom can refer either to the special friends of the groom or to all of the wedding guests, but the point of the illustration is valid in either case [NIGTC].
  1. They are the restricted group of the bridegroom's attendants [BAGD, BECNT, BNTC, Hb, ICC, Lns, NTC, Sw, WBC; NASB]. These are the bridegroom's friends who provided whatever was necessary for the wedding ceremony [ICC]. In the preceding verse the criticism was directed at the disciples who accompanied Jesus, and they would correspond to the attendants of the bridegroom [BECNT].
  2. They are the wedding guests in general [AB2, CGTC, EBC; ESV, GW, NET, NLT, NRSV, TEV].

As-long-as[a] they-have[b] the bridegroom with them they-are- not -able to- fast.

LEXICON—a. ὅσον χρόνον (LN **67.139**) (BAGD 1. p. 586): This phrase is translated 'as long as' [AB2, BAGD, BECNT, BNTC, **LN**, Lns, WBC; ESV, GW, KJV, NCV, NET, NRSV, REB, TEV], 'so long as' [NTC; NASB, NIV], 'while' [AB1, LN], not explicit [CEV, NLT]. The phrase ὅσον χρόνος 'so long a time (as)' means 'as long as, while' and refers to an extent of time of the same length as another extent or unit of time [LN].
  b. pres. act. indic. of ἔχω (LN 90.65) (BAGD I.3. p. 333): 'to have' [LN], 'to have in one's company' [BAGD]. The phrase 'they have...with them'

[BECNT, WBC; ESV, GW, KJV, NASB, NET, NIV, NRSV] is also translated 'they have...in their own company' [Lns]. The subject is changed from 'they' to 'the bridegroom': 'is with them' [AB1, AB2, BNTC, NTC; NCV, NLT, REB, TEV], 'is still with them' [CEV]. This verb means to experience a state or condition that generally involves duration [LN].

QUESTION—What relationship is indicated by the phrase ὅσον χρόνον 'as long as'?

'As long as' indicates the condition that makes it impossible to fast, and it also hints that this condition may not last [BNTC, Hb, NIGTC]. The time when fasting is appropriate should be determined by the circumstances in which one finds himself and not by following some fixed schedule [ICC, Lns]. The question is not whether they could fast but whether they would want to fast [TH]. They *are not able* to fast means that it would *not be appropriate* to fast [ICC, NIGTC]. It is unthinkable that they would fast during the joy and activity of a wedding [NICNT].

2:20 But there-will-come days[a] when the bridegroom is-taken-away[b] from them, and then they-will-fast in that day.

LEXICON—a. ἡμέρα (LN 67.142, 67.178) (BAGD 4.b. p. 347): 'day' [LN (67.178)], 'time' [BAGD, LN (67.142)], 'period' [LN (67.142)]. The phrase 'there will come days' [Lns] is also translated 'the days will come' [AB2; ESV, KJV, NASB, NRSV; similarly BECNT], 'the days are coming' [NET; similarly WBC], 'days will arrive' [NTC], 'the day will come' [TEV], 'the time will come' [AB1, BNTC; CEV, GW, NCV, NIV, REB], 'someday' [NLT]. Whether grammatically singular or plural, this noun denotes an indefinite unit of time that is not particularly long [LN (67.142)], or a definite period of time beginning at sunset and ending at the following sunset [LN (67.178)].

b. aorist pass. subj. of ἀπαίρω (LN 15.177) (BAGD p. 79): 'to be taken away' [AB2, BAGD, BECNT, BNTC, LN, Lns, NTC; ESV, GW, KJV, NASB, NLT, NRSV, REB, TEV], 'to be taken' [AB1, WBC; CEV, NCV, NET, NIV], 'to be taken off, to be led away' [LN]. This verb means to lead or take away from a particular point [LN].

QUESTION—What relationship is indicated by δέ 'but'?

This conjunction contrasts one period of time with another period of time [WBC].

QUESTION—Is there significance in the difference between the plural noun in 'there will come *days*' and the singular noun in the next phrase 'in that *day*'?

1. The two phrases are just literary variations that refer to a period of time [BECNT, ICC, WBC; KJV, NLT, TEV; probably CEV, GW, NCV]. Some translate the plural ἡμέραι 'days' as a singular noun [NLT, TEV]. Another translates the singular ἡμέρᾳ 'day' as a plural noun, 'in *those days*' [KJV]. The use of the adverb τότε 'then' in the clause 'and then in that day' makes the phrase 'in that day' redundant [BECNT], so some let

'then' carry the meaning and omit the phrase 'in that day' [CEV, GW, NCV, NLT, TEV]. The phrase 'in that day' is omitted in Matt. 9:15 and is changed to 'in those days' in Luke 5:35. The phrase 'in that day' refers to the same time period as the phrase 'there will come days' [WBC].
2. The two phrases are different and 'that day' refers to a specific day that will come [AB1, AB2, Hb, NTC]. It means 'at that particular time' fasting will be in order [NTC]. The phrase 'there will come days' stresses the nature of the days characterized by Jesus having been 'taken away' from them, while the phrase 'in that day' emphatically points to that coming day when his removal becomes a reality [Hb].

QUESTION—What is meant by the bridegroom being 'taken away' from them?
The allegorical application is made obvious because a bridegroom would not be expected to be removed or killed at his wedding celebration [WBC]. The verb does not indicate whether his removal will be sudden and violent or natural [NICNT, TH]. Some think the verb implies a violent removal from them [CGTC, Hb, PNTC, Tay, WBC]. This verb suggests force, and in this verse it refers to his violent death [AB1, BECNT, NIGTC, NTC, TRT]. The context implies he will have a violent death that will cause sorrow and fasting [TH]. Jesus was referring to the crucifixion that awaited him [Hb].

QUESTION—Why will they fast when the bridegroom is taken away from them?
The mention of fasting has to do with the sorrow they will experience when Jesus is taken away from them [BECNT, Gnd, Hb, NICNT, NTC, Tay, TH]. When Jesus is arrested and crucified, his disciples will mourn for him and express their sorrow by fasting [BECNT, Hb, NTC]. The resurrection of Jesus will end their sorrow and fasting [BECNT]. After Pentecost, the joyful situation of 'God *within* us' makes such fasting inappropriate for Christians [BECNT, NTC].

2:21 No-one sews a-patch[a] of-unshrunken[b] cloth on[c] an-old[d] garment.[e]

LEXICON—a. ἐπίβλημα (LN 6.157) (BAGD p. 290): 'patch' [AB2, BAGD, BNTC, LN, Lns, NTC, WBC; NASB, NCV, NET, NIV, REB], 'piece' [AB1, BECNT; ESV, KJV, NRSV]. This noun is also translated as a verb phrase: 'no one patches…(by sewing on) a piece' [CEV; similarly GW], 'uses a piece…to patch up' [TEV], 'who would patch' [NLT]. This noun denotes a piece of cloth that is sewed on clothing to repair a hole or a tear [LN].

b. ἄγναφος (LN 48.8) (BAGD p. 10): 'unshrunk' [AB1, AB2; ESV, NASB, NCV, NET, NIV, NRSV, REB], 'unshrunken' [BAGD, BECNT, LN, WBC], 'not as yet shrunken' [LN], 'that will shrink' [GW], 'unwashed' [BNTC], 'unbleached' [BAGD], 'new' [BAGD, Lns, NTC; CEV, KJV, NLT, TEV]. This adjective describes the unshrunken condition of cloth before it has been washed and dried [LN].

c. ἐπί (LN 84.20): 'on' [AB1, AB2, LN, Lns, WBC; CEV, ESV, KJV, NASB, NET, NIV, NRSV, REB], 'upon' [BECNT], 'onto' [BNTC, LN],

'into' [NTC], 'over (a hole)' [NCV], not explicit [GW, TEV]. This preposition refers to an extension to a goal, and it implies contact on a horizontal surface [LN].
  d. παλαιός (LN 58.75) (BAGD 1. p. 605): 'old' [BAGD, LN; all translations]. This adjective describes that which is old or obsolete and inferior [LN].
  e. ἱμάτιον (LN 6.162) (BAGD 1. p. 376): 'garment' [AB2, BECNT, BNTC, Lns, NTC, WBC; ESV, KJV, NASB, NET, NIV, REB], 'coat' [GW, NCV, TEV], 'himation' [AB1], 'cloak' [NRSV], 'clothes' [CEV], 'clothing' [LN; NLT], 'apparel' [LN]. This noun denotes any kind of clothing [LN]. It refers to an outer garment [AB1, CGTC]. It is an outer cloak made from the hair of goats or camels [AB1].

QUESTION—How do verses 21–22 relate to the preceding verses?

These two verses indicate the reason why they cannot fast [AB2]. The wedding feast in 2:19 involved the wearing of special clothing and drinking wine, so it was appropriate to refer to those two features of a wedding in order to explain why the coming of Jesus calls for joy and celebration, a situation that is incompatible with the fasting of John's disciples and the Pharisees [BECNT, Gnd]. If the disciples were to follow the same practice of fasting, they would be like people who put a new unshrunk piece of cloth on an old garment or who put new fermenting wine into old wineskins [NICNT]. The question of fasting was only a part of a greater truth, and these illustrations show that the new life of following Jesus cannot simply be confined to the old forms of Judaism [Hb, NICNT]. The point of adding the two parables is the incompatibility of the old and the new orders; fasting and wedding celebrations do not go together [WBC]. Since there are destructive consequences of trying to mix the old with the new, the newness of Jesus' mission cannot be contained in the old forms of Judaism. An attempt to do so would be disastrous for both [AB2]. The new clothes and the new wine represent the new teachings of Jesus that are accompanied by the new vitality experienced by the people he brings into the kingdom of God. The old clothes and old wineskins represent the existing religious traditions taught by the Pharisees. Attempts to contain Jesus in such restraints had already proved futile, and his followers must be prepared to break free from those old restraints [NIGTC].

QUESTION—What is unshrunken cloth?

It is cloth fresh from the loom [Lns] and still untreated [AB1]. It is new unbleached cloth that has not been cleaned and combed to remove its natural oils. It will shrink with its first washing [NIGTC].

But if not,[a] the patch will-take-away[b] (something) from it, the new from the old, and a-worse tear[c] is-made.

LEXICON—a. εἰ δὲ μή (BAGD VI. 3.b. p. 220): The phrase εἰ δὲ μή 'but if not' is translated 'otherwise' [BAGD, LN, Lns, NTC, WBC; GW, NASB, NET, NRSV], 'else' [KJV], 'if one/he does' [BECNT, BNTC; ESV, NIV,

REB], 'for if he does' [AB2], 'for' [NLT], 'because' [TEV], not explicit [CEV, NCV]. After negative clauses the phrase has the meaning 'otherwise' [BAGD]. It introduces a hypothetical result [WBC].
  b. pres. act. indic. of αἴρω (LN 20.43) (BAGD 4. p. 24): 'to take something away' [BAGD], 'to destroy, to do away with' [LN]. The clause αἴρει τὸ πλήρωμα ἀπ' αὐτοῦ 'the patch will take away (something) from it' is translated 'the filling tears something away from it' [Lns], 'the fullness takes out from it' [AB2], 'the patch pulls away from it' [NTC; NASB, NET, NRSV], 'the patch tears away from it' [BECNT, BNTC; ESV, REB], 'the patch would tear away from it' [WBC]. The clause 'the patch will take away something from it, the new from the old' is translated 'the new patch will tear off some of the old cloth' [**LN** (19.28)], 'the new patch will shrink and tear off some of the old cloth' [TEV], 'the new patch will shrink and rip away some of the old cloth' [GW], 'the new patch would shrink and rip away from the old cloth' [NLT], 'the new patch that filled it up taketh away from the old' [KJV], 'the new piece will pull away from the old' [NIV], 'the new patch will tear away from it' [AB1], 'the patch will shrink and pull away—the new patch will pull away from the old coat' [NCV]. The whole clause is translated 'the new piece would shrink and tear a bigger hole' [CEV]. This verb means to destroy and implies that there is a removal and doing away of something [LN].
  c. σχίσμα (LN **19.28**) (BAGD 1. p. 797): 'tear' [BECNT, LN, NTC; ESV, GW, NASB, NET, NIV, NRSV], 'rent' [Lns; KJV], 'rip' [AB2, WBC]. The phrase 'a worse tear is made' is translated 'making an even greater tear' [**LN**], 'leaving an even bigger tear than before' [NLT], 'making an even bigger hole' [TEV], 'then the hole will be worse' [NCV], 'tear a bigger hole [CEV], 'leaves a bigger hole' [REB]. This noun denotes the condition resulting from splitting or tearing [LN].

QUESTION—Why will the patch pull away from the old garment?
  A new piece of cloth used for a patch would shrink when washed, but an old outer garment or cloak that has already been washed several times would no longer shrink [BECNT]. The new patch will tear the old cloth as it shrinks [NLTfn]. When a patch of unshrunk wool or cloth sewn onto a worn garment gets wet and shrinks, the bordering cloth of the old garment will be pulled to pieces [NTC].

QUESTION—What is the point of this illustration?
  Traditional things like fasting are inappropriate for the new life of a Christian [ICC]. Both illustrations show that the new message of the kingdom of God is incompatible with the existing forms of religion [NAC, NIGTC, Tay, WBC], and compromise between the two has destructive results [NIGTC]. Old practices of the old covenant are not compatible with the new arrival of God's Kingdom, so the fasting of the old cannot be mixed with the feasting of the new [NLTfn].

2:22 And no-one pours new[a] wine into old[b] wineskins.[c]

LEXICON—a. νέος (LN **6.198**) (BAGD 1.a.α. p. 536): 'new' [AB1, AB2, BAGD, BECNT, BNTC, LN, Lns, NTC, WBC; all versions]. The phrase οἶνος νέος 'new wine' is a set phrase that refers to newly pressed grape juice that is either unfermented or just in the initial stages of fermentation [LN]. New wine is wine that is still fermenting [BAGD]. 'New' means that it is freshly made in reference to time [Sw, Tay].

b. παλαιός (LN 58.75) (BAGD 1. p. 605): 'old' [AB2, BAGD, BECNT, BNTC, LN, Lns, NTC, WBC; all versions except TEV], 'used' [TEV], 'discarded' [AB1]. This adjective describes something that is old and obsolete [LN]. It refers to something that has been in existence for a long time and implies that it is antiquated or worn out [BAGD]. 'Old' means that it is worn out [Sw].

c. ἀσκός (LN 6.132) (BAGD p. 116): 'wineskin' [AB1, AB2, BAGD, BECNT, LN, Lns, NTC, WBC; all versions except KJV, NCV], 'skins' [BNTC], 'leather bag' [BAGD; NCV], 'bottle' [KJV]. This noun denotes a bag made of skin or leather and all occurrences of this word in the NT refer to the bags used as wineskins [LN].

QUESTION—What is new wine?

The new wine commonly used by the Jews was a slightly alcoholic drink made from grapes [TRT]. *New* wine is wine that is fresh from the vat [Hb] and still in the process of fermenting [AB1, Lns, NIGTC, NTC, TH]. The first stage of fermentation was carried out in a vat. Then the wine was strained to remove the sediment and placed in jars or skins to complete the fermentation [NIGTC].

QUESTION—What is a wineskin?

Wineskins were containers for liquids that were made from partly tanned goat skins [Hb]. After the goat's skin was removed without slitting it, the openings at the feet and tail were tied shut so that only the opening at the neck was left [Lns].

But if not, the wine will-burst[a] the wineskins and the wine is-lost[b] and the wineskins. Instead new wine (is poured)[c] into new[d] wineskins."

TEXT—Manuscripts reading ὁ οἶνος ἀπόλλυται καὶ οἱ ἀσκοί 'the wine is lost and the wineskins' are given a C rating by GNT to indicate that choosing it over a variant text was difficult. A variant reading is ὁ οἶνος ἐκχεῖται καὶ οἱ ἀσκοί ἀπολοῦνται 'the wine is poured out and the wineskins will be lost' and it is followed by KJV. Other variant readings are ὁ οἶνος ἐκχεῖται καὶ οἱ ἀσκοί 'the wine is poured out and the wineskins', and ὁ οἶνος ἐκχυθήσεται καὶ οἱ ἀσκοὶ ἀπολοῦνται 'the wine will be poured out and the wineskins will be lost'. Some manuscripts omit this clause.

TEXT—Manuscripts reading ἀλλὰ οἶνον νέον εἰς ἀσκοὺς καινούς 'instead new wine into new wineskins' are given a C rating by GNT to indicate that choosing it over a variant text was difficult. A variant reading is ἀλλὰ οἶνον νέον εἰς ἀσκοὺς καινοὺς βλητέον 'instead new wine must be put into new wineskins' and it is followed by KJV. Another variant reading is ἀλλὰ οἶνον νέον εἰς ἀσκοὺς καινοὺς βάλλουσιν 'instead new wine they put into new wineskins'. Other manuscripts omit this clause and they are followed by Lns.

LEXICON—a. fut. act. indic. of ῥήγνυμι (LN 19.31) (BAGD 1. p. 735): 'to burst' [AB1, AB2, BAGD, BECNT, BNTC, LN, Lns, NTC, WBC; all versions except NCV], 'to tear' [BAGD, LN], 'to rip' [LN], 'to break' [NCV]. The phrase 'will burst the wineskins' is translated 'would swell and burst the old skins' [CEV]. This verb means to tear, rip, or burst, either from internal or external forces that involve a sudden and forceful action [LN].

b. pres. mid. indic. of ἀπόλλυμι (LN 20.31) (BAGD 2.a.β. p. 95): 'to be lost' [AB1, AB2, BAGD, BNTC, Lns, NTC; CEV, GW, NASB, NIV, NLT, NRSV, REB], 'to be ruined' [LN; NCV, TEV], 'to be destroyed' [BECNT, LN, WBC; ESV, NET], 'to be spilled' [KJV]. The phrase 'the wine is lost and the wineskins' is translated 'the wine would be lost, and the skins would be ruined' [CEV]. This verb means to destroy or to cause the destruction of persons, objects, or institutions [LN]. The wine is lost by being spilled, and the wineskin is lost by being destroyed [Tay].

c. The implied verb is 'to pour' [NTC; GW, NET, NIV, TEV], 'to put' [WBC; CEV, KJV, NASB, NCV, NRSV], 'to go into' [BNTC; REB], 'is for' [BECNT; ESV], 'to call for' [NLT].

d. καινός (LN 58.71) (BAGD 1. p. 394): 'new' [AB1, AB2, BAGD, BECNT; LN, WBC; CEV, KJV, NCV, NET, NIV, NLT], 'unused' [BAGD], 'fresh' [BNTC, NTC; ESV, GW, NASB, NRSV, REB, TEV]. This adjective describes something that is new or recent, and hence superior to that which is old [LN].

QUESTION—Why would the new wine burst the old wineskin?

The soft pliable skin of a new wineskin would become brittle after constant use and then it would burst from the pressure of fermentation [AB2, NIGTC, TH]. Already having been stretched to its fullest by previous fermentations, it would not be able to contain the pressure of the fermentation of the new wine [BECNT]. Instead of stretching to accommodate the pressure of fermenting wine, the dried-up skin would burst. The wine would be spilled and the container would be ruined [Hb].

QUESTION—What is the point of this illustration?

This illustration reinforces the first one [NTC]. It shows the foolishness of putting the new religion into the old forms [ICC]. Behavior that had been appropriate for the old age before Jesus arrived was now inappropriate in the new age [BECNT]. The new religion cannot be contained within Judaism [BNTC]. The irresistible expansion of the new wine illustrates the irresistibility of Jesus' new teaching [Gnd].

DISCOURSE UNIT—2:23–3:6 [EBC, Hb; NIV]. The topic is the controversies about Sabbath observance [Hb], the Lord of the Sabbath [EBC; NIV].

DISCOURSE UNIT—2:23-28 [CBC, EBC, Hb, NICNT; CEV, ESV, GW, NASB, NCV, NET, NLT, NRSV, TEV]. The topic is the fourth controversy: Jesus' disciples violate the Sabbath [CBC], picking/plucking grain on the Sabbath [EBC, Hb], a question about the Sabbath [CEV, TEV; similarly NASB], a discussion about the Sabbath [NLT], a pronouncement about the Sabbath [NRSV], Sabbath infringement and the Lord of the Sabbath [NICNT], the Lord of the Sabbath [NET], Jesus is Lord of the Sabbath [ESV, NCV], Jesus has authority over the day of worship [GW].

2:23 And it-happened-that on the Sabbath[a] he was-passing[b] through the grainfields,[c] and his disciples began to-make (their) way[d] picking[e] the heads-of-grain.[f]

LEXICON—a. σάββατον (LN 67.184) (BAGD 1.b.β. p. 739): 'Sabbath' [BAGD, LN], 'Saturday' [LN]. This plural form τοῖς σάββασιν 'the Sabbaths' is translated as a singular noun: 'the Sabbath' [AB2, BECNT, Lns; NASB], 'the Sabbath day' [KJV], 'one Sabbath' [AB1, BNTC; CEV, ESV, NIV, NRSV, REB], 'one Sabbath day' [NCV, NLT], 'a Sabbath' [NTC, WBC; NET, TEV], 'a day of worship' [GW]. This noun denotes the last day of the week, the day consecrated to the worship of God by the Jews [LN]. This was the seventh day of the week in the Jewish calendar, and it was observed by resting from work and by special religious ceremonies [BAGD]. Here the plural form 'Sabbaths' is used for a single Sabbath day [BAGD, TH; all versions]. This word occurs at 1:21; 2:23, 24, 27, 28; 3:2, 4; 6:2; 16:1.

b. pres. mid./pass. (deponent = act.) infin. of παραπορεύομαι (LN 15.28) (BAGD 2. p. 621): 'to pass through' [NTC; NASB], 'to go through' [AB1, AB2, BAGD, Lns, WBC; ESV, GW, KJV, NET, NIV, NRSV, REB], 'to walk through' [BNTC; CEV, NCV, NLT, TEV], 'to walk by' [BECNT], 'to pass by, to go by' [LN]. This verb means to move past a reference point [LN]. Jesus was walking through the field on a footpath that had grain on both sides [EGT; Hb].

c. σπόριμος, σπόριμα (LN 43.7) (BAGD p. 763): 'grain field' [AB2, BAGD, BECNT, **LN**, WBC; ESV, GW, NASB, NET, NIV, NLT], 'field of grain' [NCV], 'field of standing grain' [NTC], 'wheat field' [AB1; CEV], 'cornfield' [BNTC; KJV, REB], 'the grain' [Lns]. This adjective is a derivative of σπείρω 'to sow', and as an adjectival noun it denotes a field of growing grain [LN].

d. ὁδός (LN 15.19) (BAGD 1.b. p. 554): 'way, journey' [BAGD, LN]. See translations of this word in the following lexical item. This noun is derived from the verb ὁδεύω 'to be in the process of traveling' and denotes a journey [LN].

e. pres. act. participle of τίλλω (LN 18.9) (BAGD p. 817): 'to pluck, to pick' [BAGD, LN]. The phrase ἤρξαντο ὁδὸν ποιεῖν τίλλοντες 'began to make their way, plucking/picking' [AB2, BECNT, BNTC, Lns, WBC] is also translated 'began to make their way along while picking' [NASB].

Some connect the verb 'began' with the participle 'picking': 'began to pick...as they made their way' [NET; similarly ESV], 'as they walked began to pluck' [AB1], 'began, as they went, to pick' [NTC], 'began to pick' [NCV], 'began, as they went, to pluck' [KJV], 'his disciples were picking...as they went along' [CEV], 'as his disciples walked along with him, they began to pick off' [**LN**; similarly GW, NIV], 'as his disciples walked along with him, they began to pick' [TEV], 'as they made their way, his disciples began breaking off' [NLT], 'as they made their way his disciples began to pluck' [NRSV], 'as they went along his disciples began to pluck' [REB]. This verb means to pluck or pick by pulling something off or out of something [LN].

f. στάχυς (LN **3.40**) (BAGD 1. p. 765): 'head of grain' [BAGD, NTC; ESV, GW, NASB, NIV, NLT, NRSV], 'head of wheat' [BAGD, **LN**, WBC; NET, TEV], 'grain of wheat' [CEV], 'grain' [BECNT; NCV], 'ear of grain' [AB2], 'ear of wheat' [AB1], 'ear' [Lns], 'ear of corn' [BNTC; KJV, REB]. This noun denotes the dense spiky cluster in which seeds of grain such as wheat grow [LN]. The word 'corn' used in the British translations BNTC, KJV, and REB does not refer to maize, but to wheat since 'corn' is a British term for whatever grain is the primary crop of a region [TH]. This word occurs at 2:23; 4:28.

QUESTION—What kind of grain was growing in the grain field?

The grain field was a field of wheat [AB1, BNTC, Hb, LN, NAC, TH, WBC; CEV, NET, TEV]. It was either wheat or barley [NIGTC].

QUESTION—Where were the disciples?

Jesus and his disciples were walking on a public path that went through a field of grain [TRT]. The singular verb 'he was passing through' refers to Jesus, but it is understood that he was accompanied by his disciples since they are the subject of the verbs in the rest of the sentence [Hb, TH]. One version makes this explicit: 'Jesus and his disciples were walking through some wheat fields. His disciples were picking' [CEV]. The verse begins with Jesus passing through the grain field, and then talks about the disciples making their way picking the heads of grain. This implies that Jesus was going along without picking the heads of grain. Therefore the Pharisees raised a question only about the conduct of the disciples [Gnd]. They asked Jesus because he was responsible for what his disciples did [CBC, NICNT].

QUESTION—What were the disciples doing?

The disciples were picking the heads of wheat, rubbing them in their hands to get rid of the chaff, and then eating the raw grain as they walked along [BECNT, BNTC, Hb, NTC].

2:24 And the Pharisees said to-him, "Look,[a] why are-they-doing on the Sabbath what is not lawful[b]?"

LEXICON—a. ἴδε (LN 91.13) (BAGD 1. p. 369): 'look' [AB2, BECNT, BNTC, LN, WBC; ESV, GW, NASB, NET, NIV, NLT, NRSV, TEV], 'behold' [KJV], 'see' [Lns], 'see here' [NTC], 'do you see' [AB1], 'listen,

pay attention' [LN], not explicit [CEV, NCV, REB]. This particle serves to draw someone's attention, and in this verse it also emphasizes the following statement [LN]. The Pharisees were excitedly drawing Jesus' attention to the objectionable act of the disciples [Hb]. This indicates their shocked disapproval of something that needed to be corrected immediately [NTC].
    b. pres. act. indic. of ἔξεστι (LN 71.32) (BAGD 1. p. 275): 'to be lawful' [BECNT, Lns; ESV, KJV, NASB, NCV, NRSV], 'to be permitted' [BAGD, NTC; GW], 'to be permissible' [AB2], 'to be possible' [BAGD], 'must, ought to' [LN]. The phrase 'what is not lawful' is translated 'what is unlawful' [NIV], 'what is forbidden' [AB1, BNTC], 'what is forbidden on the sabbath' [REB], 'what is illegal' [WBC], 'what is against the law' [NET], 'it is against our Law...to do that on the Sabbath' [TEV], 'they are breaking the law by harvesting grain' [NLT], 'they are not supposed to do that' [CEV]. This verb means that something is obligatory, and with a negative particle means 'it ought not to be done' [LN]. This word occurs at 2:24, 26; 3:4; 6:18; 10:2; 12:14.

QUESTION—What is the function of this question?

This is a rhetorical question used to accuse the disciples of wrongdoing [TH, TRT]. The question indicates the Pharisee's disapproval and also functions as an accusation [NTC]. This question demanded that Jesus explain why he had permitted such an unlawful activity [Hb, Lns].

QUESTION—Why was it wrong to pick the heads of grain?

By itself, this action was not unlawful since the law in Deut. 23:25 says 'When you go into the ripe grain fields of your neighbor you may pluck off the kernels with your hand, but you must not use a sickle on your neighbor's ripe grain' [NET]. However, the Pharisees were objecting to this being done on a Sabbath day since they considered it to be doing work on the day of rest [BECNT, Hb, WBC]. The Law forbids work on the Sabbath, and the Pharisees considered reaping, threshing, and winnowing to be work that was prohibited on the Sabbath. So they regarded the actions of the disciple to be threshing [EGT, Lns, NTC, WBC], harvesting [BECNT, Gnd, NIVfn, TRT], and reaping [AB1, Lns, NAC, NCBC, NICNT, NIGTC, NTC, PNTC, Sw, Tay, TH, WBC]. They considered picking the heads of wheat to be reaping, and rubbing the heads to be threshing [EGT, Hb], and perhaps blowing away the chaff to be winnowing [Hb]. The Pharisees considered the disciples to be guilty of breaking the law that prohibited the preparation of food on the Sabbath [Tay].

2:25 **And he says to-them, "Have-you- never -read what David did when he-had need[a] and he-was-hungry, he and the (ones) with him,**
    LEXICON—a. χρεία (LN 57.40) (BAGD 2. p. 885): 'need, lack' [BAGD, LN], 'what is needed' [LN]. The phrase 'to have need' [BECNT, Lns, WBC; KJV] is also translated 'to be in need' [AB2, BNTC, NTC; CEV, ESV, GW, NASB, NET, NIV], 'to be in need of food' [NRSV], 'to need food'

[NCV]. The phrase 'he had need and he was hungry' is translated 'he and his men were hungry and had nothing to eat' [AB1; REB], 'he and his companions were hungry' [NLT], 'he needed something to eat' [TEV]. This noun denotes that which is lacking and is particularly needed [LN]. 'He had need' is a general term, while 'he was hungry' refers to the specific type of need [Hb].

QUESTION—What kind of question is this?

It is a rhetorical question [TH, TRT]. Since there was no doubt that the Pharisees had read this account in 1 Samuel 21:1–6, this counter-question accuses them of not understanding what they have read [TH]. It implies that they had failed to see the significance of what David did in connection with the case before them [Hb]. For the moment, Jesus concedes their point about working on the Sabbath and goes on to point out that such rules allow exceptions [Sw]. The law of need takes precedence over the law of ceremonial laws [WBC]. The fact that scripture does not condemn David shows that the rigidity of the Pharisees about the ritual law was not supported by scripture [CGTC].

2:26 how[a] he-entered into the house[b] of-God during (the time of)[c] Abiathar (the) high-priest[d]

LEXICON—a. πῶς (LN 92.16) (BAGD 2.a. p. 732): 'how' [AB2, BECNT, LN, Lns, WBC; KJV], 'that' [BAGD]. Some translate this as an interrogative 'how' and connect this verse with the preceding question with a colon [NTC; ESV], a semi-colon [NASB], or a dash [NET]. Another repeats the beginning of the question from the preceding verse: 'haven't you read how…' [GW]. Some omit this conjunction and translate the verse as a statement [AB1, BNTC; CEV, NCV, NIV, NLT, NRSV, REB, TEV]. This conjunction is an interrogative reference to means [LN]. This interrogative conjunction is used in indirect questions, but here the conjunction clearly has the same meaning as ὅτι 'that' [BAGD].

b. οἶκος (LN 7.2) (BAGD 1.a.β. p. 560): 'house' [AB1, AB2, BAGD, BECNT, BNTC, LN, Lns, NTC, WBC; all versions], 'temple' [BAGD, LN], 'sanctuary' [LN]. This noun denotes a building consisting of one or more rooms and normally refers to a dwelling place. The extension of the meaning of οἶκος to include temples may be the result of speaking of a temple as the dwelling place of God [LN].

c. The words supplied here are: 'the time of' [AB2, BECNT, BNTC, Lns, WBC; CEV, ESV, NASB, NCV, REB], 'the days of' [NTC; KJV, NIV]. The phrase 'during the time of Abiathar the high priest' is also translated 'when Abiathar was high priest' [AB1; GW, NET, NLT, NRSV, TEV].

d. ἀρχιερεύς (LN 53.89): 'high priest' [AB1, AB2, BECNT, BNTC, Lns, NTC, WBC; all versions except GW], 'chief priest' [LN; GW]. This noun denotes a principal priest who belonged to one of the high-priestly families [LN].

QUESTION—What was the house of God?

The phrase 'house of God' is a generic term that referred to the tent or tabernacle in which the Jews first worshiped, and then later referred to the temple when it was built. Here it refers to the tent where God was worshipped [ICC]. 'House' was an appropriate name for this tabernacle since in a sense God dwelt there and manifested his presence in the inner shrine [ICC]. This does not mean that David entered the Holy Place or the sanctuary of the tabernacle itself. It means that he entered the outside courts of the tabernacle or tent, a place that he could freely enter [Hb, Lns, NTC].

QUESTION—Who was the high priest who gave the bread to David?

At the time David entered the house of God, the high priest who gave him the bread was Ahimelech (1 Sam. 21:1–4). Ahimelech's son was Abiathar who is first mentioned in 1 Sam. 22:20, and he was the high priest during all of David's reign [NICNT]. Mark may have used Abiathar's name to indicate the section of the Samuel manuscript that contained this story about Ahimelech and David [NICNT]. Perhaps the son was also present with his father at the time [Lns]. The simplest solution is that the text simply means 'during the lifetime of Abiathar the high priest' [Hb, Lns].

and he-ate the loaves-of-bread of the presentation,[a] which is- not -lawful[b] to-be-eaten except by-the priests, and he-gave (some) also to-the (ones) with him?"

LEXICON—a. πρόθεσις (LN 53.26) (BAGD 1. p. 706): 'presentation, setting forth, putting out' [BAGD]. The phrase τοὺς ἄρτους τῆς προθέσεως 'the loaves of bread of the presentation' is translated 'the loaves of presentation' [AB2, BAGD], 'the bread offered to God' [LN; TEV], 'the consecrated bread' [LN, NTC; NASB, NIV], 'the loaves of shewbread' [WBC], 'the showbread' [Lns; KJV], 'the bread of the Presence' [AB1, BECNT; ESV, GW, NRSV], 'the sacred bread' [BNTC; NET, REB], 'the sacred loaves of bread' [CEV, NLT], 'the holy bread' [NCV]. The phrase ἄρτοι τῆς προθέσεως 'bread of the presentation' was the bread that was set out as an offering in the presence of God in the Tabernacle and later in the Temple. In some languages it has been translated 'bread placed before God' and 'bread placed in the presence of God' [LN].

b. pres. act. indic. of ἔξεστι (LN 71.32) (BAGD 1. p. 275): 'to be permitted, to be possible' [BAGD], 'must (not), ought (not) to' [LN]. The phrase 'which is not lawful' [Lns; ESV, KJV, NASB; similarly NRSV] is also translated 'which is unlawful' [BECNT], 'which is not allowed' [AB1], 'which were illegal' [WBC], 'which is against the law' [NET]. The clause 'which is not lawful to be eaten except by the priests' is translated 'which is lawful only for priests to eat' [NCV, NIV], 'which it is forbidden to eat—except for the priests' [BNTC], 'that only priests are allowed to eat' [CEV; similarly NTC; REB], 'He had no right to eat those loaves. Only the priests have that right.' [GW], 'and broke the law by eating the sacred loaves of bread that only the priests are allowed to eat' [NLT], 'according to our Law only the priests may eat this bread' [TEV]. This verb means to be obligatory, and with a negative particle it means 'ought not to' [LN]. This word occurs at 2:24, 26; 3:4; 6:18; 10:2; 12:14.

QUESTION—What were the 'loaves of bread of the presentation'?

In the OT, the Hebrew text refers to this as 'the bread of the Presence', meaning that the bread was displayed before the presence of God. In many languages, the closest equivalent would be 'the bread set before God' [TH]. Every week priests set out twelve loaves of bread before God on a table located in the holy place of the tabernacle and those loaves were replaced every Sabbath [ICC]. The loaves probably symbolized God's presence with his people as their Sustainer [Hb], or the fellowship of the people with God [NTC].

QUESTION—When did the priests eat that bread?

The priests were allowed to eat the bread after it had been replaced with fresh bread [ICC], so the bread that David ate was bread that had already been replaced [Lns]. It is assumed that David did this on the Sabbath since that was the day that the sacred bread was replaced [NICNT, NIGTC].

QUESTION—What is the point Jesus was making with his counter question?

David's act of breaking the Law is recorded in Scripture with apparent approval, and Jesus had an authority at least as great as that of David [NIGTC]. If David could do something unlawful, how much more does the Son of Man have authority to do so [BECNT]. David was allowed to break the law because he had a special status in Judaism. Jesus had an even greater status, so he could allow his disciples to break that law [CGTC]. The Law allowed for an exception in the case of David, so it also allows an exception in the present situation in spite of the overly stringent interpretation of the Law by the Pharisees [NICNT]. Human need such as hunger comes before the ritual keeping of the Law [Hb]. A different explanation is that Jesus would not have argued that any necessity could excuse breaking God's Law. His argument is that since Scripture did not condemn David for his action, the rigidity of the interpretation of ritual laws by the Pharisees was not in accordance with Scripture [CGTC].

2:27 And he-said to-them, "The Sabbath was-made[a] for[b] man and not (that) man (was made) for the Sabbath.

LEXICON—a. aorist mid. (deponent = act.) indic. of γίνομαι (LN 13.80) (BAGD I.2.α. p. 158): 'to be made' [AB1, BAGD, BECNT, BNTC, NTC, WBC; all versions], 'to be created' [AB2], 'to come to be' [Lns], 'to be formed, to come to exist' [LN], 'to be established' [BAGD]. This verb means to come into existence [LN]. The word ἐγένετο 'was made' is used differently in the cases of God making the Sabbath and God making man. God *instituted* the Sabbath and God *created* man [TH].

  b. διά (LN **90.38**) (BAGD B.II.1. p. 181): 'for' [AB2, BECNT, BNTC, NTC; ESV, GW, KJV, NASB, NIV, NRSV, REB], 'for the good of' [CEV], 'for the sake of' [AB1, BAGD, LN, WBC], 'for the benefit of'

[LN], 'on behalf of' [LN], 'on account of' [Lns], 'because of' [BAGD]. Some give different meanings of this preposition in the two clauses 'The Sabbath was made for the good of human beings; they were not made for the Sabbath' [TEV], 'The Sabbath day was made to help people; they were not made to be ruled by the Sabbath day' [NCV], 'The Sabbath was made to meet the needs of people, and not people to meet the requirements of the Sabbath' [NLT]. This preposition indicates a participant who is benefited by an event or for whom an event occurs [LN].

QUESTION—What is meant by the noun ἄνθρωπος 'man' in this saying?

In the context of the account of creation in Genesis 1, the Sabbath was created for the benefit of the *human creature* [WBC] and this noun is translated 'man' [ESV, KJV, NASB, NIV, REB], 'people' [CEV, GW, NCV, NET, NLT], 'human beings' [TEV], 'humankind' [NRSV].

QUESTION—What is meant by God establishing the Sabbath διά 'for' man and not creating man διά 'for' the Sabbath?

God ordered, ordained, or set aside the Sabbath to be a day of rest for the sake of the people he had brought into existence. God did not create people in order that they keep the laws about the Sabbath day of rest [TH]. The Sabbath was established in order to be a blessing of physical rest for people so that they could attend to their spiritual needs [Lns]. The arbitrary regulations of the Pharisees made man a slave to the Sabbath with the result that the Sabbath observances were a burden rather than a blessing [Hb]. Since it was instituted for the benefit of people, the application of the Sabbath law must be elastic enough to promote their welfare [Hb, NTC]. God's purpose for the establishment of the Sabbath was not affected by plucking the grains of wheat [NICNT].

2:28 Therefore[a] the Son of Man[b] is lord[c] even/also[d] of-the-Sabbath."

LEXICON—a. ὥστε (LN 89.52) (BAGD 1.a. p. 899): 'therefore' [AB1, BNTC, LN; KJV], 'as a result' [LN], 'so' [AB2; CEV, ESV, NASB, NIV, NLT, NRSV, REB, TEV], 'so then' [LN; NCV], 'so that' [BECNT, LN, Lns, WBC], 'for this reason' [GW, NET], 'consequently' [NTC]. This conjunction indicates the result, and often implies the intended or indirect purpose [LN].

b. υἱὸς τοῦ ἀνθρώπου (LN 9.3) (BAGD 2.e. p. 835): This title is translated 'the Son of Man' [BAGD, LN; all translations except AB1], 'The Man' [AB1]. See 2:10 for a discussion of this title.

c. κύριος (LN 37.51) (BAGD 1.a.α. p. 459): 'lord' [AB1, AB2, BAGD, LN, Lns, WBC; ESV, NET, NRSV, REB], 'Lord' [BECNT, BNTC, NTC; CEV, KJV, NASB, NCV, NIV, NLT, TEV], 'master' [BAGD, LN], 'ruler' [LN]. This noun is also translated as a verb: 'has authority over' [GW]. This noun denotes one who rules or exercises authority over others [LN].

d. καί (BAGD II.2. p. 393): 'even' [AB1, BAGD, BNTC, LN, Lns, NTC; ESV, NASB, NCV, NET, NIV, NLT, REB, TEV], 'also' [BECNT, LN, WBC; KJV], 'and also, in addition' [LN]. The phrase καὶ τοῦ σαββάτου 'even of the Sabbath' is translated 'even over the Sabbath' [AB1; NLT], 'over the Sabbath' [CEV, GW]. This conjunction functions as the emphatic adverb 'even' [BAGD].

QUESTION—Who is speaking in this verse, and what relationship is indicated by ὥστε 'therefore'?

1. This continues the words spoken by Jesus [AB1, AB2, BECNT, BNTC, Gnd, Hb, ICC, Lns, NTC, WBC; all versions]. Jesus states the conclusion to be drawn from the Sabbath principle he had just stated [Hb, Lns, WBC]. The conclusion to be drawn from David's action is not that anyone could do what David had done, but that David had done what he did just because he was David, thus setting a precedent for the actions of someone who had greater authority than David [NIGTC].
2. This is a comment added by Mark [CGTC, NCBC, NICNT, Tay]. Mark adds the conclusion to be drawn from what Jesus said in the previous verse about the Sabbath [CGTC]. From the incident given in 2:23-27, Mark drives home the theological point that Jesus is the Lord of the Sabbath [NICNT].

QUESTION—What relationship is indicated by καί 'even, also'?

1. This conjunction means 'even' [EGT, Lns, NTC; ESV, NASB, NCV, NET, NIV, NLT, REB, TEV]. Since Jesus is Lord over all, then of course he is Lord of the Sabbath [NTC]. He was Lord of all things, even of the Sabbath that was so inviolable in the eyes of the Pharisees [EGT].
2. This conjunction means 'also' [ICC, My, Tay, WBC; KJV]. He was Lord of the Sabbath as well as Lord over all the other things belonging to the life of man [ICC].

DISCOURSE UNIT—3:1-12 [NASB]. The topic is Jesus healing on the Sabbath.

DISCOURSE UNIT—3:1-6 [CBC, EBC, Hb, NICNT; CEV, ESV, GW, NCV, NET, NLT, NRSV, TEV]. The topic is the fifth controversy: Jesus heals on the Sabbath [CBC], Jesus heals on the Sabbath [NLT], Jesus heals on the day of worship [GW], healing on the Sabbath [EBC], the man with a paralyzed hand [TEV], a man with a withered hand [Hb; ESV, NRSV], a man with a crippled hand [CEV], healing a withered hand [NET], Jesus heals a man's hand [NCV], the decision that Jesus must be destroyed [NICNT].

3:1 And he-entered again into the synagogue, and a-man was there having (a) withered[a] hand.

LEXICON—a. perf. pass. participle of ξηραίνομαι, ξηραίνω (LN 23.172) (BAGD 2.b. p. 548): 'to be stiff, to be paralyzed' [LN], 'to be withered' [BAGD]. This adjectival participle is translated 'withered' [AB1, AB2, BECNT, BNTC, WBC; ESV, KJV, NASB, NET, NRSV, REB], 'shriveled' [NTC; NIV], 'paralyzed' [GW, TEV], 'crippled' [CEV, NCV], 'deformed' [NLT]. This verb is a figurative extension of ξηραίνομαια 'to dry up' [LN (79.81)], and it means to become stiff to the point of not being able to move [LN]. It means to be incapable of motion [BAGD]. The verb 'to be dried up' may be a figurative expression for being paralyzed [AB2].

QUESTION—How is this verse connected with the preceding event?

This verse seems to suggest that this happened right after the incident in the cornfield [NIGTC, Sw] and Matthew 12:9 appears to support such a sequence [Sw]. Some point out that Luke 6:6 says this occurred 'on another Sabbath' [Hb, Lns, Sw]. The connection with the preceding four incidents about conflict is topical rather than temporal and these five conflict stories serve to bring out the growing antagonism toward Jesus [EBC, Hb, NLTfn]. This is about another event that had taken place on a different Sabbath day [EGT, Hb, NICNT, WBC]. The word 'again' may refer to the Sabbath incidences of 1:21 and 2:23 [BECNT, BNTC, Gnd, NLTfn, Tay, TH, WBC], or it may simply mean 'here is another example' [BNTC, NCBC]. No details of time or location are given [EBC]. This could have taken place in the synagogue of any town in Galilee [NICNT], but probably it happened in Capernaum [NLTfn]. Jesus entered into a synagogue again, as was his habit on Sabbath days [EGT]. Some translations start out 'the *next time* that Jesus went into the meeting place' [CEV], '*another time* when Jesus went into a synagogue' [NCV; similarly NIV], '*on another occasion* when he went to synagogue' [AB1; REB].

QUESTION—What was the matter with the man's hand?

This adjectival participle describes a stiffness that prevented the man from using his hand [TH]. His hand had withered and become paralyzed [CBC, EBC, NETfn]. He had a stiff and deformed hand [PNTC]. The passive participle indicates that it was a prolonged illness [BECNT, EGT]. The perfect passive participle 'having been withered' indicates that the man had not been born with that condition [Hb, ICC, Lns, Sw]. This participle gives no more information than the adjective ξηράν 'withered' in 3:3 [CGTC, NTC, Tay, TH]. It does not indicate whether his paralysis was from birth or due to an accident [AB1, CGTC, Tay, TH] or disease [ICC]. Here the word 'hand' probably refers to the man's hand, wrist, and possibly his forearm, since withering often involves various areas of a person's arm [TH].

3:2 And they-were-watching[a] him (to see) if he-would-heal him on the Sabbath, in-order-that they-might-accuse[b] him.

LEXICON—a. imperf. act. indic. of παρατηρέω (LN 24.48) (BAGD 1.a.α. p. 622): 'to watch' [BAGD, BNTC; CEV, ESV, NASB, NRSV, REB], 'to watch closely' [AB1, AB2, BECNT, LN, WBC; GW, KJV, NCV, NET, NIV, NLT, TEV], 'to covertly watch' [Lns]. This verb means to watch closely or diligently [LN]. It means to watch someone in order to see what

he is doing [BAGD]. The imperfect tense indicates that this was an act in progress [ICC].
b. aorist act. subj. of κατηγορέω (LN 33.427) (BAGD 1.a. p. 423): 'to accuse' [BECNT, LN, Lns; ESV, KJV, NASB, NCV, NET, NIV, NRSV], 'to bring an accusation against' [AB1], 'to bring a charge against' [BNTC, NTC; REB], 'to bring charges against' [AB2, BAGD, LN], 'to charge' [WBC]. This verb is also translated as a verb phrase: 'to accuse Jesus/him of doing something wrong' [CEV, GW; similarly TEV], 'to accuse him of working on the Sabbath' [NLT]. This verb means to bring serious charges or accusations against someone, perhaps in a legal or court context [LN]. This is a legal technical term meaning to bring charges in court [BAGD].

QUESTION—Who were the people who were watching Jesus in order to accuse him?

A subject is supplied in some translations: 'some people' [CEV, NCV], 'the people' [GW], 'Jesus' enemies' [NLT], 'the Pharisees' [CEV]. In this context it does not refer to people in general, but to the Pharisees who wanted to be able to accuse Jesus of wrongdoing [AB1, BNTC, CGTC, EBC, Gnd, NIVfn, NTC, Tay, TH]. This identification is made certain in verse 6 were it refers to them as 'the Pharisees' [ICC, Tay].

QUESTION—What could the Pharisees accuse Jesus of doing?

These Pharisees did not doubt that Jesus had the ability to heal a person, so they were watching to see if he would heal someone on the Sabbath. If he did, they would accuse him of breaking their laws about healing on the Sabbath [BECNT, EBC, Gnd]. Healing the man with a withered hand on the Sabbath would be considered a violation of the Sabbath law that prohibited work on the Sabbath [NIGTC, NLTfn]. The Rabbis had established the rule that the sick or injured could only be treated on the Sabbath if their life was actually in danger, so healing the man's withered hand would be breaking the Sabbath law [CGTC, EBC, Hb, NIGTC, Sw]. They would charge Jesus of unnecessarily practicing medicinal therapy on the Sabbath [NTC].

3:3 **And he-says to-the man, the (one) having the withered hand, "Stand-up in the middle.**[a]**"**

LEXICON—a. μέσος (LN 83.10) (BAGD 2. p. 507): 'in the middle' [BAGD, LN], 'in the midst' [LN]. The command 'stand up in the middle' is translated 'stand up in the midst' [Lns], 'get up and come to the middle of the room' [AB2], 'rise and stand in the center of the synagogue' [BECNT], 'stand in the center of the synagogue' [GW], 'stand here in the middle' [WBC], 'stand up here in the middle of everyone' [NCV], 'stand up in front of everyone' [NIV], 'stand up among all these people' [NET], 'stand forth' [KJV], 'rise and come forward' [NTC], 'get up and come forward' [NASB], 'come here' [ESV], 'come forward' [NRSV], 'come and stand out here' [AB1, BNTC; REB], 'come up here to the front' [TEV], 'come and stand in front of everyone' [NLT]. This is also translated as an indirect quotation: 'Jesus told the man to stand up where everyone could see him' [CEV]. This adjectival substantive refers to a position in the middle of an area, such as an object in the midst of other objects [LN].

QUESTION—Where was the man to stand?

Jesus wasn't telling him to come stand beside him, but to stand in the midst of the people [Hb, Lns, NICNT, TH; CEV, GW, NET, NIV]. He was to stand up right where he was sitting [Lns]. Or, it is implied that to get to the middle of the onlookers the man would have to move to another location [CGTC, EGT, ICC, Sw]. Or, the man was to come up where Jesus was [AB1, AB2, BNTC, TH, WBC; ESV, NCV, REB, TEV; probably NTC; NASB, NLT, NRSV which include the word 'come']. Jesus had the man stand up where everyone could see what he was going to do for him [EBC, Hb, NTC, TH].

3:4 And he-says to-them, "Is-it-lawful[a] on-the Sabbath to-do good[b] or to-do-harm,[c] to save[d] life or to-kill[e]?" But they were-silent.

LEXICON—a. pres. act. indic. of ἔξεστι (LN 71.32) (BAGD 1. p. 275): 'to be permitted, to be proper' [BAGD]. The question is translated 'is it lawful' [BECNT, Lns; ESV, KJV, NASB, NCV, NET, NIV, NRSV], 'does the law permit' [NLT], 'what does our Law allow us to do' [TEV], 'is it legal' [WBC], 'is it permitted' [BNTC; REB], 'is it permissible' [AB2], 'is it allowed' [AB1], 'is it right' [NTC; GW], 'should (we...)' [CEV]. This verb means that something is obligatory, and with a negative particle means 'it ought not to be done' [LN]. The standard of reference is the Mosaic Law [AB1, TH]. This word occurs at 2:24, 26; 3:4; 6:18; 10:2; 12:14.

b. ἀγαθός (LN 88.1): 'good, a good act' [LN]. The phrase ἀγαθὸν ποιῆσαι 'to do good' [AB1, AB2, BECNT, BNTC, Lns, NTC; WBC; all versions except CEV, NLT, TEV] is also translated 'do good deeds' [CEV; similarly NLT], 'to help' [TEV]. This adjective refers to positive moral qualities of the most general nature [LN].

c. aorist act. infin. of κακοποιέω (LN 20.12, **88.112**) (BAGD 1. or 2. p. 397): 'to do harm' [LN (20.12), Lns, NTC; ESV, NASB, NRSV], 'to harm' [BAGD (2.); TEV], 'to do evil' [AB1, AB2, BECNT, BNTC, **LN (88.112)**, WBC; GW, KJV, NCV, NET, NIV, NLT, REB], 'to do evil deeds' [CEV], 'to be an evil-doer' [BAGD (1.)], 'to do wrong' [BAGD (1.), LN (88.112)]. This verb means to do harm [LN (20.12)], or to do that which is evil or wrong [LN (88.112)].

d. aorist act. infin. of σῴζω (LN 21.18, 23.136) (BAGD 1.a. p. 798): 'to save' [BAGD], 'to deliver, to rescue, to make safe' [LN (21.18)], 'to heal, to cure, to make well' [LN (23.136)]. The phrase ψυχὴν σῶσαι 'to save life' [AB1, AB2, BECNT, BNTC, Lns, NTC; ESV, KJV, NIV, NLT, NRSV, REB] is also translated 'to save a life' [BAGD, WBC; NASB, NCV, NET], 'to save someone's life' [CEV, TEV], 'to give a person back his health' [GW]. The verb means to rescue from danger and to restore someone to a former state of safety and well-being [LN (21.18)], or to cause someone to become well again after having been sick [LN (23.136)]. It means to preserve or rescue from natural dangers and afflictions [BAGD].

    e. aorist act. infin. of ἀποκτείνω (LN 20.6) (BAGD 1.a. p. 94): 'to kill' [AB1, AB2, BAGD, BECNT, BNTC, LN, Lns, NTC, WBC; ESV, KJV, NASB, NCV, NIV, NRSV, REB], 'to destroy' [CEV, NET, NLT, TEV], 'to let die' [GW]. This verb means to cause someone's death, usually with violence [LN].

QUESTION—What is meant by doing 'good' or doing 'harm/evil'?

    1. These are adjectival nouns that refer to the application of dong good or evil in regard to people who need help [EGT, Hb, ICC, NICNT, NTC, TH; ESV, NASB, NRSV, TEV]: *to do good to people or to harm them*. It is clear that the answer to this rhetorical question is 'to do good' [ESVfn]. The alternatives imply that failure to do good is to do harm [Hb]. Instead of a question about right and wrong, this is about benefit and injury, and therefore not doing what is good to a person is the same as doing what is evil to him [ICC].

    2. These are adjectival nouns that refer to the moral aspects of one's actions [AB1, AB2, BECNT, BNTC, CGTC, **LN**, Lns, My, NIGTC, PNTC, Sw, Tay, WBC; CEV, GW, KJV, NCV, NET, NIV, NLT, REB]: *to do good or to do evil*. When good deeds need to be done, failure to do those good deeds is to do evil. Therefore it is right to do the good deed of healing on the Sabbath, whether or not it is 'lawful' according to the scribes [PNTC].

QUESTION—What is meant by the alternatives 'to save life or to kill'?

When Jesus was speaking about 'doing good or doing harm' he was referring to preserving a man's life or destroying it [TH]. This statement uses hyperbole to make its point since delaying a healing for one day would not be doing evil, nor would it amount to destroying a life [NIGTC]. Using their own method of scribal legal arguments, it could be argued that the man's withered hand could be considered to be threatened by death or even considered to be already dead, so restoring that hand to health would count as saving life [Gnd]. Some point out that the reference to killing was just the fate Jesus' enemies had in mind for him [BECNT, BNTC, EBC, NIVfn, NTC, Sw, Tay, TRT], and it is better to save a life (i.e., to restore it to health) than to plot to kill someone as the Pharisees were doing (3:6) [EBC].

QUESTION—Why were they silent?

They did not want to be drawn into a discussion that viewed the matter from an ethical standpoint instead of a legal one [Hb]. To answer the question by affirming the positive virtues would undermine their whole approach to the Sabbath, yet to answer in the negative would be impossible to defend, and it would draw disapproval from the congregation [NIGTC].

3:5 And having-looked (at) them with anger,[a] being-deeply-grieved[b] at the hardness[c] of-their hearts he-says to-the man, "Stretch-out[d] the hand." And he-stretched- it -out and his hand was-restored.[e]

TEXT—Manuscripts ending this verse with ἀπεκατεστάθη ἡ χεὶρ αὐτοῦ 'his hand was restored' are followed by GNT, which does not mention any variant reading. A variant reading is ἀπεκατεστάθη ἡ χεὶρ αὐτοῦ ὑγιὴς ὡς ἡ ἄλλη 'his hand was restored sound as the other' and it is followed by KJV.

LEXICON—a. ὀργή (LN 88.173) (BAGD 1. p. 579): 'anger' [AB1, AB2, BAGD, BECNT, BNTC, LN, Lns, NTC, WBC; ESV, KJV, NASB, NET, NIV, NRSV, REB], 'indignation, wrath' [BAGD], 'fury' [LN]. The noun is also translated as a verb: 'was angry' [CEV, GW, NCV, TEV]; as an adverb: '(he looked around at them) angrily' [NLT]. This noun denotes a relative state of anger [LN]. This was a holy indignation against evil, not the kind of a human anger that is malignant and vindictive [Hb]. The aorist tense indicates that looking around in anger was a momentary act [EBC].

b. pres. pass. participle of συλλυπέομαι, συλλυπέω (LN **25.276**) (BAGD p. 777): 'to be deeply grieved' [BAGD], 'to feel sorry for' [LN]. The participle 'being deeply grieved' [NTC; similarly WBC] is also translated 'very grieved' [BECNT], 'grieved' [AB2, BNTC; ESV, NASB, NET; similarly Lns; KJV, NRSV], 'deeply distressed' [NIV], 'he was deeply hurt' [GW], 'sorrowing' [AB1], '(with anger) and sorrow' [REB], 'and he felt very sad' [NCV], 'and was deeply saddened' [NLT], 'but at the same time he felt sorry for them' [**LN**; TEV], 'yet he felt sorry for them' [CEV]. This verb means to feel sorrow or grief [LN]. This compound stem has no other force than to strengthen the simple verb so that it means '*deeply* grieved' [BAGD]. The present tense indicates a prolonged feeling of grief concerning such men [EBC, EGT, Hb, NTC].

c. πώρωσις (LN 27.52) (BAGD p. 732): 'hardening, dullness, insensibility, obstinacy' [BAGD], 'unwillingness to learn, mental stubbornness, closed mind' [LN]. The phrase 'the hardness of their hearts' [AB2, Lns; KJV, NET], is also translated 'their hardness of heart' [BNTC, WBC; ESV, NASB, NRSV; similarly BECNT], 'their hard hearts' [NLT], 'the hardening of their hearts' [NTC], 'their stubborn hearts' [NIV], 'their obstinate stupidity' [REB], 'their obdurate stupidity' [AB1], '(because) they were so stubborn' [CEV; similarly NCV], '(because) they were so stubborn and wrong' [TEV], '(because) their minds were closed' [GW]. This noun denotes a stubborn unwillingness to learn [LN]. See this word in relation to hearts at 3:5, 6:52, 8:17.

d. aorist act. impera. of ἐκτείνω (LN **16.19**) (BAGD 1. p. 245): 'to stretch out' [AB2, BECNT, BNTC, **LN**, Lns, NTC; CEV, ESV, NASB, NET, NIV, NRSV, REB, TEV], 'to stretch forth' [KJV], 'to extend' [BAGD, LN, WBC], 'to reach out' [LN], 'to hold out' [BAGD; GW, NCV, NLT]. This verb means to cause an object to extend in space [LN].

e. aorist pass. indic. of ἀποκαθίστημι (LN 13.65) (BAGD 1. p. 92): 'to be restored' [AB2, BAGD, BECNT, LN, NTC, WBC; ESV, KJV, NASB, NET, NLT, NRSV, REB], 'to be completely restored' [Lns; NIV], 'to be restored to normal' [BNTC], 'to become normal again' [GW], 'to become well again' [TEV], 'to be healed' [CEV, NCV]. This verb means to change to a previously good state [LN].

QUESTION—Why did Jesus look around at them with anger?

Jesus looked around at them to see whether at least one man would respond, and their total silence explains his anger [Gnd, Lns]. Jesus looked to see who would answer him, and he was angry at their sullen refusal to respond to the truth [Hb]. In the name of piety, they had become insensitive to the purposes of God and to the sufferings of people [NICNT]. This was a righteous indignation, such as a good man would feel in the presence of such stark evil [EBC].

QUESTION—What relationship is indicated by the use of the participial clause 'being deeply grieved at the hardness of their hearts'?

1. The participle indicates an attendant circumstance [AB1, AB2, BNTC, CBC, Gnd, Hb, ICC, Lns, NICNT, NTC, Sw; CEV, NCV]. His anger was mingled with grief at their sinful attitude [CBC, Hb]. His anger was tempered by his godly sorrow for the men [NICNT, NTC, Sw]. 'Yet/but' he was grieved at their hardness of heart [AB1; CEV, TEV]. Jesus was both angry and grieved at their deliberate blindness [BNTC, ICC]. 'And' he was grieved at their hardness of heart [AB2; NCV, NIV, NLT].
2. The participle indicates the reason for his anger [BECNT, EBC, NIGTC, TH; probably GW]: *because* he was grieved at their hardness of heart. It explains his anger [BECNT].

QUESTION—What was involved in Jesus' command for the man to stretch out his hand?

The man's response would show whether or not he had faith that his hand would be restored [Hb]. Some think he had been able to stretch out his hand before he was healed [CBC, CGTC, Hb]. With his hand stretched out in plain view, all could see its withered condition, and they could watch it being healed [CBC, Hb]. Others think he had been unable to stretch out his hand and the healing took place in the very act of stretching it out [BNTC, Gnd]. Since the word for 'hand' can also mean 'arm', perhaps his whole limb was paralyzed, so when he stretched out his formerly immobile limb as an act of faith he found that he was already cured [BNTC].

3:6 **And going-out the Pharisees immediately held consultation[a] with the Herodians against him as-to-how they-might-destroy[b] him.**

LEXICON—a. συμβούλιον (LN **30.74**) (BAGD 1. p. 778): 'consultation' [BAGD, LN], 'plan' [LN]. The phrase 'to hold consultation' is translated 'to hold counsel' [ESV], 'to take counsel' [AB2, Lns, NTC, WBC; KJV], 'to conspire' [BECNT; NASB, NRSV], 'to plot' [AB1, BNTC; GW, NET, NIV, NLT, REB], 'to make plans' [CEV, NCV, TEV]. This noun

denotes joint planning in order to devise a course of common action, and often it is done with a harmful or evil purpose in mind [LN].
  b. aorist act. subj. of ἀπόλλυμι (LN 20.31) (BAGD 1.a.α. p. 95): 'to destroy' [AB2, BAGD, BECNT, BNTC, LN, Lns, NTC, WBC; ESV, KJV, NASB, NRSV], 'to kill' [BAGD; CEV, GW, NCV, NIV, NLT, TEV], 'to assassinate' [NET], 'to put to death' [BAGD], 'to bring about (Jesus') death' [REB]. This verb means to destroy or to cause the destruction of persons, objects, or institutions [LN]. The verb 'destroy' means to put to death [TH], to kill [BECNT].

QUESTION—What did the Pharisees go out of?

They went out of the synagogue [Gnd, Hb, NIGTC, Sw, TH]. This does not necessarily mean that they stalked out the moment the man was healed. The service was now ended and everybody left the synagogue at the same time [Lns].

QUESTION—Who were the Herodians and why would the Pharisees consult with them about how to destroy Jesus?

The word 'Herodian' is built on the name *Herod*, and to that name is added the Latin suffix *–ians*, which indicates that they were party adherents of Herod or of the Herodian dynasty [Hb]. They were neither a religious sect nor a political party [EBC]. The Herodians were the political followers and supporters of Herod Antipas, a Galilean tetrarch (the ruler of the fourth part of a country or province in the Roman Empire) [CGTC, Gnd, Hb, ICC, NAC, NIGTC, Tay, TH]. They were influential men who supported Herod Antipas in a country where a large number of the people resented Herod's rule over them [EBC, NICNT]. Because the Pharisees had failed to devise a theological accusation against Jesus, they went to the Herodians for political help [Gnd]. Since Jesus was a subject of Herod, it was important to turn Herod against him [NTC]. Probably the Herodians considered Jesus to be a threat to the peace and stability of the country and therefore lent their support to the Pharisees [NIGTC]. The religious Pharisees and the political Herodians were united in wanting to kill Jesus [CBC]. Probably they didn't arrive at a definite plan of action at this meeting, but they agreed to oppose Jesus and when the time was ripe, to silence him [NIGTC]. If it could be established that Jesus was willfully breaking the Sabbath law, then capital punishment would be the proper course [Lns, NIGTC].

DISCOURSE UNIT—3:7–6:13 [EBC, NICNT]. The topic is the later Galilean ministry [EBC], the later phases of Jesus' ministry in Galilee [NICNT].

DISCOURSE UNIT—3:7–19 [NLT]. The topic is the expansion of Jesus' ministry.

DISCOURSE UNIT—3:7–12 [CBC, EBC, Hb, NICNT, NIGTC; CEV, ESV, GW, NASB, NCV, NET, NIV, NLT, TEV]. The topic is a summary of Jesus' early ministry [CBC], Jesus' ministry to the multitudes [Hb], the wide recognition of Jesus' authority to heal [NIGTC], the crowds follow Jesus [NIV, NLT], a great crowd follows Jesus [ESV], large crowds come to Jesus [CEV], many people follow Jesus [NCV], many people are cured [GW], a withdrawal to the sea [NICNT], withdrawal to the lake [EBC], a crowd by the lake [TEV], crowds by the sea [NET], a multitude at the seaside [NASB].

3:7 And Jesus with his disciples went-away[a] to the lake, and a-large crowd[b] from Galilee followed, and from Judea 3:8 and from Jerusalem and from Idumea and beyond the Jordan and around Tyre and Sidon, a-large crowd hearing all he-was-doing came to him.

TEXT—Manuscripts reading ἠκολούθησεν καὶ ἀπὸ τῆς Ἰουδαίας ⁸καὶ ἀπὸ Ἱεροσολύμων καὶ ἀπὸ τῆς Ἰδουμαίας 'followed; and from Judea and from Jerusalem and from Idumea' are given a C rating by GNT to indicate that choosing it over a variant text was difficult. Variant readings are ἠκολούθησεν αὐτῷ καὶ ἀπὸ τῆς Ἰουδαίας καὶ ἀπὸ Ἱεροσολύμων καὶ ἀπὸ τῆς Ἰδουμαίας 'followed him both from Judea and from Jerusalem and from Idumea', ἠκολούθησεν αὐτῷ καὶ ἀπὸ Ἱεροσολύμων καὶ ἀπὸ τῆς Ἰουδαίας 'followed him both from Jerusalem and from Judea', ἠκολούθησαν αὐτῷ καὶ ἀπὸ τῆς Ἰουδαίας καὶ ἀπὸ Ἱεροσολύμων καὶ ἀπὸ τῆς Ἰδουμαίας '(they) followed him both from Judea and from Jerusalem and from Idumea', καὶ ἀπὸ τῆς Ἰουδαίας ἠκολούθησαν καὶ ἀπὸ Ἱεροσολύμων καὶ ἀπὸ τῆς Ἰδουμαίας 'and from Judea they followed, and from Jerusalem and from Idumea', καὶ ἀπὸ Ἱεροσολύμων ἠκολούθησαν αὐτῷ καὶ ἀπὸ τῆς Ἰουδαίας καὶ ἀπὸ τῆς Ἰδουμαίας 'and from Jerusalem they followed him, and from Judea and from Idumea', and καὶ τῆς Ἰουδαίας καὶ ἀπὸ Ἱεροσολύμων καὶ τῆς Ἰδουμαίας 'and Judea and from Jerusalem and Idumea'.

TEXT—In 3:8, manuscripts reading πλῆθος πολύ 'a large crowd' are given an A rating by GNT to indicate it was regarded to be certain. A variant reading omits these words.

LEXICON—a. aorist act. indic. of ἀναχωρέω (LN 15.53) (BAGD 2.b. p. 63): 'to go away' [AB1, LN; NET, REB, TEV], 'to leave' [GW, NCV], 'to depart' [NRSV], 'to withdraw' [AB2, BECNT, BNTC, LN, Lns, NTC, WBC; ESV, KJV, NASB, NIV], 'to go off' [LN], 'to go out' [NLT], 'to retire' [BAGD, LN]. The phrase 'Jesus with his disciples went away to the lake' is translated 'Jesus led his disciples down to the shore of the lake' [CEV]. This verb means to move away a considerable distance from a location [LN].

b. πλῆθος (LN 11.1) (BAGD 2.b.α. p. 668): 'crowd' [BAGD, LN], 'multitude' [LN]. The phrase 'a large crowd' [NTC, WBC; GW, NCV, NIV, NLT, TEV] is also translated 'a great crowd' [AB2, Lns; ESV], 'great crowds' [AB1], 'large crowds' [CEV], 'a great multitude' [BECNT; KJV, NASB, NET, NRSV], 'great numbers' [REB], 'a huge number of people' [BNTC]. This noun denotes a casual non-membership group of people, fairly large in size that is assembled for some purpose [LN].

QUESTION—Why did Jesus go away to the lake?

Jesus preferred to teach and heal in the greater quiet of the lakeside where he would be away from the controversies that occurred in the synagogue [BNTC, Tay]. The verb ἀνεχώρησεν 'he went away' may simply indicate that Jesus was getting away from the crowds, or it may refer to a tactical withdrawal to get away from his opponents [NIGTC]. It may imply that Jesus was withdrawing or retreating from danger [AB1, EBC, Gnd, Hb, Lns, Sw], but if so, his reason for doing this was not due to fear, but to prudence [Lns]. Jesus withdrew to avoid a direct confrontation with Jewish leaders in order to be freely accessible to the crowds [EBC, Hb]. He went away to extend his ministry, not to retreat from danger [AB1, BECNT, BNTC, CGTC, NAC, Tay, WBC]. Instead of continuing his ministry in the towns and synagogues, he now went to minister to the people in the open air by the side of the Lake of Galilee and in adjacent districts [Tay]. Since Capernaum is located right on the shore of the Lake of Galilee, the words 'went away to the lake' must mean they left Capernaum to go farther north to the more deserted stretches of shore close to where the Jordan river entered the lake [PNTC].

QUESTION—What is significant about the placement of the phrase 'with his disciples'?

In Greek, this phrase occurs in an emphatic position before the verb. This indicates that we are about to hear something about the disciples, and the information about the crowd is just a prelude to that [EGT]. It shows that Jesus' disciples shared in his alienation from the Jewish leaders [Hb].

QUESTION—How many crowds are mentioned in these two verses?

1. There is one crowd in view [AB1, BNTC, CGTC, Gnd, Lns, PNTC, Sw, Tay, TRT, WBC; CEV, ESV, GW, NLT, REB, TEV]: *there followed him a great crowd from Galilee and Judea and Jerusalem and Idumea. etc. This great crowd came to him because they heard about all he was doing.* Jesus' response in 3:10 does not distinguish between two groups [WBC]. This was one crowd composed of people from all of the places that are listed [TRT].

2. There are two crowds in view [BECNT, EGT, Hb, ICC, NAC, NIGTC, NTC; NASB, NET, NIV, NRSV]: *a great crowd from Galilee followed him. And from Judea, Jerusalem, Idumea…a great crowd came to him when they heard about all he was doing.* The use of two different verbs ἠκολούθησεν 'followed (him)' and ἦλθον 'came (to him)' separates the Galilean crowd that was already present from the other crowd that later came from more distant regions [NIGTC]. Both verbs are in the aorist tense to state the historical fact that they were with Jesus, but the time relationship between the two events is not specified [Hb].

3:9 And he told his disciples that a-small-boat[a] should-stand-ready[b] for-him because-of[c] the crowd, in-order-that they- not -crush[d] him;

LEXICON—a. πλοιάριον (LN **6.42**) (BAGD p. 673): 'small boat' [BAGD, LN, Lns, NTC, WBC; NET, NIV], 'small ship' [KJV], 'boat' [AB1, AB2, BECNT, BNTC; all versions except KJV, NET, NIV]. This noun is a diminutive form of πλοῖον 'boat, ship', but in some contexts it is possible that the diminutive aspect is not relevant [LN].

b. pres. act. subj. of προσκαρτερέω (LN 35.28) (BAGD 1. p. 715): 'to stand ready' [BAGD], 'to be in personal attendance' [LN]. The phrase 'that a small boat should stand ready' is translated 'that a boat should stand ready' [NASB], 'that a small ship should wait upon him' [KJV], 'that a small boat should be constantly attending him' [Lns], 'that a small boat should be kept in readiness' [NTC], 'that a boat should be made ready' [BECNT], 'to get/have a boat ready' [AB1, BNTC; CEV, ESV, GW, NCV, NLT, NRSV, REB, TEV], 'to have a small boat ready' [NET, NIV], 'to prepare a small boat' [WBC], 'to prepare a boat' [AB2]. This verb means to serve in a close personal relationship [LN]. The present tense of the verb indicates that they were to have the boat constantly ready for Jesus to use [BECNT, ICC, Lns].

c. διά (LN 90.44): 'because of' [AB2, BECNT, BNTC, LN, NTC; ESV, KJV, NASB, NET, NIV, NRSV], 'on account of' [LN, Lns, WBC], 'so that' [AB1; GW, NLT]. The phrase 'because of the crowd' is translated 'The crowd was so large that (he told…)' [TEV]. The phrase 'because of the crowd in order that they would not crush him' is translated 'to keep him from being crushed by the crowds' [CEV], 'to save him from being crushed by the crowd' [REB], 'to keep people from crowding against him' [NCV]. This preposition indicates the person constituting the cause or reason for an event or state [LN].

d. pres. act. subj. of θλίβω (LN 19.44) (BAGD 1. p. 362): 'to press upon' [BAGD, Lns, WBC], 'to press toward' [NET], 'to press against' [LN], 'to crush' [AB2, BECNT, BNTC, NTC; CEV, ESV, GW, NLT, NRSV, REB, TEV], 'to crowd' [BAGD; NASB, NIV], 'to crowd against' [LN; NCV], 'to throng' [KJV]. This verb is also translated passively: 'to be crushed by' [AB1]. This verb means to crowd in hard against someone [LN].

QUESTION—What kind of a boat was to be made ready for Jesus?

The noun πλοιάριον is a diminutive form of πλοῖον 'boat', and means a 'little boat', probably something like a rowboat instead of a regular fishing boat [Hb, Sw]. It probably was a small boat even though the noun doesn't have to refer to a 'small' boat [Lns, NTC, Sw, WBC; KJV, NET, NIV]. Mark, however, has a tendency to use colloquial terms and this noun need not be distinguished from the regular fishing boat, πλοῖον, that is referred to in verses 4:1 and 36 [AB1, CGTC, NIGTC, NTC, Tay, TH]. The boat probably belonged to one of the disciples [BECNT, NLTfn] and this boat will be used in 4:1–2 [BNTC].

QUESTION—What was involved in having the boat stand ready for Jesus?
The boat would be moored close to the shore so that the disciples could move it along as Jesus walked along the shore [Sw]. The boat would always to be in position for Jesus to escape from the crush of the crowd by getting into it and moving out a short distance from the shore [EBC, Lns, NTC]. He would then be able to address the crowd of people left standing on the beach [Lns, NTC]. Jesus did not seem to have used it on this occasion [Sw].

3:10 because[a] he-had-healed many, with-the-result-that[b] as-many-as[c] had afflictions[d] pressed-around[e] him in-order-that they-might-touch him.

LEXICON—a. γάρ (LN 89.23). 'for' [AB2, BECNT, BNTC, Lns, NTC, WBC; ESV, KJV, NASB, NET, NIV, NRSV, REB], not explicit [AB1; CEV, GW, NCV, NLT, TEV]. This conjunction indicates a cause or reason between events [LN].

b. ὥστε (LN 89.52) (BAGC 2.a.β. p. 900): 'as a result' [LN], 'with the result that' [NASB], 'so that' [AB1, AB2, BAGD, BECNT, BNTC, LN, Lns, WBC; ESV, NET, NRSV], 'that' [NTC; GW, REB], 'insomuch that' [KJV], 'so' [NCV, NLT], 'therefore, so then, and so' [LN], 'and' [TEV], not explicit [CEV, NIV]. This conjunction indicates result [LN].

c. ὅσος (LN 59.7) (BAGD 2. p. 586): 'as many as' [BAGD, LN]. The phrase 'as many as had afflictions' [AB2] is also translated 'all those who had afflictions' [NASB], 'all who were afflicted with diseases' [NET], 'all those who had diseases' [AB1, BECNT, BNTC; ESV, NRSV], 'those with diseases' [NIV], 'everyone with a disease' [GW], 'all who were suffering' [WBC], 'all those who were suffering from illnesses' [NTC], 'all the sick people' [NLT; similarly LN (19.42); NCV, REB, TEV], 'the other sick people' [CEV], 'as many as had scourges' [Lns], 'as many as had plagues' [KJV]. This adjectival pronoun refers to a comparative quantity of objects or events [LN].

d. μάστιξ (LN 23.153) (BAGD 2. p. 495): 'affliction' [AB2, WBC; NASB], 'disease' [AB1, BECNT, BNTC, LN; ESV, GW, NIV, NRSV], 'illness' [BAGD, NTC], 'scourge' [Lns], 'plague' [KJV]. This noun is also translated as an adjective: 'sick' [CEV, NCV, NLT, REB, TEV]; as a verb phrase: 'who were afflicted with diseases' [NET], 'who were suffering' [WBC]. This noun denotes the state of being diseased [LN]. The noun literally means 'whip, scourge, torment' and it was used to denote a sickness that was regarded to be a chastisement from God [CGTC, Sw, Tay, TH]. However, it had become a general term for any disease [CGTC, NIGTC, TH]. This word occurs at 3:10; 5:29, 34.

e. pres. act. infin. of ἐπιπίπτω (LN **19.42**) (BAGD 1.b. p. 297): 'to press about' [BAGD], 'to press around' [ESV, NASB], 'to press upon' [BECNT], 'to press against, to push against' [LN], 'to push toward' [**LN**; NCV], 'to push forward' [NIV, NLT], 'to push their way to' [TEV], 'to press toward' [**LN**; NET], 'to press upon' [KJV, NRSV], 'to crowd around' [REB], 'to crowd in upon' [AB1, BNTC, NTC], 'to rush up to'

[GW], 'to fall upon' [AB2, Lns], not explicit [CEV]. This verb means to press or push against [LN].

QUESTION—What relationship is indicated by γάρ 'because'?

This conjunction indicates the reason for telling the disciples to get a boat ready as mentioned in the preceding verse [BECNT, BNTC, Hb, Lns, TH]. The sense is '*Jesus did this because* he had healed many, and as a result all who had afflictions pressed around him' [TH].

QUESTION—Does the statement 'he had healed *many*' imply that there were some whom he had failed to heal?

'Many' does not mean 'some' as though there were others who were not healed. It means all of the many sick people [AB1, BECNT, NLTfn, Sw, Tay]. Of course 'all' doesn't include those who were not in need of healing [AB1]. Jesus healed all who came to him for healing [Lns].

QUESTION—Why did the people want to touch Jesus?

It is implied that those who touched Jesus would be healed [Lns]. In Luke 6:17 it says that power came out of Jesus and healed them all [AB1, Tay]. Physical contact with Jesus was thought to be a condition for being healed [Hb, ICC, NIGTC, Sw]. They thought that a touch was effective, whether Jesus touched them or they touched him [Sw]. They did not wait for Jesus to touch them, they crowded around Jesus in order to touch him [NTC].

3:11 And whenever[a] the unclean[b] spirits saw him they-would-fall[c] before him and would-cry-out[d] saying "You are the Son of God.[e]"

LEXICON—a. ὅταν (LN **67.36**) (BAGD 2.c. p. 588): 'whenever' [AB2, BAGD, BECNT, BNTC, **LN**, Lns, NTC, WBC; all versions except KJV, NCV, REB], 'when' [AB1, BAGD; KJV, NCV, REB], 'as often as' [LN]. This conjunction indicates indefinite and multiple points of time that are simultaneous with other corresponding points of time [LN].

b. ἀκάθαρτος (LN 12.39) (BAGD 2. p. 296): 'unclean' [AB1, AB2, BECNT, BNTC, LN, Lns, NTC, WBC; ESV, KJV, NASB, NET, NRSV, REB], 'evil' [CEV, GW, NCV, NIV, NLT, TEV]. The phrase πνεῦμα ἀκάθαρτον 'unclean spirit' denotes an evil supernatural spirit that is ritually unclean and any person possessed by an unclean spirit is considered to be ceremonially unclean also [LN]. The term 'unclean spirits' refers to evil spirits [BAGD, NETfn]. Evil spirits are called 'unclean spirits' at 1:23, 26, 27; 3:11, 30; 5:2, 8, 13; 6:7; 7:25; 9:25.

c. imperf. act. indic. of προσπίπτω (LN 17.22) (BAGD 1. p. 718): 'to fall down before' [BAGD, LN], 'to fall down at the feet of' [BAGD], 'to prostrate oneself before' [LN]. The phrase 'to fall before him' [AB1, BECNT, WBC; KJV] is also translated 'to fall down before him' [AB2, Lns; ESV, NASB, NCV, NET, NIV, NRSV, TEV], 'to fall down in front of him' [GW], 'to fall down at his feet' [NTC], 'to fall at his feet' [BNTC; REB], 'to fall to the ground' [CEV], '(the spirits) would throw them to the ground in front of him' [NLT]. This verb means to prostrate oneself

before someone in supplication [LN]. The imperfect tense refers to repeated instances [Hb]. This word occurs at 3:11; 5:33; 7:25.
   d. imperf. act. indic. of κράζω (LN 33.83) (BAGD 2.a. p. 447): 'to call out' [BAGD], 'to cry out' [BECNT, WBC; ESV, NET, NIV], 'to cry aloud' [BNTC; REB], 'to cry' [KJV], 'to shout' [CEV, GW, NASB, NCV, NRSV], 'to yell' [Lns], 'to yell out' [AB2], 'to scream' [AB1, LN, NTC; TEV], 'to shriek' [NLT]. This verb means to shout or cry out [LN].
3. υἱὸς τοῦ θεοῦ 'Son of God' is a title applied to Jesus. It is parallel in semantic structure to phrases consisting of υἱός 'son' followed by the genitive of class or kind. It means one who has the essential characteristics and nature of God [LN]. This title appears in 1:1; 3:11; 15:39.

QUESTION—Who were falling before Jesus?
Demon-possessed people fell before Jesus, their actions being directed by the unclean spirits controlling them [BECNT, CGTC, Hb, ICC, NCBC, NIGTC]. Some translations makes this clear: 'And whenever those possessed by evil spirits caught sight of him, the spirits would throw them to the ground in front of him shrieking...' [NLT], 'And whenever the people who had evil spirits in them saw him, they would fall down before him and scream...' [TEV]. 'Falling before a person' was an action of an inferior person prostrating himself in homage before one who is superior [BECNT, BNTC, PNTC], but in this verse this action signaled the fear of the unclean spirits, not their commitment to him [NAC]. It was an acknowledgement of Jesus' power over them [Lns].

QUESTION—How did the unclean spirits know that Jesus was the Son of God?
The demons had supernatural knowledge about Jesus' true identity, so they reluctantly submitted to him through the actions of the people whom they possessed [BECNT].

QUESTION—Did Jesus heal the people possessed by the unclean spirits?
It is assumed that Jesus cast out those unclean spirits [NIGTC]. This is not made explicit here because the point Mark wants to make is the identity of Jesus as the Son of God [Gnd].

3:12 And he sternly commanded^a them that they- not -make him known.^b
LEXICON—a. imperf. act. indic. of ἐπιτιμάω (LN 33.331, 33.419) (BAGD 1. p. 303): 'to command' [LN (33.331)], 'to rebuke' [LN (33.419)], 'to warn, to reprove' [BAGD]. The phrase 'to sternly command' [NLT] is also translated 'to sternly order' [NET, NRSV, TEV], 'to strictly order' [ESV], 'to give strict orders' [NIV], 'to give orders' [GW], 'to give strict instructions' [BNTC], 'to straightly charge' [KJV], 'to insist' [AB1; REB], 'to strongly warn' [NCV], 'to earnestly warn' [NASB], 'to warn' [CEV], 'to rebuke' [LN (33.419)], 'to sharply rebuke' [AB2, BECNT], 'to rebuke severely' [LN (33.331)], 'to silence' [WBC]. This verb means to give a command that carries with it an implied threat against disobeying it

[LN (33.331)], or to express strong disapproval of someone [LN (33.419)].

b. φανερός (LN 28.28) (BAGD 1. p. 852): 'known' [BAGD], 'well known, widely known' [LN]. The phrase 'not to make him known' [AB1, AB2, BECNT, Lns; ESV, KJV, NET, NRSV, REB; similarly WBC] is also translated 'not to tell who he was' [CEV, NASB, NCV, NIV, TEV; similarly GW], 'not to reveal who he was' [NLT]. This adjective refers to being widely and well known [LN]. To make someone 'known' means to inform people what he really is and to reveal his identity [BAGD].

QUESTION—Why did Jesus command the unclean spirits not to make his true identity known?

Jesus silenced the demons because the time for a clear revelation of his relationship with God had not yet come, and demons were not appropriate heralds to make such an announcement [EBC]. The Roman authorities would not have tolerated a movement in which its leader proclaimed the arrival of God's kingdom and whose followers regarded him to be the long-awaited Messiah and King of Israel. In the Roman empire, there was no room for another kingdom or for a messianic rescuer from Roman occupation. However, Jesus had come to give his life as ransom for many, not to lead a rebellion against Rome [NLTfn].

DISCOURSE UNIT—3:13–6:6a [CBC]. The topic is the teaching about the mystery-filled kingdom and miracles of power yield rejection.

DISCOURSE UNIT—3:13–4:34 [PNTC]. The topic is the insiders and outsiders.

DISCOURSE UNIT—3:13–35 [NIGTC; NASB]. The topic is the varying responses to Jesus by supporters and opponents [NIGTC], the twelve are chosen [NASB].

DISCOURSE UNIT—3:13–21 [ESV]. The topic is the twelve Apostles.

DISCOURSE UNIT—3:13–19 [CBC, EBC, Hb, NICNT, NIGTC; CEV, GW, NCV, NET, NIV, NLT, TEV]. The topic is the Twelve [NIGTC], the selection of the Twelve [EBC], the choosing of the Twelve [CBC, NICNT], Jesus chooses his twelve Apostles [CEV, NCV, NLT, TEV], the appointment of the Twelve [Hb], the appointing of the twelve Apostles [NET, NIV], Jesus appoints twelve Apostles [GW].

3:13 And[a] he goes-up to[b] the mountain and he-summons[c] whom he wanted, and they-came to him.

LEXICON—a. καί (LN 89.87): 'and' [AB2, BECNT, LN, Lns, WBC; ESV, KJV, NASB], 'and then' [LN], 'then' [AB1, BNTC; NCV, REB, TEV], 'now' [NET], 'afterward' [NLT], not explicit [NTC; CEV, GW, NIV, NRSV]. This conjunction indicates a sequence of closely related events [LN].

b. εἰς (LN 84.16): 'to, toward, in the direction of' [LN], 'on' [BECNT; CEV, ESV, NASB, NCV, NLT], 'into' [Lns, NTC; KJV]. The phrase 'goes up to the mountain' is translated 'went up the/a mountain' [AB2, BNTC, WBC; GW, NET, NRSV], 'went up on a mountainside' [NIV], 'went up a hill' [TEV], 'went up into the hill-country' [REB]. This preposition indicates extension toward a special goal [LN].

c. pres. mid. indic. of προσκαλέομαι, προσκαλέω (LN 33.308) (BAGD 1.a. p. 715): 'to summon' [BAGD; BNTC; NASB, REB], 'to call to oneself' [AB2, BAGD, BECNT, Lns, NTC; ESV, KJV, NCV, NIV, NRSV, TEV], 'to call out someone' [NLT], 'to call for' [NET], 'to call' [LN, WBC; GW], 'to ask (to go…with him)' [CEV]. This verb means to call someone [LN]. Here this has the special meaning of selecting them [BECNT, WBC]. This word also occurs at 6:7.

QUESTION—What relationship is indicated by the beginning conjunction καί 'and'?

This conjunction indicates a further significant event, but does not necessarily imply a close chronological sequence [Hb]. Mark's account seems to be continuous [Sw].

QUESTION—Why did Jesus go up to the mountain, and did he go up there before he summoned the disciples?

Luke 6:12 says that Jesus went up the mountain to spend the night in prayer and the next morning he summoned his disciples to choose twelve of those disciples to be his apostles [EBC, Hb, NTC, Sw, Tay]. That the men 'came to (πρός) him' suggests that Jesus was already on the mountain and the men heeded his summons from a distance [Gnd]. It is not indicated if Jesus went down to personally speak to each individual he wanted to go up with him or if Jesus sent some disciples to notify the ones he wanted to come up to where he was [EGT]. Mark focused on the authority of Jesus' summons and did not bother with the practical questions concerning the timing and the means of the summons in relation to Jesus going up the mountain ahead of the others [Gnd]. There is one translation that seems to say that the disciples accompanied Jesus when he first went up to the mountain; 'Jesus decided to ask some of his disciples to go up on a mountain with him, and they went' [CEV].

QUESTION—Who were the people Jesus summoned?
1. Jesus summoned a group of his disciples to himself and then appointed twelve from that group to accompany him as his apostles [AB1, EGT, Hb, Lns, Sw, Tay; CEV, NLT]. From a crowd of people gathered together to listen to Jesus, Jesus summoned certain ones of them to leave that crowd and take their stand with him as his disciples [Hb]. Out of those who answered his summons, Jesus selected twelve [Sw].
2 Jesus summoned just twelve disciples to himself and appointed them to accompany him as his apostles [BECNT, BNTC, My, NICNT, NIGTC, NTC, PNTC, WBC]. Only twelve disciples are in focus from the very beginning of this account. Jesus summoned the twelve disciples to come

to him and appointed them to accompany him as his apostles. The words 'he summoned' was a statement of their election, and the following words 'he appointed twelve' refers to what that summons signified [NICNT].

3:14 And he-appointed[a] twelve, whom also he-named[b] apostles,[c] so-that they-might-be with[d] him and so-that he-might-send them to preach[e]

TEXT—Manuscripts reading δώδεκα, οὓς καὶ ἀποστόλους ὠνόμασεν, ἵνα ὦσιν μετ' αὐτοῦ 'twelve, whom also named apostles, in order that they would be with him' are given a C rating by GNT to indicate that choosing it over a variant text was difficult. A variant reading is δώδεκα, ἵνα ὦσιν μετ' αὐτοῦ 'twelve, in order that they would be with him' and it is followed by AB1, AB2, BNTC, Hb, Lns, Tay; KJV, NASB, REB. Another variant reading is δώδεκα μαθητὰς ἵνα ὦσιν μετ' αὐτοῦ, οὓς καὶ ἀποστόλους ὠνόμασεν 'twelve disciples in order that they would be with him, whom also he named apostles'.

LEXICON—a. aorist act. indic. of ποιέω (LN 37.106): 'to appoint' [AB2, BECNT, BNTC, NTC, WBC; ESV, GW, NASB, NET, NIV, NLT, NRSV, REB], 'to assign to a task' [LN], 'to choose' [CEV, NCV, TEV], 'to ordain' [KJV], 'to make' [Lns]. This verb means to cause someone to assume a particular type of function, such as assuming responsibilities for some task [LN].

b. aorist act. indic. of ὀνομάζω (LN **33.127**) (BAGD 1. p. 573): 'to name' [BAGD, BECNT, NTC, WBC; ESV, NET, NRSV, TEV], 'to designate' [NIV], 'to call' [BAGD, **LN**; GW, NCV, NLT]. The phrase 'whom also he named apostles' is translated '(he chose…) to be his apostles' [CEV]. This verb means to give a name or title to someone [LN].

c. ἀπόστολος (LN 53.74) (BAGD 3. p. 99): 'apostle' [BAGD, LN; all translations except AB1, AB2, BNTC; KJV, NASB, REB which follow a different text that does not include this word], 'special messenger' [LN]. This noun denotes someone who fulfills the role of being a special messenger [LN]. It designates a group of highly honored believers who had a special function [BAGD]. This word occurs at 3:14; 6:30.

d. μετά (LN 89.108) (BAGD A.II. 1.c.α. p. 508): 'with' [AB1, AB2, BAGD, BECNT, BNTC, LN, NTC, WBC; all versions except GW, NLT, REB], 'in company with' [Lns]. The phrase 'they might be with him' is translated 'they were to accompany him' [GW, NLT], 'to be his companions' [REB]. This preposition refers to an associative relation that often involves joint participation in some activity [LN].

e. pres. act. infin. of κηρύσσω (LN 33.256) (BAGD 2.b.β. p. 431): 'to preach' [AB2, BAGD, BECNT, BNTC, LN, NTC, WBC; all versions except GW, NRSV, REB], 'to proclaim' [BAGD], 'to proclaim the message' [NRSV], 'to proclaim the gospel' [REB], 'to spread the Good News' [GW], 'to act as heralds' [Lns], 'to make the Proclamation' [AB1]. This verb means to publicly announce religious truths and principles while urging acceptance and compliance [LN].

QUESTION—What is odd about the clause 'whom he named apostles'?

The inclusion of this clause is grammatically awkward in that it interrupts the thought that 'he appointed twelve…so that they might be with him' [Gnd]. The clause 'whom he named apostles' is a parenthetical remark added by Mark to accent the appointment of the Twelve and it does not mean that Jesus told them at that time that they would be called 'apostles' [WBC]. Some translations that include this phrase enclose it within parenthesis marks [ESV, NET], em dashes [NTC; NIV], or just commas [BECNT, WBC; NRSV]. Others begin a new sentence after this clause [GW, NCV, NLT, TEV]: 'Then he appointed twelve of them and called them his apostles. They were to accompany him and he would send them out to preach' [NLT]. One translation adjusts the syntax so as to make a proper sentence by making this an appointment to be apostles: 'Then he chose twelve of them to be his apostles, so that they could be with him' [CEV].

QUESTION—What relationship is indicated by the two conjunctions ἵνα 'so that'?

The two conjunctions indicate the twofold purpose for which the Twelve were appointed [BECNT, EBC, Gnd, Hb, ICC, NAC, NIGTC, Tay, TH, WBC]. First they were to live with Jesus in order to be trained by him, and later Jesus would send them out to preach the Good News and drive out demons as related in 6:7 [EBC].

QUESTION—What is meant by the twelve apostles being appointed to be 'with' Jesus?

These men would begin a personal relationship with Jesus that included sharing in his life and ministry [WBC]. They would live with Jesus, travel with him, talk with him, and learn from him [EBC]. They would learn his teachings and witness what he did in order to be equipped to serve as his apostles and witnesses [BECNT, Tay]. Jesus would train them for the active ministry they would later have when they were sent out to preach [NIGTC].

QUESTION—What were they to preach?

We can assume that they would preach the message of the Kingdom referred to in 1:14–15 [BECNT, NAC, WBC]. They would preach a message of salvation through Jesus Christ [NTC].

3:15 and to-have authority to-cast-out^a demons.

TEXT—Manuscripts reading ἐκβάλλειν τὰ δαιμόνια 'to cast out demons' are followed by GNT, which does not mention any variant reading. A variant reading is θεραπεύειν τὰς νόσους καί ἐκβάλλειν τὰ δαιμόνια 'to heal the sicknesses and to cast out demons' and it is followed by KJV.

LEXICON—a. pres. act. infin. of ἐκβάλλω (LN 53.102) (BAGD 1. p. 237): 'to cast out' [AB1, AB2, BECNT, LN, Lns, WBC; ESV, KJV, NASB, NET, NLT, NRSV], 'to make to go out, to exorcise' [LN], 'to drive out' [BAGD, BNTC; NIV, REB, TEV], 'to expel' [BAGD, NTC], 'to force out' [CEV], 'to force out of people' [GW, NCV]. This verb means to cause a demon to no longer possess or control a person [LN]. In reference to 'casting' out demons, this verb occurs at 1:34, 39; 3:15, 22, 23; 6:13; 7:26; 9:18, 28, 38; 16:9, 17.

QUESTION—What is the problem with the syntax of the three infinitives in the statement 'so that he might send them *to preach* and *to have* authority *to cast out* demons'?

The infinitive phrase 'to cast out demons' seems to parallel the first infinitive phrase 'to preach', so these two phrases could be expressed 'so that he might send them to preach and to cast out demons'. The inclusion of the infinitive phrase 'to have authority' complicates the syntax and makes no sense with the verb 'to send' since a person is sent to perform an action, not to have an ability [BECNT, Gnd, WBC]. Most translations follow the Greek syntax. Some make adjustments in the syntax: 'to be sent out to proclaim the gospel, *with authority* to drive out demons' [REB; similarly AB1], 'he would send them out to preach, *giving them authority* to cast out demons' [NLT], 'I will also send you out to preach, and *you will have authority* to drive out demons.' [TEV], 'They were…to be sent out by him to spread the Good News. *They also had the authority* to force demons out of people.' [GW]. One leaves the idea of authority implicit: 'He wanted to send them out to preach and to force out demons.' [CEV].

QUESTION—What is significant about being given authority to cast out demons?

The coming of the kingdom of God would be demonstrated by their casting out demons [NAC]. That they were to 'have authority' implies they were given both the power and the right to expel demons [BECNT, NTC, TH]. This authority to cast out demons is representative of all the miracles that they would do in their ministry [Hb, ICC]. It is taken for granted that they also were given the lesser power of healing diseases, since Matt. 10:8 includes healing the sick, raising the dead, and cleansing lepers [Lns]. In 6:13 it indicates that healing would take place along with preaching and casting out demons [NIGTC].

3:16 And he-appointed the Twelve, and he gave (the) name Peter to-Simon, 3:17 and James the (son) of-Zebedee and John the brother of-James and he-gave to-them (the) names Boanerges, which is,[a] Sons[b] of Thunder.

TEXT—Manuscripts reading καὶ ἐποίησεν τοὺς δώδεκα, καί 'and he appointed the Twelve, and' are given a C rating by GNT to indicate that choosing it over a variant text was difficult. A variant reading is καί 'and' and it is followed by CGTC, Tay; KJV. Other variant readings are πρῶτον Σίμωνα καί 'first Simon and' and καὶ περιάγοντας κηρύσσειν τὸ εὐαγγέλιον. καί 'and going around to preach the gospel. And'.

LEXICON—a. ὅ ἐστιν (LN 89.106) (BAGD II.3. p. 224): The phrase ὅ ἐστιν 'which is' [Lns; KJV] is also translated 'which means' [BAGD, BECNT, LN, WBC; CEV, NASB, NCV, NIV, TEV], 'that is' [AB2, LN, NTC; GW, NET, NRSV], 'that is to say, which is the equivalent of' [BAGD], not explicit [AB1; NLT, REB]. This phrase introduces an explanation or

clarification in the same or different language [LN]. This phrase occurs at 3:17; 7:11.
b. υἱός (LN 9.4) (BAGD 1.c.δ. p. 834): 'son' [BAGD, LN], 'person' [LN]. The phrase Υἱοὶ Βροντῆς 'Sons of Thunder' [AB1, AB2, BECNT, BNTC, Lns, NTC, WBC; all versions except CEV, GW, TEV] is also translated 'Men of Thunder' [TEV], 'Thunderbolts' [CEV, GW]. This noun denotes a person of a class or kind that is specified by the following genitive construction [LN]. It is a Hebraism that denotes one who shares in the specified thing [BAGD].

QUESTION—What is the significance of giving Simon the name Πέτρος 'Peter'?

The name given to Simon is Πέτρος, a Greek equivalent of the Aramaic *kepa* 'rock' [EBC, NLTfn]. Since the Greek word πέτρος 'rock, stone' was not used as a proper name in either Aramaic or Greek, naming him 'the stone' was done as a descriptive designation [Hb, NIGTC], which could function as a nickname [NIGTC]. This name might have been picked to describe Peter's character as having a rock-like firmness or to describe his official function as a foundation rock in the building of the church [Hb]. Since Simon did not display a rock-like firmness in Galatians 2:11–12, the name must denote the part he would play as the spokesman and representative of the Twelve while Jesus was with them [CGTC]. Whether Simon was given the name 'Peter' as a nickname or not, Mark uses Πέτρος 'Peter' as a proper name throughout this book [BECNT]. Having introduced Simon's better-known name 'Peter', Mark then uses 'Peter' throughout the rest of the book except at 14:37 where Jesus addresses him by the name Simon [NIGTC]. This does not mean that the name Peter was first given to Simon at this time, since John 1:42 describes how Jesus gave Simon that name when they first met [Hb, NTC, Sw, Tay].

QUESTION—What is the significance of giving James and John the names Boanerges (a plural name meaning 'Sons of Thunder')?

This name is probably meant to symbolize their impetuous and ardent natures [Hb], their tempers [PNTC], their rashness [Gnd], their fiery and vehement temperament [ICC, NICNT, NTC, TH], or the fiery zeal for the Lord that they would manifest [Lns]. However, the NT does not give enough information to indicate how this term might fit their characters [CBC, NIGTC]. The plural word ὀνόματα 'names' refers to just the one name *Boanerges*. The word 'names' is plural in order to include both James and John [Gnd]. Some translations change the plural noun 'names' to its singular form 'name': he gave them the *name* 'Boanerges' [AB1, AB2, BNTC, WBC; NASB, NET, NIV, NRSV].

3:18 **And Andrew and Philip and Bartholomew and Matthew and Thomas and James the (son) of-Alphaeus and Thaddaeus and Simon the Cananaean**[a] **3:19 and Judas Iscariot who also betrayed**[b] **him.**

TEXT—Manuscripts reading καὶ Θαδδαῖον 'and Thaddaeus' are given an A rating by GNT to indicate it was regarded to be certain. A variant reading is καὶ Λεββαῖον 'and Lebbaeus'. Another manuscript omits this phrase.

LEXICON—a. Καναναῖος (LN 11.88) (BAGD p. 402): 'Cananaean' [BAGD], 'zealot' [BAGD, LN], 'nationalist' [LN]. The phrase 'Simon the Cananaean' [BECNT, NTC; ESV, NRSV] is also translated 'Simon the Kannanite' [AB2], 'Simon the Canaanite' [KJV], 'Simon the Zealot' [BNTC, WBC; GW, NASB, NCV, NET, NIV, NLT, REB], 'Simon, known as the Eager One' [CEV], 'Simon the member of the zealot party' [AB1], 'Simon the Patriot' [TEV]. This noun is the Aramaic equivalent of ζηλωτής 'zealot, nationalist' and is not in any way related to the geographical names Cana or Canaan. It denotes a member of a Jewish nationalistic group seeking independence from Rome [LN].

b. aorist act. indic. of παραδίδωμι (LN 37.111) (BAGD 1.b. p. 614): 'to betray' [AB1, AB2, BECNT, BNTC, LN, NTC, WBC; all versions except NCV], 'to hand over, to turn over to' [BAGD, LN], 'to turn against' [NCV]. This verb means to deliver a person into the control of someone else by either handing over a presumably guilty person to the authorities for punishment or handing over an individual to an enemy who will presumably take undue advantage of the victim [LN].

QUESTION—Who was Μαθθαῖος 'Matthew'?

1. This is the same disciple who appeared in 2:14–17 with the name Levi [AB1, CGTC, EBC, EGT, Hb, ICC, NICNT, NIGTC, NLTfn, NTC, PNTC, Sw, Tay, TRT, WBC]. This toll collector is identified as Matthew in Matt. 9.9, and also in the parallel event in Mark 2:14 where the toll collector is called Levi [BECNT, ICC, WBC; NLT].

2. This disciple was not Levi [BNTC]. Matthew was one of the Twelve, and Levi was in a circle of disciples wider than the Twelve [BNTC].

QUESTION—Who was Θαδδαῖος 'Thaddaeus'?

Thaddaeus is the only name that does not occur in all of the lists of apostles in the Gospels. Apparently he had three names. He is called Thaddaeus in the lists of Matthew and Mark. In Luke and Acts he is called 'Judas the son of James'. In John 14:22 he is called 'Judas (not Iscariot)' [EBC, ICC, Lns, NTC]. Since there were three apostles with the name Judas, the substitution of a secondary name in the case of one of them is natural [Sw].

QUESTION—What is meant by the name τὸν Καναναῖον 'the Cananaean'?

The name 'the Cananaean' does not mean that Simon was a Canaanite or that he was from the village of Cana [BAGD, Hb, LN, Tay, TRT, WBC]. Here the name 'the Cananaean' is a transliteration of an Aramaic word that is given its Greek equivalent ζηλωτήν 'zealot' in Luke 6:15 [Hb].

1. Simon probably was called 'the Zealot' to indicate that he belonged to the Zealot party of the Jews [AB1, BECNT, BNTC, CBC, CGTC, EBC, ICC,

Lns, NIGTC, NLTfn, NTC, Tay, WBC; probably TEV]. He is identified as being a fervent nationalist [NIGTC], an anti-government activist [NLT]. The members of the Zealot party hated their foreign ruler and were involved in fomenting rebellion against the Roman government [NTC]. His connection with the party was before he became a disciple [CBC].
   2. Simon probably was called 'the Zealot' to describe his zealous personal disposition [NICNT, Sw; CEV]. He was zealous for the honor of God [NICNT]. He was zealous for what he considered to be right or true [Sw].
QUESTION—What is meant by Judas' other name Ἰσκαριώθ 'Iscariot'?
   It identifies Judas with the village of Kerioth [BNTC, CGTC, EBC, Hb, ICC, LN, Lns, NAC, NICNT, NIVfn, NLTfn, NTC, PNTC, Sw, Tay, WBC] located in southern Judea [LN (93.181)]. Another takes the word to be a nickname describing Judas as being reddish-brown or ruddy [AB1].

DISCOURSE UNIT—3:20-35 [EBC, Hb, NICNT; NLT]. The topic is the mounting opposition to Jesus [Hb], the character of Jesus' family [NICNT], Jesus, his family, and Satan [NLT], Jesus, his family, and the Beelzebub controversy [EBC].

DISCOURSE UNIT—3:20-30 [CBC, Hb, NIGTC; CEV, NCV, NET, NIV, NLT, TEV]. The topic is Jesus and the ruler of demons [CEV], Jesus and the prince of demons [NLT], Jesus and Beelzebul [NET, TEV], Jesus and Beelzebub [NIV], a charge of collusion with Beelzebub [Hb], some people say Jesus has a devil [NCV], scribes from Jerusalem [NIGTC], the debate over Jesus' power: Is his power from Satan or from God? [CBC].

DISCOURSE UNIT—3:20-21 [EBC, Hb, NICNT; NLT]. The topic is the anxiety of Jesus' friends [Hb], charged with insanity [EBC], a charge that Jesus is deranged [NICNT], Jesus' family thinks he is crazy [NLT].

3:20 **And he-goes into a house. And the crowd gathers again, so-that they-were- not -able even to-eat bread.**ᵃ

TEXT—Manuscripts reading ἔρχεται 'he goes' are given a B rating by GNT to indicate it was regarded to be almost certain. A variant reading is ἔρχονται 'they go' and it is followed by KJV.
LEXICON—a. ἄρτος (LN 5.1): 'bread' [Lns; KJV], 'food' [AB2, LN]. The phrase 'to eat bread' is translated 'to eat a meal' [NTC, WBC], 'to eat' [AB1, BECNT; all versions except KJV]. This noun denotes any kind of food or nourishment [LN, Tay]. The expression 'to eat bread' involves more than just bread and simply means 'to eat' [BECNT].
QUESTION—Where did Jesus go?
   While some translate the noun οἶκον 'a house' by saying that Jesus went into *a house* [AB2; KJV, NIV, NLT, REB] or *the house* [AB1], other translations say that Jesus went into *his* house [WBC] or Jesus went *home* [EGT, Lns; CEV, ESV, GW, NASB, NCV, NET, NRSV, TEV]. One commentary says that the phrase is ambiguous and merely says that Jesus

went *indoors* [BNTC]. The house is probably the one in Capernaum that is referred to in 2:1 [CGTC, EBC, ESVfn, Gnd, Hb, NCBC, NIGTC, PNTC, TRT], where it probably refers to the house of Simon and Andrew mentioned in 1:29 [CGTC, EBC, Gnd, NAC, NCBC, NICNT, NIGTC, NIVfn, PNTC, TRT] or Jesus' own home in Capernaum [ICC, Lns; probably NTC]. Another view is that if Mark wanted the readers to assume that it was Peter's house he could easily have said 'Peter's house'. Neither does it seem likely that it was Jesus' own home since it would be strange for his mother and brothers to be standing outside asking for him (3:31–32). Mark just didn't think it was important to identify the owner of the house [BECNT].

QUESTION—What is meant by the crowds gathering *again*?

The adverb 'again' refers to similar occurrences of crowds gathering around Jesus at a house in 1:29 [NICNT], and in 2:2 [Hb, ICC, NICNT, Sw]. It could refer back to the crowds gathering around Jesus at the lake at 3:7 [Tay]. It does not mean that the very same members of a previous crowd gathered again, but that it happened again that a crowd gathered around Jesus [TH].

QUESTION—Who are the referents of 'they', and why couldn't they eat?

The pronoun 'they' refers to Jesus and the twelve Apostles [BECNT, Gnd, NIGTC] or Jesus and his disciples [CGTC, EBC, TH, TRT]. The crowd was so large and intrusive that it filled the house in such numbers that there was no opportunity for Jesus and his disciples to take time to eat [Hb, Lns, NIGTC]. The reason they couldn't eat is not mentioned, but probably it was because Jesus was too busy teaching the crowd, healing the sick, and casting out demons [Gnd].

3:21 And having-heard, the (ones) beside[a] him went-out to-take-hold-of[b] him. Because they-were-saying, "He-has-lost-his-senses.[c]"

TEXT—Manuscripts reading ἀκούσαντες οἱ παρ' αὐτοῦ 'having heard the ones beside him' are given an A rating by GNT to indicate it was regarded to be certain. Variant readings are ἀκούσαντες ὑπὲρ αὐτοῦ 'having heard about him', and ὅτε ἤκουσαν περὶ αὐτοῦ οἱ γραμματεῖς καὶ οἱ λοιποί 'when the scribes and the rest heard concerning him'.

LEXICON—a. παρά (LN **10.9**) (BAGD I.4.b.β. p. 610): 'beside' [LN]. The phrase οἱ παρ' αὐτοῦ 'the ones beside him' is translated 'his family' [AB1, BAGD, BECNT, BNTC, **LN**; all versions except KJV, NASB], 'his people' [WBC], 'his own people' [NASB], 'his relatives' [AB2], 'his kinsmen' [Lns], 'his friends' [NTC; KJV]. The idiom 'those beside him' refers to the associates of a person, including family, neighbors, and friends [LN].

b. aorist act. infin. of κρατέω (LN **18.6**) (BAGD 1.b. p. 448): 'to lay hold of' [Lns], 'to take hold of, to grasp' [BAGD], 'to hold on to' [LN], 'to lay hold on' [KJV], 'to restrain' [NET, NRSV], 'to seize' [AB2, BECNT, LN; ESV], 'to take custody of' [NASB], 'to take into custody' [WBC], 'to take charge of' [AB1, BNTC, NTC; NIV, REB, TEV], 'to get' [GW,

NCV], 'to get under control' [CEV], 'to take away' [NLT]. This verb means to hold onto an object [LN].
c. aorist act. indic. of ἐξίστημι (LN **30.24**) (BAGD 2.a. p. 276): 'to lose one's senses' [NASB], 'to lose one's mind' [BAGD, Lns], 'to be out of one's mind' [AB1, AB2, BECNT, BNTC, LN, NTC, WBC; ESV, GW, NCV, NET, NIV, NLT, REB], 'to be out of one's senses' [BAGD], 'to not be in one's right mind, to be mad' [LN], 'to be besides oneself' [KJV], 'to go out of one's mind' [NRSV], 'to go mad' [TEV], 'to be insane' [**LN**], 'to be crazy' [CEV]. This verb means to think or reason in a completely irrational manner [LN].

QUESTION—Who were οἱ παρ' αὐτοῦ 'the ones beside him' who went to take hold of Jesus?
  1. They were Jesus' own family [AB1, BECNT, BNTC, CBC, CGTC, EBC, Gnd, Hb, ICC, LN, My, NAC, NCBC, NICNT, NIGTC, Sw, Tay, TH, WBC; all versions except KJV]. This is a colloquial expression that could mean family, relatives, or friends. But in view of 3:31–35, this group of people is further defined as the mother and brothers of Jesus [BECNT, BNTC, Gnd, Hb, ICC, NAC, NICNT, NIGTC, Sw, WBC]. Even though this includes his mother, it does not mean that Mary also thought that Jesus was out of his mind. Her presence with his brothers indicates that her faith was not sufficient to resist the determination of her sons to restrain Jesus and bring him home [CGTC, NICNT]. They were the relatives of Jesus [AB2, Lns].
  2. They were people who knew and cared for Jesus [EGT, NTC, Tay; KJV]. Because there is no reason to think that Mary's faith in God's revelation regarding Jesus was ever removed to the extent that she regarded her son as having lost his mind, these people could have been some of his friends he had grown up with in Nazareth. Perhaps some were those in his outer circle of disciples [NTC]. This group consisted of Jesus' friends and family [Tay].

QUESTION—What did they hear?
They heard that Jesus was constantly ministering to the crowds without even taking time off to eat [BECNT, Hb, NIGTC]. What they heard was not confined to the event described in 3:20. They had been hearing reports about Jesus during his whole Galilean ministry as he dealt with the huge crowds and healed great numbers of people [EGT]. They mistook his zeal for God to be madness [NICNT].

QUESTION—What did they go out of?
They left their home in Nazareth to go to where Jesus was ministering in Capernaum [BECNT, BNTC, CGTC, Gnd, Hb, NICNT, NIGTC, Sw, Tay, TRT, WBC]. The incident related in 3:22–30 takes place between the family's departure from Nazareth and their arrival in Capernaum in 3:31 [Sw].

QUESTION—Why did they want to seize Jesus?

They were going to take hold of Jesus in order to control his actions [CGTC, EBC, Tay]. They wanted to take him under control for his own sake and also for their own reputations [NIGTC]. They intended to bind Jesus and take away his freedom [PNTC]. This does not mean that they were angry with Jesus and would handle him roughly. They just wanted to do what was necessary to rescue Jesus from the crowds [TRT]. They wanted to forcefully persuade him to go back home with them [NTC]. Although they did this because they were concerned for Jesus' safety, their interpretation of Jesus' zeal implied their lack of faith in him [Sw].

QUESTION—Who were the people who said that Jesus had lost his senses?

They were the people who went out to take hold of Jesus [CGTC, EBC, EGT, Gnd, Hb, ICC, Lns, My, NCBC, NICNT, NTC, Tay, WBC]. This is an indefinite reference to people in general [TEV].

QUESTION—What is meant by their words 'He has lost his senses'?

They felt that Jesus was not acting rationally when he let himself be constantly imposed upon by the crowds [Hb]. Jesus' urgent drive to minister and his failure to eat and sleep brought them to this conclusion [NICNT]. They feared that overwork had affected Jesus mentally [EBC]. They probably thought that Jesus was insane [AB2].

DISCOURSE UNIT—3:22–30 [EBC, NICNT; ESV, GW]. The topic is the source of Jesus' power [NLT], the charge that Jesus is possessed [NICNT], charged with demon possession [EBC], Jesus is accused of working with Beelzabul [GW], blasphemy against the Holy Spirit [ESV].

DISCOURSE UNIT—3:22–27 [NLT]. The topic is the source of Jesus' power.

3:22 And the scribes, the (ones) having-come-down from Jerusalem, were-saying, "He has^a Beelzebul^b" and "By^c the ruler^d of-the demons^e he casts-out the demons."

LEXICON—a. pres. act. indic. of ἐνέχομαι, ἔχω (LN 90.65) (BAGD 1.2.e.α. p. 332): 'to have' [AB2, BAGD, LN, Lns; KJV, NRSV], 'to be possessed by' [AB1, BAGD, BECNT, BNTC, NTC, WBC; ESV, NASB, NET, NIV, NLT, REB], 'to be under the power of' [CEV]. The phrase 'he has Beelzebul' is translated 'he has Beelzebul in him' [TEV], 'Beelzebul is in him' [GW], 'Beelzebul is living inside him' [NCV]. This verb means to experience a state or condition [LN]. Here it means to be possessed by a demon [BAGD, NIGTC, TH]. This verb is a common expression for being possessed, and is used in similar contexts at 3:30, 5:15, 7:25, and 9:17 [BECNT, EBC, Tay, WBC]. Beelzebul is pictured as being inside the soul of Jesus, not just exerting his influence from the outside [NTC]. The present tense indicates a continuing condition [Hb]. A reference to 'having' a demon occurs at 3:22, 30; 5:15; 7:25; 9:17.

b. Βεελζεβούλ (LN 93.68): 'Beelzebul' [LN; all translations except KJV, NIV, NLT], 'Beelzebub' [KJV, NIV], 'Satan' [NLT]. This noun refers to

MARK 3:22 163

the Devil's name in his role as the prince of the demons [LN]. Because the name Beelzebul occurs in no other Jewish writings, it could just be a passing colloquialism for 'the ruler of the demons' [NICNT]. The variant spelling 'Beelzebub' (KJV, NIV) is found in Syriac manuscripts and in the Latin Vulgate [BNTC, WBC].

c. ἐν (LN 90.6): 'by' [AB1, AB2, BECNT, BNTC, LN, NTC, WBC; ESV, KJV, NASB, NET, NIV, NRSV, REB], 'in connection with' [Lns], 'with the help of' [CEV, GW], 'he uses the power of' [NCV], '(that's where) he gets the power' [NLT], '(it is...) who gives him the power to...' [TEV]. This preposition indicates the agent and often implies that the agent is being used as an instrument [LN].

d. ἄρχων (LN 37.56) (BAGD 3. p. 114): 'ruler' [AB2, BAGD, BECNT, LN, Lns; CEV, GW, NASB, NET, NRSV], 'prince' [AB1, BECNT, NTC, WBC; ESV, KJV, NIV, NLT, REB]. The phrase 'by the ruler' is translated 'he uses power from the ruler' [NCV], 'with the help of the ruler' [GW; similarly CEV], 'it is the chief of the demons who gives him the power' [TEV]. This noun denotes one who rules or governs [LN].

e. δαιμόνιον (LN 12.37): 'demon' [LN; all translations except KJV], 'devil' [KJV], 'evil spirit' [LN]. This noun denotes an evil supernatural being or spirit [LN]. This word occurs at 1:34, 39; 3:15, 22; 6:13; 7:26, 29, 30; 9:38; 16:9, 17.

QUESTION—How is this section related to the preceding one?

This account happened after the people left Nazareth to travel the 20 miles to Capernaum (3:21) but before their arrival at the location where Jesus was teaching the crowd (3:31) [EBC, Hb, Sw].

QUESTION—Who were the scribes that came down from Jerusalem?

This was a delegation of scribes from Jerusalem who had greater authority than the local scribes previously mentioned [AB1, BECNT, BNTC, CGTC, EGT, Gnd, Hb, PNTC]. Perhaps they had been sent by the Sanhedrin to examine Jesus' miracles and determine if he was an apostate preacher [BNTC, ICC, NCBC, NICNT, PNTC]. They were sent to neutralize Jesus' influence [Hb].

QUESTION—Why does it say the scribes came *down* from Jerusalem?

The elevation of Jerusalem is about 2,400 feet above sea level [NTC] and the scribes had to descend to reach the shore of the Lake of Galilee [EBC, Gnd, ICC, NTC, TRT], which is about 600 feet below sea level [NTC]. Since Jerusalem was the capital city, it was customary to say that one went up to the capital city or came down from it [TH].

QUESTION—Who is Beelzebul and how is he connected with 'the ruler of the demons'?

1. Beelzebul is another name for Satan and he is called the ruler of the demons in the next clause [AB2, BECNT, BNTC, CBC, EBC, Gnd, Hb, ICC, Lns, NETfn, NIGTC, NTC, PNTC, Tay, TRT, WBC; CEV, NLT]. Beelzebul, 'the ruler of the demons', and Satan (verses 22 and 26) are the same entity [Gnd].

2. Beelzebul is a name of an evil spirit, but the ruler of the demons is Satan [CGTC, Tay]. There are two charges here. In the first charge, Beelzebul is the name of an evil spirit that is not otherwise known to us, and the second charge refers to acting under the instrumentality of Satan [Tay].

QUESTION—What is meant by the charge that Jesus cast out demons ἐν 'by' the ruler of the demons?

They could not deny the fact that Jesus was casting out demons, but they said that his supernatural power came from Satan [BNTC, CBC, NAC, PNTC]. The preposition 'by' means that they accused Jesus of casting out demons by the help of, in the name of, and under the authority of the ruler of the demons [CGTC]. They said that Jesus cast out demons by the power of Satan, who is the ruler of the demons [NTC, Tay]. The phrase 'by the power of' indicates instrumentality [Hb, NIGTC], so this says that Jesus was in alliance with Satan, subordinate to him, and dependent on Satan's power to cast out demons [Hb].

3:23 And having-called them he-was-speaking in parables^a to-them, "How is-it-possible (for) Satan^b to-cast-out^c Satan?

LEXICON—a. παραβολή (LN 33.15) (BAGD 2. p. 612): 'parable' [BAGD, BECNT, BNTC, LN, Lns, NTC; ESV, KJV, NASB, NET, NIV, NRSV, REB, TEV], 'illustration' [BAGD; GW, NLT], 'story' [NCV], 'figure, allegory' [LN], 'riddle' [CEV]. This noun denotes a relatively short narrative that has symbolic meaning [LN]. The word 'parables' is used in the usual sense of comparisons [NIVfn]. In this context, Jesus is either making a comparison or is speaking proverbially [EBC]. This word occurs at 3:23; 4:2, 10, 11, 13, 30, 33, 34; 7:17; 12:1, 12; 13:28.

b. Σατανᾶς (LN 12.34) (BAGD p. 744): 'Satan' [BAGD, LN; all translations], 'devil' [LN]. 'Satan' is a title for the Devil, and the word literally means 'slanderer' [LN]. This title denotes the 'Adversary' in the special sense of being the enemy of God and of all those who belong to God [BAGD]. Satan is the Hebrew name for the devil, the one who rules over the demons [ICC].

c. pres. act. infin. of ἐκβάλλω (LN 53.102) (BAGD 1. p. 237): 'to cast out' [AB2, BECNT, LN, Lns, NTC, WBC; ESV, KJV, NASB, NET, NLT, NRSV], 'to force out' [GW], 'to drive out' [AB1, BAGD, BNTC; NIV, REB, TEV], 'to expel' [BAGD], 'to make to go out, to exorcise' [LN]. The question, 'How is it possible for Satan to cast out Satan?' is translated 'How can Satan force himself out?' [CEV]. It is also translated as a statement: 'Satan will not force himself out of people' [NCV]. This verb means to cause a demon to cease possessing or controlling a person [LN]. In reference to 'casting' out demons, this verb occurs at 1:34, 39; 3:15, 22, 23; 6:13; 7:26; 9:18, 28, 38; 16:9, 17.

QUESTION—What kind of question is this?

It is a rhetorical question that assumes the answer would be negative: it is not possible that Satan would do that [AB2, WBC]. Jesus had just cast out demons. If he had done this by Satan's power, then Satan was actually working against himself, but that would be absurd [EBC, EGT, Gnd, Hb, NAC]. The question destroys the scribes' case against Jesus by showing that an attack on Satan's domain is a threat to Satan's power, not a sign of collusion with him [NIGTC].

QUESTION—What is meant by Satan casting out Satan?

1. This doesn't mean that one Satan is casting out another Satan, but that Satan is casting out himself [EBC, EGT, NCBC, TH; CEV]: *how can Satan cast himself out?* There are not two Satans, it is about Satan driving out himself and he would be doing this if he were to drive out the demons who comprise his empire [TH]. Satan would be undoing his own work [NTC].
2. The name Satan is used in two senses, the second occurrence of 'Satan' standing for the demons who represented Satan [BECNT, CGTC, Gnd, ICC, Lns, Sw, WBC]: *How can Satan cast out his own demons?* The demons are referred to as 'Satan' since they are regarded as Satan's representatives and his instruments [Sw]. Since the demons are Satan's servants, it is illogical to say that he is casting out his own servants [WBC].

3:24 And if a-kingdom is-divided[a] against itself, it-is- not -possible (for) that kingdom to-stand.[b]

LEXICON—a. aorist act. subj. of μερίζω (LN 63.23) (BAGD 1.a. p. 504): 'to be divided' [AB1, AB2, BAGD, BECNT, BNTC, LN, Lns, NTC, WBC; ESV, GW, KJV, NASB, NET, NIV, NRSV, REB], 'to be disunited' [LN]. The phrase 'a kingdom is divided against itself' is translated 'a kingdom that is divided' [NCV], 'a nation whose people fight each other' [CEV], 'a kingdom divided by civil war' [NLT], 'a country divides itself into groups which fight each other' [TEV]. This verb means to divide into separate parts [LN].

b. aorist pass. infin. of ἵσταμαι, ἵστημι (LN 13.90) (BAGD II.1.d. p. 382): 'to stand' [AB1, AB2, BAGD, BECNT, BNTC, Lns, NTC, WBC; ESV, KJV, NASB, NET, NIV, NRSV, REB], 'to continue' [LN; NCV], 'to continue to be, to keep on existing' [LN], 'to last' [GW], 'to last long' [CEV]. The phrase 'it is not possible for that kingdom to stand' is translated 'will collapse' [NLT], 'that country will fall apart' [TEV]. This verb means to continue to exist [LN].

QUESTION—How are the three 'if' examples in 3:24, 25, and 26 connected with verse 3:23?

The three conditional statements express the logical result of assuming that the scribes are correct in saying that Jesus heals people by Satan's power. If the scribes were correct, then Satan's kingdom will not stand. Therefore their accusation makes no sense since Satan would not seek to cast out the very demons he ruled [NETfn]. Just as a kingdom (3:24) or a house (3:25) cannot

stand if it is divided against itself or opposes itself, so Satan would be
bringing about his own destruction by working against himself (3:26) [EBC].
QUESTION—What is the point of bringing up the example of a kingdom being
divided against itself?
This hypothetical example points out the unreality of the principle stated in
the preceding verse [Hb]. This first example uses the illustration of a
kingdom because the scribes had referred to the ruler of the demons [Gnd,
Lns]. This verse is a generic statement of the preceding principle since Satan
and his subjects constitute a kingdom [ICC], and what is true of any
kingdom can be applied to them [ICC, Lns]. When there is a civil war in a
kingdom, it will not stand because it is an easy prey for invaders [CBC,
Gnd].

3:25 And if a-house[a] is-divided against itself, that house will- not -be-able to-stand.

LEXICON—a. οἰκία (LN 10.8) (BAGD 2. p. 557): 'house' [AB1, BECNT, Lns, NTC; ESV, KJV, NASB, NET, NIV, NRSV], 'household' [AB2, BAGD, BNTC, LN; GW, REB], 'family' [BAGD, LN; CEV, NCV]. The whole sentence is translated 'And a family that fights won't last long either.' [CEV], 'If a family divides itself into groups which fight each other, that family will fall apart.' [TEV], 'Similarly, a family splintered by feuding will fall apart.' [NLT]. This noun denotes a family consisting of those related by blood and marriage, as well as slaves and servants, living in the same house or homestead [LN].

QUESTION—How is 'house' used here?
The word 'house' is used by metonymy for the family members living in it [ICC, TH]. This is made clear in some of the above translations [CEV, NLT, TEV]. In the context of a kingdom, this could refer to strife within a royal family that enables a usurper to get control of the kingdom [Gnd].

3:26 And if Satan rose-up[a] against himself and was-divided, he is- not able to-stand, but he-has an-end.[b]

LEXICON—a. aorist act. indic. of ἀνίσταμαι, ἀνίστημι (LN 39.34) (BAGD 2.c. p. 70): 'to rise up' [BAGD, BECNT, Lns, NTC, WBC; ESV, KJV, NASB, NET, NRSV], 'to rise' [AB2], 'to revolt, to engage in insurrection' [LN], 'to fight' [NLT], 'to rebel' [BNTC, LN; GW, REB], 'to be in rebellion' [AB1], 'to oppose (himself)' [NIV]. The clause 'if Satan rose up against himself and was divided' is translated 'if Satan fights against himself' [CEV], 'if Satan's kingdom divides into groups' [TEV], 'if Satan is against himself and fights against his own people' [NCV]. This verb means to rise up in open defiance of authority, and the implied intention is to overthrow it or to act in complete opposition to its demands [LN]. The tenses are aorist because, according to the scribes, this must have already occurred [Lns].

b. τέλος (LN 67.66) (BAGD 1.a. p. 811): 'end' [BAGD, LN; KJV], 'termination, cessation' [BAGD]. The clause 'but he has an end' [Lns; KJV] is also translated 'but is coming to an end' [ESV; similarly TEV], 'that will be the end of him' [CEV, GW; similarly NCV, REB], 'his end has come' [NET, NIV, NRSV], 'but has met his end' [BECNT], 'but would have met his end' [WBC], 'he would never survive' [NLT], 'he is finished' [NTC; NASB], 'that is the end of him' [BNTC], 'that is the end of his power' [AB1]. This noun denotes a point of time that marks the end of some duration [LN].

QUESTION—How is this verse related to the preceding verses?

Following the two preceding illustrations, the argument now reaches its climax [AB1, BECNT, Hb, Lns, Tay]. It shows the actual implication of the charge made by the scribes in 3:22 [EBC, Gnd, Tay]. The scribes' charge was that Satan has actually risen up against himself, and if that had happened, he and his kingdom would be a divided force [Hb]. Since Satan remains strong, their charge must be false [NICNT]. Instead of being in collusion with Satan, Jesus was actually destroying Satan's work [EBC].

QUESTION—What is meant by Satan coming to an end?

It does not refer to the end of Satan's personal existence but to Satan's position as ruler of the demonic world [CBC, Hb, TH]. He would no longer be ruling over them [TRT]. Satan would be coming to the end of his career [Gnd].

3:27 But no-one having-entered into the house of-the strong[a] (man) is-able to-plunder[b] his possessions,[c] unless first he-ties-up[d] the strong (man), and then he-will-plunder his house.

LEXICON—a. ἰσχυρός (LN 79.63) (BAGD 1.a. p. 383): 'strong' [all translations], 'mighty, powerful' [BAGD]. This adjective refers to being physically strong and vigorous [LN].
  b. aorist act. infin. of διαρπάζω (LN **57.238**) (BAGD p. 188): 'to plunder' [AB2, BECNT, BNTC, **LN**, Lns, WBC; ESV, NASB, NLT, NRSV], 'to plunder thoroughly' [BAGD], 'to rob' [LN], 'to steal' [CEV, GW, NCV, NET], 'to carry off' [NIV], 'to make off with' [REB], 'to take away' [AB1; TEV], 'to spoil' [KJV]. This verb means to plunder something thoroughly and completely [LN].
  c. σκεῦος (LN **57.20**) (BAGD 1.a. p 754): 'possessions' [BECNT, WBC; NIV], 'belongings' [AB1, **LN**, TH; TEV], 'property' [GW, NASB, NET, NRSV], 'goods' [BNTC, LN, Lns; ESV, KJV, NLT, REB], 'things' [AB2, BAGD; CEV, NCV], 'household furnishings' [**LN**]. This noun denotes objects that are possessed [LN]. Here it denotes all that one has [BAGD].
  d. aorist act. subj. of δέω (LN 18.13) (BAGD 1.b. p. 177): 'to tie up' [AB1, AB2, BAGD, LN; all versions except ESV, KJV, NASB], 'to bind' [BAGD, BECNT, BNTC, Lns, WBC; ESV, KJV, NASB]. This verb means to tie objects together [LN].

QUESTION—What relationship is indicated by the conjunction ἀλλά 'but'?
This offers a contrary explanation of why demons are being cast out in Jesus' ministry [BECNT, NIGTC, NLTfn]. It contradicts the charge made by the scribes that Jesus was acting in the name of the ruler of the demons [EGT, Hb, TH].

QUESTION—Who is represented by the strong man who owns the house?
The strong man represents Satan [AB1, AB2, BECNT, BNTC, CBC, CGTC, EBC, Gnd, Hb, ICC, Lns, NAC, NETfn, NICNT, NIGTC, Sw, Tay, TRT, WBC].

QUESTION—What is represented by the possessions of the strong man that Jesus plunders?
There is no need to allegorize either the possessions or the house in this illustration since they merely complete the picture in which someone (Jesus) overpowers the strong man (Satan) [Gnd, Tay]. We shouldn't try to press the details of the parable by identifying the possessions or the time of the binding since the parable is given as a challenge to faith to recognize the hidden power of God at work in the ministry of Christ, the 'stronger one' [NCBC]. If this refers to Jesus coming into the world to tie up Satan and deliver those who are under Satan's control, then Satan is now on a long chain and will not be finally defeated until the End Time [EBC]. However, some do try to identify the possessions.

1. The strong man's possessions represent the victims of Satan's rule, the people who were possessed by demons [AB2, BECNT, BNTC, CGTC, Gnd, Hb, Lns, NAC, NICNT, NIGTC, NTC, WBC]. Jesus plundered the possessions of the strong man by taking away demon-possessed people from out of Satan's power [Lns]. Jesus, the stronger one, has come to restrain Satan's activity and release those who have been enslaved by Satan [NICNT]. Luke tells how the strong man is armed and guarding his possessions [Lns]. Satan is pictured as a strong bandit who stores his plunder in his house. His possessions are the demon-possessed people he has in his power, but Jesus is taking those demoniacs away from Satan [Hb, Lns].

2 The strong man's possessions represent the utensils in his house, and they represent the demons as being Satan's instruments that are cast out by Jesus [Gnd, ICC, PNTC].

QUESTION—What is the point of verse 27?
The correct conclusion to be drawn from the fact that Jesus has cast out demons is that a stronger one than Satan has come and bound him [CGTC; ESV]. The binding of the strong man does not refer to any particular event such as what happened at the time of the temptation. The binding simply pictures Jesus as being the one who is stronger than Satan and able to plunder Satan's possessions at will [BECNT]. Nothing can be seized from the strong man until he is bound, so each individual confrontation with Satan in which Jesus casts out demons involves a power encounter in which Jesus demonstrates his superior authority by plundering Satan's possessions

[NIGTC]. Jesus' acts of healing indicate that the war is being won and the kingdom of God is coming [NETfn].

3:28 Truly[a] I-say to-you that all (things) will-be-forgiven[b] the sons[c] of-men, the sins and the blasphemies what ever they-may-blaspheme.[d]

LEXICON—a. ἀμήν (LN 72.6) (BAGD 2. p. 45): 'truly' [AB1, BAGD, BECNT, BNTC, LN; ESV, NASB, NRSV, REB], 'indeed, it is true that' [LN], 'verily' [KJV], 'amen' [AB2, Lns]. The phrase 'truly I say to you' is translated 'I tell you the truth' [NCV, NET, NIV, NLT], 'I assure you' [WBC; TEV], 'I can guarantee this truth' [GW], 'I solemnly declare to you' [NTC], 'I promise you' [CEV]. This particle makes a strong affirmation of what is declared [LN]. It is an assertive particle that begins a solemn declaration [BAGD]. The phrase 'truly I say to you' also occurs at 8:12; 9:1, 41; 10:15, 29; 11:23; 12:43; 13:30; 14:9, 18, 25, 30.

b. fut. pass. indic. of ἀφίημι (LN 40.8) (BAGD 2. p. 126): 'to be forgiven, to be pardoned' [BAGD, LN], 'to be cancelled, to be remitted' [BAGD]. The phrase 'will/shall be forgiven' [AB2, BECNT, BNTC, Lns, NTC, WBC; ESV, GW, KJV, NASB, NET, NIV, NRSV] is also translated 'can be forgiven' [AB1; CEV, NCV, NLT, REB, TEV]. This verb means to remove the guilt resulting from wrongdoing [LN].

c. υἱός (LN **9.2**) (BAGD 1.e.β. p. 833): 'son' [BAGD, LN]. The phrase τοῖς υἱοὶ τῶν ἀνθρώπων 'the sons of men' [BAGD, BNTC, Lns, NTC; KJV, NASB] is also translated 'the children of men' [ESV], 'men' [AB1; NIV], 'people' [AB2, **LN**; GW, NCV, NET, NRSV, TEV], 'human beings' [BECNT], 'every human being' [WBC], 'you' [CEV], not explicit [NLT, REB]. The phrase 'sons of men' is a Semitic idiom for 'human beings' [Hb, LN, NIGTC].

d. aorist act. subj. of βλασφημέω (LN 33.400) (BAGD 2.b.α. p. 142): 'to blaspheme' [BAGD, LN], 'to revile, to defame' [LN]. The phrase αἱ βλασφημίαι ὅσα ἐὰν βλασφημήσωσιν 'the blasphemies what ever they may blaspheme' is translated 'the blasphemies that they blaspheme' [AB2, BECNT], 'blasphemies wherewith soever they shall blaspheme' [KJV], 'the blasphemies, as many as they may blaspheme' [Lns], 'whatever/all blasphemies that they utter' [NTC, WBC; ESV, NASB, NRSV], 'even all the blasphemies they utter' [NET], 'the blasphemies they use' [AB1], 'blasphemies of every kind' [BNTC], 'all (the sins and) blasphemies' [NIV], 'all (sin and) blasphemy' [NLT], 'every (sin and) slander' [REB], 'all the evil things they may say' [TEV], '(the sinful things) you say...no matter how terrible those things are' [CEV], 'for (any sin or) curse' [GW], 'all the things people say against God' [NCV]. This verb means to speak against someone in such a way as to harm or injure his or her reputation, and this can be directed against people as well as against God [LN].

QUESTION—What is being confirmed by the declaration, 'truly I say to you'?
1. The word ἀμήν 'amen' refers to the statement that follows [CGTC, EBC, Gnd, Hb, ICC, Tay, TH; all translations]: *Truly I say to you that....* The word ἀμήν 'truly' is a Hebrew word meaning 'truth', and here it means 'surely' or 'truly'. The word 'amen' is always followed by the words 'I say to you' to indicate that Jesus is speaking from his own authority [Hb]. He solemnly guarantees the truth of what he is about to say [CGTC]. It adds emphasis and solemnity to what follows [ICC, Tay, TH]. Jesus has shown the scribes the absurdity of their second charge that he casts out demons by the ruler of the demons, and now he will show them the seriousness of their charge that he has Beelzebul [Gnd].
2. The word ἀμήν 'amen' refers to what Jesus had said in the preceding verse [TRT]: *Yes, what I said is true. And now I say to you that....* Everywhere in the OT and everywhere in the NT except the Gospels the word 'Amen' is clearly used in the Hebrew way of emphasizing the importance of something that has just been said or done, and it often shows that the speaker agrees with it. In the Gospels, Jesus used 'amen' in the same Hebrew way to refer back to what he wants to teach or say more about and then he adds the words 'I say to you' to point forward to what he wants to say about whatever 'Amen' refers back to. This could be translated, 'Amen/Yes, that is why I'm able to throw his evil spirits out of people, and I tell you all sins will/can be forgiven...' [TRT].

QUESTION—What is meant by the statement 'all things will be forgiven'?
The divine passive 'will be forgiven' expresses God's role as the forgiver [BECNT, WBC], and the future tense points to the final judgment [WBC].
1. There is a *potential* forgiveness for all sins [BECNT, Hb, NICNT, NTC, TH; CEV, NCV, NLT, REB, TEV]. Of course it doesn't mean that all sins will be forgiven by God regardless of whether or not people change or repent. The context makes clear that all sins and blasphemies except the blasphemy against the Holy Spirit are *capable* of being forgiven [BECNT, Hb, TH]. Repentance is an implied condition for forgiveness [NTC, TH].
2. There is a *potential* forgiveness for the sin of slandering. Instead of referring to all kinds of sins and all kinds of blasphemies, the phrase '*the sins* and *the blasphemies* whatever they may blaspheme' is a figure of speech called a hendiadys in which one of the two nouns connected by 'and' is subordinate to the other, so that the phrase means 'however many sins they commit *by slandering*' [Gnd].

QUESTION—Why are βλασφημίαι 'blasphemies' singled out and what does blasphemy involve?
Blasphemies are the specific class of sins that the context has brought into focus [NIGTC, NTC], and in the next verse the one exception to forgiveness of all blasphemies will be made, the blasphemy against the Holy Spirit [ICC]. In a general sense, blasphemy refers to insolent language directed against either God or people, and it includes defamation, railing, and reviling [NTC]. The word means 'injurious speech', and when directed towards God

it is speech that is derogatory to his divine majesty [ICC]. In this context, blasphemy refers to words that are spoken directly or indirectly against God [WBC]. Here it is the denial of the power and greatness of God [BNTC].

3:29 **But whoever blasphemes against[a] the Holy Spirit does- not -have forgiveness into[b] the age, but is guilty[c] of-an-eternal[d] sin."**

TEXT—Manuscripts reading ἁμαρτήματος 'sin' are given a B rating by GNT to indicate it was regarded to be almost certain. A variant reading is κρίσεως 'judgment' and it is followed by KJV. Another variant reading is κρίσεως καὶ ἁμαρτίας 'judgment and sin' and one manuscript reads κολάσεως 'punishment'.

LEXICON—a. εἰς (LN 90.59) (BAGD 4.c.α. p. 229): 'against' [BAGD], 'toward' [LN]. The phrase 'whoever blasphemes against' [AB1, AB2, BECNT, BNTC, Lns, WBC; ESV, NASB, NET, NIV, NRSV] is also translated 'whoever utters blasphemies against' [NTC], 'he that shall blaspheme against' [KJV], 'anyone who blasphemes' [NLT], 'whoever curses' [GW], 'whoever slanders' [REB], 'whoever says evil things against' [TEV], 'anyone who speaks against' [NCV], 'if you speak against' [CEV]. This preposition indicates the object of the verb [LN]. It indicates the goal, in a hostile sense [BAGD].

b. εἰς (LN 67.95) (BAGD 2.b. p. 229): 'into' [LN], 'throughout' [BAGD]. The phrase εἰς τὸν αἰῶνα 'into the age' is translated 'forever' [BAGD, LN], 'always, forever and ever, eternally' [LN]. The clause 'does not have forgiveness into the age' is translated 'has no remission for the eon' [NTC], 'never has forgiveness' [ESV, KJV, NASB; similarly WBC; NRSV], 'never gains forgiveness' [AB2], 'will never be forgiven' [BECNT, BNTC; GW, NCV, NET, NIV, NLT, TEV], 'will never receive forgiveness' [NTC], 'can never be forgiven' [AB1; REB; similarly CEV]. The idiom 'into the age' refers to an unlimited future duration of time [LN].

c. ἔνοχος (LN 88.313) (BAGD 2.b.β. p. 268): 'guilty' [BAGD, LN; all translations except CEV, KJV, NLT, TEV], 'answerable, liable' [BAGD]. See the following lexical item for translations by CEV, KJV, NLT, TEV. This adjective describes someone as being guilty and therefore deserving of some particular penalty [LN].

d. αἰώνιος (LN 67.96) (BAGD 3. p. 28): 'eternal' [AB1, AB2, BAGD, BECNT, BNTC, LN, WBC; ESV, NASB, NET, NIV, NRSV, REB], 'everlasting' [NTC; GW]. The clause 'but is guilty of an eternal sin' is translated 'but is guilty of an eternal sinful act' [Lns], 'he is guilty of a sin that continues forever' [NCV], 'this is a sin with eternal consequences' [NLT], 'that sin will be held against you forever' [CEV], 'but is in danger of eternal damnation' [KJV], 'because he has committed an eternal sin' [TEV]. This adjective pertains to an unlimited duration of time [LN]. It is eternal in the sense that it has no end [BAGD].

QUESTION—What is meant by blasphemy against the Holy Spirit?

As explained by the following verse, this blasphemy is the act of attributing acts of healing wrought by the power of the Holy Spirit to be wrought instead by the power of Beelzebul (3:22), and thus deliberately denying the power and greatness of the Holy Spirit [Tay]. It is the sin of attributing the work of the Holy Spirit through Jesus to demonic forces [CGTC, EBC, NLTfn, WBC]. This sin is a conscious and deliberate rejection of God's saving power and grace released through Jesus' word and act [NICNT].

QUESTION—Why can't this sin of blasphemy be forgiven?

There can be no forgiveness because a person with such an attitude is incapable of seeking it [Hb]. Such a man has made up his mind not to pay attention to the promptings of the Spirit [NTC]. Resisting and denouncing the work of God in this way prevents the convicting work of the Spirit that leads to repentance and saving faith in God [Hb, NLTfn]. The person who persists in hardening his heart against the work of the Holy Spirit and against the provision of Christ as Savior is outside the reach of God's provision for forgiveness and salvation [ESVfn].

QUESTION—What is meant by an eternal sin?

It is a sinful act that has eternal consequences [BECNT, CBC, CGTC, NAC, WBC]. It is a sin that remains unforgiven forever, and its guilt has unending consequences [Hb, NIGTC]. This speaks of the ultimate fate of such a person [NIGTC]. Probably the sin is eternal in that it affects the person's very nature, and such a sinful state is fixed beyond recovery [ICC]. His attitude is so fixed and obstinate that a permanent obstacle has been formed between him and God [BNTC]. To blaspheme the work of the Holy Spirit, who seeks to lead a person to faith, is unforgivable because it makes faith impossible [BECNT]. It is not that the sin is eternally repeating itself, but that the sin is unpardonable, perhaps because the sinner will never repent [EGT].

3:30 Because[a] they-were-saying, "He-has[b] an-unclean spirit."

LEXICON—a. ὅτι (LN 89.33): 'because' [AB2, BAGD, Lns; KJV, NASB, NET], 'for' [BECNT, WBC; ESV, NRSV]. This conjunction is translated as a phrase: 'Jesus/he said this because' [AB1, BNTC, NTC; CEV, GW, NCV, NIV, REB, TEV]. 'he told them this because' [NLT].

b. pres. act. indic. of ἔχω (BAGD 1.2.e.α. p. 332): 'to have' [BAGD; ESV, GW, KJV, NASB, NET, NIV, NRSV], 'to be possessed by' [NLT, REB]. The clause 'he has an unclean spirit' is translated 'he has an evil spirit in him' [CEV, TEV], 'he had an evil spirit inside him' [NCV]. This verb means to have as one's own. It can refer to having an illness, and also being demon possessed [BAGD]. This verb means the same as 'he has Beelzebul' in 3:22 and 'he has a demon' in 1:34 [TH].

QUESTION—What relationship is indicated by the conjunction 'because'?

Mark is explaining the reason for the solemn assertion made by Jesus in 3:28–29 [EBC, Gnd, Hb, NTC, WBC]. Mark explains that Jesus had spoken about the sin of blasphemy against the Holy Spirit because the scribes were saying that Jesus had an unclean spirit [EGT]. The reason given in this verse virtually repeats the substance of the scribes' accusation in 3:22 [NICNT]. This indicates that the blasphemy Jesus referred in 3:29 was the scribes' accusation in 3:22 where they said he was possessed by Beelzebul [CGTC, Gnd, Lns, NIGTC, WBC]. Beelezebul is called an 'unclean spirit' here in order to contrast him with the holiness of the Holy Spirit [Gnd].

QUESTION—What is the significance of the use of the imperfect tense of the verb ἔλεγον 'they were saying'?

The imperfect tense implies that the scribes were repeatedly making this accusation [CBC, Hb, NICNT], and this fixed attitude of mind had brought them to the brink of unforgivable blasphemy [NICNT]. It is the Holy Spirit who works repentance, and his work ceases when he is made out to be a demon [Lns].

QUESTION—Are the words 'He has an unclean spirit' a direct quotation or an indirect quote?

These words are translated as a direct quotation [AB1, AB2, BECNT, BNTC, Lns, NTC, WBC; ESV, KJV, NASB, NET, NIV, NLT, NRSV, TEV] and as an indirect quote [CEV, GW, NCV, REB].

DISCOURSE UNIT—3:31-35 [CBC, Hb, NICNT, NIGTC; CEV, ESV, GW, NASB, NCV, NET, NIV, NLT, TEV]. The topic is Jesus' mother and brothers [CEV, ESV, NIV, TEV], Jesus' true family [EBC, NICNT], the true family of Jesus [GW, NCV, NET, NLT], the true kindred of Jesus [NASB], the identity of his true kindred [Hb], Jesus' true family is those who do God's will [CBC], 'insiders and outsiders' [NIGTC].

3:31 **And his mother comes and his brothers, and standing outside they-sent[a] to him, summoning[b] him.**

LEXICON—a. aorist act. indic. of ἀποστέλλω (LN 15.67) (BAGD 1.b.α. p. 98): 'to send word, to send a message' [LN], 'to send out someone' [BAGD]. The phrase 'they sent to him' [BECNT; ESV, KJV, NRSV; similarly Lns], is also translated 'they sent word to him' [NASB, NET; similarly NLT], 'they sent a message to him' [AB2, BECNT, WBC], 'and sent in a message' [AB1; REB, TEV], 'they sent someone' [CEV, GW], 'they sent someone in' [NCV, NIV], 'they sent someone to him' [NTC]. This verb means to send a message, presumably by some person [LN].

b. pres. act. participle of καλέω (LN 33.307) (BAGD 1.d. p. 399): 'to summon' [BAGD, LN], 'to call' [LN]. The phrase 'summoning him' is translated 'to summon him' [WBC; NET], 'to call him' [NTC; NIV; similarly AB2, Lns; ESV, KJV, NASB], 'and called him' [BECNT; NRSV], 'asking for him' [AB1; TEV], 'to ask him to come out' [GW], 'asking him to come out to them' [REB], 'with a message for him to come out to them' [CEV], 'to tell him to come out' [NCV; similarly BNTC], 'for him to come out and talk with them' [NLT]. This verb means to communicate directly or indirectly with someone who is at a distance in order to tell that person to come [LN].

QUESTION—What relationship is indicated by the conjunction καί 'and' at the beginning of this verse?

Mark now turns back to the family of Jesus after having allowed time for them to travel from Nazareth to Capernaum [EBC]. They began their journey in 3:21 and now they have arrived [BECNT, BNTC, EGT, Hb, ICC, NICNT, NIGTC, NLTfn, Sw, WBC]. Matthew 12:46 explicitly joins this narrative to a different narrative by beginning 'While he was still speaking to the crowds, behold his mother and brothers stood outside' [Hb].

QUESTION—Who were the ἀδελφοί 'brothers' of Jesus?

There are three main explanations: (1) they were the sons of Mary and Joseph, (2) they were sons of Joseph by a former wife, or (3) they were cousins of Jesus, sons of Mary's sister [AB1, BECNT, CGTC, Hb]. The first is the most simple and probable explanation [BECNT, CBC, CGTC, Hb, ICC, Lns, NIGTC, NTC, WBC], and it is consistent with the fact of the virgin birth of Jesus [CGTC]. The other two explanations are due to the belief that Mary remained a perpetual virgin [CGTC, Lns, WBC]. The plural form, 'brothers' could also include his sisters in light of the following verse in which some manuscripts include the words 'and sisters' [BAGD (p. 15)].

QUESTION—What were they standing outside of?

1. They were standing outside of the house where Jesus was teaching and they were not able to enter because it was so filled with listeners [AB2, BECNT, CGTC, EBC, Gnd, Hb, ICC, NICNT, NIGTC, NTC, PNTC, WBC]. This is probably the house mentioned in 3:20 [AB2, Gnd, PNTC].
2. Since no house is mentioned, probably they were standing on the outskirts of the crowd that surrounded Jesus [Lns].

3:32 And a-crowd was-sitting around him, and they-are-saying to-him, "Behold,[a] your mother and your brothers and your sisters (are) outside asking-for[b] you."

TEXT—Manuscripts reading καὶ αἱ ἀδελφαί σου 'and your sisters' are followed by AB2; CEV, NRSV, TEV and by GNT, which gives it a C rating to indicate that choosing it over a variant text was difficult. The phrase is omitted by AB1, BECNT, BNTC, CGTC, EBC, Gnd, Lns, NTC, PNTC, Tay, WBC; ESV, GW, KJV, NASB, NCV, NET, NIV, NLT, REB.

LEXICON—a. ἰδού (LN 91.13): 'behold' [NTC; KJV, NASB], 'look' [AB2, BECNT, LN; NET, TEV], 'listen, pay attention' [LN], 'lo' [Lns], not explicit [AB1, BNTC, WBC; CEV, ESV, GW, NCV, NIV, NLT, NRSV, REB]. This particle is a prompter for attention [LN]. It emphasizes the words that follow [BECNT].

b. pres. act. indic. of ζητέω (LN 33.167) (BAGD 1.b. p. 338): 'to ask for' [AB1, BNTC; NRSV, REB], 'to ask earnestly for, to demand' [LN], 'to look for' [BAGD, NTC; GW, NASB, NET, NIV, NLT], 'to seek' [BAGD, BECNT, Lns, WBC; ESV, KJV]. The phrase 'asking for you' is translated 'want to see you' [CEV], 'want you' [TEV], 'are waiting for you' [NCV]. This verb means to ask for something that is being especially sought [LN]. They were not 'looking' for Jesus since they already knew that he was there [TH].

QUESTION—Who told Jesus about his mother and siblings being outside looking for him?

The pronoun 'they' refers to the crowd, since the singular noun 'crowd' can be used as the plural subject of the verb λέγουσιν 'they are saying' [WBC]. Jesus' relatives had given their message for Jesus to someone at the outside of the crowd and then the message was passed along from person to person until it reached someone near to Jesus who could speak to him [Hb, Lns, NICNT, NTC, Sw, Tay]. Perhaps when the message reached a person near Jesus, that person waited until there was a pause and then informed him [Hb].

3:33 And answering^a them he-says, "Who is my mother and my brothers?"
3:34 And having-looked-around at-the (ones) sitting in-a-circle^b around him he says, "Behold^c my mother and my brothers.

TEXT—In 3:33, manuscripts reading καὶ οἱ ἀδελφοί μου 'and my brothers' are followed by GNT, which does not mention any variant reading. A variant reading is ἢ οἱ ἀδελφοί μου 'or my brothers' and it is followed by KJV.

TEXT—In 3:34, manuscripts reading περιβλεψάμενος τοὺς περὶ αὐτὸν κύκλῳ καθημένους 'having looked around at the (ones) *sitting in a circle around him*' are followed by GNT, which does not mention any variant reading. A variant reading is περιβλεψάμενος κύκλῳ τοὺς περὶ αὐτὸν καθημένους '*having looked around in-a-circle* at the (ones) sitting around him' and it is followed by KJV.

LEXICON—a. aorist pass. (deponent = act.) participle of ἀποστοματίζω (LN 33.28, 33.184): 'to speak, to declare, to say' [LN (33.28)], 'to answer, to reply' [LN (33.184)]. The phrase 'answering them he says' is translated 'answering them he said' [NASB], 'answering he says to them' [Lns; similarly NTC], 'he answered them and said' [NET; similarly AB2]. 'he answered them' [WBC; ESV, KJV], 'he replied to them' [GW], 'Jesus/he replied' [NLT, NRSV, REB], 'Jesus/he answered' [AB1, BNTC; TEV], 'Jesus/he asked' [CEV, NIV], 'he says to them' [BECNT]. This verb occurs regularly with λέγω 'to say' to introduce or continue a somewhat formal discourse [LN (33.28)], or it means to respond to a question asking for information [LN (33.184)]. There are 15 instances of the phrase 'answering...he says' in Mark and an English translation needs only to communicate the sense 'he answered' [TH].

b. κύκλῳ (LN **83.19**) (BAGD 1.a. p. 457): 'in a circle' [**LN**], 'around' [BAGD, LN], 'all around' [BAGD]. The phrase 'sitting in a circle around him' [BECNT; similarly AB2; GW, NIV, REB] is also translated 'sitting around/about him in a circle' [BNTC, Lns; NET; similarly WBC], 'sitting in a circle about him' [NTC], 'sitting around him' [CEV, NASB, NCV,

TEV; similarly ESV, NRSV], 'those around him' [NLT], 'sitting with him' [AB1]. This adverb indicates a position completely encircling an area or object [LN].

c. ἴδε (LN 91.13) (BAGD 3. p. 369): 'behold' [KJV, NASB], 'look' [AB2, LN; TEV], 'see' [AB1, BECNT, Lns], 'look, (these are)' [NLT]. Some replace the interjection Ἰδού 'behold' with a verb phrase: 'here are/is' [BAGD, BNTC, NTC; CEV, ESV, NCV, NET, NIV, NRSV, REB], 'these are' [WBC]. This verb functions as a prompter for attention [LN].

QUESTION—Who were the people referred to by 'them' in the phrase 'and answering them'?

Jesus was answering the ones who had informed him, not his family standing outside the crowd [Hb, Sw]. Jesus directed his answer to the man who told him that his relatives were seeking him, and then looking around at all those seated about him, he told them who his relatives really are [Lns].

QUESTION—Why did Jesus ask this question?

Jesus asked this rhetorical question in order to set up the answer he was about to give [CGTC, Gnd, NICNT, WBC]. Of course it does not mean that Jesus didn't know who his mother and brothers were [TRT].

QUESTION—Who were the people that were his mother and brothers?

Jesus referred to the twelve apostles who were seated nearest to him [EBC, NICNT]. The Twelve had responded to his call to accompany him and now there were spiritual ties between Jesus and the Twelve that were closer than blood ties [EBC]. Probably Jesus was referring to all of his disciples among the group around him [Hb, Lns, Sw, Tay]. The description 'the ones sitting in a circle around him' refers to his disciples and probably distinguishes them from the rest of the people standing on the fringes who might not have been disciples [AB1, Tay]. Since those sitting around him were mostly men, calling them his mother and brothers indicates that he was speaking of something higher than ties of blood [Lns]. This doesn't mean that Jesus only included males as members of his spiritual family since the next verse includes women [NTC].

QUESTION—Why is the verb ἐστιν 'is' singular in the question 'Who is my mother and my brothers?'

The use of the singular form gives special prominence to Mary by singling her out above his brothers. This is slightly unnatural in English since the predicate nominative is plural, so a plural verb can be used in the translation: 'Who are my mother and my brothers?' [NETfn]. Some follow the Greek and translate with the singular verb: 'who *is* my mother and my brothers' [BECNT, Lns, WBC; KJV]. Some change the singular verb 'is' to 'are': 'who *are* my mother and my brothers?' [AB2, BNTC, Gnd; ESV, NASB, NCV, NET, NIV, NRSV, REB, TEV]. Some use separate forms of the verb: 'who *is* my mother and who *are* my brothers' [AB1, NTC; CEV, GW, NLT, TEV].

3:35 Because whoever does the will[a] of-God, this (one) is my brother and sister and mother."

TEXT—Manuscripts reading ὃς γὰρ ἄν 'because whoever' are given an equivalent of a C rating by GNT, which encloses γάρ 'because' in brackets to indicate that it was difficult to decide whether or not to keep γάρ 'because' in the text. The conjunction is not translated by some translations either for stylistic reasons or because they are following the variant reading [BNTC; CEV, GW, NCV, NIV, NLT, NRSV, REB, TEV].

LEXICON—a. θέλημα (LN 30.59) (BAGD 1.c.γ. p. 354): 'will' [AB1, AB2, BAGD, BECNT, BNTC, LN, Lns, NTC, WBC; ESV, KJV, NASB, NET, NIV, NLT, NRSV, REB], 'intent, purpose, plan' [LN]. The phrase 'does the will of God' is translated 'does what God wants' [GW, NCV, TEV], 'obeys God' [CEV]. This noun denotes that which is purposed, intended, or willed [LN]. It denotes what one wishes to bring about by the actions of others [BAGD].

QUESTION—What relationship is indicated by γάρ 'because'

Jesus explains the meaning of his answer in verse 34 [BECNT, Lns, WBC].

QUESTION—What is the will of God?

In this book, the will of God has been described by the command 'to repent and believe the gospel' (1:15), and to follow Jesus (1:18, 20) [BECNT, NLTfn].

QUESTION—What did Jesus mean when he said 'this one is my brother and sister and mother'?

The singular verb ἐστίν 'is' combines all three comparisons into one concept so as to indicate an intimate spiritual connection closer than blood ties. It does not mean that male disciples were his brothers, and female disciples of various ages were his sisters or mothers [Lns]. Even though 'sister' does not appear in 3:32, it is added here because women were present in the crowd. It does not imply that his sisters were outside with his mother and brothers [Sw]. By adding sister, he emphasizes the rightful place of women in the Christian fellowship [PNTC]. 'Father' is not mentioned since they have only one Father, their Father in heaven [BECNT, Hb, PNTC].

DISCOURSE UNIT—4:1–34 [EBC, Hb, NICNT, NIGTC; NLT, REB]. The topic is parables [REB], Jesus teaches in parables [NLT], parabolic teaching to the crowd [Hb], parables about/concerning the kingdom of God [EBC, NICNT], explanatory discourse: the paradox of the kingdom of God [NIGTC].

DISCOURSE UNIT—4:1–20 [CBC; GW, NIV, NLT]. The topic is a story about a farmer [GW], the parable of the sower [CBC; NIV], the parable of the farmer scattering seed [NLT].

DISCOURSE UNIT—4:1–12 [NASB, NLT]. The topic is the parable of the sower and the soils [NASB], the parable of the farmer scattering seed [NLT].

DISCOURSE UNIT—4:1–9 [EBC, NICNT; CEV, ESV, NCV, NET, NRSV, TEV]. The topic is the parable of the sower [EBC, NICNT; ESV, NET, NRSV, TEV], a story about a farmer [CEV], a story about planting seed [NCV].

DISCOURSE UNIT—4:1–2 [Hb]. The topic is the setting for the teaching.

4:1 And again he-began to-teach beside the lake. And a-large crowd gathered[a] to him, so[b] he got into a-boat[c] to-sit on[d] the lake, and all the crowd were beside the lake on the land.

LEXICON—a. pres. pass. indic. of συνάγω (LN 15.125) (BAGD 2. p. 782): 'to gather together' [BAGD, LN]. The phrase συνάγεται πρὸς αὐτὸν 'gathered to him' [NASB], is also translated 'was gathered unto him' [KJV], 'gathered around him' [GW, NCV, NET, NIV, NLT, NRSV, REB, TEV], 'gathered about him' [ESV], 'gathered' [CEV]. This verb means to come together [LN]. The passive has the reflexive sense of 'to gather, to gather together' [BAGD].

   b. ὥστε (LN 89.52): 'so' [BNTC, LN; GW, NCV, NLT], 'so then, therefore, as a result' [LN], 'so that' [AB2, BECNT, LN, Lns, WBC; ESV, KJV], '(was so large) that' [AB1, NTC; CEV, NIV, REB, TEV], '(such a very large crowd gathered) that' [NASB, NET, NRSV]. This conjunction indicates result [BECNT, LN, Lns].

   c. πλοῖον (LN 6.41) (BAGD 2. p. 673): 'boat' [AB1, AB2, BAGD, BECNT, BNTC, LN, Lns, NTC, WBC; all versions except KJV], 'ship' [KJV]. This noun denotes any kind of boat from the small fishing boats on Lake Galilee to large seagoing vessels [LN]. Here it denotes a small fishing vessel [BAGD].

   d. ἐν (LN 83.47): 'on' [AB2, LN, WBC], 'in' [BECNT, Lns; KJV]. The phrase 'got into a boat to sit on the lake' is translated 'he got into a boat and sat in it on the sea' [ESV; similarly NIV], 'he got into a boat in/on the sea and sat down' [NASB, NRSV], 'he got into a boat on the lake and sat there' [BNTC; NET; similarly REB], 'he had to sit in a boat out on the lake' [CEV], 'stepped into a boat and sat in it out on the sea' [NTC], 'he got into a boat and sat in it. The boat was in the water' [GW, TEV], 'he went into a boat on the lake. There he sat' [AB1], 'he got into a boat. Then he sat in the boat' [NLT], 'he sat down in a boat near the shore' [NCV]. This preposition indicates a position on the surface of an area [LN].

QUESTION—What relationship is indicated by the adverb πάλιν 'again'?
   'Again' refers to the similar account at 3:7–12 when Jesus had arranged for a boat to stand by while he taught the crowd [AB1, BECNT, CGTC, ICC, Lns, NAC, NIGTC, NTC, Sw, Tay, WBC], and also at 2:13 [BECNT, Gnd, ICC, Lns, NTC, Sw, Tay, TRT] and 1:16 [ICC].

QUESTION—What is meant by Jesus getting into the boat 'to sit *on* the lake'?
   The boat was not filled with water [TRT]. The boat was floating on the water and Jesus was sitting in the boat, not in the water [TH]. This indicates that the boat was launched rather than just being on the beach [NIGTC]. Jesus sat

in the boat and was encircled by the lake since the boat had been rowed a little way from the shore [Hb].

QUESTION—In the last clause, why is the noun phrase πᾶς ὁ ὄχλος 'all the crowd' singular in number but the accompanying verb ἦσαν 'were' is plural in number?

The plural verb 'were' agrees with the plural sense of the noun 'crowd' rather than its grammatical singular form [BECNT]. Translations vary greatly, but make the grammatical numbers of the noun and verb agree: 'the whole crowd was' [AB2, BECNT, BNTC, WBC; ESV, NASB, NET, NRSV; similarly KJV], 'all the people were' [NTC; NIV], 'the entire crowd lined' [GW], 'the crowd stood' [TEV], 'the people stood' [CEV], 'all the people stayed' [NCV], 'all the people remained' [NLT], 'with the whole crowd on the shore' [AB1; REB].

4:2 And he-was-teaching them many (things) with parables,[a] and he-was-saying[b] to-them in[c] his teaching,

LEXICON—a. παραβολή (LN 33.15) (BAGD 2. p. 612): 'parable' [BAGD, LN; all translations except CEV, GW, NCV, NLT], 'illustration' [BAGD], 'story' [CEV, NCV], 'stories in the form of parables' [NLT], '(he used) stories as illustrations' [GW], 'figure, allegory' [LN]. This noun denotes a relatively short narrative with symbolic meaning [LN]. This word occurs at 3:23; 4:2, 10, 11, 13, 30, 33, 34; 7:17; 12:1, 12; 13:28.

b. imperf. act. indic. of λέγω (LN 33.69): 'to say' [AB1, AB2, BECNT, BNTC, LN, Lns, WBC; all versions except CEV, NLT], 'to talk, to tell, to speak' [LN]. The phrase 'he was saying to them in his teaching' is translated 'this is part of what he taught' [CEV], 'such as this one' [NLT]. This verb means to speak or talk about something [LN].

c. ἐν (67.136) (BAGD II.3. p. 260): 'in' [AB1, AB2, BECNT, BNTC, Lns, WBC; ESV, GW, KJV, NASB, NET, NIV, NRSV], 'in the course of' [LN, WBC], 'during' [BAGD, LN], 'while' [BAGD; GW], not explicit [NCV, TEV]. The phrase 'he was saying to them in his teaching' is translated 'this is part of what he taught' [CEV], 'as he taught he said' [REB], 'such as this one' [NLT]. This preposition indicates the extent of time within a unit [LN]. The sense of διδαχή 'teaching' is active and refers to the act of teaching, so this can be translated 'as he was teaching them' [TH].

QUESTION—What were the 'many things' Jesus was teaching?

He was teaching them many things about the kingdom of God [NIGTC, PNTC, WBC]. The things he taught are described in the following verses 4:3–32 [BECNT]. Jesus taught many things, but only a fragment of a larger discourse is given here [Hb, NICNT].

QUESTION—What relationship is indicated by the preposition ἐν 'with' in the phrase 'with parables'?

This preposition indicates the means by which Jesus taught [BECNT, TH, WBC]. 'He used stories to teach them many things, and this is part of what he taught' [CEV]. 'He taught them by telling many stories in the form of parables, such as this one' [NLT].

QUESTION—What are parables?

A parable is basically a comparison that comes in various forms. Here it is presented as a narrative [Hb]. Parables can come in the form of stories (Luke 15:11–32; 18:1–8), proverbs (3:24; Luke 4:23), similes and metaphors (Matt. 5:14; 10:16), riddles (7:15; 14:58), comparisons (Matt. 13:33; Luke 15:3–7), examples (Luke 10:30–35; 12:16–21), and allegories (4:3–9; 12:1–12) [NLTfn].

DISCOURSE UNIT—4:3–32 [Hb]. The topic is the content of the teaching.

DISCOURSE UNIT—4:3–20 [Hb]. The topic is the parable of the sower.

4:3 "Listen.[a] Behold,[b] the (one) sowing[c] went-out[d] to sow.

LEXICON—a. pres. act. impera. of ἀκούω (LN 24.52) (BAGD 1.c. p. 32): 'to listen' [BAGD], 'to hear' [BAGD, LN]. The imperative form is translated 'Listen!' [AB1, AB2, BECNT, BNTC, NTC, WBC; all versions except CEV, KJV, NASB], 'Now listen!' [CEV], 'Listen to this!' [NASB], 'Harken!' [KJV], 'Give heed!' [Lns].

b. ἰδού (LN 91.13): 'behold' [BECNT; KJV, NASB], 'look' [AB2, LN], 'lo' [Lns], 'listen' [LN; NIV], 'pay attention' [LN], 'see' [WBC], 'once upon a time' [NTC], not explicit [AB1, BNTC; all versions except KJV, NASB]. This particle prompts attention and serves to emphasize the following statement [LN].

c. pres. act. participle of σπείρω (LN 43.6) (BAGD 1.a.α. p. 761): 'to sow' [LN], 'to sow seed' [BAGD]. The phrase ὁ σπείρων 'the one sowing' is translated 'the sower' [Lns; NTC; NASB], 'a sower' [AB2, BECNT, BNTC, WBC; ESV, KJV, NET, NRSV, REB], 'a farmer' [CEV, GW, NCV, NLT], 'a man' [TEV]. This verb means to scatter seed over tilled ground [LN]. The article in the phrase '*the* sower' gives the participle 'sowing' a generic or representative sense [ICC, Lns]. This describes a typical sower [Tay]. It designates the particular sower in this parable [Sw].

d. aorist act. indic. of ἐξέρχομαι (LN 15.40): 'to go out of, to depart out of, to leave from within' [LN]. The phrase 'went out to sow' [AB2, BECNT, BNTC, Lns, NTC, WBC; ESV, KJV, NASB, NET, NRSV, REB] is also translated 'went to sow' [AB1], 'went out to sow grain' [TEV], 'went out to sow his seed' [NIV], 'went out to scatter seed in a field' [CEV], 'went to plant seed' [GW; similarly NCV], 'went out to plant some seed' [NLT]. This verb means to move out of an enclosed or well-defined two or three-dimensional area [LN].

QUESTION—What is the function of the opening word ἀκούετε 'listen'?
This is a summons to pay close attention to what Jesus was about to teach them [CGTC, EGT, Hb, Lns, NIGTC, WBC]. It emphasizes the importance of the teaching [BNTC, CBC]. It is a solemn call to be attentive since a superficial hearing may miss the point [NICNT]. This introductory command ἀκούετε 'listen/hear' is to be connected with the closing command, 'let the one who has ears to hear, let him hear' (4:9) [CGTC, EBC, Gnd, NAC, NCBC, PNTC], and together they suggest that the meaning of the parable may not be self-evident [EBC].

QUESTION—What is the function of the next word ἰδού 'behold'?
This command grabs attention [Gnd]. When joined with 'listen', the words doubly emphasize the importance of heeding the parable that will follow [BECNT]. It simply strengthens the urgency of the preceding word 'listen' [TH] and many translations omit it [AB1, BNTC; all versions except KJV, NASB]. The word 'behold' focuses attention on the development of the whole story, not just the fact that a sower went out to sow [NTC].

QUESTION—What did the man go out of?
He went out from his house in the village to go to his field in the open country [Hb].

QUESTION—What did the man sow and how did he sow the seeds?
The sower was sowing seeds of either wheat or barley, scattering them by hand from a leather bag tied to his waist [Hb]. The seeds would later be plowed into the ground by a wooden plow that did not cut deeply into the ground [BNTC]. The wooden plow was drawn by a pair of oxen [Hb]. It was the custom in Palestine to plow the fields after the seeds had been sown on top of the soil [AB2, BNTC, CBC, EBC, ESVfn, Hb, NCBC, NICNT, NIGTC]. Others think that the ground would have been plowed before the seeds were sown [BNTC, NTC, PNTC]. Another says that farmers frequently plowed the ground before they sowed the seeds, and then plowed the ground again in order to cover the seeds [PNTC].

4:4 **And it-happened[a] during[b] the sowing one/one-(portion) fell[c] along[d] the road, and the birds came and devoured[e] it.**

TEXT—Manuscripts reading τὰ πετεινά 'the birds' are followed by GNT, which does not mention any variant reading. A variant reading is τὰ πετεινά τοῦ οὐρανοῦ 'the birds of heaven' and it is followed by KJV.

LEXICON—a. aorist mid. (deponent = act.) indic. of γίνομαι (LN 13.107) (BAGD I.3.f. p. 159): 'to happen' [AB1, BECNT, BNTC, LN, NTC, WBC; REB], 'to occur, to come to be' [LN], 'to take place' [BAGD], 'to come to pass' [AB2, Lns; KJV], not explicit [all versions except KJV, REB]. This verb means 'to happen' and implies that what happens is different from a previous state [LN]. This word also occurs at 1:9; 2:23.
  b. ἐν (LN 67.136) (BAGD II.3. p. 260): 'during' [BAGD, LN], 'while, when' [BAGD], 'in the course of' [LN]. The phrase ἐν τῷ σπείρειν 'during the sowing' is translated 'in the sowing' [AB2, Lns], 'while he

was sowing' [BECNT, WBC], 'as he sowed' [AB1, BNTC; ESV, KJV, NET, NRSV, REB; similarly NTC; NASB], 'as he was scattering the seed' [NIV; similarly NLT, TEV], 'as he scattered the seed in the field' [TEV], 'while the farmer was scattering the seed' [CEV], 'while he was planting' [NCV], not explicit [GW]. This preposition refers to the extent of time within a unit [LN]. It introduces an activity whose time is stated [BAGD]. The Greek phrase 'in the sowing' is a Semitic construction that is also found in Greek [TH].

- c. aorist act. indic. of πίπτω (LN 15.118) (BAGD 1.a. p. 659): 'to fall' [AB1, AB2, BAGD, BECNT, BNTC, LN, Lns, NTC; WBC; all versions except GW], 'to be planted' [GW]. This verb means to fall from one height to another [LN].
- d. παρά (LN 83.25) (BAGD III.1.d. p. 611): 'along' [Lns, NTC; CEV, ESV, GW, NET, NIV, REB, TEV], 'at, alongside' [LN], 'beside' [AB2, BNTC, LN; NASB], 'by' [BECNT; KJV, NCV], 'on' [AB1, BAGD, WBC; NLT, NRSV]. This preposition indicates a position near another location or object, and it usually implies being alongside something or close to it [LN].
- e. aorist act. indic. of κατεσθίω (LN 23.11) (BAGD 1. p. 422): 'to devour' [BAGD, LN, WBC; ESV, GW, KJV, NET], 'to eat up' [AB1, AB2, BAGD, BECNT, LN, Lns; NASB, NCV, NIV, NRSV, REB, TEV], 'to eat' [BNTC; NLT], 'to gobble up' [NTC]. The active form is also translated as passive: 'was eaten (by the birds)' [CEV]. This verb means to devour something completely [LN].

QUESTION—What is meant by the phrase 'and it happened'?

This calls attention to something that happened during the process of sowing that was not part of the sower's purpose [Hb].

QUESTION—Why do the references to the seed in the first three accounts about the sowing of the seeds occur in the singular forms of the adjectives, verbs, and pronouns: (4) ὃ ἔπεσεν...αὐτό 'one fell...it', (5-6) ἄλλο ἔπεσεν 'another fell...it did not have...it sprang up...it did not have', it was scorched...it did not have...it withered, (7) ἄλλο ἔπεσεν...αὐτό 'another fell...it came up...choked it...it did not give'?

1. These three accounts describe the fate of a single seed in each of the three types of soil [Gnd, NIGTC, WBC]: *one (seed) fell...it, another (seed) fell, another (seed) fell...it.* A single seed happened to fall on the edge of the path, another seed happened to fall on the rocky ground, and still another seed happened to fall among the thorns. The fate of the three seeds that fell on poor soil are then matched by the fate of three other seeds that fell on good soil, each of them producing different levels of yield [Gnd, NIGTC].
2. These three accounts describe the fate of a portion of the seeds in each of the three types of soil [AB2, BECNT, Lns, Sw, Tay]: *one (portion of the seeds) fell...it, another (portion of the seeds) fell, another (portion of the seeds) fell...it.* This parable is not about a total of just six seeds. It would

be ridiculous to talk about a single seed falling on the road and then being devoured by a number of birds [BECNT].
3. These three accounts describe what happened to many seeds that were sown in each type of soil. [AB1, ICC, NTC; CEV, ESV, GW, NCV, NET, NIV, NLT, NRSV, REB, TEV]. The implied singular noun 'seed' is a collective noun referring to 'seeds', and the series could be translated 'some seeds' and 'other seeds' [TH].
3.1 The implied noun 'seed' is used collectively [AB1, ICC, NTC; ESV, NCV, NET, NIV, NLT, NRSV, REB, TEV]: *some of the seed fell...it, others of the seed fell...it, others of the seed fell...it.* This parable uses the collective singular to refer to the seed throughout. But the parallel passage in Matt. 13:1–9 begins with plural pronouns in 13:4 and then switches to the collective singular for the rest of the verses [NETfn].
3.2 The implied plural noun 'seeds' is used in the translation and the verbs and pronoun are changed to their plural forms [CEV, GW]: *some seeds fell...they, other seeds fell...they, other seeds fell...they.*
QUESTION—Where did the scattered seeds land?
The seeds fell on the road [AB1, NICNT, TH, WBC; NLT, NRSV], on the edge of the road [BECNT, Gnd], beside the road [AB2, BNTC, LN; NASB], by the road [Sw; KJV, NCV]. The road upon which the seeds landed was either a road that went alongside the field or a footpath that crossed the open field [Hb, TRT]. It was unavoidable that some seeds would land along a footpath that crossed through the field [Gnd, NTC]. The seed may have been deliberately sown on a path through the field since afterwards the whole field would be plowed to cover the seeds [EBC, NICNT]. If the road was a permanent path along the boundary of the field, the seed sown alongside that road would unintentionally land on the road itself [BNTC]. Such a road would not be plowed at all and the seeds along it would remain exposed to the birds [NIGTC].

4:5 **And another/another-(portion) fell upon the rocky-ground[a] where it-did- not -have much soil,[b] and immediately[c] it-sprang-up[d] because it-did- not -have depth of-soil.**

LEXICON—a. πετρῶδες (LN 2.22) (BAGD p. 655): 'rocky ground' [AB1, AB2, BAGD, BECNT, LN, NTC, WBC; ESV, GW, NASB, NCV, NET, NRSV, REB, TEV], 'rocky places' [NIV], 'stony ground' [BNTC; KJV], 'thin, rocky ground' [CEV], 'shallow soil with underlying rock' [NLT], 'rock-soil' [Lns]. This noun denotes a rocky substance or bedrock covered by a thin layer of earth [BAGD, LN].
b. γῆ (LN 2:14) (BAGD 1. p. 157): 'soil' [AB1, BAGD, BECNT, BNTC, LN, NTC, WBC; all versions except KJV, NCV], 'dirt' [NCV], 'ground' [LN], 'earth' [AB2, BAGD, Lns; KJV].
c. εὐθύς (LN 67.53): 'immediately' [AB2, BECNT, LN, Lns, NTC, WBC; ESV, KJV, NASB], 'quickly' [AB1; CEV, GW, NIV, NLT, NRSV, REB], 'at once' [NET], 'straight away' [BNTC], 'right away, then' [LN],

'soon' [TEV], '(grew) very fast' [NCV]. This adverb indicates a point of time immediately following a previous point of time but the actual interval of time depends upon the nature of the events and the manner in which the sequence is presented by the writer [LN].
- d. aorist act. indic. of ἐξανατέλλω (LN **23.195**) (BAGD p. 272): 'to spring up' [AB2, BECNT, Lns, NTC; ESV, KJV, NASB, NET, NIV, NRSV], 'to sprout' [AB1, BNTC, **LN**, WBC; GW, NLT, REB, TEV], 'to sprout leaves' [LN], 'to start growing' [CEV], 'to grow' [NCV]. This verb means to begin vegetative growth and there is an emphasis on the sprouting of leaves [LN].

QUESTION—What was the rocky ground?

This ground was part of the field where the sowing took place. 'Rocky ground' means that there was bedrock close to the surface with only a thin layer of soil covering it [BECNT, CGTC, Hb, ICC, LN, Lns, NIGTC, Sw, Tay, TH, WBC]. This was an area in the field where a thin layer of soil covered an unseen ledge of limestone [Hb, NCBC, NETfn, NICNT, WBC]. The layer of rock was not apparent since it did not show above the surface of the field [NICNT].

QUESTION—Why would the seed spring up quickly?

A thin layer of soil over bedrock warms faster than deep soil, and this condition allows for a more rapid germination of the seed [BNTC, Hb, Lns, TH, WBC]. Since it was near the surface, the shoots would appear above ground more quickly [BNTC].

4:6 **And when the sun rose[a] it-was-scorched[b] and because it-did- not -have root[c] it-withered.[d]**

LEXICON—a. aorist act. indic. of ἀνατέλλω (LN 15.104) (BAGD 2. p. 62): 'to rise' [AB2, BAGD, BECNT, LN, Lns, WBC; ESV, NASB, NCV, NRSV, REB], 'to come up' [AB1, BNTC, LN, NTC; CEV, GW, NET, NIV, TEV], 'to move upward' [LN], 'to be up' [KJV]. The phrase 'when the sun rose' is translated 'under the hot sun' [NLT]. This verb means to move up and is often used to describe the upward movement of the sun and the stars [LN]. This refers to the time of day when the sun is high enough in the sky for its heat to be felt [TH].
- b. aorist pass. indic. of καυματίζω (LN 14.68) (BAGD p. 425): 'to be scorched' [AB1, AB2, BAGD, BECNT, BNTC, LN, Lns, NTC; CEV, ESV, GW, KJV, NASB, NET, NIV, NRSV, REB], 'to be burned' [BAGD], 'to be burned up' [WBC], 'to be harmed by heat' [LN], 'to wilt' [NLT], not explicit [NCV]. This passive verb is translated actively: 'it burned the young plants' [TEV]. This verb means to cause something to suffer from an intense heat [LN].
- c. ῥίζα (LN 3.47) (BAGD 1.a. p. 736): 'root' [LN]. The phrase 'it did not have root' is translated 'it/they had no root' [AB1, BECNT, BNTC, NTC, WBC; ESV, KJV, NASB, NIV, NRSV, REB; similarly AB2], 'they didn't have any roots' [GW; similarly Lns], 'they did not have enough roots'

[CEV], 'it did not have sufficient root' [NET], 'they/it did not have deep roots' [NCV, NLT], 'the roots had not grown deep enough' [TEV]. This noun denotes the underground part of a plant [LN].
  d. aorist pass, indic. of ξηραίνομαι, ξηραίνω (LN 79.81) (BAGD 2.a. p. 548): 'to wither' [AB2, BAGD, WBC; GW, KJV, NET, NIV], 'to wither away' [AB1, BECNT, BNTC, NTC; ESV, NASB, NRSV, REB], 'to dry up' [BAGD, LN, Lns; CEV, NCV, TEV], 'to die' [NLT]. This verb means to become dry [LN].

QUESTION—Does the statement 'when the sun rose it was scorched' imply that this all happened in one day?

The plant must have grown over a longer period than one day, so the sun would have risen many times. This probably refers to an occasion when the heat of the sun had became too intense [NIGTC]. It does not refer to the next day after the seeds were planted, but to the hot days when the plants were young [TRT]. 'But the plant soon wilted under the hot sun' [NLT].

QUESTION—What is meant by the phrase 'it did not have root'?

This statement is not describing a miraculous plant that grew without any roots at all [TH]. It means it did not have deep roots [NLTfn, TH], enough roots [CEV], sufficient roots [NET]. 'The roots had not grown deep enough' [TEV]. Because the plant's growth had been concentrated upward, it hadn't established a system of deep roots [BECNT]. The reason it was scorched was that the plant was unable to draw moisture from below [Hb].

4:7 **And another/another-(portion) fell among the thorns,^a and the thorns grew^b and choked^c it, and it-did- not -produce^d grain.^e**

LEXICON—a. ἄκανθα (LN 3.17) (BAGD p. 29): 'thorn' [AB2, BECNT, Lns, NTC; ESV, KJV, NASB, NET, NIV, NLT, NRSV], 'thorn plant' [BAGD, LN], 'thorn bush' [CEV, GW, TEV], 'thorny weed' [NCV], 'thistle' [AB1, BAGD, BNTC, LN, WBC; REB], 'brier' [LN]. This noun denotes any kind of a thorny plant [LN]. Palestinian thorns could grow up to six feet in height and have major root systems [NETfn].
  b. aorist act. indic. of ἀναβαίνω (LN **23.196**) (BAGD 1.b. p. 50): 'to grow' [NCV], 'to grow up' [AB1, BECNT; all versions except NASB, NCV], 'to sprout and grow' [**LN**], 'to come up' [AB2, BAGD, Lns; NASB], 'to shoot up' [NTC], 'to spring up' [BNTC], 'to rise up' [WBC]. This verb means to grow, and can refer to the growth of plants from the time they sprout until they reach their mature size [LN]. The verb means to move upward [BAGD]. This verb is a synonym for ἐξανατέλλω 'to spring up, to sprout' in verse 5 [TH].
  c. aorist act. indic. of συμπνίγω (LN 13.128, **23.120**) (BAGD 1. p. 779): 'to choke' [AB1, AB2, BAGD, BECNT, BNTC, Lns, NTC, WBC; all versions except CEV, NLT], 'to choke out' [CEV, NLT], 'to cause to die' [**LN**]. This verb means to cause the death of plants by other plants crowding them out or overshadowing them [LN]. Plants are choked when

their food and light are cut off by weeds [BAGD]. Thorns choked the plants by crowding them out [NETfn].
  d. aorist act. indic. of δίδωμι (LN 13.128, **23.199**) (BAGD 4. p. 193): 'to produce' [BECNT, BNTC, LN (13.128, **23.199**); CEV, GW, NCV, NET, NLT, REB], 'to yield' [AB2, BAGD, LN, NTC; ESV, KJV, NASB, NRSV], 'to bear' [AB1; NIV, TEV], 'to give' [Lns, WBC]. This verb means to cause to happen [LN (13.128)], and the phrase καρπὸν δίδωμι 'to give fruit' means to produce either fruit or seed [LN (23.199)].
  e. καρπός (LN 3.33) (BAGD 1.a. p. 404): 'grain' [AB1, BECNT, NTC; CEV, ESV, NET, NIV, NLT, NRSV, TEV], 'crop' [NASB, NCV, REB], 'fruit' [AB2, BAGD, LN, Lns, WBC; KJV], 'anything' [GW; similarly BNTC]. The noun denotes any fruit part of plants, including both grains and pulpy fruit [LN]. It refers to crops and the fruit of trees or vines, and the singular form can be used collectively [BAGD].

QUESTION—Why would the seeds have been scattered among thorns?
The seeds were not scattered among thorn bushes, but onto soil that still contained the roots of thorn bushes that had been previously burned away [Hb, Lns, NTC, Tay, TH]. The thorn seeds were already in the ground when the farmer scattered the grain seeds [Gnd, ICC]. Some seeds could have fallen among the weeds outside the area of the prepared land [BNTC].

QUESTION—Why didn't the seeds produce grain?
When the thorns and the scattered seeds grew up together, the thorns grew faster and higher until they deprived the grain of the light and moisture it needed [Hb, Lns, NIGTC, NTC, Sw, TH]. Although the seeds might have developed into plants with green heads, they lacked the energy to produce grain [Hb]. Although the grain plants ultimately died off, the point is that they did not produce grain [Sw].

4:8 And others fell on the good[a] soil and sprouting[b] and growing[c] it-was-producing[d] grain,

TEXT—Manuscripts reading καὶ αὐξανόμενα 'and increasing (neuter accusative middle plural)' are given a C rating by GNT to indicate that choosing it over a variant text was difficult. Variant readings are καὶ αὐξανόμενον 'and increasing (masculine accusative middle singular)', or καὶ αὐξάνοντα 'and increasing (neuter accusative active plural)'. Some manuscripts omit this phrase.

LEXICON—a. καλός (LN 65.22) (BAGD 2.a. p. 400): 'good' [BAGD, LN; all translations except Lns; NLT], 'fine' [LN], 'excellent' [Lns], 'fertile' [NLT]. This adjective describes something as having acceptable characteristics or functioning in an agreeable manner, often focusing on the outward form or appearance [LN]. It refers to the quality of something [BAGD].
  b. pres. act. participle of ἀναβαίνω (LN 23.196) (BAGD 1.b. p. 50): 'to sprout' [GW, NET, NLT, TEV], 'to spring up' [BNTC; KJV], 'to come up' [AB1, AB2, NTC, WBC; NIV, REB], 'to begin to grow' [NCV], 'to

grow up' [ESV, NASB, NRSV], 'to rise up' [BAGD, BECNT], 'to sprout and grow' [LN], 'to go up' [Lns], 'to ascend' [BAGD]. The phrase 'sprouting and increasing' is translated 'the plants grew' [CEV]. This verb means to grow, and can refer to the growth of plants from the time they sprout until they reach their mature size [LN]. The verb means to move upward [BAGD]. In this verse, it describes the seed breaking through the soil while the following verb 'growing' refers to its development into a mature plant [Gnd].

c. pres. pass. participle of αὐξάνω (LN 23.188) (BAGD 2. p. 121): 'to grow' [AB1, AB2, BAGD, BECNT, BNTC, LN, NTC; NET, NIV, NLT, REB, TEV], 'to increase' [Lns, WBC; ESV, KJV, NASB, NRSV], 'to get taller' [NCV], not explicit [CEV, GW]. This verb means to grow or to increase in size, and it applies to both animate beings and plants [LN].

d. imperf. act. indic. of δίδωμι (LN 13.128, 23.199) (BAGD 4. p. 193): 'to produce, to make, to cause, to give' [LN (13.128)], 'to yield' [BAGD]. The phrase δίδωμι καρπόν 'to produce grain' [AB1, BECNT; ESV, NET] is also translated 'to produce a crop' [BNTC; NCV, NIV, REB], 'to yield a crop' [NASB], 'to bring forth grain' [NRSV], 'to bear grain' [TEV], 'to yield fruit' [AB2, Lns; KJV], 'to bear fruit' [NTC], 'to give fruit' [WBC], not explicit [CEV, GW, NLT]. This verb means to cause to happen [LN (13.128)], and the phrase καρπὸν δίδωμι 'to give fruit' means to produce either fruit or seed [LN (23.199)].

QUESTION—Why has the singular form ἄλλο 'another/another-(portion)' used in verses 5 and 7 now changed to the plural form ἄλλα 'others' in this verse?

In verses 5 and 7, the singular forms describe the fate of a *single* or *typical* seed, but here in verse 8 the fates of three individual seeds must be distinguished since each produced a different yield [NIGTC]. Another explanation is that the singular form 'another' is used in verses 5 and 7 because the seeds in both scenes were thought of *collectively*, but now in verse 8 the three different results refer to three different seeds [AB1, CGTC, ICC, NTC, Tay].

QUESTION—What is significant about the plants sprouting, growing, and producing grain?

This sequence pictures the steady growth of the plants in the good soil. The seeds on the path did not even sprout, those sown in the rocky ground sprouted but did not grow up, and those sown among the thistle plants grew up but did not produce grain [Hb]. We can assume that the farmer would have sown the great bulk of the seeds in the good soil [Tay, WBC].

and one produced[a] thirty and one sixty and one one-hundred."

LEXICON—a. aorist act. indic. of φέρω (LN 23.199) (BAGD 2. p. 855): 'to produce' [LN], 'to yield' [BAGD, LN], 'to bear' [BAGD]. The phrase 'and produced one thirty' is translated 'and produced some thirty' or 'and produced thirty times...what was planted' [**LN**], 'and yielding thirty...fold' [NRSV; similarly BECNT, NTC; ESV], 'the yield was thirtyfold' [AB1; REB], 'and produced thirty...fold' [NASB], 'bore thirty...respectively' [WBC], 'multiplying thirty...times' [NIV], 'some yielded thirty times as much' [NET], 'some bore thirty grains' [BNTC], 'some had thirty grains' [TEV], 'and they were bearing thirty fold' [AB2], 'and produced a crop that was thirty...times as much as had been planted' [NLT], 'and went on to bring up to thirty' [Lns], 'Some plants made thirty times more' [NCV], 'and brought forth, some thirty' [KJV], 'and produced thirty...times as much as was planted' [GW], 'produced thirty...times as much as was scattered' [CEV]. This verb means to produce fruit or seed of plants [LN]. This word also occurs at 4:7.

QUESTION—Why did the seeds produce different amounts and how could some seed yield a hundred?

Different areas of the good soil varied in their fertility [Hb]. Even though the average yield in the United States is twenty to thirty times what is sown, in Israel a hundred times was possible [BNTC], and not extravagant [NIGTC, Sw, TRT, WBC]. A different view is that a yield of a hundred times what is sown would be exceptional [BNTC, NCBC], unusual [NIVfn], and astounding [PNTC].

4:9 And he-was-saying,[a] "Who has ears to-hear,[b] let-him-hear.[c]"

LEXICON—a. imperf. act. indic. of λέγω (LN 33.69): 'to say, to talk, to tell' [LN]. The phrase 'and he was saying' [BECNT; NASB] is also translated 'and he said' [AB1, AB2, BNTC, NTC, WBC; ESV, NET, NRSV; similarly KJV], 'then Jesus/he said' [CEV, NCV, NIV, NLT], 'he went on to say' [Lns], 'he added' [GW, REB], 'and Jesus concluded' [TEV]. This verb means to speak or talk about something [LN].

b. pres. act. infin. of ἀκούω (LN 32.1): 'to understand, to comprehend' [LN]. The phrase 'who has ears to hear' [LN, NTC; ESV, NASB, NET, NIV; similarly AB2, BECNT, BNTC, WBC; GW, KJV, NLT, NRSV, REB], is also translated 'if you have ears' [CEV, TEV], 'if you have ears that are good for listening' [AB1], 'you people who can hear me' [NCV]. This verb means to hear and understand a message [LN].

c. pres. act. impera. of ἀκούω (LN 31.56): 'to hear' [AB2, BECNT, BNTC, Lns, NTC, WBC; ESV, KJV, NASB, NIV, REB], 'to listen' [AB1; GW, NCV, NET, NRSV, TEV], 'to understand' [NLT], 'to pay attention' [CEV], 'to accept, to listen to, to listen and respond, to pay attention and respond, to heed' [LN]. This verb means to believe something and to respond to it on the basis of having heard [LN].

QUESTION—What is meant by this admonition?

The listeners must hear and heed what Jesus was teaching [Hb]. It is a warning that they must think deeply about this parable and not dismiss it lightly [Lns]. There is more to the parable than appears on the surface [EBC, Lns, NICNT]. It implies that not all who have listened to the parable will benefit from it, a fact that is made explicit in the following section [NAC, NCBC, NIGTC, WBC]. The twofold use of the word 'hear' is a play on words so that the second 'hear' means to 'heed' and is directed to the disciples who will be able to heed the teaching [BECNT]. The third person imperative 'let him hear' is not just giving permission to listen to the words, but has the force of 'He had better listen!' [NETfn].

DISCOURSE UNIT—4:10–20 [ESV, NET, NRSV]. The topic is the purpose of the parables.

DISCOURSE UNIT—4:10–12 [EBC, NICNT; CEV, NCV, NLT, TEV]. The topic is the purpose of the parables [TEV], Jesus' purpose for teaching in parables [NLT], why Jesus used stories [CEV], Jesus tells why he used stories [NCV], the fulfillment of the purpose of God [NICNT], the secret of the kingdom of God [EBC].

4:10 **And when he-was alone,ᵃ the (ones) around him with the twelve were-asking him (about) the parables.**

LEXICON—a. μόνος (LN 58.50) (BAGD 3. p. 528): 'alone' [BAGD, LN; all translations]. This adverb means the only entity in a class [LN (58.50)], and the idiom κατὰ μόνας 'alone' refers to the only item of a class in a place [LN (58.51)].

QUESTION—In what sense was Jesus alone?

1. Jesus was alone with his twelve disciples and some other disciples [BECNT, Hb, ICC, Lns, Tay, TH, TRT; CEV, GW, NLT, REB]. 'Alone' is not used in the absolute sense since there was a group of his disciples around him. This means that Jesus had withdrawn from the crowd to speak privately with these disciples. It may have to be translated 'when he was no longer with the crowd' or 'when the crowd was no longer there' [TH]. Jesus was alone in the sense that he was free from the presence of the crowd that he had been teaching [BECNT, Hb, ICC, Lns, Tay]. Jesus was 'alone with the twelve apostles and some others' [CEV; similarly GW, NLT, REB].
2. Jesus was alone by himself and then his twelve disciples and others came to him. 'When Jesus was alone, some of those who had heard him came to him with the twelve disciples' [TEV].

QUESTION—What happened to the large crowd that was listening to Jesus as he taught them from the boat in 4:1–9?

The text seems to imply that the whole chapter occurred in a single day, but there is a problem in fitting in the things Jesus did [NIGTC]. Jesus was seated in a boat talking to the large crowd, then suddenly he is at a private meeting with some of his disciples in 4:10, and after an account of teaching more parables he is back in the boat in 4:35 [WBC].

1. Mark interrupted his account of Jesus teaching parables to a large crowd in order to let his readers in on a private meeting Jesus had with his disciples on another occasion when he told them his purpose for teaching with parables and explained the meaning of the parable he had told about sowing the seeds [AB2, BECNT, BNTC, CGTC, Gnd, Hb, ICC, NAC,

NCBC, NICNT, NLTfn, PNTC, Sw, Tay, WBC]. This private meeting occurred either while they were in a house or while they were walking along [Tay].
2. Verses 1 and 35–36 indicate that all this happened on the same day [Lns, TRT]. Jesus merely took a short break from speaking to the large crowd to teach his followers in the privacy of the boat [TRT]. There was ample time for Jesus to give his disciples private instruction at his house during the afternoon and then return to the boat to cross the lake when evening came [Lns].

QUESTION—Who were τοῖς δώδεκα 'the twelve'?

They were the twelve disciples Jesus had appointed to be his apostles in 3:14 [TH], and some translations supply a noun: 'the twelve apostles' [CEV, GW, NCV], 'the twelve disciples' [NLT, TEV]. Instead of simply indicating the number of disciples involved, the phrase 'the twelve' is used as a title [TH], and some show this by capitalizing the number: 'the Twelve' [BECNT, BNTC, Lns; NIV, REB].

QUESTION—Who were the ones around Jesus besides the Twelve, and who were asking the question?

These were a wider group of disciples than the Twelve [AB2, BECNT, CGTC, EBC, EGT, Hb, ICC, Lns, My, NCBC, NICNT, Sw, Tay]. These people are distinguished from the multitude that had departed and also from the Twelve who were there with them. We know that they were disciples since Jesus was going to explain the mystery of the kingdom that was kept secret from the outsiders (4:11) [ICC]. The word order in Greek, 'were asking him the ones around him with the twelve' clearly indicates that Jesus was questioned about the parables by the twelve apostles and the other disciples who were clustered around him [NICNT, NTC, TH].

QUESTION—What is implied by the plural form τὰς παραβολάς 'the parables'?

The plural form implies that Jesus had taught the crowd more than just the one parable reported in 4:5–8 [EBC, Hb]. Verse 2 says that Jesus 'was teaching them many things with *parables*', so we are to understand that Mark recorded the parable of the sower as an example of Jesus' wider parabolic teaching [NIGTC]. Assuming that this conversation with the disciples occurred at another occasion, it refers to all of the parables that had been included in Jesus' teachings that day [EGT, ICC]. The plural form includes the preceding parable in 4:3–8 and the following parables in 4:13–32 [BECNT]. When Jesus speaks about 'this parable' in 4:13 it seems to indicate that the disciples were specifically concerned about the meaning of the parable of the sower. Perhaps when they asked about 'the *parables*', they were asking why Jesus didn't express his thoughts to the crowds in a more direct way than through parables [NICNT; probably Sw]. They wanted to know his purpose for using parables [EBC].

4:11 And he-was-saying to them, "To-you has-been-given^a the secret^b of-the-kingdom^c of-God.

TEXT—Manuscripts reading δέδοται 'has been given' are followed by GNT, which does not mention any variant reading. A variant reading is δέδοται γνῶναι 'has been given to know' and it is followed by KJV.

LEXICON—a. perf. pass. indic. of δίδωμι (LN 57.71): 'to be given' [AB1, AB2, BECNT, BNTC, LN, Lns, NTC, WBC; ESV, KJV, NASB, NET, NIV, NRSV, REB, TEV], 'to be imparted' [**LN**]. The phrase 'to you has been given the secret' is translated 'you are permitted to understand the secret' [NLT] 'you can know the secret' [NCV], 'to you has been imparted the mystery' [**LN**], 'the mystery...has been given directly to you' [GW], 'I have explained the secret...to you' [CEV]. This verb means to give an object, usually implying that what is given is valuable [LN].

b. μυστήριον (LN 28.77) (BAGD 1. p. 530): 'secret' [AB1, BAGD, BNTC, LN; all versions except GW, KJV, NASB], 'mystery' [AB2, BAGD, BECNT, LN, Lns, NTC, WBC; GW, KJV, NASB]. This noun denotes the content of that which had not been known before but which has been revealed to the in-group [LN]. In Scripture, this word denotes the secret thoughts, plans, and dispensations of God that are hidden from human reason and must be revealed to those for whom they are intended [BAGD].

c. βασιλεία (LN 37.64) (BAGD 3.b., 3.g. p. 135): 'kingdom, royal reign' [BAGD], 'reign, rule' [LN]. This noun denotes the act of ruling with complete authority [LN]. For translations of the phrase 'the kingdom of God' see 1:15.

QUESTION—Who has given them the secret?

The passive form of the verb 'has been given' is a Jewish circumlocution to avoid using the name 'God', and this means that God has given them the privilege of knowing the secret [AB2, BECNT, BNTC, CGTC, Gnd, Hb, Lns, NAC, NETfn, NIGTC, NIVfn, PNTC, TH, WBC]. God chose to reveal himself in a veiled way, and only by faith could they recognize that the lowly person of Jesus of Nazareth was the Son of God [CGTC, NICNT]. At that time they did not understand all that was involved about the kingdom being embodied in Jesus, but they would come to understand in the future [Hb]. That it was *given* them to know the secret points out their privilege to know it [CBC, Gnd] but stops short of saying that the disciples had already understood the secret [Gnd]. Verses 4:13–20 are part of what was 'given' them to know [NIGTC]. They will know that the kingdom of God has truly come as the miracles of healing and exorcisms manifested its presence [BECNT].

QUESTION—What is meant by the term μυστήριον 'secret'?

This secret is a truth about the Kingdom that human minds could not have discovered by themselves, and that is what Jesus is making known [Hb, ICC, NTC]. Although some translate μυστήριον as 'mystery', it does not mean that it is inherently hard to understand [ICC, NIGTC]. It is better translated 'secret' since it is privileged information that is not hard to grasp after it has been explained [NIGTC]. The secret is proclaimed to all, but only those who have faith can really understand it [EBC].

QUESTION—What is meant by the genitive construction τὸ μυστήριον τῆς βασιλείας τοῦ θεοῦ 'the secret of the kingdom of God'?

It means the secret *concerning* the kingdom of God [BECNT, TH]. The secret is that the kingdom of God has come in the person of Jesus Christ, the Son of God, who was right there in their midst [CGTC, EBC, NAC, NIVfn, NLTfn]. The kingdom was imminent and already exerting its power [Tay]. These parables concern the nature and development of the kingdom [Hb]. In regard to this group of parables, the secret is that there will be only a partial success in the early stage [ICC].

But to-the (ones) outside[a] all (things) come[b] in parables,

LEXICON—a. ἔξω (LN 11.10) (BAGD 1.a.β. p. 279): 'outside' [LN]. The phrase τοῖς ἔξω 'the ones outside' is translated 'those who are outside' [BAGD, BNTC; NASB, REB; similarly WBC], 'those on the outside' [AB1; GW, NIV], 'those outside' [AB2, BECNT, Lns; ESV, NET, NRSV], 'the others, who are on the outside' [TEV], 'them that are without' [KJV], 'the outsiders' [LN, NTC; NLT], 'other people' [NCV], 'others' [CEV]. This adjective refers to a position that is not contained within a particular area [LN]. It refers to those who did not belong to the circle of disciples [BAGD].

b. pres. mid./pass. (deponent = act.) indic. of γίνομαι (LN 13.107) (BAGD I.3.b.γ. p. 159): 'to come to be' [LN]. The phrase ἐν παραβολαῖς τὰ πάντα γίνεται 'all things come in parables' [Lns] is also translated 'everything comes in parables' [BECNT, NTC; NRSV], 'everything comes through parables' [AB1], 'everything comes by way of parables' [REB], 'everything is in parables' [BNTC], 'everything happens in parables' [AB2], 'all these things are done in parables' [KJV], 'get everything in parables' [NASB], 'everything is in parables' [ESV, NET], 'everything is said in parables' [NIV], 'receive everything in parables' [BAGD], 'hear all things by means of parables' [TEV], 'it is given in stories' [GW], 'all things come in riddles' [WBC], 'I tell everything by using stories' [NCV], 'I use parables for everything I say' [NLT], 'I can use only stories' [CEV]. This verb means 'to happen', and implies that what happens is different from a previous state [LN].

QUESTION—Who are the ones who are outside?

These are the people who do not belong to the immediate group of disciples to whom Jesus was explaining the meaning [TH]. They are the people outside the circle of Jesus' followers [BAGD, Hb]. It refers to all the people who remain outside the kingdom of God [AB2, ICC, Sw, TH]. They are the people who have rejected Jesus' ministry [WBC], the non-disciples [Gnd, Sw]. It refers to the Pharisees [Lns, NTC, PNTC] and their followers [NTC], all those who hear only carelessly and do not bear fruit [PNTC], those hardened by unbelief [EBC], all unbelievers [NAC].

QUESTION—What is meant by πάντα 'all things'?

'All things' in this context are the contents of Jesus' teaching concerning the kingdom of God [BECNT, TH]. It refers not only to Jesus' teachings but also his whole ministry [EBC, NICNT, NIGTC]. It is the revelation that the kingdom was embodied in the person, words, and work of Jesus [Hb].

QUESTION—What is involved in all things coming to the outsiders in *parables*?

Christ's teaching had to be presented to outsiders in parabolic form [NTC]. In this statement, 'all things' is hyperbolic since Jesus did not use only parables in his teaching, but it is especially applicable in reference to parables. A parable is a metaphor or analogy that requires a person to deduce its meaning [BECNT]. At times parables function as riddles [BECNT, EBC, Hb, WBC]. The message conveyed by these stories is not apparent to outsiders who do not have the key to their interpretation [Hb, ICC]. The teaching about the kingdom of God was that the kingdom had come and Christ, the Son of God, was in their midst. Since this was a teaching that would make the Roman authorities very uneasy, teaching in parables helped defuse the issue for the time being [NLTfn].

4:12 **so-that^a seeing^b they-may-see and not perceive,^{c} and hearing^d they may hear and not understand,^{e}**

LEXICON—a. ἵνα (LN 89.49, 89.59) (BAGD II.2. p. 378): 'so that' [AB1, LN (89.49, 89.59); ESV, NASB, NCV, NET, NIV, REB, TEV], 'in order that' [AB2, BECNT, BNTC, Lns; NRSV], 'in order to, for the purpose of' [LN], 'so as a result' [LN (89.49)], 'that' [LN (89.49), Lns; KJV], 'the reason is' [CEV], 'that is' [WBC], 'so that (the Scriptures might be fulfilled:)' [NLT], not explicit [GW]. This conjunction indicates the *purpose* for events and states [LN (89.59)], or it indicates *result*, sometimes implying an underlying or indirect purpose [LN (89.49)]. In many cases, purpose and result cannot be clearly differentiated so that ἵνα can be used for the result that follows from the purpose of God [BAGD].

b. pres. act. participle of βλέπω (LN 24.41): 'to be able to see' [LN]. The phrase βλέποντες βλέπωσιν 'seeing they may see' [KJV] is also translated 'seeing they see' [WBC], 'while seeing, they may see' [NASB], 'in their looking they may look' [AB2], 'they may indeed look' [NRSV], 'although they look, they may look (but)' [NET; similarly Lns], 'they/these people will look and look' [CEV, NCV, REB; similarly BNTC; TEV], 'they may see and see' [NTC], 'they may go on looking' [AB1], 'they may be ever seeing' [NIV], 'they see clearly' [GW], 'they may indeed see' [ESV], 'they may see' [BECNT], 'when they see what I do' [NLT]. This verb means to have the faculty of sight [LN].

c. aorist act. subj. of ὁράω (LN 32.11): 'to perceive, to see, to understand, to recognize' [LN]. The phrase 'and/but not perceive' [BECNT, NTC; ESV, KJV, NASB, NRSV; similarly GW] is also translated 'but never perceiving' [NIV], 'yet perceive nothing' [BNTC], 'but/yet not see' [AB1, AB2, Lns; NET, TEV], 'but do not see' [WBC], 'but never see' [CEV], 'but see nothing' [REB], 'but they will not learn' [NCV], 'they will learn nothing' [NLT]. This verb means to come to understand as the result of perception [LN].

d. pres. act. participle of ἀκούω (LN 24.52) (BAGD 1.b.α. p. 32): 'to hear' [BAGD, LN]. The phrase ἀκούοντες ἀκούωσιν 'hearing they may hear' [KJV] is also translated 'hearing they hear' [WBC], 'while hearing, they may hear' [NASB; similarly AB2], 'although they hear they may hear (but)' [NET], 'they may indeed listen' [NRSV], 'they may listen and listen' [BNTC; REB, TEV], 'they will listen and listen' [CEV, NCV], 'and hear and hear' [NTC], '(they may be) ever hearing' [NIV], 'they hear clearly' [GW], 'may indeed hear' [ESV], 'they may hear' [BECNT], 'go on hearing' [AB1], 'when they hear what I say' [NLT].

e. pres. act. subj. of συνίημι (LN **32.5**) (BAGD p. 790): 'to understand' [BAGD, **LN**], 'to comprehend, to have insight into' [BAGD, LN], 'to perceive' [LN]. The phrase 'and/but/yet not understand' [AB1, AB2, BECNT, Lns, NTC; ESV, KJV, NASB, NET, NRSV, TEV; similarly WBC] is also translated 'but never understand' [CEV; similarly NIV], 'but they will understand' [GW, NCV, NLT], 'but understand nothing' [BNTC; REB]. This verb means to use one's capacity for understanding and thus arrive at insight [LN]. This word occurs at 4:12; 6:52; 7:14; 8:17, 21.

QUESTION—Why did Jesus refer to this passage in the OT?

This verse quotes part of the Septuagint Greek translation of Isaiah 6:9–10 [EBC, ESVfn]. (In the Septuagint passage, God says to Isaiah, "Go, and say to this people, 'You shall hear indeed, but you shall not understand; and you shall see indeed, but you shall not perceive.' For the heart of this people has become gross, and their ears are dull of hearing, and their eyes have they closed; lest they should see with their eyes, and hear with their ears, and understand with their heart, and be converted, and I should heal them.") The passage in Isaiah pronounced God's judgment upon the people of Isaiah's time [NLTfn]. Jesus compared his preaching in parables to the ministry of Isaiah who exposed the hardhearted resistance of many to God's warning and appeal [NIVfn]. By referring to the hard-heartedness of the people of Israel during the time of Isaiah, Jesus indicated that he was speaking in parables to the outsiders as a form of prophetic warning of the serious consequences for all who do not open their hearts to him [ESVfn].

QUESTION—What relationship is indicated by the conjunction ἵνα 'so that'?

1. The conjunction ἵνα means 'so that' and indicates the purpose for teaching with parables [AB2, BECNT, BNTC, CGTC, EBC, EGT, ESVfn, Gnd, ICC, Lns, My, NICNT, NTC, PNTC, Sw, Tay, TH, TRT,

WBC; NLT]: *to the ones outside all things come in parables in order that they may not understand.* Jesus was carrying out God's judicial sentence of blindness pronounced on those who refused to see [Lns, NTC, PNTC, Sw]. God's original purpose was that people should see and understand in order to be converted and obtain remission of their sins. Yet when people persist in unbelief, God's judicial purpose is to block actual seeing and understanding so that they will not turn and be saved [Lns]. Jesus spoke in parables to outsiders as a form of *prophetic warning* of the serious consequences for those who do not accept him [ESVfn]. One reason Jesus taught in parables was to conceal the truth from persistent unbelievers so that they would not understand the full significance of his teaching about the kingdom of God and bring false charges against him before the Roman government. He also knew that in some cases understanding would result in more sin when the truth was not accepted. It is also a fact that God in his wisdom hardens persistent unbelievers in order to carry out his purposes [EBC]. People are excluded from being further instructed in the mystery of the kingdom so long as their unbelief continues [NICNT].

2. The conjunction ἵνα means 'so that' and indicates the consequence of teaching in parables [Hb, NAC; probably AB1]: *to the ones outside all things come in parables with the result that they do not understand.* Jesus taught in parables to provoke thought and to invite commitment [NAC]. Jesus did not want to hide the truth from the people, so he used parables in an effort to get their attention and stimulate reflection upon the truth contained in the parables. Depending on the attitude of the hearers, the parables either served to veil the truth or to unveil it. The scribes' persistent rejection of Jesus concealed the message from them and as a result, the parables became an instrument of judgment upon those self-blinded enemies of Christ [Hb].

lest[a] they-should-turn[b] and it-should-be-forgiven[c] them."

LEXICON—a. μήποτε (LN 89.62) (BAGD 2.b.α. p. 519): 'lest' [AB2, BAGD, BECNT, LN, Lns, NTC; ESV], 'lest at any time' [KJV], 'otherwise' [AB1, BNTC; NASB, NIV, NLT, REB], 'that...not' [BAGD], 'in order that...not' [LN], 'so that...not' [LN; NRSV], 'so' [NET], not explicit [GW]. This is also translated as a conditional phrase: 'if they did' [WBC; CEV], 'if they did learn and understand' [NCV], 'for if they did' [TEV]. This indicates a negative purpose and often implies apprehension [LN].

b. aorist act. subj. of ἐπιστρέφω (LN **41.51**) (BAGD 1.b.β. p. 301): 'to turn' [AB2, BAGD, BECNT, BNTC, Lns; ESV, NIV], 'to turn back, to turn around' [BAGD], 'to turn again' [NTC; NRSV], 'to turn to God' [AB1, **LN**; CEV, REB, TEV], 'to turn (to me)' [NLT], 'to return' [GW, NASB], 'to come back (to me)' [NCV], 'to repent' [WBC; NET], 'to change one's ways' [LN], 'to be converted' [KJV]. This verb means to change one's manner of life in a particular direction, and is used in relation to turning

back to God [LN]. This is a figurative meaning of 'to turn' and refers to a change of mind or course of action [BAGD].
  c. aorist act. subj. of ἀφίημι (LN 40.8): 'to be forgiven' [AB2, BECNT, BNTC, LN, NTC, WBC; all versions except CEV, KJV, TEV], 'to be pardoned' [LN], 'to be remitted' [Lns]. The phrase 'it should be forgiven them' is translated 'their sins should be forgiven them' [KJV], 'and he would forgive them' [AB1; CEV, TEV]. This verb means to remove the guilt resulting from wrongdoing [LN]. The passive voice implies that it is God who has not forgiven them [BECNT].

QUESTION—What relationship is indicated by the conjunction μήποτε 'lest'?
  1. Following the preceding ἵνα 'so that' clause, this gives the negative purpose for teaching in parables [AB1, AB2, BNTC, CGTC, ICC, Lns, NTC, Sw, Tay, TH]. God's judicial sentence of blindness is being fulfilled on those who choose not to see [Sw].
  2. This indicates the purpose of those people who will not perceive and understand. It implies that they refuse to see and hear because they want to avoid turning from their sin. It is not God's intention to keep them from turning away from sin [Hb].

QUESTION—What is meant by turning?
This refers to turning from their sin of rejecting the truth [Hb]. Turning means to repent [BECNT; NET], to be converted [Lns; KJV], to come back to God [NCV], to turn to God [NLT].

DISCOURSE UNIT—4:13–25 [NASB]. The topic is an explanation of the parable.

DISCOURSE UNIT—4:13–20 [EBC, NICNT; CEV, NCV, NLT, TEV]. The topic is the interpretation of the parable of the sower [EBC, NICNT], the interpretation of the parable of the farmer scattering seed [NLT], Jesus explains the parable of the sower [TEV], Jesus explains the story about the farmer [CEV], Jesus explains the seed story [NCV].

4:13 And he-says to-them, "Do-you- not -understand[a] this parable? And how will-you-understand[b] all[c] the parables?

LEXICON—a. perf. act. indic. of οἶδα (LN 32.4) (BAGD 4. p. 556): 'to understand' [AB1, BAGD, BECNT, BNTC, LN, WBC; all versions except KJV], 'to comprehend' [LN], 'to grasp' [WBC], 'to know' [AB2, Lns, NTC; KJV], 'to recognize, to come to know, to experience' [BAGD]. This verb means to comprehend the meaning of something, with the focus upon the resulting knowledge [LN].
  b. fut. mid. (deponent = act.) indic. of γινώσκω (LN 32.16) (BAGD 3.a. p. 161): 'to understand' [AB1, BAGD, BECNT, BNTC, NTC; all versions except KJV], 'to comprehend' [BAGD, LN], 'to know' [AB2, Lns; KJV], 'to come to understand, to perceive' [LN]. This verb means to come to an understanding as the result of the ability to experience and learn [LN].

c. πᾶς (LN 59.23) (BAGD 1.d.α p. 632): 'all' [BAGD, LN;], 'every, each' [LN]. The phrase 'all the parables' [AB2, Lns, NTC, WBC; ESV, KJV, NASB, NRSV] is also translated 'all of the other parables' [AB2, BECNT; NLT], 'any parable' [AB1; NET, NIV, REB, TEV], 'any of the parables' [BNTC], 'any story' [NCV], 'any of the stories I use as illustrations' [GW], 'any others' [CEV]. This adjective refers to the totality of any object, mass, or extension [LN].

QUESTION—How is this verse connected with what precedes?

'Them' refers to the disciples mentioned in 4:10 [TRT]. The disciples had asked Jesus about the parables in verse 10, and now Jesus explains the parable he had told them in 4:3–8 [BECNT, BNTC, Lns, My, NCBC, PNTC]. Jesus answers their question by giving them an example of interpretation instead of general rules [Hb].

QUESTION—What is the function of these two rhetorical questions?

The first question assumes that the disciples did not understand the parable about sowing the seeds [Hb, Lns] and it rebukes them for not understanding it [AB2, EBC, EGT, NIGTC, Sw, TH, WBC]. It also implies that they should give attention to what Jesus was going to say about the parable [AB2]. The second question infers that since they couldn't understand the first parable, they will not be able to understand the rest of the parables [ICC, WBC]. The first question can be taken as a condition to the second question [Gnd, TRT; NLT]: 'If you can't understand the meaning of this parable, how will you understand all the other parables?' [NLT]. Removing the question forms altogether, it comes out, 'If you don't understand this story, you won't understand any others' [CEV].

QUESTION—If they don't understand the parable about the sower, why will they not be able to understand other parables?

It implies that understanding the first parable is the key to understanding other parables about the kingdom of God [BNTC, CGTC, Hb, NIGTC]. The other parables are of a similar nature, so the disciples wouldn't be able to understand them any better [ICC]. The words 'all the parables' refer to all of the parables that Jesus will teach in his ministry [Sw, Tay], or all the parables that he had taught that day [EGT].

QUESTION—What is the distinction between the verb οἴδατε 'do you (not) understand' in the first question and γνώσεσθε '(how) will you understand' in the second question?

The first verb refers to knowing by intuition while the second verb refers to knowing by experience [AB1, NTC, Tay, TH]. Some translate the verbs differently: 'know what it means…understand' [NTC], 'grasp…understand' [WBC]. However, we should not try to make a strict distinction here between these verbs [TH]. Most translate both verbs the same [AB1, AB2, BECNT, BNTC, NICNT, TH; all versions].

4:14 The (one) sowing[a] sows the word.[b]

LEXICON—a. present active participle of σπείρω (LN 43.6) (1.b.β. p. 761): 'to sow' [BAGD, LN]. The phrase 'the one sowing' is translated 'the sower' [AB1, AB2, BECNT, BNTC, Lns, NTC, WBC; KJV, NASB, NRSV, REB, TEV], 'the/a farmer' [CEV, ESV, GW, NCV, NET, NIV, NLT]. This verb 'sowing' means to scatter seed over tilled ground [LN].

b. λόγος (LN 33.260) (BAGD 1.b.β. p. 478): 'word' [AB1, AB2, BECNT, BNTC, Lns, NTC, WBC; ESV, GW, KJV, NASB, NET, NIV, NRSV, REB], 'God's word' [NLT], 'God's message' [NCV, TEV], 'the message about the kingdom' [CEV], 'the gospel' [LN]. This noun denotes the content of what is preached about the good news and about Christ [LN].

QUESTION—What is the 'word' that is represented by the seed being sown in the parable?

In the explanation of this parable in Matthew 13:19, Jesus says that the seed is 'the word of the kingdom' [CBC, EBC, Hb, Lns, WBC; CEV]. In Luke 8:11 the seed is identified as 'the word of God' [Hb; NLT]. The 'word' is God's message [NCV, TEV], the gospel [BECNT, BNTC], the gospel of salvation [Lns], the Christian message [AB1, NCBC, Tay, TH]. The word of the kingdom concerns the coming of the reign of God in the person and work of Jesus [EBC]. The seed is the message that Jesus had been teaching in Galilee, and this parable focuses on the effects this message has on the different types of people represented by the four types of soil [NIGTC].

QUESTION—Who does the man who sows the word represent?

Since the parable is about what happens to the seeds, the 'sower' is merely a part of a story about seeds being sown in various types of soil [Tay]. Although the sower is not identified, the seed is Jesus' word as he proclaims the kingdom of God [NICNT], so the sower of the word is Jesus [BECNT, BNTC, EBC, ESVfn, Lns, NICNT, NTC]. In Matt. 13:37, the parable of the tares is another story about a man sowing seeds in a field, and there the man is identified as being the Son of Man, so probably that identification also holds for this parable [NTC]. The ambiguity about whether the sower is God, Christ, or a Christian preacher may be intentional [AB2]. The sower could represent every person who proclaims the word [BNTC, ESVfn, NCBC, NLTfn]. In any case, the emphasis is placed on the proclamation of the word and the reception it receives, not on the sower who is mentioned only in verses 3 and 14 [BECNT].

4:15 And these are the (ones) along the road where the word is-sown and when they-hear (it), immediately Satan comes and takes-away[a] the word (that) has-been sown in[b] them.

TEXT—Manuscripts reading εἰς αὐτούς 'in them' are given a C rating by GNT to indicate that choosing it over a variant text was difficult. A variant reading is ἐν ταῖς καρδίαις αὐτῶν 'in their hearts' and it is followed by KJV. Other variant readings are ἐν αὐτοῖς 'in them' and ἀπὸ τῆς καρδίας αὐτῶν 'from their heart'.

LEXICON—a. pres. act. indic. of αἴρω (LN 20.43): 'to take away' [AB1, AB2, BECNT, BNTC, Lns, NTC, WBC; all versions except CEV, NET, REB], 'to snatch' [NET], 'to snatch away' [CEV], 'to carry off' [REB], 'to destroy, to do away with' [LN]. This verb means to destroy and it implies the removal and doing away with something [LN].

b. εἰς (LN 83.13): 'in' [AB1, AB2, BECNT, BNTC, LN (83.13), NTC, WBC; all versions except CEV, NLT, TEV], 'into' [LN (84.22), Lns], 'inside, within' [LN (83.13)], not explicit [CEV, NLT, TEV]. This preposition refers to a position defined as being within certain limits [LN].

QUESTION—What element in the four stories of the seeds sown in different locations represents the people referred to by οὗτοι 'these'?

In all four stories, the demonstratives ('these, others, those, the ones, them'), the prepositional phrases, and the participles are not neuter as they would be if they referred to the neuter gender noun σπέρμα 'seed'. Instead, they are masculine nouns that refer to the men or people who are the listeners that receive the word proclaimed to them [TH]. Neither Matthew, Mark, or Luke have a perfectly logical structure [NIGTC]. There is some confusion [ICC] and inconsistency [CGTC, TH]. In 4:14, the seed that is sown is said to be the word, but the exact identification of the seed becomes confusing as the parable continues [BECNT]. It speaks of people being sown, so that the seeds now seem to refer to the different kinds of people who receive the word [AB2]. The focus of the parable is not on the seeds but on the listeners who receive the word proclaimed to them [TH].

1. The soils upon which the seeds are sown represent different kinds of people [AB1, BECNT, ESVfn, Hb, ICC, NIGTC, NLTfn, NTC, TH, TRT; probably EGT]. The seed cannot be both the word and the soil since the word 'seed' is in the singular and the demonstratives 'these, others, those' are in the plural to refer to the people who are represented by the kinds of soil. These people could be called 'the beside-the-path-people', 'the rocky-soil people', 'the thorny-soil people', and 'the good-soil people' in whom the word is sown [BECNT]. The focus is on the effect of the seed (the word) on the different types of soil (the people) [NIGTC]. In each case, the seed is the word of God and the soil is the heart of a person [NTC]. The stories about different kinds of soils illustrate the different attitudes people have toward Jesus and explain the indifference and opposition that Jesus encountered [Hb]. In the Greek, it appears to say that different kinds of people are sown, but of course it is the word that is sown, and the different types of soil are the various types of people. A translation that does justice to the Greek is: 'Those on the path are those in whom the Word is sown.... Then there are those in whom the message is sown on rocky ground.... And there are those who receive the word among thistles.... But there are those who receive the seed on good ground' [AB1].

2. The seeds that are sown represent the different kinds of people in all or some of the four illustrations.

2.1 The seeds in all four illustrations represent people who hear the word [CBC, My, NCBC, PNTC, WBC]. There are two different kinds of seed in the parable. First there is the seed that is extraneous to the details of the parable and represents the word that is sown by the sower in 4:14, taken away by Satan in 4:15, and choked in 4:18–19. The second kind of seed is at the core of the parable and represents the four types of hearers of the word [CBC, WBC].

2.2 The seed represents the word in 4:15, but represents the different kinds of people in 4:16–17, 4:18–19, and 4:20 [BNTC, NIGTC]. The differences are not in the seed, but in the nature of the responses to it [BECNT].

2.3 The seed represents both the hearers and the word [CBC, CGTC, Gnd, Sw]. Sometimes the seed represents both the word and the different kinds of people [CGTC]. There is a confusion between the seed and the soil [ICC]. The seed sown by the sower is the word, yet the masculine plural word οὗτοι 'these' refers to people who are like the seed sown in different kinds of soil [Gnd]. The seed is the word when it is sown, but that seed becomes the plants (people) that bear fruit or fail to do so. Also the hearer of the gospel is both the plant and the soil [Sw]. In the three stories of 4:16, 18, and 20 the hearers are clearly identified with the seed, while in 4:15 it appears that they are identified with both the seed and the soil [CGTC].

3. The stories concerning seeds sown in certain kinds of soil are about how the word affects different kinds of people [EBC, EGT, NIGTC; NCV]. This is a symbolic story describing the fate of a seed when it is sown on a particular kind of soil. The parable describes the kind of reception the word of the kingdom receives [EBC]. A pedantic interpreter would need to say something like this: 'The fate of the seed sown in the rocky soil represents what happens to the word when it is preached among people who…' [NIGTC]. Each illustration is identified by stating where the seed fell, and then it tells what happens to the different kinds of people: 'Sometimes the teaching falls on the road. This is like the people who hear the teaching of God, but Satan quickly comes and takes away the teaching that was planted in them' [NCV].

QUESTION—How does Satan take away the word from these people?

Satan takes it away from their minds and hearts [ICC, Lns]. He removes it by the power of suggestion or persuasion [Hb]. It is implied that the people did not receive the Word [Tay].

4:16 **And these are the (ones) being-sown upon the rocky-ground, who when they-hear the word immediately they-receive[a] it with joy,**

LEXICON—a. pres. act. indic. of λαμβάνω (LN 31.50) (BAGD 1.e.β p. 464): 'to receive' [AB1, AB2, BAGD, BECNT, BNTC, LN, Lns, WBC; ESV, KJV, NASB, NET, NIV, NLT, NRSV, TEV], 'to accept' [LN, NTC; CEV, GW, NCV, REB], 'to come to believe' [LN]. This verb means to come to believe something and to act in accordance with such a belief [LN].

QUESTION—What is meant by seeds being sown on rocky ground?

The seeds were not just thrown down on top of rocks. The plural πετρώδη 'rocky ground' indicates that there were several places in the field where there was an underlying rock ledge [Hb].

QUESTION—How did they receive the word with joy?

Regarding the word to be desirable and attractive, they responded with enthusiasm without considering its implications [Hb].

4:17 **and they-do- not -have[a] a-root in themselves but are temporary,[b] then (when) trouble[c] comes or persecution[d] because of the word immediately they-fall-away.[e]**

LEXICON—a. pres. act. indic. of ἔχω (LN 57.1): 'to have' [LN]. The clause 'they do not have a root in themselves' [WBC] is also translated 'they have no root in themselves' [BECNT, NTC; ESV, KJV, NET; similarly AB2, BNTC, Lns], 'they have no firm root in themselves' [NASB], 'they have no root' [NIV, NRSV], 'they don't have any roots' [CEV], 'they don't have deep roots' [NLT], 'they don't develop any roots' [GW], 'it strikes no root in them' [AB1; REB], 'it does not sink deeply into them' [TEV], 'they don't allow the teaching to go deep into their lives' [NCV]. This verb means to have or possess objects [LN].

b. πρόσκαιρος (LN 67.109) (BAGD p. 715): 'temporary' [BAGD, LN], 'transitory, lasting only a little while' [BAGD], 'not long, for a little while, for a while' [LN]. The phrase 'are temporary' is translated 'are temporary' [AB2; similarly NASB], 'are only transient' [Lns], 'they last for a short time' [WBC; GW; similarly NTC; NIV], 'they are short-lived' [BNTC], 'they keep it (the teaching) only a short time' [NCV], 'they don't last very long' [CEV; similarly NLT, TEV], 'they have no stability' [AB1], 'they have no staying power' [REB], 'they do not endure' [NET], 'they only endure for a short time' [BECNT], 'they endure for a while' [ESV; similarly KJV, NRSV]. This adjective describes something as having a relatively short period of time, and there is an emphasis upon its temporary nature [LN].

c. θλῖψις (LN 22.2) (BAGD 1. p. 362): 'trouble' [AB1, BNTC, LN; NCV, NET, NIV, NRSV, REB, TEV], 'suffering' [LN; GW], 'oppression' [BAGD], 'affliction' [BAGD, Lns, NTC, WBC; KJV, NASB], 'tribulation' [AB2, BAGD, BECNT; ESV], 'persecution' [LN]. The phrase 'when trouble comes' is translated 'as soon as they have problems' [NLT], 'as soon as life gets hard' [CEV]. This noun denotes trouble that involves direct suffering [LN]. It denotes stress that is brought about by outward circumstances [BAGD].

d. διωγμός (LN 39.45) (BAGD p. 201): 'persecution' [AB1, AB2, BAGD, BECNT, BNTC, LN, Lns, NTC, WBC; all versions except CEV, NLT]. The phrase 'persecution because of the word' is translated 'are persecuted

for believing God's word' [NLT], 'the message gets them in trouble' [CEV]. This noun denotes a program organized to systematically oppress and harass people [LN].
- e. pres. pass. indic. of σκανδαλίζομαι, σκανδαλίζω (LN 31.77) (BAGD 1.a. p. 752): 'to fall away' [AB2, BAGD, BECNT, BNTC, NTC, WBC; ESV, NASB, NET, NIV, NLT, NRSV], 'to fall (from faith)' [GW], 'to give up' [AB1; CEV, NCV, TEV], 'to cease believing, to give up believing' [LN] 'to lose faith' [REB], 'to be offended' [KJV], 'to be caught' [Lns]. This verb is a figurative extension of 'falling into a trap' and means to give up believing what is right and believing what is false [LN].

QUESTION—What is meant by 'not having root in themselves'?

Having no root means that the plant does not have a sufficient root system [Gnd]. The picture is of the plants growing in shallow soil so that the roots do not grow as deeply as they should, and this symbolizes people who have no deep convictions and therefore lack stability and endurance [TH]. The message did not penetrate into their inner life, so it did not transform their nature [Hb].

QUESTION—What is meant by θλῖψις 'trouble'?

This refers to tribulation and trials caused by pressure from various providential experiences [Hb]. It is a crushing sorrow of any kind [Sw]. The troubles are difficulties and hardships brought about by either people or circumstances [TH].

QUESTION—What is meant by διωγμός 'persecution'?

Persecution is the result of human hatred and enmity [TH]. These people are persecuted on account of the word [BNTC]. It refers to any social pressure against the Jesus movement when it challenges the norms of society [NIGTC]. Because they professed to accept the word, they are harassed by enemies of the word [Hb].

QUESTION—What is meant by such people σκανδαλίζονται 'falling away'?

The verb pictures people being lured into a trap or snare, which indicates that they have been lured into sin and have fallen away [NTC]. The shame they feel in being persecuted overcomes their commitment to the word [CBC]. These troubles cause them to sin by giving up their profession of faith [Hb]. They are offended [Lns, TH], and repelled so that they abandon their faith in the word, either temporarily or permanently [TH]. In the NT this verb means that someone is caused to stumble or to fall away [EBC]. It may be a moral stumbling that falls short of apostasy [Sw]. Or, this refers to permanent apostasy caused by giving way to the constant pressure of persecution [NIGTC].

4:18 And others are the (ones) being-sown among the thorns. These are the (ones) having-heard the word, **4:19** and the worries[a] of-the age and the seduction[b] of-wealth and the desires[c] for the other (things) coming-in choke[d] the word and it-becomes unfruitful.[e]

LEXICON—a. μέριμνα (LN 25.224) (BAGD p. 504): 'worry, anxiety' [BAGD, LN], 'anxious concern' [LN]. The phrase αἱ μέριμναι τοῦ αἰῶνος 'the worries of the age' is translated 'the anxieties of this age' [WBC], 'the anxieties of this life' [AB1], 'the cares of this age' [BECNT; similarly AB2], 'the cares of this/the world' [ESV, KJV, NRSV], 'the cares of this present world' [NTC], 'the worries of the world' [NASB], 'the worries of this eon' [Lns], 'the worries of this life' [NCV, NIV, NLT; similarly GW], 'the worries about this life' [TEV], 'worldly cares' [BNTC; NET, REB], 'they start worrying about the needs of this life' [CEV]. This noun denotes a feeling of apprehension or distress in view of possible danger or misfortune (LN).

b. ἀπάτη (LN **31.12**) (BAGD 1. p. 82): 'seduction' [BAGD], 'deception' [LN], 'deceitfulness' [BAGD]. The phrase ἡ ἀπάτη τοῦ πλούτου 'the seduction of wealth' [BNTC] is also translated 'the seductiveness of wealth' [NET], 'the lure of wealth' [NLT, NRSV], 'the love for riches' [TEV], 'the deceitfulness of riches/wealth' [AB2, BECNT; ESV, KJV, NASB, NIV], 'the deceit of wealth' [Lns, WBC], 'the deceitful pleasures of riches' [GW], 'the deceitful glamour of riches' [NTC], 'the deceptive attraction of riches' [AB1], 'the false glamour of wealth' [REB], 'the temptation of wealth' [NCV], 'being misled by riches' [**LN**], 'they are fooled by the desire to get rich' [CEV]. This noun denotes misleading or erroneous views concerning the truth [LN].

c. ἐπιθυμία (LN 25.12) (BAGD 1. p. 293): 'desire' [BAGD]. The phrase αἱ περὶ τὰ λοιπὰ ἐπιθυμίαι 'the desires/desire for other things' [AB2, BAGD, BECNT, NTC, WBC; ESV, GW, NASB, NET, NIV, NLT, NRSV] is also translated 'the lusts of other things' [KJV], 'the lusts concerning the remaining things' [Lns], 'evil desires of all kinds' [REB], '(they are fooled by) the desire to have all kinds of other things' [CEV], 'desires of other kinds' [BNTC], 'all other kinds of desires' [AB1; TEV], 'many other evil desires' [NCV]. This noun denotes a deep desire to do or have something [LN].

d. pres. act. indic. of συμπνίγω (LN 22.22) (BAGD 1. p. 779): 'to choke' [BAGD], 'to cause severe hardship, to oppress, to overwhelm' [LN]. The phrase 'choke the word' [AB1, BECNT, BNTC, Lns, NTC, WBC; ESV, GW, KJV, NASB, NET, NIV, NRSV, REB] is also translated 'choke the message' [TEV], 'strangle the word' [AB2], 'so the message gets choked out' [CEV], 'all too quickly the message is crowded out' [NLT], 'keep the teaching from growing' [NCV]. This verb is a figurative extension of the verb πνίγω 'to choke' and means to cause serious trouble to something, and implies that there will be dire consequences, probably resulting in a weakened state [LN]. Its meaning 'to crowd together and choke' concerns plants whose food and light is cut off by weeds [BAGD].

e. ἄκαρπος (LN 65.34) (BAGD 2. p. 29): 'unproductive, useless' [BAGD, LN]. The phrase 'it becomes unfruitful' [AB2, BECNT, Lns, NTC; NASB] is also translated 'it is unfruitful' [WBC], 'it proves unfruitful' [ESV], 'making it unfruitful' [NIV], 'so no fruit is produced' [NLT], 'it yields nothing' [BNTC; NRSV], 'it will not yield anything' [AB1], 'it can't produce anything' [GW], 'it produces nothing' [NET], 'it proves barren' [REB], 'they never produce anything' [CEV], 'they don't bear fruit' [TEV], '(keep the teaching from) producing fruit in their lives' [NCV]. This adjective describes something as being useless in the sense of being unproductive [LN].

QUESTION—What are the 'worries of the age'?

It refers to the anxieties, worries, and cares of this world [TH]. They are the anxieties arising out of the particular times and circumstances [AB1]. It concerns the worries of the age in which one lives, with every age having its own types of worries [Lns]. These worries drew their minds in different directions so that they neglected spiritual and eternal concerns [Hb].

QUESTION—What is the seduction of wealth?

This word has elements of deceitfulness and pleasure in a bad sense [EBC, TH].. It is deceitful because it gives a false sense of security [EBC]. Wealth deceives by promising a satisfaction it cannot bring [Lns]. They were enticed to strive for the delights promised by wealth, a goal they will never realize [Hb]. They imagine that if they were richer they would then be satisfied [NTC].

QUESTION—What are the desires for other things?

It refers to desires for all those things that are not included in the worries about wealth [Lns, NIGTC]. This is an all-inclusive statement that includes everything else that would prevent the word from being productive [EBC]. This is the essence of materialism, the constant desire for more [NIGTC].

QUESTION—What is meant by choking the word so that it becomes unfruitful?

The things that people crave in this life force their way into the heart after the word had found lodgment there and compete with the word in their thoughts until they take the place the word had [Hb]. The word is prevented from being productive in one's life [EBC]. This is not spelled out, but it involves a lack of conformity to the principles of the kingdom and a lack of opposition to worldly values [NIGTC].

4:20 And those are the (ones) having-been sown on the good soil, who hear the word and accept[a] (it) and bear-fruit,[b] one thirty and one sixty and one one-hundred."

TEXT—Manuscripts reading the neuter ἓν 'one' with each different amount are given a C rating by GNT to indicate that choosing it over a variant text was difficult. A variant reading is the preposition ἐν 'in' with each of the amounts. One manuscript reads τὸ ἕν 'the one' with each amount. Another manuscript has the combination ἐν...ἕν...ἕν... 'in...one...one...'.

LEXICON—a. pres. mid./pass. (deponent = act.) indic. of παραδέχομαι (LN 31.52) (BAGD 1. p. 614): 'to accept' [AB2; BAGD, BNTC, LN, NTC; all versions except CEV, KJV, NET], 'to receive' [AB1, BAGD, LN, Lns, WBC; KJV, NET], 'to welcome' [BECNT; CEV]. This verb means to come to believe something to be true and then respond accordingly [LN].

   b. pres. act. indic. of καρποφορέω (LN 23.199) (BAGD 2. p. 405): 'to bear fruit' [AB1, AB2, BAGD, BECNT, BNTC, LN, Lns, NTC, WBC; ESV, NASB, NET, NRSV, REB, TEV], 'to produce crops/a crop' [GW, NIV], 'to produce a harvest' [NLT], 'to produce fruit' [LN; NCV], 'to bring forth fruit' [KJV], 'they produce (thirty...times) as much as was planted' [CEV], 'to produce seed, to yield' [LN]. This verb means to produce fruit or seed [LN]. To bear fruit in one's inner life is used figuratively of resolving to do what is right [BAGD].

QUESTION—What is meant by 'receiving' the word?

It means that when they heard the word, they believed and accepted it [TH]. They welcomed the word and allowed it to work out its purpose in their lives [Hb]. They put the word into practice [NTC].

QUESTION—In what way do people bear fruit?

The parable leaves it up to the reader to decide what sort of fruit is in view and what affects the different rates of yield [NIGTC]. The readers of this Gospel would have thought that the amount of yield involved a person's faithfulness to Jesus and his teaching [BECNT]. People bear fruit by obeying the word of the kingdom of God [Gnd]. They put the message into practice and they bear the fruit of faith, love, joy, etc. [NTC]. As they receive the word and submit to its demands, their lives are characterized by personal goodness and power for continued service to God's glory [Hb]. The fruit involves faithfulness to Jesus and his teachings [BECNT]. Bearing fruit may refer to a deepening loyalty to the word, or to spreading the word through the example of their own obedience to it [NCBC]. The word multiplies by spreading from one heart to another and causes the hearers to bear fruit in regards to repentance, faith, Christian virtues, and works [Lns].

DISCOURSE UNIT—4:21–25 [CBC, EBC, Hb, NICNT; CEV, ESV, GW, NASB, NCV, NET, NIV, NLT, TEV]. The topic is the parable of the lamp [CBC; NET, NLT], a story about a lamp [GW], a lamp under a basket [ESV], a lamp under a bowl [TEV], a lamp under a bushel basket [NASB], a lamp on a stand [NIV], light [CEV], the parables of the lamp and the measures [EBC], the responsibility of the hearers [Hb], exhortation to true hearing [NICNT], use what you have [NCV].

4:21 And he-was-saying to-them, "The lamp[a] does- not -come[b] in-order-that it-may-be-placed under the basket[c] or under the couch/bed[d] (does it)? Is it not in-order-that it-may-be-placed upon the lampstand[e]?

LEXICON—a. λύχνος (LN **6.104**) (BAGD 1. p. 483): 'lamp' [AB1, AB2, BAGD, BECNT, BNTC, **LN**, Lns, NTC, WBC; all versions except KJV], 'candle' [KJV]. This noun denotes a relatively small vessel that produces light from a burning wick saturated with oil [LN].

    b. pres. mid./pass. (deponent = act.) indic. of ἔρχομαι (LN **15.7**) (BAGD I.1.c.β. p. 311): 'to come' [BAGD, LN]. The phrase Μήτι ἔρχεται ὁ λύχνος 'The lamp does not come...does it?' is translated 'A lamp certainly doesn't come...does it?' [**LN**], 'A lamp is not brought...is it?' [NTC; NASB, NET], 'Do you hide a lamp under...? No!' [NCV], 'Would anyone light a lamp and then...? Of course not!' [NLT], 'Does the lamp come' [AB2, BECNT], 'Is a lamp brought in' [ESV, NRSV, REB; similarly KJV], 'Does anyone bring in the lamp' [AB1; similarly NIV, TEV], 'Does anyone bring a lamp into a room' [GW], 'Do you fetch a lamp' [BNTC], 'Certainly the lamp does not come' [Lns], 'You don't light a lamp and put it...' [CEV]. This verb means to move from one place to another, either coming or going, but because the subject is a lamp, which would not move by its own force, it would need to be brought into the room by someone. It often needs to be translated 'no one brings a lamp' [LN]. Saying that the lamp 'comes' is a colloquial personification [Hb]. In relation to things, this verb has the sense of 'to be brought' [BAGD, TH]. 'Come' describes the light being brought in by a servant [Lns]. Or, the use of the verb 'come' is understandable if Jesus was speaking of himself as the lamp that has come [BECNT, BNTC, EBC, NAC, NICNT, PNTC, TRT]. However, the other meaning of ἔρχομαι, 'to be brought', is not so unnatural as to require a connection to the coming of Jesus [NIGTC].

    c. μόδιος (LN 6.151) (BAGD p. 525): 'basket' [BECNT, LN; ESV, GW, NASB, NET, NLT], 'box, bucket' [LN], 'clay pot' [CEV], 'bowl' [LN; NCV, NIV, TEV], 'measuring bowl' [AB1; REB], 'measure' [BNTC], 'bushel' [AB2, WBC; KJV], 'bushel basket' [NRSV], 'peck-measure' [Lns, NTC]. This noun denotes a container for dry matter and it has a capacity of about two gallons [LN].

    d. κλίνη (LN 6.106) (BAGD p. 436): 'bed' [AB1, AB2, BAGD, BECNT, BNTC, LN, Lns, NTC, WBC; all versions], 'cot' [LN], 'couch' [BAGD, LN]. This noun denotes any piece of furniture that is used for reclining or lying on [LN].

    e. λυχνία (LN 6.105) (BAGD p. 483): 'lampstand' [AB1, AB2, BAGD, BECNT, BNTC, LN, Lns, NTC, WBC; CEV, GW, NASB, NCV, NET, NRSV, REB, TEV], 'a/its stand' [ESV, NIV], 'candlestick' [KJV]. The phrase 'in order that it may be placed upon the lampstand' is translated 'a lamp is placed on a stand, where its light will shine' [NLT]. This noun denotes a stand that is designed to hold a single lamp or a series of lamps [LN]. Lamps were either placed on a stand or hung from it [BAGD].

QUESTION—To whom was Jesus speaking?

The phrase 'and he was saying to them' usually indicates a change of subject, but these sayings are quite appropriate to the same limited group mentioned in 4:10 [BECNT, BNTC, Hb, ICC, Lns, NTC, WBC]. This was the group to whom the mystery of the kingdom had been given [WBC]. It is a sample of parabolic teaching to the crowds at the Lake of Galilee [NICNT, PNTC, TRT]. The following admonition to understand the teaching recalls verses 3 and 9, so probably the same crowd is again present [NICNT].

QUESTION—What kind of answers do these two rhetorical questions call for?

The first question is a double one that expects a no answer for the first, and the second question expects a yes answer [AB2, BECNT, BNTC, Hb, Lns, NIGTC, NTC, TH, WBC]. To cover the lamp would be absurd [Gnd, Lns, NTC]. Such answers indicate that the true function of a lamp is to give light [Tay] and to give as much light as possible [NIGTC].

QUESTION—What kind of lamp is this parable speaking about?

It was a shallow bowl containing a wick and filled with oil [TH]. Probably it was a small closed terracotta bowl with a hole in the top to pour in a small amount of olive oil. It had a handle and a spout for the wick [Hb, Lns, NTC].

QUESTION—What is a μόδιος 'basket'?

It originally referred to a bushel measure but came to mean a measure of any size [NICNT]. It held a little more than a peck [Hb]. It was probably a large bowl for holding and measuring grain [TH]. It was a common two-gallon bowl [PNTC, Tay, TRT]. It had to be large enough to cover a lamp [TRT].

QUESTION—What is a κλίνη 'couch'?

It was something used for reclining, and in this context it probably refers to a dining couch [Gnd, Hb, My, TH], or a bench [NICNT], or a bed [AB1, AB2, BAGD, BECNT, BNTC, LN, Lns, NTC, PNTC, WBC; all versions]. It could be a bed that was high enough so that it wouldn't be in danger of catching on fire from the lamp [EGT, TRT]. It is apparent that it would be foolish to put it under a bed and set the bed on fire [Gnd].

QUESTION—What was a λυχνία 'lampstand'?

It was a projection from the wall on which a lamp could be placed [Hb]. It might have been a shelf attached to a pillar in the center of the room or just a stone projecting from the wall [NTC].

QUESTION—Is the presence of the article 'the' before each piece of furniture significant?

The article is properly used with these nouns since usually Galilean homes would have just one of each of these items of furniture [AB1, NTC]. No significance is to be attached to this article [Gnd, WBC]. The phrase '*the* lamp' might suggest that the lamp refers to something definite, probably to the coming of the kingdom of God in the person of Jesus [BECNT].

4:22 Because there is not (anything) hidden[a] except in-order-that it-be-revealed,[b] nor has-it-become secret[c] but in-order-that it-may-come into (the) open.[d]

LEXICON—a. κρυπτός (LN 28.69) (BAGD 1. p. 454): 'hidden' [AB1, BAGD, BECNT, BNTC, LN, Lns, WBC; all versions except TEV], 'hid' [AB2], 'hidden away' [TEV], 'concealed' [NTC], 'secret' [BAGD, LN]. This adjective describes something that is not able to be seen or known [LN].
- b. aorist pass. subj. of φανερόω (LN 28.36) (BAGD 1.b. p. 852): 'to be revealed' [BAGD, BNTC, LN, WBC; GW, NASB, NET], 'to be made manifest' [AB2, BECNT, Lns; ESV], 'to be manifested' [KJV], 'to be made known, to be made plain, to be brought to the light' [LN], 'to become known, to become visible' [BAGD], 'to be disclosed' [AB1, LN, NTC; NIV, NRSV, REB], 'to be brought into the open' [NLT; similarly TEV], 'to be made public' [CEV], 'to be made clear' [NCV]. This verb means to cause something to be fully known by revealing it clearly and in some detail [LN].
- c. ἀπόκρυφος (LN 28.70) (BAGD p. 93): 'secret' [BECNT, LN, WBC; CEV, ESV, GW, KJV, NASB, NCV, NLT, NRSV], 'hidden' [AB2, BAGD], 'hidden away' [Lns], 'concealed' [BNTC; NET, NIV, REB], 'covered' [AB1], 'covered up' [NTC; TEV]. This adjective describes something as not being able to be known [LN].
- d. φανερός (LN 28.58) (BAGD 2. p. 852): 'the open' [BAGD], 'clearly known, easily known, evident, plain, clear' [LN]. The phrase 'to come into the open' [WBC] is also translated 'to be bought into the open' [BNTC; REB; similarly NIV, 'to be brought to light' [NET, NLT], 'to come to light' [AB1, BAGD, Lns, NTC; ESV, GW, NASB, NRSV], 'to be made known' [NCV], 'to be made manifest' [BECNT], 'might come to manifestation' [AB2], 'to be uncovered' [TEV], 'to be well known' [CEV], 'to come abroad' [KJV]. This adjective pertains to being clearly and easily known [LN].

QUESTION—What relationship is indicated by γάρ 'because'?

This conjunction explains the point of the figurative language in the preceding verse [Hb, Lns, Sw]. The point in verse 21 is that no one would bring in a lamp in order to cover it, but in the broader context of chapter 4, it is assumed that the lamp has been intentionally covered until the time comes to carry out its expected purpose [CGTC, WBC]. Although the example concerning the lamp does not explicitly say that the lamp was actually hidden, it refers to a time of being hidden [CGTC]. Jesus used parables to hide truth from the outsiders in order that he might reveal it through his explanations to the insiders [Gnd].

QUESTION—What is the relationship between the two clauses in this verse?

This is a case of synonymous parallelism in which the two clauses say the same thing with slightly different wording [BECNT, CGTC, NIGTC, TH, WBC].

QUESTION—What relationship is indicated by the use of the conjunction ἵνα 'in order that' in each clause?

The conjunctions indicate the purposes for something being hidden and for being made secret [BECNT, BNTC, Hb, ICC]. Although one normally hides something in order that it will not be seen and generally known, the purpose for hiding it is the opposite here [Lns]. It is planned that what is hidden is going to be made known, but this does not tell when it will happen or who will make it known [NIGTC].

QUESTION—How is this verse about hiding something in order to reveal it at a later time to be applied?

1. This is connected with 4:11–12 where it says that God did not want outsiders to understand the mystery of the kingdom and be forgiven. Although God has hidden this mystery at the present time, it will be revealed later [AB2, BECNT, CGTC, Hb, ICC, Lns, NAC, NIGTC, PNTC, Tay, WBC]. The parabolic teachings now hid the mystery of the kingdom from those who were outsiders, but Jesus' intention was that after his death and resurrection the disciples he had taught about the kingdom would make it known [Hb, Tay]. There is a clue in 9:9, where Jesus orders Peter, James, and John not to tell anyone about his transfiguration *until after* he had risen from the dead. It was then that the missionary activity of the disciples would take place [NIGTC]. The disciples are to be like lamps placed on a lampstand to shine forth the mystery of the gospel in the world [Lns]. Others think that the mystery will not be completely revealed until God's rule will become supreme [CBC, NAC, WBC]. Jesus was fully revealed after his resurrection, but the kingdom will not be fully revealed until after the final consummation of all things [NAC].
2. What has been hidden in parables spoken to the large crowds will be made known to Jesus' disciples in private explanations [Gnd].
3. The lamp represents Jesus who ἔρχεται 'comes'. As the purpose of the lamp is to be put on a lampstand, so the present hiddenness of Jesus will come to an end and he will be manifested in all his glory at the Second Coming. [EBC].
4. Although men may try to cover up sinful things, they will not get away with it since God will bring their evil thoughts, plans, words, and actions out into the open [NTC].

4:23 If anyone has ears to-hear, let-him-hear.[a]"

LEXICON—a. See the similar clause 'Who has ears to hear, let him hear' at 4:9.

4:24 And he-was-saying to-them, "Consider[a] what you-hear. By what measure[b] you-measure[c] it-will-be-measured to-you and it-will-be-added[d] to-you.

TEXT—Manuscripts reading καὶ προστεθήσεται ὑμῖν 'and it shall be added to you' are given an A rating by GNT to indicate it was regarded to be certain. Variant readings are καὶ προστεθήσεται ὑμῖν τοῖς ἀκούουσιν 'and it shall be added to you the ones hearing' and τοῖς ἀκούουσιν 'the ones hearing'. Some manuscripts omit this phrase.

LEXICON—a. pres. act. impera. of βλέπω (LN **27.58**) (BAGD 4.c. p. 143): 'to consider' [BAGD], 'to consider carefully' [NIV], 'to take notice of' [AB1], 'to pay attention to' [AB2, BECNT, BNTC, **LN**, WBC; ESV, GW, NRSV, TEV], 'to pay close attention' [NLT], 'to listen carefully' [CEV], 'to think carefully about' [NCV], 'to note, to direct one's attention to' [BAGD], 'to take note' [REB], 'to take heed' [KJV], 'to give heed' [Lns], 'to take care' [NASB, NET], 'to be careful about' [NTC], 'to beware of, to watch out for' [LN]. This verb means to be ready to learn about future dangers or needs, and implies being prepared to respond appropriately [LN].

b. μέτρον (LN 81.1) (BAGD 1.a. p. 515): 'measure' [AB1, AB2, BAGD, BECNT, BNTC, LN, Lns, NTC, WBC; ESV, KJV, NET, NIV, NRSV, REB], 'standard of measure' [NASB], not explicit [CEV, GW, NCV, NLT, TEV]. This noun denotes a unit of measurement, either of length or volume [LN].

c. pres. act. indic. of μετρέω (LN **57.92**) (BAGD 2. p. 514): 'to give' [LN], 'to give out, to deal out' [BAGD], 'to apportion' [BAGD, LN]. The clause ἐν ᾧ μέτρῳ μετρεῖτε μετρηθήσεται ὑμῖν 'by what measure you measure it will be measured to you' is taken in the following ways: (1) It is translated as a general rule: 'by/with what measure you measure it will be measured to you' [AB2, BECNT, WBC], 'the measure with which you measure is the measure by which you will receive' [BNTC], 'with the measure you use, it will be measured to you' [ESV, NIV, NRSV], 'the measure you use will be the measure you receive' [NET], 'with what measure ye mete, it shall be measured to you' [KJV], 'in accordance with the measure whereby you measure it shall be measured back to you' [NTC], 'in what measure you go on measuring it shall be measured to you' [Lns], 'the measure you give will be the measure you get' [BAGD, **LN**; similarly REB], 'by your standard of measure it will be measured to you' [NASB]; (2) It is translated in relation to receiving knowledge: 'knowledge will be measured out to you by the measure of attention you give' [GW], 'the closer you listen, the more understanding you will be given' [NLT]; (3) It is translated in regard to personal relationships: 'the way you give to others is the way God will give to you' [NCV], 'the way you treat others will be the way you will be treated' [CEV], 'he will deal with you in the manner that you deal with others' [**LN**], 'the measure you use in judgment will be the same measure which judges you' [AB1], 'the same rules you use to judge others will be used by God to judge you' [TEV]. This verb means to give a measured portion to someone [LN].

d. fut. pass. indic. of προστίθημι (LN 59.72) (BAGD 1.a. p. 719): 'to be added' [BAGD, LN]. The clause προστεθήσεται ὑμῖν 'it will be added to you' is translated (1) in relation to a general rule: 'and still more will be added to you' [ESV; similarly AB2; NET], 'and will be further added to you' [BECNT], 'and more besides shall be given to you' [NTC], 'and more besides' [BNTC], 'and even more' [NIV], 'and still more will be given you' [NRSV], 'and given additionally to you' [WBC], 'and more will be given you besides' [NASB], 'and more shall be added for good measure to you' [Lns], 'with something more besides' [REB], 'and unto you that hear shall more be given' [KJV]; (2) in relation to receiving knowledge: 'this is the way knowledge increases' [GW], 'and you will receive even more' [NLT], (3) in relation to personal relationships: 'but God will give you even more' [NCV], 'and with something more besides' [AB1], 'and even worse' [CEV], 'but with even greater severity' [TEV]. This verb means to add something to an existing quantity [LN].

QUESTION—What is meant by the command, 'Consider what you hear'?

1. This is an admonition to carefully consider the meaning of what Jesus was teaching them [AB1, CGTC, EGT, Gnd, Hb, ICC, Lns, My, NICNT, NIGTC, Sw, TH, WBC]. The amount of attention they give to Jesus' teaching will be the measure of the profit they will receive from that teaching [Sw]. It stresses the importance of how one hears [NIGTC]. The reason for doing so is given in the next sentence [Tay, WBC].

2. This is a warning to consider the kind of things they listen to [AB2, NTC]. They are to recognize the source of what they listen to. In this world there is not only the word of God but also the deceitful words of Satan that claim to be God's word [AB2]. They must listen attentively and judiciously to what they hear in order to determine what is to be accepted and what is to be rejected [NTC].

QUESTION—What is meant by ἐν ᾧ μέτρῳ μετρεῖτε μετρηθήσεται ὑμῖν 'by what measure you measure it will be measured to you'?

This is a proverbial saying that can be applied to a variety of situations [EBC, Lns, NIGTC, PNTC, Sw].

1. This refers to paying attention to Jesus' teaching and responding to it [BECNT, BNTC, CBC, CGTC, EGT, ESVfn, Gnd, Hb, ICC, Lns, My, NAC, NCBC, NICNT, NIGTC, NLTfn, Sw, TRT, WBC]. Jesus used this maxim in Matt. 7:2 to warn about the danger of judging others [Hb, WBC], but here the maxim is applied to the reward one derives from diligent effort [Hb], and it functions as a promise instead of a threat [WBC]. In the context of hearing, it means that the amount of attention they give to Jesus' message affects the profit they will gain from it [AB2, BNTC, Hb, Lns, Sw]. This maxim is used in the context of hearing Jesus' message, so it probably means that the blessings they derive from his message will depend upon the way they respond to it [BNTC, CGTC]. God will generously give a blessing that is disproportionately large [CGTC]. The more one listens to the word of Jesus with spiritual perception and appropriates it, the more the truth about Jesus will be revealed [EBC]. It pays to listen carefully since the reward of attention is knowledge [EGT].

2. This has the same meaning as the identical passage in Matt. 7:2 where it refers to judging others [AB1, NTC; CEV, TEV]. When a person listens to something he should not be hearing, such as malicious gossip, he will be inclined to wrongly measure people and condemn them instead of being kind and judging favorably. Such a person must be warned that the measure he gives will be the measure he will get [NTC].

QUESTION—What is meant by the addition 'and it will be added to you'?

The passive voice implies that God will measure it out and even add to it [AB2, BECNT, CGTC, NICNT, PNTC, TRT; TEV]. God will not give just in proportion to one's effort, but because of his overwhelming grace he will give additional understanding concerning the person and work of Jesus and the arrival of his kingdom [BECNT].

4:25 Because whoever has[a], it-will-be-given[b] to-him. And whoever does-not -have, even what he-has will-be-taken-away[c] from him."

LEXICON—a. pres. act indic. of ἔχω (LN 57.1) (BAGD I.2.a. p. 332): 'to have' [AB1, AB2, BECNT, BNTC, LN, Lns, NTC, WBC; ESV, KJV, NASB, NET, NIV, NRSV, REB], 'to possess' [BAGD, LN]. The phrase 'whoever has' is translated 'everyone who has something' [CEV; similarly TEV], 'those who have understanding' [NCV], 'those who understand these mysteries' [GW], 'to those who listen to my teaching' [NLT]. This verb means to have or possess objects or property in the technical sense of having control over the use of such objects [LN].

b. fut. pass. indic. of δίδωμι (LN 57.71): 'to be given' [BECNT, LN, Lns, NTC, WBC; KJV]. The phrase δοθήσεται αὐτῷ 'it will be given to him' is translated 'to him more shall be given' [NASB; similarly ESV], 'will be given more' [AB1, BNTC; CEV, NCV, NET, NIV, NRSV, REB, TEV; similarly AB2], 'will be given more knowledge' [GW], 'more understanding will be given' [NLT]. This verb means to give an object, usually something of value [LN].

c. fut. pass. indic. of αἴρω (LN 90.96) (BAGD 4. p. 24): 'to be taken, to be removed' [BAGD, LN]. The clause 'even what he has will/shall be taken away from him' [AB2, BECNT, Lns; NASB; similarly NTC, WBC; ESV, KJV, NCV, NET, NIV, NRSV] is also translated 'will lose even what he has' [AB1], 'will have what he has taken away' [BNTC], 'will forfeit even what they have' [REB], 'will have taken away from them even the little they have' [TEV], 'will lose what little they have' [CEV], 'even what they have will be taken' [WBC], 'even what they understand will be taken away from them' [GW], 'even what little understanding they have will be taken away from them' [NLT]. The phrase αἴρω ἀπό 'to take from' is an idiom that means to cause someone to no longer experience something [LN].

QUESTION—What relationship is indicated by γάρ 'because'?

The preceding proverbial saying is explained by quoting another proverbial saying [BECNT, BNTC, Gnd, Hb, Lns, My, NTC, WBC]. It supports the command to *hear* with the promise of receiving an abundant understanding and a greater experience of the kingdom [WBC]. The idea in the preceding verse of more being given to those who already 'have' is reinforced and then contrasted with what happens to those who do not 'have' [NIGTC].

QUESTION—What does the person have?

The person has a knowledge of the word [CGTC], and an understanding of the kingdom [BECNT, BNTC, CGTC, PNTC, WBC]. When a person receives and assimilates the truth, his capacity to receive more truth is enlarged [CGTC, Hb, Lns, Sw, WBC]. Those who already know that Christ has come to establish the kingdom of God will have their understanding of this increase even more [BECNT]. The more a person thinks about this, the more he will understand [EGT]. One must listen to the teachings with attentiveness, and since knowledge is a series of successive steps, each step depends on the preceding one [ICC]. Another view is that those who have accepted the word about the secret of the kingdom will receive all of the joys of the kingdom [BNTC]. Those who have made a beginning in the faith are assured of further progress in knowledge, love, holiness, joy, etc., with every blessing is a guarantee of further blessings to come [NTC].

QUESTION—Who is the actor of the passive verb 'it will be given him'?

God is the one who gives it [NICNT, TH, TRT]. It will be given to him even more by God [NICNT].

QUESTION—How can a person be deprived of that which he does not possess?

This hyperbole means that he who has *very little* will have even that little taken away from him [Lns, TH]. It describes the person who depends on his own resources without receiving the word [ESVfn]. Even a superficial acquaintance with spiritual matters will be taken away [NTC]. The one who was not given insight into the mystery of the kingdom of God will have the little knowledge about the kingdom he does have taken away from him [AB2]. Some apply this to anyone, including disciples [EGT, Gnd, Hb]. The less a person thinks, the less his ability to understand will be [EGT]. Those who fail to listen to parabolic teaching in the right way will lose the parable in the sense that they will miss out on its explanation [Gnd]. The person who does not use his ability to understand the truth blunts his ability to understand it. So if the disciples do not use their knowledge of the mystery of the kingdom, their knowledge will diminish until they lose even the knowledge they now possess [Hb].

DISCOURSE UNIT—4:26–29 [CBC, EBC, Hb, NICNT; CEV, ESV, GW, NASB, NCV, NET, NIV, NLT, NRSV, TEV]. The topic is the parable of the growth of the seed [NICNT], the parable of the growing seed [CBC; NET, NIV, NLT, NRSV, TEV], the parable of the seed growing [Hb; ESV], the parable of the secretly growing seed [EBC], a story about seeds that grow [GW], another story about seeds [CEV], the parable of the seed [NASB], Jesus uses a story about seed [NCV].

4:26 And he-was-saying, "Thus[a] is the kingdom of God, like a-man might-throw[b] the seed upon the soil

LEXICON—a. οὕτως (LN 61.10) (BAGD 2. p 598): 'thus, in this way' [BAGD], 'the following' [LN], 'as follows' [BAGD, LN]. The words οὕτως ἐστὶν...ὡς 'thus is...like' is translated 'is like what happens' [CEV], 'is like this' [BNTC; REB, TEV], 'is like' [AB1; GW, NASB, NCV, NET, NLT], 'is as if' [NTC, WBC; ESV, NRSV], 'so is...as when' [Lns], 'so is...as if' [KJV], 'this is what...is like' [NIV], 'is like this. It is as if' [AB2, BECNT]. This adverb refers to that which follows [BAGD, LN]. It is placed forward in the sentence for emphasis [Lns].
   b. aorist act. subj. of βάλλω (LN 15.215) (BAGD 1.a. p. 130): 'to throw' [AB2, BAGD, LN], 'to cast' [Lns, WBC; KJV, NASB], 'to scatter' [AB1, BAGD, BECNT, BNTC, NTC; CEV, ESV, GW, NIV, NLT, NRSV, REB, TEV], 'to spread' [NET], 'to plant' [NCV]. Here the verb 'throw' refers to a man sowing seeds by scattering them upon the ground [TH]. The aorist tense indicates that the seed is cast only once upon the ground, and the following present subjunctives indicate that the rest of the activities in the parable are continuous [BECNT, CGTC, My, NCBC, NTC, WBC].

QUESTION—What relationship is indicated by the introductory phrase 'and he was saying'?
   This phrase resumes the account of Jesus' public teaching mentioned in 4:1–9 [Hb, Lns, My, NTC, Sw]. The intervening verses 4:10–25 are a parenthetical account of Jesus' private teaching to the group named in 4:10 [Hb, Sw].

QUESTION—What is the kingdom of God like?
1. The kingdom is compared to the seed [AB2, BECNT, CBC, EBC, NIGTC, PNTC, Tay, WBC]. At first it seems like the kingdom of God is being compared to a man who sows seed, but in 4:30–31 it says it is to be compared to the seed [NIGTC]. The placement of this parable in the midst of seed parables favors taking this to be of the same kind [BECNT, WBC]. The parable emphasizes the seed's mysterious power to produce a crop [EBC].
2. This does not say that the kingdom is like either a seed or a man. Here the kingdom is compared to the entire *action* described in these verses [Lns, NIGTC, TRT; CEV, REB, TEV]. Some translations indicate this more clearly than others: 'This is what the kingdom of God is like' [NIV], 'The kingdom of God is like this' [REB, TEV]. 'The kingdom of God is like what happens when a farmer scatters seed in a field' [CEV]. The kingdom is compared to the contrast between sowing and harvest. As seedtime is followed later by harvest, so the present hiddenness of the kingdom of God will be followed by its glorious manifestation [CGTC].

QUESTION—Why is the word σπόρος 'seed' in the singular form in this parable?

This is a generic use of the word 'seed' and the parable refers to throwing many seeds upon the soil so that they will sprout and grow [TH]. In English translations, most keep the generic term 'seed' in both 4:26 and 27 [all translations except CEV, GW, TEV]. Some who translate it as 'seed' in 4:26 think it is necessary to use the plural form 'seeds' in 4:27 [CEV, TEV]. Another translation uses the plural form in both verses [GW].

4:27 **and he-sleeps and rises**[a] **night and day, and the seed sprouts and grows how**[b] **he-does- not -know.**

LEXICON—pres. pass. subj. of ἐγείρομαι, ἐγείρω (LN 23.74) (BAGD 2.a. p. 215): 'to rise' [AB2, BECNT, Lns, NTC, WBC; ESV, KJV, NRSV], 'to get up' [AB1, BNTC; NASB, NET, NIV, REB], 'to wake up' [BAGD, LN], 'to awaken' [BAGD], 'to be awake' [LN; GW, NCV, NLT], 'to be up and around/about' [CEV, TEV]. This verb means to become awake after sleeping [LN]. The passive voice means to awaken from sleep and get up [BAGD].
  b. ὡς (LN 89.86) (BAGD I.1. p. 897): 'how' [BAGD, LN; all translations except NLT, TEV], 'in what manner' [LN], 'how it happens' [NLT, TEV]. This conjunction indicates how something took place [LN].

QUESTION—Why does this talk about the farmer sleeping and rising night and day?

It describes the ordinary routine of a farmer's life as he sleeps at night and then rises when day begins, and all the time the seeds just keep on growing [Hb, TH]. The order *night and day* may be Semitic since the Jewish day begins at sunset [AB2, BECNT, BNTC, CGTC, Hb, NTC, PNTC, WBC]. Probably night is mentioned first because the process begins at the close of that first busy day of planting [NCBC]. This means that he sleeps in the night and rises in the day [BNTC, TH], not that throughout the night and the day he is constantly getting awakened as he tries to get some sleep [TH].

QUESTION—What doesn't the farmer know?

The man doesn't know how the process of germination and growth of the seed takes place [TH]. The listeners would understand that this means he doesn't know how the seed sprouts and grows [BECNT, Gnd, TRT]. This emphasizes the mysterious power of the seed [EBC].

QUESTION—Does this imply that the farmer does nothing about the plants after sowing the seeds?

This describes the life of a man who has nothing to do with the growth as he waits for the result of that first day of planting [EGT]. The fact that a farmer cultivates the field and does other farm work is not in view [Gnd, ICC] because those activities have no effect on the growth of the seeds [BNTC, Hb]. In real life, this apparently laid-back approach to farming is not a true picture of agriculture. In the parable, however, the farmer's inactivity points out that the kingdom of God does not depend on human effort to achieve it

[NIGTC]. The independence of the seed's growth is emphasized. It teaches that the consummation of God's kingdom is not dependent on human action [BECNT].

4:28 By-itself[a] the soil produces-a-crop,[b] first a-stalk[c] then a-head[d] then full grain[e] in the head.

LEXICON—a. αὐτόματος (LN 89.21) (BAGD p. 122): 'by itself' [AB1, BAGD, BNTC, LN, NTC; ESV, GW, NASB, NCV, NET, REB], 'all by itself' [AB2; NIV], '(the soil) itself' [TEV], 'of itself' [NRSV; similarly KJV], 'on its own' [NLT], 'of its own accord' [BECNT], 'without visible cause' [WBC], 'without any cause, without something to cause it' [LN], 'automatically' [Lns], not explicit [CEV]. This adjective describes something as being self-caused, or not having an evident cause [LN]. The adjective is used almost as if it were an adverb [CGTC, NICNT, Tay] with the meaning 'spontaneously, of its own accord' [NICNT, Tay]. It does so as a matter of course [Lns]. Its position at the beginning of the sentence makes this word emphatic [Hb, Tay].

b. pres. act. indic. of καρποφορέω (LN 23.199) (BAGD 1. p. 405) 'to bear fruit, to produce fruit, to produce seed, to yield' [LN]. The clause 'the soil produces a crop' is translated 'the earth produces a crop' [BNTC, WBC; similarly NLT], 'the ground produces a crop' [REB], 'the earth/soil produces crops/grain' [NTC; GW, NASB, NCV, NIV; similarly ESV, NET], 'the ground bears grains' [BECNT], 'the soil makes the plants grow' [TEV], 'the earth produces' [NRSV], 'it is the ground that makes the seeds sprout and grow' [CEV], 'the earth bringeth forth fruit' [KJV], 'the earth yields fruit' [AB2], 'the earth bears fruit' [Lns]. This verb means to produce fruit or the seeds of plants [LN].

c. χόρτος (LN **3.18**) (BAGD p. 884): 'stalk' [NET, NIV, NRSV], 'slender stalk' [AB1], 'shoot' [AB2], 'sprout' [LN], 'blade' [BECNT, BNTC, LN, NTC, WBC; ESV, KJV, NASB, REB], 'green blade' [**LN**; GW], 'grass blade' [NTC], 'grass' [BAGD]. This noun is also translated as a verb phrase: 'the seeds sprout' [CEV], 'the tender stalk appears' [TEV], 'the leaf blade pushes through' [NLT], 'the plant grows' [NCV]. This noun denotes the young growth of a plant rising from a germinating seed [LN]. It refers to stalks of grain in their early grass-like stages [BAGD]. It means the green grass-like stalk with leaves [Hb], the part of the grain that is like grass before the grain heads form [ICC].

d. στάχυς (LN 3.40) (BAGD 1. p. 765): 'head' [WBC; GW, NASB, NCV, NET, NIV, NRSV, TEV], 'head of wheat' [BAGD, LN], 'ear' [AB1, AB2, BAGD, BECNT, BNTC, LN, Lns, NTC; ESV, KJV, REB]. This noun is also translated as a verb phrase: 'heads of wheat are formed' [NLT], 'grow into plants' [CEV]. This noun denotes the dense spiky cluster in which the seeds of grain such as wheat grow [LN]. It refers to the green, unfilled head [Hb]. This word occurs at 2:23; 4:28.

e. σῖτος (LN 3.41) (BAGD p. 752): 'wheat, grain' [BAGD, LN]. The phrase 'full grain' [AB2, BECNT, BNTC, Lns, NTC; ESV, NET, NRSV, REB] is also translated 'whole grain' [WBC], 'full corn' [KJV], 'full kernel' [NIV], 'all the grain' [NCV], 'mature grain' [NASB], '(the head) full of grain' [GW, TEV], 'the grain (in the ear)' [AB1]. This phrase is also translated as a verb phrase: 'the grain ripens' [NLT], '(plants) that produce grain' [CEV]. This noun denotes any kind of edible grain, but it generally refers to wheat [LN]. It refers to the soft, pulpy kernel of grain as it swells to full size and then hardens as it ripens [Hb]. The full grain is grain that is full grown, mature, and ripe [EGT, TH].

QUESTION—How does the soil produce a crop by itself?
The earth is the medium for the living powers of the seeds to work [Hb, Lns] The plant germinates in the ground [NICNT]. The land itself contains the elements needed for the nourishment and growth of the plant [ICC]. The phrase 'by itself' means that the crops grow apart from any human help or visible cause [ESVfn, NTC, TH, WBC].

4:29 But/then when the crop allows,[a] immediately he-sends[b] the sickle, because the harvest[c] has-come."

LEXICON—a. aorist act. subj. of παραδίδωμι (LN **13.142, 23.200**) (BAGD 4. p. 613): 'to allow' [LN (13.142)], 'to give' [BAGD]. The phrase 'the crop allows' is translated 'the crop permits' [WBC; NASB], 'the fruit allows' [Lns], 'the condition of the crop permits' [BAGD, NTC], 'the condition of the fruit allows it' [AB2, **LN** (13.142)], 'the harvest is ripe' [**LN** (23.200)], 'the crop/grain is ripe' [BECNT, BNTC; CEV, ESV, NET, NIV, NRSV, REB, TEV], 'the crop/grain is ready' [AB1; GW, NCV, NLT], 'the harvest time has come' [LN], 'the fruit is brought forth' [KJV. This verb means to grant the opportunity or occasion to do something [LN (13.142)]. The phrase 'the fruit/crop allows' is an idiom for the ripening of fruit being a sign for the harvest to begin [LN (23.200)]. The phrase literally is 'when the fruit allows or permits' and it means 'when the fruit is ripe' [Lns, TH].
b. pres. act. indic. of ἀποστέλλω (LN **42.17**) (BAGD 2. p. 99): 'to send' [LN], 'to put in' [BAGD]. The phrase 'he sends the sickle' is translated 'he sends forth the sickle' [AB2], 'he sends in the sickle' [NET], 'he puts in the sickle' [NTC, WBC; ESV, KJV, NASB], 'he puts the sickle to it' [NIV], 'he commissions the sickle' [Lns], 'he wields the sickle' [BECNT], 'he cuts it with a sickle' [GW], 'the man starts cutting it with his sickle' [TEV], 'the farmer cuts it' [NCV], 'the farmer cuts it with a sickle' [CEV], 'he begins working with the sickle' [AB1], 'he sets to work with the sickle' [BNTC], 'he goes in with his sickle' [NRSV], 'the farmer comes and harvests it with a sickle' [NLT], 'he begins to harvest the grain' [**LN**], 'he starts reaping' [REB]. The words ἀποστέλλω τὸ δρέπανον 'to send a sickle' is an idiom that means to begin to harvest a crop by cutting the ripe grain with a sickle [LN].

218   MARK 4:29

c. θερισμός (LN 43.14) (BAGD 1. p. 359): 'harvest' [BAGD, LN], 'reaping' [LN]. The phrase παρέστηκεν ὁ θερισμός 'the harvest has come' [AB2, BECNT, Lns, NTC; ESV, KJV, NASB, NET, NIV, NRSV] is also translated 'harvest season comes' [CEV], 'harvest time has come' [BNTC; GW, NLT, REB, TEV], 'harvest time has arrived' [AB1], 'the harvest is ready' [WBC], 'this is the harvest time' [NCV]. This noun denotes the harvest that results from cutting the ripe grain and gathering it into bundles [LN]. It denotes the time and process of harvesting [BAGD].

QUESTION—What relationship is indicated by the conjunction δέ 'but/then'?
1. It indicates contrast [AB1, AB2, BNTC, NTC, Tay, WBC; ESV, KJV, NASB, NRSV, REB]: the soil produces a crop: first…then…, and then…, *but* when the crop ripens, immediately he puts forth the sickle. The contrastive conjunction 'but' with 'immediately' serves to bring the normal process to its climax [Tay, WBC].
2. It indicates the sequence of closely related events [BECNT, Lns; CEV, GW, NET, NLT]: the soil produces a crop: first…then…, and then…, *and then* when the crop ripens, immediately he puts forth the sickle.

QUESTION—What is meant by the statement 'he sends the sickle'?
1. This means that the man begins cutting the grain [AB1, BECNT, BNTC, WBC; CEV, ESV, GW, KJV, NASB, NCV, NIV, NRSV, TEV]: *the man cuts it with a sickle.*
2. This means that the man sends workmen into the fields to do the work of harvesting [ICC, TH]: *the man sends out the reapers.* The sickle is used as a metonymy for the reapers who use the sickle [ICC].

QUESTION—What does this parable teach?
There are many interpretations of this unexplained parable. As seed time is followed by harvest, so will the present hiddenness of the kingdom of God be followed by its glorious manifestation [CGTC, EBC, Gnd, NIGTC, NLTfn, PNTC]. Although the kingdom of God seems to be inactive, it really is growing and the harvest will come in God's way and at his time [NTC]. The focus is on the seed and its ultimate growth [BECNT]. The inevitable growth of the seed shows that the consummation of God's kingdom does not depend on human action [NLTfn]. Some think the act of putting forth the sickle for the harvest refers to Joel 3:13 where there is an eschatological harvest representing the coming judgment of the world [BNTC, CBC, Hb, NAC, NICNT, Sw, TRT, WBC]. Although the harvest represents the end of the age, the parable is concerned with the manifestation of those who are righteous, not the condemnation of the wicked [NAC]. Christ came to sow, and in the future he will come to reap. The growth results from the invisible working of the Spirit in the church and in the soul [Sw]. Others specifically reject this idea [BECNT, NIGTC; probably AB2]. Another view is that the harvest is the hidden growth of the fruit of sanctification coming to its consummation in glory. It will happen to an individual at death, and to the church at the last day [Lns].

DISCOURSE UNIT—4:30–34 [CBC; ESV, GW, NASB, NCV, NIV, TEV]. The topic is a story about a mustard seed [GW, NCV], the parable of the mustard seed [ESV, NASB, NIV, TEV], the mustard seed and a summary on parables [CBC].

DISCOURSE UNIT—4:30–32 [EBC, Hb, NICNT; CEV, NET, NLT, NRSV]. The topic is a mustard seed [CEV], the parable of the mustard seed [EBC, Hb, NICNT; NET, NLT, NRSV].

4:30 And he-was-saying, "How[a] shall-we-compare[b] the kingdom of-God or by what parable can-we-explain[c] it?

LEXICON—a. πῶς (LN 92.16) (BAGD 1.e. p. 732): 'how?' [BAGD, LN], 'by what means?' [LN], 'in what way?' [BAGD]. See the following lexical item for translations of this word. This is an interrogative particle that refers to means [LN].
  b. aorist act. subj. of ὁμοιόω (LN **64.5**) (BAGD 2. p. 567): 'to compare' [BAGD, LN]. The question πῶς ὁμοιώσωμεν 'how shall we compare' [**LN**, WBC] is also translated 'to what can we compare' [NET], 'with what can/shall we compare' [NTC; ESV, NRSV], 'what comparison can we find' [BAGD (1.e. p. 732)], 'how can/shall we picture' [BNTC; NASB, REB], 'how shall we make a likeness of' [Lns], 'how shall we form a likeness for' [AB2], 'to what shall we liken' [BECNT], 'whereunto shall we liken' [KJV], 'how shall we describe' [AB1], 'how can I describe' [NLT]. The question 'How should we compare the kingdom of God?' is translated 'How can we show what the kingdom of God is like?' [GW], 'What shall we say the kingdom of God is like?' [NIV, TEV], 'How can I show you what the kingdom of God is like?' [NCV], 'What is God's kingdom like?' [CEV]. This verb means to consider something to be like something else [LN].
  c. aorist ac. subj. of τίθημι (LN **33.151**) (BAGD I.1.b.ε. p. 816): 'to explain' [**LN**; CEV, NCV, TEV], 'to make clear' [LN], 'to describe' [AB1, BECNT; NIV, REB], 'to present' [BAGD, NTC; NASB, NET], 'to set forth' [Lns], 'to illustrate' [NLT], 'to compare' [GW, KJV]. The clause 'by what parable can we explain it' is translated 'in what parable shall we put it?' [AB2], 'what parable shall we use for it?' [BNTC; ESV; similarly NRSV]. This verb means to explain something by putting forward additional or different information [LN].

QUESTION—What is the function of these two questions?
  With the use of 'we' this question is phrased as though Jesus was asking the hearers to join him in a search for finding appropriate comparisons. However he already had a comparison ready to explain this to them [Hb, NTC, Sw]. These two rhetorical questions were asked to arouse their interest and get them to listen carefully to his explanation [NTC].

QUESTION—Why are there two questions?
Both questions mean the same thing, so the conjunction 'or' does not indicate something opposite, but a parallel statement that defines the first [Lns]. This is a form of Hebrew parallelism [NCBC].

4:31 **(It is) like a-mustard^a seed, which when it-is-sown on the ground, is-smaller (than) all of-the seeds on the earth.^b**

LEXICON—a. σίναπι (LN 3.20) (BAGD p. 751): 'mustard' [BAGD, LN]. The phrase κόκκῳ σινάπεω 'a mustard seed' [AB1, BECNT, BNTC, NTC, WBC; all versions except CEV, ESV, KJV] is also translated 'a grain of mustard seed' [ESV, KJV], 'a kernel of mustard' [Lns], 'a mustard grain' [AB2]. The clause 'it is like a mustard seed which when it is sown on the ground' is translated 'it is like what happens when a mustard seed is planted in the ground' [CEV]. This noun denotes a mustard plant, a large herb noted for its very small seeds. Some can grow to a height of about ten feet [LN]. This probably refers to the common black mustard plant *sinapsis nigra* [Hb, Lns, TH], which was grown for its leaves and seed [Hb], or *brassica nigra*, which was grown as a condiment and also for its oil [NIGTC].

b. γῆ (LN 1.39): 'earth, world' [LN]. The phrase 'is smaller than all of the seeds on the earth' is translated 'is the smallest seed in all the world' [CEV; similarly TEV], 'is the smallest of all the seeds on the earth' [AB1, BECNT; ESV, NRSV], 'is the smallest of all seeds of the earth' [WBC], 'is smaller than all the seeds on earth' [Lns], 'is smaller than all the other seeds on earth' [AB2], 'is one of the smallest seeds on earth' [GW], 'is less than all the seeds that be in the earth' [KJV], 'is the smallest of all the seeds on/in the ground' [NTC; NET], 'is smaller than all the seeds that are upon the soil' [NASB], 'is the smallest seed you plant in the ground' [NCV, NIV], 'is smaller than any other seed' [BNTC; REB], 'is the smallest of all seeds' [NLT]. This noun denotes the surface of the earth as the dwelling place of mankind [LN].

QUESTION—How can it be said that the kingdom of God is like a mustard seed?
One important aspect of God's kingdom is illustrated by a tiny mustard seed that grows into a very large plant [Hb, NLTfn]. The kingdom of God is not an object like a mustard seed, but its beginning and ending are likened to what happens to a mustard seed [EBC, NICNT]. The comparison is to the whole situation that is described in this parable [AB2].

QUESTION—Does this mean that there is no seed smaller than a mustard seed?
A mustard seed is about the size of the head of a pin [WBC]. There are smaller seeds on earth [AB2, Hb, WBC], such as the orchid seed [AB2, BECNT], but the mustard seed was the smallest seed known to the people of Galilee [WBC], or the smallest seed that they sowed in their fields [Hb]. The mustard seed was used proverbially to indicate anything that was very small

[BECNT, BNTC, CBC, EBC, Gnd, Hb, NAC, NCBC, NICNT, NTC, PNTC, Tay, WBC].

4:32 But/and[a] when it-is sown, it-grows-up and becomes larger-than all of the garden-plants[b] and makes large[c] branches, so-that the birds of-(the)-air[d] can nest[e] under its shade."

LEXICON—a. καί (LN 91.12, 89.87): 'but' [AB2; CEV, KJV, NCV, NLT, REB], 'yet' [AB1, LN (91.12), NTC; ESV, NASB, NIV, NRSV], 'however' [GW], 'and' [BECNT, BNTC, LN (89.97), WBC], 'and then' [LN (89.97)], 'after a while' [TEV], 'even' [Lns], not explicit [NET]. This conjunction indicates emphasis and suggests surprise and unexpectedness [LN (91.12)], or it indicates a sequence of closely related events [LN (89.87)].

b. λάχανον (LN 3.29) (BAGD p. 467): 'garden plant' [LN; CEV, ESV, GW, NASB, NCV, NET, NIV, NLT], 'garden herb' [NTC], 'edible garden herb' [BAGD], 'vegetable' [BAGD, Lns], 'herb' [KJV], 'plant' [BNTC; REB, TEV], 'shrub' [AB1, AB2, BECNT; NRSV]. This noun denotes any one of the smaller plants such as herbs and vegetables that are cultivated in a garden [LN].

c. μέγας (LN 79.123) (BAGD 1.a. p. 497): 'large' [AB1, AB2, BNTC, LN, NTC; ESV, GW, NASB, NCV, NET, NRSV, REB, TEV], 'long' [NLT], 'great' [BAGD, BECNT, LN, Lns; KJV], 'big' [LN; CEV, NIV]. This adjective describes something as being of a large size relative to the norm for the class of objects in question [LN]. It is large in regard to its extension in space in all directions [BAGD].

d. οὐρανός (LN 4.41) (BAGD 1.d. p. 594): 'sky' [LN], 'heaven' [BAGD]. The phrase τὰ πετεινὰ τοῦ οὐρανοῦ 'the birds of the air' [BNTC, NTC; ESV, NASB, NIV, NRSV] is also translated 'birds of heaven' [AB2, BECNT, Lns], 'fowls of the air' [KJV], 'birds' [AB1, LN; CEV, GW, NLT, REB, TEV], 'wild birds' [LN; NCV, NET]. The phrase 'birds of the air' is an idiom that denotes wild birds in contrast to domesticated birds such as chickens [LN, NETfn]. In this verse the noun οὐρανός denotes the atmosphere [BAGD].

e. pres. act. infin. of κατασκηνόω (LN 6.147) (BAGD 2. p. 418): 'to nest' [BAGD, LN, WBC; CEV, GW, NASB, NET], 'to make nests' [AB1, LN; ESV, NCV, NLT, NRSV, TEV], 'to build nests' [BNTC], 'to dwell' [BECNT], 'to lodge' [AB2, NTC; KJV, NASB], 'to go tenting' [Lns], 'to perch' [NIV], 'to roost' [REB]. This verb is derived from the noun κατασκήνωσις 'nest' and refers to making a nest [LN]. This does not mean that birds had their nests on the ground underneath the plant, but that they made their nests in its branches under its shade [TH]. Or it means to nest on the ground under the tree [BECNT].

QUESTION—Does the verb κατασκηνόω mean that the birds 'make nests' in its shade or merely that they 'perch' in its shade?
1. The verb κατασκηνόω means that the birds make nests in its shade [BECNT, BNTC, Hb, ICC, Lns, NCBC, NIGTC, NTC, TH, TRT, WBC; all versions except NIV, REB]. The birds not only perched on its branches but actually made their nests there [Hb]. The birds nest in the branches under its shade, or perhaps the reference to shade implies that they nest on the ground underneath the plant [TH].
2. The birds perch in its shade [EBC, NICNT; NIV, REB]. They take shelter in the branches [EBC].

QUESTION—Why is the comment added about the birds nesting under the shade of its branches?

The fact that the branches are large enough for the birds to nest in them emphasizes the large size of the plant [EBC, Gnd, NICNT, WBC]. The mustard plant grows to look almost like a tree since it reaches a height of ten to fifteen feet [BECNT, NTC], eight to twelve feet [Tay, TRT], eight to ten feet [WBC]. However, it would be an exaggeration to call this large shrub a tree [BECNT].

QUESTION—What is the teaching of this parable?

This parable contrasts the small and apparently insignificant beginning of the kingdom with its later glorious manifestation [AB2, BECNT, BNTC, CGTC, EBC, EGT, ICC, Lns, NAC, NICNT, NIGTC, NLTfn, NTC, PNTC, Sw, TRT, WBC]. The focus is on the contrast between an insignificant beginning and the impressive final size [ESVfn, NIGTC, NLTfn]. Another point included in the parable is the gradual growth of the kingdom [ESVfn, ICC]. It teaches that a small beginning and gradual growth is not inconsistent with a great result [ICC]. Those who have witnessed the beginning proclamation of the kingdom of God must not despise its small beginning nor should they be impatient for the final full majesty of his kingdom to be revealed [NIGTC]. Although the emphasis is on the large size of the plant [EBC, Gnd, NICNT, WBC], some also refer to the OT references of Ezekiel's two cedars and Nebuchadnezzar's tree in which the birds nesting in their branches represented the great nations that enjoyed the benefits of the great empire [AB1, BNTC, ESVfn, NIGTC]. Perhaps the birds symbolize the Gentiles [AB2, BNTC, NAC, PNTC, Tay]. The nesting of birds in the shadow of the grown bush points to God's blessings [ESVfn]. This is concerned with the visible vital growth of the kingdom, not with any outward organization [Lns]. A very different view is that the parable pictures an abnormal development of the kingdom as it begins as a small, insignificant movement that develops into a huge worldly-minded organization exercising imperial power. That it becomes like a tree indicates something foreign to its nature, and the birds picture evil forces that embrace Christianity for various reasons and find shelter in its branches. Under Constantine the church gained world recognition, but then corrupting forces invaded the professing church and altered its original spiritual nature [Hb].

DISCOURSE UNIT—4:33-34 [EBC, Hb, NICNT; CEV, NET, NLT, NRSV]. The topic is a summary of the parabolic section [Hb], a summary statement on parables [EBC], a summary of Jesus' parable ministry [NLT], the reason for teaching with stories [CEV], the use of parables [NET, NRSV], parabolic utterance and private interpretation [NICNT].

4:33 **And with-many similar parables he-was-speaking the word to-them as they-were-able to-hear.**[a]

LEXICON—a. pres. act. infin. of ἀκούω (LN **32.1**) (BAGD 5, 7. p. 32): 'to listen' [BAGD (5.)], 'to understand' [BAGD (7.), LN], 'to comprehend' [LN]. The phrase καθὼς ἠδύναντο ἀκούειν 'as they were able to hear' [AB2, BECNT, Lns, NTC, WBC; ESV, KJV, NET, NRSV] is also translated 'to the extent they were able to hear it' [WBC], 'so far as they were able to hear it' [AB1; NASB], 'so far as they were able to receive it' [REB], 'as far as they could grasp it' [BNTC], 'to the extent they could understand' [**LN**], 'as much as they could understand' [CEV, NCV, NIV, NLT, TEV], 'in this way people could understand what he taught' [GW]. This verb means to hear and understand a message [LN].

QUESTION—What was the 'word' Jesus was speaking to them in parables?
   The instrumental use of the dative case of πολλαῖς 'with/by-means-of many (similar parables)' indicates that the parable were a means of teaching the 'word' [BECNT]. This word was the word about the messianic kingdom of God (4:11) [CBC, ESVfn, Hb, ICC, NCBC, NICNT, NIGTC, Sw]. The mystery he was teaching them at this time concerned the gradual establishment of the kingdom. On other occasions he did not confine himself to just this one subject [ICC].

QUESTION—In what way was Jesus speaking the word to the people 'as they were able to hear'?
   1. This means that Jesus limited his teaching to what the crowds were capable of understanding [AB1, AB2, BECNT, BNTC, CGTC, EBC, ICC, My, NCBC, NICNT, NIGTC, NTC, WBC; all versions except GW]. 'To hear' is used in the sense of hearing so as to remember [Lns]. 'To hear' means to hear and respond to the message [WBC]. Their prejudices and inability to understand his person were taken into account as he used a form they were morally qualified to accept [Hb]. Jesus adapted his teaching to the people's level of understanding. If he had spoken to the crowds in a direct manner about making a decision to enter the kingdom of God from the start, their wrong ideas about such a kingdom would have resulted only in unbelief and rejection [CGTC, NICNT]. The crowd would understand that Jesus was talking about the kingdom of God, but they would not be able understand the full relationship Jesus had with the kingdom [CGTC]. The parables kept the people's attention even though they could not comprehend the inner doctrinal meaning of the parables [NTC].

2. This means that Jesus used parables in order to help people understand [EGT, NAC; GW]. Jesus used the parables to make the truth plain [EGT]. 'Jesus spoke God's word to them using many illustrations like these. In this way people could understand what he taught' [GW].
3. This means that Jesus taught as much as he could in the time available [Gnd, PNTC]. Since Jesus was teaching a crowd that included his disciples, the qualification 'as they were able to hear' does not refer to either good hearing or bad hearing. It refers to their attention span or the amount of time they had to attend the teaching sessions [Gnd, PNTC].

4:34 And[a] without[b] a-parable he-was- not -speaking to-them, yet privately[c] he-was-explaining[d] all (things) to-his-own disciples.

LEXICON—a. δέ (LN 89.87) (BAGD 4.b. p. 171): 'and' [AB1, BECNT, LN, Lns, NTC; NASB], 'and also' [BAGD], 'and then' [LN], 'but' [KJV], 'in fact' [NLT], 'indeed' [AB2], not explicit [BNTC, WBC; all versions except KJV, NASB, NLT]. This conjunction indicates a sequence of closely related events [LN]. Following a καί 'and' (4:33) the combination means 'and also' [BAGD].

  b. χωρίς (LN 89.120) (BAGD 2.b.β. p. 890): 'without' [AB2, LN, Lns, NTC; CEV, ESV, GW, KJV, NASB, NET, NIV, TEV], 'apart from' [BECNT, LN, WBC], 'without making use of' [BAGD], 'except in' [AB1; NRSV, REB]. The phrase 'without a parable he was not speaking to them' is translated 'he always used stories to teach them' [NCV], 'he never spoke to them without a parable' [BNTC], 'in his public ministry he never taught without using parables' [NLT]. This preposition indicates negatively linked elements [LN].

  c. κατ' ἰδίαν (LN 28.67): The phrase κατ' ἰδίαν 'according to that which is private' means 'privately' [AB1, AB2, BECNT, LN, NTC, WBC; ESV, NASB, NET, NRSV, REB], 'in private' [Lns], 'when alone with' [CEV, GW, NIV, NLT; similarly KJV, NCV, TEV], 'when they were on their own' [BNTC]. This phrase is an idiom pertaining to what occurs in a private context or setting, and it has the sense of not being made known publicly [LN].

  d. imperf. act. indic. of ἐπιλύω (LN **33.4**) (BAGD 1. p. 296): 'to explain' [AB1, AB2, BECNT, BNTC, LN, NTC, WBC; all versions except KJV], 'to expound' [KJV], 'to solve' [Lns]. This verb means to explain the meaning of something that is difficult or complex [LN].

QUESTION—What is the function of this verse?

This negative statement adds emphasis to the preceding positive statement [Lns, NCBC, Tay], and also makes it clear that Jesus often used parables when he was teaching [ESVfn, Lns, NTC]. Some think that it means that Jesus spoke exclusively with parables [Sw, WBC], but only at this stage of his ministry [Sw]. It is probably taking this general statement too literally to think that Jesus only told a string of parables whenever he taught in Nazareth (6:2) and other places (6:6, 34). It is limited to this particular occasion [Hb,

NAC] as he spoke about God's kingdom [TRT]. Jesus did not confine himself to parables on other subjects and occasions [ICC]. It is evident in many passages that Jesus' teaching was not limited to parables, so probably Mark used hyperbole here in order to emphasize that much of Jesus' teaching was in parables [BECNT].

QUESTION—Why did Jesus speak only in parables to this crowd?

Jesus used parables to stimulate their thinking and awaken their spiritual perception because they were not ready for a direct revelation of the truth [EBC]. If Jesus had spoken in a direct manner to the crowds at that point, they would only have responded in unbelief and rejection [NICNT]. Jesus used graphic images from everyday life to get the attention of those in his audiences who really wanted to understand his message [PNTC].

QUESTION—What were the 'all things' he was explaining to his disciples?

Jesus told them what the parables meant [AB2, TH]. The 'things' would be more than the veiled mystery of the kingdom in the parables. It would include Jesus' mission [Hb, NICNT, WBC].

DISCOURSE UNIT—4:35–9:50 [Hb]. The topic is the withdrawals from Galilee.

DISCOURSE UNIT—4:35–6:29 [Hb]. The topic is the first withdrawal and return.

DISCOURSE UNIT—4:35–6:6a [PNTC; REB]. The topic is miracles [REB], Who then is this? [PNTC].

DISCOURSE UNIT—4:35–5:43 [EBC, NICNT, NIGTC; NLT]. The topic is further revelations of Jesus' unique authority [NIGTC], the vanquishing of powers hostile to God [NICNT], triumph over hostile powers [EBC], Jesus is Lord over all [NLT].

DISCOURSE UNIT—4:35–41 [CBC, EBC, Hb, NICNT; ESV, GW, NASB, NCV, NET, NIV, NLT, NRSV, TEV]. The topic is a storm [CEV], the stilling of a storm [NET], calming the storm [EBC], Jesus calms/stills a storm [CBC; ESV, NCV, NIV, NLT, NRSV, TEV], Jesus calms/stills the sea [GW, NASB], the subduing of the sea [NICNT], stilling the tempest [Hb].

4:35 And he-says to-them on that day when-it-became evening, "Let-us-go-over to the other-side[a]"

LEXICON—a. πέραν (LN 83.43) (BAGD 1. p. 643): 'on the other side' [BAGD, LN], 'opposite, across from' [LN]. The phrase 'to the other side' [AB1, AB2, BECNT, BNTC, Lns, NTC, WBC; ESV, GW, KJV, NASB, NIV, NRSV] is also translated 'to the other side of the lake' [NET, NLT, REB, TEV], 'to the east side' [CEV], 'across the lake' [NCV]. This adjective means a position opposite another position, with something intervening [LN].

QUESTION—What day was ἐκείνῃ τῇ ἡμέρᾳ 'that day'?
This was the day on which Jesus taught the parables to the crowd [ICC, Lns, NCBC, NICNT, NIGTC, NTC, Sw, WBC]. The trip across the lake started at sundown and the storm came up during the evening [Hb, Lns, NTC, TH].

QUESTION—Where was 'the other side' and why did Jesus want to go there?
The other side was the eastern side of the Lake of Galilee [AB1, CGTC, Hb, NLTfn, NTC, TRT; CEV]. Since this was an area where there were no large cities, it indicates that Jesus wanted to get away from the crowds after such an exhausting day [EBC, EGT, Hb, ICC]. Jesus either wanted to escape the crowd or to expand his ministry [NAC].

4:36 And leaving the crowd they-take[a] him as he-was in the boat, and other boats were with[b] him.

LEXICON—a. pres. act. indic. of παραλαμβάνω (LN 15.168) (BAGD 1. p. 619): 'to take along' [BAGD, LN], 'to take with' [BAGD]. The phrase 'they take/took him as he was in the boat' [BNTC, WBC] is also translated 'they take him along as he was in the boat' [Lns], 'they took him along, just as he was, in the boat' [NET, NIV], 'they took him even as he was in the ship' [KJV], 'they took him/Jesus along in a boat just as he was' [NTC; GW], 'they took him in the boat just as he was' [NCV], 'they took him with them in the boat, just as he was' [AB1, BECNT; ESV, NRSV; similarly NASB], 'they…took him with them in the boat in which he had been sitting' [REB], 'the disciples got into the boat in which Jesus was already sitting, and they took him with them' [TEV], 'they took Jesus in the boat and started out' [NLT], 'they took him off, when he had gotten back in the boat' [AB2], 'his disciples started across the lake with him in the boat' [CEV]. This verb means to take or bring someone along [LN].

b. μετά (LN 89.108): 'with, in the company of, together with' [LN]. The phrase 'were with him' [AB2, BECNT, NTC, WBC; ESV, GW, NET, NRSV] is also translated 'were also with him' [KJV], 'were accompanying him' [AB1, BNTC], 'were in his company' [Lns], 'went with him' [REB], 'were with them' [NCV, NIV], 'were there too' [TEV], 'followed along' [CEV], 'followed' [NLT]. This preposition indicates an associative relation that usually implies being in the company of someone [LN].

QUESTION—What crowd did they leave?
They were leaving the large crowd mentioned in 4:1 [BECNT, Gnd, ICC, NIGTC, WBC]. They left the crowd behind as they set out onto the lake [NCV, NIV, NLT, NRSV].

QUESTION—Who took Jesus along in the boat?
Jesus' disciples took Jesus along with them in the boat [TH]. It is proper to say that the disciples *took Jesus along with them* since some of disciples were the owners of the boat [Hb], and the boat was crewed by the disciples as it crossed the lake [Gnd, Hb, Lns, NTC, Sw] while Jesus slept [Gnd].

QUESTION—What is meant by taking Jesus ὡς ἦν ἐν τῷ πλοίῳ 'as he was in the boat'?

1. The phrase ὡς ἦν 'as he was' is a separate statement, while ἐν τῷ πλοίῳ 'in the boat' is to be connected with 'they take him' [AB1, BECNT, BNTC, EBC, Gnd, Hb, ICC, Lns, NAC, NTC, PNTC, Sw; ESV, GW, NASB, NCV, NET, NIV, NRSV; probably CEV]: *they took him with them in the boat just as he was*. The disciples left with Jesus in the boat as he was, that is, Jesus was already in the boat and he did not go ashore to make any preparations for the trip [CGTC, EBC, Hb, ICC, Lns, Sw], they left without delay [ICC]. 'As he was' could mean 'immediately' or 'without going ashore' [BECNT]. They took him without Jesus having to disembark to get in another boat [BNTC, CGTC, NAC], because he was already in the boat he had entered at 4:1 [BNTC, EBC, NAC]. Another answer is that they took Jesus along just as he was, that is, exhausted after a hard day of work and in need of rest and sleep [Lns, NTC].
2. The phrase ὡς ἦν ἐν τῷ πλοίῳ 'as he was in the boat' is a single idea that means that he was already in the boat [My, NIGTC, TH, TRT, WBC; probably REB, TEV]: *they took him along with them since he was already in the boat*. The conjunction ὡς 'as' indicates a comparison not of Jesus' appearance but of his location [TH]. This means that Jesus was in the same boat in which he had entered to teach the crowd in 4:1 [TH, WBC]. 'They took Jesus with them in the boat were he was' or 'they joined Jesus in the boat he was in' [TRT].
3. The phrase ὡς ἦν ἐν τῷ πλοίῳ means 'when he was in the boat' [AB2] *they took him along with them when he had gotten back in the boat.* The Greek word ὡς 'as' can also mean 'when' [AB2].

QUESTION—What is the significance of the information that other boats were with Jesus?

It simply means that some other boats followed the boat that was taking Jesus away from the crowd [NLT]. The other boats must have been filled with friends of Jesus who were eager to remain with him [Hb]. This emphasizes Jesus' popularity and fame [BECNT, NLTfn]. With the experienced crew in the boat with Jesus, they soon left the other boats far behind [NICNT]. Jesus' miracle of calming the storm probably affected all the boats on the lake [WBC], but the other boats are not mentioned any more because they have no relevance to the rest of the story [BNTC, NIGTC, WBC]. It is not clear why those other boats are mentioned [BNTC, EBC].

4:37 And there-arose a-great windstorm[a] of-wind and the waves were-beating[b] into the boat, so-that already the boat was-being-filled.[c]

LEXICON—a. λαῖλαψ (LN 14.6) (BAGD p. 463): 'windstorm' [LN], 'squall' [LN], 'whirlwind' [BAGD, LN]. The phrase 'a great windstorm of wind' is translated 'a great windstorm' [AB2, BECNT, WBC; ESV, NRSV], 'a violent windstorm' [GW], 'a heavy storm' [NTC], 'a fierce storm' [NLT], 'a strong wind' [LN; NCV, TEV], 'a fierce gale of wind' [NASB], 'a fierce gust of wind' [BAGD], 'a fierce squall' [REB], 'a furious squall' [NIV], 'a heavy squall' [BNTC], 'a great storm of wind' [KJV], 'a great hurricane of wind' [Lns]. The phrase 'there arose a great windstorm of wind' is translated 'a great windstorm developed' [NET], 'a very strong windstorm began to blow' [AB1], 'a windstorm struck the lake' [CEV]. This noun denotes the sudden and violent gusts of winds that often came from varied directions [LN].

b. imperf. act. indic. of ἐπιβάλλω (LN **14.21**) (BAGD 2.a. p. 290): 'to beat upon' [BAGD], 'to splash into' [**LN**]. The phrase 'were beating into' is translated 'beat into' [KJV, NRSV], 'beat against' [WBC]. 'crashed into' [Lns], 'were breaking into' [AB2; ESV, GW, NET, NLT], 'were breaking over' [NASB; similarly AB1, BNTC; NIV, REB], 'were beginning to break over' [BECNT], 'were dashing into' [NTC], 'splashed into' [**LN**], 'started splashing into' [CEV], 'came over the sides and into' [NCV], 'began to spill over into' [TEV]. This verb means to strike upon and into a boat when referring to the action of waves [LN]. The imperfect tense indicates that the waves were repeatedly coming into the boat [Hb, WBC]. Others think the verb has an inceptive imperfect tense, which would indicate that the waves were just *beginning* to do this [BECNT; CEV, TEV].

c. pres. pass. infin. of γεμίζω (LN 59.42) (BAGD 3. p. 153): 'to be filled' [BAGD, LN]. The verb 'was being filled' is translated 'was already filling' [Lns; ESV], 'was already filling up' [NTC; NASB], 'was already filling with water' [BECNT], 'it began to fill with water' [NLT; similarly AB2], 'it was about to fill with water' [TEV], 'was quickly filling up' [GW], 'it quickly filled with water' [BNTC], 'it was now full' [KJV], 'it was already full of water' [NCV], 'was being swamped' [WBC], 'was already being swamped' [NRSV], 'was nearly swamped' [NET, NIV], 'it was all but swamped' [REB], 'it was almost swamped' [AB1], 'was about to sink' [CEV]. This verb means to be filled with some substance [LN]. The present tense indicates an act in progress [ICC]. The description focuses not so on much the violence of the waves, but on the waves filling the boat [CGTC, ICC, Sw].

4:38 And he was in the stern[a] sleeping on the cushion.[b] And they-wake him and they-say to-him, "Teacher does-it- not -concern[c] you that we-are-perishing[d]?"

LEXICON—a. πρύμνα (LN 6.47) (BAGD p. 724): 'stern' [AB1, AB2, BAGD, BECNT, BNTC, LN, Lns, NTC, WBC; ESV, NASB, NET, NIV, NRSV, REB], 'the hinder part' [KJV], 'the back of the boat' [CEV, GW, NCV, NLT, TEV]. This noun denotes the back part of a boat. In languages lacking technical terms for the bow and stern of a boat, one can speak of 'the front of a boat' for πρῷρα 'prow', and 'the back of the boat' for πρύμνα 'stern' [LN].

b. προσκεφάλαιον (LN **6.110**) (BAGD p. 715): 'cushion' [AB1, AB2, BAGD, BECNT, BNTC, **LN**, WBC; all versions except CEV, KJV, TEV], 'pillow' [BAGD, LN, Lns; CEV, KJV, TEV], 'headrest' [NTC]. This noun denotes an object upon which one may lay his head [LN].

c. pres. act. indic. of μέλει (LN 25.223) (BAGD 3. p. 500): 'to be concerned' [BAGD, LN], 'to be anxious about' [LN], 'to care' [AB1, AB2, BECNT, BNTC, Lns, NTC, WBC; all versions]. This verb means to be particularly concerned and apprehensive about something [LN].

d. pres. mid. indic. of ἀπόλλυμαι, ἀπόλλυμαι (LN 23.106) (BAGD 2.a.α. p. 95): 'to perish, to die' [BAGD, LN]. The verb ἀπολλύμεθα 'we are perishing' [BECNT, Lns, NTC; ESV, NASB, NRSV; similarly WBC; KJV] is also translated 'we are about to perish' [AB1], 'we are about to die' [AB2; NET, TEV], 'we're going to die' [GW], 'we are drowning' [NCV], 'we are going to drown' [NLT], 'we are sinking' [BNTC; REB], 'we're about to sink' [CEV], 'if we drown' [NIV]. This verb means to die [LN]. The present tense probably indicates that they were about to perish [TH].

QUESTION—What was the cushion?

It probably was a leather cushion on the steersman's seat [BNTC, Hb, WBC]. Probably it was a rowers' leather seat, and the definite article, '*the* cushion', probably indicates that it was the only one in the boat [CGTC, EBC, Sw, Tay]. It could have been a cushion kept as a seat of honor at the back of the boat [CGTC]. Perhaps it was a sandbag used for ballast that served as a pillow for Jesus [AB2, BECNT, CBC, NLTfn]. The cushion was being used as a headrest [Tay, TH].

QUESTION—Why would Jesus be sleeping during this terrible storm?

Jesus was exhausted from his busy day [CGTC, EBC, Hb, ICC]. Being physically exhausted, he could go to sleep in the storm, confident of his Father's care [BNTC, CBC, NAC, PNTC, Tay] and omnipotence [NIGTC]. He also knew that he himself was sovereign and therefore secure [WBC]. He could trust in his own abilities since he was the Son of God [Gnd].

QUESTION—What did they mean by asking Jesus 'Does it not concern *you* that *we* are perishing?'

Their words 'we are perishing' in the present tense probably indicates that they thought they were just about to die [Hb, TH]. The Greek language does not make a distinction between the inclusive 'we' and the exclusive 'we'. However many languages require that such a distinction be made. If a translation uses the inclusive form, they would be saying 'Does it not concern you that *we disciples and also you* are perishing?', perhaps thinking that since Jesus had been asleep he was unaware of the danger to himself and his disciples. If the exclusive form is used, they would be saying 'Does it not concern you that *we disciples* are perishing?', perhaps thinking that Jesus would make a miraculous escape and leave them behind. Translators usually choose the inclusive form [TH].

QUESTION—What is implied by their question?
  This was a definite reproach [AB1, BNTC, CGTC, EBC, NAC, NCBC, NICNT, NTC, PNTC, Sw, Tay, TH, TRT, WBC]. They resented Jesus' apparent indifference to their peril [Hb, Tay]. Their question implied that they thought Jesus didn't care about their survival [NTC, WBC]. They thought it was unbelievable that Jesus should not care [Lns]. They had been with him long enough to presume that he would have the solution to this problem that was beyond their control [NIGTC]. Since the use of οὐ 'not' in their question anticipates a positive answer, this was a request for help [BECNT, CBC, Gnd]. Yet they seemed to lack faith that he would save them from destruction [Gnd].

4:39 **And having-been-awakened**[a] **he-rebuked**[b] **the wind and he-said to-the lake, "Be-still,**[c] **be-silenced.**[d]**"**

LEXICON—a. aorist pass. participle of διεγείρω (LN 23.77) (BAGD p. 194): 'to be awakened' [BAGD, LN], 'to be caused to wake up' [LN], 'to be aroused' [WBC]. This passive verb is translated actively: 'he woke up' [BNTC; NLT, NRSV; similarly Lns], 'he awoke' [AB1, BECNT, ESV, KJV, REB], 'he roused himself' [AB2], 'he got up' [NTC; CEV, GW, NASB, NET, NIV], 'he stood up' [NCV, TEV]. This verb means to cause someone to awaken [LN].

  b. aorist act. indic. of ἐπιτιμάω (LN 33.331) (BAGD 1. p. 303): 'to rebuke' [AB1, AB2, BAGD, BECNT, Lns, NTC, WBC; ESV, KJV, NASB, NET, NIV, NLT, NRSV, REB], 'to reprove' [BAGD, BNTC], 'to censure' [BAGD], 'to command' [LN; NCV, TEV], 'to order' [CEV]. The phrase 'he rebuked the wind' is translated 'he ordered the wind to stop' [GW]. This verb means to command, and there is an implied threat for disobedience [LN].

  c. pres. act. impera. of σιωπάω (LN **14.24**) (BAGD 2.b. p. 752): 'to become calm' [LN], 'to become still' [**LN**]. This imperative is translated 'Be still!' [WBC; GW], 'Hush!' [NTC; NASB], 'Be quiet!' [AB1; NET, TEV], 'Quiet!' [BECNT, BNTC; NCV, NIV], 'Be silent!' [Lns], 'Silence!' [AB2; NLT, REB], 'Peace!' [ESV, KJV, NRSV]. The two imperatives 'be still, be silenced' are translated 'ordered the wind and the waves to be quiet' [CEV]. In connection with the wind and waves in a storm, the verb 'to become quiet' is used figuratively [BAGD]. This figurative extension of the verb 'to be silent' refers to the process of the water becoming calm after a storm. Since there is a change in state, it may be necessary to translate this 'become still' or 'cease to be stormy' [LN]. It can denote quietness, inactivity, or calmness [TH].

  d. perf. pass. impera. of φιμόω (LN **14.86**) (BAGD 2. p. 862): 'to be silenced' [BAGD], 'to become still, to become quiet' [**LN**]. The imperative is translated 'be still' [AB1, BECNT, NTC; ESV, KJV, NASB, NCV, NIV, NLT, NRSV, REB, TEV], '(be still,) absolutely still' [GW], 'remain quiet' [WBC], 'be silent' [BNTC], 'shut up' [AB2], 'calm down' [NET], 'put the muzzle on and keep it on' [Lns]. This verb means to cause something to cease making a sound [LN]. This was the same command given to an unclean spirit in 1:25 [TH].

QUESTION—How did Jesus rebuke the wind?

The wind and waves were addressed as though they were rational agents who had gone beyond their legitimate bounds [Hb, NIGTC]. This is a figurative or poetic manner of speaking [NTC]. Jesus ordered the wind to stop blowing [GW], and become quiet [CEV, TEV].

QUESTION—Why did Jesus give these commands to the lake?

The lake is personified and addressed as though it were able to obey the command [My, PNTC]. Jesus spoke as though the storm was a force threatening him and his disciples [NICNT].

QUESTION—To what are the two commands 'Be still, be silenced' directed?

1. Both commands were addressed to the lake [AB1, AB2, BNTC, Gnd, NTC, PNTC, TH, WBC; all versions except CEV, TEV]. 'He…rebuked the wind, and said to the sea, "Be quiet! Calm down!"' [NET]. Jesus addressed the wind and the lake separately by rebuking the wind and then saying to the lake, 'Hush! Be still!' The results of the two commands are then indicated separately [NTC].
2. The command 'Be quiet!' was addressed to the wind, and the command 'be silenced' was addressed to the waves [BECNT, EBC, Hb; TEV]. The two commands were directed to the wind and the waves separately [BECNT]. 'Be silent' was directed at the howling wind, and 'be silenced' was directed at the raging waves [Hb]. 'Jesus…commanded the wind, "Be quiet!" and he said to the waves, "Be still!"' [TEV].
3. Both commands were addressed to the wind and the lake [Lns; CEV; probably NCBC]. 'Jesus…ordered the wind and the waves to be quiet' [CEV]. The rebuke to the wind goes with the command to the lake since wind and lake acted together [Lns].

And the wind died-down^a and there-was a-great calm.^b

LEXICON—a. aorist act. indic. of κοπάζω (LN 68.42) (BAGD p. 443): 'to die down' [AB2; NASB, NIV, TEV], 'to abate' [BAGD, WBC], 'to drop' [AB1, BNTC; REB], 'to fall' [NTC], 'to cease' [BAGD, BECNT, LN; ESV, KJV, NRSV], 'to stop' [BAGD, LN; CEV, NCV, NET, NLT], 'to stop blowing' [GW], 'to grow tired' [Lns]. This verb means to cease, in reference to some type of movement [LN].

b. γαλήνη (LN **14.23**) (BAGD p. 150): 'calm' [BAGD, **LN**, WBC]. The phrase 'a great calm' [AB1, AB2, BECNT, BNTC, Lns, WBC; ESV, KJV, NLT, TEV] is also translated 'a dead calm' [NET, NRSV, REB], 'a deep calm' [NTC], '(was/became) completely calm' [NASB, NCV, NIV], '(became) very calm' [GW], '(was) calm' [CEV]. This noun denotes a calm and unruffled surface of a body of water [LN].

4:40 And he-said to-them, "Why are-you cowardly[a]? Do-you- still not have-faith[b]?"

TEXT—Manuscripts reading Τί δειλοί ἐστε; οὔπω ἔχετε πίστιν; 'Why are you cowardly? Do you still not have faith?' are given an A rating by GNT to indicate it was regarded to be certain. Variant readings are Τί δειλοί ἐστε οὕτως; ἔχετε πίστιν; 'Why are you thus cowardly? Do you have faith?', Τί οὕτως δειλοί ἐστε; οὔπω ἔχετε πίστιν; 'Why are you thus cowardly? Do you not yet have faith?', Τί δειλοί ἐστε οὕτως; πῶς οὐκ ἔχετε πίστιν; 'Why are you thus cowardly? How do you not have faith?', Τί δειλοί ἐστε, ὀλιγόπιστοι; οὔπω ἔχετε πίστιν; 'Why are you cowardly, little faith ones? Do you still not have faith?', and Τί δειλοί ἐστε, ὀλιγόπιστοι; οὕτως ἔχετε πίστιν; 'Why are you cowardly little faith ones? Do you thus have faith?'.

LEXICON—a. δειλός (LN 25.268) (BAGD p. 173): 'cowardly' [BAGD, LN]. The question Τί δειλοί ἐστε; 'Why are you cowardly?' [AB2; NET] is also translated 'Why are you so cowardly?' [BNTC], 'Why are you such cowards?' [GW, REB], 'Why are you afraid?' [BECNT, NTC; CEV, NASB, NCV, NLT, NRSV], 'Why are you so afraid?' [ESV, NIV], 'Why are ye so fearful?' [KJV], 'Why are you frightened?' [AB1; TEV]. Some translate the present tense of the verb ἐστε 'are' in the past tense: 'Why were you frightened?' [WBC], 'Why were you afraid?' [CEV]. This question is translated as an exclamation: 'How frightened you are!' [Lns]. This adjective pertains to being cowardly [LN].

b. πίστις (LN 31.85) (BAGD 2.b.α. p. 663): 'faith' [BAGD]. The question οὔπω ἔχετε πίστιν 'Do you still not have faith?' [NET] is also translated 'Have you still no faith?' [NTC; ESV, NRSV], 'Do you still have no faith?' [NCV, NIV, NLT, TEV], 'Do you not yet have faith?' [BECNT, WBC; similarly AB2, BNTC, Lns; GW], 'Have you no faith, even now?' [AB1; REB], 'Don't you have any faith?' [CEV], 'How is it that you have no faith?' [KJV, NASB]. This noun denotes a complete trust and reliance in someone [LN]. In this context, faith refers to a belief and trust in the Lord's help when there is physical and spiritual distress [BAGD].

QUESTION—What is implied by the question 'Why are you cowardly?'

The question is a rebuke for being so afraid in the face of the storm's danger [BNTC, EBC, Hb, Lns, NAC, Sw, WBC]. Seeing their fearful and cowardly actions, Jesus expressed his surprise at their lack of faith [Lns]. They should not have been fearful after all they had seen and heard during their association with Jesus [EBC, Hb].

QUESTION—What is implied by the question 'Do you still not have faith?'?

This is an expansion on the previous question since their fear had exposed their lack of faith [Hb, NICNT, WBC]. It is a rebuke [CGTC, NAC, NIGTC, Tay] for not responding to a crisis with a firm confidence in God or in Jesus [NIGTC]. The text does not state whether this faith is in God or in Jesus himself [BECNT, TH].

1. Here it refers to having faith in Jesus [BECNT, CGTC, EBC, Hb, ICC, My, NAC, NICNT, NIGTC, TRT, WBC]. This faith refers to a practical confidence in Jesus' supernatural power [Hb, NIGTC]. They should have had faith that God's helping power was present in Jesus [CGTC, EBC, NAC, NICNT, WBC]. It is faith in Jesus, both in his power and in his disposition to care for them. Their appeal to Jesus in the boat had not been the calm request of trust in his power, rather it had been a frightened reproach by men whose faith had been overcome by the danger they faced [ICC]. They still did not understand that the kingdom was present in the person and work of Jesus and their fear during the storm implied that they lacked a strong faith in him and his power [Hb].
2. It refers to their faith in God [AB1, Tay, TH]. This refers to faith in God's providential care [AB1]. It is faith in God's care, the kind of faith Jesus displayed while he slept in the boat [Tay].

QUESTION—What is implied by saying that they οὔπω 'still' do not have faith?

In spite of what they have seen and heard, they still did not understand and believe what should have been apparent in the ministry of Jesus [BNTC]. By this time they should have learned something about the secret that the kingdom of God has come in the person and work of Jesus [CGTC]. Jesus expected a more mature faith by this time [EBC].

4:41 And they-were-afraid[a] with-a-great fear and they-were-saying to one-another, "Who then is this (person) that even the wind and the lake[b] obeys[c] him?"

LEXICON —a. aorist pass. indic. of φοβέομαι, φοβέω (LN 25.252) (BAGD 1.a. p. 862): 'to be afraid' [BAGD, LN], 'to fear' [LN]. The phrase ἐφοβήθησαν φόβον μέγαν 'they were afraid with a great fear' is translated 'they feared a great fear' [AB2; similarly Lns], 'the followers were very much afraid' [NCV], 'they became very much afraid' [NASB], 'they were terribly afraid' [TEV], 'they were terrified' [BNTC; NIV], 'the disciples were absolutely terrified' [NLT], 'they feared exceedingly' [KJV], 'they were filled with great fear' [ESV], 'they were overcome with fear' [GW], 'they were overwhelmed by fear' [NET], 'they were more afraid than ever' [CEV], 'they were awestruck' [AB1, NTC, WBC; REB], 'they were filled with awe' [BECNT], 'they were filled with great awe' [NRSV]. This verb means to be in a state of fear [LN].
  b. θάλασσα (LN 1.70): 'lake' [LN], 'sea' [AB1, AB2, BECNT, BNTC, LN, Lns, NTC, WBC; ESV, GW, KJV, NASB, NET, NRSV, REB]. Some refer to the particular part of the lake that had been affected: 'waves' [CEV, NCV, NIV, NLT, TEV]. This noun denotes a particular body of water, normally rather large [LN].
  c. pres. act. indic. of ὑπακούω (LN 36.15) (BAGD 1. p. 837): 'to obey' [BAGD, LN; all translations]. This verb means to obey on the basis of having paid attention to a command [LN]. The verb is singular in order to

indicate that both the wind and the lake acted in unity [EGT, Hb, ICC, Sw]. The present tense indicates that they obey him as a matter of course [Lns].

QUESTION—Why did the disciples have such a great fear?

This is a different fear than they had in the boat when they were afraid of drowning [AB2, BECNT, Gnd, Hb, Lns, NIGTC, NTC, Sw, Tay, WBC]. They had been scared of the wind and waves, but here they were filled with a reverential fear of Jesus [Gnd]. This is the kind of fear that is the appropriate response to a display of divine power or glory [AB2, BECNT, EBC, NIGTC]. The disciples were not afraid of Jesus [Lns]. They regarded him with the greatest awe [BECNT, CBC, EBC, Hb, Lns, NAC, Sw; NRSV, REB]. It was a reverential awe [AB1, NCBC, Tay, WBC] that came from understanding that the divine had met them in Jesus [NAC].

QUESTION—What relationship is indicated by the conjunction ἄρα 'then' in their question 'who then is this person?'

This conjunction refers to the logical deduction to be made from what they had just seen Jesus do when he caused the wind and waves to obey his command [Gnd].

QUESTION—What is the force of the ascensive καί 'even'?

Not only diseases and demons obeyed Jesus, even the elements themselves obeyed him [ICC, Sw].

QUESTION—What is implied by their question?

This indicates that they were left wondering about the source and character of Jesus' authority [BNTC]. They realized that they did not yet understand who Jesus really was [Hb]. They were beginning to realize that Jesus was far greater than they had previously imagined [Gnd, NTC]. It is a rhetorical question that was not asked in search of an answer [BECNT, EBC, Gnd, WBC]. The disciples were making an exclamation about Jesus' greatness, not asking what his name is [TRT]. They were making a positive expression of the greatness of Jesus [BECNT]. The implied answer is 'He is the strong Son of God' [EBC]. Instead of being left in confusion and doubt about who Jesus was, their reverential awe indicates that they had recognized that Jesus was accomplishing God's work by stilling the storm and calming the lake [WBC].

DISCOURSE UNIT—5:1–20 [CBC, EBC, Hb, NICNT; CEV, ESV, GW, NASB, NCV, NET, NIV, NLT, NRSV, TEV]. The topic is a man with evil spirits [CEV], the Gerasene demoniac [NASB], a man with demons inside him [NCV], the Gerasene demoniac: the subduing of the demoniac [NICNT], the healing of a demoniac [NET], the healing of a demon-possessed man [EBC; NIV], the cure of the Gerasene demoniac [Hb], the healing of the Gerasene demoniac [CBC], Jesus cures a demon-possessed man [GW], Jesus heals a man with a demon [ESV], Jesus heals the Gerasene demoniac [NRSV], Jesus heals a man with evil spirit [TEV], Jesus exercises authority over demons [NLT].

5:1 **And they-came to the other-side of-the lake to the region[a] of-the Gerasenes.**

TEXT—Manuscripts reading Γερασηνῶν 'Gerasenes' are given a C rating by GNT to indicate that choosing it over a variant text was difficult. A variant reading is Γαδαρηνῶν 'Gadarenes' and it is followed by ICC; KJV. Another variant reading is Γεργεσηνῶν 'Gergesenes' and it is followed by Gnd. Still another variant reading is Γεργυστηνῶν 'Gergustenes'.

LEXICON—a. χώρα (LN 1.79) (BAGD 1.b. p. 889): 'region' [AB2, BAGD, LN, WBC; CEV, NET, NIV, NLT], 'territory' [BECNT, LN; GW, TEV], 'district' [BAGD, BNTC], 'country' [AB1, Lns, NTC; ESV, KJV, NASB, NRSV, REB], 'place' [BAGD], 'area' [NCV], 'land' [LN]. This noun refers to an area occupied by some ethnic group or to a geographical center. This area does not necessarily constitute a unit of governmental administration [LN].

QUESTION—Who are the referents of the verb 'they came'?

This refers to Jesus and his disciples [AB2, BECNT, Gnd, Hb, Lns, TRT; CEV, NCV, TEV]. They had completed the trip they began in 4:35 [NLTfn]. The men in the other boats that had set out in 4:36 are no longer in the story [Lns].

QUESTION—Where was the region of the Gerasenes?

Since the boat came to *the other side* of the lake, this region was located on the eastern side of the Lake of Galilee [EBC, WBC]. It was the region of τῶν Γερασηνῶν 'the Gerasenes', the people who lived east of the Jordan in Gerasa, a city in Peraea [LN (93.450)]. Yet the exact identification of the region is disputed [TH]. Textual variants arose because the city of Gerasa was not located on the shore of the lake, but southeast of the lake about thirty miles inland [EBC]. The *region* of the Gerasenes probably refers to the entire district extending from Gerasa down to the lake [BECNT, EBC, Lns, NIGTC, PNTC]. Another possibility is that the name Gerasenes does not refer to the people of the city of Gerasa but to the small town of Kersa (also called Gersa) which was near the lake about midway along the eastern shore [CGTC, EBC, Hb, NAC, NICNT]. In Matt. 8:28 it is called 'the country of Gadarenes' [Hb, Lns]. The presence of the herds of pigs indicates that it was an area populated by Gentiles [AB1, EBC].

5:2 **And he having-come[a] out of-the boat immediately a-man with[b] an-unclean[c] spirit met[d] him from-out-of the tombs,[e]**

LEXICON—a. aorist act. participle of ἐξέρχομαι (LN 15.40) (BAGD 1.a.α. p. 274): 'to come out of' [AB2, BECNT, WBC; KJV, NET], 'to get out of' [BAGD, BNTC, LN, NTC; CEV, NASB, NCV, NET, NIV, TEV], 'to climb out of' [NLT], 'to go out of' [LN, Lns], 'to depart out of' [LN], 'to leave' [AB1], 'to step out of' [ESV, GW, NRSV], 'to step ashore' [REB]. This verb means to move out of an enclosed or well-defined two or three-dimensional area [LN].

b. ἐν (LN 13.8) (BAGD 1.5.d. p. 260): 'with' [AB1, BECNT, BNTC, LN, Lns, NTC, WBC; CEV, ESV, KJV, NASB, NCV, NET, NRSV, TEV], 'in' [AB2]. The phrase 'with an unclean spirit' is translated 'possessed by an unclean spirit' [REB], 'possessed by an evil spirit' [NIV, NLT], 'was controlled by an evil spirit' [GW], 'had an evil spirit in him' [TEV]. This preposition indicates being in some state or condition [LN]. It designates a close personal relationship, and the phrase 'to be in a spirit' means to be under the special influence of a spirit, even a demonic spirit [BAGD]. The preposition ἐν has the force of the Hebrew b^e 'having' [TH]. The phrase 'with an unclean spirit' also occurs at 1:23 where there is a discussion about the meaning of the phrase.

c. ἀκάθαρτος (LN 12.39) (BAGD 2. p. 29): 'unclean' [AB1, AB2, BAGD, BECNT, BNTC, LN, Lns, NTC, WBC; ESV, KJV, NASB, NET, NRSV, REB], 'impure' [BAGD], 'evil' [CEV, GW, NCV, NIV, NLT, TEV]. Evil spirits are called 'unclean spirits' at 1:23, 26, 27; 3:11, 30; 5:2, 8, 13; 6:7; 7:25; 9:25.

d. aorist act. indic. of ὑπαντάω (LN 15.78) (BAGD p. 837): 'to meet' [AB1, AB2, BAGD, BECNT, LN, Lns, NTC, WBC; ESV, GW, KJV, NASB, NET, NLT, NRSV, TEV], 'to meet up with, to draw near' [LN], 'to come up to' [REB], 'to come to meet' [BNTC], 'to come' [NCV]. The phrase 'immediately there met him' is translated 'quickly ran to him' [CEV]. This verb means to come near to and meet someone, either in a friendly or hostile sense [LN]. This means that he encountered this man [Hb, TH]. Jesus was confronted by this man as soon as he stepped out of the boat [EBC].

e. μνημεῖον (LN **7.75**) (BAGD 2. p. 524): 'tomb' [AB1, AB2, BAGD, BECNT, BNTC, **LN**, Lns, NTC, WBC; ESV, GW, KJV, NASB, NET, NIV, NRSV, REB], 'burial cave' [NCV, TEV], 'grave' [BAGD, LN]. The phrase 'from out of the tombs' is translated 'from the graveyard' [CEV], 'from a cemetery' [NLT]. The noun denotes a construction for the burial of the dead [LN]. This word occurs at 5:2; 6:29; 15:46; 16:2, 3, 5, 8.

QUESTION—What were the tombs the man came from?

Probably these were small caves hewn in the limestone walls of cliffs [AB2, EBC, Hb, ICC, Lns, NCBC, TH; NCV, TEV], or natural caverns that served as tombs [EBC, ICC, TH]. These tombs could also provide shelter for a man who had no other place to go [AB2, EBC].

5:3 who had his dwelling-place[a] in the tombs,[b] and no-one no-longer was-able to-bind[c] him not-even with-a-chain[d]

LEXICON—a. κατοίκησις (LN 85.70) (BAGD p. 424): 'dwelling place' [LN], 'dwelling' [AB2, BAGD, LN, Lns; KJV, NASB], 'living quarters' [NTC], 'a place to dwell' [**LN**]. The phrase 'had his dwelling place' is translated 'had made his home' [BNTC], '(he) lived' [AB1, WBC; ESV, GW, NCV, NET, NIV, NLT, NRSV, TEV], 'was dwelling' [BECNT], 'where he had made his home' [REB], 'where he had been living' [CEV]. This noun is derived from the verb κατοικέω 'to dwell' and denotes a place of dwelling, whether an object or area [LN].

b. μνᾶμα (LN 7.75) (BAGD p. 524): 'tomb' [BAGD, LN], 'grave' [BAGD, LN]. The phrase 'in the tombs' [AB1, BAGD, LN, Lns; NIV] is also translated 'among the tombs' [AB2, BECNT, BNTC, NTC, WBC; ESV, GW, KJV, NASB, NET, NRSV, REB, TEV], 'in the caves' [NCV], 'among the burial caves' [NLT]. The plural form 'tombs' is translated 'grave yard' [CEV]. The noun denotes a construction for the burial of the dead. This verb is in the same semantic domain as μνημεῖον 'tomb' in 5:2 [LN]. This word occurs only at 5:3, 5.

c. aorist act. infin. of δέω (LN 18.13) (BAGD 1.b. p. 177): 'to bind' [BAGD, BECNT, BNTC, Lns, NTC, WBC; ESV, KJV, NASB, NET, NIV], 'to tie, to tie together' [LN], 'to tie up' [AB2, LN; CEV, NCV], 'to keep him tied' [TEV], 'to restrain' [GW, NLT, NRSV], 'to control' [AB1; REB]. This verb means to tie objects together [LN].

d. ἅλυσις (LN 6.16) (BAGD 1. p. 41): 'chain' [BAGD, LN; all translations]. The phrase 'not even with a chain' is translated 'even chains were useless' [REB]. This noun denotes a linked, metal instrument used for binding someone [LN].

QUESTION—Why did this man have a dwelling place in the tombs?
This man used to live in a town until he had become demon-possessed (Luke 8:39), and then he was no longer allowed to live in town [EGT, NTC]. Now he lived in abandoned burial caves hewn in the sides of the cliffs [Lns, NTC]. Burial caves had room enough to stand and to move around in them [BECNT]. The statement that he dwelt in the 'tombs' (plural) implies that he moved about to find shelter in various tombs [Hb]. Or the plural form 'tombs' could just be referring to a graveyard [CEV, NET].

QUESTION—Why did people need to bind the demoniac?
This does not state whether their reason for binding the man was to keep him from hurting himself or from hurting others since it is not essential to the story [BECNT]. They bound him in order to protect themselves from his violence [NICNT, NTC]. It is implied that they were not able to bind him for long because the next verse tells how he tore apart the chains that bound him [AB2].

QUESTION—What is implied by the phrase 'no longer'?
This implies that his case had grown worse [Hb, Sw], or that his strength had increased [Gnd]. His abnormal strength could now overcome all attempts to keep him bound [Hb].

5:4 because[a] he often had-been-bound with-shackles[b] and chains and the chains had-been-torn-apart[c] by him and the shackles had been smashed,[d] and no-one was-strong (enough) to-subdue[e] him.

LEXICON—a. διά (LN 89.26): 'because' [BECNT, LN; KJV, NASB], 'for' [AB2, BNTC; ESV, NET, NIV, NRSV, REB], 'on account of' [LN, Lns], not explicit [AB1, NTC; CEV, GW, NCV, NLT, TEV]. The conjunction indicates a cause or reason [LN].

b. πέδη (LN **6.17**) (BAGD p. 638): 'shackles' [BAGD, **LN**, NTC, WBC; ESV, NASB, NET, NLT, NRSV], 'fetters' [AB2, BAGD, BECNT, BNTC, LN, Lns; KJV], 'leg irons' [CEV]. The phrase 'he had been bound with shackles and chains' is translated 'he had been chained hand and foot' [GW, NIV], 'his feet and hands had been tied' [TEV], 'people had used chains to tie the man's hands and feet' [NCV], 'he had been fettered' [AB1; REB]. This noun denotes a shackle for the feet and normally consisted of chains with special links prepared to go around the ankles [LN].

c. perf. pass. infin. of διασπάω (LN **19.29**) (BAGD p. 188): 'to be torn apart' [AB2, BAGD, **LN**, NTC, WBC; NASB], 'to be wrenched apart' [BECNT], 'to be pulled apart' [LN], 'to be plucked asunder' [KJV], 'to be broken' [Lns]. This passive verb is also translated actively: 'he broke the chains' [CEV, TEV], 'he broke them off' [NCV], 'he tore the chains apart' [NIV; similarly BNTC; NET], 'he wrenched the chains apart' [ESV; similarly NRSV], 'he had snapped his chains' [AB1; REB], 'he snapped the chains off his hands' [GW], 'he snapped the chains from his wrists' [NLT]. This verb means to pull or tear an object apart [LN].

d. perf. pass. infin. of συντρίβω (LN 19.39) (BAGD 1.a. p. 793): 'to be smashed' [AB2, BAGD, LN], 'to be smashed in pieces' [WBC], 'to be shattered' [BAGD, LN], 'to be broken into/in pieces' [BECNT, LN, NTC; KJV, NASB], 'to be torn to pieces' [Lns]. This passive verb is also translated actively: 'he smashed the shackles/fetters' [BNTC; NLT], 'he smashed the leg irons' [CEV], 'he smashed the irons on his feet' [TEV], 'he had broken the fetters' [AB1; REB], 'he broke the shackles in pieces' [ESV, NET; similarly NRSV], 'he broke them off' [NCV], 'he broke the irons on his feet' [NIV], 'he broke the chains from his feet' [GW]. The verb means to break or shatter a solid object into pieces [LN].

e. aorist act. infin. of δαμάζω (LN **37.1**) (BAGD 1. p. 170): 'to subdue' [AB2, BAGD, BECNT, BNTC, NTC, WBC; ESV, NASB, NET, NIV, NLT, NRSV], 'to get control of' [**LN**], 'to control' [LN; CEV, GW, NCV, TEV], 'to bring under control' [LN], 'to master' [AB1; REB], 'to tame' [Lns; KJV]. This verb means to bring someone under control and continue to restrain him [LN].

QUESTION—What relationship is indicated by the conjunction διά 'because'?

It indicates the grounds for saying that no one was able to bind him [Gnd, Hb, ICC, My, NTC, Sw]. It explains the present situation by relating the past circumstances [CGTC, Tay]. It indicates both the reason and the evidence for saying that no one was able to bind him [Lns].

QUESTION—What were the shackles used for and how were they smashed?

The shackles were foot or ankle chains [TRT]. Perhaps they were leg irons consisting of a pair of metal rings around the ankles and connected with a chain [NTC]. Since the chains on the wrists were 'torn apart' and the shackles were 'smashed', perhaps the difference in the actions of the verbs indicates that the shackles were made of a different material than that of the iron used on the wrists [EGT, My]. Shackles were used to bind the man's feet and his legs [BECNT, EGT, Gnd, Hb, TH]. The man smashed the shackles with stones or by slamming them against rocks on the ground [TH]. They were broken to pieces [BECNT, Gnd, Tay].

QUESTION—What were the chains used for and how were they torn apart?
They were hand or wrist chains [TRT] that served as handcuffs [BECNT]. The chains were used to bind the hands and arms [BECNT, EGT, Gnd, TH]. They were broken by being pulled apart [Gnd, ICC, TH, TRT]. The man violently wrenched them apart [BECNT, TH].

5:5 And through[a] all (the) night and day among the tombs and in the mountains[b] he-was-crying-out[c] and cutting[d] himself with-stones.

LEXICON—a. διά (LN 67.86) (BAGD A.II.1.a. p. 179): 'through, during' [BAGD, LN]. The phrase διὰ παντός 'through all' is translated 'always' [BAGD, LN, Lns, NTC; ESV, KJV, NRSV], 'constantly' [BAGD, LN; NASB], 'continuously' [AB2], 'continually' [BAGD, LN], 'unceasingly' [REB], 'each (night and day)' [NET], 'all (night and day)' [WBC], not explicit [AB1, BECNT, BNTC; CEV, GW, NCV, NIV, NLT, TEV]. The idiom 'through all' denotes a duration of time without limits that may be continuous or episodic [LN].

b. ὄρος (LN 1.46) (BAGD p. 582): 'mountain', [AB2, BAGD, BECNT, LN, Lns, WBC; ESV, KJV, NASB, NET, NRSV], 'mountain side' [GW], 'hill' [BAGD, LN, NTC; CEV, NCV, NIV, NLT, TEV], 'hillside' [AB1, BNTC; REB]. This noun denotes a high elevation of land that is higher than a βουνός 'hill' (1.48) [LN].

c. pres. act. participle of κράζω (LN 33.83) (BAGD 1. p. 447): 'to cry out' [BAGD, BECNT; ESV, NET, NIV], 'to cry aloud' [BNTC; REB], 'to cry' [KJV], 'to shriek' [AB2, BAGD], 'to shout' [LN], 'to scream' [AB1, BAGD, LN, NTC, WBC; GW, NASB, NCV, TEV], 'to yell' [Lns; CEV], 'to howl' [NLT, NRSV]. This verb means to shout or cry out, perhaps with an unpleasant sound [LN]. This refers to loud cries without words that were capable of being understood, the kind of cries made by insane persons, epileptics, or evil spirits living in them [BAGD]. He was crying out in agony for help [BECNT].

d. pres. act. participle of κατακόπτω (LN **19.21**) (BAGD 1. p. 412): 'to cut' [AB1, AB2, BAGD, BECNT, BNTC, LN, Lns; all versions except NASB, NRSV, REB], 'to gash' [NTC; NASB, REB], 'to beat' [BAGD, WBC], 'to bruise' [BAGD; NRSV]. This verb means to cut severely with a sharp instrument or object [LN]. Some have interpreted κατακόπτω in Mark 5:5 to mean 'to bruise severely' [WBC; NRSV] on the basis that stones would only bruise a person rather than cut him, but this inference seems unnecessary [LN, Tay].

QUESTION—What is meant by 'through all the night and day'?

This means at intervals during each night and day [NICNT, Sw, Tay]. He habitually did this at intervals [NTC]. There were no long intervals between his frenzied actions [Hb, Sw]. He did this all night and all day long [NTC].

QUESTION—What is the connection between the tombs and the mountains?

Day and night his restlessness spurred him to action. He would sit among the tombs for a while, but soon he would be going about through the mountains in the area [Hb]. He was always in the tombs or in the mountains [CEV].

QUESTION— Why would he cut himself with sharp stones?

Demons always injured the people they possessed [Lns]. When he cut himself with the sharp points of stones, it demonstrated the life-destroying aim of the demon who possessed him [ESVfn, Gnd, NIVfn, TRT]. This shows that the man wanted to kill himself to end his unbearable existence [NICNT].

5:6 And having-seen Jesus from afar[a] he-ran and bowed-down-before[b] him.

LEXICON—a. μακρόθεν (LN 83.30) (BAGD p. 488): 'far, at a distance, some distance away, far away' [LN]. The phrase ἀπὸ μακρόθεν 'from afar' [BECNT, BNTC, Lns; ESV] is also translated 'afar off' [KJV], 'far away' [NCV], 'from far away' [AB2], 'from a distance' [BAGD, NTC; NASB, NET, NIV, NRSV], 'at a distance' [WBC; GW], 'in the distance' [AB1; CEV, REB], 'some distance away' [NLT, TEV]. This adjective refers to a position at a relatively great distance from another position [LN].

b. aorist act. indic. of προσκυνέω (LN 17.21) (BAGD 5. p. 717): 'to prostrate oneself before' [BAGD, LN], 'to fall down before' [ESV, NCV], 'to fall on one's knees in front of/before' [NTC; NIV, TEV], 'to fling oneself down before' [REB], 'to throw oneself down before' [AB1, AB2, BNTC], 'to bow before' [WBC], 'to bow down before' [NASB, NET, NRSV], 'to bow low before' [NLT], 'to bow down in front of' [GW], 'to kneel down before' [BECNT], 'to kneel down' [CEV], 'to do obeisance to' [BAGD], 'to make obeisance to' [Lns], 'to worship' [KJV]. This verb means to prostrate oneself before someone as an act of reverence, fear, or supplication [LN].

QUESTION—What relationship is indicated by the initial καί 'and'?

The conjunction 'and' connects the description of the man's past with his conduct on this occasion when he encountered Jesus [Hb]. The account of Jesus' encounter with the demon-possessed man began in 5:1–2 and now it is being resumed after having been interrupted by the parenthetical history of the man in 5:3–5 [BECNT, BNTC, CGTC, Hb, NCBC, NICNT, NIGTC, Tay, WBC].

QUESTION—What is the function of verse 6?

Before going on with the account, Mark paused to describe the details of his short summary statement in 5:2, 'there met him…a man with an unclean spirit' [CGTC, EBC, Gnd, Hb]. The participle 'having seen' is temporal:

'And *when* he saw Jesus afar off' [AB1, BNTC, Hb, NTC; CEV, ESV, NET, NIV, NLT, NRSV, REB, TEV]. The man came running towards the boat's destination point in order to accost Jesus as soon as he stepped ashore [NTC, Tay]. He intended to make Jesus go away [Gnd].

QUESTION—Why did the man bow down before Jesus?

When the man fell on his knees in front of Jesus, it was an act of homage paid to one who was his superior, not an act of worship and devotion [EBC, Lns, WBC]. The demon recognized Jesus' superior power [EBC, Gnd, NCBC, NICNT], and was in awe of his divine majesty [Gnd, NTC]. It was the demon possessing the man who caused him to approach Jesus and bow before him in acknowledgement of Jesus' true nature [EBC, Hb]. Or perhaps the man recognized Jesus' superior power, and against the wishes of the demons [BECNT], he approached Jesus and bowed down in hope of receiving help [BECNT, NLTfn].

5:7 And crying-out[a] (with) a–loud voice he-says, "What to-me and to-you,[b] Jesus Son of-the Highest[c] God? I-implore[d] you by-God, don't torture[e] me."

LEXICON—a. aorist act. participle of κράζω (LN 33.83) (BAGD 2.a. p. 447): 'to call out loudly' [BAGD], 'to shout, to scream' [LN]. The phrase κράξας φωνῇ μεγάλῃ λέγει 'crying out with a loud voice he says' [BECNT; ESV] is translated 'cried with a loud voice, and said' [KJV], 'shouting with a loud voice, he said' [NASB], 'screaming with a loud voice, he said' [WBC], 'yelling with a loud voice, he says' [Lns], 'shrieking with a loud voice he said' [AB2], 'with a shriek, he screamed' [NLT], 'cried out with a loud voice' [NET], 'cried/shouted in a loud voice' [BNTC; NCV], 'screamed in a loud voice' [TEV], 'shouted loudly' [AB1], 'he shouted at the top of his voice' [NIV, NRSV; similarly REB], 'at the top of his voice he yelled' [NTC], 'he shouted' [CEV, GW]. This verb means to shout or cry out [LN].

b. τί ἐμοί καὶ σοί 'what to me and to you' is an idiom used to express a protest against hostile measures [BAGD (p. 217)]. Here this idiom is translated 'What have I to do with you?' [BAGD, Lns; KJV; similarly AB2], 'What have you to do with me?' [NRSV; similarly ESV], 'What do we have in common?' [BAGD, WBC], 'What business do we have with each other…?' [NASB], 'What do you want with me?' [AB1, BECNT, BNTC; CEV, NCV, NIV, REB, TEV], 'Why are you bothering me now?' [GW; similarly NTC], 'Why are you interfering with me?' [NLT], 'Leave me alone!' [BAGD; NET].

c. ὕψιστος (LN 12.4) (BAGD 2. p. 850): 'Highest, Supreme' [LN], 'Most High' [BAGD, LN]. The phrase θεοῦ τοῦ ὑψίστου 'the Highest God' is translated 'God the Highest' [Lns], 'the Most High God' [AB2, BECNT, BNTC, NTC, WBC; all versions except CEV], 'God most high' [AB1], 'God in heaven' [CEV]. This adjective is used as a title to refer to God's status as the one who is supreme [LN].

d. pres. act. indic. of ὁρκίζω (LN 33.467) (BAGD p. 581): 'to implore, to adjure' [BAGD], 'to put under oath, to insist that one take an oath, to require that one swear' [LN]. The phrase ὁρκίζω σε τὸν θεόν 'I implore you by God' [BAGD; NASB, NET] is also translated 'I adjure you by God' [AB2, BECNT, Lns, WBC; ESV, KJV, NRSV], 'I command you in God's name' [NCV], 'Promise me in God's name' [CEV], 'Swear to God that' [NTC; GW, NIV], 'In God's name' [AB1, BNTC; REB], 'In the name of God, I beg you' [NLT], 'I ask you to swear by the name of God' [LN], or more idiomatically, 'for God's sake, I ask/beg you' [**LN**; TEV]. This verb means to demand that a person take an oath as to the truth of what is said or as to the certainty that one will carry out a request or command [LN].

e. aorist act. subj. of βασανίζω (LN 38.13) (BAGD 2.a. p. 134): 'to torture' [AB2, BAGD, LN, NTC; CEV, GW, NCV, NIV, NLT], 'to torment' [AB1, BAGD, BECNT, BNTC, LN, Lns, WBC; ESV, KJV, NASB, NET, NRSV, REB], 'to punish' [TEV]. This verb means to punish by physical torture or torment [LN]. It is used figuratively to refer to any severe distress [BAGD]. It means 'to cause to suffer' [TH].

QUESTION—How does the participle '*crying out*' and the verb '*he says*' relate to the words that follow in the quotation?

1. These are two events. The man first cried out with a loud voice and then said the following words [Hb]: *having cried out with a loud voice, he said*. Since the participle κράξας 'having cried out' is in the aorist tense, it means that the man screamed before he began to speak to Jesus. His scream gave evidence that he was possessed by a demon [Hb].

2. This is one event. The man cried out the following words with a loud voice [AB1, EBC, NTC; CEV, GW, NCV, NET, NIV, NLT, NRSV, REB, TEV].

QUESTION—Who was speaking to Jesus, and who is the referent of the singular pronouns 'I' and 'me' in the words that were spoken?

The man with the unclean spirit (5:2) had run up to Jesus and bowed down before him, and in all translations it appears that the man was now speaking to Jesus. Some translations specify that it was the *man* speaking: 'the man said this because' (5:8) [CEV], and 'the man answered' (5:9) [CEV, TEV]. However, the man was speaking under the influence of the demons and identified himself with them [ICC]. The explanation in 5:8 indicates that Jesus had just spoken directly to the unclean spirit and ordered that spirit to come out of the man, so these words are the response of the unclean spirit speaking through the voice of the man [NICNT]. The leader of the demons used the man's vocal cords to speak to Jesus [BECNT, CBC, EBC, NCBC, NIVfn, NTC]. The legion of demons were speaking as one [Lns].

QUESTION—What is meant by the words 'I implore you by God'?

This request is made to Jesus along with a call upon God to witness the request [TH]. This is a request for Jesus to make a binding oath that he would leave the demons alone [NIGTC, NTC]. It means, 'Swear to God that you won't torture me' [EBC].

QUESTION—How did the demon think Jesus would torture him?

1. The demon was referring to the torture of the final judgment that awaits all evil spirits [CGTC, EBC, Hb, NAC, NICNT, NLTfn, NTC, Sw, WBC]. This refers to being sent into the abyss ahead of the final judgment [Lns]. The representative of the demons was afraid that Jesus would hurl him and his partners into the abyss of hell (Luke 8:32) before the appointed time (Matt. 8:29) [Hb, NLTfn, NTC].
2. This punishment consisted of banishment from the spirit's home in the man [BECNT, BNTC, Gnd, WBC]. The torment would be the pain that both the unclean spirit and the demoniac would feel at the moment of the expulsion [EGT, Gnd].

5:8 **Because he-was-saying**[a] **to-him, "Come-out**[b] **unclean spirit from the man."**

LEXICON—a. imperf. act. indic. of λέγω (LN 33.69) (BAGD II.1.c. p. 469): 'to say' [AB1, AB2, BNTC, LN, Lns, NTC, WBC; all versions], 'to tell' [LN], 'to order, to command' [BAGD]. This verb means to speak or talk about something [LN]. The generic word 'to say' is used in special types of saying, and in this verse it means 'to order' [BAGD].

b. aorist act. impera. of ἐξέρχομαι (LN 15.40) (BAGD 1.a.δ. p. 274): 'to come out' [AB1, AB2, BAGD, BECNT, BNTC, NTC, WBC; all versions], 'to go out of, to depart out of, to leave from within' [LN], 'Out!' [Lns]. This verb means to move out of an enclosed or well-defined two or three-dimensional area [LN].

QUESTION—What relationship is indicated by the conjunction γάρ 'because'?

This conjunction indicates the reason for the demon's protest [ICC]. Mark has interrupted his account in order to explain what had brought about the demon's request in verse 7 [BECNT, CGTC, EBC, Hb, Lns, NICNT, NIGTC, Tay, WBC]. This verse is parenthetical [BNTC], and some translations use parenthesis marks [AB2; NET, TEV].

QUESTION—When had Jesus commanded the unclean spirit to leave the man?

Some translations use the past tense, 'he/Jesus had said', in order to show that the command had already taken place [AB2, BECNT, NICNT, WBC; NET, NIV, NRSV]: 'Jesus had already said' [NLT], 'Jesus had already told' [CEV], 'he had been saying' [NASB]. Jesus' command probably followed the man's words 'What to me and to you, Jesus Son of God the Highest?' [NTC, Sw]. The imperfect tense ἔλεγεν 'he was saying' [AB1, BNTC; ESV, NCV, REB, TEV] could indicate that the demon interrupted Jesus as he was ordering the unclean spirit to come out of the man or that Jesus was repeating his command [TH]. Some, think that the imperfect tense has the sense of the pluperfect, 'he had been saying' [BECNT, CGTC, Gnd, NTC, Sw, Tay; NASB], and it does not mean that he was now repeating it [Tay].

5:9 And he-was-asking him, "What (is) your name?" And he-says to-him, "Legion[a] (is) my name, because we-are many.[b]"

LEXICON—a. λεγιών (LN 55.8) (BAGD p. 468): 'Legion' [BAGD, LN; all translations except CEV, TEV], 'army' [LN], 'Lots' [CEV], 'Mob' [TEV]. This noun denotes a Roman army unit of about six thousand soldiers [LN].

b. πολύς (LN 59.1) (BAGD I.1.a.α. p. 687): 'many' [AB2, BAGD, BECNT, BNTC, LN, Lns, WBC; all versions except CEV], 'numerous' [BAGD], 'a great deal of, a great number of' [LN]. The phrase 'we are many' is translated 'we are many spirits' [NCV], 'there are so many of us' [AB1; REB, TEV], 'there are many of us inside this man' [NLT], 'I have "lots" of evil spirits' [CEV]. This adjective indicates a relatively large quantity of objects or events [LN].

QUESTION—What relationship is indicated by καί 'and' at the beginning of the verse?

This indicates a resumption of the conversation after Mark's explanation in 5:8 [Hb].

QUESTION—Whom was Jesus addressing?

1. Jesus was speaking to the unclean spirit in the man [AB1, Hb, Lns, NAC; NCV, NLT, REB, TEV]. The unclean spirit replied, 'My name is Legion, because there are many of us inside this man' [NLT]. The singular pronoun 'him' refers to the unclean spirit mentioned in 5:8 [Lns, WBC]. This one evil spirit had the name 'Legion' because of all of the other evil spirits associated with him [Lns].
2. Jesus was speaking to the man [EBC, WBC; CEV]: 'The man answered, "My name is Lots, because I have 'lots' of evil spirits."' [CEV]. Perhaps the man felt he was possessed by thousands of demons or that the many demons in him had combined to form one unified force [EBC].

QUESTION—What is indicated by the use of the imperfect tense of ἐπηρώτα 'he was asking'?

The imperfect tense either indicates that the demon was reluctant to give his name and Jesus had to repeatedly ask the question, or perhaps it was merely a way of viewing the conversation as a process [Hb]. This verb is translated in the past tense [all versions except ESV,NASB]. It just carries on the narrative of the conversation [Sw].

QUESTION—Whose name was 'Legion'?

It is not clear whether 'Legion' is the name of the demon in the man or a description of the man's terrible domination by demons. At this point in the account, there is a vacillation between the singular and the plural terms referring to the demoniac. When the man is in the forefront, it uses the singular forms 'he/him' (5:9, 10, 18, 19, 20), 'the demoniac' (5:15, 16), 'the (one) having' (5:15, 18, 19), and 'you/you' (5:19). When the demons are in the forefront, the text uses the plural forms 'we/us' (5:9, 12), and 'they/them' (5:10, 12, 13) [BECNT].

1. Legion was the name of the particular unclean spirit Jesus was addressing [AB2, EGT, Hb, Lns, NTC, WBC]. 'Legion is *my* name' implies that this was the name of the one unclean spirit who spoke to Jesus in 5:7 and 5:9–10 [Hb, WBC]. He was the spokesman for all of the unclean spirits inhabiting the man [Hb, NTC]. The unclean spirit said *his* name was Legion because all of the other spirits were associated with him [EGT, Lns]. There is a fluctuation between the singular and the plural because sometimes the demons are considered as a unit and at other times as individuals [NAC].
2. Legion was the name of the man who was possessed by the unclean spirits [AB1, EBC, EGT, Sw; CEV]: 'The man answered, "My name is Lots, because I have 'lots' of evil spirits."' [CEV]. The demoniac may have felt as if he was possessed by thousands of demons, or he may have had an unfortunate experience with a Roman legion that had caused his madness [EBC].

QUESTION—Why was his name Legion?

'Legion' is a military term for the largest unit in the Roman army. It consisted of 6,000 men [AB1, BNTC, ESVfn, Gnd, Hb, ICC, LN, Lns, Tay, TH; GW]. Because a legion was not always at full strength, the number of men might be 5,000 [BECNT, Sw], 4,000 [CGTC, NAC, WBC], 3,600 [AB2], or 3,000 [CBC]. The use of the name 'Legion' is not to be taken literally to mean that there were 6,000 unclean spirits in control of the man [NTC]. 'Legion' is to be taken figuratively for a very large number [ESVfn, ICC, Lns, NCBC, NLTfn, NTC]. There were 'lots' of unclean spirits [CEV]. The term 'legion' may also have been used to suggest an army of occupation with its cruelty and destruction [NTC].

5:10 And he-was-imploring him greatly[a] that he- not -send them out of-the region.[b]

LEXICON—a. πολλά, πολύς (LN 67.11) (BAGD I.2.b.β. p. 688): 'greatly' [AB2, BAGD], 'loudly' [BAGD], 'earnestly' [AB1, BAGD, BECNT, Lns; ESV, NASB, NRSV], '(begged) hard' [BNTC], 'often' [BAGD, LN], 'many times' [LN, WBC], 'repeatedly' [NET], 'again and again' [NTC; NCV, NIV, NLT], 'much' [KJV]. The phrase 'he was imploring him greatly' is translated 'he kept begging' [TEV], 'he implored' [REB], 'he begged' [CEV, GW]. This adverb refers to a number of related points of time [LN]. The imperfect tense of the verb, 'he was imploring' indicates repeated action [AB2, CBC, ICC], and the addition of the adverb 'greatly, many times' stresses the fact that he was repeatedly imploring Jesus not to send them away [NTC; NCV, NET, NIV, NLT]. He probably kept doing this because his pleas were unsuccessful [AB2].

b. χώρα (LN 1.79) (BAGD 1.a. p. 889): 'region' [AB1, BAGD, LN, WBC; NET, TEV], 'district' [BAGD, BNTC; REB], 'area' [NTC; NCV, NIV], 'territory' [BECNT, LN], 'land' [AB2, LN], 'country' [Lns; ESV, GW, KJV, NASB, NRSV], 'place' [BAGD]. The clause 'that he not send them out of the region' is translated 'not to send them away' [CEV], 'not to send them to some distant place' [NLT]. This noun denotes a region of the earth normally associated with some ethnic group or geographical center [LN].

QUESTION—Who is the subject of the singular verb form 'he was imploring him (that he not send *them*…)'?

1. The singular form refers to the man himself [AB1, CGTC, EBC, ICC, NCBC, NICNT, NIGTC, Sw, TH; CEV, TEV]: *the man was imploring him*. The man is the one who actually speaks, even if he is only the mouthpiece of the demons [CGTC, TH]. This is probably Mark's way of indicating that the demons were speaking through the lips of the demon-possessed man [EBC, NCBC]. Notice the plural form of this verb '*they implored* him (saying, "Send *us*…)' in verse 12 where it definitely refers to the demons speaking [TH]. Since Mark used plural verbs for the demons in 5:12-13, this verse could mean the man remains the subject as the voice used by the demons. Nevertheless, the man is speaking for the demons and it is with the demons, not the man, that Jesus must deal with [NIGTC]. The man requested this on behalf of the demons who possessed him [AB1].

2. The singular form refers to the unclean spirit that Jesus was directly speaking to in verse 9 [EGT, Hb, Lns, NTC, Sw, WBC; all versions except CEV, NLT, TEV]: *the evil spirit was imploring him*. The leading demon who called himself 'Legion' pleaded not only for himself but for the other demons as well [EGT, Hb]. The singular pronoun 'he' refers to the spirits, still regarded as a single ego, who were speaking through the voice of the man [Sw].

3. All of the unclean spirits were imploring Jesus [AB2, Tay; NLT]: *they were imploring him*. The singular verb 'he was imploring' is translated as a plural form to agree with αὐτά 'them' [AB2, Tay; NLT]: 'the evil spirits begged him again and again not to send them to some distant place' [NLT].

QUESTION—Why didn't the demons want to leave that region?

The text is not clear as to why the demons begged to remain in that region [NIGTC]. The account of this encounter in Luke 8:31 says that the demons begged Jesus not to send them to the abyss [Lns, NIVfn, TRT]. The demons not only wanted to avoid the punishment of the abyss, they wanted to remain in that particular location because they felt at home in a place of tombs, skeletons, death, and destruction [CBC, NTC]. The demons wanted to stay in their home territory instead of being banished to a wilderness that lacked other human hosts [Gnd].

5:11 Now there-was a-large herd of-pigs feeding there on the mountain.[a]

LEXICON—a. ὄρος (LN 1.46) (BAGD p. 582): 'mountain' [BAGD, LN], 'hill' [BAGD]. The phrase πρὸς τῷ ὄρει 'on the mountain' [AB2, BECNT; NASB] is also translated 'on a hill' [NCV], 'on the hillside' [AB1, BNTC,

NTC; CEV, ESV, NET, NIV, NLT, NRSV, REB, TEV], 'on a mountainside' [GW], 'over against the mountain' [Lns], 'near the mountain' [WBC], 'nigh unto the mountains' [KJV]. This noun denotes a high elevation of land that is higher than a βουνός 'hill' (1.48) [LN].

QUESTION—What relationship is indicated by δέ 'now'?

This conjunction indicates a transition to the parenthetical remark given in verse 11 [Hb, Lns, Tay].

QUESTION—Where were the pigs in relation to the mountain?

The pigs were 'on' the mountain [AB2, BECNT, CGTC, EGT, Gnd, ICC, NTC; GW, NASB, NCV], that is, on the side of it [EGT, Sw, TRT; CEV, ESV, GW, NET, NIV, NLT, NRSV, REB, TEV]. The pigs were near a mountain, which was in sight [Sw]. They were on a sloping plateau that stretched toward the mountain towering in the background [Hb].

5:12 And they-implored him saying, "Send[a] us into/to the pigs, that into them we-may-enter."

TEXT—Manuscripts reading παρεκάλεσαν αὐτόν 'they implored him' are followed by GNT, which does not mention any variant reading. A variant reading is παρεκάλεσαν αὐτόν πάντες οἱ δαίμονες 'all the demons implored him' and it is followed by KJV. Translations following the GNT text identify the speakers of the verb 'they implored him' to be the demons [GW, NASB, NCV, NIV], the spirits [NLT, REB, TEV], the unclean spirits [NRSV], the demonic spirits [NET], or the evil spirits [CEV].

LEXICON—a. aorist act. impera. of πέμπω (LN 15.66) (BAGD 1. p. 642): 'to send' [AB1, AB2, BAGD, BECNT, BNTC, LN, Lns, WBC; all versions].

This verb means to cause someone to depart for a particular purpose [LN].

QUESTION—Who were the ones who implored Jesus?

The plural forms 'they implored' and 'us' refer to all of the demons speaking through the man's voice [CGTC, ICC, Lns, Sw, TH]. The unclean spirits were only concerned about themselves since their hold over the man was at an end [Hb, Sw].

QUESTION—What relationship is indicated by the word ἵνα 'that' and what are the meanings of the preposition εἰς 'to/into' which occurs in each of the two clauses that are connected by ἵνα 'that': 'Send us εἰς 'into/to' the pigs, that (ἵνα) εἰς 'into' them we may enter'?

1. The conjunction ἵνα means 'in order that' and indicates purpose.

   1.1 The second clause indicates the purpose for the command given in the first clause [TH, WBC]: Send us *to* the pigs, *in order that* we may enter *into* them. If this conjunction indicates purpose, then the first εἰς must mean '*to* the pigs' since the second εἰς clearly means '*into* the pigs' [TH].

   1.2 Some translate the conjunction to indicate purpose, but translate the two εἰς prepositions with the same meaning 'into' [AB2, BECNT, Gnd, Hb, Lns, NTC; KJV, NASB]. This is an example of duality in Mark where the plea turns more specific: 'Send us *into* the pigs in order that *into* them we may enter' [Gnd]. The second clause gives a fuller statement of what they wanted [Hb]. Translations that probably follow this duality are: 'Send us *into* the pigs/swine so that we may *enter* them' [AB2; KJV, NASB], 'Send us *into* the swine, in order that we might enter *into* them' [BECNT; similarly Lns], 'Allow us to go *into* the pigs, so that we may *enter* them' [NTC].

2. The word ἵνα 'into' has an imperative sense and indicates the contents of a second command.

2.1 The second clause is a repetition of the first clause with the preposition εἰς meaning the same in each phrase [CGTC, Tay; CEV, GW, NCV, NET, NLT, NRSV]. 'Send us εἰς 'into' those pigs! Let us go εἰς 'into' them!' [CEV, NCV]. 'Send us into the/those pigs! Let us enter them!' [GW, NET, NLT; similarly NRSV]. This is a redundancy for the sake of style [CGTC].

2.2 The two occurrences of the preposition εἰς 'into' have different meanings so that the second clause is a separate plea [AB1; ESV, NIV, REB, TEV]: Send us εἰς 'to' the pigs. Let us enter εἰς 'into' them. The first use of εἰς is to be translated 'to' the pigs [ESV, TEV] or 'among' the pigs [AB1; NIV, REB].

5:13 And he-permitted[a] them. And having-come-out, the unclean spirits entered into the pigs, and the herd rushed[b] down the slope[c] into the lake, about two-thousand (of them), and they-were-drowning[d] in the lake.

TEXT—Manuscripts reading ἐπέτρεψεν αὐτοῖς 'he permitted them' are followed by GNT, which does not mention any variant reading. A variant reading is ἐπέτρεψεν αὐτοῖς εὐθέος ὁ Ἰησοῦς 'immediately Jesus permitted them' and it is followed by KJV.

LEXICON—a. aorist act. indic. of ἐπιτρέπω (LN 13.138) (BAGD 1. p. 303): 'to permit' [AB2, LN, Lns], 'to give permission' [AB1, BECNT, LN, NTC, WBC; ESV, NASB, NET, NIV, NLT, NRSV], 'to give leave' [BNTC; KJV, REB], 'to allow' [BAGD, LN; NCV], 'to let' [LN]. The phrase 'permitted them' is translated 'let them go' [CEV, TEV], 'let them do this' [GW]. This verb means to allow someone to do something [LN].

b. aorist act. indic. of ὁρμάω (LN 15.222) (BAGD p. 581): 'to rush' [AB1, BAGD, BECNT, BNTC, LN, Lns, WBC; all versions except KJV, NLT], 'to rush headlong' [AB2, NTC], 'to run' [LN], 'to run violently' [KJV], 'to plunge' [NLT]. This verb means to make a fast movement from one place to another [LN].

c. κρημνός (LN 1.50) (BAGD p. 450): 'steep slope' [BAGD, LN; NET], 'steep hillside' [NLT], 'steep bank' [BAGD, BECNT, BNTC, Lns, WBC; CEV, NASB, NIV, NRSV], 'steep place' [KJV], 'cliff' [AB2, NTC; GW], 'the side of the cliff' [TEV], 'edge' [AB1; REB], 'hill' [NCV]. This noun denotes the steep side of a hill [LN].

d. imperf. pass. indic. of πνίγομαι, πνίγω (LN 23.119) (BAGD 1.d. p. 679): 'to be drowned' [AB1, BNTC, LN, WBC; ESV, NASB, NCV,

NET, NIV, NRSV, REB, TEV], 'to drown' [BECNT, NTC; CEV, GW, NLT], 'to be choked' [BAGD, Lns; KJV], 'to choke to death' [AB2]. This verb means to die as the result of drowning [LN]. The imperfect tense describes the pigs sinking into the lake as one after another plunged into the water and drowned [Hb].

QUESTION—What did Jesus permit the unclean spirit to do?
Jesus let him 'do this' [GW, NCV], he let them 'go' [TH; CEV, TEV]. He permitted them to carry out their request to enter into the pigs [Hb].

QUESTION—How did the pigs get into the lake?
The place where the pigs were feeding ended in a steep bank at the edge of the water [Hb]. The pigs careened over a cliff into the lake [AB2].

QUESTION—What were the consequences of the pigs drowning in the lake?
The drowning of the pigs thwarted the plans of the demons [AB2, BECNT, Gnd, NAC, NIGTC], and the demons were left homeless after all [NIGTC]. Probably the demons perished along with the pigs [BECNT, Gnd, NAC]. Perhaps the demons destroyed the pigs because they were not allowed to destroy the man [EBC, ESVfn, Lns, NICNT]. This was tangible evidence to all that the demons had actually left the man and that their purpose had been to destroy the man just like they had destroyed the pigs [EBC].

5:14 **And the (ones) tending**[a] **them fled**[b] **and told**[c] **(it) in the city and in the countrysides/hamlets.**[d]

LEXICON—a. pres. act. participle of βόσκω (LN 44.1) (BAGD 1. p. 145): 'to tend' [BAGD, WBC; NIV], 'to feed' [BAGD, Lns; KJV], 'to graze' [AB2], 'to take care of' [LN; CEV, GW, TEV], 'to be in charge of' [AB1, BNTC, NTC; REB], 'to herd, to look after' [LN], 'to watch over' [BECNT]. The phrase οἱ βόσκοντες αὐτοὺς 'the ones tending them' is translated 'the herdsmen' [ESV, NASB, NCV, NET, NLT], 'the swineherds' [NRSV]. This verb means to herd animals so as to provide them with adequate pasture and to take care of what other needs may be involved [LN].

b. aorist act. indic. of φεύγω (LN 15.61) (BAGD 1. p. 855): 'to flee' [AB1, BAGD, BECNT, LN, Lns, NTC, WBC; ESV, KJV, NLT], 'to run away' [AB2, LN; GW, NASB, NCV, TEV], 'to run off' [NET, NIV, NRSV], 'to run' [CEV], 'to take to their heels' [BNTC; REB]. This verb means to move quickly from a point or area in order to avoid presumed danger or difficulty [LN]. It means to seek safety in flight [BAGD].

c. aorist act. indic. of ἀπαγγέλλω (LN 33.198) (BAGD 1. p. 79): 'to tell' [BAGD, LN; ESV, KJV, NCV, NRSV], 'to report' [BAGD, Lns; GW, NASB, NIV], 'to inform' [LN], 'to announce' [BAGD, BECNT, WBC], 'to spread the news' [AB2, NTC; CEV, NET, NLT, TEV], 'to carry the news' [AB1; REB], 'to bring the news' [BNTC]. This verb means to announce or inform [LN].

d. ἀγρός (LN 1.93, 1.87) (BAGD 3. p. 14): 'countryside' [AB1, BECNT, BNTC, LN (1.87), NTC; GW, NCV, NET, NIV, REB], 'surrounding countryside' [NLT], 'country' [ESV, KJV, NASB, NRSV], 'rural area' [LN (1.87)], 'farm' [BAGD, LN (1.93)], Lns, WBC; CEV, TEV], 'farm settlement' [LN (1.93)], 'hamlet' [BAGD, LN (1.93)], 'village' [AB2]. This noun denotes a relatively small village, or even just a cluster of farms [LN (1.93)], or it is a rural area in contrast to a population center [LN (1.87)].

QUESTION—Why did the herdsmen flee?
The herdsmen panicked at what had happened and ran to report their loss to the owners [Lns, NICNT, NTC, WBC], so they would not be blamed for the loss of the pigs [Lns, NTC]. They reported the news of the miracle to everyone they met [AB2, BECNT, Gnd, NTC].

QUESTION—What were τοὺς ἀγρούς 'the countrysides/hamlets'?
1. This refers to the countryside [AB1, BECNT, BNTC, EGT, Hb, ICC, Lns, My, NTC, PNTC, Sw, WBC; all versions]. They went to the farms [EGT, ICC, Lns, My, WBC; CEV, TEV]. They told the news to people working in the fields [Hb].
2. This refers to hamlets or country towns [AB2, CGTC, Gnd, NICNT, Tay]. These were hamlets surrounding the city [Tay].

And they-came to-see^a what is the (thing) having-happened.^b

LEXICON—a. aorist act. infin. of ὁράω (LN 27.5): εἶδον (BAGD 1.c. p. 220): 'to see' [AB1, AB2, BAGD, BECNT, BNTC, Lns, NTC, WBC; all versions], 'to learn about, to find out about' [LN]. This verb means to acquire information [LN].
   b. perf. act. participle of γίνομαι (LN 13.107) (BAGD I.3.a. p. 158): 'to happen' [AB1, AB2, BAGD, BNTC, LN, NTC, WBC; all versions except KJV], 'to take place' [BAGD, BECNT], 'to be done' [KJV]. This verb means 'to happen' and implies a change from a previous state [LN].

5:15 And they come to Jesus and they-see the (one) being-demon-possessed^a sitting, clothed and being-of-sound-mind,^b the (one) having-had^c the legion, and they-were-afraid.^d

LEXICON—a. present mid. pass. (deponent = active) participle of δαιμο (LN 12.41) (BAGD p. 169): 'to be demon possessed' [BAGD, LN]. This verb is translated with the demon possession being in the present time: 'who was possessed with the devil' [KJV] 'the demon-possessed man' [NTC, WBC; ESV, NET], 'the demoniac' [BNTC, Lns; NRSV], 'the madman' [REB]. It is translated in the past tense: 'who had been demon-possessed' [NASB], 'who had been demonized' [AB2, BECNT]. The two phrases 'the one being demon-possessed...the one having had the legion' are translated as a single phrase: 'the man who had been possessed by the legion of demons' [AB1; GW, NIV, NLT], 'the man who used to have the mob of demons in him' [TEV], 'the man who had once been full of demons' [CEV], 'the man who used to have the many evil spirits' [NCV]. This verb means to be possessed by a demon [LN]. This word occurs at 1:32; 5:15, 16, 18.

b. pres. act. participle of σωφρονέω (LN 30.20) (BAGD 1. p. 802): 'to be of sound mind' [BAGD], 'to be in one's right mind' [BAGD, BECNT, BNTC, LN, Lns, NTC, WBC; all versions except NLT], 'to be sane' [AB2, LN], 'to be perfectly sane' [NLT], 'to think straight, to reason correctly' [LN]. This verb means to be able to reason and think properly in a sane manner [LN].

c. perf. act. participle of ἔχω (LN 90.65) (BAGD 1.2.e.α. p. 332): 'to have' [BAGD, LN], 'to be possessed by' [BAGD]. See translations of this word at 3:22. This verb means to experience some state or condition [LN]. A reference to 'having' a demon occurs at 3:22, 30; 5:15; 7:25; 9:17.

d. aorist pass. indic. of φοβέομαι (LN 25.252): 'to be afraid' [AB2, BECNT, BNTC, LN, Lns, WBC; ESV, KJV, NET, NIV, NLT, NRSV, REB, TEV], 'to be frightened' [NTC; GW, NASB, NCV], 'to be terrified' [CEV]. This verb means to be in a state of fearing [LN].

QUESTION—Why is the man still referred to as being demon possessed?

This simply identifies the man and does not mean that he was still possessed by demons [TH]. This description reflects the local people's point of view even though it was no longer true [AB1, CGTC, Sw, Tay]. It was the familiar title by which they had known him [BECNT, NIGTC]. Many translations use the past tense since it is clear that he was no longer demon-possessed [AB1, AB2, BECNT; CEV, GW, NASB, NCV, NIV, NLT, TEV].

QUESTION—What is implied by reporting that the man was seated and clothed?

This emphasizes the contrast between the man's present peaceful condition with his previous condition [Hb, Lns, NICNT, WBC]. 'Sitting' contrasts his present peaceful condition with the days when he had been a raving maniac [Hb]. The man was seated at the feet of Jesus as any disciple would be [TH]. The fact that he was clothed implies that he had gone around naked (as stated in Luke 8:27) when he had been demon-possessed [EGT, TH].

QUESTION—Why were the people afraid?

The miraculous change that had taken place caused their fear. They were filled with awe at being in the presence of something supernatural [Hb, Sw, Tay]. Their fear was caused by being in the presence of the one who had power to perform such a miracle [EBC, EGT, Lns, NAC, NCBC]. This fear was a paralyzing dread [CBC]. Some even thought the exorcism was the work of the devil [AB2].

5:16 And the (ones) having-seen (it) described[a] to-them what had-happened to-the-demon-possessed (man) and about the pigs.

LEXICON—a. aorist mid./pass. (deponent = act.) participle of διηγέομαι (LN 33.201) (BAGD p. 195): 'to describe' [AB2, BAGD, BNTC, Lns; ESV, NASB], 'to tell' [AB1, BAGD, NTC, WBC; CEV, GW, KJV, NCV, NIV, NLT, REB, TEV], 'to explain' [BECNT], 'to relate' [BAGD, LN], 'to report' [NET, NRSV], 'to inform, to tell fully' [LN]. This verb means to provide detailed information in a systematic manner [LN].

QUESTION—Who were the 'ones having seen it'?
The ones who saw the miracle were the twelve disciples [BECNT, Hb, Lns, NTC, Sw], the men who had come in the other boats (4:36) [Lns], and the herdsmen who were telling their story again [BECNT, EGT, Gnd, Hb, NICNT, NTC]. Perhaps people thought that the herdsmen would lie about what happened in order to shield themselves from blame for the loss of the pigs, so they sought out others who had also seen the miracle [Lns].

5:17 And they-began to-implore^a him to-leave from their regions.^b

LEXICON—a. pres. act. infin. of παρακαλέω (LN 33.168) (BAGD 3. p. 617): 'to implore' [BAGD; NASB], 'to entreat' [BAGD], 'to beg' [AB1, BECNT, BNTC, NTC; CEV, ESV, GW, NCV, NRSV, REB], 'to plead' [AB2, LN; NIV, NLT], 'to beseech' [Lns], 'to appeal to' [BAGD, LN, WBC], 'to request' [BAGD, LN], 'to ask' [NET, TEV], 'to earnestly ask for' [LN], 'to pray (them to depart)' [KJV]. This verb means to ask for something earnestly and with propriety [LN]. This same verb is used again in 5:18.

b. ὅριον (LN 1.79) (BAGD p. 581) 'region' [AB2, BECNT, LN; ESV, NET, NIV, NRSV], 'their part of the country' [CEV], 'district' [AB1, BNTC, NTC; REB], 'area' [NCV], 'neighborhood' [NRSV], 'territory' [LN, WBC; GW, TEV], 'land' [LN], 'borders' [Lns], 'coasts' [KJV]. The phrase 'to leave from their regions' is translated 'to go away and leave them alone' [NLT]. This noun always occurs as a plural noun and refers to an area occupied by some ethnic group or to a geographical center. This area does not necessarily constitute a unit of governmental administration [LN]. It is translated in the singular [all versions except KJV, NLT]. This word occurs at 5:17; 7:24, 31; 10:1.

QUESTION—Who began to implore Jesus to leave?
They were not just the local eyewitnesses referred to in the preceding verse, but people in general [EBC, TH], the inhabitants [WBC], the townspeople [AB2]. The pronoun 'they' includes the owners of the pigs [Hb]. Everyone present implored Jesus to leave [Gnd]. Luke says that this was the unanimous request of the inhabitants of that area [Hb].

QUESTION—What is implied by the phrase 'they *began* to implore him'?
This suggests that after some started to ask Jesus to leave, others joined in [Lns].

QUESTION—Why would these people want Jesus to leave their regions?
They were upset by the loss of their pigs [CGTC, EBC, Lns, Tay]. They didn't object to the demonic being restored to normality, but they did object to the loss of the pigs [NIGTC]. They were probably afraid to have someone with such great power in their midst [BNTC, CBC, EBC, NAC, NCBC, NICNT, PNTC, Sw]. After the loss of their pigs, they feared what Jesus might do next [WBC]. They were afraid to have such a dangerous man in their district [AB1, EGT].

5:18 And while he is-getting[a] into the boat, the (one) having-been-demon-possessed was-imploring him that he-might-be with[b] him. **5:19** And/but he- did- not -allow[c] him,

LEXICON—a. pres. act. participle of ἐμβαίνω (LN 15.95) (BAGD p. 254): 'to get into' [AB2, BAGD, BECNT, BNTC, LN, NTC, WBC; all versions except GW], 'to go into' [Lns], 'to step into' [GW], 'to embark' [AB1, BAGD, LN]. This verb means to go into or onto something [LN].
- b. μετά (LN 89.108): 'with, in the company of, together with' [LN]. The phrase ἵνα μετ' αὐτοῦ ᾖ 'that he might be with him' [AB2, BECNT, WBC; ESV, KJV, NRSV] is also translated 'that he might accompany him' [NASB], 'to be in his company' [Lns], '(begged/asked) to go with him' [AB1, BNTC, NTC; CEV, NCV, NET, NIV, NLT, REB], '(he begged him,) "Let me stay with you."' [GW], '(begged him,) "Let me go with you!"' [TEV]. This preposition indicates an associative relationship, which usually implies being in the company of someone [LN].
- c. aorist act. indic. of ἀφίημι (LN 13.140) (BAGD 4. p. 126): 'to allow' [BAGD, BNTC, LN; GW], 'to let' [BAGD, LN, Lns; CEV, NASB, NCV, NIV, REB, TEV], 'to permit' [AB1, AB2, BAGD, BECNT, WBC; ESV, NET], 'to suffer' [KJV]. The phrase 'he did not allow him' is translated 'he/Jesus refused' [NTC; NRSV]. This verb means to leave it up to someone to do something [LN].

QUESTION—What is implied by beginning this verse with Jesus getting into the boat?

This passes over anything Jesus might have said to the people [Gnd]. It assumes that Jesus meekly accepted the local people's desire for him to depart from their region [Hb, NIGTC, WBC]. Jesus was not going to force himself on people who did not want him [EBC, Hb]. Jesus left because his work was completed, not because of the townspeople's rejection of his ministry. Their request had simply given an occasion for beginning a new phase of his ministry [WBC].

QUESTION—Why did the man want to be with Jesus?

This man wanted to go along with Jesus in the boat [CBC, CGTC, EBC, EGT, Gnd, Lns, My, NAC, NCBC, NICNT, NTC, PNTC, Sw, Tay, TH]. No one had ever showed this man such love and compassion [EBC]. He felt so indebted to his benefactor that he wanted to serve him in whatever way he could [NTC]. He also might have wanted to get away from the reactions of his countrymen [CGTC, Hb]. In 3:14, Jesus had chosen the twelve apostles that *they might be with* him in a close personal relationship for personal training as apostles, and now this man implored *that he might be with* Jesus. This similar expression indicates that he wanted to accompany Jesus in the same personal relationship shared exclusively by the twelve apostles [AB2, BECNT, WBC; probably BNTC, NIGTC]. Jesus didn't refuse this request because he doubted the man's sincerity or commitment, he just hadn't called this man to belong to the circle of the twelve [AB2, WBC]. Jesus gave this man a task more suited to his situation [AB2].

QUESTION—What relationship is indicated by the beginning conjunction καί 'and/but' of verse 19?
1. This conjunction indicates the beginning of a new sentence [LN (91.1)] since this is the usual discourse connector that Mark uses [AB1, AB2, BECNT, ICC, Lns, WBC; ESV, NASB]: *and* he did not allow him.
2. This indicates a contrast with what the man wanted [BNTC, NTC; CEV, GW, NCV, NLT, NRSV, REB, TEV]: *but instead of granting his request* he did not allow him to be with him.

instead he-says to-him, "Go to your house to the (ones who are) yours[a] and tell them how-much[b] the Lord has-done for-you and (how) he-had-mercy-upon[c] you."

LEXICON—a. σός (LN 92.8): 'your, of you' [LN]. The phrase τοὺς σοὺς 'the ones who are yours' is translated 'your family' [CEV, GW, NCV, NIV, NLT, TEV], 'your people' [AB2, NTC, WBC; NASB, NET], 'your own people' [AB1, BNTC; REB], 'your relatives' [Lns], 'your friends' [BECNT; ESV, KJV, NRSV]. This pronominal adjective refers to the receptor of something [LN].

b. ὅσος (LN 59.7) (BAGD 2. p. 586): 'how much' [BAGD, BNTC, WBC; CEV, ESV, GW, NCV, NIV, NRSV, TEV], 'all that' [BECNT], 'everything' [BAGD; NLT], 'what' [AB1; NET, REB], 'how great things' [KJV], 'what great things' [AB2, Lns, NTC; NASB]. This refers to a comparative quantity of objects or events, 'as many as, as much as' [LN]. It concerns quantity and number [BAGD]. 'How much' may refer to the details about his new state of being seated, clothed, and sane (5:15) [Gnd].

c. aorist act. indic. of ἐλεάω or ἐλεέω (LN 88.76) (BAGD p. 249): 'to have mercy on, to be merciful toward, to show mercy' [BAGD, LN], 'to help someone out of pity' [BAGD]. The phrase 'and how he had mercy on you' [AB1, AB2, BECNT, BNTC, NTC; ESV, NCV, NIV; similarly NASB] is also translated 'and how he has been merciful to you' [WBC], 'and how merciful he has been to you' [GW, NLT], 'and did have mercy on you' [Lns], 'and hath compassion on thee' [KJV], 'and what mercy he has shown you' [NRSV], 'that he had mercy on you' [NET], 'and how kind he has been to you' [TEV], 'and how good he has been to you' [CEV]. The sentence 'tell them how much the Lord has done for you and how he had mercy upon you' is translated 'tell them what the Lord in his mercy has done for you' [REB]. This verb means to show kindness or concern for someone who is in serious need [LN]. This phrase specifies the character of the things he has done for the man [Gnd].

QUESTION—What relationship is indicated by the conjunction ἀλλά 'instead'?
This conjunctive indicates that along with the refusal of the man's request to accompany him, Jesus had something positive for him to do [AB2, BECNT, Gnd, NICNT, NIGTC]. The reason Jesus refused his request is now revealed when Jesus commands him to go home and tell all the people there what the Lord had done for him [Hb, NICNT, NIGTC, Sw].

QUESTION—Who are 'the ones who are yours' whom Jesus told the man to go to?

At a minimum, it includes the man's family he had had been separated from when he went to live among the tombs [BNTC, Gnd, Hb, Lns, PNTC, TH]. The reference to both his house and to his family is Mark's typical use of dual expressions [Gnd]. This includes both the immediate and extended family of the man [TH]. It refers to a circle wider than the man's family and includes his friends also [AB1, BECNT, CGTC, Hb, My, NICNT, NTC, Sw, Tay, TRT, WBC; ESV, KJV, NRSV]. It refers to all of the people in his area [WBC].

QUESTION—To whom does ὁ κύριος 'the Lord' refer?

1. Jesus was referring to God [AB1, AB2, BNTC, CBC, CGTC, EGT, Gnd, Hb, ICC, Lns, My, NAC, NCBC, NIGTC, Tay, TH, TRT, WBC]. In Luke 8:39, Jesus explicitly says, 'tell what God did for you' [BNTC, ICC, NIGTC]. This refers to the God of the OT [Hb, Lns]. God did this through Jesus [AB2, NIGTC]. Jesus implied that he was the Lord's agent [Gnd, NAC].
2. Jesus was referring to himself [BECNT, EBC, NTC, PNTC]. In the next verse, the man told people what *Jesus* had done for him, showing that he understood 'Lord' to mean Jesus [NTC, PNTC]. In writing this account, Mark also used 'Lord' to refer to Jesus [BECNT].

QUESTION—Is there a difference between telling people 'what the Lord has done (perfect active indicative)' for the man and how the Lord 'had mercy' (aorist active indicative) upon him?

The aorist tense 'had mercy' refers to the initial and decisive act of the exorcism while the perfect tense 'what the Lord has done' refers to a completed action with its effects continuing on into the present [AB1, BECNT, EGT, Sw]. By the one act of mercy (aorist tense) of casting out the demons, the Lord has done (perfect tense) something permanent for this man [Lns]. But whether the aorist tense 'had mercy' has a different nuance from the perfect tense 'has done' is doubtful since no occurrence of a perfect tense of 'to have mercy' seems to be known [Tay]. The miracle of healing the man was the expression of God's mercy [EGT, Hb, Lns, My, NICNT, Tay; NET, REB, TEV]. The two are united in the translation 'tell them what the Lord in his mercy has done for you' [REB].

5:20 And he-left and began to-proclaim[a] in the Decapolis[b] how-much Jesus did for-him, and everyone was-amazed.[c]

LEXICON—a. pres. act. infin. of κηρύσσω (LN **33.207**) (BAGD 2.a. p. 431): 'to proclaim' [AB2, BAGD, BECNT, BNTC, **LN**, NTC, WBC; ESV, NASB, NET, NLT, NRSV], 'to publish' [KJV], 'to spread the news' [AB1], 'to tell' [LN; CEV, GW, NCV, NIV, TEV], 'to make known' [REB], 'to to speak of, to mention publicly' [BAGD]. This verb means to announce extensively and publicly [LN]. This verb is used with the same meaning at 1:45; 5:20; 7:36.

b. Δεκάπολις (LN 93.40) (BAGD p. 174): 'Decapolis' [BAGD, LN]. The phrase 'in the Decapolis' [AB2, BECNT, Lns, NTC, WBC; ESV, NET, NIV, NRSV] is also translated 'in Decapolis' [KJV, NASB], 'throughout the Decapolis' [BNTC; REB], 'in the ten cities' [GW], 'in the Ten Towns' [NCV], '(to visit) the Ten Towns of that region' [NLT], 'all through the Ten Towns' [AB1; TEV], 'into the region near the ten cities known as Decapolis' [CEV]. This noun denotes a league of ten cities in the region east of the Jordan [BAGD, LN]. This was the territory of a league of ten free Greek cities under the protection of the governor of Syria [CGTC]. All but one of these ten Greek cities were located east of the Jordan River [Hb].

c. θαυμάζω (LN 25.213) (BAGD 1.a.α p. 352): 'to be amazed' [AB1, AB2, BAGD, NTC, WBC; all versions except ESV, KJV], 'to be astonished' [BAGD], 'to marvel' [BAGD, BECNT, BNTC, LN, Lns; ESV, KJV], 'to wonder' [BAGD, LN]. This verb means to wonder or marvel at some event or object [LN]. This word occurs at 5:20; 6:6; 15:5, 44.

QUESTION—If ὁ κύριος 'the Lord' refers to God in the previous verse, why did the man tell how much Jesus had done for him?

Jesus had told the man to tell how much the LORD God had done for him and the man attributed his healing to the *agency* of Jesus [NIGTC]. What Jesus did is what God did [BNTC]. The man felt that by praising Jesus he was praising God [Lns]. Mark intended to identify Jesus with God in this account [Gnd, NCBC].

DISCOURSE UNIT—5:21–43 [CBC, Hb; CEV, ESV, GW, NASB, NCV, NET, NIV, NLT, NRSV, TEV]. The topic is Jesus' two miracles upon returning [Hb], Jesus heals a woman and Jairus' daughter [ESV], Jesus gives life to a dead girl and heals a sick woman [NCV], Jairus' daughter and a woman with chronic bleeding [GW], Jairus' daughter and the woman who touched Jesus' cloak [TEV], a dying girl and a sick woman [CEV], a dead girl and a sick woman [NIV], a girl restored to life and a woman healed [NASB], the woman with the hemorrhage and Jairus' daughter [CBC], Jesus heals in response to faith [NLT], miracles and healing [NASB], restoration and healing [NET].

DISCOURSE UNIT—5:21–24 [EBC, Hb, NICNT; NLT]. The topic is the plea of Jairus [Hb, NICNT; NLT], Jairus' plea in behalf of his daughter [EBC].

5:21 **And Jesus having-crossed-over in the boat again to the other-side a-large crowd was-gathered-together to**[a] **him, and he-was beside the lake.**

TEXT—Manuscripts reading ἐν τῷ πλοίῳ 'in the boat' are given a C rating by GNT to indicate that choosing it over a variant text was difficult. A variant reading omits this phrase.

TEXT—Manuscripts reading πάλιν εἰς τὸ πέραν συνήχθη '(crossed over) again to the other side (a large crowd) was gathered' are followed by GNT, which does not mention any variant reading. A variant reading is εἰς τὸ πέραν πάλιν συνήχθη '(crossed over) to the other side (a large crowd) again was gathered' and it is followed by ICC, Tay.

LEXICON—a. ἐπί (LN 83.46, 84.17) (BAGD III.1.a.γ. p. 288): 'to' [BAGD, LN], 'toward' [LN]. The phrase συνήχθη...ἐπ' αὐτόν 'was gathered together to him' is translated 'gathered unto him' [KJV], 'assembled unto him' [Lns], 'gathered together around him' [AB2], 'gathered around him' [AB1; BECNT, BNTC, WBC; all versions except ESV, KJV], 'gathered about him' [NTC; ESV]. This preposition indicates an extension toward a goal and usually implies that the goal is reached [LN]. Literally 'gathered on top of him', the preposition means 'gathered around him' [AB1]. It means that they pressed closely to his person [Hb]. The crowd came together at the first sight of Jesus arriving in the boat and swarmed down upon him as soon as he had landed [Sw].

QUESTION—Where was the other side of the lake?

After crossing the Lake of Galilee from its western side in 5:1, Jesus arrived at the region of the Gerasenes located on the eastern side of the lake. In this verse, the other side where the crows gathered was again on the western side of the lake [BECNT, EGT, Gnd, Lns, NTC, PNTC, Sw, Tay, TRT], probably near Capernaum [CGTC, Hb, NAC, NICNT, NIGTC, Sw]. Although it is not mentioned, Jesus was accompanied by his disciples who will take part in the following account [BECNT, Gnd, TRT].

QUESTION—When did the crowd gather around Jesus at the lakeside?

There is no indication whether a crowd immediately gathered about Jesus when he arrived at the shore or if they gathered after an extended period of time [EGT, NICNT, Tay]. Mark has picked this event to come next in order to contrast Jesus' reception here with the reception he had received on the eastern shore where those people told him to depart from their region [NIGTC].

1. All translations seem to have the crowd gather as soon as the boat arrived and most commentaries seem to take this view. People had been waiting for Jesus, and they immediately gathered on the beach when they saw his boat approaching (Luke 8:40) [Hb, Sw]. This large crowd gathered about Jesus as soon as he got out of the boat [AB2, BECNT, BNTC, Gnd, Sw, Tay] Jairus approached Jesus at this time [Gnd, Hb, Sw, WBC], probably before Jesus could begin preaching to the crowd [Hb]. In view of the parallel account in Matt. 9:14–18, the disciples of John the Baptist were among those waiting for Jesus to land, and they were talking with Jesus about fasting when Jairus approached Jesus with his request [NTC].

2. This does not say that a great multitude *immediately* gathered around Jesus when he landed. [EBC, EGT, ICC, Lns]. Thematic interests have probably determined the sequence of events [EBC]. Sequence and situation was not the purpose for placing this account here [EGT, Lns]. The statement that Jesus 'was beside the lake' implies that after he had come ashore, he had been involved in other things before he went back beside the lake when this crowd gathered. We learn from Matthew 9 that

after Jesus left the boat he healed a paralyzed man, called Matthew to be his disciple, and later dined at Matthew's house, which was beside the Lake of Galilee [ICC, Lns]. Jairus interrupted Jesus while he was busy speaking to the crowd [EBC].

5:22 **And comes one of-the synagogue-leaders, Jairus by-name, and having-seen him he-falls-down**[a] **at his feet 5:23 and he-begs him earnestly saying, "My little-daughter is at-the-final-point.**[b] **Come in-order-that you-may-put (your) hand on-her in-order-that she-may-be-healed and live."**

TEXT—At the beginning of 5:23, manuscripts reading καί 'and' are followed by GNT, which does not mention any variant reading. A variant reading is καὶ ἰδού, 'and behold' and it is followed by EGT; KJV.

LEXICON—a. pres. act. indic. of πίπτω (LN 17:22) (BAGD 1.b.α. p. 659): 'to fall down' [BAGD, LN], 'to prostrate oneself' [LN]. The phrase 'he falls down at his feet' is translated 'he fell at his feet' [AB2, BECNT, BNTC, NTC, WBC; ESV, KJV, NASB, NCV, NET, NIV, NLT, NRSV; similarly Lns], 'he threw himself down at his feet' [AB1; REB, TEV], 'he quickly bowed down in front of him' [GW], 'he knelt at Jesus' feet' [CEV]. This verb means to prostrate oneself in supplication before someone [LN]. It means to throw oneself to the ground before a high-ranking person [BAGD]. It was an act of respect [TRT] or an act of a supplication [BAGD, CGTC, Gnd]. This act indicates that Jairus considered Jesus to be superior to himself [Hb, NCBC]. By now Jesus was a respected teacher in the town with a reputation of having a miraculous power to heal [NIGTC].

b. ἐσχάτως (LN **23.151**) (BAGD p. 314): 'at an extreme' [LN], 'finally' [BAGD]. The phrase ἐσχάτως ἔχει 'is at the final point' is translated 'is at the last' [Lns], 'is at the point of death' [BAGD, BECNT, NTC; ESV, NASB, NRSV; similarly KJV], 'is dying' [BNTC; GW, NCV, NIV, NLT], 'is about to die' [AB2, LN; CEV], 'is near death' [WBC; NET], 'is close to death' [AB1], 'is at death's door' [REB], 'is very sick' [**LN**; TEV]. The idiom 'to be at an extreme' means to be so very sick that death is imminent [LN].

QUESTION—What did a leader in a synagogue do?

The synagogue leader was in charge of the administrative duties of the synagogue [TH]. One of his responsibilities was to arrange for a speaker at the services [BECNT, CBC, CGTC, EBC, NICNT, PNTC, WBC]. All of the Jewish synagogues had 'synagogue leaders' and Jairus was one of such leaders [Hb, PNTC, TH, WBC]. The reference to 'one' of the leaders could mean that this particular synagogue had more than one leader [AB2, Hb, WBC]. Probably he was one of the men in the governing body of his synagogue but not the chief official [NIGTC].

QUESTION—How old was his daughter and what was wrong with her?

The account in Luke 8:42 says that she was his only daughter and was about twelve years old [Hb, NIGTC]. Because she was at the point of death, Jairus wanted Jesus to go and heal her before she died [Hb, Lns, NIGTC]. The account in Matthew 9:18 says that Jairus told Jesus that his daughter had just died, but this was probably because Matthew was writing an abbreviated account that left out the detail about messengers coming from the house to tell the leader that his daughter had died before he could bring Jesus to her [Hb].

QUESTION—Why did Jairus want Jesus to put his hand on the girl?

Jesus frequently put his hand on those he healed and this act had become expected as the normal gesture used in healing [BECNT, BNTC, Hb, NAC, NIGTC, Sw, Tay]. It was a gesture that implied the transmission of a healing power [WBC].

5:24 **And he-went with him. And a-large crowd was-following him and they-were-pressing-against**[a] **him.**

LEXICON—a. imperf. act. indic. of συνθλίβω (LN **19.45**) (BAGD p. 790): 'to press in, to crowd around' [LN], 'to press upon' [BAGD]. The phrase 'they were pressing against him' [AB2; similarly WBC] is also translated 'pressing in on him' [AB1; NASB, NRSV], 'were pressing upon him' [BECNT, NTC], 'pressed around him' [NET, NIV, REB], 'pressed him on every side' [GW], 'were pressing him on all sides' [Lns], 'pushed very close around him' [NCV], 'crowding round him' [NLT], 'kept crowding around' [CEV], 'were crowding him from every side' [**LN**; TEV], 'thronged him' [KJV], 'thronged about him' [ESV]. This verb means to press in hard from all sides [LN].

QUESTION—Where is the paragraph break?

1. There is a paragraph break in the middle of this verse after the first sentence, 'And he went with him.' [BECNT, NAC, NICNT, TH, TRT; CEV, ESV, NCV, NIV, NRSV].
2. This verse is connected with the preceding verses and ends the paragraph [AB2, BNTC, Lns, NTC; NASB, NET, REB].
3. This verse begins a new paragraph that continues with the following verses [NLT].
4. This verse is a separate paragraph by itself [GW, TEV].

DISCOURSE UNIT—5:25-34 [EBC, Hb, NICNT]. The topic is the woman with the flow of blood [Hb], the woman with the hemorrhage [NICNT], healing a woman with a hemorrhage [EBC].

5:25 **And (there was) a-woman being with a-flow**[a] **of-blood twelve years**

LEXICON—a. ῥύσις (LN **23.182**) (BAGD p. 738): 'flow' [LN]. The phrase ῥύσει αἵματος 'a flow of blood' [AB2] is also translated 'an issue of blood' [Lns; KJV], 'a discharge of blood' [ESV], 'a loss of blood, a menstrual flow, bleeding' [LN]. The phrase 'being with a flow of blood' is translated 'had been bleeding' [CEV, NCV], 'had been subject to bleeding' [NIV], 'had a hemorrhage' [WBC; NASB], 'who was hemorrhaging' [BECNT], 'had been subject to hemorrhages' [NTC], 'had suffered from a hemorrhage' [BNTC; NET], 'had been suffering from hemorrhages' [AB1; NRSV; similarly REB], 'had suffered from severe bleeding' [TEV], 'had been suffering from chronic bleeding' [GW], 'had suffered with constant bleeding' [NLT], 'suffered from menstrual bleeding' [**LN**]. The idiom 'a flow of blood' refers to the loss of blood through menstrual bleeding [LN]. It refers to a hemorrhage [TH].

QUESTION—What was wrong with this woman?

This does not say what caused the flow of blood [Lns, NICNT, NIVfn]. It probably was a chronic uterine hemorrhage [AB2, EBC, Hb], a vaginal bleeding [BNTC, CBC, NETfn] of a menstrual nature [ICC, LN, NIGTC, PNTC, TH]. The present participle οὖσα '*being* with a flow of blood' indicates a condition that had begun in the past and was still present, but it does not mean that the bleeding had never stopped for twelve years. The point is that she had suffered from this abnormal bleeding during the twelve years without being cured [TH]. She had a problem with her monthly period, but she was not constantly bleeding [TRT]. This was a condition that made her ceremonially unclean (Lev. 15:25–27) [AB1, BECNT, CBC, CGTC, Hb, Lns, NICNT, NIGTC, TH, TRT, WBC] and caused everything she touched to be unclean also [AB1, WBC].

5:26 **and having-suffered**[a] **much from/under many physicians and having-spent**[b] **everything she had**

LEXICON—a. aorist act. participle of πάσχω (LN 24.78) (BAGD 3.b. p. 634): 'to suffer' [BAGD, LN], 'to be in pain' [LN]. The phrase πολλὰ παθοῦσα ὑπὸ πολλῶν ἰατρῶν 'having suffered much from/under many physicians' is translated 'having suffered much by many physicians' [Lns], 'had suffered much under many physicians' [ESV], 'had suffered much at the hands of many doctors' [BECNT], 'had suffered a great deal under the care of many doctors' [NIV], 'had endured much under many physicians' [NRSV], 'had endured a great deal under the care of many doctors' [NET], 'had suffered many things of many physicians' [KJV], 'had suffered much from many physicians' [NTC, WBC; similarly NCV, NLT], 'she had been treated by many doctors' [AB1], 'she had gone to many doctors, and they had not done anything except cause her a lot of pain' [CEV], 'had endured much at the hands of many physicians' [BNTC; NASB], 'had been under the care of many doctors' [GW], 'even though she had been treated by many doctors' [AB2; TEV], 'in spite of long treatment by many doctors' [REB]. This verb means to suffer pain [LN]. This word occurs at 5:26; 8:31; 9:12.

b. aorist act. participle of δαπανάω (LN 57.146) (BAGD 1. p. 171): 'to spend, to pay out, to pay expenses' [LN]. The phrase δαπανήσασα τὰ παρ' αὐτῆς πάντα 'having spent everything she had' is translated 'had spent all that she had' [AB1, BECNT, BNTC; NTC, WBC; ESV, KJV, NASB, NET, NIV, NRSV, REB; similarly NCV], 'having spent everything from her own means' [Lns], 'had spent all her money' [LN;

GW, TEV], 'had spent all her money on them' [AB2], 'had paid them all the money she had' [CEV], 'over the years she had spent everything she had to pay them' [NLT]. This verb means to pay out money in order to obtain future benefits or to pay for benefits already received [LN]. She spent all of her money to pay the doctors [AB2, TRT; CEV, NLT].

QUESTION—What was the cause of this woman's suffering?
1. The woman had suffered much *from being treated by* many physicians [BECNT, BNTC, CGTC, Gnd, ICC, My, NTC, PNTC, Sw, Tay, WBC; CEV, KJV, NASB, NCV, NLT, NRSV, REB]. She had suffered much *from* the physicians [NTC, WBC; CEV, NCV, NLT, REB], had endured much *under* them [NRSV], *at* their hands [BECNT, BNTC, CGTC, Gnd, ICC, Sw, Tay; NASB]. The varied remedies prescribed by the physicians were often severe and loathsome, and instead of curing her, they caused additional suffering [Hb]. Her condition grew worse partly because of the care the doctors had bestowed on her [NTC].
2. The woman had suffered much *from her flow of blood* even though she had been under the care of many physicians [AB1, AB2, NCBC; GW, TEV; probably ESV, NET, NIV].

and having-benefited[a] nothing but rather having-come to a-worse[b] (condition),
LEXICON—a. aorist pass. participle of ὠφελέω (LN 35.2) (BAGD 1.a. p. 900): 'to be helped' [LN]. The phrase 'having benefited nothing' is translated 'having in no way been benefited' [Lns], 'hadn't benefited a bit' [AB2], 'was nothing bettered' [KJV], 'was no better' [BNTC; ESV, NRSV], 'had not been helped' [BECNT], 'was not helped at all' [NASB; similarly GW], 'to no avail' [WBC], 'she had gotten no better' [NLT], 'instead of getting better' [AB1; NTC; CEV, NET, NIV, TEV; similarly REB], 'instead of improving' [NCV]. This verb means to provide assistance [LN].
b. χείρων (LN **23.150**, 65.29) (BAGD p. 881): 'worse' [BAGD, LN]. The phrase εἰς τὸ χεῖρον ἐλθοῦσα 'having come to a worse condition' is translated 'having come to worse' [Lns], 'grew worse' [ESV, KJV, NET, NIV, NRSV; similarly AB1, BNTC; NASB], 'she had become worse' [BECNT; GW, REB; similarly WBC], 'had gotten worse' [AB2], 'she only got worse' [CEV; similarly NCV, NLT], 'had grown worse' [NTC], 'she got worse all the time' [TEV], 'became more sick' [**LN** (23.150)]. This adjective describes something as being less satisfactory than something else [LN (65.29)].

5:27 having-heard about Jesus, having-come behind (him) in the crowd she-touched his garment.[a]
LEXICON—a. ἱμάτιον (LN 6.172) (BAGD 1. p. 376): This singular form is translated 'garment' [AB2, BAGD, BECNT, BNTC, Lns, NTC; ESV, KJV], 'cloak' [LN; NASB, NET, NIV, NRSV, REB], 'coat' [LN; NCV],

'robe' [LN; NLT], 'clothing' [WBC], 'clothes' [AB1; CEV, GW, TEV]. This noun denotes any type of outer garment [LN].

QUESTION—What relationship is indicated by the use of the aorist active participle ἀκούσασα 'having heard'?

The seven connected participial constructions in verses 25 and 26 introduce this woman who touches Jesus' garment. The participle 'having heard' may be taken in two ways.
1. The participle 'having heard' indicates when she went to touch his garment [Hb, NTC, WBC; KJV, NASB, NCV, NET, NIV]: *when she heard about Jesus, she came behind him and touched his garment*.
2. The participle indicates the reason she came behind him to touch his garment [AB1, EBC, Hb, TRT; GW, NLT, TEV]: *because she heard about Jesus, she came behind him and touched his garment*. The reports she had heard of Jesus' healing powers made her believe that he could heal her also [Hb, Sw].

QUESTION—What had the woman heard about Jesus?

She had heard about the miracles of his healing ministry [AB1, BECNT, EBC, Hb, ICC, Lns, NCBC, NICNT, Sw, Tay, TH, TRT, WBC]. She had also heard of his teachings about the kingdom of God [BECNT].

QUESTION—Why did she come up behind Jesus in the crowd?

The woman wanted to avoid a public disclosure of her condition, so she tried to keep from being noticed [Hb, Lns]. She thought that not even Jesus would notice her [Lns].

QUESTION—What part of Jesus' clothing did the woman touch?

Matt. 9:18 and Luke 8:44 say that she touched the fringe of Jesus' robe [Hb, Lns, Sw, Tay]. The fringe may refer to one of the tassels attached to the four corners of the outer garment worn by all observant Jews (Num. 15:38–39; Deut. 22:12) [Hb, Lns, NLTfn, NTC, PNTC, Sw, Tay]. His robe was square and two of its corners were thrown back over the shoulders so that the tassels on two of the corners were hanging down at his back [Lns].

5:28 Because she-was-saying,[a] "If I-might-touch even his garments[b] I-will-be-healed.[c]"

LEXICON—a. imperf. act. indic. of λέγω (LN 33.69) (BAGD I.1.b.α. p. 468): 'to say' [BAGD, LN], 'to speak' [LN]. The phrase 'she was saying' is translated 'she kept saying' [Lns; NET], 'she said' [AB2, BNTC, NTC; ESV, GW, KJV, NRSV, REB], 'she thought' [NASB, NCV, NIV], 'she thought to herself' [NLT], 'she had said to herself' [AB1; CEV], 'was saying to herself' [BECNT; TEV]. This verb means to speak or talk about something [LN].
   b. ἱμάτιον (LN 6.172) (BAGD 1. p. 376): 'garment' [BAGD], 'cloak, coat, robe' [LN]. This plural form is translated 'garments' [BECNT; ESV, NASB, NCV, NET], 'clothes' [AB1, BECNT, BNTC, NTC, WBC; CEV, GW, KJV, NIV, NRSV, REB, TEV], 'robes' [Lns], 'robe' [NLT]. This noun denotes any type of outer garment [LN].

c. fut. pass. indic. of σῴζω (LN 23.136) (BAGD 1.c. p. 798): 'to be healed' [LN; NCV, NET, NIV, NLT, REB], 'to be cured' [AB1, AB2, LN], 'to be made well' [LN, WBC; ESV, NRSV], 'to be free from disease' [BAGD], 'to be saved' [BAGD, BECNT, BNTC, Lns]. This passive verb is also translated in the active voice: 'to be well' [CEV], 'to get well' [NTC; GW, NASB, TEV], 'to be whole' [KJV]. This verb means to cause someone to become well again after having been sick [LN]. Here σῴζω 'saved' means to be restored [Lns].

QUESTION—What relationship is indicated by the conjunction γάρ 'because'?
This conjunction indicates the reason why the woman touched Jesus' garment [BECNT, Hb, Lns, TH]. This verse is inserted into the story as a parenthesis in order to explain why the woman touched Jesus' garment [BECNT, Tay, TH, WBC].

QUESTION—How was she saying these words?
It is obvious that the woman was speaking to herself since she was trying to remain unnoticed by the crowd [TH]. She spoke within herself (Matt. 9:21) [AB1, BECNT, CGTC, EBC, Gnd, Hb, Sw, Tay, TRT; CEV, NCV, NLT, TEV] because she did not want to inform others of her condition or intentions [Hb]. The imperfect tense indicates that this thought was uppermost in her mind as she made her way through the crowd [Hb, Lns, WBC].

QUESTION—Why did she want to touch Jesus' garments?
Most people thought that touching a healer's garments would bring about healing [AB1, BECNT, CBC, EBC, NIGTC]. They thought there was some sort of power resident in the body of a healer and healing would result from contact with his garments [AB2]. It was a popular belief that the dignity and power of a person transferred to what that person was wearing [NICNT].

QUESTION—Why is 'garment' in the plural here instead of singular as in 5:27?
The plural form probably indicates that she thought that contact with any part of any of Jesus' garments would serve for her healing [Hb].

5:29 And immediately the fountain[a] of her blood was-dried-up and she-knew[b] in her body that she-had-been-cured[c] from the affliction.[d]

LEXICON—a. πηγή (LN **23.183**) (BAGD 1. p. 655): 'fountain' [BAGD, LN]. The phrase 'the fountain of her blood was dried up' [KJV; similarly AB2] is also translated 'the well of her blood was dried up' [WBC], 'the spring of her blood was dried up' [Lns], 'the flow of her blood was dried up' [NASB; similarly BNTC; ESV, REB], 'the flow of blood stopped' [AB1], 'the/her bleeding stopped' [**LN**, NTC; CEV, GW, NCV, NET, NIV, NLT, TEV], 'her hemorrhage stopped' [NRSV], 'the hemorrhaging ceased' [BECNT]. The idiom 'a fountain of blood' refers to the loss of blood through menstrual bleeding [LN].

b. aorist act. indic. of γινώσκω (LN 28.1) (BAGD 4.c. p. 161): 'to know, to know about, to have knowledge of' [LN], 'to perceive, to notice, to realize, to feel' [BAGD]. The phrase 'she knew in her body' [AB2,

BECNT, WBC] is also translated 'she realized in her body' [Lns], 'she knew in herself' [AB1; REB], 'she knew' [CEV], 'she felt in her body' [BNTC, NTC; ESV, KJV, NASB, NCV, NET, NIV, NRSV], 'she could feel in her body' [NLT], 'she had the feeling inside herself' [TEV], 'she felt (cured)' [GW]. This verb means to possess information about something [LN].

c. perf. pass. indic. of ἰάομαι (LN 23.136) (BAGD 1. p. 368): 'to be cured' [AB1, BAGD, LN; GW, REB], 'to be healed' [AB2, BAGD, BECNT, LN, Lns, NTC, WBC; ESV, KJV, NASB, NCV, NET, NLT, NRSV, TEV], 'to be freed' [NIV], 'to be made well' [LN; CEV]. This verb means to cause someone to become well again after having been sick [LN].

d. μάστιξ (LN 23.153) (BAGD 2. p. 495): 'affliction' [AB1, BECNT, BNTC; NASB, REB], 'disease' [LN; ESV, NCV, NET, NRSV], 'suffering' [BAGD, WBC; NIV], 'illness' [NTC; GW], 'plague' [KJV], 'scourge' [AB2, Lns], 'terrible condition' [NLT], 'trouble' [TEV]. The phrase 'she has been cured from the affliction' is translated 'she was well' [CEV]. This noun denotes the state of being diseased [LN]. The word literally means a 'whip' and it is used figuratively to refer to the lashing of a disease [AB2]. Calling it a whip or scourge emphasizes the severity of her affliction [Gnd]. This word occurs at 3:10; 5:29, 34.

QUESTION—What relationship is indicated by the initial καί 'and'?

This conjunction connects the touching of Jesus' garment in verse 27 to the instant result that came from that touch [Hb]. Since this follows the parenthetical comment in verse 28, the act of touching Jesus' garment is repeated: 'As soon as she touched them, her bleeding stopped' [CEV]. Another translation moves the act of touching Jesus' garment from verse 27 to this verse: 'She touched his cloak, and her bleeding stopped' [TEV].

QUESTION—What is meant by saying the woman 'knew in her body' that she had been cured?

The instantaneous healing caused a definite physical sensation [Hb, ICC, NTC, Sw; probably ESV, GW, KJV, NASB, NCV, NET, NIV, NLT, NRSV, TEV which use the verb 'she felt']. She had a feeling of being strong and well [EBC, My]. How she knew is not explained here [BECNT].

5:30 And immediately Jesus having-perceived[a] within himself the power[b] having-gone-out[c] from him having-turned-around in the crowd he-was-saying, "Who touched my garments?"

LEXICON—a. aorist act. participle of ἐπιγινώσκω (LN 28.2) (BAGD 2.c. p. 291): 'to perceive' [BAGD, WBC; ESV, NASB], 'to notice' [BAGD], 'to realize' [Lns; NIV, NLT], 'to know' [AB2, BECNT, BNTC; KJV, NET, TEV], 'to know about' [LN], 'to be aware' [AB1; NRSV, REB], 'to be well aware' [NTC], 'to feel' [CEV, GW, NCV]. This verb means to possess information about something [LN].

b. δύναμις (LN 76.1): 'power' [LN; all translations except KJV, NLT], 'healing power' [NLT], 'virtue' [KJV]. This noun denotes the potentiality to exert force in performing some function [LN]. This power was a mighty supernatural force that accomplished his mighty works [WBC]. It refers to the healing power that dwelled in Jesus [Tay].

c. aorist act. participle of ἐξέρχομαι (LN 15.40) (BAGD 2.b.γ. p. 275): 'to go out of' [AB1, AB2, BNTC, LN, Lns; GW, KJV, REB, TEV], 'to go out from' [CEV, ESV, NCV, NET, NIV, NLT], 'to go forth' [BECNT; NRSV], 'to proceed from' [WBC; NASB], 'to issue from' [NTC], 'to depart out of, to leave from within' [LN], 'to come out' [BAGD]. This verb means to move out of an enclosed or well-defined two or three-dimensional area [LN].

QUESTION—What does the phrase ἐξ αὐτοῦ 'from him' modify in the statement τὴν ἐξ αὐτοῦ δύναμιν ἐξελθοῦσαν 'the *from him* power having gone out'?

1. 'From him' is to be connected with the verb ἐξελθοῦσαν 'having gone out' [AB1, AB2, EBC, Hb, ICC, TH; all versions except NASB]: the power *had gone out from him*. Jesus knew that power had gone forth from him [TH].
2. 'From him' is to be connected with the noun δύναμιν 'power' [BNTC, CGTC, Gnd, NCBC, NTC, Sw, Tay, WBC; NASB]: *the power that resides in him* had gone forth. It was the power that issued from Jesus that had gone forth from him [NTC]. Jesus was the source of the power, not simply the channel of that power [BNTC]. It does not mean that Jesus' power left him when it went forth to heal the woman [Sw].

QUESTION—What is meant by Jesus 'perceiving within himself' that the power had gone out from him?

Jesus sensed that power had gone out from him [ESVfn, Sw, Tay, TH]. It appears that the healing of the woman was not the result of a conscious act of Jesus [CGTC, EBC, ICC, My, NICNT, NTC, Tay, TRT, WBC]. If the healing of the woman was unknown to Jesus until the miracle occurred, it was due to a limitation imposed by his humanity [WBC]. Since Jesus was God's representative, it was the power of God that healed the woman through Jesus [BNTC, CGTC, EBC, NICNT]. The power went out from him independent of his will [Gnd]. Although the statement seems to imply that the healing was not accomplished by the will of Jesus, it may have been. If so, Jesus may have felt the woman's touch, understood its meaning, and then consented to heal her [EGT]. When Jesus perceived the significance of the woman's touch and willed to honor her faith, he was conscious of the power going our from him since it cost him spiritual energy to heal people [Hb]. This healing power was always under the control of Jesus' conscious will. When the woman touched him he knew what her ailment was and willed her healing [Lns].

QUESTION—What is indicated by the use of the plural form 'my garments'?

It is not likely that she touched more than one article of clothing, so in many languages it must be translated with the singular form 'garment' as it is in 5:27 [TH]. Some translate this with the noun 'clothes', which does not distinguish between singular and plural [CEV, GW, KJV, NIV, NRSV, REB, TEV].

QUESTION—Didn't Jesus really know who had touched him?

Jesus didn't know who had touched him [CGTC, EBC, Gnd, ICC, My, NCBC, NICNT, NIGTC, NTC]. He wanted to know who it was in order to correct the imperfect faith of the person who sought healing from his clothing rather than from him personally [CGTC]. Others think that Jesus knew who it was [Hb, Lns] but asked the question so the woman would interact with him and receive more than just physical healing [Hb].

5:31 And his disciples were-saying to-him, "You-see the crowd pressing-against[a] you, and you-say, 'Who touched me?'" **5:32** And he-was-looking-around[b] to-see the (one) having-done this.

LEXICON—a. pres. act. participle of συνθλίβω (LN 19.45) (BAGD p. 790): 'to press against' [AB2, WBC; NET], 'to press around' [BNTC; ESV, NLT, REB], 'to press upon' [BECNT], 'to press in on' [LN; NASB, NRSV; similarly AB1, NTC], 'to press on all sides' [Lns], 'to press' [GW], 'to push against' [NCV], 'to crowd against' [NIV], 'to crowd around' [LN; CEV], 'to crowd' [TEV], 'to throng' [KJV]. This verb means to press in hard from all sides [LN]. This word also occurs at 5:24.

b. imperfect mid. indic. of περιβλέπομαι, περιβλέπω (LN 24.11) (BAGD 1. p. 646): 'to look around' [AB1, AB2, BAGD, BECNT, BNTC, LN, Lns, NTC, WBC; all versions except CEV, NRSV], 'to look all around' [NRSV], 'to turn' [CEV]. This verb means to look or to glance around, but not necessarily in a complete circle [TH]. The imperfect tense refers to a long, searching gaze from face to face [EGT, Hb, Lns, NTC, Sw, Tay] as he continued to look around [AB2, EGT, PNTC, Sw].

QUESTION—Did each of the disciples individually ask this question and what did the question imply?

In Luke 8:45, it says that Peter acted as their spokesmen [Hb, Lns, NTC, Sw]. This comment was ironic [TH], sarcastic [NAC], and disrespectful [CGTC] because they all thought that Jesus' question was absurd [BNTC] and ludicrous [BECNT]. They thought the question to be unreasonable since numerous people had been inadvertently pressing against Jesus as they crowded around him [AB2, BECNT, CBC, Hb, Lns, NICNT, NTC, WBC]. It was impossible to locate any particular person who might have touched him [AB2].

QUESTION—Why is the feminine gender used with the pronoun τήν 'the (female-one)' in the statement 'he was looking around to see the (female) having done this' if Jesus didn't know who had touched him?

The fact that 'the one' he was looking for was a woman is from Mark's viewpoint, and does not necessarily imply that Jesus knew whether the person was a man or a woman [AB1, CGTC, ICC, My, NICNT, NTC, Tay, TH]. It could be that Jesus supernaturally knew that it was a woman who had touched him [AB2, BECNT]. Jesus may even have known the identity of the woman who had touched him and was looking about to locate her in the crowd [CBC, Hb, Lns]. Jesus was not looking around to see *who* had done this, he was looking around to find the very woman who had touched him [Lns].

5:33 Now the woman was-afraid[a] and was-trembling,[b] having-known what had-happened to-her. She-came and fell-down-before[c] him and told him the whole truth.[d]

LEXICON—a. aorist pass. participle of φοβέομαι, φοβέω (LN 25.252) (BAGD 1.a. p. 862): 'to be afraid' [BAGD, LN, Lns, WBC], 'to be frightened' [NLT], 'to be fearful' [BNTC], 'to fear' [AB2, BECNT, LN; KJV, NASB]. The phrase 'was afraid and was trembling' is translated '(came) in fear and trembling' [ESV, NRSV; similarly NET], '(came) shaking with fear' [CEV; similarly NCV], 'trembling with fear' [AB1, NTC; NIV, REB, TEV; similarly GW]. This verb means to be in a state of fearing [LN].

b. pres. act. participle of τρέμω (LN 16.6) (BAGD p. 825): 'to tremble' [BAGD, LN; all translations except CEV, NCV], 'to quiver' [BAGD, LN], 'to shake' [Hb, LN; CEV, NCV]. This verb means to shake or tremble, often because of fear or consternation [LN]. This verb can be used figuratively to mean 'to be afraid, to fear' [BAGD].

c. aorist act. indic. of προσπίπτω (LN **17.22**) (BAGD 1. p. 718): 'to prostrate oneself before' [AB1, **LN**], 'to fall down before' [AB2, BAGD, BECNT, LN, Lns, NTC, WBC; ESV, KJV, NASB, NET, NRSV; similarly BNTC], 'to fall at his feet' [NCV, NIV, REB], 'to fall to her knees in front of' [NLT], 'to kneel down in front of' [CEV], 'to kneel at his feet' [TEV], 'to bow in front of' [GW]. This verb means to prostrate oneself before someone, usually in supplication [LN]. This word occurs at 3:11; 5:33; 7:25.

d. ἀλήθεια (LN **72.2**) (BAGD 2.a. p. 35): 'truth' [BAGD, **LN**]. The phrase πᾶσαν τὴν ἀλήθειαν 'the whole truth' [all translations except Lns; CEV, KJV, NLT] is also translated 'all the truth' [Lns; KJV], 'the whole story' [CEV], 'what she had done' [NLT]. This noun denotes the content of that which is true and thus in accordance with what actually happened [LN].

QUESTION—Why was the woman afraid and trembling?

The participial phrase 'having known what had happened to her' indicates the reason for her fear [AB1, BECNT, CGTC, Hb, Lns, NTC, Tay, TH; NLT, REB, TEV]: the woman was afraid *because* she knew what had happened to her. She was afraid because what had happened to her bore witness to the supernatural power of Jesus [BNTC, CGTC, Gnd, NCBC], and his question 'Who touched me' revealed his supernatural knowledge of her act [Gnd]. Perhaps she was also afraid that Jesus would be angry with her [CGTC, Hb] since she had secured her healing without his consent [Hb, NIGTC], and her touch had made Jesus ceremonially unclean until evening (Lev. 15:19) [AB1, Hb]. She was afraid she had offended Jesus by her secrecy and disregard of ceremonial law [CBC, EGT]. She was not only afraid to speak before a crowd, but she was also afraid that everyone would learn about her problem of bleeding [NIGTC, NTC]. Her fear may also be due to her awe in the presence of the miraculous healer [BNTC, NIGTC].

QUESTION—Why did the woman fall down before Jesus?
She prostrated herself before Jesus [TH] to express both her humility and her reverence toward Jesus [Hb].

QUESTION—What was 'the *whole* truth she told Jesus'?
Mark has already recorded in verses 25–29 the 'whole truth' she revealed about her illness, her desire to be healed, and the reason she touched his garment to be healed [BECNT, Hb, NTC, TH].

5:34 And he said to-her, "Daughter,[a] your faith has healed[b] you. Go in peace[c] and be healed[d] from you affliction.[e]"

LEXICON—a. θυγάτηρ (LN 9.47) (BAGD 2.a. p. 364): 'daughter' [AB2, BAGD, BECNT, BNTC, LN, Lns, NTC, WBC; all versions except CEV, NCV, TEV], 'my daughter' [AB1; TEV], 'lady, woman' [LN], 'dear woman' [NCV], not explicit [CEV]. This noun is a figurative extension of the word 'daughter' and denotes a woman for whom there is some affectionate concern [LN]. 'Daughter' is used figuratively as a friendly greeting to girls and women [BAGD].

b. perf. act. indic. of σῴζω (LN 23.36) (BAGD 1.c. p. 798): 'to heal' [LN; NIV, REB], 'to cure' [AB1, LN], 'to make well' [LN, Lns, WBC; ESV, GW, NASB, NET, NLT, NRSV, TEV], 'to make whole' [KJV], 'to save or free from disease' [BAGD], 'to save' [AB2, BECNT, BNTC, Lns]. The phrase 'your faith has healed you' is translated 'you are now well because of your faith' [CEV], 'you are made well because you believed' [NCV]. In this context, the verb means to cause someone to become well again after having been sick [LN]. The verb means to save from death [BAGD]. 'Saved' is used in the sense of making a person well [BECNT, WBC]. The word 'saved' goes beyond her physical healing to include her restoration to society [BNTC].

c. εἰρήνη (LN 22.42) (BAGD 2. p. 227): 'peace' [AB1, AB2, BAGD, BECNT, BNTC, LN, Lns, NTC, WBC; all versions except CEV], 'tranquility' [LN]. The clause 'go in peace' is translated 'May God give you peace!' [CEV]. This noun denotes a set of favorable circumstances involving peace and tranquility [LN].

d. ὑγιής (LN 23.129) (BAGD 1.a. p. 832): 'healed' [BECNT, NTC, WBC; ESV, NASB, NCV, NET, NRSV, TEV], 'cured' [GW], 'freed' [NIV], 'free' [AB1, BECNT; REB], 'whole' [KJV], 'well' [AB2, Lns], 'healthy' [BAGD, LN]. The phrase 'be healed from your affliction' is translated 'your suffering is over' [NLT], 'you are healed, and you will no longer be in pain' [CEV]. This adjective pertains to being in a state of health [LN].

e. μάστιξ (LN 23.153) (BAGD 2. p. 495): 'affliction' [AB1, BECNT, BNTC; NASB, REB], 'disease' [LN; ESV, NCV, NET, NRSV], 'illness'

[NTC; GW], 'suffering' [BAGD, WBC; NIV, NLT], 'pain' [CEV], 'trouble' [TEV], 'scourge' [AB2, Lns], 'plague' [KJV]. This noun denotes being in a state of disease [LN]. This word occurs at 3:10; 5:29, 34.

QUESTION—Why did Jesus call the woman 'daughter'?

This was a term of endearment [Hb, NTC, TH]. It expresses his tender compassion [PNTC] and loving concern for someone [Lns]. It could be used as a respectful and affectionate way of addressing a woman regardless of her age or relationship [BECNT]. Jesus spoke to her as a father would to his child [AB2, EGT, NTC] even though she may not have been younger than he was [EGT, NTC]. It assured her of the spiritual relationship to him that she had entered into [Hb]. By calling her 'daughter', he signified that she was a member of his new family of disciples [Gnd].

QUESTION—How had her faith healed her?

The woman's faith had been the channel through which her cure had been accomplished [NTC]. Because of her faith, she touched Jesus who then healed her by his power [Lns, NTC]. Her faith was the reason she was healed by the power that had proceeded from Jesus [Sw, Tay]. Her faith was her belief that Jesus had the power to heal her [Hb, NICNT].

QUESTION—What is meant by the words ὕπαγε εἰς εἰρήνην 'Go in peace'?

This was a Jewish idiomatic expression used in saying farewell [AB1, BECNT, EBC, ICC, NCBC, Tay, TH, TRT, WBC]. The meaning of 'peace' includes the ideas of soundness, wholeness, and well-being [AB1, NTC, TH]. These parting words express a wish that this woman would continue to remain free from her former affliction [AB2]. This farewell wished her the blessing of well-being, and may also imply being at peace with God [TRT]. The word 'peace' signified more than a release from agitation or a fear of recrimination since after touching Jesus she was experiencing the feeling of well-being that accompanies salvation from God [NICNT].

QUESTION—What is meant by Jesus' parting statement, 'be healed from your affliction'?

This assured her that her healing was permanent [BECNT, Gnd, Hb, Lns, NICNT, NTC, Tay]. She was not cured by these words since she had already been healed when she touched Jesus [ICC]. This confirmed that the healing had already happened [NIGTC, WBC]. Jesus put into words what she had already experienced [CGTC, PNTC]. Instead of repeating the cure, it means 'be healthy' [BNTC].

DISCOURSE UNIT—5:35–43 [EBC, Hb, NICNT]. The topic is the raising of Jairus' daughter [EBC, Hb, NICNT], the subduing of death [NICNT].

5:35 **(While) he still is-speaking they-come from the (house) of-(the) synagogue-leader saying, "Your daughter died.[a] Why are-you- still -bothering[b] the teacher?"**

LEXICON—a. aorist act. indic. of ἀποθνῄσκω (LN 23.99) (BAGD 1.a.α. p. 91): 'to die' [BAGD, LN]. The aorist verb ἀπέθανεν 'died' is translated 'has died' [AB1, AB2, BECNT; CEV, GW, NASB, NET, REB,

TEV], 'did die' [Lns], 'is dead' [BNTC, NTC, WBC; ESV, KJV, NCV, NIV, NLT, NRSV]. This verb refers to the process of dying [LN]. The aorist tense states the historical fact that she died [Hb, Lns]. The perfect tense would have been more natural and here the tense does not just mean that she 'died', but stresses that now she 'is dead' [CGTC, NTC, Tay].
- b. pres. act. indic. of σκύλλω (LN **22.23**) (BAGD 2. p. 758): 'to bother' [AB1, AB2, BAGD, **LN**, NTC, WBC; CEV, GW, NCV, NIV, TEV], 'to trouble' [BAGD, BECNT, BNTC, LN, Lns; ESV, KJV, NASB, NET, NLT, NRSV, REB], 'to annoy' [BAGD]. Some translate this rhetorical question as a statement: 'There is no need to bother the teacher anymore' [NCV], 'There's no use troubling the Teacher now' [NLT]. This verb means to cause trouble or harassment [LN].

QUESTION—Who were the people who came to meet Jairus and where did they come from?

The verb ἔρχονται 'they come' is an impersonal plural form for 'men came' [BECNT, Tay, TH]. Since these men felt free to tell Jairus what he should do, they were probably his friends or relatives [Hb, Lns, TRT]. The text says they come ἀπὸ τοῦ ἀρχισυναγώγου 'from the synagogue leader', but since they were bringing a message *to* the synagogue leader who was already with Jesus, it means that they came from *the house/home of* the synagogue leader where the daughter had died [CGTC, ICC, TH; all translations].

QUESTION—What is meant by 'bothering' the teacher?

Because the messengers thought that the girl's death had ended all hope that Jesus could help the girl, they presumed there was no need to have such a busy teacher take time to come to the house [Hb]. It would be a waste of time for Jesus to continue on to the house [TRT].

5:36 **But having-overheard/ignoring[a] the word being-spoken Jesus says to-the synagogue-leader, "Do- not -be-afraid,[b] only believe.[c]"**

TEXT—Manuscripts reading παρακούσας 'having overheard/ignoring' are given a B rating by GNT to indicate it was regarded to be almost certain. A variant reading is εὐθέως ἀκούσας 'immediately having heard' and it is followed by KJV. Another variant reading is ἀκούσας 'having heard'.

LEXICON—a. aorist act. participle of παρακούω (LN **24.66**, **30.37**) (BAGD 1. p. 619): 'to overhear' [AB1, BAGD, BNTC, **LN** (23.66); ESV, GW, NASB, NLT, NRSV, REB], 'to ignore' [AB2, BAGD, BECNT, LN (30.37), NTC, WBC; NIV], 'to pay no attention to' [BAGD, **LN** (30.37); NCV, NET, TEV], 'to disregard' [Lns]. This verb means to hear something without the speaker's knowledge [LN (23.66)], or to pay no attention to something [LN (30.37)].
- b. pres. pass. impera. of φοβέομαι, φοβέω (LN **25.252**) (BAGD 1.a. p. 862): 'to be afraid' [AB1, AB2, BAGD, BECNT, BNTC, LN, WBC; all versions except CEV, ESV, NRSV], 'to fear' [LN, Lns, NTC; ESV, NRSV], 'to worry' [CEV]. This verb means to be in a state of fearing [LN].

c. pres. act. impera. of πιστεύω (LN 31.85) (BAGD 2.c. p. 662): 'to believe' [AB1, AB2, BAGD, BECNT, BNTC, LN, Lns, NTC, WBC; all versions except CEV, NLT, REB], 'to have faith' [LN; CEV, NLT, REB], 'to trust, to have confidence' [BAGD, LN]. This verb means to believe something with complete trust and reliance [LN]. This special kind of faith is being confident that God or Christ is in a position to help the supplicant out of his distress [BAGD].

QUESTION—Should the verb παρακούσας be translated 'having overheard' or 'ignoring'?

Each alternative implicitly includes the other sense. Jesus overheard what was said and spoke in response to that message, ignoring what they told Jairus to do [Gnd, Hb, PNTC].

1. It means that Jesus *overheard* what the messengers told Jairus [AB1, BNTC, CGTC, EGT, Hb, ICC; ESV, GW, NASB, NLT, NRSV, REB]: *but when Jesus overheard what they said.* It is best to be guided by the parallel passage in Luke 8:50 which says, 'when Jesus heard this' [CGTC, Hb]. Jesus overheard the message given to Jairus and then responded to that message [Hb]. Jesus is frequently described as acting on what he hears [AB1]. Jesus did not ignore the message, since it caused him to give these two commands to Jairus [BNTC].
2. It means that Jesus *ignored* what the messengers told Jairus [AB2, BECNT, CBC, EBC, Lns, My, NCBC, NICNT, NIGTC, NTC, Sw, Tay, WBC; NCV, NET, NIV, TEV]: *but Jesus ignored what they said.* Even though Jesus heard what the messengers said, he continued on his mission to help Jairus [CBC]. Jesus spoke to Jairus because he ignored the message. Those who translate it 'overheard' still have to infer that Jesus was not deterred by the message [Tay].

QUESTION—What was Jairus afraid of?

Jairus feared that it was too late to do anything about his daughter [Hb]. The present imperative 'do not be afraid' indicates he was presently afraid [BECNT, CGTC, Lns, Tay].

QUESTION—What was Jairus to believe?

Jairus must continue to believe Jesus would heal his daughter so that she would live [AB2, CGTC, Hb, NICNT]. He must *go on believing* in Jesus' power [Lns]. Jairus must believe that all would end well [NAC]. The present imperative 'believe' indicates that he must keep on believing [AB2, BECNT, BNTC, CBC, CGTC, EGT, Hb, ICC, Lns, PNTC, Tay].

5:37 And he-did- not -allow[a] anyone to-follow[b] (along) with him except Peter and James and John, the brother of James.

LEXICON—a. aorist act. indic. of ἀφίημι (LN 13.140) (BAGD 4. p. 126) 'to allow' [AB1, BAGD, BNTC, LN, Lns, NTC; ESV, GW, NASB, NRSV, REB], 'to permit' [BAGD, BECNT, WBC], 'to let' [AB2, BAGD, LN; CEV, NCV, NET, NIV, TEV], 'to suffer' [KJV]. The phrase 'did not allow anyone to follow along with him' is translated 'stopped the crowd

and wouldn't let anyone go with him' [NLT]. This verb means to leave it up to someone to do something [LN].
  b. aorist act. infin. of συνακολουθέω (LN 15.157) (BAGD p. 783): 'to follow' [AB2, BAGD, LN, Lns, WBC; ESV, KJV, NET, NIV, NRSV], 'to accompany' [BAGD, BECNT, BNTC, LN, NTC; NASB, REB], 'to go' [AB1; CEV, GW, NCV, NLT], 'to go on' [TEV]. This verb means to accompany someone [LN, TH].

QUESTION—Wasn't the girl's father allowed to follow along with Jesus?
  It is assumed that Jairus accompanied Jesus [CGTC, TRT]. At this point Jesus separated himself from the crowd following him [EBC].
QUESTION—Where was Jesus at this time?
  This took place where the messengers met them, probably still some distance from the house [Hb].

5:38 And they-come to[a] the house of-the synagogue-leader, and he-sees a-commotion[b] and weeping[c] and wailing[d] loudly,[e]

LEXICON—a. εἰς (LN 84.16): '(come) to' [BNTC, LN, Lns, NTC, WBC; all versions except CEV, TEV], '(arrived) at' [AB1; TEV], '(enter) into' [BECNT], '(went) into' [AB2]. The phrase 'they come to the house of' is translated 'they went home with' [CEV]. This preposition indicates extension toward a special goal [LN]. Although this preposition can be translated 'came to the house' or 'came into the house', it has to mean that they came *to* the house since the next verse speaks about entering the house [TH]. Another view is that they went 'into the house' [AB2, BECNT, Gnd] and the same action is mentioned again in the next verse in order to set the stage for throwing the mourners out of the house [Gnd].
  b. θόρυβος (LN 14.79) (BAGD 3.a. p. 363): 'commotion' [AB2, BECNT, BNTC, WBC; ESV, NASB, NIV, NLT, NRSV, REB], 'great commotion' [AB1], 'confusion' [**LN** (25.139); TEV], 'noisy confusion' [NET], 'din' [Lns], 'hubbub' [NTC], 'clamor, noise' [LN], 'tumult' [KJV], 'turmoil, excitement, uproar' [BAGD], not explicit [CEV, GW, NCV]. This noun denotes a noise or clamor marked by confusion [LN]. It refers to the turmoil of a crowd milling about in a house of mourning [BAGD].
  c. pres. act. participle of κλαίω (LN 25.138) (BAGD 1. p. 433): 'to weep' [AB2, BECNT, BNTC, LN, NTC, WBC; ESV, KJV, NASB, NET, NLT, NRSV], 'to cry' [AB1; GW, NIV, REB, TEV], 'to sob' [Lns], 'to wail, to lament' [LN]. The clause 'weeping and wailing' is translated 'crying' [CEV, NCV]. This verb means to weep or wail with much noise [LN].
  d. pres. act. participle of ἀλαλάζω (LN **25.139**): 'to wail' [AB1, AB2, BECNT, BNTC, LN, Lns, WBC; all versions except CEV, GW, NCV], 'to weep loudly' [**LN**], 'to sob' [GW]. See the preceding lexical item [CEV, NCV]. This verb means to cry or weep intensely with wailing [LN].
  e. πολύς (LN 78.3) (BAGD I.2.b.β. p. 688): 'loudly' [AB2, BAGD, NTC; ESV, GW, NASB, NET, NIV, NRSV], 'loud' [AB1, BNTC; CEV, REB]

'greatly' [BAGD, LN, Lns; KJV], 'much' [BECNT, LN, WBC; NLT], 'a great deal of' [LN], 'a lot of' [CEV, NCV]. This adverb or adjective indicates the upper range of a scale of extent [LN]. One has this adverb modify only 'wailing' [BNTC], some have it modify both 'weeping and wailing' [AB1, BECNT, NTC, WBC; GW, NASB, REB, TEV], some seem to have it modify 'commotion' [CEV, NLT], and most leave the word in its ambiguous position [AB2, BNTC, Lns; ESV, KJV, NCV, NET, NIV, NRSV].

QUESTION—What is the function of the first conjunction καί 'and' in the clause 'he sees a commotion *and* weeping and wailing loudly'?

1. The clause 'and weeping and wailing loudly' explains what is meant by the noun 'commotion' [AB1, AB2, BNTC, CGTC, EGT, Gnd, My, Sw, TH; ESV, GW, NCV, NIV, NRSV]: he saw a commotion consisting of people weeping and wailing. The uproarious people within the house were the mourners [Sw]. This is translated 'saw the commotion—weeping and loud wailing' [BNTC], 'saw a commotion, people weeping and wailing loudly' [ESV, NRSV], 'saw a noisy crowd there. People were crying and sobbing loudly' [GW], 'found many people there making lots of noise and crying loudly' [NCV], 'found a great commotion, loud crying, and wailing' [AB1], 'saw the commotion made by the people weeping and wailing loudly' [AB2], 'saw the people crying and making a lot of noise' [CEV].

2. It is not clear in some translations whether the conjunction 'and' explains what is meant by 'commotion', or just mentions the two main features of this commotion [AB1, EGT, NTC, WBC; NASB, NIV, REB]. He saw a multitude of people making a confused din in which sounds of weeping and howling without restraint were distinguishable [EGT]. This is translated 'saw a commotion, with people crying and wailing loudly' [NIV], 'found a commotion with much weeping and wailing' [WBC], 'noticed the hubbub, with people loudly weeping and wailing' [NTC], 'found a great commotion, with loud crying and wailing' [REB], 'saw a commotion, and people loudly weeping and wailing' [NASB].

3. The conjunction connects the two events of what he saw with what he heard [LN; TEV]. This is translated 'saw the confusion and (heard) all the crying and loud weeping' [**LN** (25.139)], 'saw the confusion and heard all the loud crying and wailing' [TEV].

4. The grammar in the Greek text is strictly followed with the three conjunctions seeming to list three separate things that he saw [BECNT, Lns, Tay; KJV, NET, NLT]. Jesus beholds the utter confusion and the weeping and wailing people [Tay]. This is translated 'saw much commotion and weeping and wailing' [NLT], 'sees a commotion and much weeping and wailing' [BECNT], 'beholds a din and people sobbing and wailing greatly' [Lns] 'saw noisy confusion and people weeping and wailing loudly' [NET], 'seeth the tumult, and them that wept and wailed greatly' [KJV].

QUESTION—Who were weeping and wailing?

It was customary to have professional mourners participate in a funeral [AB1, AB2, BECNT, EBC, ESVfn, Hb, ICC, Lns, NCBC, NICNT, NIVfn, NTC, PNTC, Sw, TRT, WBC]. The members of the household and relatives would be mourning over the death of the girl, but Matt. 9:23 says that there were also flute players and a 'crowd' making a commotion. It was the custom for a family to show its esteem for the departed one by hiring musicians and mourners [BECNT, Hb]. According to custom, flute players and professional mourners performed during the first part of a funeral with music and wailing [NICNT]. Usually a woman was hired to lead in antiphonal singing or chanting accompanied by flutes and percussion instruments [WBC].

5:39 And having-entered he-says to-them, "Why are-you-making-a-commotion/are-you-distressed[a] and weeping? The child did- not -die but is-sleeping."

LEXICON—a. pres. pass. indic. of θορυβέω, θορυβέομαι (LN 39.44, 25.234) (BAGD 2. p. 363): 'to make a commotion' [AB2, BECNT, BNTC, WBC; ESV, NASB, NRSV; similarly AB1], 'to cause an uproar' [LN (39.44)], 'to make a din' [Lns], 'to make a hubbub' [NTC], 'to make so much noise' [GW, NCV], 'to carry on' [CEV], 'to make this ado' [KJV], 'to be distressed' [BAGD, LN; NET], 'to be troubled' [BAGD, LN (25.234)], 'to be upset' [LN (25.234)]. The phrase 'why are you making a commotion' is translated 'why all this commotion?' [NIV, NLT, REB], 'why all this confusion?' [TEV]. The verb form θορυβέω means to cause people to riot against something [LN (39.44)] while the form θορυβέομαι means to be emotionally upset because of concern or anxiety, although it is possible to interpret it as referring to some evident commotion [LN (25.23)].

b. aorist act. indic. of ἀποθνῄσκω (LN 23.99) (BAGD 1.a.α. p. 91): 'to die' [BAGD, LN]. The phrase οὐκ ἀπέθανεν 'did not die' [Lns] is also translated 'has not died' [AB2, BECNT; NASB], 'is not dead' [AB1, BNTC, NTC, WBC; all versions except NASB]. This verb refers to the process of dying [LN].

QUESTION—What did Jesus enter?

The next verse tells about a further entering into the room where the child was located, so in this verse Jesus might have entered the courtyard [AB1, Sw], or one of the rooms inside the house [Lns, TH]. In Luke 8:51 it says that Jesus entered the house [CGTC; GW]. Upon his arrival at the house, he watched the uproar from the doorway, and now he entered the house [Hb].

QUESTION—What kind of a question did he ask?

It was a rhetorical question indicating that he had no patience with their superficial mourning [Hb]. It implies that their mourning was out of place [Lns, NTC], and he will go on to tell them why they had no reason to mourn [WBC].

QUESTION—Does the verb θορυβεῖσθε refer to making a commotion or to being distressed?
1. It refers to making a commotion [AB1, AB2, BECNT, BNTC, EBC, Gnd, ICC, Lns, My, NICNT, NIGTC, NTC, Tay, TH, TRT, WBC; all versions except NET]. This word refers to the noun θόρυβον 'commotion' in the previous verse [TH].
2. It refers to being distressed [NET].

QUESTION—Why did Jesus say that the child was sleeping?
This was the reason their mourning was unwarranted [Hb, NICNT]. Although she was dead, her death was no more permanent than being asleep [CBC, CGTC, EBC, Gnd, Hb, ICC, NIGTC, Sw, WBC]. Her temporary experience of death would be so short that it will seem as though she had only taken a short nap [BECNT]. In spite of her death, she had not been delivered over to the realm of death with all its consequences [NICNT].

5:40 And they-were-laughing-at[a] him. But he having-put-out[b] everyone takes the father of the child and the mother and the (ones) with him and goes-into where the child was.

TEXT—Manuscripts reading ὅπου ἦν τὸ παιδίον 'where the child was' are followed by GNT, which does not mention any variant reading. A variant reading is ὅπου ἦν τὸ παιδίον ἀνακείμενον 'where the child was lying' and it is followed by KJV.

LEXICON—a. imperf. act. indic. of καταγελάω (LN 33.410) (BAGD 1. p. 409): 'to laugh at' [AB1, AB2, BAGD, BNTC, LN; all versions except KJV, NET, TEV], 'to laugh (in his face)' [NTC], 'to laugh to scorn' [Lns, NTC; KJV], 'to ridicule' [BAGD, BECNT, LN, WBC], 'to make fun of' [LN; NET, TEV]. This verb means to make fun of someone or to ridicule someone by laughing at him [LN].

b. aorist act. participle of ἐκβάλλω (LN 14.44): 'to put out' [AB1, Lns, WBC; KJV, NASB, NIV, TEV], 'to put outside' [BECNT; ESV, NET, NRSV], 'to turn out' [BNTC, NTC; REB], 'to throw out' [AB2; NCV], 'to make (them) go outside' [GW], 'to make (them) leave' [NLT], 'to send out' [CEV], 'to send away, to drive out, to expel' [LN]. This verb means to cause someone to go out or leave, and often force is involved [LN]. The verb implies a forcible ejection [AB1, NETfn, Tay].

QUESTION—Why did the people laugh at Jesus?
They understood Jesus' words in a literal sense and they knew that the girl had really died [CGTC, EBC, Hb, ICC, Sw, WBC]. They presumed that Jesus couldn't accept the reality of death [ESVfn]. They intended to ridicule him [BECNT, CBC, TH, WBC].

QUESTION—Why did Jesus put the people who were laughing at him out of the house?
Their role as mourners for a dead person was no longer appropriate [WBC]. Their irreverence showed that they were unfit to share in the miracle that was about to take place [Hb]. The dignity of Jesus and the miracle that he was

going to perform demanded silence [Lns]. The miracle was intended to be kept secret (5:43) [BNTC].

QUESTION—Who were the 'ones with him'?

The 'ones with him' were the three disciples he had allowed to accompany him in 5:37 [EBC, EGT, Gnd, ICC, Lns, NICNT, NIGTC, Tay, TH, TRT, WBC; CEV, NCV].

QUESTION—Where was the child?

The verb εἰσπορεύεται 'goes into' indicates that they went into an inner room where the child was lying [AB2, IIb, TH, TRT].

5:41 And having-grasped[a] the hand of the child he-says to-her, "Talitha koum," which being-translated means, "Little-girl, I-say to-you, Get-up.[b]"

LEXICON—a. aorist act. participle of κρατέω (LN 18.6) (BAGD 1.b. p. 448): 'to grasp' [BAGD, BNTC, Lns, NTC], 'to take hold of' [BAGD, WBC; NCV, REB], 'to hold' [NLT], 'to take (by the hand)' [CEV, ESV, KJV, NASB, NET, NIV, NRSV, TEV], 'to take' [AB1, AB2, BECNT; GW], 'to hold onto, to retain in the hand, to seize' [LN]. This verb means to hold on to an object [LN].

b. pres. act. impera. of ἐγείρω (LN **17.9**) (BAGD 1.b. p. 214): 'to get up' [AB1, BAGD, BNTC, **LN**, NTC; all versions except ESV, KJV], 'to arise' [BECNT, Lns, WBC; ESV, KJV], 'to rise' [AB2], 'to stand up' [LN; NCV]. This verb means to get up from a lying or reclining position [LN]. In this context, it means to stand up [TH].

QUESTION—Why did Jesus grasp the child's hand?

He took hold of her hand to help her get up [Gnd, Lns], not to heal her [Gnd]. Jesus established a physical contact with the child for the benefit of the witnesses, but she didn't really need help to get up [Hb]. Jesus' words, not his touch, brought about her healing [WBC].

QUESTION—What language was the command 'Talitha koum'?

'Talitha koum' is a transliteration of the Aramaic words Jesus spoke to the girl [CGTC, EBC]. Aramaic was the language of Palestine and it probably was the language that Jesus normally spoke [EBC]. *Talitha* is the feminine form of the word meaning 'lamb', used here as a term of endearment for a child [CGTC, Hb, NIGTC]. Instead of the Mesopotamian form of the imperative verb *koum* 'get up', some manuscripts have the Palestinian form *kumi* 'get up' and it is not clear which form Mark transliterated [CGTC]. This verb is transliterated from the Greek text as 'koum' [CEV, GW, NCV, NET, NIV, NLT, TEV], 'kum' [NASB], 'cum' [NRSV, REB], 'cumi' [ESV, KJV].

QUESTION—Where are the Aramaic words for 'I say to you'?

This phrase is merely Mark's interpretive addition to the Aramaic words used by Jesus [Hb, Lns, NTC, PNTC, WBC]. He added this for the benefit of his Greek speaking readers in Rome [PNTC]. It brings out the spirit of the command [Hb]. Although these words are in the Greek text, they are omitted in some translations [AB1; CEV, NLT].

QUESTION—Why did Mark include the Aramaic words if he was going to translate them anyway?

These were the actual words Jesus said to the girl in their native language, and probably when Mark learned the story in Rome, it was related to him in Aramaic [NLTfn]. This reinforces the eyewitness quality of this Gospel account [AB1, ESVfn].

5:42 And immediately the girl got-up and she-was-walking-around,ª because she-was twelve years-old. And immediately they-were-amazedᵇ with-a-great amazement.

LEXICON—a. imperf. act. indic. of περιπατέω (LN 15.227) (BAGD 1.c. p. 649): 'to walk around' [AB2, NTC, WBC; CEV, NET, NIV, NLT, TEV], 'to walk about' [AB1, BAGD, BNTC; NRSV, REB], 'to walk' [BAGD, BECNT, LN, Lns; ESV, GW, KJV, NASB, NCV]. This verb means to walk along or around [LN]. The imperfect tense indicates that she *started* walking around [Lns, NTC, TH, TRT; CEV, GW, TEV], she *began* walking [AB2, BECNT; ESV, NASB, NCV, NET, NRSV]. The imperfect tense indicates that the girl *kept on* walking about [AB1, Hb, Sw, Tay].

b. aorist act. indic. of ἐξίστημι (LN 25.220) (BAGD 2.b. p. 276): 'to be amazed, to be astonished' [BAGD], 'to be astonished greatly, to be greatly astounded, to be astounded completely' [LN]. The phrase ἐξέστησαν ἐκστάσει μεγάλῃ 'they were amazed with a great amazement' [Lns] is also translated 'they were astonished with a great astonishment' [KJV], 'they were overcome with amazement' [ESV, NRSV, REB], 'they were overwhelmed and totally amazed' [NLT], 'they were completely astounded/astonished' [NASB, NET, NIV], 'they were completely amazed' [AB1; TEV; similarly NCV], 'they were utterly astounded/astonished' [BNTC], 'they were utterly amazed' [BECNT, WBC], 'they were greatly amazed' [AB2], 'everyone was greatly surprised' [CEV], 'they were astonished' [GW]. This verb means to cause someone to be so astounded as to be practically overwhelmed [LN]. This intransitive form describes a feeling of astonishment mingled with fear caused by events that are miraculous or difficult to understand [BAGD]. This word occurs at 2:12; 5:42; 6:51.

QUESTION—What is the purpose of mentioning that the girl was walking around?

This demonstrated that she was completely restored to life [Hb, PNTC]. The girl had immediately regained her full strength [EBC, EGT, Sw].

QUESTION—What relationship is indicated by γάρ 'because'?

Since the words for 'child' and 'little girl' are not precise in regard to the age of the child, this explains why the girl could get up and walk about [BECNT, BNTC, EGT, Gnd, ICC, NCBC, NTC, TRT, WBC].

QUESTION—Who were so amazed?
> This refers to the parents and the disciples who were in the girl's room [BECNT, EBC, Hb]. Others who saw her afterwards would also be amazed [NTC].

5:43 And he- strictly -gave-orders[a] to-them that no-one should-know-about[b] this, and he-said (something) should-be-given her to-eat.

LEXICON—a. aorist mid. indic. of διαστέλλομαι, διαστέλλω (LN 33.323) (BAGD p. 188): 'to give orders' [BAGD], 'to order' [BAGD, LN], 'to command' [LN]. The phrase 'he strictly gave orders to them' is translated 'he strictly ordered them' [WBC; NET, NRSV], 'he strictly charged them' [BECNT, NTC; ESV], 'he/Jesus gave them strict orders/instructions' [BNTC; NASB, NCV, NIV, NLT, REB, TEV], 'he gave them strict injunction' [AB1], 'he charged them straitly' [KJV], 'he charged them much' [Lns], 'Jesus ordered them' [CEV, GW], 'he commanded them urgently' [AB2]. This verb means to state with force and authority what others must do [LN]. This verb occurs at 5:43; 7:36; 8:15; 9:9.

b. aorist act. subj. of γινώσκω (LN 28.1) (BAGD 2.a. p. 161): 'to know about' [LN; NASB, NET, REB], 'to know' [AB1, AB2, BECNT, Lns, NTC, WBC; ESV, KJV, NRSV], 'to have knowledge of' [LN], 'to learn of, to find out' [BAGD]. The phrase 'no one should know about this' is translated 'not to tell anyone' [TEV], 'not to tell anyone what had happened' [CEV, NLT], 'not to tell people about this' [NCV], 'not to let anyone know about this' [GW, NIV], 'to let no one know what had happened' [BNTC]. This verb means to possess information about something [LN].

QUESTION—Why didn't Jesus want the parents to tell others about this miracle?
> There were a great many people outside the house and Jesus wanted time to be on his way in order to avoid being detained by an excited crowd when they learned about the miracle [Gnd, Lns, NAC, NICNT, Sw]. After he departed, the facts would be apparent when the child appeared in public [Gnd, Hb, Lns, NICNT].

QUESTION—What is the significance of ending this account with Jesus' instructions to give the girl something to eat?
> The girl's need of food confirmed the reality of the miraculous healing [NCBC]. The girl's parents were overcome with joy and had to be reminded that their daughter needed some food since she had not been able to eat for a long time because of her illness [NTC]. The passive verb 'should be given' implies that her mother would be the one who would supply the food [Hb].

DISCOURSE UNIT—6:1–8:26 [NCV, NLT]. The topic is Jesus being misunderstood.

DISCOURSE UNIT—6:1–13 [NCV]. The topic is Jesus going to his hometown.

MARK 6:1 279

DISCOURSE UNIT—6:1–6 [CBC, Hb, NIGTC; ESV, NASB, NET]. The topic is that not everyone is impressed by Jesus [NIGTC], rejection at Nazareth [NET], Jesus faces rejection at Nazareth [CBC], Jesus rejected at Nazareth [Hb; ESV], teaching at Nazareth [NASB].

DISCOURSE UNIT—6:1–6a [EBC, NICNT; CEV, GW, NIV, NLT, NRSV, TEV]. The topic is the rejection of Jesus at Nazareth [EBC, NICNT; NLT, NRSV, TEV], Nazareth rejects Jesus [GW], the people of Nazareth turn against Jesus [CEV], a prophet without honor [NIV].

6:1 **And he-came-out^a from-there and comes into his hometown,^{b} and his disciples are-following^c him.**

LEXICON—a. imperf. pass. indic. of ἐξέρχομαι (LN 15.40) (BAGD 1.a.α. p. 274): 'to go out' [AB2, LN, Lns; KJV, NASB], 'to get out' [BAGD, LN], 'to leave' [AB1, BNTC, NTC; CEV, GW, NCV, NET, NIV, NLT, NRSV, TEV], 'to depart out of' [LN], 'to depart' [BECNT, WBC], 'to go away' [ESV]. The phrase 'he came out from there and comes into' is translated 'from there he went to' [REB]. This verb means to move out of an enclosed or well-defined two or three-dimensional area [LN].
  b. πατρίς (LN 1.81) (BAGD 2. p. 637): 'hometown' [AB2, BAGD, BECNT, BNTC, **LN**, NTC, WBC; all versions except KJV], '(his) own country' [KJV], '(his) native place' [AB1, Lns]. This noun denotes the region or population center from which a person *comes*, that is to say, the place of one's birth, childhood, or family origin [LN].
  c. pres. act. indic. of ἀκολουθέω (LN 15.156): 'to follow' [AB2, BECNT, BNTC, Lns, NTC, WBC; ESV, GW, KJV, NASB, NET, NRSV], 'to go with' [NCV], 'to accompany as a follower, to go along with' [LN]. The active voice is translated passively: 'followed by' [AB1; TEV], 'accompanied by' [NIV, REB]. The phrase 'and his disciples followed him' is translated 'with his disciples' [CEV, NLT]. This verb means to follow or accompany the one who takes the lead in determining the direction and route of movement [LN]. In this verse, it means to go along with someone, but without the specialized sense of following Jesus as a disciple [TH]. Jesus was returning as a noted teacher accompanied by an organized band of twelve disciples [Hb, NAC, PNTC, Sw]. These disciples are the ones who will be sent out on the mission in 6:7–13 [Hb, NCBC].

QUESTION—What did Jesus 'come out' of?
  Jesus came out of Jairus' house in Capernaum where he had brought the child to life (5:21–43) [BECNT, Gnd, Sw, Tay, WBC]. Jesus came out of the city of Capernaum [Hb, Lns, NICNT, NTC, Sw, Tay, WBC].

QUESTION—Where was Jesus' hometown?
  Jesus' hometown was the small town of Nazareth [BNTC, CGTC, EBC, EGT, ESVfn, Gnd, Hb, ICC, Lns, NAC, NICNT, NIVfn, NTC, PNTC, Sw, TH, WBC]. Jesus was born in Bethlehem in Judea [CGTC, EBC], but this refers to the town in Galilee where he spent his childhood [CGTC, EBC,

Lns, NTC]. Jesus came from his home in Nazareth to be baptized by John in 1:9, and later he is called 'Jesus the Nazarene' by the demon in 1:24 [BECNT, Gnd, Hb, NCBC, NICNT, WBC]. Nazareth was located in the hill country of Galilee about twenty-five miles from the large town of Capernaum on the shore of Lake Galilee [NIGTC, PNTC].

6:2 And (the) Sabbath having-come, he-began to-teach in the synagogue, and many listening were-amazed[a] saying, "From-where[b] (did) this (one) (learn) these (things), and what (is) the wisdom[c] given to-this (one), and the miracles[d] such-as[e] are-taking-place through his hands?

TEXT—Manuscripts reading καὶ πολλοὶ ἀκούοντες 'and many listening' are followed by GNT, which does not mention any variant reading. A variant reading is καὶ οἱ πολλοὶ ἀκούοντες 'and the many listening' and it is followed by Hb; NASB, REB, TEV.

TEXT—Manuscripts reading καὶ αἱ δυνάμεις 'and the miracles' are given a C rating by GNT to indicate that choosing it over a variant text was difficult. A variant reading is ὅτι καὶ δυνάμεις 'that/because even the miracles' and it is followed by Lns; KJV, NIV.

LEXICON—a. imperf. pass. indic. of ἐκπλήσσομαι, ἐκπλήσσω (LN 25.219) (BAGD 2. p. 244): 'to be amazed' [AB2, BAGD, BECNT; CEV, GW, NCV, NIV, NLT, REB, TEV], 'to be astonished' [AB1, BECNT, BNTC, NTC; ESV, KJV, NASB, NET], 'to be astounded' [LN; NRSV], 'to be overwhelmed' [WBC], 'to be dumbfounded' [Lns]. This verb means to be so amazed that one is practically overwhelmed [LN]. The imperfect tense indicates that they remained astonished all through his teaching [Gnd]. This word occurs at 1:22; 6:2; 7:37; 10:26; 11:18.

b. πόθεν (LN 84.6) (BAGD 2. p 680): 'from where?, whence?, where?' [BAGD, LN]. The question Πόθεν οὕτω ταῦτα 'From where this one these things?' lacks a verb and is translated 'Whence these things to this man?' [Lns], 'From whence hath this man these things?' [KJV], 'Where did this man/he get all this?' [AB1, BECNT; NRSV; similarly TEV], 'Where did/does this man get these things?' [NTC, WBC; ESV, NASB, NIV], 'Where does this man get these things from?' [AB2], 'Where did he come by all this?' [BNTC], 'Where does he get it from?' [REB], 'Where did this man get these ideas?' [GW; similarly NET], 'Where did this man get these teachings?' [NCV], 'How can he do all this?' [CEV]. This question is combined with the other two questions: 'Where did he get all this wisdom and the power to perform such miracles?' [NLT]. This word indicates an extension from a source [LN]. They expressed their surprise by exclaiming, 'How has he learned so much?' [TH].

c. σοφία (LN 32.32) (BAGD 3. p. 760): 'wisdom' [BAGD, LN]. The question 'What is the wisdom given to this one?' is translated 'What is the/this wisdom given to him?' [ESV, NASB; similarly BECNT, Lns; NCV, NET, NIV, NRSV, REB], 'What wisdom has been given this man?' [WBC], 'What wisdom is this that has been given him?' [AB1, BNTC;

TEV; similarly KJV], 'What sort of wisdom is it that has been given to him?' [NTC], 'Where did he get all this wisdom?' [NLT], 'Where did he get such wisdom?' [CEV], 'Who gave him this kind of wisdom?' [GW]. This rhetorical question is translated as an exclamation: 'What wisdom has been given to him!' [AB2]. The noun denotes the capacity to understand well enough to act wisely [LN]. The noun 'wisdom' refers to both the process of learning and the application of one's mental faculties. On this occasion they were surprised at all that Jesus had learned [TH].

d. δύναμις (LN 76.7): 'miracle' [AB1, LN, NTC; CEV, GW, NCV, NET, NLT, REB], 'mighty deed' [LN], 'mighty work' [BECNT, BNTC, WBC; CEV, KJV], 'work/deed of power' [AB2, Lns; NRSV]. This noun denotes a deed that manifests a power so great that it could only be supernatural [LN].

e. τοιοῦτος (LN 92.31) (BAGD 2.a.α. p. 821): 'of such a kind' [BAGD, LN], 'of a kind such as this' [LN], 'such as this' [BAGD]. The phrase 'and the miracles such as are taking place through his hands' is translated 'and such works of power occurring through his hand' [Lns], 'and such miracles as these performed by his hands?' [NASB], 'What are these miracles that are done through his hands?' [NET], 'And what are these mighty works being accomplished through his hands?' [BECNT; similarly BNTC], 'How are such mighty works done by his hands?' [ESV], '...so that even miracles are done by his hands?' [NTC], 'How does he work/perform such miracles?' [AB1; REB], 'How do such mighty works happen through him?' [WBC], 'and the ability to do such great miracles?' [GW], 'and the power to perform such miracles?' [NLT], 'Where did he get the power to work these miracles?' [CEV; similarly NCV]. This question is also translated as an exclamation: 'What deeds of power are being done by his hands!' [NRSV], 'And such works of power are performed by his hands!' [AB2]. Following the variant reading, it is translated 'that even such mighty works are wrought by his hands?' [KJV], 'that he even does miracles!' [NIV]. This adjective refers to the miracles being of the kind that is identified in the context [LN]. The text does not tell of any miracles being performed in Nazareth, but the people had heard of the miracles Jesus had been performing in other places and likely there were people present in the synagogue who had witnessed some of those miracles [Lns].

QUESTION—What is implied by the verb ἤρξατο 'he began' to teach?

Mark uses the verb 'to begin' numerous times and he often uses it with the main verb to introduce some development in the narrative as in 1:45; 2:23; 4:1, etc. [NIGTC, Sw]. Mark's characteristic phrase 'he began to teach' also occurs in 4:1; 6:34; 8:31 [BECNT, WBC] and the phrase 'he began to say/speak' occurs in 10:32; 12;1; 13:5 [BECNT]. On this occasion it could be that the verb 'he began' suggests that his teaching remained unfinished when he was interrupted by the crowd's reaction in verses 2–3 [Hb, Lns,

NIGTC]. It also implies that Jesus did not begin any public teaching in his hometown until that Sabbath day [EGT, Hb].

QUESTION—Does the statement '*many* listening were amazed' mean that some of those listening weren't amazed?

1. This means that all of the many people present were amazed [BECNT, BNTC, CGTC, Gnd, Hb, NAC, NCBC, NICNT, NTC, TH, WBC; NASB, NCV, REB, TEV]. No matter whether the text reads 'and many listening' or 'and *the* many listening', it means that all present were amazed [BNTC, WBC]. In Semitic speech, 'many' often means 'all', and here the forward position of 'many' emphasizes the fact there were many people present [Gnd]. The entire audience found his teaching more than they could comprehend in view of their knowledge about him [WBC].
2. This refers to many of those present, but not all of them [EBC, Hb, ICC, NAC, Sw, Tay]. The wording of many translations appears to imply that 'many' does not include all of the people present [AB1, AB2, EBC, Hb, ICC, Lns, Sw, Tay; CEV, ESV, GW, KJV, NET, NIV, NLT, NRSV]. There was an undercurrent of dissatisfaction [EBC, Sw].

QUESTION—What kind of questions are being asked?

These are rhetorical questions that function to express their surprise and astonishment as they listened to his teaching [NICNT, TH]. Astonished to hear Jesus expound the reading from the Law and the Prophets, they voiced their puzzlement about the source of his knowledge and also the source of his power to work the miracles of healing and exorcism they had heard about [NICNT]. They recognized Jesus' wisdom in his teaching and they had learned about the miracles Jesus had worked in 4:35–5:43 [Lns, WBC]. The context does not suggest that the people were inclined to recognize Jesus' God-given ministry or abilities, so in languages where the grammar requires that an agent of a passive verb be supplied, the sentence structure might have to be altered to express the intended meaning, 'How has he learned so much?' [TH].

QUESTION—Did each person ask all three questions?

The different questions were asked by different people [Hb, ICC, TRT].

QUESTION—What is implied by the people calling Jesus τούτῳ 'this one'?

1. 'This one' is a disparaging term [Gnd, Hb, ICC, Lns, NIGTC, NTC, PNTC, TH, WBC]. 'This one' has the contemptuous connotation of 'this guy' [Gnd]. It expresses their resentment [TH]. Although their first reaction was favorable, their enthusiasm was replaced by criticism as they asked 'Where did this fellow get these things?'. An ordinary, unschooled villager like the rest of them had no business teaching them 'this kind of wisdom' [NTC].
2. The positive nature of similar questions in 1:27 and 4:41 suggests that the people referred to Jesus as 'this one' with reverential fear and amazement. Their changed attitude begins in the following verse as they think about his education and family [BECNT].

QUESTION—What is meant by the miracles taking place διά 'through' his hands?
1. This refers to the way Jesus laid his hands on sick people as he healed them [My; probably ESV, KJV, NASB, NET, NRSV which include a reference to his hands].
2. The phrase 'through his hands' is a Hebrew idiom meaning 'wrought by him' and does not mean that Jesus actually laid his hands on the sick people [CGTC, Lns, NICNT, NTC, Sw, Tay, WBC; probably CEV, GW, NCV, NIV, NLT, REB, TEV which do not refer to his hands]. Jesus was the agent through whom God worked [WBC]. Jesus did not always use his hands to touch the people he healed and the phrase simply means 'through his agency' [Lns, NTC].

6:3 Is not this (one) the carpenter, the son of Mary and brother of-James and of-Joses and of-Judas and of-Simon? And are not his sisters here with us?" And they-were-taking-offense[a] at him.

TEXT—Manuscripts reading ὁ τέκτων, ὁ υἱὸς καὶ τῆς Μαρίας 'the carpenter, the son of Mary' are given an A rating by GNT to indicate it was regarded to be certain. A variant reading is ὁ τοῦ τέκτονος υἱὸς τῆς Μαρίας 'the son of the carpenter and of Mary'.

TEXT—Manuscripts reading καὶ Ἰωσῆτος 'and of Joses' are given a B rating by GNT to indicate it was regarded to be almost certain. A variant reading is καὶ Ἰωσήφ 'and of Joseph' and it is followed by AB1; CEV, KJV, NCV, NIV, NLT, TEV. 'Joses' is a variant form of 'Joseph' [Hb].

LEXICON—a. imperf. pass. indic. of σκανδαλίζομαι (LN 25.180, 31.77) (BAGD 1.b. p. 752): 'to take offense' [AB1, BAGD, BECNT, LN (25.180), NTC; ESV, GW, NASB, NET, NIV, NRSV], 'to be offended' [BNTC, LN (25.180); KJV], 'to be scandalized' [AB2], 'to cease believing, to give up believing' [LN (31.77)], 'to be entrapped' [Lns]. The phrase 'they were taking offense at him' is translated 'the people were very unhappy because of what he was doing' [CEV], 'they turned against him' [REB], 'they rejected him' [TEV], 'they were deeply offended and refused to believe in him' [NLT], 'they refused to believe in him' [WBC]. This is a figurative extension of the verb 'to fall into a trap' and means to be offended because of some action [LN (25.180)], or to give up believing what is right and let oneself believe what is false [LN (31.77)]. They refused to believe in him [BAGD]. This verb refers to a loss of faith in 4:17, but here they reacted with jealousy and personal animosity [TH]. They were repelled by him [NTC]. They considered Jesus to be just one of them and their amazement turned to jealousy [Sw]. It was more than jealousy. They refused to consider the implications of his teaching, wisdom, and miracles [WBC].

QUESTION—What is the function of these two questions?
They are rhetorical questions that are hostile and derogatory in nature [EBC, NICNT]. They thought that a mere carpenter could not possibly know about

prophetic interpretation and fulfillment [NTC]. Some translate these questions as statements, 'He is just the/a carpenter…' [NCV, NLT]. Calling him a carpenter placed Jesus on a level with themselves, he was no better than they were [Hb]. The questions point out that Jesus was just a common worker with his hands as they all were [NICNT].

QUESTION—Why did they take offense at Jesus?

They took offense because of his lowly origins [ESVfn, NAC]. They were prejudiced against him because of their familiarity with him and his family [Gnd]. They saw no reason to believe that he was any different from them [NIVfn]. Jesus was just a common laborer like themselves [NETfn]. They thought Jesus was claiming to be someone he could not possibly be [NLTfn]. They were unable to explain him, so they rejected him [Hb].

6:4 And Jesus was-saying to-them, "A-prophet[a] is not unhonored[b] except in his hometown and among his relatives[c] and in his house.[d]"

LEXICON—a. προφήτης (LN 53.79) (BAGD 1. p. 723) 'prophet' [BAGD, LN; all translations], 'inspired preacher' [LN]. This noun denotes one who proclaims inspired utterances on behalf of God [LN]. It denotes someone who proclaims and interprets the divine revelation [BAGD]. In this verse, the sense of 'prophet' probably is 'inspired teacher' [EBC]. This word occurs at 1:2; 6:4, 15; 8:28; 11:32.

b. ἄτιμος (LN 87.72) (BAGD 1. p. 120): 'unhonored' [BAGD], 'without honor' [BECNT, BNTC, NTC, WBC; ESV, KJV, NASB, NET, NRSV], 'lacking in honor' [LN], 'honorless' [Lns], 'dishonored' [AB2, BAGD, LN]. The negative statement, 'a prophet is *not* unhonored *except*' is translated 'a prophet is honored everywhere except' [NCV, NLT], 'prophets are honored by everyone, except' [CEV], 'a prophet is respected, except' [AB1], 'prophets are respected everywhere except' [TEV], 'a prophet never lacks honor except' [REB], 'the only place a prophet isn't honored is' [GW], 'only (in his hometown…) is a prophet without honor' [NIV]. This adjective describes someone as being of low status on the basis of not having honor or respect [LN]. It refers to not receiving one's due honor and respect [TH]. The force of being *dishonored* is much more than just being without honor [Gnd].

c. συγγενής (LN 10.6) (BAGD p. 772): 'relative' [AB1, AB2, BECNT, LN, NTC, WBC; CEV, ESV, GW, NASB, NET, NIV, NLT, TEV], 'kinsman' [LN, Lns], 'kin' [KJV, NRSV], 'own people' [NCV], 'relation' [BAGD; REB], 'family' [BNTC]. This noun denotes a person who belongs to the same extended family or clan [LN].

d. οἰκία (LN **10.8**) (BAGD 2. p. 557): 'house' [Lns, WBC; GW, KJV, NET, NIV, NRSV], 'home' [BNTC; NCV], 'household' [AB2, BAGD, LN; ESV, NASB], 'family' [AB1, BAGD, BECNT, **LN**, NTC; CEV, NLT, REB, TEV]. The extended meaning of the noun 'house' denotes a family consisting of those related by blood and marriage living in the same house or homestead [LN].

QUESTION—Does this imply that a prophet is honored everywhere outside his hometown?

Some translations state that a prophet is honored everywhere else [CEV, GW, NCV, NLT, TEV]. Some leave the location of where the prophet is honored open [ESV, KJV, NASB, NET, NRSV]: *is not without honor*. Instead of meaning that a prophet is honored and respected everywhere else, it means that wherever a prophet might be honored, it certainly would not be in his hometown [NTC]. Those who know a prophet best tend to think the least of him [Hb, Lns]. This is based on the principle that familiarity breeds contempt [EBC].

QUESTION—Why did Jesus state this proverbial saying?

Jesus was comparing his own experience to that of the prophets who were dishonored by their own people [Hb, NICNT]. People were already speaking of Jesus and John the Baptist as being prophets (6:15; 8:28; 11:32), and Jesus accepted the designation 'prophet' [AB1, AB2, BECNT, ESVfn, Lns, NIGTC, NTC, Tay] even though it was less than the whole truth [NIGTC] and was an inadequate term for him [AB2, BECNT, NAC, Tay]. Jesus used this proverb even though he was not claiming to be a prophet. Actually, his teachings and miracles showed him to be more than a prophet [WBC].

6:5 **And he-was- not -able to-do any miracles there, except having-laid**[a] **(his) hands on-a-few sick-people he-healed (them).**

LEXICON—a. aorist act. participle of ἐπιτίθημι (LN 85.51) (BAGD 1.a.α. p. 303): 'to lay on, to place on' [BAGD, LN], 'to put on' [LN]. The participial phrase 'having laid/placed his hands on' [Lns] is also translated 'to lay his hands on' [GW, NET; similarly NIV], 'to place his hands on' [NLT], 'he laid his hands on' [BECNT, NTC, WBC; ESV, NASB, NRSV; similarly AB2; KJV], 'he put his hands on' [AB1, BNTC; REB], 'he placed his hands on' [TEV]. Some translate this to show that the participle indicates the means of healing: 'by placing his hands on' [CEV], 'by putting his hands on' [NCV]. This verb means to place something on something [LN].

QUESTION—Why wasn't Jesus able to do any miracles except for a few sick people?

Jesus was not able to miraculously heal many people because they did not come to him for healing. It does not imply that Jesus tried to heal some people and failed to do so [Lns, NICNT, WBC]. Jesus was not powerless to work miracles when a person lacked faith, but he could not heal in the absence of faith in accordance with the purpose of his ministry [CGTC]. Jesus had the power to perform miracles at Nazareth but he chose not to heal in such a climate of unbelief [EBC, NIVfn]. This was a moral inability since Jesus required faith [Hb, ICC, NAC], and Jesus would not force himself upon those who did not want him [ESVfn, Hb]. The reason is supplied in one translation: 'because of their unbelief' [NLT]. Nevertheless, Jesus did heal the few people who had faith enough to come to him for healing [NTC,

WBC]. Perhaps those few people did not have 'saving' faith, but they did have faith that Jesus could heal them [NTC].

6:6a And he-was-amazed[a] because-of[b] their unbelief.[c]

LEXICON—a. imperf. act. indic. of θαυμάζω (LN 25.213) (BAGD 1.a.β. p. 352): 'to be amazed' [LN, NTC, WBC; GW, NCV, NET, NIV, NLT, NRSV], 'to marvel' [BECNT, BNTC, LN, Lns; ESV, KJV], 'to be astonished' [REB], 'to be surprised' [CEV], 'to be greatly surprised' [AB1; TEV], 'to be dumbfounded' [AB2], 'to wonder' [BAGD, LN; NASB]. This verb means to wonder or marvel at some event or object [LN]. This word occurs at 5:20; 6:6; 15:5, 44.

b. διά (LN 89.26): 'because of' [LN; ESV, KJV, NET, TEV], 'on account of, by reason of' [LN], 'at' [AB2, BECNT, BNTC, Lns, NTC, WBC; NASB, NCV, NIV, NLT, NRSV, REB], 'by' [AB1], 'that' [CEV], not explicit [GW]. This preposition indicates cause or reason and focuses on the instrumentality of objects or events [LN].

c. ἀπιστία (LN 31.97) (BAGD 2.a. p. 85): 'unbelief' [BAGD, BECNT, LN, Lns, NTC, WBC; ESV, GW, KJV, NASB, NET, NRSV], 'lack of belief' [BAGD, BNTC; NIV], 'want of faith' [AB1; REB]. This noun is also translated with a verb phrase: 'the people did not have any faith' [CEV; similarly TEV], '(at) how many people had no faith' [NCV]. This noun denotes a refusal to put one's trust or reliance in something or someone [LN].

QUESTION—What relationship is indicated by the preposition διά 'at/because of'?

1. This preposition indicates the object of Jesus' amazement [AB1, AB2, BECNT, BNTC, EBC, Lns, WBC; CEV, GW, NASB, NCV, NIV, NLT, NRSV, REB]: he was amazed *at* their unbelief.
2. The preposition indicates the reason for his surprise [TH; ESV, KJV, NET, TEV]: he was amazed on account of their unbelief. Instead of taking διά to indicate the object of the Jesus' surprise as most English translations do, it indicates the cause for his surprise [TH].

QUESTION—Why did their unbelief amaze Jesus?

Jesus apparently had not anticipated this reaction from the people in his hometown [EBC, NICNT]. Since the people had been amazed at his wisdom and miracles, Jesus was amazed at their continued unbelief [CBC, Gnd]. There was reason to expect that the people of Nazareth would have faith in him by now since Nazareth was located in the midst of the very area where Jesus had been ministering to great crowds of people [NTC]. This amazement was a part of Jesus' humanity [ICC, NAC, NIGTC, Sw, Tay, WBC].

DISCOURSE UNIT—6:6b–8:26 [CBC]. The topic is a challenge, misunderstanding, and confession.

DISCOURSE UNIT—6:6b–7:23 [PNTC]. The topic is the witness to Jews.

DISCOURSE UNIT—6:6b–29 [REB]. The topic is the death of John the Baptist.

DISCOURSE UNIT—6:6b–13 [CBC, EBC, NICNT; CEV, GW, NLT, NRSV, TEV]. The topic is the sending out of the twelve [CBC, EBC], Jesus sends out the Twelve [GW], Jesus sends out the twelve disciples [NLT, TEV], instructions for the twelve Apostles [CEV], the mission of the twelve [NRSV], the mission of the twelve in Galilee [NICNT].

6:6b And he-was-traveling-about the villages[a] around[b] teaching.

LEXICON—a. κώμη (LN 1.92) (BAGD 1. p. 461): 'village' [BAGD, LN; all translations], 'small town' [BAGD]. This noun denotes a relatively unimportant population center [LN]. This word occurs at 6:6, 36, 56; 8:23, 26. 27; 11:2.

b. κύκλῳ (LN 83.19) (BAGD p. 458): 'around, in a circle' [BAGD, LN], 'all around' [BAGD]. This word is translated as an adverb modifying the verb 'he was traveling about': 'he went about among the villages' [NTC; ESV, NRSV], 'he went around among the villages' [BAGD; NET], 'he went round about the villages' [Lns; KJV], 'he was going around the villages' [NASB; similarly REB], 'Jesus went from village to village' [NLT], 'Jesus went around teaching from village to village' [NIV], 'he went around to the villages' [GW]. This word is translated as an adjective modifying 'villages': 'the villages around there' [AB1, LN; TEV], 'the villages round about' [BNTC], 'the neighboring villages' [CEV], 'other villages in that area' [NCV; similarly AB2], 'the villages nearby' [WBC]. This adverb indicates a position completely encircling an area or object [LN]. Mark expected his readers to supply the location: 'around *his hometown of Nazareth*' [BECNT].

QUESTION—What is the function of this clause?
  1. It begins a new discourse unit by giving the background for the account about sending the Twelve [AB1, AB2, BECNT, CBC, CGTC, EGT, Gnd, ICC, NAC, NICNT, NTC, PNTC, Sw, Tay; CEV, NCV, NIV, NLT, NRSV, REB, TEV]. This verse gives the general occasion for sending out the disciples [Gnd]. It connects the mission of the disciples with the period during which Jesus was moving from village to village [Tay]. As a result of his village ministry, Jesus decided to send out the Twelve to increase his own ministry through them [EBC].
  2. It ends the paragraph 6:1–6 [ICC, NCBC, NIGTC; NET]. If 6:1–6 is a discourse unit, then it ends with Jesus' decision to inaugurate a village ministry as a result of his rejection at Nazareth [EBC].
  3. It is a transitional sentence that is translated as a separate paragraph [BNTC, Hb, WBC; ESV, GW, NASB]. It gives the outcome of the visit to Nazareth and also sets the background for the mission of the Twelve [Hb].

DISCOURSE UNIT—6:7–30 [NIGTC]. The topic is the extension of Jesus' mission through the disciples.

DISCOURSE UNIT—6:7–13 [Hb; ESV, NASB, NET, NIV]. The topic is sending out the twelve Apostles [NET], Jesus sends out the twelve Apostles [ESV], Jesus sends out the twelve [NIV], the Twelve sent out [NASB], the mission of the twelve [Hb].

6:7 And he summons^a the Twelve and he-began^b to-send- them -off two (by) two and he-was-giving them authority^c (over) the unclean spirits,

LEXICON—a. pres. mid. indic. of προσκαλέομαι, προσκαλέω (LN 33.308) (BAGD 1.a. p. 715): 'to summon' [AB1, AB2, BAGD, BNTC; NASB, REB], 'to call' [BECNT, LN, WBC; ESV, GW, NLT, NRSV], 'to call to himself' [BAGD, Lns, NTC; KJV, NIV], 'to call together' [CEV, NCV, NLT, TEV]. This verb means to call to someone [LN]. The middle voice indicates that he called them to himself [Lns]. That he *summoned* the Twelve does not imply that they had not been traveling with him. It only means that he got them together to give them this authority over unclean spirits before sending them out [Gnd].

  b. aorist mid. indic. of ἄρχομαι, ἄρχω (LN 68.1) (BAGD 2.a.α p 113): 'to begin' [AB2, BAGD, BECNT, BNTC, LN, Lns, NTC, WBC; ESV, KJV, NASB, NET, NLT, NRSV], 'to commence' [LN], 'to get ready' [NCV], not explicit [AB1; NIV, REB, TEV]. The phrase 'he began to send them off two by two and he was giving them authority' is translated: 'and sent them out two by two with authority/power' [CEV, REB]. This verb means to initiate an action, process, or state of being [LN].

  c. ἐξουσία (LN 76.12) (BAGD 3. p. 278): 'authority' [AB1, AB2, BAGD, BECNT, BNTC, Lns, NTC, WBC; all versions except CEV, KJV], 'power' [BAGD, LN; CEV, KJV]. This noun denotes the power to do something, and it may have the added implication of authority [LN]. To be given authority means to be given the right to do something along with the power to carry it out [Lns].

QUESTION—Who were the 'Twelve'?

'The Twelve' is a title for the twelve apostles who have been referred to in 3:14, 16 [TH]. They are called οἱ ἀπόστολοι 'the Apostles' when they return in 6:30 [NIGTC]. Some translate this phrase 'the/his twelve apostles' [CEV, ESV, NLT], or 'his twelve followers' [NCV].

QUESTION—What is meant by ἤρξατο 'he began' to send them off two by two?

'Began' indicates the beginning of a new method of using the disciples [Hb]. The words 'he began to send them off two by two' may also imply that each pair was individually commissioned to go out as his representatives [Hb, WBC]. Jesus had called the Twelve in 3:14 *in order that* he might send them out and now he is actually beginning to send them [BECNT, BNTC, EGT, ESVfn]. One translation says that Jesus 'got ready to send them out' [NCV] since they did not actually leave until after Jesus had given them the instructions recorded in 6:8–11 [TRT]. Sending men out in pairs was a common Jewish practice [AB1, AB2, CBC, EBC, NAC, PNTC, Tay].

Traveling in pairs provided them mutual support and companionship [BECNT, NIGTC, NIVfn, NLTfn, NTC]. Sending them out in pairs also fulfilled the OT requirements in Deut. 17:6 and 19:15 for an authentic testimony [BECNT, BNTC, EBC, Gnd, Hb, My, NAC, NICNT, NIVfn, NLTfn, NTC, PNTC, TRT]. Each pair would go off in different directions [TH] and thus spread the gospel even further [ESVfn, ICC].

QUESTION—What is meant by being given 'authority' over the unclean spirits?

They were given the power to cast unclean spirits out of demoniacs while on their mission [EBC, TH; NLT]. They were given both the right and the power to cast out the demons [NTC]. Giving them authority to cast out demons in the name of Jesus would authenticate their message [Hb]. The imperfect tense ἐδίδου 'he was giving' them authority may indicate that as Jesus sent each pair on its way he gave them this authority [BECNT, Gnd, Tay, TRT].

QUESTION—Weren't these disciples supposed to heal sick people also?

The greatest and most dramatic gift Jesus was giving to the apostles is named, but it is taken for granted that they would also receive the lesser gift of healing [Gnd, Lns]. In 6:12–13 it says that their ministry included preaching, casting out demons, and healing the sick [BECNT, WBC]. Mark also mentioned casting out evil spirits in other places as if it were by itself, but this was a representative miracle since it is evident that it was accompanied by other miracles of healing at 1:39; 3:15 [ICC].

6:8 **and he-commanded them that they-should-take nothing on (the) road except a staff[a] only, no bread,[b] no bag,[c] no copper-coins[d] inside the belt,[e]**

LEXICON—a. ῥάβδος (LN **6.218**) (BAGD p. 733): 'staff' [AB1, AB2, BECNT, Lns, NTC, WBC; ESV, KJV, NASB, NET, NIV, NRSV], 'traveler's staff' [BAGD], 'walking stick' [**LN**; CEV, GW, NCV, NLT, TEV], 'stick' [BNTC, LN; REB]. This noun denotes a stick or rod. It could be used for a number of different purposes, such as an aid for walking, herding animals, or beating people [LN]. A staff was used for walking and for protection [AB2, BECNT, PNTC] from wild animals, bandits, and so forth [AB2].

b. ἄρτος (LN 5.1) (BAGD 1.a. p. 110): 'bread' [BAGD; all translations except CEV, GW, NLT], 'food' [BAGD, LN; CEV, GW, NLT]. This noun denotes any kind of food or nourishment [LN].

c. πήρα (LN 6.145) (BAGD p. 656): 'bag' [AB1, BECNT, BNTC, WBC; ESV, NASB, NCV, NET, NIV, NRSV], 'traveling bag' [CEV, GW], 'traveler's bag' [BAGD, LN, NTC; NET], 'knapsack' [BAGD], 'provision bag' [AB2], 'pack' [REB], 'pouch' [Lns], 'scrip' [KJV], 'beggar's bag' [TEV]. This noun denotes a bag used by travelers or beggars to carry their possessions [LN].

d. χαλκός (LN 6.72) (BAGD p. 875): 'copper, brass, bronze' [BAGD], 'copper coin' [BAGD, LN], 'bronze money' [LN], 'money' [AB1,

BECNT, NTC, WBC; all versions], 'silver' [Lns], 'small change' [AB2, BAGD]. This noun denotes coins of bronze or copper, hence coins of little value [LN].

e. ζώνη (LN 6.178), (BAGD p. 342): 'belt' [AB1, BAGD, BECNT, BNTC, LN, Lns, NTC, WBC; ESV, NASB, NET, NIV, NRSV, REB], 'girdle' [BAGD, LN], 'pocket' [GW, NCV, TEV], 'money belt' [AB2], 'purse' [KJV], not explicit [CEV, NLT]. This noun denotes a band of leather or cloth worn around the waist outside of one's clothing. A belt was normally quite wide and could be readily folded [LN]. Money was often carried in such belts [BAGD, LN, WBC].

QUESTION—What is the grammatical construction of verse 8?

Verse 8 starts out with an indirect quotation: 'he commanded them *that* they should take nothing on the road'. Then an exception is immediately made: 'except a-staff only'. Then there is a *list* of three specific things they were not to take: 'no bread, no bag, no copper coins inside the belt'. This list is translated in different ways. It is begun with an em-dash [AB1, AB2, BNTC; ESV, NASB, NET, NIV, NLT, REB, TEV], a colon [BECNT], a semi-colon [WBC; NRSV], or a comma [Lns, NTC]. Others supply a verb to begin a new sentence: 'They were not to take any food…' [GW], 'Take no bread…' [NCV], 'But don't carry food…' [CEV]. Some translate all of the instructions in verses 8–11 as a direct quotation using second person forms because the instructions to these twelve disciples change in the second clause of verse 9 from an indirect quotation using third-person forms to the direct quotation using second-person forms, "Do not put on two tunics." and then verse 10 begins 'And he was saying to them, "Wherever you enter into a house…"' with the direct quotation continuing on to the end of the instructions in verse 11 [CEV, NCV, NIV].

QUESTION—What was a staff?

The staff was a walking stick that most travelers used in their journeys [AB2, Hb, Lns, PNTC, Sw]. Walking sticks aided people to walk on rocky terrain and also served as weapons against wild animals or bandits [TRT]. The disciples were already using walking sticks as they accompanied Jesus, so he told them to take them along when they went on their assignments. In Matthew 10:9–10, the command not to κτήσησθε 'acquire' a walking stick directed them not to bother looking for a new stick for the trip [ESVfn, Hb]. No new staff was to be provided since the disciples were to go as they were [Lns, NTC].

QUESTION—Why shouldn't they take bread or a traveler's bag, or money along with them?

They were to rely completely on receiving hospitality from the people they meet during their journeys [CGTC, EBC, NICNT, NIGTC, NIVfn, NLTfn, TRT]. Their provisions would come from the people who accepted their messages [ESVfn]. They were to take no food as they started off, no bag to carry provisions given them during the trip, and no money to buy anything.

This would prevent them from having any sense of self-sufficiency [WBC]. It would be a lesson in trust [Hb, NTC].

QUESTION—What was a traveler's bag?
1. This was a bag that a person filled with the supplies he thinks might be needed while traveling [AB2, Hb, ICC, Lns, NIGTC, NTC, Sw, TRT; CEV, GW, NLT, REB]. It was usually made of leather [AB2, ICC]. It probably would be used for carrying food [NIGTC]. It doesn't refer to a beggar's bag since Jesus and his disciples never traveled as beggars [Lns, TRT].
2. This refers to a beggar's bag [BNTC, CBC, CGTC, NCBC, NICNT, TH, WBC; TEV]. It would be pointless to add that they were not to take a bag for provisions just after telling them not to take food, so it must refer to a beggar's bag [TH]. A beggar's bag would be used for carrying supplies they received along the way [WBC].

QUESTION—What was a belt with copper money inside it?
The folds of a traveler's girdle were used to hold money [Hb]. By winding or wrapping a belt a few times around the body, folds were made that could be used as pockets for money [NTC].

6:9 but having-put-on[a] sandals, and "Do- not –put-on[b] two tunics.[c]"

LEXICON—a. perf. mid. participle of ὑποδέομαι, ὑποδέω (LN **49.17**) (BAGD p. 852): 'to put on' [BAGD, LN], 'to tie on, to wear' [LN]. See the various translations of this verb in the answers to the first question below. This verb means to put on and wear footwear such as shoes, boots, or sandals [LN].
  b. aorist mid. impera./subj. of ἐνδύω (LN 49.1) (BAGD 2, p. 263): 'to put on, to clothe oneself' [BAGD, LN], 'to wear' [BAGD]. See the various translations of this verb in the answers to the first question below. This verb means to put on clothes, without implying any particular article of clothing [LN].
  c. χιτών (LN 6.176) (BAGD p. 882): 'tunic' [AB1, AB2, BAGD, BECNT, BNTC, LN, Lns, NTC; ESV, NASB, NET, NIV, NRSV], 'shirt' [BAGD, LN], 'coat' [WBC; KJV, REB], 'clothes' [CEV, GW, NCV, NLT]. This noun denotes a garment that is worn under the cloak [LN]. It is a garment worn next to the skin [BAGD].

QUESTION—What are the grammatical features of verse 9?
Verse 9 begins with the conjunction ἀλλά 'but' which would seem to continue the indirect quotation of verse 8 except it is followed by a participial phrase 'having put on sandals' instead of a main verb. This is followed by the conjunction καί 'and' and then a direct quotation with a second-person imperative clause, "Do not put on two tunics." Because of the shift in grammatical form, the passage must be recast to fit the requirements of the receptor language [TH]. English translations of this verse have been recast in various ways. Only Lns retains the participial form of the first verb.

1. One translation moves the participial phrase to verse 8 to join the one other exception, and supplies information to account for the second-person imperative clause in verse 9: '⁸He instructed them to take nothing for the journey except simply a staff and sandals strapped on;...⁹and he instructed them, "Do not wear two coats."' [WBC].
2. One translation follows the Greek text quite closely by changing the participle to an infinitive and supplying information to account for the direct quotation: 'but to wear sandals; and *he added*, "Do not put on two tunics."' [NASB].
3. Some connect the conjunction ἀλλά 'but' with the participial phrase ὑποδεδεμένους σανδάλια 'having put on sandals'. Some keep the translation in the third person form of indirect quotes: 'but having been shod with sandals, and not to clothe themselves with two tunics' [Lns], 'but to wear sandals, and not to put on two tunics' [NTC; NRSV; similarly ESV], 'but they were to wear sandals and not to wear two tunics' [BECNT]. Some use the second person form of the direct quotation of the last clause for the whole verse: "but have your sandals strapped up, and don't put on two tunics" [AB2], "But be shod with sandals, and not put on two coats" [KJV].
3. Others connect the conjunction 'but' with the imperative clause that follows, and translate 'having put on sandals' with an active verb. Some keep the translation in the third person form of indirect quotes: 'and to put on sandals but not to wear two tunics' [NET], 'They might wear sandals, but not an additional tunic' [AB1; similarly BNTC; TEV], 'They could wear sandals but could not take along a change of clothes' [GW], 'He allowed them to wear sandals but not to take a change of clothes' [NLT], 'They might wear sandals, but not a second coat' [REB]. Some have used the second person form of the direct quotation of the last clause for all of Jesus' command in verses 8 and 9: '⁸This is what Jesus commanded them: "Take nothing for your trip.... ⁹Wear sandals, but take only the clothes you are wearing."' [NCV], '⁸These were his instructions: "Take nothing for the journey.... ⁹Wear sandals but not an extra tunic."' [NIV], '⁸He told them, "You may take along a walking stick.... ⁹It's all right to wear sandals, but don't take along a change of clothes."' [CEV].

QUESTION—What is a tunic and why shouldn't they put on two tunics?

The tunic was a shirt worn under the robe next to the skin [Hb, Lns, NTC]. It was worn with or without a robe over it [TRT]. It reached almost to the knees or ankles [AB2, NTC, TRT]. Travelers often had two or more tunics in order to have a change of clothes [AB2, Lns]. The command 'Do not put on two tunics' implies that they were not to take along an extra tunic [BNTC, Hb, Lns, NIGTC; CEV, GW, NCV, NLT]. Two tunics were evidence of comparative wealth and the disciples were to have no more than what an ordinary man would have [Hb]. Without a second tunic to be used as a covering from the chilly night air, they would have to trust God to provide hospitality for each night [EBC].

6:10 And he-was-saying to-them, "Where[a] ever you-enter[b] into a-house, stay there until you-depart[c] from-there.

LEXICON—a. ὅπου (83.5) (BAGD 1.a.δ. p. 576): 'where' [BAGD, LN (83.5)]. The phrase ὅπου ἐάν 'where ever' is translated 'wherever' [BAGD, Lns, NTC, WBC; NASB, NET, NIV, NLT, NRSV, TEV], 'whenever' [BECNT, BNTC; ESV, GW], 'when' [AB1; CEV, NCV, REB], 'whatever' [AB2], 'in what place soever' [KJV]. This particle indicates a position in space and is often used with ἐάν 'ever' to mark an indefinite and unrestricted position in space [LN].

  b. aorist act. subj. of εἰσέρχομαι (LN 15.93): 'to enter' [BECNT, BNTC, LN, NTC, WBC; ESV, KJV, NASB, NCV, NET, NIV, NRSV, REB], 'to go into' [AB1, AB2, LN, Lns; GW]. The phrase 'where ever you enter into a house' is translated 'when you are welcomed into a home' [CEV; similarly TEV], 'when you are admitted to a house' [AB1], 'into whatever house you go' [Lns], 'wherever you go' [NLT]. This verb means to move into a two-dimensional or three-dimensional space [LN].

  c. aorist act. subj. of ἐξέρχομαι (LN 15.40) (BAGD 1.a. p. 274): 'to depart out of, to go out of, to leave from within' [LN], 'to go away' [BAGD]. The phrase 'until you depart from there' [ESV] is also translated 'until you go out from thence' [Lns], 'till ye depart from that place' [KJV], 'until you leave from there' [BECNT], 'until you leave the/that place' [BNTC, WBC; NRSV, TEV], 'until you are ready to leave that place' [GW], 'until you leave that town' [NTC; CEV, NCV, NIV; similarly NASB, NLT], 'until you leave those parts' [AB1], 'until you leave the area' [NET], 'until you leave that district' [REB]. This verb means to move out of an enclosed or well-defined two or three-dimensional area [LN].

QUESTION—Does this command mean that when they enter any house after they arrive in a village, they are not to go outside that house until they depart from the village?

  That is the impression given in many translations, but the meaning is 'when you enter a house *as a guest*, do not change residence until you leave the town' [TH]. This refers to whatever house they are invited to stay in as guests as they travel from town to town [BNTC, Hb; CEV, TEV]. It does not mean that they were to stay inside that one house the whole time they were in town [TRT]. They were to be grateful guests [PNTC] and not change their residence while they remain in that town [EGT, NICNT, PNTC, TH]. Once they accept the hospitality of some home they were not to seek better accommodations for their stay in the town [BNTC, Hb, Lns, NAC, NLTfn, WBC]. They are not to dishonor the home by moving somewhere else in the same village [CGTC]. This would help avoid conflicts between householders who wanted the privilege of having these visitors staying in their homes [WBC].

6:11 **and what ever place does- not -welcome[a] you nor do-they-listen[b] to-you, departing[c] from-there shake-off[d] the dust under[e] your feet for a-testimony[f] to-them/against-them.**

TEXT—Manuscripts reading ὃς ἂν τόπος μὴ δέξωνται 'what ever place does not welcome' are followed by GNT, which does not mention any variant reading. A variant reading is ὅσοι ἂς μὴ δέξηται 'whoever may not welcome' and it is followed by KJV.

TEXT—Some manuscripts add αμην λεγω υμιν ανεκτοτερον εσται Σοδομοις η Γομορροις εν ησμερα κρισεως η τη πολει εκεινη 'Truly I tell you, it shall be more tolerable for Sodom or Gomorrah in the day of judgment, than for that city' at the end of this verse, and this reading is followed by KJV.

LEXICON—a. aorist mid. (deponent = act.) subj. of δέχομαι (LN 34.53) (BAGD 1. p. 177): 'to welcome' [BAGD, BECNT, LN, NTC; CEV, GW, NCV, NET, NIV, NLT, NRSV, TEV], 'to receive' [AB1, BAGD, BNTC, LN, Lns, WBC; ESV, KJV, NASB, REB], 'to accept' [AB2, LN], 'to have as a guest' [LN]. This verb means to accept the presence of a person with friendliness [LN]. It means to give hospitality [Sw].

b. aorist act. subj. of ἀκούω (LN 31.56) (BAGD 5. p. 32): 'to listen' [AB1, BAGD, BECNT, BNTC, LN, NTC, WBC; all versions except CEV, KJV, NRSV], 'to hear' [AB2, Lns; KJV, NRSV], 'to accept, to listen and respond, to pay attention and respond, to heed' [LN]. The phrase 'do not listen to you' is translated 'won't listen to your message' [CEV]. This verb means to believe something and then respond to it on the basis of having heard it [LN].

c. pres. mid./pass. (deponent = act.) participle of ἐκπορεύομαι (LN 15.40) (BAGD 1.b. p. 244): 'to depart out of' [LN], 'to go out of' [BAGD, LN]. The participial phrase 'departing from there' is translated 'as you go out from there' [NET; similarly Lns], 'as you leave' [AB1, BNTC; NLT, NRSV, REB], 'when you leave' [AB2, NTC, WBC; ESV, NIV], 'when ye depart thence' [KJV]. Some translate this participle as an imperative: 'leave' [BECNT; CEV, GW, NCV, TEV]. This verb means to move out of an enclosed or well-defined area [LN].

d. aorist act. impera. of ἐκτινάσσω (LN 16.8) (BAGD 1. p. 246): 'to shake off' [AB1, AB2, BAGD, BECNT, LN, Lns, WBC; all versions except CEV, GW, NLT], 'to shake (from)' [BNTC, LN, NTC; CEV, GW, NLT]. This verb means to shake something out or off of something in order to get rid of it [LN].

e. ὑποκάτω (LN 83.52) (BAGD p. 844): 'under' [AB2, BAGD, LN; KJV], 'on' [LN], not explicit [AB1; all versions except KJV, NASB, NRSV]. The phrase 'shake off the dust under your feet' [**LN**] is also translated 'shake off the dust from under your feet' [BECNT, WBC], 'shake the dust from/off the soles of your feet' [NTC; NASB], 'shake off the dust on your feet' [**LN**; similarly NRSV]. This preposition indicates a position on the undersurface of an object [LN].

f. μαρτύριον (LN 33.264) (BAGD 1.a. p. 493): 'testimony' [BAGD, LN], 'witness' [LN], 'that which serves as a testimony or proof' [BAGD]. The phrase εἰς μαρτύριον αὐτοῖς 'for/as a testimony to them' [BNTC, Lns, NTC] is also translated 'as a warning to them' [AB1; CEV, GW, NCV], 'as a solemn warning' [REB], 'This will be a warning to them!' [TEV]. The dative case of αὐτοῖς 'them' can also mean 'as/for a testimony against them' [ESV, KJV, NASB, NET, NIV, NRSV], 'as a witness against them' [AB2, BECNT, WBC], 'to show that you have abandoned those people to their fate' [NLT]. This noun denotes the content of what is witnessed or said [LN]. It refers to an action that serves as a testimony or proof [BAGD].

QUESTION—What is meant by a τόπος 'place' that does not welcome them?

This 'place' refers to whatever town or city they visit where the people living in it do not welcome or listen to the disciples' message [BECNT, Hb, Lns, TH; CEV]. The subject changes from the *place* to the *people* living in that place [BECNT, EGT, Hb, ICC]. It is the people of the place who refuse to listen to the disciples [TH]. Some translate it so that it refers to the inhabitants of that place: 'a town where people do not welcome you' [TEV], 'if the people in a certain place refuse to welcome you' [NCV], 'wherever people don't welcome you' [GW].

QUESTION—What relationship is indicated by the use of the participle ἐκπορευόμενοι 'departing'?
   1. It indicates a temporal relationship [AB2, NTC, WBC; ESV, KJV, NIV]: *when* you depart, shake off the dust.
   2. It indicates a circumstantial relationship [AB1, BNTC, Hb, Lns; NET, NLT, NRSV, REB]: *as* you depart, shake off the dust. While in the act of leaving, they should shake off the dust that was stuck to their sandals [Hb].
   3. It has an imperative sense [BECNT, TH; CEV, GW, NCV, TEV]: *Depart* and shake off the dust! In the context of the imperative main verb 'shake off', the participle should be translated '*Leave* and shake off the dust!' [TH].

QUESTION—What would be indicated by shaking off the dust from their feet?

When pious Jews returned from visiting a heathen land, it was their custom to carefully remove the dust of that land from their feet and clothing before they stepped back onto Jewish territory so as not to defile it [CGTC, EBC, NAC, NCBC, NTC, PNTC, WBC]. When the disciples shake off the dust from their feet, it will be a symbolic declaration that the place that rejected them was a heathen place [CGTC, EBC, My, PNTC, Tay]. It would be a symbolic act to declare a complete end to further fellowship with them [AB2, CGTC, Hb]. It probably symbolized several things: (1) the place was declared to be pagan, (2) there would be no further contact with the place, and (3) the messengers had done their job and now washed their hands of any further responsibility for the people living there [WBC].

QUESTION—What kind of testimony would this be?

This symbolic act indicated the seriousness of rejecting God's messengers. It announced that the disciples had been in the town and had been forced to leave as unwelcome guests when the people who lived there rejected their message [Lns]. This testimony was a public declaration that God's displeasure rested on that village because its people had refused the gospel [NTC]. This action declared the village to be pagan in character [CGTC, NICNT]. The dative case of the pronoun αὐτοῖς 'them' could be (1) the *dative of advantage*: the testimony is given *to them* as a warning to repent and be saved, or it could be (2) the *dative of disadvantage*: the testimony is given as a witness against them that would be used at the day of the final judgment [AB2, BECNT].

1. This was a testimony *to* them [AB1, CGTC, Hb, ICC, NIVfn, NTC, Tay; CEV, GW, NCV, REB, TEV]. Since this testimony was publicly given *to* the people of the village, it served as a last call to repentance. This testimony was not to be taken as a curse, but as a warning to the people to change their hearts [AB1; probably CEV, GW, NCV, REB, TEV which call this a 'warning']. This act was intended to cause them to think about the greatness of their guilt in rejecting the message of the gospel [Hb, Tay]. The warning summoned them to repentance [CGTC, NTC, Tay].
2. This was a testimony *against* them [AB2, BECNT, CBC, EBC, Gnd, NCBC, NICNT, NIGTC, NLTfn, WBC; ESV, KJV, NASB, NET, NIV, NRSV]. It indicates that the disciples have abandoned the people to their fate [CBC, NLTfn]. The town had rejected the disciples and their message, and the dust shaken off from the disciples' shoes would serve as incriminating evidence against the villagers at the final judgment [AB2, NIGTC, WBC]. That dust indicated that judgment awaited them at the last day [BECNT, Gnd].
3. Perhaps both meanings are included [BNTC, CGTC, NAC, Sw]. The effect of this action would either lead to reflection and perhaps repentance on the part of the villagers, or at least it would justify God's future judgment [Sw].

6:12 And having-gone-out^a they-preached^b that (people) should-repent,^c
6:13 and they-were-casting-out many demons, and they-were-anointing^d with oil many sick (people) and healing (them).

LEXICON—a. aorist act. participle of ἐξέρχομαι (LN 15.40): 'to go out' [AB1, AB2, BECNT, Lns, NTC; all versions except CEV, GW, REB], 'to go' [GW], 'to leave' [CEV], 'to set out' [BNTC; REB], 'to depart' [WBC]; 'to go out of, to depart out of, to leave from within' [LN]. This verb means to move out of an enclosed or well-defined two or three-dimensional area [LN]. The phrase 'having gone out' means they started on their journey [TH].

  b. aorist act. indic. of κηρύσσω (LN 33.256) (2.b.β. p. 431): 'to preach' [BAGD, BECNT, LN, NTC, WBC; KJV, NASB, NCV, NET, NIV,

TEV], 'to proclaim' [AB1, AB2, BAGD, BNTC, Lns, NTC, WBC; ESV, NRSV, REB], 'to herald' [Lns], 'to tell people/everyone' [CEV, GW, NLT]. This verb means to publicly announce religious truths and principles while urging acceptance and compliance [LN]. The aorist tense summarizes their activity [Hb].
  c. pres. act. subj. of μετανοέω (LN 41.52) (BAGD p. 512): 'to repent' [AB1, AB2, BAGD, BECNT, BNTC, LN, Lns, WBC; ESV, KJV, NASB, NET, NIV, NRSV], 'to be converted' [NTC], 'to change one's way' [LN], 'to change one's mind' [BAGD]. The phrase 'they preached that people should repent' is translated 'proclaimed the need for repentance' [REB], 'preached that people should turn away from their sins' [TEV], 'preached that people should change their hearts and lives' [NCV], 'telling everyone they met to repent of their sins and turn to God' [NLT], 'started telling everyone to turn to God' [CEV], 'told people that they should turn to God and change the way they think and act' [GW]. This verb means to change one's way of life as the result of a complete change of thought and attitude with regard to sin and righteousness [LN]. See 'repent' and 'repentance' at 1:4, 15.
  d. imperf. act. indic. of ἀλείφω (LN 47.14) (BAGD 1. p. 35): 'to anoint' [BAGD, LN]. The clause καὶ ἤλειφον ἐλαίῳ πολλοὺς ἀρρώστους καὶ ἐθεράπευον 'and they were anointing with oil many sick people and healing them' [NASB; similarly NTC] is also translated 'and anointed with oil many who were sick and healed them' [ESV; similarly KJV, NRSV], 'and anointed many sick people with oil and healed/cured them' [BNTC; NET, NIV, REB; similarly AB2, BECNT, WBC], 'and proceeded to anoint with oil many sick and to heal them' [Lns], 'and put olive oil on many sick people and healed them' [NCV], 'and many sick people they anointed with oil and cured them' [AB1], 'and healed a lot of sick people by putting olive oil on them' [CEV], 'and healed many sick people, anointing them with olive oil' [NLT], 'and poured oil on many who were sick to cure them' [GW], 'and rubbed olive oil on many sick people and healed them' [TEV]. This verb means to anoint with a liquid which usually was oil [LN].
QUESTION—Why did they anoint people with oil and how was it done?
  This oil was the common olive oil used for food, anointing, sacrifice, lamp fuel, and medicine [PNTC]. It is assumed that the cure came immediately after the anointing [Hb]. Olive oil was widely used as a medicine, but in the context of supernatural healing, anointing the sick person with oil was a symbolic act and not therapeutic [AB1, BECNT, CGTC, Hb, ICC, NAC, NCBC, NTC, PNTC, TH, WBC]. Since olive oil was a well-known healing agent, it was an appropriate visible symbol of God's power that miraculously healed people [Hb, ICC]. The oil was a symbol of God's presence, his grace, and his power [NAC]. It symbolized that God was present and working [TRT]. The oil was probably rubbed on the head [TH, TRT]. The imperfect

tenses indicate that there were repeated instances of these healing acts [Gnd, Hb].

DISCOURSE UNIT—6:14–8:30 [EBC, NICNT]. The topic is the withdrawal from Galilee [EBC], the withdrawals beyond Galilee [NICNT].

DISCOURSE UNIT—6:14–32 [NASB]. The topic is recalling John's fate.

DISCOURSE UNIT—6:14–29 [CBC, Hb; CEV, ESV, GW, NCV, NET, NIV, NLT, NRSV, TEV]. The topic is the reaction of Antipas to the reports about Jesus [Hb], the death of John the Baptist [CBC; CEV, ESV, NET, NRSV, TEV], Herod and the death of John the Baptist [NLT], how John the Baptist was killed [NCV], John the Baptist beheaded [NIV], recalling John's death [GW].

DISCOURSE UNIT—6:14–16 [EBC, Hb, NICNT]. The topic is the excited reaction of Herod Antipas [Hb], popular estimates of the identity of Jesus [EBC, NICNT].

6:14 **And king Herod heard, because his name[a] had-become known, and they-were-saying, "John the (one) baptizing has-been-raised[b] from (the) dead and because-of this the (miraculous) powers[c] are-at-work in him."**

TEXT—Manuscripts reading καὶ ἔλεγον 'and they were saying' are given a B rating by GNT to indicate it was regarded to be almost certain. A variant reading is καὶ ἔλεγεν 'and he was saying' and it is followed by EGT, Hb, ICC, Lns; KJV. Another variant reading is καὶ ἐλέγοσαν 'and they said'.

LEXCON—a. ὄνομα (LN 33.265) (BAGD IV. p. 573): 'name, reputation' [BAGD, LN]. The phrase 'his name had become known' [NASB; similarly Lns] is also translated 'his name was spread abroad' [KJV], 'Jesus' name had become known/well-known' [AB2, BECNT, WBC; ESV, GW, NET, NIV, NRSV], 'Jesus became so well known' [CEV], 'Jesus' fame had become known' [WBC], 'his fame had spread' [BNTC; REB], 'Jesus' reputation had spread everywhere' [AB1; TEV], 'everyone was talking about him' [NLT]. This noun denotes that which is said about a person on the basis of an evaluation of his conduct [LN].

b. perf. pass. indic. of ἐγείρω (LN 23.94) (BAGD 2.c. p. 215): 'to be raised' [BAGD], 'to be raised to life, to be made to live again' [LN]. The phrase 'has been raised from the dead' [BECNT, BNTC; ESV, NET, NIV, NRSV, REB; similarly NLT] is also translated 'had been raised from among the dead' [AB2], 'has been raised to life' [AB1], 'has risen from the dead' [Lns, WBC; NASB, NCV; similarly NTC; KJV], 'has come back to life' [GW, TEV; similarly CEV]. This verb means to be caused to live again after having died [LN]. The perfect tense indicates that John had been raised and was now alive and active [Hb].

c. δύναμις (LN 76.1, 76.7) (BAGD 1. p. 207): 'power' [LN (76.1)], 'mighty deed, miracle' [LN (76.7)]. The phrase 'the powers are/were at work in him' [AB2] is also translated 'mighty works do show forth themselves in him' [KJV], 'the works of power operate in him' [Lns], 'these powers are at work in him' [BNTC, WBC; NRSV; similarly BECNT], 'these miraculous powers are at work in him' [AB1, NTC; ESV, NASB, NIV, REB; similarly NET], 'with the power to work miracles' [CEV], 'he has the power to perform these miracles' [GW; similarly TEV], 'he can work these miracles' [NCV], 'he can do such miracles' [NLT]. This noun denotes the potentiality to exert force in performing some function [LN (76.1)], or it denotes a deed that manifests great power, probably involving a supernatural force [LN (76.7)].

QUESTION—Who was King Herod?

At least four rulers bear the name Herod in the NT [PNTC]. The ruler mentioned here was Herod Antipas who ruled as tetrarch of Galilee and Peraea from the time of the death of his father, Herod the Great, until A.D. 39 [CGTC, EBC, ESVfn, WBC]. This Herod is called a tetrarch in Mathew 14:1 and Luke 9:7. A tetrarch was appointed by Rome to be a governor of one of four divisions of a country, so Mark probably reflects local custom when he calls this tetrarch a 'king' [AB1, AB2, BECNT, BNTC, CBC, CGTC, ESVfn, Lns, NCBC, NETfn, NTC, Tay, WBC]. The title 'King' was freely used in Rome for all eastern rulers [Hb]. The title βασιλεύς 'king' is also translated as 'ruler' [CEV].

QUESTION—What did Herod hear?

The preceding discourse unit suggests that Herod had heard about Jesus sending out the Twelve [NTC] and the increased preaching activity in Galilee [AB2, BECNT, BNTC, NLTfn, NTC]. However, the reason clause 'because his name had become well known' focuses on Jesus, so the king was reacting to what 'he heard' about the activities of Jesus rather than news about the Twelve [BNTC, EBC, EGT, Hb, ICC, Lns, NICNT, NTC, Tay, WBC]. What had especially caught Herod's attention were the different opinions being publicly expressed about Jesus [EBC, Sw, WBC]. Some translate 'heard' as 'heard *about him*' [CEV; similarly KJV], 'heard *about/of Jesus*' [BNTC; GW, NCV, NLT, REB].

QUESTION—What is meant by the statement, John 'has been raised from the dead'?

The agent of the passive verb ἐγήγερται 'has been raised' is not identified, and it would be too specific to translate this as 'God has raised him from the dead' at this point in the narrative. Some who have to translate this with an active verb end up with something like 'he got up and left the dead' [TH]. Most translations say that Jesus has been raised 'from the dead' [BECNT, BNTC, NTC, WBC; all versions except CEV, GW, TEV]. One says this means he was raised from the realm of the dead [AB2]. The adjective νεκρῶν 'dead' lacks an article, so instead of being raised from among *dead persons*, the adjective refers to the condition of death and means that John was raised from *death* without reference to other dead people [Lns]. Some omit the reference to death: he has been raised to life [AB1], he has come back to life [CEV, GW, TEV]. The people who identified Jesus with John the Baptist would not have known about Jesus prior to his present ministry in

Galilee [EBC, NICNT] and probably thought Jesus was someone who had appeared suddenly upon earth a short time after John's death [NICNT].

QUESTION—Why did Herod think a risen John would have αἱ δυνάμεις 'the powers' at work in him?

The δυνάμεις 'powers' in verses 2 and 5 refer directly to miracles, but in this verse the 'powers' refer to 'miraculous powers', that is, the 'power to perform miracles' [AB1, CGTC, EBC, Lns, NAC, NTC, Tay, WBC]. Miraculous powers might be expected of someone who had been raised from the dead [AB2, BECNT, EBC, Gnd, NIGTC]. Perhaps John was so highly esteemed that the ability to perform miracles had been ascribed to him [NTC]. This may even indicate that John the Baptist had also accomplished mighty works in his role as a prophet before his death [BECNT, WBC].

6:15 **But others were-saying, "He is Elijah." And others were-saying, "(He is) a-prophet like one of-the prophets."**

QUESTION—What made them think Jesus was the prophet Elijah?

Malachi 4:5 quotes the LORD as saying "Behold, I will send you Elijah the prophet before the great and awesome day of the LORD comes." [ESV]. These people thought that Jesus was Elijah who had returned to announce the day of the Lord [BNTC, WBC]. Since Elijah had been taken up into heaven without dying, there was no need for a resurrection [BNTC].

QUESTION—What is meant by εἷς τῶν προφητῶν 'one of the prophets'?

The phrase 'one of the prophets' is generally taken to refer to προφήτης τις τῶν ἀρχαίων 'some prophet of the ancients' as Luke 9:8 puts it [CGTC, NTC, Tay, TH]. This seems to be a lower estimate of Jesus than the two previous views [EBC]. Many translations supply the information that this refers to the ancient prophets: 'the prophets of old' [BECNT, BNTC; ESV, NASB, NRSV, REB], 'the prophets from the past' [NET], 'the prophets of long ago' [NIV, TEV], 'the prophets who lived long ago' [NCV], 'the former prophets' [AB1], 'the other great prophets of the past' [NLT], 'a prophet in the Scriptures' [AB2], 'some other prophet who had lived long ago' [CEV]. The words 'one of the prophets' distinguish Jesus from contemporary 'prophets' of the first-century and link him to the prophets of the OT, whose prophetic line was considered to have ceased until the end times [AB2].

QUESTION—Why did these people think that Jesus was like one of those prophets?

These people recognized the similarity of divine enablement between Jesus and the OT prophets [Gnd]. They were ready to accept Jesus as being in the general category of prophets [Hb]. He was another prophet in the succession of prophets who spoke and acted for God in Israel's history [NICNT]. They thought that the long-suspended line of OT prophets had now restarted [BNTC, Hb, My]. But since both of the first two speculations involved a resurrection or return of an ancient prophet, this too relates to the return of another of the OT prophets [NIGTC].

6:16 And having-heard, Herod was-saying, "John, whom I beheaded,ᵃ this (one) has-been-raised.ᵇ"

TEXT—Manuscripts ending the verse with ἠγέρθη 'has been raised' are followed by GNT, which does not mention any variant reading. A variant reading is ἠγέρθη ἐκ νεκρῶν 'has been raised from the dead' and it is followed by KJV.

LEXICON—a. aorist act. indic. of ἀποκεφαλίζω (LN 20.80) (BAGD p. 93): 'to behead' [BAGD, LN], 'to cut the head off' [LN]. The phrase 'whom I beheaded' [AB1, WBC; ESV, KJV, NASB, NET, NRSV, REB; similarly Lns; NIV] is also translated 'the man I beheaded' [NLT], 'I killed John by cutting off his head' [NCV], 'I had his head cut off' [CEV, TEV; similarly GW]. This verb means to kill someone by beheading him, an act of capital punishment [LN].

b. aorist pass. indic. of ἐγείρω (LN 23.94) (BAGD 2.c. p. 215): 'to be raised' [BAGD; ESV, KJV, NET, NRSV], 'to be raised to life' [AB1, LN], 'to be raised from the dead' [BECNT, WBC; NIV, REB], 'to be made to live again' [LN]. This passive verb is also translated actively: 'did rise again' [Lns], 'has risen' [NASB], 'has come back to life' [CEV, GW, TEV], 'has come back from the dead' [NLT], 'has risen from the dead' [NCV]. This verb means to be caused to live again after having once died [LN]. The passive tense implies that God had raised him [AB2, BECNT].

QUESTION—What had Herod heard?
1. Herod heard what Jesus was doing [EBC, Lns, NCBC, NIGTC, TH; CEV]. After the comment about the popular views about Jesus, the clause 'and king Herod heard (of this)' in 6:14 is now resumed, and Herod gives his own conclusion, which agrees with the first view [EBC, NCBC, NIGTC, WBC]. There is no suggestion that Herod's response to the identity of Jesus was formed in the light of the popular opinions just expressed [NCBC].
2. Herod heard the opinions expressed in the previous verse [EGT, Gnd, Hb, ICC, Lns, Sw, Tay]. Herod heard the three different opinions and then fastened on the first one [Lns]. Another view is that the imperfect tense 'was saying' suggests that whenever he heard of some person's view, Herod responded with his own view of the identity of Jesus [Hb].

QUESTION—Who beheaded Jesus?
The grammatical subject is Herod, but it means that Herod had caused it to be done through someone else, so this could be translated 'Herod caused John to be beheaded', or 'Herod ordered men to cut off his head' [TH]. The actual beheading had been accomplished by Herod's bodyguard (6:27) [AB2].

QUESTION—Why did Herod think Jesus was John the Baptist?
Herod's uneasy conscience and superstitions made him afraid that John had come back to haunt him [NCBC, NICNT, NIVfn, NTC]. Herod must have known that Jesus and John were contemporaries before John was beheaded,

so perhaps Herod thought that just like Elijah's spirit came to rest upon Elisha (2 Kings 2:1–15), so the spirit of John had come to rest on Jesus [BECNT]. Or he could have meant, 'This is John the Baptist all over again!' [BECNT, BNTC, Tay].

DISCOURSE UNIT—6:17-29 [EBC, Hb, NICNT]. The topic is an explanatory account of John's death [Hb], the imprisonment and death of John [NICNT], the death of John the Baptist [EBC].

6:17 Because (it was) Herod himself[a] (who), having-sent,[b] arrested John and bound[c] him in prison on-account-of[d] Herodias the wife of-Philip his brother, because he-married her.

LEXICON—a. αὐτός (LN 92.11): 'himself' [AB2, BECNT, Lns, WBC; KJV, NASB, NCV, NET, NIV, NRSV], not explicit [AB1, BNTC, NTC; CEV, GW, NLT, REB, TEV]. This pronoun refers to the definite person spoken or written about [LN]. The forefronted pronoun αὐτός 'himself' distinguishes Herod from John, who has just been referred to at the end of the previous verse by the pronoun οὗτος 'this (one) has been raised' [Gnd]. Αὐτός 'himself' is emphatic in order to make the point that the first step was taken by Herod himself [Hb, ICC, Sw]. Others think it is merely redundant and could be left untranslated [CGTC, Tay, TH].

   b. aorist act. participle of ἀποστέλλω (LN 15.66) (BAGD 1.d. p. 99): 'to send' [LN]. The phrase ἀποστείλας ἐκράτησεν τὸν Ἰωάννην 'having sent, arrested John' is translated 'having sent forth, arrested John' [Lns], 'had sent and arrested John' [AB1], 'had sent out and arrested John' [AB2], 'had sent and seized John' [BNTC; ESV; similarly BECNT], 'had sent men, arrested John' [NET], 'had sent forth and laid hold upon John' [KJV], 'had sent and had John arrested' [NASB], 'had sent and had John taken into custody' [WBC], 'had John arrested' [BAGD], 'arrested John' [CEV], 'had sent men who had arrested John' [GW, NRSV], 'had sent men to arrest John' [REB; similarly NLT], 'had ordered his soldiers to arrest John' [NCV], 'had ordered John's arrest' [TEV], 'had given orders to have John arrested' [NIV], 'by order of Herod, John had been arrested' [NTC]. This verb means to cause someone to depart for a particular purpose [LN]. When this verb is used with other verbs, it often means that the action in question has been performed by someone else [BAGD]. 'Sent' indicates that Herod had his subordinates tie up John and put him into prison [Gnd].

   c. aorist act. indic. of δέω (LN 18.13, 37.114) (BAGD 1.b. p. 177): 'to bind' [BAGD], 'to tie, to tie together, to tie up' [LN (18.13)], 'to imprison, to put in jail' [LN (37.114)]. The phrase ἔδησεν αὐτὸν ἐν φυλακῇ 'bound him in prison' [AB2, BECNT, BNTC, Lns; ESV, KJV, NET; similarly WBC; NASB] is also translated 'tied him up and put him in prison' [GW], 'had him tied up and put in prison' [TEV], 'had him bound and put in prison' [NIV; similarly NRSV], 'put him in prison' [AB1; CEV, NCV, REB]. 'had sent soldiers (to arrest and) imprison' [NLT]. This is also translated with John as the subject: 'John had been arrested, bound, and put in prison' [NTC]. This verb means to tie objects together [LN (18.13)], or to confine someone in prison [LN (37.114)]. It refers to the actual binding and imprisonment of prisoners [BAGD]. John's hands were probably bound, and his ankles could also have been bound together with a loose rope or chain [TRT].

d. διά (LN **90.44**) (BAGD B.II.1. p. 181): 'on account of' [AB1, AB2, BECNT, BNTC, LN, Lns, NTC, WBC; NASB, NET, NRSV], 'because of' [AB2, BAGD, **LN**; NIV, TEV], 'for the sake of' [ESV, KJV], 'for' [GW], 'at the instance of' [REB] 'in order to please' [CEV, NCV], 'as a favor to' [NLT]. This preposition refers to the participant constituting the cause or reason for an event or state [LN].

QUESTION—What relationship is indicated by the initial conjunction γάρ 'because'?

This introduces an explanation of what brought about the beheading of John the Baptist mentioned in verse 16 [BECNT, Hb, NICNT, NTC, WBC]. The conjunction γάρ 'because' seems to turn verses 17–29 into an extended footnote [Gnd] since these verses are a parenthetical account of the events that caused the people in verse 14 to think that Jesus was John the Baptist risen from the dead [Gnd, TH].

QUESTION—When was John bound ?

1. John was arrested and bound, and then put into prison [BECNT, Gnd, NTC, TH; GW, NIV, NRSV, TEV].
2. John was arrested, brought to prison, and then bound [Hb, Lns; probably KJV, NASB, NET which translate it 'bound him in prison']. John was kept bound while in prison [Hb, Lns] to prevent his escape [Lns].
3. Binding is not mentioned in some translations [CEV, NCV, NLT, REB] since the verb does not always include the literal meaning of 'to bind' [TH].

QUESTION—What relationship is indicated by the prepositional phrase 'on account of Herodias'?

This indicates that in some way Herodias was the reason Herod had John imprisoned [BECNT, Gnd, ICC, NTC, WBC]. The reason could be because of what Herodias had done, asked, or wanted [TH]. Herod imprisoned John because John rebuked him for marrying Herodias, his brother's wife [BECNT, EBC]. Herodias wanted John punished because she was included in that rebuke [NTC]. Herod imprisoned John because he wanted to please Herodias [Gnd, NTC; CEV, NCV, NLT, REB]. Herod had mixed motives for imprisoning John [NICNT] and 6:19–20 says that Herod imprisoned John in order to protect him from Herodias who wanted to get him killed [AB2, NICNT, TRT].

QUESTION—What relationship is indicated by the ὅτι reason clause 'because he married her'?

This states more exactly the connection between Herodias and the imprisonment of John [BECNT, ICC]. It stresses the fact that Herod's marriage to Herodias had been the basis for John's rebuke [Hb]. This reason is amplified with another reason clause in verse 18 [WBC].

6:18 Because John was-saying[a] to Herod, "It-is- not -lawful[b] for-you to-have[c] the wife of-your brother."

LEXICON—a. imperf. act. indic. of λέγω (LN 33.69): 'to say, to tell, to speak' [LN]. The imperfect tense 'was saying' [BECNT, Lns] is also translated 'kept telling' [NTC; TEV], 'had been saying' [ESV, NASB, NIV], 'had been telling' [GW, NCV, NLT, NRSV], 'had repeatedly told' [NET], 'had said' [AB2, WBC; KJV], 'had told' [AB1, BNTC; CEV, REB]. This verb means to speak or talk about something [LN].

b. pres. act. indic. of ἔξεστι (LN 71.32) (BAGD 2.p. 275): 'to be permitted, to be possible, to be proper' [BAGD], 'must, ought to' [LN]. With the negative particle, it is translated 'it is not lawful' [BECNT, Lns; ESV, KJV, NASB, NCV, NET, NIV, NRSV], 'it is not right' [BNTC, NTC; CEV, GW, TEV], 'it is illegal' [WBC], 'you have no right' [AB1; REB], 'you're not allowed' [AB2], 'it is against God's law' [NLT]. This verb means that something is obligatory, and when accompanied by a negative particle it means 'it ought not to be done' [LN]. This word occurs at 2:24, 26; 3:4; 6:18; 10:2; 12:14.

c. pres. act. infin. of ἔχω (LN 57.1) (BAGD I.2.b.α. p. 332): 'to have' [BAGD, BECNT, BNTC, LN, Lns, NTC, WBC; ESV, KJV, NASB, NRSV], 'to take' [CEV, REB], 'to marry' [AB1, AB2, BAGD; NET, NLT, TEV], 'to be married to' [GW, NCV]. This verb means to have or possess objects [LN]. It means to have as one's own, and the verb was used to speak of persons to whom one has close relationships [BAGD]. This means 'to have or possess as a wife' [Lns, TH].

QUESTION—What relationship is indicated by the initial conjunction γάρ 'because'?

This conjunction is another explanatory note explaining the reason why Herod had imprisoned John [BECNT, Hb, TH]. The rather vague reason 'because he married her' at the end of the preceding verse is now amplified to explain that it was John's pronouncements about the legality of that marriage that caused Herodias to get Herod to put John in prison [WBC].

QUESTION—What is indicated by the use of the imperfect tense of ἔλεγεν 'was saying'?

John was saying this *repeatedly* [CGTC, Hb, NIGTC, NTC, WBC; NET, TEV]. In this context, the imperfect tense may be the equivalent of the pluperfect tense, 'he had been saying' [AB1, AB2, BNTC, CGTC, Hb, NTC, Tay, TH, WBC; ESV, GW, NASB, NCV, NET, NIV, NLT, NRSV]. This could mean John had a private meeting with Herod to rebuke him, or John had sent his disciples to rebuke Herod, or John had publicly stated this during his preaching [Hb, Sw, Tay].

1. John had directly rebuked Herod [Hb, NIGTC; perhaps CEV, KJV, REB which translate the imperfect tense as though it referred to one occasion].

John had a private confrontation with Herod on more than one occasion in his ministry [Hb]. This seems to say that John had repeatedly spoken to Herod, suggesting John had gained personal access to Herod before he was arrested by Herod [NIGTC].

2. John had been saying this to the crowds in the course of his preaching, and reports of this preaching had come to Herod and Herodias [Lns, Sw].

QUESTION—Why wasn't it lawful for Herod to have Herodias as his wife?

The Mosaic law in Lev. 18:16 and 20:21 prohibited marriage to a brother's wife if the brother was still alive [AB1, AB2, BECNT, BNTC, EBC, Hb, HNTC, NAC, NCBC, NICNT, NIGTC, NTC, Sw, Tay, TRT, WBC]. This relationship was not only a violation of the law against marrying a brother's wife, it was also an act of adultery (Lev. 20:10) [Lns, NETfn, NLTfn, NTC].

6:19 And[a] Herodias was-bearing-a-grudge[b] against him and wanted to-kill[c] him, and she-could not.

LEXICON—a. δέ (LN 89.87): 'and' [LN; ESV, NRSV], 'and then' [LN], 'so' [GW, NCV, NET, NIV, NLT, TEV], 'therefore' [KJV], not explicit [CEV, NASB, REB]. This conjunction indicates a sequence of closely related events [LN].

b. imperf. act. indic. of ἐνέχω (LN **88.169**) (BAGD 1. p. 265): 'to have a grudge against' [AB1, BAGD, BNTC, LN; CEV, ESV, NASB, NRSV], 'to hold a grudge against' [BECNT, **LN**; GW, TEV], 'to bear a grudge against' [NLT], 'to nurse a grudge against' [NET, NIV, REB], 'to have a quarrel against' [KJV], 'to have it in for (him)' [AB2, Lns, NTC, WBC], 'to be resentful against' [LN], 'to hate' [NCV]. This verb means to feel resentful because of what someone has done [LN].

c. aorist act. infin. of ἀποκτείνω (LN 20.61) (BAGD 1.a. p. 94): 'to kill' [AB1, AB2, BAGD, BECNT, BNTC, LN, Lns, NTC, WBC; all versions except ESV, NASB], 'to put to death' [ESV, NASB]. This verb means to cause someone's death, normally by violent means, with or without intent or legal justification [LN]. When a language requires a translation to distinguish between the primary and secondary agency, the phrase 'she wanted to kill him' means that she wanted *to cause* John to be killed by someone else [TH].

QUESTION—What relationship is indicated by δέ 'so/but Herodias'?

1. This conjunction indicates the result of John's accusations [AB1, Gnd, NTC, TRT; GW, KJV, NCV, NET, NIV, NLT, TEV]: *so Herodias bore a grudge against him.*

2. This conjunction indicates a contrast between Herod's act of only imprisoning John with Herodias' desire to have John killed [Gnd].

QUESTION—What relationship is indicated by the conjunction καί 'and' in the phrase 'and she could not'?

Here the conjunction has the adversative sense of 'but' [CEV, ESV, NCV, NET, NIV, NLT, NRSV, REB, TEV]. She could not have John killed without Herod's approval [NLT]. The imperfect tense of 'she could not' may indicate that she was going to persist until she found a way of killing John [Hb, Lns].

6:20 Because Herod was-fearing/respecting[a] John, having-known him (to be) a-righteous[b] and holy[c] man, and he-was-protecting[d] him,

LEXICON—a. imperf. pass. indic. of φοβέομαι, φοβέω (LN 87.14) (BAGD 1.b.α. p. 863): 'to fear' [BAGD, BECNT, BNTC, LN, Lns, WBC; ESV, KJV, NIV, NRSV], 'to be afraid of' [AB1, AB2, NTC; CEV, GW, NASB, NCV, TEV], 'to stand in awe of' [NET], 'to go in awe of' [REB], 'to respect' [NLT], 'to show great respect for' [LN]. This verb means to have such awe or respect for a person that there is some fear of that person as well [LN]. The imperfect tense indicates that this was an ongoing fear of John, or respect for him [NETfn].
- b. δίκαιος (LN 88.12) (BAGD 1.b. p. 195): 'righteous' [AB2, BAGD, BECNT, BNTC, LN, Lns, NTC; ESV, NET, NIV, NRSV], 'just' [BAGD, LN, WBC; KJV, NASB], 'upright' [BAGD], 'good' [AB1; CEV, NCV, NLT, REB, TEV], 'fair' [GW]. This adjective describes someone as being in accordance with what God requires [LN]. John was approved by God [Lns, NTC].
- c. ἅγιος (LN 53.46) (BAGD 1.b.α. p. 9): 'holy' [AB1, AB2, BAGD, BECNT, BNTC, **LN**, Lns, NTC, WBC; all versions], 'devout, godly, dedicated' [LN], 'consecrated to God' [BAGD]. This adjective describes someone as being dedicated to the service of God [Hb, LN, Lns]. He was a man of upright conduct who was consecrated to God [NTC]. This means that John was morally pure and was committed to serving God, but it does not imply that he was perfect and sinless [TRT].
- d. imperf. act. indic. of συντηρέω (LN 13.33) (BAGD 1. p. 792): 'to protect' [AB2, BAGD, BECNT, WBC; CEV, GW, NCV, NET, NIV, NLT, NRSV], 'to give him protection' [REB], 'to defend' [BAGD], 'to preserve' [LN], 'to keep (him) safe' [Lns, NTC; ESV, NASB, TEV], 'to keep (him) in safety' [BNTC], 'to keep in safe custody' [AB1], 'to observe' [KJV]. This verb means to cause something to continue along with something else [LN]. It means to protect someone from harm [BAGD].

QUESTION—What relationship is indicated by the initial conjunction γάρ 'because'?

This indicates the reason why Herodias could not carry out her desire to have John killed [AB1, Gnd, Lns, Tay, WBC; CEV, NASB, NCV, NET, NIV, NLT, NRSV, REB]: Herodius could not have John killed *because King Herod feared John and protected him.*

QUESTION—Does the verb ἐφοβεῖτο mean that Herod 'feared' John or 'respected' John?

Most translations say that Herod feared John [AB1, AB2, BAGD, BECNT, BNTC, EBC, EGT, Gnd, Hb, ICC, Lns, WBC; CEV, ESV, GW, KJV, NASB, NCV, NIV, NRSV, TEV]. John's righteousness made Herod afraid

[ICC]. He was awed by John's character and feared him in the same way those who are bad fear the good [EBC, Sw]. Herod had mixed feelings of superstitious fear and awed respect [EGT, Hb, NICNT, NIGTC]. Some think that instead of focusing on fear, this should be a statement of John's respect for Jesus [NCBC, TH, TRT; NLT], and some translations say that Herod was in awe of John [NET, REB]. Instead of being scared of him, Herod respected him very much [TRT]. Herod held John in awe and had a great deal of respect for him [TH].

QUESTION—What relationship is indicated by the use of the participle εἰδώς 'having known'?

The participle is causal [Gnd, Hb, Lns, TH, TRT; NET, TEV]: Herod feared and respected John *because he knew* that John was a righteous and holy man.

QUESTION—Why did Herod have to protect John?

Herodias wanted to kill John, so Herod protected John from her [BECNT, BNTC, CGTC, Gnd, Lns, Tay, TH, TRT] and refused to have John put to death [EBC]. He protected John from Herodias by keeping John in prison [Lns].

and having-heard him many-(times)/greatly[a] he-was-perplexed,[b] and-yet[c] gladly[d] he-was-listening[e] to-him.

TEXT—Manuscripts reading πολλὰ ἠπόρει, καί 'many/greatly he was perplexed, and' are given a C rating by GNT to indicate that choosing it over a variant text was difficult. A variant reading is πολλὰ ἐποίει, καί 'he was doing many things, and' and it is followed by WBC; KJV. Another variant reading is πολλὰ ἃ ἐποίει, καί 'many things that he was doing, and'. Two manuscripts omit this phrase.

LEXICON—a. πολύς (LN 59.1, 78.3) (BAGD I.2.b.α., I.2.b.β. p. 688): 'many' [BAGD (I.2.b.α.), LN (59.1)], 'a great number of' [LN (59.1)], 'greatly' [BAGD (I.2.b.β.), LN (78.3)]. This adverb modifies the preceding verb ἀκούσας 'having heard': 'often' [CEV], 'much, (i.e., at length)' [Lns]. This adverb modifies the following verb ἠπόρει 'he was perplexed': 'greatly' [AB1, AB2, BECNT, BNTC, NTC; ESV, NIV, NLT, NRSV, REB, TEV], 'very' [GW, NASB], 'thoroughly' [NET], 'always' [NCV]. This adverb indicates a relatively large quantity of events (or objects) [LN (59.1)], or the upper range of a scale of extent [LN (78.3)].

b. imperf. act. indic. of ἀπορέω (LN 32.9) (BAGD p. 97): 'to be perplexed' [AB1, AB2, BECNT, NTC; ESV, NASB, NRSV; similarly Lns], 'to be baffled' [NET], 'to be puzzled' [NIV], 'to be confused' [CEV], 'to be disturbed' [BAGD, BNTC; GW, NLT, REB, TEV], 'to be at a loss, to be uncertain, to be in doubt' [BAGD, LN], 'to be anxious' [LN], 'to be bothered' [NCV]. This verb means to be perplexed about something [LN]. The imperfect tense indicates that he continued to be perplexed [Lns].

c. καί (LN 91.12): 'and yet' [AB2; GW, NET, NRSV], 'yet' [LN; ESV, NIV], 'but' [NASB], 'but even so' [NLT], 'still' [NTC], 'and' [BECNT, Lns], 'although' [REB]. This unexpectedness is also indicated by

beginning the preceding clause '*even though* Herod was afraid of John...,
he was glad to listen to him' [CEV; similarly NCV, TEV], 'though...'
[AB1, BNTC]. This conjunction indicates surprise and unexpectedness
[LN].

d. ἡδέως (LN 25.129) (BAGD p. 343): 'gladly' [BAGD, BECNT, LN, Lns, WBC; ESV, KJV], 'happily' [LN], 'eagerly' [AB2]. This adverb is translated as a verb phrase: 'he was glad' [CEV], 'he liked (to listen to)' [AB1, BNTC; GW, NET, NIV, NLT, NRSV, REB, TEV], 'he enjoyed (listening to)' [NTC; NCV; similarly NASB]. This adverb relates to experiencing happiness that is based primarily upon the pleasure derived from doing something [LN]. Herod was fascinated with the authoritative preaching of this holy man [NICNT].

e. imperf. act. indic. of ἀκούω (LN 31.56): 'to listen to' [AB1, AB2, BNTC, LN, NTC; all versions except ESV, KJV], 'to hear' [BECNT, Lns, WBC; ESV, KJV], 'to listen and respond, to pay attention and respond, to accept, to heed' [LN]. This verb means to believe something and to respond to it on the basis of having heard [LN].

QUESTION—What relationship is indicated by the use of the participle ἀκούσας 'having heard'?

This is a temporal participle indicating time [AB2, Lns, NTC, WBC; ESV, GW, KJV, NASB, NET, NIV, NLT, NRSV, REB, TEV]: *when* he heard him. Herod had John brought before him at various times so that he could talk with him [Hb].

QUESTION—What caused Herod to be so perplexed?

Although Herod liked to listen to John, he puzzled about what he heard [EBC]. He would like to live the godly life described by John, yet he couldn't bring himself to leave his present life style [Lns]. He felt compelled to keep listening to John even though he was too weak to follow John's counsel [NICNT]. Herod was disturbed with indecision about what to do in regard to his guilty conscience and his passion for Herodias [EGT, Hb, ICC, Lns]. Even though Herod opposed John because of John's accusation in 6:18, he was nervous about what to do with him [BECNT].

6:21 And having-come an-opportune[a] day when on-his birthday[b] Herod gave a-banquet for-his nobles[c] and the military-commanders[d] and the important[e] (ones) of Galilee,

LEXICON—a. εὔκαιρος (LN **67.6**) (BAGD p. 321): 'opportune' [AB2, BECNT], 'suitable' [BAGD; NET], 'favorable' [LN], 'appropriate' [WBC], 'good' [LN], 'convenient' [KJV], 'strategic' [NASB]. The phrase 'an opportune day' is translated 'the opportune time' [NIV], 'a favorable time' [**LN**], 'the right day' [Lns], 'an opportunity' [BNTC, NTC; ESV, GW, NRSV]. The phrase 'having come an opportune day' is translated 'Herodias found her opportunity' [AB1; REB], 'finally Herodias got her chance' [TEV], 'Herodias got her chance' [CEV], 'Herodias's chance finally came' [NLT], 'the perfect time came for Herodias to cause John's death' [NCV]. This adjective refers to a favorable occasion for some event [LN].

b. γενέσια (LN 51.12) (BAGD p. 154): 'birthday' [AB1, AB2, BECNT, BNTC, NTC, WBC; all versions except CEV], 'birthday celebration' [BAGD, LN, Lns], 'birthday festival' [LN]. The phrase 'on his birthday Herod gave a banquet' is translated 'Herod gave a great birthday celebration' [CEV]. This noun denotes a celebration or a festivity marking the anniversary of someone's birth [LN].

c. μεγιστάν (LN **87.41**) (BAGD p. 498): 'noble' [ESV], 'nobleman' [BECNT], 'important person' [**LN**], 'very important person, great person' [LN], 'great man, magnate' [BAGD], 'courtier' [BAGD; NRSV], 'official' [CEV], 'chief official' [BNTC; REB], 'top official' [GW], 'high official' [NIV], 'high civil official' [NTC], 'court official' [NET], 'lord' [AB2; KJV, NASB], 'dignitary' [Lns], 'political magistrate' [WBC], 'most important government leader' [NCV], 'top government official' [TEV], 'high government official' [NLT], 'principal official' [AB1]. This noun denotes a person of particularly great importance and high status [LN]. It refers to the important people at Herod's court [BAGD, LN].

d. χιλίαρχος (LN 55.15) (BAGD p. 882): 'commanding officer, general' [LN], 'chiliarch' [LN, Lns], 'military tribune' [BAGD], 'military commander' [AB2, BNTC, NTC, WBC; ESV, NASB, NET, NIV], 'military chief' [TEV], 'military officer' [BECNT], 'commander' [AB1; REB], 'commander of his army' [NCV], 'army officer' [CEV, GW, NLT], 'officer' [NRSV], 'high captain' [KJV]. This noun denotes a military officer normally in command of a thousand soldiers [LN]. This compound word literally means 'the leader of a thousand soldiers', but it was used to refer to a commander of a cohort of about 600 men or just to high ranking officers in general [BAGD]. This term was used for any military leader of high rank [CGTC, NTC, Tay, TH].

e. πρῶτος (LN **87.45**) (BAGD 1.c.β. p. 726): 'important' [LN], 'prominent' [BAGD, LN], 'great, foremost' [LN]. The phrase τοῖς πρώτοις 'the important ones' is translated 'the important people' [**LN**], 'the most important people' [GW, NCV], 'the leading men' [AB1, BECNT, BNTC; ESV, NASB, NIV, REB], 'the leading citizens' [NLT, TEV], 'the leaders' [CEV, NET, NRSV], 'the prominent men' [WBC], 'the chief men' [NTC], 'the first men' [Lns], 'the magnates' [AB2], 'chief estates' [KJV]. This adjective describes especially prominent men of high rank [LN]. These guests were probably socially prominent friends who did not hold any civil or military positions [NTC].

QUESTION—What relationship is indicated by the beginning conjunction καί 'and'?

This conjunction shifts the scene from John in prison to a banquet hall [WBC]. Since 6:20 is a parenthetical explanation of why Herodias was not able to kill John the Baptist, this verse logically follows verse 19 [CGTC, NICNT].

QUESTION—In what way was this an opportune day?
This day was suitable for Herodias to carry out her plan to kill John because there was now an opportunity to make it happen [AB1, AB2, BECNT, BNTC, CGTC, EBC, EGT, ICC, Lns, My, NAC, NICNT, NTC, Sw, TH, TRT, WBC; CEV, NCV, NLT, REB, TEV].

6:22 and the daughter[a] of-him of-Herodias having-entered and having-danced, pleased[b] Herod and the (ones) reclining-at-table-with (him). The king said to-the girl,[c] "Ask- me -for[d] what ever you-desire[e] and I-will-give (it) to-you."

TEXT—Manuscripts reading τῆς θυγατρὸς αὐτοῦ Ἡρῳδιάδος 'the daughter of-him of-Herodias' are given a C rating by GNT to indicate that choosing it over a variant text was difficult. This text has good manuscript support, but it is the most difficult reading to accept since it may describe Herodias as being Herod's daughter [NETfn]. This reading is translated 'his daughter Herodias' [AB2, WBC; NET, NRSV], 'his daughter, also named Herodias' [NLT]. Or it is translated so that it speaks of his step-daughter: 'his daughter, that is, Herodias' daughter' [GW]. A variant reading is τῆς θυγατρὸς αὐτῆς τῆς Ἡρῳδιάδος 'the daughter of-her Herodias' and this is translated 'the daughter of Herodias herself' [Lns, NTC; NASB], 'the daughter of the said Herodias' [KJV]. Another variant reading is τῆς θυγατρὸς τῆς Ἡρῳδιάδος 'the daughter of-Herodias' and this is translated 'the daughter of Herodias' [CEV, NCV, NIV, TEV], 'Herodias' daughter' [BNTC; ESV], 'her daughter' [AB1; REB].

LEXICON—a. θυγάτηρ (LN 10.46) (BAGD 1. p. 364): 'daughter' [BAGD, LN; all translations]. This noun denotes an immediate female offspring [LN].
  b. aorist act. indic. of ἀρέσκω (LN 25.90) (BAGD 2.a. p. 105): 'to please' [AB2, BAGD, BNTC, LN, Lns, WBC; all versions except GW, REB], 'to delight' [AB1; GW, REB], 'to fascinate' [NTC]. This verb means to cause someone to be pleased with someone or something [LN].
  c. κοράσιον (LN 9.40) (BAGD p. 444): 'girl' [AB1, AB2, BAGD, BNTC, LN, Lns, NTC, WBC; all versions except CEV, KJV], 'damsel' [KJV], not explicit [CEV]. This noun is a diminutive derivative of κόρη 'girl', a word that does not occur in the NT. It seems to have lost the diminutive meaning and just referred to a girl close to the age of puberty. In 5:42, this noun refers to a girl about twelve years old [LN]. The context suggests that this girl was probably about twelve years old [BECNT], beyond puberty [TH], in her mid-teens [CBC, NICNT, TRT], about twenty years old [AB1, Sw].
  d. aorist act. subj. of αἰτέω (LN 33.163) (BAGD p. 26): 'to ask for' [LN, NTC; all versions except ESV, KJV], 'to ask' [AB1, AB2, BAGD, BNTC, Lns, WBC; ESV, KJV], 'to demand' [LN]. This verb means to ask for with urgency, even to the point of demanding [LN].

e. pres. act. subj. of θέλω (LN 25.1) (BAGD 2. p. 355): 'to desire' [LN], 'to want' [AB2, BAGD, LN, Lns; GW, KJV, NASB, NCV, NET, NIV], 'to wish' [BAGD, BECNT, LN, NTC, WBC; ESV, NRSV], 'to like' [BNTC; NLT, REB], 'to like to have' [TEV]. The phrase 'ask me for whatever you desire' is translated 'ask for anything' [CEV]. This verb means to desire to have or experience something [LN].

QUESTION—How was the dancing girl related to King Herod?

The choice of the Greek text to follow has much to do with determining her relationship, and even the best-supported text has alternative interpretations.

1. She was the daughter of Herodias, making her the step-daughter of Herod [AB1, BNTC, CGTC, EBC, Gnd, Hb, ICC, Lns, My, NAC, NICNT, NIGTC, NTC, PNTC, Sw, Tay, TRT; all versions except NET, NLT, NRSV].

    1.1 Since the story clearly indicates that the girl is the daughter of Herodias (6:24, 28; Matt 14:6), many translations follow texts that are different from the best attested reading [AB1, BNTC, Lns, NTC; CEV, ESV, KJV, NASB, NCV, NIV, REB, TEV]. The usual rule for making decisions about the original text is that if two texts both have substantial support, the hardest text to account for should be accepted. But here the hardest text says that the girl was the daughter of Herod and her name was Herodias, which conflicts with the context. Therefore another text must be adopted [NTC]. Most Greek manuscripts and the clear parallel account at Matt. 14:6 say that the girl was the daughter of Herodias [NIGTC]. Her name is not given in the text, but the historian Josephus has provided the name 'Salome' [NAC, NICNT, PNTC].

    1.2 Even the best-attested reading τῆς θυγατρὸς αὐτοῦ Ἡρῳδιάδος, literally 'the daughter of-him of-Herodias', is followed by some who take it to mean that the girl was the daughter of Herodias and therefore the step daughter of Herod [WBC; GW]. With the genitive form Ἡρῳδιάδος 'of Herodias', the phrase can be correctly translated 'his daughter, *that is,* Herodias' daughter' [GW]. Another interpretation takes the words 'his daughter' to mean that she was part of Herod's *extended* family, actually his step-daughter. So calling her 'Herodias' was just a mistake caused by confusing her name with her mother's name [WBC].

2. She was the natural daughter of Herod [BECNT; NET, NLT, NRSV]. The girl's name was Herodias, the same name as Herod's wife [BECNT; NET, NLT, NRSV]. This is likely the original reading because of it's attestation and the fact that it is the most likely text that would give rise to the other readings as scribes sought to correct it [NETfn].

6:23 And he-swore[a] to-her much, "What ever you-ask of-me I-will give you up-to[b] half of-my kingdom."

TEXT—Manuscripts reading ὤμοσεν αὐτῇ πολλά 'he swore to her much' are given a C rating by GNT to indicate that choosing it over a variant text was difficult. Variant readings are ὤμοσεν αὐτῇ 'he swore to her', ὤμοσεν πολλά 'he swore much', and ὤμοσεν 'he swore'. The adverb πολλά 'much' is omitted or not translated by AB1, AB2, BNTC, Lns, NTC; CEV, ESV, GW, KJV, NASB, NCV, NET, NIV, NLT, REB.

TEXT—Manuscripts reading ὅ τι ἐάν 'whatever' (which in manuscripts without word-spacing is indistinguishable from ὅτι ἐάν 'that if') are given a C rating by GNT to indicate that choosing it over a variant text was difficult. Variant readings are ὅτι ὃ ἐάν 'that whatever', and εἴ τι ἐάν 'if anything'.

LEXICON—a. aorist act. indic. of ὀμνύω (LN 33.463) (BAGD p. 566): 'to swear' [AB2, BAGD, LN, WBC; KJV, NASB, NET, NRSV, TEV], 'to swear an oath' [BNTC; GW], 'to make an oath' [LN, Lns], 'to take an oath' [BAGD], 'to say on oath' [REB], 'to vow' [AB1; ESV, NLT], 'to promise' [NCV], 'to promise with an oath' [NIV], 'to promise on oath' [NTC]. Those who follow the GNT reading ὤμοσεν αὐτῇ πολλά 'he swore to her *much*' translate it 'he solemnly swore to her' [NRSV], 'he swore a strong oath to her' [BECNT], 'he repeatedly swore to her' [WBC], 'with many vows he said to her, "I swear that..."' [TEV]. This verb means to affirm the truth of a statement by calling on a divine being to execute sanctions against that person if the statement in question is not true [LN].

b. ἕως (LN 59.21) (BAGD II.4. p. 335): 'up to' [AB2, BECNT, BNTC, LN, NTC, WBC; all versions except CEV, NRSV, TEV], 'unto' [Lns], 'as much as' [BAGD, LN; CEV], 'even as much as' [TEV], 'even to' [AB1], 'even' [NRSV]. This preposition indicates the extent of some quantity [LN]. It indicates the upper limit [BAGD].

QUESTION—Why did Herod add this vow?

The girl probably hesitated to give her request, so Herod confirmed his promise with an oath [Hb, Lns, NTC]. When he swore to do this, he was asking God to be his witness that he would carry out his oath and should punish him if he broke this oath [TRT]. This addition was not intended to limit his previous rash promise, but to show how very generous he was [Hb].

QUESTION—Why would Herod promise to give the girl whatever she asked for?

In order to impress his guests with his generosity, Herod imitated the style of Oriental monarchs, such as the king in Esther 5:6 and 7:2. Since he did not actually have a 'kingdom' to give away, everyone understood it to be an absurd exaggeration to indicate his generous mood [BECNT, Hb, NICNT, NIGTC, NTC, PNTC]. This hyperbole meant that Herod would give her whatever she asked for without considering the cost [NTC]. Perhaps he was drunk when he made this extravagant promise [NIGTC].

6:24 And having-gone-out she-said to her mother, "What should-I-ask-for?" And she-said, "The head of John the (one) baptizing."

QUESTION—What did the girl go out of?

She went out of the room [TH]. Leaving the banquet room, she rejoined her mother in the women's quarters [Hb].

QUESTION—Why did her mother tell her to ask for John's head?

That would be tangible proof that John had really been put to death [Hb].

6:25 And having-entered immediately with haste[a] to the king she-asked saying, "I-desire that at-once you-give me upon a-platter[b] the head of John the Baptist."

LEXICON—a. σπουδή (LN **68.79**) (BAGD 1. p. 763): 'haste' [BAGD, LN], 'speed' [BAGD]. The phrase 'having entered immediately with haste' is translated 'having gone in immediately with haste' [Lns], 'immediately having entered with haste' [BECNT], 'immediately entering in a hurry' [WBC], 'she came in immediately with haste' [ESV], 'she came in straightway with haste' [KJV], 'immediately she came in a hurry' [NASB], 'immediately she hurried back' [NET], 'immediately she rushed back' [NRSV], 'she rushed right back' [NTC], 'she hurried back in straight away' [BNTC], 'the girl hurried back at once' [TEV], 'the girl hurried back' [AB1; CEV, GW, NLT], 'the girl hurried straight back' [REB], 'at once the girl hurried in' [NIV], 'at once the girl went back' [NCV], 'she went in (to the king) with haste and immediately (made her request)' [AB2]. This noun denotes doing something hurriedly [LN]. Perhaps the haste was to get back before the king's mood should change [ICC].

b. πίναξ (LN **6.134**) (BAGD p. 658): 'platter' [AB1, AB2, BAGD, BECNT, LN, Lns, NTC, WBC; CEV, ESV, GW, NASB, NCV, NET, NIV, NRSV], 'tray' [NLT], 'plate' [**LN**; TEV], 'dish' [BAGD, BNTC; REB], 'charger' [KJV]. This noun denotes a relatively flat, large dish [LN]. It refers to any kind of bowl or dish on which food was served [AB1].

QUESTION—Why would the girl ask to have John's head delivered on a platter?

This implies that she was asking that John be beheaded [Hb]. The setting of the banquet suggested the use of a platter [Sw]. John's head would be clearly seen by all those present at the banquet and they would recognize her triumph in having John killed [TH]. A translation must not suggest that she wanted to eat the head [TRT].

6:26 And being very-sorry[a] the king did- not -want to-refuse[b] her because-of the oaths and the (people) reclining-at-table.

LEXICON—a. περίλυπος (LN 25.277) (BAGD p. 648): 'very sorry' [CEV, NASB], 'exceedingly sorry' [ESV, KJV], 'very sad' [AB2, BAGD, LN, WBC; NCV], 'very distressed' [BECNT], 'greatly distressed' [NIV, REB], 'deeply distressed' [LN], 'greatly disturbed' [AB1], 'deeply grieved' [BAGD, BNTC, Lns; NRSV]. The phrase 'being very sorry' is

translated 'this made the king very sad' [TEV], 'it grieved the king deeply' [NET], 'the king deeply regretted his promise' [GW], 'the king deeply regretted what he had said' [NLT]. This adjective describes someone as being very sad or deeply distressed [LN].
   b. aorist act. infin. of ἀθετέω (LN 76.24) (BAGD 1.b. p. 21): 'to refuse' [AB1, BAGD, BECNT, BNTC, WBC; GW, NASB, NIV, NLT, NRSV, REB, TEV], 'to turn down' [Lns], 'to deny' [AB2], 'to break faith with' [BAGD], 'to break (the promise)' [CEV], 'to reject' [BAGD, LN; KJV]. The phrase 'did not want to refuse her' is translated 'did not want to refuse what she asked' [NCV], 'did not want to reject her request' [NET], 'did not want to break his word to her' [ESV]. This verb means to refuse to recognize the validity of something [LN].

QUESTION—What relationship is indicated by the participial phrase 'being very sorry'?

The participle indicates concession [AB2, BECNT, BNTC, EGT, ICC, Lns, NTC; NASB, NCV, NET]: *although he was very sorry, the king did not want to refuse her.* Some show this by translating this participial phrase as a statement followed by a 'but/yet' clause [AB1, WBC; CEV, ESV, GW, KJV, NIV, NLT, NRSV, REB, TEV]: *the king was very sorry, but he did not want to refuse her.*

QUESTION—What was the king very sorry about?

The king was sorry that he had made that oath [CEV, GW, NLT]. He was sorry that he was forced to execute John contrary to his own desires [ESVfn, Hb, Lns]. This sorrow was connected with his attitude towards John that is described in verse 20 [Tay].

QUESTION—What is meant by using the plural form, ὅρκους 'oaths'?

The plural form could refer to only one oath or to multiple oaths [EGT, Hb].
   1. This is translated with the plural form, 'oaths' [AB1, AB2, BECNT, BNTC, Lns, NTC, Tay; ESV, NASB, NIV, NLT, NRSV, TEV]. It appears that Herod had repeated his oath [AB1, Lns, Tay].
   2. This is translated with the singular form, 'oath' [WBC; CEV, GW, KJV, NCV, NET, REB].

6:27 And immediately the king having-sent an-executioner^a ordered^b (him) to-bring his head. And having-left he-beheaded^c him in the prison 6:28 and he-brought his head upon a-platter and gave it to-the girl, and the girl gave it to-her mother.

LEXICON—a. σπεκουλάτωρ (LN 20.70) (BAGD p. 761): 'executioner' [BAGD, BECNT, LN, NTC, WBC; ESV, KJV, NASB, NIV, NLT], 'guard' [AB1, BNTC; CEV, GW, TEV], 'bodyguard' [AB2, Lns], 'soldier' [NCV], 'soldier of the guard' [NRSV, REB], 'courier' [BAGD]. This noun denotes one who carries out official executions on the basis of orders from military or government officials [LN]. He was Herod's bodyguard who did whatever Herod commanded him, including performing executions [CBC].

b. aorist act. indic. of ἐπιτάσσω (LN 33.325) (BAGD p. 302): 'to order' [BAGD, LN, Lns, NTC, WBC; CEV, ESV], 'to command' [AB2, BAGD, BECNT, LN; KJV], 'to give orders, to instruct, to tell' [LN], not explicit [NCV, NLT, NRSV]. This verb is translated as a noun phrase: '(sent…) with orders' [AB1, BNTC; ESV, NIV, NRSV, REB, TEV]. This verb means to give detailed instructions as to what must be done [LN].

c. aorist act. indic. of ἀποκεφαλίζω (LN 20.80) (BAGD p. 93): 'to behead' [AB1, AB2, BAGD, BECNT, BNTC, LN, Lns, NTC, WBC; ESV, KJV, NASB, NET, NIV, NLT, NRSV, REB], 'to cut the head off' [LN; CEV, GW, NCV, TEV]. This verb means to kill by beheading, and it is normally an act of capital punishment [LN].

QUESTION—What is the temporal sequence of sending the executioner and commanding him to bring John's head?

Some translations keep the literal sequence of the Greek text: he *sent* an executioner *and ordered* him to bring his head [AB2, NICNT, WBC; GW, KJV, NASB]. However, Herod would have given the order to the executioner before sending him off to behead John and the literal wording could be confusing in other languages [TH]. The wording of most translations makes the temporal sequence clear: he *sent for* an executioner *and ordered* him to bring his head [BECNT], he *sent* an executioner *with orders to* bring his head [AB1, BNTC, LN (20.17); ESV, NIV, NRSV, REB, TEV], he *sent* an executioner to bring his head [NCV, NET, NLT], he *ordered* an executioner to bring his head [NTC; similarly CEV].

6:29 And having heard, his disciples came and carried-away his corpse[a] and placed it in a-tomb.[b]

LEXICON—a. πτῶμα (LN **8.7**) (BAGD p. 728): 'corpse' [LN, Lns, WBC; KJV], 'body' [AB1, AB2, BECNT, BNTC, NTC; all versions except KJV], 'dead body' [**LN**]. This noun denotes a dead body of a human being or an animal [LN]. In this case, the corpse was the headless body of John the Baptist [Hb].

b. μνημεῖον (LN 7.75) (BAGD 2. p. 524): 'tomb' [AB1, AB2, BAGD, BECNT, BNTC, LN, Lns, NTC, WBC; all versions except TEV], 'grave' [BAGD, LN]. The phrase 'placed it in a tomb' is translated 'buried it' [TEV]. This noun denotes a construction in which to bury the dead [LN]. This was probably one of the rock tombs in Samaria [Sw, Tay]. This word occurs at 5:2; 6:29; 15:46; 16:2, 3, 5, 8.

QUESTION—What relationship is indicated by the use of the participle 'having heard'?

This is a circumstantial participle indicating the time when the disciples came [AB1, BECNT, NTC, WBC; all versions]: *when* they heard of it, his disciples came.

QUESTION—What had the disciples heard?

Some translations make explicit what the disciples had heard: 'heard this' [NCV, NET, NIV], 'heard about this' [GW, NASB, TEV], 'heard of/about it' [AB1, AB2, BECNT, NTC; ESV, KJV, NRSV], 'heard what had happened' [NLT], 'heard the news' [REB], 'learned that he had been killed' [CEV].

QUESTION—Whose disciples came and carried away the corpse?
Although the phrase 'his disciples' usually refers to the disciples of Jesus, here it refers to John's disciples [TH]. Some translations identify them as *John's* disciples [BECNT, NTC, WBC; CEV, GW, NCV, NET, NIV, NLT, REB, TEV]. They probably were located close to the king's fortress at the time [Hb]. It is assumed that John's disciples first went to Herod and asked for his permission to take away John's body [NICNT, TRT].

DISCOURSE UNIT—6:30–8:26 [REB]. The topic is the miracles of feeding and their significance.

DISCOURSE UNIT—6:30–7:23 [Hb]. The topic is the second withdrawal and return.

DISCOURSE UNIT—6:30–44 [CBC, EBC, Hb; CEV, ESV, GW, NCV, NET, NIV, NLT, NRSV, TEV]. The topic is the feeding of the five thousand [EBC, Hb; NET, NRSV], Jesus feeding five thousand [CBC; CEV, ESV, GW, NIV, NLT, TEV], more than five thousand fed [NCV].

DISCOURSE UNIT—6:30–34 [NICNT]. The topic is the provision of rest in the wilderness.

6:30 **And the apostles[a] gathered[b] to Jesus and reported[c] to him all (the things) which they-did and which they-taught.**

LEXICON—a. ἀπόστολος (LN 53.74) (BAGD 3. p. 99): 'apostle' [BAGD, LN; all translations]. This noun denotes someone who fulfills the role of being a special messenger [LN]. It designates a group of highly honored believers who had a special function [BAGD]. This word occurs at 3:14; 6:30.

b. pres. pass. indic. of συνάγω (LN 15.125) (BAGD 2. p. 782): 'to gather together' [BAGD, LN]. The phrase συνάγονται πρὸς τὸν Ἰησοῦν 'gathered to Jesus' is translated 'gathered themselves together unto Jesus' [KJV], 'gathered together with Jesus' [NASB], 'gathered around Jesus' [BECNT, NTC, WBC; GW, NCV, NET, NIV, NRSV], 'congregated before Jesus' [AB2]. 'rejoined Jesus' [REB], 'returned to Jesus' [AB1, BNTC; CEV, ESV, NLT], 'returned and met with Jesus' [TEV]. This verb means to cause to come together [LN]. This passive has a reflexive sense of 'to gather, to gather together' [BAGD].

c. aorist act. indic. of ἀπαγγέλλω (LN 33.198) (BAGD 1. p. 79): 'to report' [AB1, BAGD, BECNT, BNTC, Lns, NTC, WBC; GW, NASB, NIV, REB], 'to inform' [LN], 'to tell' [AB2, BAGD, LN; CEV, ESV, KJV, NCV, NET, NLT, NRSV, TEV]. This verb means to announce or inform [LN].

MARK 6:30 317

QUESTION—What is the setting of this section?
After being sent by Jesus on a mission to the Galilean villages (6:7–13), the apostles returned to report how they have fulfilled that mission [NICNT]. It is likely that Jesus had set a time and place for their return [Lns].

QUESTION—What is meant by the designation οἱ ἀπόστολοι 'the apostles'?
This term is related to the verb ἀποστέλλειν 'to send' in 6:7 where it says 'Jesus began to send them off two by two', so the designation 'the apostles' refers to their role as 'the sent ones' [Tay, WBC]. They were authorized agents who represented Jesus [BNTC]. When these men reported to Jesus, the word 'apostle' only described their function as being commissioned to work in association with Jesus himself [AB1], and all translations of this verse use the lower case in reference to 'the apostles'. Since these men were returning from doing their apostolic work, it was appropriate for Mark to call them apostles [EBC, ICC]. In the broader context of the early Christian church, the word ἀπόστολος 'apostle' became a technical term for 'the *Apostles*' to denote an official, authorized representative or agent of Jesus or of a local group [WBC]. It is possible that Mark used the word in the technical sense it had by the time he was writing [CGTC], but Mark may have used the term in order to distinguish them from the disciples of John the Baptist mentioned in 6:29 [BECNT, Gnd, NETfn].

QUESTION—What did the apostles do and teach?
Their actions included the exorcisms and healings mentioned in 6:12 [BECNT, WBC]. Their teaching would have been preaching about the kingdom [Lns], and the need for repentance (6:7, 12–13) [BECNT].

DISCOURSE UNIT—6:31–56 [NIGTC]. The topic is the sequence of miracles around the lake: Who is Jesus?

6:31 And he-says to-them, "You yourselves come privately[a] to an-uninhabited[b] place and rest[c] a-little." Because the (ones) coming and the (ones) going were many, and they-did- not -have-opportunity[d] to-eat. **6:32** And they-departed in the boat to a-lonely place privately.

LEXICON—a. κατ᾽ ἰδίαν (LN 28.67): The phrase κατ᾽ ἰδίαν 'according to that which is private' is an idiom pertaining to what occurs in a private context or setting, and it has the sense of not being made known publicly [LN]. See translations of this phrase in the following lexical item.
  b. ἔρημος (LN 1.86): 'lonely place, desert, wilderness' [LN]. The phrase κατ᾽ ἰδίαν ἔρημον τόπον 'privately to an uninhabited place' is translated 'privately to an isolated/deserted place' [AB2; NET], 'in private to a lonely place' [Lns], 'by yourselves, to some remote place' [REB], 'by yourselves to a quiet place' [NIV], 'by yourselves to an uninhabited/ desolate/lonely/secluded place' [NTC, WBC; ESV, NASB, NCV; similarly AB1], 'apart into a desert place' [KJV], 'to a deserted place all by yourselves' [NRSV], 'to a lonely place by yourselves' [BNTC], 'alone by yourselves to a deserted place (with me)' [BECNT], 'a place where we can be alone' [CEV, GW], '(let's go off) by ourselves to a quiet place'

[NLT], '(let's go off) by ourselves to some place where we will be alone' [TEV]. This adjective describes a mostly uninhabited region, usually having little vegetation. In the NT, the word ἔρημος focuses primarily upon the lack of population [LN]. This adjective occurs at 1:35, 45; 6:31, 32, 35.

    c. aorist mid. impera. of ἀναπαύομαι, ἀναπαύω (LN **23.80**) (BAGD 2. p. 59): 'to rest' [BAGD, LN]. The phrase ἀναπαύσασθε λίγον 'rest a little' [Lns; REB] is also translated 'rest awhile' [**LN**, Lns, NTC; ESV, GW, KJV, NASB, NET, NLT, NRSV, TEV], 'rest for a while' [BNTC, WBC], 'rest for a little while' [BECNT], 'rest up a little' [AB2], 'get some rest' [CEV, NIV]. This verb means to become physically refreshed after ceasing one's activity or work [LN]. The aorist tense indicates that the rest would be just a short one [Hb].

    d. imperf. act. indic. of εὐκαιρέω (LN **67.4**) (BAGD p. 321): 'to have opportunity' [BAGD, BNTC], 'to have an opportunity' [BECNT, WBC], 'to have time' [BAGD, **LN**; NASB, NCV, NET, NLT, REB, TEV], 'to have an appropriate time for, to have an occasion to' [LN], 'to have a chance' [LN, NTC; CEV, GW, NIV], 'to have leisure' [Lns; ESV, KJV, NRSV]. This verb means to experience an appropriate occasion for some activity [LN].

QUESTION—Who didn't have time to eat?

The third person verb '*they* did not have opportunity to eat' refers to the apostles [NICNT, WBC], and also to Jesus [TH; CEV]. The constant departures and arrivals left no opportunity for them to take time to eat [Sw].

QUESTION—What is designated by the article in the phrase τῷ πλοίῳ '*the* boat'?

The boat refers to the same boat that they had used before in 5:1–2 [Hb, Lns]. It could refer to the same boat mentioned in 3:9, 4:1, and 5:2, in which case the article would not be designating any particular boat [NTC], and some translate it simply as 'a boat' [AB2, NTC; CEV, GW, NCV, NET, NIV, TEV]. Probably it just means that they went away 'by boat', in agreement with the parallel passage ἐν πλοίῳ 'by boat' in Matt. 14:13 [AB1, NTC; KJV, NLT, REB].

DISCOURSE UNIT—6:33–44 [NASB]. The topic is the feeding of the five thousand.

6:33 **And many (people) saw them going and knew,[a] and on-foot from all of-the towns they-ran-together there and arrived-before them.**

    TEXT—Manuscripts reading εἶδον αὐτοὺς ὑπάγοντας καὶ ἐπέγνωσαν πολλοί 'many saw them going and knew' are followed by GNT, which does not mention any variant reading. A variant reading is εἶδον αὐτοὺς ὑπάγοντας οἱ ὄχλοι, καί ἐπέγνωσαν αὐτοὺς πολλοί 'the crowds saw them going and many knew him' and it is followed by KJV.

    TEXT—Manuscripts reading συνέδραμον ἐκεῖ καὶ προῆλθον αὐτούς 'they ran together there and arrived before them' are given a B rating by GNT to indicate it was regarded to be almost certain. A variant reading is συνέδραμον ἐκεῖ καὶ προῆλθον αὐτοὺς καὶ συνῆλθον πρὸς αὐτόν 'they ran together there and arrived before them and came together to him' and it is followed by KJV.

LEXICON—a. aorist act indic. of ἐπιγινώσκω (LN 27.61, 28.2) (BAGD 2.b. p. 291): 'to know' [BAGD, LN (28.2)], 'to recognize' [BAGD, LN (27.61)]. The aorist tense ἐπέγνωσαν '(they) knew' is translated 'knew him' [KJV], 'recognized them' [AB2, BECNT, NTC, WBC; all versions except CEV, KJV, TEV], 'knew at once who they were' [TEV], 'figured out where they were going' [CEV], 'found out about it' [AB2], 'understood' [Lns]. This verb means to identify newly acquired information with what had been previously learned or known [LN (27.61)], or to possess more or less definite information about something [LN (28.2)].

QUESTION—What is the grammatical function of the adjectival noun πολλοί 'many' that is last in the Greek sentence, 'And they saw them going and they knew *many*'?

1. 'Many' is the subject of both verbs [AB1, BECNT, BNTC, HNTC, Lns, My, NTC, TRT, WBC; all versions except KJV, NASB]: *many saw them going and they knew*.
2. 'Many' is the subject of only ἐπέγνωσαν 'knew' [AB2, CGTC, Hb, ICC, Tay; KJV, NASB]: *they (the people) saw them going and many (of them) knew*. The first verb εἶδον 'saw' is an impersonal verb meaning '*they saw*' [Hb].

QUESTION—What was known by the people who saw them in the boat?

1. They knew who the occupants of the boat were [BECNT, BNTC, Gnd, Hb, ICC, NICNT, NTC, Sw, Tay, TH; all versions except CEV]: *they recognized who they were*. Seeing that it was Jesus and his disciples in the boat, they realized what was taking place [Hb]. The boat went along the shore, all the time in sight of the crowds along the shore [BECNT, NICNT, NLTfn; WBC].
2. They knew where the boat was going to land by noting the course the boat was steering [EGT, Lns, My, NIGTC, Sw; CEV].

QUESTION—How could so many people get to the landing place ahead of the boat?

1. The people arrived ahead of the boat [BECNT, BNTC, EBC, Gnd, Hb, NAC, NIVfn, PNTC, Sw, TH, TRT, WBC]. If there was hardly any wind, the people could get there before the sail boat did [Sw]. Probably there were even strong headwinds [EBC, Hb, NIVfn] that slowed the sailing boat enough for people to walk around the lake and arrive at the landing place ahead of it [EBC, Sw]. The younger and stronger people outran the crowd that had started out and the phrase 'from all of the towns they ran together' pictures people from towns along the shore joining those runners so that there was a large crowd waiting for Jesus when he got out of the

boat [EGT, Gnd, Hb]. In order for the crowd to keep up with the boat, the boat must have crossed only one of the corners of the lake [NAC].
2. It was not possible for the crowd to outrun the boat and be waiting on the shore when Jesus arrived [Lns, NTC]. The straight distance by boat was about four miles while going along the shore would have been about ten miles [NTC]. Jesus arrived first and spent at least a few hours with his disciples in private on a hillside retreat [Lns]. Jesus had left to go 'to a lonely place and rest a little' (6:32) [NTC], so it wasn't until he left that place of seclusion that he saw the crowd that had gathered along the shore of the lake [Lns, NTC].

6:34 And having-got-out[a] he-saw a-large crowd and he-had-compassion[b] on them, because they-were like sheep not having a-shepherd, and he-began to-teach them many-things/much.

LEXICON—a. aorist act. participle of ἐξέρχομαι (LN 15.40): 'to go out of' [LN]. The participle ἐξελθών 'having got out' is translated 'when he came out' [KJV], 'when he/Jesus got out of the boat' [AB2, BECNT, WBC; CEV, GW, TEV], 'as he stepped from the boat' [NLT], 'when Jesus landed' [NIV; similarly BNTC], 'when he/Jesus went/came ashore' [AB1; ESV, NASB, REB], 'as he/Jesus came/went ashore' [NET, NRSV], 'when he arrived' [NCV]. Instead of getting out of the boat, some refer to coming out of a place of seclusion: 'having come out' [Lns, NTC]. This verb means to move out of an enclosed or well-defined two or three-dimensional area [LN].

b. aorist pass. (deponent = act.) indic. of σπλαγχνίζομαι (LN 25.49) (BAGD p. 762): 'to have/feel compassion for/on' [BECNT, LN, Lns, WBC; ESV, NASB, NET, NIV, NLT, NRSV], 'to be moved with compassion toward' [KJV], 'to have great affection for' [LN], 'to feel sorry for' [CEV, GW, NCV], 'to have pity for, to feel sympathy for' [BAGD], 'to take pity on' [AB2], 'to be full of pity for' [BNTC], 'to be moved with pity' [AB1], 'his heart was filled with pity for' [TEV], 'his heart went out to' [NTC; REB]. This verb means to experience great affection and compassion for someone [LN]. This word occurs at 1:41; 6:34; 8:2; 9:22.

QUESTION—In what way were the people like sheep without a shepherd?
This is a metaphor [NIGTC]. It pictures the crowd of people as being like a flock of untended sheep which lacked a shepherd to care for them [NIGTC, TH]. Sheep without a shepherd will stray helplessly and then perish [Lns]. When the people eagerly gathered to listen to Jesus' teaching, it was apparent that they were eager to follow someone who could offer them something their religious leaders did not supply [Sw]. These people lacked spiritual guidance [ICC] since their religious leaders were not meeting their needs [Hb, NTC]. Teaching this crowd was the way Jesus met their need for a shepherd [NLTfn].

QUESTION—What did Jesus teach the crowd when he taught them πολλά 'many things/much'?
1. The word πολλά is adjectival and means 'many' [AB1, AB2, BECNT, BNTC, LN, Lns, NTC, PNTC, WBC; all versions except GW]: Jesus taught them *many things*. Jesus expressed his compassion for the people by teaching them many things [NETfn, PNTC]. In Luke 9:11, it says that Jesus taught the crowds about the kingdom of God [Lns].
2. The word πολλά is adverbial and means 'much, at length' [CGTC, Hb, NICNT, Tay; GW; probably Gnd]: Jesus taught them *at length*. It is not that Jesus taught them many different things, but that he persistently taught the one message of the kingdom of God [CGTC]. He 'spent a lot of time teaching them' [GW]. His teaching continued until the day was far advanced [Hb].

DISCOURSE UNIT—6:35–44 [NICNT]. The topic is the provision of bread in the wilderness.

6:35 **And already it-was-becoming a-late hour, (and) approaching him his disciples were-saying, "Uninhabited[a] is the place and already (it is) a-late[b] hour. 6:36 Send- them -away,[c] in-order-that having-gone to the surrounding[d] farms and villages they-may-buy for-themselves what they-may-eat."**
TEXT—At the end of 6:36, manuscripts reading τί φάγωσιν 'what they may eat' are followed by GNT, which does not mention any variant reading. A variant reading is ἄρτους· τί γὰρ φάγωσιν οὐκ ἔχουσιν 'bread; for they do not have anything to eat' and it is followed by KJV.
LEXICON—a. ἔρημος (LN 1.86) (BAGD 1.a. p. 309): 'uninhabited' [WBC], 'desolate' [BAGD, ESV, NASB], 'lonely' [AB1, BNTC, LN, NTC; TEV], 'empty' [BAGD], 'deserted' [AB2, BECNT; NRSV], 'isolated' [NET], 'remote' [NIV, NLT, REB], 'desert' [Lns; KJV], 'like a desert' [CEV]. The phrase 'uninhabited is the place' is translated 'no one lives around here' [GW], 'no one lives in this place' [NCV]. This adjective describes a place as being a largely uninhabited region [LN]. This adjective occurs at 1:35, 45; 6:31, 32, 35.
b. πολύς (LN **67.77**) (BAGD I.2.b.α. p. 688): 'much, many things' [BAGD]. The phrase 'a late hour' is an idiom ὥρα πολλή 'much hour' and it is translated 'much time (has gone)' [Lns], 'the hour is late' [AB2, BECNT, WBC; ESV], 'the hour is now very late' [NRSV], 'it is very late' [**LN**; NCV, NET, NIV, REB, TEV], 'it is quite late' [NASB], 'it is late' [AB1, BNTC; CEV, GW], 'it is getting late' [NLT], 'the time is far passed' [KJV], 'the day is drawing to a close' [NTC]. This idiom refers to a point of time relatively late in view of the circumstances and could refer to the late afternoon or evening [LN].
c. aorist act. impera. of ἀπολύω (LN 15.43) (BAGD 2.b. p. 96): 'to send away' [AB1, AB2, BAGD, BECNT, BNTC, WBC; all versions except CEV, GW, REB], 'to send to' [GW], 'to send off' [REB], 'to dismiss' [BAGD, LN], 'to release' [Lns], 'to let (them) go away' [LN], 'to let (the

crowds) leave' [CEV]. This verb means to cause a person or persons to leave a particular location [LN]. This has the idea of urging the people to go and provide for themselves [TH]. In relation to crowds, this word occurs at 6:36, 45; 8:3, 9.
- d. κύκλῳ (LN 83.19) (BAGD 1.b. p. 457): 'around' [BAGD, LN], 'around here' [NCV], 'surrounding' [BECNT, WBC; ESV, NASB, NET, NIV, NRSV], 'round about' [Lns, NTC; KJV, REB], 'in a circle' [LN], 'nearby' [AB1, BNTC], 'neighboring' [AB2, BAGD; NLT, TEV], 'closest' [GW], 'near here' [CEV]. This adjective refers to a position completely encircling an area or object [LN].

QUESTION—What time of day was 'a very late hour'?

Here it must refer to the late afternoon [AB1, BECNT, NCBC, NIGTC, NTC, Tay, TH, WBC] since there was still time to find the village market places open [TH]. There were a number of things that would be done before dark [BECNT]. It was mid-to-late afternoon [Gnd], about 3 p.m. [TRT]. After the people were fed and dismissed, it speaks of the evening 'having come' in verse 47 [BECNT, WBC].

QUESTION—What kind of a place was this uninhabited place?

Since the disciples suggested that the people be sent to the surrounding farms and villages, this uninhabited place must have been located somewhere in the fields and slopes along the northwest corner of the Lake of Galilee [BECNT]. Later, the people will be reclining to eat on the green grass that grew there [Gnd, NICNT].

6:37 But answering he said to-them, "You- yourselves -give them (something) to-eat." And they-say to-him, "Having-gone should-we-buy loaves-of-bread[a] for-two-hundred denarii[b] and give (it) to-them to-eat?"

LEXICON—a. ἄρτος (LN 5.8) (BAGD 1.a. p. 110): 'loaf of bread' [BAGD, LN], 'bread' [AB2, BAGD, BECNT, BNTC, Lns, NTC, WBC; ESV, GW, KJV, NASB, NCV, NET, NIV, NRSV, TEV], 'food' [AB1; NLT, REB], 'something to eat' [CEV]. This noun denotes a relatively small round loaf of bread similar to a roll or bun [LN]. Probably this refers to barley loaves [EBC, Hb, NCBC, TH]. A loaf of bread was round and flat [BNTC, Lns, NAC, NCBC, TRT], perhaps eight inches across and an inch thick [BNTC].
- b. δηνάριον (LN 6.75) (BAGD p. 179): 'denarius' [BAGD, LN]. The phrase 'two hundred denarii' [AB1, AB2, BECNT, BNTC, Lns, NTC, WBC; ESV, NASB, NRSV, REB] is also translated 'two hundred silver coins' [NET, TEV], 'two hundred pennyworth' [KJV], 'eight months of a man's wages' [NIV], 'almost/about a year's wages' [CEV, GW; similarly NCV, NLT]. This noun denotes a Roman silver coin having a value equivalent to a day's wage for a common laborer [BAGD, LN].

QUESTION—What is implied by this question?

This is a rhetorical question that indicates the disciples thought Jesus was demanding something impossible to accomplish [EBC, Hb, NICNT, TH,

WBC]. It expresses their astonishment [NICNT, Tay] and frustrated amazement [Hb]. They thought this command was foolish [TH], absurd [AB2], and unreasonable [PNTC]. This question is translated as a statement: 'We would all have to work a month to earn enough money to buy that much bread!' [NCV], 'With what? We'd have to work for months to earn enough money to buy food for all these people!' [NLT].

QUESTION—Why is the price of two hundred denarii mentioned?

It was a sum impossible for the disciples to come up with [Hb]. This large amount of money was what it would take a common workman about eight months to earn [Hb, NICNT; NIV], or about a year [CEV, GW, NCV, NLT].

6:38 And he says to-them, "How-many loaves-of-bread do-you-have? Go see.ᵃ" And having-found-outᵇ they say, "Five, and two fish."

LEXICON—a. aorist act. impera. of ὁράω, εἶδον (LN 27.5) (BAGD 1.e. p. 221): 'to see' [AB1, AB2, BAGD, BECNT, BNTC, Lns, NTC, WBC; all versions except NASB, NLT], 'to look' [NASB], 'to find out' [LN; NLT]. This verb means to acquire information [LN].

b. aorist act. participle of γινώσκω (LN **27.2**) (BAGD 1.a. p. 160): 'to find out' [AB1, AB2, BECNT, BNTC, **LN**; all versions except KJV, NLT], 'to learn' [LN], 'to know' [BAGD, Lns, NTC, WBC; KJV], 'to ascertain, to come to know' [BAGD], not explicit [NLT]. This verb means to acquire information by whatever means available [LN]. 'Having found out' indicates they had gone about through the crowd to find someone who still had some food left [Hb, Lns]. John 6:8–9 gives the information that Andrew found a young boy who had five barley loaves and two fish [NTC]. Probably this boy had brought bread and fish to sell and still had this much left [Lns].

QUESTION—What were the loaves of bread like?

The loaves of bread were small flat loaves made from barley (John 6:9) and one could easily eat several of them at a meal [EBC]. Five loaves were enough to feed two people [TRT].

QUESTION—What were the fish like?

The fish were cooked. They could have been dried, smoked, salted, or pickled in order to preserve them [TRT]. The fish had been prepared to serve as a relish for bread, and were probably either cooked, pickled, or smoked [HNTC, NCBC, TH]. They were either dried or roasted [Lns]. They probably were salted and dried [AB2].

6:39 And he-ordered them to-have- everyone -reclineᵃ groups (by) groupsᵇ on the green grass. 6:40 And they reclinedᶜ groups (by) groupsᵈ in hundreds and in fifties.

LEXICON—a. aorist act. infin. of ἀνακλίνω (LN 17.24) (BAGD 1.b. p. 56): 'to recline' [AB2, BAGD, LN, Lns], 'to sit down' [AB1, BECNT, BNTC, LN, NTC, WBC; all versions]. This verb means to cause someone to assume a reclining or sitting position in order to eat [LN]. This was a customary position for eating [BECNT, Hb, WBC].

b. συμπόσιον (LN **11.5**) (BAGD p. 780): 'group' [BAGD, LN]. The phrase συμπόσια συμπόσια 'groups by groups' is translated 'eating-group by eating-group' [AB2], 'in groups' [BNTC, **LN**; ESV, GW, NCV, NET, NIV, NLT, NRSV, REB], 'by groups' [BNTC; NASB; similarly TEV], 'company by company' [Lns, NTC], 'in companies' [BECNT, WBC], 'by companies' [KJV], not explicit [AB1; CEV]. This noun denotes a group of persons engaged in eating together. The repetition 'group by group' refers to a series of groups distributed over the area [LN].

c. aorist act. indic. of ἀναπίπτω (LN 7.23) (BAGD 1. p. 59): 'to recline, to eat, to be at table, to eat, to dine, to sit down to eat' [LN]. See translations of this verb in the following lexical item. This verb means to be in a reclining position as one eats [LN]. Reclining was the usual position for meals [Hb, WBC], and this word is especially appropriate when eating outside on the grass where there were no tables [Hb]. This word occurs at 6:40; 8:6.

d. πρασιά (LN 11.6) (BAGD p. 698): 'group' [BAGD, LN]. The phrase συμπόσια συμπόσια 'groups by groups' is translated 'group by group' [WBC], 'cluster by cluster' [AB2], 'by groups' [WBC], 'in groups' [BECNT; ESV, GW, NASB, NCV, NET, NIV, NLT, NRSV], 'in rows' [REB, TEV], 'in ranks' [KJV], 'rank by rank' [Lns], 'in companies' [BNTC], 'in groups (of a hundred) and groups (of fifty)' [LN; CEV]. This noun is a figurative extension of meaning of πρασιά 'garden plot' and denotes a group of persons arranged in an orderly fashion. This noun speaks of 'groups' as does the noun συμπόσιον in verse 39, but the words συμπόσια συμπόσια 'groups by groups' includes the idea of an orderly arrangement of the groups. It gives a picture of the people sitting down in orderly groups of a hundred and groups of fifty, or sitting down in rows by groups of a hundred and groups of fifty [LN].

QUESTION—Who are αὐτοῖς 'them' to whom Jesus gave this command?
1. Jesus commanded his disciples to have the people sit in groups [AB2, BECNT, Gnd, Hb, LN (11.5), Lns, NIGTC, Sw, TRT; CEV, KJV, NCV, NIV, NLT, NRSV, REB, TEV]. 'He told the disciples to have the people sit down in groups' [NLT],
2. Jesus commanded the crowd to sit down [BNTC, NTC, TH, WBC; ESV, GW, NASB, NET]. 'He commanded them all to sit down in/by groups' [BNTC; ESV, NASB]

QUESTION—What was the purpose of this seating arrangement?
Seating the crowd in groups secured order and made it easier to serve so many people [CGTC, EBC, ICC, NTC, PNTC, Sw]. If the huge crowd had remained standing, they would have crowded around those who were distributing the food, making it impossible to distribute the food in an orderly manner [Hb, Sw]. This arrangement provided lanes between groups so that the disciples could move about to serve the food [CBC, Lns].

QUESTION—What is the significance of mentioning that the grass was green? Since the grass was green, we know that this took place in the springtime [AB2, BECNT, EBC, Hb, Lns, NIGTC, Sw, TH], near the Passover season (John 6:4) [Lns].

6:41 **And having-taken**[a] **the five loaves-of-bread and the two fish, having looked-up to heaven**[b] **he-blessed**[c] **and broke**[d] **the loaves-of-bread**

LEXICON—a. aorist act. participle of λαμβάνω (LN 18.1): 'to take hold of, to grasp' [LN], 'to take' [AB1, AB2, BNTC, Lns, NTC, WBC; all versions]. This verb means to take hold of something [LN]. The bread and fish were probably brought to Jesus in a basket that he held in his hands as he prayed [Sw].

b. οὐρανός (LN 1.11) (BAGD 2.a. p. 594): 'heaven' [LN]. The phrase ἀναβλέψας εἰς τὸν οὐρανὸν 'having looked up to heaven' [BECNT; similarly Lns, NTC] is also translated 'he looked up to/toward heaven' [AB1, BNTC, WBC; CEV, ESV, GW, KJV, NLT, NRSV, REB, TEV; similarly AB2; NASB, NCV, NET, NIV]. This noun denotes the supernatural dwelling place of God and of other heavenly beings. The noun contains a component denoting that which is 'above' or 'in the sky', but the element of 'abode' is evidently more significant than its location above the earth [LN]. Looking up to heaven was a common posture when praying [AB1, CGTC, Hb, Lns, NTC, Sw, Tay, TH]. It signaled that God was the object of praise [Gnd], and that one's thoughts were above the present world to where God dwelled in heaven [Hb].

c. aorist act. indic. of εὐλογέω (LN 33.356) (BAGD 1, or 2.b. p. 322): 'to give thanks' [BAGD (1.)], 'to praise, to speak well of' [BAGD (1.), LN], 'to consecrate' [BAGD (2.b.)]. The verb εὐλόγησεν 'he blessed' [BECNT, WBC; KJV, NRSV] is also translated 'he said the/a blessing' [AB2, Lns; ESV, REB], 'he blessed God' [BNTC], 'he gave thanks' [AB1, NTC; NET, NIV], 'he gave thanks to God' [TEV], 'he thanked God for the food' [NCV], 'he blessed the food' [CEV, GW, NASB], 'he blessed them' [NLT]. This verb means to praise or speak well of someone in favorable terms [LN]. It means to give thanks and praise [BAGD (1.)], or to call down God's gracious power to bless things in the sense of consecrating them [BAGD (2.b.)]. This word occurs at 6:41; 8:7; 11:9, 10; 14:22.

d. aorist act. indic. of κατακλάω (LN **19.38**) (BAGD p. 411): 'to break into pieces' [BAGD, **LN**, Lns; NLT], 'to break' [AB1, BECNT, BNTC, NTC, WBC; CEV, ESV, KJV, NASB, NET, NRSV, REB, TEV], 'to break apart' [GW], 'to divide' [NCV]. This verb means to break into pieces [LN, TH]. Jesus prepared the flat barley loaves for distribution by breaking each into several pieces [Hb]. He broke off pieces of edible size [NTC] by snapping the loaves apart into pieces [Gnd].

QUESTION—What is the object of the verb εὐλόγησεν 'blessed' and what does 'blessed' mean?

The words 'having looked up to heaven' suggest that this is the traditional Jewish grace given before meals when a person blesses (praises) God. But the sequence 'he blesses and broke the bread' suggests that Jesus blessed the loaves before he broke them. It is not certain which meaning is intended here [AB2]. The verb εὐλογέω is a compound word consisting of the morphemes εὐ- 'well' and λογέω 'to speak'. It is easy to understand that Jesus would 'speak well' of God by 'praising' and 'extolling' him. In connection with receiving food from God's providential care, it means 'to give thanks' to God or 'to praise' God for providing the food [BAGD (1.)]. The verb is used in other contexts of 'blessing' people by calling down God's gracious power on them [BAGD (2.a.)]. But this verb can also refer to blessing things by consecrating them (to make or declare something sacred by dedicating them to a religious or divine purpose) [BAGD (2.b.)]. When God is the subject of the verb, it means that God provides someone with benefits [BAGD (3)].

1. Jesus 'blessed' God [BNTC, CGTC, EBC, Gnd, NICNT, NIGTC, PNTC, Sw, Tay, WBC] in the sense that he praised God by thanking him [AB1, Hb, HNTC, Lns, NAC, NTC, TH, TRT; NCV, NET, NIV, TEV]: *he thanked God and then broke the bread.* Every prayer before a Jewish meal began with this blessing of the name of God: 'Praise unto thee, O Lord our God, King of the world, who makes bread to come forth from the earth' [NICNT, Sw; similarly CGTC, Tay, WBC]. He praised God for providing the fish and bread [Gnd]. Here the verb expresses one's gratitude to God. In the parallel passage at John 6:11, John used the verb εὐχαριστήσας 'having given thanks' [Hb, NTC]. The verbs 'blessed' and 'gave thanks' were used as virtual synonyms, so the 'blessing' in Mark is a form of giving thanks [Hb]. There is a tendency to interpret any blessing of an object to mean that the object is being consecrated or sanctified in order to cause it to be holy. To avoid an incorrect interpretation that Jesus was using a magical ritual to increase the food, it is best to translate this, 'he spoke to God on behalf of the food' or more explicitly, 'he gave thanks to God for the food' [TH].
2. Jesus blessed the food [NLTfn; CEV, GW, NASB, NLT]: *he blessed the bread and broke it.*

and he-was-giving (it) to-his disciples in-order-that they-might-distribute[a] (it) to-them, and the two fish he-divided[b] among (them) all.

TEXT—Manuscripts reading τοῖς μαθηταῖς αὐτοῦ 'to his disciples' are given a C rating by GNT to indicate that choosing it over a variant text was difficult. A variant reading is τοῖς μαθηταῖς 'to the disciples' and it is followed by AB1, BECNT, WBC; ESV, GW, NASB, NLT, NRSV, REB.

LEXICON—a. pres. act. subj. of παρατίθημι (LN 57.116) (BAGD 1.a. p. 622): 'to give food to, to provide with food' [LN], 'to set before' [BAGD]. The clause 'in order that they might distribute it to them' is translated 'so that they might distribute (them) to them (the people)' [BECNT], 'so they could distribute it to the people' [NLT], 'in order that they might distribute them' [AB2], 'to distribute to the people' [TEV], 'to distribute' [AB1; REB], 'to give to the people' [CEV, GW, NCV], 'to set before the people/them' [BNTC, NTC; ESV, KJV, NASB, NIV, NRSV], 'in order that they might set before them' [Lns], 'to serve the people' [NET; similarly WBC]. This verb means to give or to provide something, and it usually refers to placing food in front of a person [LN]. This word occurs at 6:41; 8:6, 7.

b. aorist act. indic. of μερίζω (LN **57.89**) (BAGD 2.a. p. 504): 'to distribute something to some people' [BAGD], 'to divide among, to distribute, to give to each in turn' [LN (57.89)]. The phrase τοὺς δύο ἰχθύαν ἐμέρισεν πᾶσιν 'he divided the two fish among them all' [BNTC, **LN**; NCV, NET, NIV, NRSV, REB, TEV; similarly AB2, NTC], 'the two fish he divided to all' [Lns], 'he divided up the two fish among them all' [NASB], 'he divided the two fish among them all' [ESV; similarly KJV], 'he divided the fishes among them' [AB1], 'he divided the two fish for all' [BECNT; similarly WBC], 'he divided the two fish, so that everyone could have some' [CEV], 'he divided the fish for everyone to share' [NLT], 'he gave pieces of the two fish to everyone' [GW]. This verb means to distribute objects to a series of persons [LN (57.89)], or to divide into separate parts [LN (63.23)].

QUESTION—What is the significance of the use of the imperfect tense ἐδίδου 'he was giving'?

The imperfect tense indicates that Jesus continued giving the broken pieces of bread to his disciples [Hb, Lns, Tay]. 'He *kept giving* the bread to the disciples' [NTC; GW, NASB, NLT]. Jesus continued giving bread to his disciples as they kept returning for more food to distribute [BECNT, NTC]. At some time between the breaking of the bread and the dividing of the fish and the reception of the bread and fish by the people, the miracle occurred [NTC]. Whether the bread increased in the hands of Jesus or in the hands the disciples as they distributed the bread is left unanswered. The text does not mention if the multitude was aware of what was taking place [NICNT]. Probably the bread multiplied in Jesus' hands as he kept giving it to the disciples [Hb, NTC]. There were always more pieces to break off as the bread grew in Jesus' hands [Lns]. The bread and fish were probably multiplied under Jesus' hands [NTC].

QUESTION—How did the disciples set the bread before them all?

The twelve disciples probably carried baskets of the broken pieces of bread to the various groups of people, and someone in each group would take the food to distribute it among all those in the group [TH].

QUESTION—Concerning the fish, what is meant by the phrase ἐμέρισεν πᾶσιν 'he divided among them all'?

The verb μερίζω can mean (1) 'to distribute something to some people' [BAGD (p. 504), LN (57.89)], or (2) 'to divide into separate parts' [BAGD (1. p. 504), LN (63.23)].

This refers to the distribution of the fish rather than to breaking the two fish into pieces [BAGD, LN]. He divided the fish for distribution to all of the people [Gnd, WBC]. Jesus divided the fish so that all of the people could have some, but this does not mean that he personally served all the people gathered there [TH]. Jesus distributed the fish by means of the apostles, just as he had with the bread [My]. It does not say whether the fish that were multiplied were raw, dried, or cooked, but they must have been in the same condition in which they were when disciples had brought them to Jesus [AB2]. This verb refers to portioning them out, but Jesus probably broke apart the fish before distributing them [Lns]. One commentary thinks that instead of referring to dividing the fish among the people, it does refer to the act of breaking apart the fish [BECNT].

6:42 And all ate and were-satisfied.[a] 6:43 And they-picked-up[b] twelve baskets[c] full of fragments,[d] and of the fish.

LEXICON—a. aorist pass. indic. of χορτάζομαι, χορτάζω (LN 23.15) (BAGD p. 884): 'to be satisfied' [AB2, BAGD, BNTC; ESV, NASB, NCV, NET, NIV, REB], 'to have enough' [AB1; TEV], 'to eat one's fill' [BAGD, LN], 'to be filled' [BECNT, Lns, NTC, WBC; KJV, NRSV]. The phrase 'they all ate and were satisfied' is translated 'everyone had eaten all they wanted' [CEV], 'all of them ate as much as they wanted' [GW, NLT]. This verb means to eat so as to be in a state of satisfaction [LN]. The hunger of all the people was satisfied to the point they desired no more [Hb]. This word occurs at 6:42; 7:27; 8:4, 8.

b. aorist act. indic. of αἴρω (LN 15.203) (BAGD 3. p. 24): 'to pick up' [AB1, BNTC, NTC, WBC; CEV, GW, NASB, NET, NIV, NLT], 'to take up' [AB2, Lns; ESV, KJV, NRSV, TEV], 'to gather up' [BECNT], 'to lift up and carry along' [BAGD], 'to carry away, to carry off, to remove, to take away' [LN]. The phrase 'picked up twelve baskets full of broken pieces' is translated 'filled twelve baskets with the leftovers pieces of bread (and fish)' [NCV], 'twelve baskets were filled with what was left of the bread (and fish)' [REB]. This verb means to lift up and carry away [LN].

c. κόφινος (LN 6.150) (BAGD p. 447): 'basket' [BAGD; all translations except AB1; CEV], 'large basket' [AB1, LN; CEV]. This noun denotes a relatively large basket used primarily for food or produce [LN]. It denotes a large, heavy basket for carrying things [BAGD]. This word occurs at 6:43; 8:19.

d. κλάσμα (LN 19.40) (BAGD p. 433): 'fragment, piece' [BAGD, LN]. The word κλάσματα 'fragments' [AB2, BECNT, Lns, NTC, WBC; KJV] is also translated 'pieces' [BNTC], 'broken pieces' [Lns, NTC, WBC; ESV, NASB, NET, NIV, NRSV], 'leftover pieces' [GW, NCV], 'leftover (bread and fish)' [CEV, NLT], 'what was left of' [REB, TEV], 'scraps of what remained' [AB1]. This noun denotes a fragment or piece resulting from the action of breaking [LN]. The word κλάσματα 'pieces' could include both bread and fish, although only the bread was κατέκλασεν 'broken' into pieces [WBC].

QUESTION—Who were πάντες 'all' who ate?

This refers to all of the people in the crowd, Jesus, and his disciples [TH].

QUESTION—Who picked up twelve baskets of the leftover food and how did they pick it up?

If the subject is to be specified, the *disciples* picked up the food [BECNT, Gnd, Lns, TH; CEV, NCV, NIV, NLT, TEV]. This doesn't mean that they picked up the food from ground. The disciples collected the leftover pieces of bread and fish from the people who had eaten all they wanted, and there was enough to fill twelve baskets [TH]. Another explanation is that after Jesus had ceased breaking the bread there were twelve baskets of food that had not been distributed [Hb].

QUESTION—What size baskets did they use?

The baskets were relatively large wicker baskets that were used for carrying provisions [Hb, TH]. Some think they were small wicker baskets that had been used to hold things such as a light lunch and odds and ends [EBC, NICNT, NIVfn]. Probably they were the baskets the disciple had used to distribute the food to the people [Hb]. They may have been larger baskets that were kept in the boat to contain fish that were caught [BECNT]. They were baskets large enough to hold a person [CBC].

QUESTION—Were the pieces of fish included in the twelve baskets full of the broken pieces of bread?

From the syntax, it could mean that they picked up twelve baskets full of bread and besides that they also picked up leftover fish in other baskets, or it could mean that they picked up leftover bread and leftover fish and filled twelve baskets with it all [EGT]. Most think the fish were in the twelve baskets along with the bread [AB2, BECNT, Hb, My, NIVfn, TH, TRT; all versions]: 'took up twelve baskets full of broken pieces and of the fish' [ESV], 'they filled twelve baskets with bread and fish' [GW; similarly NCV, NIV], 'picked up twelve large baskets of leftover bread and fish' [CEV].

6:44 **And the (ones) having-eaten the loaves-of-bread were five-thousand men.**

TEXT—Manuscripts reading τοὺς ἄρτους 'the loaves of bread' are given a C rating by GNT to indicate that choosing it over a variant text was difficult. A variant reading omits this phrase.

TEXT—Manuscripts reading πεντακισχίλιοι 'five thousand' are followed by GNT, which does not mention any variant reading. A variant reading is ὡσεί πεντακισχίλιοι 'about five thousand' and it is followed by KJV.

QUESTION—How many people ate the loaves of bread?

The noun ἄνδρες 'men' refers to adult males as distinguished from women and children. By saying 'the ones having eaten the loaves of bread were five thousand men' instead of 'five thousand males ate the loaves' does not seem to leave open the possibility that women and children also ate the food [Gnd]. It is possible that this indicates an all male gathering [NIGTC]. However, many refer to the parallel passage at Matt. 14:21 where it says 'about five thousand men *apart from* the women and children' and presume that this was intended here also [BECNT, CBC, EGT, Hb, ICC, Lns, NAC, NTC, PNTC, Sw, TH, TRT, WBC]. It is probable that there were not as many women and children as there were men [EBC, Hb]. Apparently it was a Jewish custom for the women and children to be grouped separately from the men for the meal [Hb]. In Matthew, it is assumed that the women and children also ate [BECNT]. The arrangement of the seating made it easy to estimate the number [EBC, NICNT].

DISCOURSE UNIT—6:45–56 [NICNT; GW, NCV, NIV]. The topic is Jesus walks on water [NCV, NIV], Jesus walks on the sea [GW], the Lord of the sea [NICNT].

DISCOURSE UNIT—6:45–52 [CBC, EBC, Hb; CEV, ESV, NASB, NET, NLT, NRSV, TEV]. The topic is walking on the water [EBC, Hb; NET], Jesus walks on the water [CBC; CEV, ESV, NASB, NLT, NRSV, TEV].

6:45 **And immediately he-made[a] his disciples get into the boat and go-ahead (of him) to the other-side to Bethsaida while he sends-away[b] the crowd.**

TEXT—Manuscripts reading εἰς τὸ πέραν 'to the other side' are given an A rating by GNT to indicate it was regarded to be certain. A variant reading omits this phrase and it is followed by NICNT, Tay.

LEXICON—a. aorist act. indic. of ἀναγκάζω (LN 37.33) (BAGD 2. p. 52): 'to make' [AB1, AB2, BECNT, BNTC, NTC; all versions except KJV, NCV, NLT], 'to insist that' [NLT], 'to urge' [WBC], 'to constrain' [KJV], 'to tell' [NCV], 'to compel' [BAGD, LN, Lns], 'to force' [BAGD, LN]. This verb means to compel someone to act in a particular manner [LN]. Here it may mean 'to urge strongly' [BECNT]. The verb implies that the disciples were unwilling to leave him. This 'compelling' was accomplished by ordering them to get in the boat [TH].

b. pres. act. indic. of ἀπολύω (LN 15.43) (BAGD 2.b. p. 96): 'to send away' [AB1, BAGD; CEV, GW, KJV, NASB], 'to dismiss' [AB2, BAGD, BECNT, BNTC, LN, Lns, NTC, WBC; ESV, NIV, NRSV, REB], 'to disperse' [NET], 'to send home' [NCV, NLT]. This verb means to cause a person or persons to leave a particular location [LN]. In relation to crowds, this word occurs at 6:36, 45; 8:3, 9.

QUESTION—Why did Jesus have to 'make' the disciples depart before he dismissed the crowds?

That Jesus ἠνάγκασεν 'made' the disciples get into the boat indicates that the disciples were unwilling to leave Jesus [Gnd, Hb, PNTC, TH]. So Jesus gently, but firmly, insisted that his disciples leave at once [Hb]. Perhaps the disciples were sent away to keep them from being involved if a messianic movement should be initiated by the crowd [EBC, Hb, NAC, PNTC]. However, there is no hint here of the crowd reacting as narrated in the parallel passage at John 6:15 where they wanted to take Jesus by force to make him king [WBC]. Jesus rapidly dismissed his disciples so that they wouldn't reveal the details of the miraculous character of the meal they had just served [CGTC, NICNT].

QUESTION—What is meant by going to *the other side* of the Lake of Galilee, to Bethsaida?

Bethsaida was a town on the northeast side of the Lake of Galilee, just east of where the Jordan River flows into the lake [AB1, AB2, BECNT, CBC, CGTC, EBC, ESVfn, Gnd, NICNT, NLTfn, Sw, Tay, TH]. Some think the feeding of the 5,000 took place at some lonely place on the eastern shore of the lake and the boat sailed along the eastern shore toward Bethsaida on the north shore of the lake [EBC, NICNT, NIVfn, NTC, Sw, Tay, TRT]. To go to the *other side* of the lake could just mean to take a short trip to the other side of a bay along the east side of the lake instead of going clear across the middle of the lake [Tay, TRT]. Since they landed at Gennesaret on the west side of the lake, a few think that they had set out for a town that is called Bethsaida of Galilee in John 12:2. Some think that the feeding of the 5,000 took place at some lonely spot on the western shore of the lake and the boat set out for Bethsaida on the northeast shore [BECNT, BNTC, Gnd, Lns, NIGTC], but the strong wind caused the boat to land at Gennesaret instead [BECNT].

6:46 And having-said-goodbye[a] to-them he-departed[b] to the mountain[c] to-pray. **6:47** And evening[d] having-come the boat was in (the) middle[e] of-the lake, and he (was) alone on the land.

TEXT—In 6:47, manuscripts reading ἦν τὸ πλοῖον 'the boat was' are given a B rating by GNT to indicate it was regarded to be certain. A variant reading is ἦν πάλαι τὸ πλοῖον 'the boat was already' and it is followed by REB.

LEXICON—a. aorist mid. participle of ἀποτάσσομαι, ἀποτάσσω (LN 33.23) (BAGD 1. p. 100): 'to say goodbye' [LN; GW, NET, TEV], 'to say farewell' [BAGD; NRSV], 'to bid farewell' [NASB], 'to take leave of' [AB1, BAGD, BECNT, BNTC, Lns, NTC, WBC; ESV, REB], 'to leave' [NIV], 'to tell (them/everyone) good-by' [CEV, NLT], 'to dismiss' [AB2], 'to send away' [KJV, NCV]. This verb means to say formalized expressions when leaving or saying farewell to someone [LN].

b. aorist act. indic. of ἀπέρχομαι (LN 15.37) (BAGD 2. p. 84): 'to depart, to go away' [BAGD, LN], 'to leave' [LN]. The phrase ἀπῆλθεν εἰς τὸ ὄρος 'he departed to the mountain' is translated 'he left for the mountain' [NASB], 'he went to the mountain' [WBC; NET], 'he went up the/a mountain' [BNTC; GW], 'he went up on the mountain' [ESV, NRSV], 'he went up on a mountainside' [NIV], 'he went up on the side of a mountain' [CEV], 'he went away to the mountain' [AB2, BECNT], 'he departed into a mountain' [KJV], 'he went away into the mountain' [Lns], 'he went up the hillside' [AB1], 'he went up the hill' [REB], 'he departed into the hill' [NTC], 'he went into the hills' [NCV, NLT], 'he went away to a hill' [TEV]. This verb means to move away from a reference point with the emphasis upon the departure [LN].

c. ὄρος (LN 1.46) (BAGD p. 582): 'mountain' [AB2, BAGD, BECNT, BNTC, LN, Lns, WBC; ESV, GW, KJV, NASB, NET, NRSV], 'mountainside' [NIV], 'the side of a mountain' [CEV], 'hill' [BAGD, NTC; NCV, NLT, REB, TEV], 'hillside' [AB1]. This noun denotes a high elevation of land that is higher than a βουνός 'hill' (1.48) [LN]. This was the mountain in the area where he had fed the people on its slopes [Hb].

d. ὀψία, ὄψιος (LN 67.197) (BAGD 2. p. 601): 'evening' [BAGD, LN]. The phrase ὀψίας γενομένης 'evening having come' is translated 'when evening had come' [AB2, WBC], 'when evening came' [AB1, BECNT, BNTC, Lns; ESV, GW, NET, NIV, NRSV, TEV], 'when even was come' [KJV], 'when it was evening' [NASB], 'when evening fell' [NTC], 'later that evening' [CEV], 'that night' [NCV]. 'late that night' [NLT], 'it was now late' [REB]. This noun denotes the period after sunset and before darkness [LN].

e. μέσος (LN 83.10) (BAGD 2. p. 507): 'in the middle' [BAGD, LN], 'in the midst' [LN]. The phrase 'in the middle of the lake' [AB1, BNTC; NASB, NIV, NLT, TEV] is also translated 'in the middle of the sea' [AB2, BECNT, NTC; GW, NASB, NET], 'in the midst of the sea' [Lns; KJV], 'somewhere in the middle of the lake' [CEV], 'out on the sea' [WBC; ESV, NRSV], 'well out on the water' [REB]. This adjectival noun denotes a position in the middle of an area, either an object in the midst of other objects or an area in the middle of a larger area [LN]. Being in the midst of the lake does not necessarily mean that the boat was in the geographical center of the lake or exactly halfway across. It means the boat was out on the lake well away from land [AB1, Hb]. The parallel passage in John 6:19 says they had rowed about 25 or 30 stadia (three or four miles), so they were indeed in the middle of the lake [NTC, Tay].

QUESTION—To whom did Jesus say goodbye?

The referent of 'them' is ambiguous in the phrase 'having said goodbye to them'. If the disciples left before Jesus dismissed the crowd, 'them' would refer to the people. It is possible that after Jesus ordered his disciples to leave, he dismissed the crowed and then turned to say goodbye to his disciples as they were getting the boat ready for the trip [TH].

1. Jesus said farewell to the crowd [AB1, AB2, CGTC, EGT, Gnd, Hb, Lns, My, Sw, Tay, WBC; NCV, NLT, TEV].

2. Jesus said farewell to his disciples [BECNT, NIGTC]. The disciples are the main focus of this account. This mention of Jesus saying farewell to his disciples prepares us for their astonishment when they later see Jesus beside the boat out on the lake [NIGTC].

QUESTION—What time of day is referred to in the phrase ὀψίας γενομένης 'evening having come'?

Some explain that the Jewish 'evening' was divided into two parts, the first evening being late afternoon [Hb, Lns], from three to six o'clock [ICC], and the second evening being when darkness set in [Hb, Lns], from six o'clock until night time [ICC]. The feeding of the people had been during the 'first' evening hours [Hb, ICC, Lns]. The story of the feeding of the crowd and the story of Jesus walking on water both have temporal settings that are essential to their narratives, and the problem of fitting them together suggests that they were originally told separately and were unrelated [BNTC, NCBC, WBC]. Yet it is not impossible that the events of 6:35–44 took place within a three-hour period [BECNT]. The participial phrase 'evening having come' gives the setting for the events that follow and many translate it '*when* the evening came' [AB1, BECNT, BNTC, Lns; ESV, GW, NET, NIV, NRSV, TEV], 'when evening fell' [NTC]. A few translations imply that the participle has the meaning '*after* the evening had come (and it was now sometime during the night)': 'that night' [NCV], 'late that night' [NLT]. The sun must have set by now [Sw]. Since it had already been 'a very late hour' (6:35) before the feeding of five thousand people began, ὀψίας 'evening' in this verse must mean 'late at night' [EBC, NIGTC, TH]. By the time Jesus finished praying it would have been the dark hours just before dawn [NICNT].

6:48 **And having-seen them distressed**[a] **in the rowing, because the wind was against**[b] **them, about (the) fourth watch**[c] **of-the night he-comes to them walking on the lake and he-intended**[d] **to-pass-by them.**

LEXICON—a. pres. pass. participle of βασανίζω (LN 38.13) (BAGD 3. p. 134): 'to be tormented, to be tortured' [LN], 'to be harassed' [BAGD]. The phrase βασανιζομένους ἐν τῷ ἐλαύνειν 'distressed in the rowing' [Lns] is also translated 'distressed while rowing' [WBC], 'they were having great difficulty in rowing' [LN (15.164)], 'they were in a lot of trouble as they rowed' [GW], 'they were in serious trouble, rowing hard' [NLT], 'making tortuous progress in their rowing' [AB2], 'being hard pressed while rowing' [BECNT], 'toiling in rowing' [KJV], 'struggling hard to row the boat' [NCV], 'rowing with difficulty' [AB1], 'straining at the oars' [BAGD, NTC; NASB, NET, NIV, NRSV, TEV], 'laboring at the oars' [BNTC; REB], 'they were making headway painfully' [ESV], 'were struggling hard because they were rowing (against the wind)' [CEV]. This verb means to punish by physical torture or torment [LN]. The verb is used figuratively to refer to any severe distress [BAGD]. This verb is literally 'tortured' and suggests both physical pains and mental distress [Hb]. It means 'to be distressed, to be troubled' [TH].

b. ἐναντίος (LN **82.11**) (BAGD 1. p. 262): 'against' [BAGD, **LN**], 'opposite, contrary' [BAGD]. The phrase 'the wind was against them' [AB2, BECNT, **LN**, NTC, WBC; ESV, NASB, NET, NIV] is also translated 'the wind was blowing against them' [BNTC, **LN**; NCV], 'the wind was contrary to them' [Lns; KJV], 'against an adverse wind' [NRSV], 'against a head wind' [AB1; REB], 'they were going against the wind' [GW], 'they were rowing against the wind' [CEV, TEV], 'struggling against the wind and waves' [NLT]. This adjective describes something as being oriented in the direction opposite to a movement [LN]. The wind was blowing from the direction in which they were heading [TH].

c. φυλακή (LN **67.196**) (BAGD 4. p. 868): 'watch' [BAGD, LN], 'a fourth of the night' [LN]. The phrase περὶ τετάρτην φυλακὴν τῆς νυκτός 'about the fourth watch of the night' [BNTC, **LN**, NTC; ESV, KJV, NASB, NIV] is also translated 'around the fourth watch of the night' [AB2, BECNT, Lns, NTC, WBC], 'about three o'clock in the morning' [NLT], 'between three and six o'clock in the morning' [GW, NCV], 'sometime between three and six o'clock in the morning' [TEV; similarly AB1; REB], 'as the night was ending' [NET], 'not long before morning' [CEV], 'early in the morning' [NRSV]. This noun denotes one of four periods of time into which the night was divided for assigning persons to be on the lookout [LN]. The Roman custom was to divide the time between 6 p.m. and 6 a.m. into four equal periods or 'watches' [BAGD, TH]. So the fourth watch would be from 3 to 6 a.m. [BECNT, CBC, EBC, EGT, Gnd, ICC, Lns, NAC, NETfn, NTC, PNTC, TH, WBC]. Jesus reached the boat at about 3 a.m. [BNTC, CBC, Hb, NCBC, NICNT, NTC, Sw, Tay; NLT].

d. imperf. act. indic. of θέλω (LN 30.58) (BAGD 2. p. 355): 'to purpose' [LN], 'to want, to be ready' [BAGD]. The phrase 'he intended to pass by them' [NASB; similarly AB2; NLT, NRSV] is also translated 'he wanted to pass by them' [BECNT; GW, NET; similarly WBC], 'he wanted to go by them' [Lns], 'he would have passed by them' [KJV], 'he wanted to walk past the boat' [NCV], 'he was going to pass by them' [AB1, BNTC; REB; similarly TEV], 'he was about to pass by them' [NTC; NIV], 'he was about to pass the boat' [CEV], 'he meant to pass by them' [ESV]. This verb means to purpose, and it is generally based upon a preference and desire [LN]. The verb is used in the weakened sense of 'he was ready to pass them by' [BAGD]. The imperfect tense indicates that something followed that altered this intention [Lns].

QUESTION—Where was Jesus when he saw them?

Jesus saw them from the hill where he was praying [AB1, CGTC, EBC, HNTC, Tay, TH]. The moon gave enough light for Jesus to see the boat out on the water [EBC, Sw]. Some think it had to be a supernatural seeing from afar since even with a full moon he would not have been able to see them from the mountain [AB2, Gnd, Hb, Lns, NAC, NTC, WBC]. It was his miraculous telescopic vision that enabled him to see so far in the dark hours of the night [WBC].

QUESTION—What relationship is indicated by the use of the participle 'having seen' in the phrase 'having seen them distressed in the rowing'?

The participle indicates the reason Jesus went to the disciples [BECNT, NICNT, NIGTC]: *because* he saw them distressed, he came to them. It indicates a temporal circumstance [NRSV]: *when* he saw them distressed, he came to them. He wanted to help them in their distress [WBC].

QUESTION—What is meant by the statement, 'he intended to go by them'?

Since Jesus was *coming to* his disciples because he had seen their distress, why would he now intend to pass by them? [BECNT]. It is best to take the statement 'he intended to pass by them' to describe how it appeared to the disciples, but not what Jesus actually planned to do [EBC, NIGTC, Tay]. The disciples *thought* that he was going to pass by them because Jesus was not walking directly toward the boat [EGT, WBC]. As Jesus approached the boat, he changed his course so as to walk past until his disciples recognized him and asked him to come into the boat with them [Hb, ICC, Lns, NTC]. He would have passed by the boat and left the disciples if they had failed to take him in [Lns]. He did this to test their faith [Hb, Lns, NCBC, NTC]. Some see this as Jesus' self-revelation to his own disciples, much like the similar language in the OT where God 'passed by' Moses and Elijah in his self revelation to them [AB1, AB2, ESVfn, Gnd, NAC, NLTfn, TRT, WBC]. Revealing himself to them by passing by them was a theophany, or rather a "Christophany" [NAC]. This would give them visible proof of his deity [ESVfn]. If this was the case, Jesus was passing by his disciples in order to assure them of his presence with them [NETfn].

6:49 **But having-seen him walking on the lake they-thought that it-was a-ghost,**[a] **and they-cried out,**[b]

LEXICON—a. φάντασμα (LN 12.42) (BAGD p. 853): 'ghost' [AB2, BAGD, BECNT, BNTC, LN, Lns, NTC, WBC; all versions except KJV], 'apparition' [AB1, BAGD], 'spirit' [KJV]. This noun denotes an apparition [LN].

b. aorist act. indic. of ἀνακράζω (LN 33.83) (BAGD p. 56): 'to cry out' [AB1, AB2, BAGD, BECNT, BNTC; all versions except CEV, GW, TEV], 'to cry out in terror' [NLT], 'to shout' [LN], 'to scream' [LN, NTC, WBC; CEV, GW, TEV], 'to shriek out' [Lns]. This verb means to shout or cry out, possibly implying that the sound was unpleasant in nature [LN]. They screamed in terror [BNTC, Hb, Sw, TH].

QUESTION—What is a φάντασμα 'ghost', and why would they think Jesus was a ghost?

When they saw a figure walking toward them on top of the water in the darkness of 3 o'clock in the morning, they thought they were seeing a disembodied spirit [NIGTC], a water spirit [EBC, NICNT, NIVfn], a phantom [Sw], a ghost [CGTC, Gnd, Hb, NAC, NIGTC, Tay]. A ghost might be the spirit of a dead person or some other kind of spirit that might harm them [TRT]. A common Jewish superstition was that the appearance of a 'spirit of the night' brought disaster [NIGTC, NIVfn]. They had not yet recognized Jesus [EBC, NIGTC]. In what little light there was, they saw the form of a man coming toward them, but they didn't believe that it really was a man since humans can't walk of water [NTC]. They did not recognize Jesus in the dark and could not believe that the figure on the water could be anything solid [ICC].

6:50 because all saw him and they-were-terrified.[a] But he immediately spoke with them, and he-says to-them, "Have-courage,[b] (it) is[c] I. Do- not -be-afraid.[d]"

LEXICON—a. aorist pass. indic. of ταράσσω (LN 25.244) (BAGD 2. p. 805) 'to be terrified' [AB1, BAGD, BECNT, BNTC, NTC, WBC; all versions except KJV, NCV], 'to be afraid' [NCV], 'to be frightened' [BAGD], 'to be troubled' [BAGD; KJV], 'to be disturbed' [AB2], 'to be distressed' [LN], 'to be upset' [Lns]. This verb means to cause acute emotional distress or turbulence [LN].

    b. pres. act. impera. of θαρσέω (LN 25.156) (BAGD p. 352): 'to be courageous, to have courage, to be bold' [LN]. The command θαρσεῖτε 'have courage' [BAGD, BECNT; NCV, NET] is also translated 'take courage' [NTC, WBC; NASB, NIV, NLT], 'Courage!' [AB1, BNTC; TEV], 'be brave' [AB2], 'don't be afraid' [BAGD], 'don't worry' [CEV], 'calm down' [GW], 'take heart' [ESV, NRSV, REB], 'cheer up' [Lns], 'be of good cheer' [KJV]. This verb means to have confidence and firmness of purpose in the face of danger or testing [LN].

    c. pres. act. indic. of εἰμί (LN 13.4) (BAGD II.5. p. 224): 'to be' [BAGD, LN]. The phrase ἐγώ εἰμι 'it is I' [AB1, BECNT, BNTC, Lns, NTC, WBC; all versions except CEV, GW, NLT] is also translated 'it's me' [GW], 'I am here' [AB2; NLT], 'I am Jesus' [CEV]. This verb means to be identical with someone [LN]. This is the ordinary Greek expression for 'it is I' [CGTC].

    d. pres. pass. impera. of φοβέομαι (LN 25.252): 'to be afraid' [AB1, AB2, BECNT, BNTC, Lns, NTC, WBC; all versions], 'to fear' [LN]. This verb means to be in a state of fearing [LN]. The present imperative form of the verb means to stop being afraid [AB1, BECNT, Gnd, Hb, Lns, NTC, Tay, TH, WBC].

QUESTION—What relationship is indicated by the conjunction γάρ 'because'? This indicates the reason the disciples cried out in fear [BECNT, EGT, Hb, Lns].

QUESTION—Do Jesus' words ἐγώ εἰμι mean 'It is I' or 'I am'?

    1. This is a normal statement of self-identification [AB2, BECNT, BNTC, CGTC, EBC, ICC, NIGTC, Sw, Tay, TRT, WBC; all translations except

NICNT]: *It is I, (Jesus)*. It was Jesus and not a ghost that approached [BECNT]. The focus is on their initial failure to recognize Jesus, so his self-identification with the normal use of colloquial Greek is appropriate. Although in its context it means 'It is I', Mark's readers may have associated it with the declaration God had made in the OT when he identified himself as 'I am' [AB2, BECNT, BNTC, CGTC, WBC]. It is clear in 6:52 that the disciples had not understood this to mean that Jesus was claiming to be God [NIGTC, WBC].
2. This is the recognized OT formula of God's self-revelation in connection with the words of Exodus 3:14, 'I Am that I Am' [Gnd, NAC, NICNT]: *I Am (God)*. In the context of walking on the water and the use of the emphatic pronoun 'I', it probably has this meaning [NICNT].

6:51 And he-went-up^a to them into the boat and the wind ceased,^b and very exceedingly^c in themselves they-were-astonished,^d

TEXT—Manuscripts reading λίαν ἐκ περισσοῦ ἐν ἑαυτοῖς 'very exceedingly in themselves' are given a C rating by GNT to indicate that choosing it over a variant text was difficult. Variant readings are λίαν ἐν ἑαυτοῖς 'very in themselves', περισσῶς ἐν ἑαυτοῖς 'exceedingly in themselves', περιέσωσεν αὐτοὺς καί 'he saved them alive and', and περιέσωσεν αὐτοὺς καὶ λίαν ἐκ περισσοῦ ἐν ἑαυτοῖς 'he saved them alive and very exceedingly in themselves'.

TEXT—Manuscripts reading ἐξίσταντο 'they were astonished' are given a B rating by GNT to indicate it was regarded to be almost certain. A variant reading is ἐξίσταντο καὶ ἐθαύμαζον 'they were astonished and they were wondering' and it is followed by KJV. Another variant reading is ἐξεπλήσσοντο 'they were amazed'.

LEXICON—a. aorist act. indic. of ἀναβαίνω (LN 15.99) (BAGD 1.a.α. p. 50): 'to go aboard' [LN], 'to embark' [BAGD, LN], 'to get into' [BAGD]. The phrase 'he went up to them into the boat/ship' [Lns; KJV] is also translated 'he came up to them, into the boat' [AB2], 'he went up with them into the boat' [NET], 'he went up into the boat with them' [AB1], 'he got into the boat with them' [CEV, ESV, GW, NASB, NCV, NRSV, TEV], 'he entered into the boat with them' [BECNT; similarly WBC], 'he climbed into the boat with them' [NIV, REB], 'he climbed into the boat to them' [NTC], 'he climbed into the boat' [BNTC; NLT]. This verb means to move up onto an object, and it has the specialized meaning of 'going aboard' in reference to boats [LN]. The unexpected verb ἀνέβη 'he went up' may imply that the side of the boat was quite high above the water on which Jesus stood [Hb].

b. aorist act. indic. of κοπάζω (LN 68.42) (BAGD p. 443): 'to cease' [BAGD, BECNT, LN; ESV, KJV, NET, NRSV], 'to stop' [BAGD, LN, Lns; NASB, NLT], 'to stop blowing' [GW], 'to die down' [AB2; CEV, NIV, TEV], 'to abate' [BAGD, WBC], 'to drop' [AB1, BNTC; REB], 'to fall' [NTC], 'to become calm' [NCV]. This verb means to cease some type of movement [LN].

c. περισσός (LN 59.51, **78.20**) (BAGD 3. p. 651): 'more than enough, beyond the norm, abundantly, superfluous' [LN (59.51)], 'abundant, profuse' [BAGD]. The clause λίαν ἐκ περισσοῦ ἐν ἑαυτοῖς ἐξίσταντο 'very exceedingly in themselves they were astonished' is translated 'they were utterly astonished within themselves' [BECNT], 'they continued greatly astonished in themselves' [Lns], 'they were completely astonished' [NET], 'they were utterly astonished' [NASB], 'they were greatly astonished' [NTC], 'they were greatly amazed within themselves' [AB2], 'they were sore amazed in themselves beyond measure' [KJV], 'they were exceedingly amazed' [**LN** (78.20)], 'they were absolutely amazed' [WBC], 'the disciples/they were completely amazed' [NIV, TEV], 'they were totally amazed' [NLT], 'the followers were greatly amazed' [NCV], 'they were utterly astounded' [BNTC; ESV, NRSV, REB], 'they were completely astounded' [AB1], 'the disciples were astounded' [GW], 'the disciples were completely confused' [CEV]. This adjective pertains to a quantity so abundant that it is considerably more than what one would expect or anticipate [LN (59.51)]. The idiom ἐκ περισσοῦ 'from excess' refers to an extremely high point on a scale of extent and implies an excess. In Mark 6:51 both λίαν 'very' (78.1) and ἐκ περισσοῦ 'from excess' are expressions of degree that reinforce one another [LN (78.20)]. They were astounded by Jesus' power [BNTC]. The imperfect tense indicates that their amazement continued on [Lns]. The phrase ἐν ἑαυτοῖ 'in themselves' describes their strong inward reaction to their experience [Hb, ICC, Sw]. They kept their amazement to themselves [ICC, My]. Although the stress is on their inward feeling, it does not mean that there wasn't also an outward expression of this reaction [Hb].

QUESTION—Why did the wind cease?

There has to be some relationship between Jesus getting into the boat and the wind ceasing because only this could explain the astonishment of the disciples [EBC]. The mere presence of Jesus in the boat was enough to cause the wind to cease [BECNT, Gnd]. Even though Mark doesn't say that the cessation of the wind was supernatural, it is clear that the wind ceased in response to the will of Jesus [Hb].

6:52 **because they-did- not -understand[a] about the loaves-of-bread, instead their heart was hardened.[b]**

TEXT—Manuscripts reading ἀλλ' ἦν αὐτῶν ἡ καρδία πεπωρωμένη 'instead their heart was hardened' are followed by GNT, which does not mention any variant reading. A variant reading is ἦν γὰρ ἡ καρδία αὐτῶν πεπωρωμένη 'for their heart was hardened' and it is followed by KJV.

LEXICON—a. aorist act. indic. of συνίημι (LN 32.5) (BAGD p. 790): 'to understand' [AB1, AB2, BECNT, BNTC, LN, WBC; ESV, GW, NCV, NET, NIV, NRSV, REB], 'to comprehend' [LN, Lns], 'to perceive, to have insight into' [LN], 'to consider' [KJV], 'to understand with regard to' [BAGD], 'to gain an insight from' [BAGD; NASB], 'to understand the significance of' [NLT], 'to grasp the significance of' [NTC], 'to understand the real meaning of' [TEV], 'to understand the true meaning' [CEV]. This verb means to use one's capacity for understanding in order to gain insight about something [LN]. This word occurs at 4:12; 6:52; 7:14; 8:17, 21.

b. perf. pass. participle of πωρόω (LN 27.51) (BAGD p. 732): 'to be hardened, dull, or obtuse' [BAGD], 'to be completely unwilling to learn, to have a closed mind' [LN]. The phrase 'their heart was hardened' [AB2; KJV, NASB] is also translated 'their heart continued as having been hardened' [Lns], 'their heart had been hardened' [BECNT], 'their hearts were hardened' [BNTC, WBC; ESV, NET, NIV, NRSV], 'their hearts were too hard to take it in' [NLT], 'their minds were closed' [AB1; CEV, GW, NCV, REB], 'their minds could not grasp it' [TEV]. This verb is a figurative extension of πωρόω 'to harden', and means to cause someone to be completely unwilling to learn and accept new information [LN]. This refers to the condition of their hearts, not the process by which they became hardened [TH]. See this word in relation to hearts at 3:5, 6:52, 8:17.

QUESTION—What relationship is indicated by the conjunction γάρ 'because'?
This indicates the reason that they were utterly astonished [BECNT, BNTC, CGTC, Hb, Tay, WBC].

QUESTION—What did they not understand about the loaves?
They must have realized that a miracle had occurred in the multiplication of the loaves of bread, but they did not realize what it implied in regard to the person of Jesus [CBC, CGTC, Hb, ICC, NICNT, NTC, WBC]. Probably the word 'heart' is in the singular form to emphasize the corporate nature of the disciples' response in this incident [BECNT]. They failed to recognize that God was acting in history through Jesus [NICNT]. If they had understood the implications of the miracle of Jesus feeding the five thousand, it would have kept them from being so amazed when the wind abated when he got into the boat [Gnd], and they would have been prepared to understand his walking on water and calming the waves [EBC]. They did not yet understand that Jesus was the Son of God, so they didn't realize how much power he possessed. If they had understood, they would not have feared the danger they had met in the boat and they would not have been surprised and astonished when he did something about it [BECNT].

QUESTION—What is meant by their hearts being hardened?
Their 'hearts' refers to their minds and their thinking [TH]. It refers to their intellectual nature in its relationship to the spiritual. Although they were still followers of Jesus, they were in a state of being spiritually imperceptive [Hb]. With their obtuseness, they were unable to draw the necessary conclusions from the miracles Jesus performed, probably because of their neglect to ponder and meditate on the miracles in connection with the nature

of the one who performed them [NTC]. This does not mean that they had the kind of hardened hearts of unbelief found in the scribes and Pharisees. It refers to the unresponsiveness of someone having just a little faith [Lns]. This refers to their failure to grasp the significance of the multiplication of the loaves. This failure to perceive was akin to moral blindness rather than willful obstinacy [Tay].

DISCOURSE UNIT—6:53–56 [CBC, EBC, Hb; CEV, ESV, NASB, NET, NLT, NRSV, TEV]. The topic is a ministry of healing among the people [Hb], healing the sick [NET], Jesus heals the sick [NLT], healing at Gennesaret [NASB], healings near Gennesaret [EBC], healing in the region of Gennesaret [NICNT], healing of the sick in Gennesaret [CBC; NRSV], Jesus heals sick people in Gennesaret [CEV, ESV, TEV].

6:53 **And having-crossed-over onto**[a] **the land they-came to Gennesaret and they-anchored.**[b]

TEXT—Manuscripts reading διαπεράσαντες ἐπὶ τὴν γῆν ἦλθον εἰς Γεννησαρὲτ 'having crossed over onto the land they came to Gennesaret' are followed by GNT, which does not mention any variant reading. A variant reading is διαπεράσαντες ἦλθον ἐπὶ τὴν γῆν Γεννησαρὲτ 'having crossed over they came onto the land of Gennesaret' and it is followed by KJV.

LEXICON—a. ἐπί (LN 84.20): 'onto, on' [LN]. The phrase 'having crossed over onto the land they came to Gennesaret' is translated 'having crossed over, they came to land, to Gennesaret' [BECNT], 'having crossed over, they came to the land in Gennesaret' [Lns], 'having crossed over, they landed at Gennesaret' [NTC], 'so they completed the crossing and landed at Gennesaret' [REB], 'Jesus and his disciples crossed the lake and brought the boat to shore near the town of Gennesaret' [CEV]. Some include the relationship indicated by the use of the participle 'having crossed over': 'when they had passed over, they came into the land of Gennesaret' [KJV], 'when they had crossed over, they came to land at Gennesaret' [BNTC; ESV, NASB, NRSV; similarly AB1, AB2; NET, TEV], 'when they had crossed the lake, they came to shore at Gennesaret' [NCV; similarly GW], 'after they had crossed the lake, they landed at Gennesaret' [NLT; similarly NIV], 'crossing to land they came to Gennesaret' [WBC]. This preposition indicates an extension to a goal [LN].

b. aorist pass. indic. of προσορμίζομαι, προσορμίζω (LN **54.20**) (BAGD p. 717): 'to moor, to anchor, to tie up' [LN], 'to come into the harbor, to come to anchor' [BAGD]. The phrase 'and they anchored' is translated 'and anchored there' [BECNT, NTC; GW, NET, NIV], 'and were anchored near the shore' [Lns], 'where they came to anchor' [AB1], 'and docked' [AB2], 'and tied the boat there' [NCV], 'where they tied up' [BNTC], 'where they tied up the boat' [**LN**; TEV], 'where they made fast' [REB], 'and moored the boat' [NRSV], 'and moored to the shore' [ESV, NASB], 'and drew to the shore' [KJV], 'they brought the boat to shore'

[NLT], 'and brought the boat to shore near the town' [CEV], 'and entered the harbor' [WBC]. This verb means to moor a ship in a safe place, either by anchoring it or drawing it up on the beach [LN]. It refers to beaching the ship [EGT, Gnd].

QUESTION—Who crossed over the lake?

Jesus was now in the boat with his disciples [PNTC; CEV].

QUESTION—Which verb does the prepositional phrase ἐπὶ τὴν γῆν 'onto the land' modify?

1. It modifies the following verb 'they came' [all translations except WBC]: they came to land at Gennesaret.
2. It modifies the preceding verb 'having crossed over' [WBC]: having crossed over to the land.

QUESTION—What was Gennesaret?

Gennesaret is the name of a plain located on the northwestern shore between Capernaum and Tiberius [AB2, BECNT, BNTC, Gnd, Hb, ICC, Lns, My, NAC, NCBC, NICNT, NTC, Sw, TH, WBC]. The Lake of Galilee is also called the Lake of Gennesaret in Luke 5:1 [Lns, NTC]. It was a densely populated fertile plain about three miles long and a mile wide [BECNT, Hb, NICNT].

QUESTION—Why did they land at Gennesaret?

The disciples had set out towards Bethsaida (6:45) at the northeast corner of the lake, but a strong wind had driven the boat southward to Gennesaret [CGTC, ESVfn, Gnd, Hb, ICC, NICNT, PNTC, Tay; possibly BECNT]. Verse 45 only means that the disciples set out πρός 'toward' Bethsaida, and John 6:17 says they were actually going to Capernaum, not Bethsaida. After spending some days in Capernaum, they had sailed to Gennesaret [Lns].

6:54 And they having-come-out from the boat immediately (the people) having-recognized[a] him 6:55 ran-about[b] that whole region

LEXICON—a. aorist act. participle of ἐπιγινώσκω (LN 27.61) (BAGD 2.a. p. 291): 'to recognize' [AB1, BECNT, BNTC, LN, Lns, NTC, WBC; all versions except KJV], 'to know' [BAGD; KJV]. This active verb is also translated as a passive: 'he was immediately recognized' [AB2]. This verb means to identify newly acquired information with what had been previously learned or known [LN]. This word also occurs at 6:33.

b. aorist act. indic. of περιτρέχω (LN **15.231**) (BAGD 2. p. 653): 'to run about' [BAGD, BNTC, LN, NTC; ESV, NASB], 'to run round about' [Lns], 'to run throughout' [BECNT, **LN**; NIV, NLT, TEV], 'to run through' [AB1, AB2, WBC; KJV, NET], 'to run everywhere' [NCV], 'to run all over' [CEV, GW], 'to rush about' [NRSV], 'to scour' [REB]. This verb means to run or go hurriedly about [LN].

QUESTION—Who recognized Jesus?

The verb is used in an impersonal sense, and the subject 'people' must be supplied [AB2, Hb, TH, WBC; ESV, NASB, NCV]. These people were the inhabitants of Gennesaret [Hb]. Although Jesus had not been in Gennesaret before, some of its people had seen and heard Jesus elsewhere [Lns]. Reports of Jesus' healings at Capernaum had spread throughout the region [NICNT].

QUESTION—Who ran around that whole region?

This is an impersonal use of the third person plural [BECNT]. People who recognized Jesus when he landed realized that this was an opportunity to bring people to Jesus to be healed. So they sent runners throughout the district to tell people to take their sick to Jesus [Lns].

and they-began to-carry-about[a] upon pallets[b] the (ones) having badly[c] (to) where they-were-hearing[d] that he-was.

LEXICON—a. pres. act. infin. of περιφέρω (LN **15.190**) (BAGD 1. p. 653): 'to carry about' [BAGD, **LN**; KJV], 'to carry around' [LN, Lns], 'to carry here and there' [BAGD; NASB], 'to carry' [GW, NIV, NLT], 'to bring' [AB1, AB2, BECNT, BNTC, NTC, WBC; CEV, ESV, NCV, NET, NRSV, REB, TEV]. This verb means to carry around from one place to another [LN].

b. κράβαττος (LN **6.107**) (BAGD p. 447): 'pallet' [AB2, BAGD, LN, Lns, NTC; NASB], 'mat' [BECNT, BNTC, WBC; CEV, NCV, NET, NIV, NLT, NRSV, TEV], 'cot' [LN; GW], 'stretcher' [AB1, LN], 'mattress' [BAGD], 'bed' [REB]. This noun denotes a relatively small and often temporary type of object on which a person could lie or recline [LN]. This word occurs at 2:4, 9, 11, 12; 6:55.

c. κακῶς (LN 23.148) (BAGD 1. p. 398): 'badly' [BAGD, LN]. The phrase τοὺς κακῶς ἔχοντας 'the ones having badly' is translated 'the sick' [AB1, AB2, BECNT; GW, NET, NIV, NRSV, TEV], 'the sick people' [BNTC; ESV, NCV, NLT], 'those who/that were sick' [KJV, NASB], 'their sick' [CEV], 'those that were ill' [Lns, NTC], 'the ill' [WBC]. The idiom 'to have badly' or 'to fare badly' means to be in a bad state, to be ill or sick [BAGD, LN]. This adverb occurs at 1:32, 34; 2:17; 6:55.

d. imperf. act. indic. of ἀκούω (LN 24.52): 'to hear' [LN]. The phrase 'to where they were hearing that he was' is translated 'to where they heard he was' [WBC; KJV], 'to the place they heard he was' [NASB], 'to wherever they heard he was' [AB2, BNTC; ESV, NCV, NIV, NLT, NRSV, TEV; similarly BECNT], 'where they would hear that he was' [Lns], 'to wherever he was rumored to be' [NET], 'to any place where they heard he was' [AB1; GW; similarly NTC], 'to any place where he was reported to be' [REB], '(they brought them) each time they heard where he was' [CEV].

QUESTION—Who began to carry the sick people on pallets?

This does not refer to the people who ran throughout the region with the news. The ones who carried the sick to Jesus were people who heard the news about his arrival in the region [TH]. This could also include those who had scoured the whole countryside for the sick [REB]. The statement 'they *began* to carry the sick' indicates that the procession of people bringing their sick people to Jesus began at once and then more and more sick people continued to be brought to him [Hb].

QUESTION—What is implied about carrying the sick to where 'they *were hearing* (ἤκουον)' that he was?

The next verse informs us that Jesus was traveling throughout the region. Before starting out, the people carrying the pallet would have made inquiries concerning Jesus' whereabouts [My]. The imperfect tense indicates that those carrying the sick were repeatedly making inquiries about where Jesus was to be found and were being informed that he was then at such and such a place [Hb, Lns]. This vividly pictures carrying the sick to where they heard Jesus was located, and if he had already gone on from there, they would go on to another place where he was likely to be [EGT, Hb].

6:56 And wherever he-was entering into villages or into cities or into country-towns,[a] they-were-putting in the marketplaces[b] the (ones) having-sicknesses[c] and they-were-begging[d] him that they might-touch even-if (only) the edge[e] of his garment. And as-many-as touched him/it were-being-healed.

LEXICON—a. ἀγρός (LN **11.93**) (BAGD 3. p. 14): 'country town' [AB1], 'farm settlement' [**LN**], 'farm' [BNTC, Lns, WBC; CEV, GW, NRSV, REB, TEV], 'hamlet' [AB2, BAGD, LN]. The plural form is translated 'countryside' [BECNT, NTC; ESV, NASB, NCV, NET, NIV, NLT], 'country' [KJV]. This noun denotes a relatively small village or even just a cluster of farms [LN]. It could refers to the open fields where many of the people would be working [Hb].

b. ἀγορά (LN 57.207) (BAGD p. 12): 'marketplace' [AB2, BAGD, BECNT, BNTC, LN, Lns, NTC, WBC; all versions except KJV], 'market' [LN], 'town center' [AB1], 'street' [KJV]. This noun denotes a commercial center containing a number of places for doing business [LN]. The marketplace would be found in towns, but apparently the word is used loosely here to include other open spaces [Sw]. This word occurs at 6:56; 7:4; 12:38.

c. pres. act. participle of ἀσθενέω (LN 23.114) (BAGD 1.a. p. 115): 'to be sick' [BAGD, LN], 'to be ill, to be disabled' [LN]. The phrase 'the ones having sicknesses' is translated 'those who were ill' [BNTC], 'the sick' [AB1, AB2, BECNT, Lns, NTC, WBC; all versions except GW, TEV], 'their sick' [GW, TEV]. This verb means to be sick and in a state of weakness and incapacity [LN].

d. imperf. act indic. of παρακαλέω (LN 33.168) (BAGD 3. p. 617): 'to beg' [AB1, BAGD, BECNT, BNTC, NTC; CEV, GW, NCV, NIV, NLT, NRSV, REB, TEV], 'to request' [BAGD, LN], 'to ask' [LN; NET], 'to appeal to' [BAGD, LN, WBC], 'to implore' [BAGD; ESV, NASB], 'to entreat' [BAGD], 'to beseech' [Lns; KJV], 'to plead' [AB2, LN]. This verb means to earnestly ask for something [LN]. The imperfect tense indicates that there were repeated requests as person after person approached him [Gnd, Lns, Sw].

e. κράσπεδον (LN 6.180) (BAGD 1. p. 448): 'edge' [AB1, BAGD, BNTC; GW, NCV, NIV, REB, TEV], 'border' [BAGD; KJV], 'hem' [BAGD], 'fringe' [AB2, LN; ESV, NASB, NLT, NRSV], 'tassel' [BECNT, Lns, NTC, WBC]. The phrase 'the edge of his garment' is translated 'his clothes' [CEV]. This noun denotes the border of a garment. It may refer to the edge of Jesus' garment, or it could refer specifically to the tassels that were worn at the four corners of the outer garment if he was strictly following the Mosaic law about clothing [BAGD, EBC, LN].

QUESTION—Who begged Jesus for permission to touch his garment?

1. The people who had brought the sick to the market places were the ones who spoke to Jesus [Lns; ESV, KJV, NASB, NET, NRSV, TEV].
2. The sick people themselves spoke to Jesus [AB2, Gnd, TH]. The following words 'and as many as touched him' refers to the people who were begging Jesus to let them touch him [AB2]. There were so many of them that they could only appeal to Jesus to come close enough for them to touch his garment as he hurried through the crowd [Gnd].

QUESTION—What is meant by the 'edge' of his garment?

1. This refers to whatever edge of his garment someone might reach out to touch [Gnd, ICC; CEV, ESV, GW, KJV, NASB, NCV, NET, NIV, NLT, NRSV, REB, TEV].
2. This refers to a tassel at a corner of his cloak [AB2, BECNT, BNTC, CBC, CGTC, HNTC, NAC, NCBC, NICNT, NIGTC, NLTfn, NTC, PNTC, TH, WBC]. Probably this has the specific sense of the tassel worn by pious Jews on each of the four corners of their cloaks [TH]. This shows that Jesus was a law-abiding Jew [AB2, BECNT, PNTC].

QUESTION—Why did they want to touch the edge of Jesus' garment?

Perhaps they had heard about the woman with a flow of blood who had been healed after touching the edge of Jesus' garment (5:27) [Hb]. Such a simple means of being healed appealed to the popular imagination and Jesus permitted its use [Sw]. People regarded Jesus as a miracle worker whose power was released through touch [NICNT]. Perhaps the fringe or tassel of Jesus' clothing was the most accessible part of his clothing [NIGTC].

QUESTION—What is indicted by the tenses of the two verbs in the clause 'as many as *touched* him *were being healed*'?

The aorist tense of the verb ἥψαντο 'touched' indicates the momentary act of touching Jesus' garment [Hb, TH]. The imperfect tense of the verb ἐσῴζοντο 'were being healed' indicates the rapid succession of people who were being healed one after another [Hb, TH]. However, some translate the imperfect tense as an aorist, 'were made well' [ESV, GW, TEV], 'were healed' [NCV, NET, NIV, NLT, NRSV, REB], 'were made whole' [KJV]. These plural verbs are translated 'everyone who did was healed' [CEV].

QUESTION—What did they touch to be healed?
1. The pronoun αὐτοῦ is to be taken as masculine: they touched 'him', that is, Jesus [AB2, BECNT, BNTC, Hb, Lns, My, NICNT, NTC, PNTC, WBC; KJV, NIV, NLT, REB]. The pronoun refers to Jesus, and no matter where they touched him they were healed [My].
2. The pronoun αὐτοῦ is to be taken as neuter: they touched 'it', that is, the edge of his garment [AB1, EBC, ESVfn, Gnd, NCBC; CEV, ESV, GW, NASB, NCV, NET, NRSV, TEV]. Even though superstition was sometimes involved, it was the faith of those who came to touch Jesus' clothes that Jesus responded to [EBC].

DISCOURSE UNIT—7:1–23 [CBC, Hb, NIGTC; GW, NCV, NET, NIV, NLT, NRSV]. The topic is a foretaste of confrontation in Jerusalem: the issue of purity [NIGTC], Jesus teaches about inner purity [NLT], controversy concerning defilement [Hb], clean and unclean [NIV], Jesus' views on cleanliness and purity [CBC], the traditions of the elders [NRSV], Jesus challenges the Pharisees' traditions [GW], breaking human traditions [NET], obey God's Law [NCV].

DISCOURSE UNIT—7:1–13 [EBC, Hb; CEV, ESV, NASB, TEV]. The topic is the teaching of the ancestors [CEV, TEV], followers of tradition [NASB], traditions and commandments [ESV], commands of God and traditions of men [EBC], condemnation of human tradition [Hb].

DISCOURSE UNIT—7:1–8 [NICNT]. The topic is defilement according to tradition.

7:1 **And were-gathered**[a] **to him the Pharisees and some of the scribes having-come from Jerusalem.**
LEXICON—a. pres. pass. indic. of συνάγω (LN 15.125) (BAGD 2. p. 782): 'to be gathered together, to be called together' [LN]. The phrase 'were gathered to him' is translated 'gathered together to him' [NTC], 'gathered to him' [Lns; ESV], 'came together unto him' [KJV], 'gathered together before him' [AB2], 'gathered around him/Jesus' [BECNT, BNTC, WBC; GW, NASB, NCV, NET, NIV, NRSV, TEV], 'came and gathered around Jesus' [CEV], 'arrived to see Jesus' [NLT], 'met him' [AB1; REB]. This verb means to be caused to come together [LN]. In the passive voice 'were gathered' could have the passive sense 'to be gathered together' or the reflexive sense 'to gather together' [BAGD]. The passive voice in this verse does not mean that someone gathered them together. They were motivated by their own inner concern to counteract the popularity of Jesus and voluntarily came to confront him [Hb].
QUESTION—Who were these Pharisees and scribes?
The word 'scribes' refers to law experts who studied, interpreted, and taught the OT Law. The word 'Pharisees' refers to a sect of Israelites who tried to live in strict accordance with scribal teaching and many of the scribes were Pharisees [NTC]. The mention of οἱ Φαρισαῖοι 'the Pharisees' does not

imply that the entire sect of Pharisees were present at this time. It means that the Pharisees who were present represented the Pharisees as a whole [BECNT]. Some translate 'the Pharisees' as 'some Pharisees' [TRT; CEV, NCV, NLT, TEV], or 'a group of Pharisees' [REB].

QUESTION—Which people had come from Jerusalem?

1. Both the Pharisees and the scribes had come from Jerusalem [EBC, Hb, ICC, Lns, NIVfn, NTC; NCV, NLT, TEV]. The parallel passage in Matt. 15:1 includes both groups in the delegation that came from Jerusalem [Hb, Lns, NTC]. The scribes would also have been Pharisees, and they are probably called 'some of the scribes' to indicate that they were especially selected to face Jesus because of their learning [Lns].

2. Only the scribes had come from Jerusalem [AB1, BECNT, HNTC, NIGTC, NTC, Sw, Tay, TH, WBC; ESV, GW, REB; probably NET, NIV]. The Pharisees were probably local residents [AB1, Tay]. These scribes had probably come from Jerusalem to investigate the teachings of Jesus and dispute them [NIGTC]. That 'some of the scribes' had come from Jerusalem implies that local scribes were also gathered there [Gnd].

7:2 **And having-seen that some of-his disciples are-eating the loaves-of-bread^a with unclean^b hands, that is, unwashed,^c**

TEXT—Manuscripts reading ἐσθίουσιν τοὺς ἄρτους 'are eating the loaves of bread' are followed by GNT, which does not mention any variant reading. A variant reading is ἐσθίουσιν τοὺς ἄρτους, ἐμέμψαντω 'are eating the loaves of bread, they found fault' and it is followed by KJV.

LEXICON—a. ἄρτος (LN 5.1) (BAGD 2. p. 110): 'loaves of bread' [AB2], 'bread' [BAGD, BECNT, BNTC; KJV, NASB, NET], 'loaves' [WBC], 'food' [AB1, BAGD, LN, NTC; NCV, NIV, REB, TEV]. The phrase ἐσθίουσιν τοὺς ἄρτους 'are eating the loaves of bread' is translated 'ate/were-eating their bread' [Lns; NASB, NET], 'ate/were-eating' [CEV, ESV, GW, NRSV; similarly NLT]. This noun denotes any kind of food or nourishment [LN]. The literal meaning 'bread' is used for food in general since bread was their most important food [BAGD]. There is probably no significance between the use of the plural noun τοὺς ἄρτους 'the loaves of bread' in this verse and the singular noun τὸν ἄρτον 'the bread' in 7:5 [NIGTC]. Perhaps '*the* loaves of bread' refer to the leftover bread of 6:43 [Gnd, Sw, TRT, WBC].

b. κοινός (LN 53.39) (BAGD 2. p. 438): 'unclean' [AB1, BECNT, BNTC; GW, NET, NIV], 'ritually unclean' [LN; TEV], 'impure' [AB2, BAGD; NASB], 'defiled' [LN, NTC, WBC; ESV, KJV, NRSV, REB], 'common' [Lns], not explicit [CEV, NLT]. The phrase 'unclean hands' is translated 'hands that were not clean' [NCV]. This adjective refers to something being ritually unacceptable, either as the result of defilement or because of the very nature of the object itself [LN]. The adjective refers to that which is ceremonially impure [BAGD]. This word occurs at 7:2, 5.

c. ἄνιπτος (LN 47.13) (BAGD p. 69): 'unwashed' [AB2, BAGD, BECNT, BNTC, LN, Lns, WBC; ESV, KJV, NASB, NET, NIV], 'unrinsed' [NTC], 'not washed' [LN; NCV], 'without washing them/their-hands' [AB1; NRSV, REB]. The phrase 'are eating…with defiled hands, that is, unwashed' is translated 'they ate without first washing their hands' [CEV; similarly GW], 'failed to follow the Jewish ritual of hand washing before eating' [NLT], 'they had not washed them in the way the Pharisees said people should' [TEV]. This adjective describes something that is not washed [LN].

QUESTION—How is verse 2 grammatically connected with the text of 7:1–5?

1. Verse 1 is a complete sentence. Verse 2 begins a new sentence that is interrupted by the parenthetical comment of verses 3 and 4. Then the sentence begun in verse 2 is completed in verse 5 [AB2, CGTC, GNT, Sw, WBC]. The parenthesis is indicated by enclosing verses 3–4 with em dashes [AB2, GNT, WBC].
2. Verses 1 and 2 form one complete sentence. Verses 3–4 are a parenthetical comment. Verse 5 is a separate sentence [AB1, Lns, My, NIGTC, NTC; ESV, NASB, NIV, NRSV, REB]. The beginning participial clause καὶ ἰδόντες… 'and having seen…' in verse 2 is coordinate with the participial clause ἐλθόντες ἀπὸ Ἱεροσολύμων 'having come from Jerusalem' at the end of verse 1. Both of these participial clauses are governed by the main verb of the sentence συνάγονται 'were gathered' at the beginning of verse 1: 'they were gathered…having come from Jerusalem and having seen…' [Lns, NIGTC]. The parenthesis is indicated by enclosing verses 3–4 with parenthesis marks [AB1; ESV, NASB, NIV, NRSV, REB] or em dashes [GNT, NTC].
3. Verses 1 and 2 are a part of one sentence that is left incomplete when interrupted by the parenthetical comment of verses 3–4. Verse 5 is a separate sentence [BECNT].
4. Verses 1 and 2 are a part of one sentence that is interrupted by the parenthetical comment of verses 3–4. Then the sentence begun in verses 1–2 is completed in verse 5 [BECNT].
5. Verses 1, 2, and 5 are each complete sentences [CEV, GW, KJV, NCV, NET, NLT, TEV]. The parenthetical comment in verses 3–4 is enclosed with parenthesis marks [GW, NCV, NET, NLT, TEV] or made into a separate paragraph [CEV].

QUESTION—Who were the disciples that were eating the loaves of bread?

They were the disciples of Jesus [Hb, NIGTC, NTC, TH; NCV, NET], probably the twelve disciples who had been with Jesus in the previous chapter [Hb, NTC]. This probably happened at a meal while they were traveling through the towns mentioned in 6:56 [Sw]. It doesn't say it was a formal meal, so probably in the midst of the pressing demands on their time, some of them had paused to eat some food [Gnd, Hb]. The reference to 'some' of the disciples does not necessarily imply that there were other disciples of Jesus who did practice the Jewish traditions about defilement [BECNT].

QUESTION—What caused their hands to be unclean?

The word 'unclean' does not refer to a failure to wash one's hands for hygienic purposes. The complaint was that they had not followed the ritual cleansing ceremonies that the Pharisees had developed. The Pharisees considered the hands of the disciples to be *ritually* unclean because they had not been ceremonially washed before eating [BECNT, Hb, NIGTC]. Such a ceremonial washing was done in order to purify one's hands by removing the defilement caused by contact with profane things [Hb].

7:3 —**because the Pharisees and all the Jews do not eat unless with-a-fist[a] they-wash their hands, holding-to[b] the tradition[c] of-the elders,[d]**

TEXT—Manuscripts reading πυγμῇ 'with a fist' are given an A rating by GNT to indicate it was regarded to be certain. A variant reading is πυκνά 'often/thoroughly' and it is followed by KJV. One ancient version reads πυκνά πυγμῇ 'with a fist often/thoroughly'. Other manuscripts omit this word altogether.

LEXICON—a. πυγμή (LN **8.35**) (BAGD 1. p. 728): 'fist' [BAGD, LN]. The phrase πυγμῇ νίψωνται τὰς χεῖρας 'with a fist they wash their hands' is translated 'they wash their hands with a/the fist' [BAGD, BECNT, BNTC, **LN**, Lns], 'they wash their hands with the hand shaped into a fist' [AB2], 'wash their hands with cupped hands' [WBC], 'they have poured water over their cupped hands' [NLT]. Some give the purpose for this washing without mentioning the fist: 'they perform a ritual washing' [NET], 'they give their hands a ceremonial washing' [NIV], 'washing their hands in a special way' [NCV], 'they wash their hands in the proper way' [CEV, TEV], 'they have properly washed their hands' [GW]. Some merely refer to the fact that they washed their hands: 'they wash their hands' [ESV; similarly AB1; REB], 'they carefully wash their hands' [NASB], 'they thoroughly wash their hands' [NRSV], 'they rinse their hands thoroughly' [NTC]. This noun denotes the clenched hand. It is a very problematic expression that occurs nowhere else in the NT and a number of translators have attempted to avoid the interpretative problem by translating 'unless they wash in the proper manner' or 'wash thoroughly' [LN]. Some translators may choose to omit a reference to the fist since its meaning is uncertain and the various alternatives obscure the meaning instead of clarifying it [TH].

b. pres. act. participle of κρατέω (LN 13.34) (BAGD 2.e.β. p. 448): 'to hold to' [BECNT; ESV, NIV], 'to hold fast to' [AB2, BAGD, Lns; NET], 'to hold' [LN; KJV], 'to cling to' [NTC], 'to keep' [LN, WBC], 'to firmly maintain' [BNTC], 'to follow' [GW, TEV], 'to observe' [NASB, NRSV], 'to obey' [CEV, NCV]. The phrase 'holding to' is translated 'as required by' [NLT], 'in obedience to' [AB1; REB]. This verb means to cause a certain state to continue on the basis of some authority or power [LN]. This word occurs with this same meaning at 7:3, 4, 8.

c. παράδοσις (LN 33.239) (BAGD 2. p. 615): 'tradition' [BAGD, LN; all translations except CEV, NCV, TEV], 'the teaching they received' [TEV], 'teaching' [LN; CEV], 'unwritten laws' [NCV]. This noun denotes the content of traditional instruction [LN]. It has the passive sense of something that is handed down, and here it refers to the tradition that was preserved by the scribes and Pharisees [BAGD]. 'Traditions' are the teachings and laws that are generally handed down in oral form from generation to generation [TH]. These unwritten traditions were not yet written down, but the Pharisees believed that they were part of God's revelation given to Moses on Mount Sinai [NLTfn]. This word occurs at 7:3, 5, 8, 9, 13.

d. πρεσβύτερος (LN 53.77) (BAGD 1.b. p. 699): 'elder' [AB2, BAGD, BECNT, BNTC, LN, Lns, NTC, WBC; ESV, KJV, NET, NIV, NRSV], 'ancestor' [CEV, GW, TEV], 'forefather' [AB1], 'the ancients' [BAGD], not explicit [NCV]. This noun is also translated as an adjective: 'ancient (traditions)' [NLT, REB]. This noun denotes a person of responsibility and authority in matters of socio-religious concerns [LN]. It refers to the 'ancient ones', the ancestors from whom the traditions had come [EGT, ICC, TH]. This refers to noted Jewish teachers of the past, not the current elders of the synagogues or the members of the Sanhedrin [Hb]. The elders were revered persons in general, such as scribes, Pharisees, and leaders of the synagogues [NAC]. This word occurs at 7:3, 5; 8:31; 11:27; 14:43, 53; 15:1.

QUESTION—How are verses 7:3-4 connected with the preceding verse?

It was not enough to explain 'unclean' hands as being 'unwashed' hands in verse 2, so Mark gives examples of ritual cleansing [Lns, NAC]. Many of the Gentile readers were unfamiliar with the Jewish practice of ceremonial washing, so Mark abruptly interrupted his story in order to explain it [EGT, Gnd, Hb, NICNT, NIGTC, NTC, Tay, TRT, WBC]. Since verses 3–4 function as a parenthetical comment, many translations signal this parenthesis with parenthesis marks [AB1, BNTC; ESV, GW, NASB, NCV, NET, NIV, NLT, NRSV, REB, TEV] or dash marks [AB2, GNT, NTC, WBC] before and after the text of verses 3–4. Some make a separate paragraph of verses 3–4 and resume the account in verse 5 [CEV, GW, TEV].

QUESTION—What is meant by washing their hands 'with a fist'?

This refers to the manner in which they washed their hands, but the exact procedure is unclear [AB2, BECNT, CBC, CGTC, Hb, NAC, NETfn, Sw, Tay, TH]. It refers to washing one's hands by twisting and turning the fist of one hand in the palm of the other hand [Lns]. Probably they used a closed hand to firmly rub the palm of the other hand in order to make sure that the part of the hand that touches the food would be clean [EGT, My]. Instead of being a tight fist, it could refer to pouring water over a cupped hand with the fingers flexed to allow the water to pass through them [Gnd, NICNT, WBC].

Perhaps the plural form 'hands' means that two cupped hands were used as a measure for the amount of water involved in the ceremony [WBC]. Another view is that this 'fist' refers to washing with just a fistful of water [CGTC]. Regardless of how it was done, it was a ceremonial washing [ESVfn, NTC].

QUESTION—Did *all* of the Jews follow this washing ceremony?

This custom originated among the Pharisees and then it became a general practice among all of the Jews [ICC, Lns]. The expression 'all of the Jews' indicates that there was a widespread adherence to this Pharisaic practice. It refers to all of those Jews who wished to be regarded as being righteous [Hb]. Using 'all' was an accepted practice of generalizing the actions of a group of people (1:5, 32, 33; 6:33; 11:11) [WBC]. 'All' is hyperbole [Gnd]. The word 'all' simply means 'very many' [NTC], or 'people in general' [BECNT, ICC, Lns, NTC]. The so-called 'sinners' (2:15) among the common people certainly were not concerned about using ritual washings [NICNT]. The phrase 'the Pharisees and all the Jews' is translated 'the Pharisees, as well as the rest of the Jews' [TEV], 'the Pharisees and many of the Jews' [WBC], 'the Pharisees and many others' [CEV], 'Pharisees and Jews in general' [REB; similarly AB1], 'the Jews, especially the Pharisees' [NLT].

7:4 **and (anyone/anything coming) from (the) marketplace**[a] **they-do- not -eat unless they-wash**[b] **(themselves/the food),**

TEXT—Manuscripts reading ἀπ' ἀγορᾶς 'from (the) marketplace' are given an A rating by GNT to indicate it was regarded to be certain. A variant reading is ἀπ' ἀγορᾶς ὅταν ἔλθωσιν 'from (the) marketplace when they come'.

TEXT—Manuscripts reading βαπτίσωνται 'they wash' are given a B rating by GNT to indicate it was regarded to be almost certain. A variant reading is ῥαντίσωνται 'they sprinkle' and it is followed by EGT, NCBC, Tay.

LEXICON—a. ἀγορά (LN 57.207) (BAGD p. 12): 'marketplace' [AB1, AB2, BAGD, BECNT, BNTC, LN, NTC, WBC; ESV, GW, NASB, NET, NIV, REB], 'market' [LN, Lns; CEV, KJV, NCV, NLT, NRSV, TEV]. This noun denotes a commercial center that contains a number of places for doing business [LN]. This word occurs at 6:56; 7:4; 12:38.

b. aorist mid./pass. subj. of βαπτίζω (LN 53.31) (BAGD 1. p. 131): 'to wash' [BAGD, LN]. 'to cleanse, to dip, to immerse' [BAGD], 'to purify' [LN]. This verb is translated in the middle or active voice to refer to people washing themselves: 'they wash themselves' [BECNT, Lns, NTC; ESV, KJV, NCV, NET, NIV; similarly GW, REB], 'they wash all over' [AB1], 'they immerse their hands in water' [NLT], 'they ceremonially wash themselves' [NTC], 'they cleanse themselves' [NASB], 'purifying themselves' [BNTC]. This verb is translated in the passive or active voice to refer to food from the marketplace: 'it is washed' [WBC; CEV], 'they wash it' [NRSV, TEV]. This verse means to wash an object in order to make it ritually acceptable: 'nor do they eat anything that comes from the market unless they wash it' Mark 7:4. It is also possible to take βαπτίσωνται 'they wash' in Mark 7:4 to be in the middle voice and mean 'they wash themselves' [LN].

QUESTION—What comes from the marketplace, and what is washed after coming from the market?

The phrase ἀπ' ἀγορᾶς 'from the marketplace' stands awkwardly outside the syntax of the rest of the sentence and requires something to be supplied. This might mean '*when they come in* from the marketplace', or '*things brought in* from the marketplace'.

1. *People* come from the marketplace, and do not eat until they wash themselves [AB1, AB2; BECNT, BNTC, CGTC, Gnd, Hb, ICC, Lns, My, NAC, NCBC, NIGTC, NTC, Sw, TH, TRT; all versions except CEV, NRSV, TEV], or sprinkle themselves [EGT, NCBC]. Those who had been mingling with all sorts of people in the marketplace would had been exposed to possible sources of ritual impurity, so they would have to purify themselves before eating [AB2, BNTC, ICC, Lns, NIGTC, NTC, Sw, TH].

1.1 This cleansing was done by immersing the whole person [ICC, NIGTC, Sw; probably AB1, AB2], by taking a bath [EGT, Hb, My]. They washed themselves all over [ICC].

1.2 This was done by ceremonially washing just their hands before eating [BNTC, Lns, NLTfn, NTC; NIV]. Their hands may have brushed against a Gentile or anything belonging to a Gentile [BNTC, Lns].

2. *Food* comes from the marketplace and that food is not eaten until it is washed [NICNT, Tay, WBC; CEV, NRSV, TEV]. This is translated 'nor do they eat anything that comes from the market unless they wash it' [LN (53.31)] 'none of them will eat anything they buy in the market until it is washed' [CEV].

3. *Food* comes from the marketplace, and people don't eat it until they wash *themselves* [NCV, NLT]. This refers to immersing their hands in water [NLT].

and there-are many other (traditions) which they-have-received[a] to-hold-to,[b]

LEXICON—a. aorist act. indic. of παραλαμβάνω (LN **27.13**) (BAGD 2.b.γ. p. 619): 'to learn from someone, to learn about a tradition, to learn by tradition' [LN]. The phrase 'traditions which they have received' [AB1, BECNT] is also translated 'traditions' [ESV, NET, NIV, NLT, NRSV], 'things which they have received' [Lns, NTC; KJV, NASB], 'rules which they have received' [TEV], 'rules' [GW], 'traditional rules' [REB], 'customs which they have received' [AB2], 'customs which they have received as tradition' [WBC], 'customs' [BNTC], 'unwritten laws' [NCV], 'teachings' [CEV]. This verb means to acquire information that is passed on by tradition [LN]. It refers to ceremonies that one receives by tradition [BAGD]. The aorist tense refers back to the time they accepted those traditions [Hb].

b. pres. act. infin. of κρατέω (LN 13.34) (BAGD 2.e.β. p. 448): 'to hold fast to' [BAGD, Lns; NET], 'to hold' [LN; KJV], 'to keep' [LN, WBC], 'to maintain' [AB1, BNTC; REB], 'to preserve' [AB2], 'to observe' [BECNT; ESV, NASB, NIV, NRSV], 'to follow' [CEV, GW, NCV, TEV], 'to cling to' [NLT]. This verb means to cause something to continue on the basis of some authority or power [LN]. This is an explanatory infinitive used to clarify what is involved in receiving tradition [CGTC]. The present tense indicates a continued effort to maintain the traditions [Hb]. This word occurs at 7:3, 4, 8 with the same meaning.

QUESTION—What is the function of this clause?

This clause serves to broaden the issue from washing one's hands to the washing of food vessels [Hb, NIGTC]. The following examples still deal broadly with defilement connected with eating food [WBC].

washing of-cups[a] and pitchers[b] and kettles[c] and couches[d]—

TEXT—Manuscripts reading καὶ χαλκίων καὶ κλινῶν 'and kettles and couches' are followed by AB2, EGT, My, Sw; ESV, GW, KJV, NET, TEV, and by GNT, which gives it a C rating to indicate that choosing it over a variant text was difficult. A variant reading is καὶ χαλκίων 'and kettles' and it is followed by AB1, BECNT, Hb, ICC, Lns, NIGTC, NTC, Tay, WBC; CEV, NASB, NCV, NIV, NLT, NRSV, REB. The inclusion of 'couch' is too difficult to accept [BECNT].

LEXICON—a. ποτήριον (LN 6.121) (BAGD 1. p. 695): 'cup' [AB1, AB2, BAGD, BECNT, BNTC, LN, Lns, NTC, WBC; all versions], 'drinking vessel' [BAGD]. This noun denotes an object from which one may drink [LN]. These were ordinary drinking vessels [Hb, Sw].

b. ξέστης (LN 6.126) (BAGD p. 548): 'pitcher' [AB2, BAGD, BECNT, LN, NTC, WBC; CEV, NASB, NCV, NLT], 'pot' [Lns; ESV, KJV, NET, NRSV, TEV], 'jug' [AB1, BAGD, BNTC; REB], 'jar' [LN; GW]. This noun denotes a small pitcher or jar [LN]. It refers to a pitcher, pot, or jug of any size [TH]. The pitchers were used to fill the cups [Hb]. They were made of wood or earthenware [Hb].

c. χαλκίον (LN **6.130**) (BAGD p. 874): 'kettle' [BAGD, NTC; NET, NLT], 'bowl' [CEV], 'pot' [NCV], 'bronze vessel' [BECNT, **LN**], 'brazen vessel' [KJV], 'bronze kettle' [NRSV], 'brass pot' [GW], 'brass vessel' [Lns], 'copper vessel' [BAGD; ESV], 'copper utensil' [AB2], 'copper pot' [WBC; NASB], 'copper bowl' [AB1, BNTC; REB, TEV]. This noun denotes a container or object made of copper, brass, or bronze [LN]. These were large metal vessels of brass or copper used for cooking [Hb, Sw].

d. κλίνη (LN 6.106) (BAGD p. 436): 'couch' [BAGD, LN], 'dining couch' [ESV, NET], 'bed' [AB2, BAGD, LN; TEV], 'cot, stretcher, bier' [LN], 'table' [KJV], 'dinner table' [GW]. This noun denotes any piece of furniture that is used for reclining or lying on [LN].

QUESTION—How is this clause related to the preceding one?

This clause gives examples of the many traditions they received. The clause is introduced with 'for example' [GW, REB], 'such as' [AB1, BECNT; CEV, ESV, NASB, NCV, NIV, NLT, TEV], and 'like' [WBC]. The focus turns from the washing of persons to the washing of food vessels, and the incongruous addition of beds serves to give an even more comprehensive account of the purification rites [NIGTC].

QUESTION—Why would eating and cooking utensils be washed?

This assured their ceremonial cleanness or purification [Hb, Sw].

QUESTION—Why would a couch be washed?

In the context of food and eating utensils, this noun refers to couches that were used when eating meals [EGT, My]. Perhaps this practice was influenced by Leviticus 15 where it speaks of beds being ceremonially unclean after diseased people had lain on them [EGT]. Although the utensils would be washed by immersion, couches would be 'washed' by sprinkling them in a purification ceremony [My].

7:5 and the Pharisees and the scribes question him, "Why don't your disciples walk[a] according-to the tradition[b] of-the elders, but with unclean[c] hands they-eat the bread[d]?"

TEXT—Manuscripts reading καί 'and' at the beginning of this verse are followed by GNT, which does not mention any variant reading. A variant reading is ἔπειτα 'then' and it is followed by KJV.

TEXT—Manuscripts reading κοιναῖς χερσίν 'unclean hands' are followed by GNT, which does not mention any variant reading. A variant reading is ἀνίπτοις χερσίν 'unwashed hands' and it is followed by KJV.

LEXICON—a. pres. act. indic. of περιπατέω (LN 41.11) (BAGD 2.a.δ. p. 649): 'to walk' [AB2, BAGD, BECNT, Lns, WBC; ESV, KJV, NASB], 'to live' [BAGD, LN, NTC; NET, NIV, NRSV], 'to behave' [LN], 'to conduct oneself' [BAGD]. The phrase περιπατοῦσιν...κατά 'walk according to' is translated 'obey' [CEV, NCV], 'observe' [BNTC], 'conform to' [AB1; REB], 'follow' [GW, NLT, TEV]. This verb means to live or behave in a customary manner [LN]. Here the verb 'to walk' has a specialized meaning of 'to live by' [WBC]. It refers to their habitual conduct [Hb]

b. παράδοσις (LN 33.239) (BAGD 2. p. 615): 'tradition' [BAGD, LN]. For translations of the phrase τὴν παράδοσιν τῶν πρεσβυτέρων 'the tradition of the elders' see the same phrase at 7:3. This word occurs at 7:3, 5, 8, 9, 13.

c. κοινός (LN 53.39) (BAGD 2. p. 438): 'unclean' [AB1, BECNT, BNTC; NIV], 'ritually unclean' [LN; TEV], 'impure' [BAGD; NASB], 'defiled' [AB2, LN, NTC, WBC; ESV, NRSV, REB], 'common' [Lns], 'unwashed' [NET]. The phrase 'with unclean hands' is translated 'with hands that are not clean' [NCV], 'with unwashed hands' [KJV], 'without washing their hands' [CEV], 'without first performing the hand-washing ceremony' [NLT]. 'they are unclean because they don't wash their hands' [GW]. This adjective refers to something being ritually unacceptable as the result of defilement or because of the very nature of the object itself [LN]. It refers to something being made common, ordinary, and profane by coming into contact with anything and everything. In this context, it refers to that which is ceremonially impure [BAGD]. This word occurs at 7:2, 5.

d. ἄρτος (LN 5.1) (BAGD 2. p. 110): 'bread' [AB2, BAGD, BECNT, Lns; KJV, NASB], 'food' [AB1, BAGD, BNTC, LN; NCV, NIV, REB]. The phrase 'they eat the bread' is translated '(they) eat' [NTC, WBC; CEV, ESV, GW, NET, NLT, NRSV, TEV]. By using the article in referring to '*the* bread' it may imply that they were pointing to the very bread the disciples were in the process of eating [Hb].

QUESTION—How is this verse connected with what precedes?

After the parenthesis in 7:3–4, the narrative continues from where it was broken off at the end of 7:2 [BECNT, NAC, NICNT, WBC]. This is shown by beginning the first word of 7:5 in the lower case [AB2, BNTC, GNT, WBC]. Mark may have forgotten that he had begun a sentence before the parenthesis, so he begins this verse with his customary καί 'and' to signal a new sentence [CGTC, Gnd, My, Sw]. Most translations begin a new sentence here with an upper case letter [AB1, BECNT, Lns, NTC; all versions]. Eating with 'unclean hands' had caught the attention of the Pharisees and scribes, but now their criticism shifts to the more important issue of following all of the traditions of the elders [NCBC, WBC].

QUESTION—What kind of question is this?

It is a rhetorical question that indicates the disciples had sinned by eating with unclean hands instead of following the traditions of the elders [Hb, NICNT]. This question was a challenge to Jesus himself [NICNT] since he was responsible for their conduct [Hb, Lns, NLTfn]. It is a challenge to the teachings of Jesus about the Law [AB1, CGTC, Tay].

7:6 **And he-said to-them, "Accurately[a] Isaiah prophesied[b] concerning you hypocrites,[c] as it-has-been-written, 'This people honors[d] me with (their) lips, but their heart is-far[e] distant from me;**

LEXICON—a. καλῶς (LN **72.12**) (BAGD 4.b. p. 401): 'accurately' [LN], 'rightly' [BAGD, **LN**; NASB, NRSV], 'correctly' [BAGD, LN; NET], 'truly' [BNTC], 'well' [BECNT, Lns; ESV, KJV]. This adverb is translated as a verb phrase: 'Isaiah was right (when he prophesied)' [AB1, NTC; CEV, GW, NCV, NIV, NLT; similarly REB, TEV]. 'Isaiah did a good job (of prophesying)' [AB2, WBC]. This adverb means being accurate and right [LN].

b. aorist act. indic. of προφητεύω (LN 33.459) (BAGD 3. p. 723): 'to prophesy' [BAGD, LN; all translations except CEV, NCV], 'to make inspired utterances' [LN], 'to foretell the future' [BAGD]. The clause is translated 'Isaiah was right when he spoke about you hypocrites. He wrote,...' [NCV], 'You are nothing but show-offs! The prophet Isaiah was right when he wrote that God had said,...' [CEV]. This verb means to speak under the influence of divine inspiration, and it may refer to present or to future events [LN]. In this verse it refers to a future event and means that long ago Isaiah spoke the truth about the hypocrites that these people were [TH]. This word occurs at 7:6; 14:65.

c. ὑποκριτής (LN 88.228) (BAGD p. 845): 'hypocrite' [AB2, BAGD, BECNT, BNTC, LN, Lns, NTC, WBC; all versions except CEV], 'pretender' [BAGD, LN], 'one who acts hypocritically' [LN]. The phrase 'you the hypocrites' is translated 'pettifogging lawyer' [AB1], 'You are nothing but show-offs!' [CEV]. This noun is derived from ὑποκρίνομαι 'to pretend' and it denotes one who pretends to be different than he really is [LN].

d. pres. act. indic. of τιμάω (LN 87.8) (BAGD 2. p. 817): 'to honor' [AB2, BAGD, BECNT, BNTC, LN, Lns, NTC, WBC; ESV, GW, KJV, NASB, NET, NIV, NLT, NRSV], 'to respect' [LN], 'to revere' [BAGD]. The phrase 'this people honors me with their lips' is translated 'this people pays me lip-service' [REB; similarly AB1], 'these people honor me with their words' [TEV], 'these people show honor to me with words' [NCV], 'all of you praise me with your words' [CEV]. This verb means to attribute high status to someone by honoring him [LN].

e. pres. act. indic. of ἀπέχω (LN 85.16) (BAGD 2. p. 85): 'to be away from, to be off from' [LN], 'to be far from, to be distant' [BAGD]. The phrase 'their heart is far distant from me' [BECNT] is also translated 'their heart is far from me' [AB1, NTC, WBC; ESV, KJV, NET, REB], 'their hearts are far from me' [GW, NCV, NIV, NLT, NRSV], 'their heart is far away from me' [BNTC; NASB], 'their heart is really far away from me' [TEV], 'their heart stands far off from me' [AB2], 'their heart keeps far away from me' [Lns], 'you never really think about me' [CEV]. The verb means to be at some distance away from someone [LN].

QUESTION—How does this respond to the rhetorical question in the preceding verse, 'Why don't your disciples walk according to the tradition of the elders?'

Jesus replied with a counter-attack on his critics [Gnd, PNTC] to deal with the basis of their criticism [BNTC]. There is sarcasm in his answer [Gnd, NIGTC, PNTC, TH] as signaled by the forward position of the adverb 'accurately' [Gnd].

QUESTION—Did the prophet Isaiah actually prophesy about these particular Pharisees and scribes who were now talking with Jesus?

What Isaiah wrote long ago concerning the people of his time was still relevant concerning the people living at the present time [NTC, WBC]. Jesus quoted the Septuagint translation of Isaiah 29:13, in which the prophet Isaiah specifically denounced the Israelite people of that time. However, those words correctly described the Pharisees and scribes who were criticizing the disciples of Jesus [BECNT, Hb, Lns, NIGTC, NTC, Sw]. The Pharisees and scribes were repeating the hypocrisy of that ancient generation [Lns]. It could be translated, 'Isaiah described people like you very well when he said…' [BECNT, Hb].

QUESTION—In what sense were these men hypocrites?

A hypocrite is a person who tries to hide his real intentions under a mask of simulated virtue, and in this case these men were honoring God with their lips even though their hearts were far from God [NTC]. It is not that these men were consciously acting a part, but there was a radical inconsistency in their lives. Their outward appearance of piety was a lie since inwardly they were godless [CGTC, Hb]. Their lofty and noble sentiments were quite different from the intentions of their hearts [PNTC]. The Pharisees and the scribes had carried their hypocrisy to the point that they actually thought they really were what they had only pretended to be [Lns].

7:7 and in-vain[a] they-worship[b] me, teaching (as) teachings[c] (the) commandments of-men.[d]'

LEXICON—a. μάτην (LN 89.54) (BAGD p. 495): 'in vain' [BAGD, BNTC, LN, Lns, NTC, WBC; ESV, KJV, NASB, NET, NIV, NRSV, REB], 'vainly' [BECNT], 'pointlessly' [AB2], 'to no avail, with no result' [LN]. This adverb is translated as a verb phrase: 'is vain' [AB1], 'is pointless' [GW], 'is worthless' [NCV], 'it is useless for you' [CEV], 'it is no use for them' [TEV], 'is a farce' [NLT]. This adverb describes an action as being without any result [LN].

b. pres. mid. indic. of σέβομαι, σέβω (LN 53.52) (BAGD 2.a. p. 746): 'to worship' [BAGD, LN; all translations except GW, NCV, NLT]. This verb is also translated as a noun: 'the worship (of me)' [GW, NCV], 'their worship' [NLT]. This verb means to express a person's allegiance to God by attitude and ritual [LN].

c. διδασκαλία (LN 33.224) (BAGD 2. p. 191): 'teaching' [BAGD, LN]. The participial phrase διδάσκοντες διδασκαλίας 'teaching as teachings' [BECNT, Lns, WBC] is also translated 'teaching as doctrines' [BNTC; ESV, NASB, NRSV], 'teaching as doctrine' [AB1; NET], 'teaching as their doctrines' [NTC], 'teaching for doctrines' [KJV], 'they teach as doctrines' [REB], 'teaching as divine teachings' [AB2] 'they teach…as though they were my laws' [TEV], 'they teach…as commands from God' [NLT], 'the things they teach' [NCV], 'you teach' [CEV], 'their teachings' [GW, NIV]. This noun denotes instruction in a formal or informal setting [LN].

d. ἄνθρωπος (LN 9.1) (BAGD 1.a.β. p. 68): 'man' [BAGD], 'human being' [BAGD, LN], 'person, individual' [LN]. The phrase ἐντάλματα ἀνθρώπων 'commandments of men' [ESV, KJV, NET, REB] is also translated 'precepts of men' [BECNT, BNTC; Lns, NTC; NASB], 'human commandments' [WBC], 'man-made commandments' [AB1], 'human precepts' [NRSV], 'human rules' [NCV, TEV], 'rules made up by humans' [CEV, GW], 'rules taught by men' [NIV], 'man-made ideas' [NLT]. This noun denotes a human being [LN].

QUESTION—What relationship is indicated by the use of the participle διδάσ-κοντες 'teaching'?
1. The participle indicates the reason why their worship is in vain [Lns, TRT, WBC; GW, NLT, REB]: they worship me in vain *because they teach the commandments of men*. Their reverence of God did not come from the heart, but only from commandments they had learned from other men [WBC].
2. The participle indicates a temporal circumstance [ICC; CEV]: they worship me in vain *when/while they teach the commandments of men*.

7:8 Having-rejected^a the commandment of-God you-are-holding-to^b the tradition of-men.^c"

TEXT—Beginning with the final word in verse 7, manuscripts reading ἀνθρώ-πων. ἀφέντες…ἀνθρώπων. 'of men. Having rejected…of men.' are given an A rating by GNT to indicate it was regarded to be certain. A variant reading is ἀνθρώπων. ἀφέντες γὰρ…ἀνθρώπων βαπτισμοὺς ξεστῶν καὶ ποτηρίων καὶ ἄλλα παρόμοια τοιαῦτα πολλὰ ποιεῖτε. 'of men. For having rejected…of men, washings of pitchers and cups and many other such similar things you do' and it is followed by KJV. Another variant reading is ἀνθρώπων, βαπτισμοὺς ξεστῶν καὶ ποτηρίων καὶ ἄλλα παρόμοια ἃ ποιεῖτε τοιαῦτα πολλὰ ἀφέντες…ἀνθρώπων. 'of men, washings of pitchers and cups and other similar things which you do many such things, rejecting…of men'. One ancient version reads ἀνθρώπων. 'of men' at the end of 7:7 and omits all of 7:8.

LEXICON—a. aorist act. participle of ἀφίημι (LN **31.63**) (BAGD 3.b. p. 126): 'to reject' [**LN**], 'to put aside' [AB1; TEV], 'to lay aside' [KJV], 'to abandon' [BAGD, BECNT, BNTC; GW, NRSV], 'to forsake' [AB2], 'to neglect' [WBC; NASB, REB], 'to ignore' [NLT], 'to dismiss' [Lns, 'to leave' [ESV], 'to let go of' [NTC; NIV], 'to give up' [BAGD], 'to stop following' [NCV], 'to disobey' [CEV], 'to have no regard for' [NET], 'to refuse to listen to' [LN]. This verb is a figurative extension of ἀπωθέομαια 'to push away' and it means to no longer pay attention to previous beliefs [LN].

b. pres. act. indic. of κρατέω (LN 13.34) (BAGD 2.e.β. p. 448): 'to hold to' [LN; ESV, NASB, NRSV], 'to hold on to' [NIV], 'to hold' [BECNT; KJV], 'to hold fast to' [AB2, BAGD, Lns; NET], 'to cling to' [NTC, 'to maintain' [BNTC; REB], 'to keep' [AB1, LN, WBC], 'to obey' [CEV, TEV], 'to follow' [GW, NCV], 'to substitute' [NLT]. This verb means to cause a state to continue on the basis of some authority or power [LN]. This word occurs at 7:3, 4, 8 with the same meaning.

c. παράδοσις (LN 33.239) (BAGD 2. p. 615): 'tradition' [BAGD, LN], 'teaching' [LN]. The phrase 'the tradition of men' [AB1, BECNT, BNTC, Lns, NTC, WBC; ESV, KJV, NASB, NIV, REB] is also translated 'the tradition of human beings' [AB2], 'what humans have taught' [CEV], 'human teachings' [TEV], 'only human teachings' [NCV], 'human tradition' [NET, NRSV], 'human traditions' [GW], 'your own tradition' [NLT]. This noun denotes the content of traditional instruction [LN]. The traditions of men were the interpretations of the scribes that had been imposed on the law of God [NAC]. This word occurs at 7:3, 5, 8, 9, 13.

QUESTION—What relationship is indicated by the use of the participial clause 'having rejected the commandment of God'?

1. The participle indicates the means by which they accomplished their desire to obey the traditions of men [AB1; CEV, GW, NET, REB]: you rejected the commandment of God *in order to* obey the traditions of men. This is confirmed in the next verse where a parallel statement use the conjunction ἵνα 'in order that'.
2. The participle indicates a coordinate circumstance [AB2; ESV, NCV, NIV, NLT, NRSV, TEV]: you rejected the commandment of God *and* obey the traditions of men.

QUESTION—Why is τὴν ἐντολήν 'the commandment' singular here?

Even though the singular form 'commandment' grammatically refers to a single commandment of God, it seems to be used in opposition to the plural form ἐντάλματα 'commandments' of men in the preceding verse, so it might be referring to the Law as a whole [Sw]. It could be a generic noun, with one command representing the entire class of laws [BECNT, Hb, Sw]. The singular form might refer to the great command in Deut. 6:4–5 about loving the Lord God with all one's heart, soul, and might [WBC]. If this does refer to a single command, it would probably be the one mentioned in the following verses about honoring one's father and mother, but it may be used generically [NTC]. Many translate this noun in its singular form [AB1, AB2, BECNT, BNTC, NTC, WBC; ESV, KJV, NASB, NET, NLT, NRSV, REB, TEV]. Some translate it with the plural form 'commandments' or 'commands' [CEV, GW, NCV, NIV]. The 'commandment of God' can be translated 'what God commanded' or 'the orders which God spoke' [TH].

DISCOURSE UNIT—7:9–13 [NICNT]. The topic is the conflict between commandment and tradition.

7:9 And he-was-saying to-them, "(How) well[a] you-have-rejected[b] the commandment of-God, in-order-that you-might-establish[c]/keep[d] your traditions.

TEXT—Manuscripts reading στήσητε 'you might establish' are followed by AB1, AB2, BECNT, BNTC, Gnd, NETfn, NICNT, NIGTC, NTC, Tay, WBC; CEV, ESV, NCV, NET, NIV, NLT, REB, TEV, and by GNT, which gives it a rare D rating to indicate that choosing it over a variant text was very difficult. A variant reading is the aorist subjunctive τηρήσητε 'you might keep' and it is followed by CGTC, Hb, Lns, PNTC, Sw, TH; GW, KJV, NASB, NIV, NRSV. Another variant reading is the present subjunctive τηρῆτε 'you might be keeping'.

LEXICON—a. καλῶς (LN 78.21) (BAGD 6. p. 401): 'well, beautifully' [BAGD], 'very well, certainly' [LN]. The phrase 'how well you have

rejected' is translated 'how well you set aside' [AB1], 'how well you nullify' [BECNT; similarly Lns], 'full well ye reject' [KJV], 'how beautifully you are setting aside' [NTC], 'you have a fine way of rejecting' [ESV, NRSV], 'you have a fine way of setting aside' [NIV], 'you have a clever way of rejecting' [TEV], 'you neatly reject' [NET], 'you do a good job of nullifying' [WBC; similarly AB2], 'you are good at rejecting' [CEV]. 'how good you are at setting aside' [BNTC]. 'how clever you are at setting aside' [REB], 'you have no trouble rejecting' [GW], 'you skillfully sidestep' [NLT], 'you cleverly ignore' [NCV], 'you are experts at setting aside' [NASB]. This adverb indicates a high degree of approval [LN], but in this verse the adverb is used ironically [BAGD].
b. pres. act. indic. of ἀθετέω (LN 76.24) (BAGD 1.a. p. 21): 'to reject' [LN; CEV, ESV, GW, KJV, NET, NRSV, TEV], 'to regard as invalid' [LN], 'to nullify' [BECNT, Lns, WBC], 'to annul' [AB2], 'to set aside' [AB1, BNTC, NTC; NASB, NIV, REB], 'to sidestep' [NLT], 'to ignore' [NCV]. This verb means to refuse to recognize the validity of something [LN]. They rejected God's commands by making a conscious choice against them [PNTC]. The present tense indicates that this was a continuing practice [Hb].
c. For the manuscripts reading στήσητε 'you might establish':
aorist act. subj. of ἵστημι (LN 76.20): 'to establish' [AB2, BECNT, BNTC, NTC, WBC; ESV], 'to maintain' [LN; REB], 'to uphold' [AB1, LN; TEV], 'to hold on to' [NIV, NLT], 'to follow' [CEV, NCV], 'to accept the validity of' [LN], 'to set up' [NET]. This verb means to acknowledge the validity of something [LN]. The present tense implies that they continued upholding their human traditions and rejecting God's commandments [PNTC].
d. For the manuscripts reading τηρήσητε 'you might keep':
aorist act. subj. of τηρέω (LN 36.19) (BAGD 5. p. 817): 'to keep' [BAGD, LN, Lns; GW, KJV, NASB, NRSV], 'to obey' [LN], 'to observe' [BAGD; NIV], 'to fulfill, to pay attention to' [BAGD]. This verb means to continue to obey orders or commandments [LN].

QUESTION—What is meant by the beginning clause 'And he was saying to them'?

Mark wanted to draw special attention to what follows [Gnd, Lns]. It may indicate a new phase of the discussion [Hb]. This implies that Jesus had paused before he went on to speak about Corban [Lns].

QUESTION—Why did Jesus say that they rejected the word of God καλῶς 'very well'?

This same adverb was used seriously with the meaning 'accurately' in verse 6, but here it is used sarcastically with the meaning 'how well' [CBC, Hb, NIGTC, TRT]. It is a case of irony in which the speaker's attitude is the opposite of the literal sense of the words [BECNT, CGTC, EGT, Gnd, ICC, Lns, My, NCBC, NICNT, Sw, TH, TRT].

7:10 Because Moses said, 'Honor[a] your father and your mother' and 'The (one) reviling[b] father or mother, by-death let-him-die.[c]'

LEXICON—a. pres. act. impera. of τιμάω (LN 87.8) (BAGD 2. p. 817): 'to honor' [BAGD, LN; all translations except CEV, TEV], 'to respect' [LN; CEV, TEV], 'to revere' [BAGD]. This verb means to attribute high status to someone by honoring that person [LN].

  b. pres. act. participle of κακολογέω (LN 33.339) (BAGD p. 397): 'to revile' [BAGD, LN, Lns; ESV], 'to speak evil of' [BAGD, BECNT, WBC; NASB, NRSV], 'to insult' [BAGD; NET], 'to say cruel things to' [NCV], 'to curse' [AB1, AB2, BNTC, NTC; CEV, GW, KJV, NIV, REB, TEV], 'to speak disrespectfully to' [NLT]. This verb means to insult someone in a particularly strong and unjustified manner [LN]. This is a quotation from Exodus 21:17. The Hebrew text uses a word that means 'to curse', but the Septuagint Greek translation of the verse used a more general word meaning 'to speak evil of a parent' and that is the word used by Mark [NAC].

  c. pres. act. impera. of τελευτάω (LN 23.102) (BAGD p. 810): 'to die' [BAGD, LN], 'to come to an end' [BAGD]. The phrase 'by death let him die' is translated 'let him die the death' [Lns; KJV], 'must certainly be put to death' [AB1, NTC], 'let him certainly die' [BECNT], 'must surely die' [NRSV], 'must die' [ESV], 'must be put to death' [GW, NCV, NET, NIV, NLT, REB; similarly BNTC, WBC; CEV], 'let him be executed' [AB2], 'is to be put to death' [NASB; similarly TEV]. This verb means 'to end' and the expression 'coming to the end of one's life' is an euphemistic way of saying that the person dies [LN]. The offender's life will come to an end when he is put to death in judicial punishment [Hb]. 'Let him die' does not mean 'permit him to die'. It is a strong statement that means he must certainly be put to death [TH].

QUESTION—What relationship is indicated by the conjunction γάρ 'because'?
This provides an example of what Jesus meant by saying they rejected the commandment of God (7:9) [BECNT, EBC, Gnd, Sw, TRT]. The conjunction is translated 'for example' [GW], 'for instance' [NLT].

QUESTION—Where are these two commands of Moses recorded?
These are two direct quotes from the Septuagint Greek translation of the Torah. The first is from Exodus 20:12 and the second is from Exodus 21:17 [CGTC, Hb, NAC, NCBC, NICNT, NIGTC, Sw, Tay, WBC]. In Judaism, one of the most important duties of a person was to honor his parents [CBC].

QUESTION—Why did Jesus include the second command from Exodus 21:17?
By pointing out the judicial punishment for disobedience to the fifth commandment, Jesus showed how seriously the law took the fifth commandment [BECNT, Hb, ICC, Lns, NICNT, NIGTC]. The sentence of death was for an extreme case of dishonoring a parent [NIGTC], but the death penalty was no longer being applied by the time of Jesus [BNTC].

QUESTION—What is meant by honoring one's father and mother?

It means more than simply obeying one's parents. Obedience is to be done in an attitude of love and respect [Hb, Lns, TH, TRT]. It refers to showing a proper esteem towards one's parents [Hb]. Honoring parents includes giving them material support in regard to food, drink, and clothing [AB2]. Part of honoring parents includes caring for them both financially and personally [ESVfn].

7:11 But you say, 'If a-man says to-the father or to-the mother, "Corban[a] (which means[b] 'a-gift[c]') (is) whatever you-might-have-benefited[d] from me"—

LEXICON—a. κορβᾶν (LN **53.22**) (BAGD p. 444): 'corban' [BAGD, BECNT, BNTC, LN, Lns, NTC, WBC; all versions except CEV, NLT], 'korban' [AB2], 'qorban' [AB1], 'offering' [LN], 'gift to God' [BAGD, LN]. This Hebrew word in the direct quote is replaced by the information provided in the explanation of its meaning [CEV, NLT]. This noun is a Greek transliteration of a Hebrew word that denotes something that has been set aside to be a gift to God, although it is still at the owner's disposal. In some languages it is important to translate corban as 'what I have promised to later give to God' [LN]. It is a gift consecrated to God that will be used for religious purposes [BAGD].

b. ὅ ἐστιν (LN 89.106) (BAGD II.3. p. 224): The phrase ὅ ἐστιν 'which means' [BAGD, BNTC, LN, WBC; TEV] is also translated 'which is' [Lns], 'which is the equivalent of' [BAGD], 'that is' [AB2, BECNT, BNTC, LN, NTC; ESV, GW, NET, NIV, NRSV, REB], 'meaning' [AB1], 'that is to say' [BAGD; KJV, NASB], not explicit [CEV, NCV, NLT]. This phrase introduces an explanation or a clarification in the same or a different language [LN]. Mark inserted an explanation of 'Corban' for his Gentile readers [BNTC]. This phrase occurs at 3:17; 7:11.

c. δῶρον (LN 57.84) (BAGD 2. p. 211): 'gift' [BAGD, LN, Lns, WBC; KJV], 'present' [BAGD, LN], 'a gift to God' [AB2, BECNT, BNTC; NCV], 'a gift for God' [NET], 'a gift set apart for God' [AB1, NTC], 'a gift devoted to God' [NIV], 'an offering to God' [GW, NRSV], 'given to God' [ESV, NASB], 'set apart for God' [REB], 'it belongs to God' [TEV]. The phrase 'corban, that is, a gift' is translated: 'I have vowed to give to God' [NLT], 'what they own has been offered to God' [CEV]. This noun denotes that which is given or granted [TH].

d. aorist pass. subj. of ὠφελέω (LN 35.2) (BAGD 1.a. p. 900): 'to benefit, to aid' [BAGD], 'to help' [BAGD, LN]. The clause 'whatever you might have benefited from me' is translated 'whatever you might be benefited from me' [WBC], 'whatever you should have benefited from me' [BECNT], 'whatever from me thou mightest have benefit' [Lns], 'whatsoever thou mightest be profited by me' [KJV], 'whatever it be by which I might benefit you' [NTC], 'anything I have which might have been used for your benefit' [REB], 'whatever you would have gained from me'

[ESV], 'whatever help you might otherwise have received from me' [NIV; similarly NET], 'whatever support you might have had from me' [NRSV], 'whatever of mine you might have benefited from' [AB2], 'what you might have received from me' [BNTC], 'what I would have given to you' [NLT], 'whatever I have that would help you' [NASB], 'I have something I could use to help you, but' [NCV]. This is also translated as a comment: 'whatever he might have used to help them' [GW], 'if people have something they could use to help their father or mother' [TEV], '(you let people get by) without helping their parents when they should' [CEV]. This verb means to provide assistance [LN]. The subjunctive form indicates a contrary to fact condition, 'whatever you might have benefited (but did not)' [TH].

QUESTION—What relationship is indicated by δέ 'but'?

This conjunction indicates contrast [AB1, AB2, BECNT, BNTC, Hb, Lns; all versions]. 'You say' is contrasted with 'Moses said' in 1:10 [AB1, BECNT, CGTC, Gnd, Lns, Sw, Tay]. It stresses the contradiction between God's command and the teachings of the Pharisees and the scribes [Hb].

QUESTION—Does the conjunction ἐάν 'if' imply that they didn't actually say this?

This illustration would be pointless unless there were actually cases of this kind [Hb, Tay].

QUESTION—What is meant by 'Corban'?

'Corban' is the English transliteration of the Greek word Κορβᾶν 'Korban', which is itself a translation of the Hebrew word meaning 'a gift'. It refers to a gift dedicated to God as an offering [NAC]. It is not clear whether the support that was due to the man's parents was already in possession of the temple and no longer available or simply vowed to the temple. Even if the gift was still in the son's possession, it was reserved for God and could not be given to his parents [BECNT]. An offering to God could be food, money, or property [NIGTC]. The money or goods a person dedicated to God by a vow was holy and could not be used for any secular purpose such as helping parents who had rightly expected support [Hb]. It seems that a person was not required to immediately turn over the property that he had declared to be Corban. He could continue to use and enjoy the property until he died. Then the remainder would go to the temple [NAC]. When the son in this illustration declared his property corban to his parents, he legally excluded his parents from the right of benefiting from it [NICNT].

7:12 No-longer[a] do-you-permit[b] him to-do anything for (his) father or (his) mother,

LEXICON—a. οὐκέτι (LN 67.130) (BAGD 1. p. 592): 'no longer' [AB1, AB2, BAGD, BECNT, BNTC, Lns, NTC, TH, WBC; ESV, GW, NASB, NCV, NET, NIV, NRSV, REB], 'no more' [KJV], not explicit [AB1; CEV, NLT, TEV]. This adverb indicates an extension of time up to a point but not beyond it [LN].

b. pres. act. indic. of ἀφίημι (LN 13.140) (BAGD 4. p. 126): 'to permit' [BAGD, BECNT, NTC; ESV, NASB, NET, NRSV], 'to let' [BAGD, LN, Lns; CEV, NCV, NIV, NLT], 'to allow' [AB1, AB2, BAGD, BNTC, LN, WBC; REB], 'to suffer' [KJV]. The phrase 'no longer do you permit him to do anything' is translated 'he no longer has to do anything' [GW], 'you excuse him from helping' [AB1], 'they are excused from helping' [TEV]. This verb means to leave it up to someone to do something [LN].

QUESTION—How is this verse connected with the previous verse?

Verse 11 starts out, "You say, 'If a man says…'" and the conditional clause continues to the end of verse 11. We would normally expect verse 12 to continue the sentence with a consequence clause something like, '*then* that man is not permitted…' Instead, verse 12 starts out with a new sentence, '*You* do not permit him…' This is an anacoluthon in which there is an abrupt change from one syntactic construction to another. Here the syntactic form shifts from a conditional clause to a new sentence that directly addresses the Pharisees [Gnd]. This anacoluthon is translated in various ways.

1. Following the Greek text, the conditional clause quoted in the words of the man to his parents in verse 11 is left without a consequence clause, and verse 12 continues with Jesus directly addressing the Pharisees [AB1, AB2, BECNT, BNTC, Lns, NTC, WBC; ESV, NASB]: 'But you say, "If a man says to his father or mother, 'Corban (…) is whatever you might have benefited from me—" ¹²No longer do you permit him to do anything for his father or his mother'. Some translations also supply the dash at the end of verse 11 to indicate that the sentence in the quote is not completed [AB2, BNTC, NTC; ESV].

2. The conditional clause has a consequence clause supplied at the end of verse 11: 'But ye say, "If a man shall say to his father or mother. 'It is Corban…, *he shall be free."* ¹²And ye suffer him no more to do ought for his father or his mother' [KJV].

3. The 'if' phrase is moved out of the quotation [AB1; NET, NIV, NRSV, REB, TEV]: 'But you say that if a man says to his father or mother: "Whatever help you might otherwise have received from me is Corban" (…), ¹²then you no longer let him do anything for his father or mother' [NIV].

4. The conditional clause is changed to an independent statement: 'But you say a person can tell his father or mother, "I have something I could use to help you, but it is Corban—a gift to God." ¹²You no longer let that person use that money for his father or his mother' [NCV].

5. The content of what 'you say' continues through the next verse by changing the subject in verse 12 from 'you' to 'he': 'But you say, "If a person tells his father or mother that whatever he might have used to help them is *corban* (…), ¹²he no longer has to do anything for his father or mother' [GW].

6. The verses are restructured and implicit information is made explicit: 'But you say it is all right for people to say to their parents, "Sorry, I can't help

you. For I have vowed to give to God what I would have given to you." ¹²In this way, you let them disregard their needy parents' [NLT], 'But you let people get by without helping their parents when they should. You let them say that what they own has been offered to God. ¹²You won't let those people help their parents' [CEV].

QUESTION—Why would the scribes not allow the son to do anything to help his parents in this case?

If a son came to regret making such a vow, the scribes would tell him that his vow was still valid and must be honored [NICNT]. Under no circumstances would the scribes of that time permit a person to annul such a vow [NAC]. Pharisaic tradition held that such a vow outweighed every other consideration and did away with every other obligation that involved money or goods [Lns]. Num. 30:2–4 supported their reasoning that any vow made to God was permanently binding [AB2].

7:13 nullifying[a] the word[b] of-God by/for-the tradition[c] of-you which you-pass-on.[d] And you-do many such similar (things).

LEXICON—a. pres. act. participle of ἀκυρόω (LN **76.25**) (BAGD p. 34): 'to make void' [BAGD], 'to disregard' [**LN**], 'to reject, to invalidate the authority of' [LN]. The participial form ἀκυροῦντες 'nullifying' is translated 'making of none effect' [KJV], 'so…you nullify' [AB1], 'thus making void' [ESV, NRSV; similarly AB2, BECNT], 'thus annulling' [WBC], 'thus you nullify' [NTC; NET, NIV], 'thus invalidating' [NASB], 'and so you cancel' [NLT], 'in this way…cancels out' [TEV], 'in this way you make (God's word) null and void' [REB] 'you have destroyed the authority of' [GW], 'you are rejecting' [NCV], 'and you ignore' [CEV]. This verb means to refuse to recognize the force or power of something [LN].

b. λόγος (LN 33.98) (BAGD 1.b.α. p. 478): 'word' [AB1, AB2, BAGD, BECNT, BNTC, LN, Lns, NTC, WBC; all versions except CEV, NCV, REB], 'saying, message, statement' [LN]. The phrase 'the word of God' is translated 'what God has said' [**LN** (76.25); similarly NCV], 'the command of God' [**LN** (76.25)], 'God's commands' [CEV, REB]. This noun denotes that which has been stated or said [LN]. The 'word of God' usually designates the Christian message, but in thus verse it refers to God's pronouncement in the fifth commandment [NIGTC].

c. παράδοσις (LN 33.239) (BAGD 2. p. 615): 'tradition' [BAGD, LN] 'teaching' [LN]. The dative form in τῇ παραδόσει ὑμῶν 'by the tradition of you' is translated 'by your tradition' [BECNT, NTC; ESV, NASB, NET, NIV, REB; similarly AB1], 'by your own rules' [NCV], 'through your tradition' [BNTC; KJV, NRSV], 'with your tradition' [WBC], 'because of your traditions' [GW], 'for your tradition' [Lns], 'for the sake of your tradition' [AB2], 'in order to follow your own teaching' [CEV], 'the teaching you (pass on to others)' [TEV], '(in order to hand down) your own tradition' [NLT]. This word occurs at 7:3, 5, 8, 9, 13.

MARK 7:13

d. aorist act. indic. of παραδίδωμι (LN 33.237) (BAGD 3. p. 615): 'to pass on' [BAGD, LN, Lns, WBC; TEV], 'to pass down' [AB2, BECNT], 'to hand on' [AB1, BNTC, NTC; NRSV], 'to hand down' [ESV, NASB, NET, NIV, NLT], 'to deliver' [KJV], 'to instruct' [LN], 'to teach' [LN; NCV], not explicit [CEV, GW]. This verb means to pass on traditional instruction [LN]. The pronoun 'you' refers to the Jews as a whole, not just the men to whom Jesus was speaking [TH].

QUESTION—What relationship is indicated by the participle 'nullifying'?

The participle indicates the result of not permitting a son to do anything for his parents [AB1, AB2, BECNT, NETfn, NTC, WBC; ESV, GW, NASB, NET, NIV, NLT]: *thus* you nullify the word of God.

QUESTION—What is meant by ἀκυροῦντες 'nullifying' the word of God?

They have dared to rule the word of God to be invalid [NIGTC]. They overruled the clear command of Scripture [BECNT] by insisting that the oath must be kept at whatever cost [BNTC]. If such a plain divine commandment as the Fourth Commandment could be robbed of its authority by these Jews, then the entire Word of God is rendered empty of authority [Lns].

QUESTION—What relationship is indicated by the use of the dative case of the noun παραδόσει 'tradition'?

1. The dative case indicates the means or the instrument by which 'nullifying the word of God' was accomplished [AB1, BECNT, CGTC, LN (76.25), NTC, Sw, Tay, TH, WBC; ESV, KJV, NASB, NCV, NET, NIV, NRSV, TEV]: you nullify the word of God *by* following your tradition.
2. The dative case indicates what was benefited by nullifying the word of God [AB2, Lns; CEV, GW, NLT]. you nullify the word of God *for the sake of* your tradition.

QUESTION—What was the problem that Jesus was addressing?

In this context, the issue was whether scribal tradition concerning an oath could nullify one of God's commandments [AB2, BECNT, BNTC, NIGTC]. The problem was not about the scribes trying to uphold the law [AB2, BNTC], and it was not about whether the law to keep one's vows took priority over the law to honor one's parents [BECNT, WBC]. The traditions of the Pharisees actually prohibited a person from keeping God's commandment about honoring one's parents [BNTC]. The scribes had actually ruled the word of God to be unlawful [NIGTC].

QUESTION—What is meant by 'many such similar things'?

This refers to other things they did that were just as bad [CEV]. Their use of Corban was just an example of what was constantly going on [NTC; NLT].

DISCOURSE UNIT—7:14–23 [EBC, Hb, NICNT; CEV, ESV, NASB, TEV]. The topic is true defilement [EBC, NICNT], what defiles a person [ESV], the things that make a person unclean [TEV], what really makes people unclean [CEV], the source of true defilement [Hb], the heart of man [NASB].

7:14 And having-summoned[a] again the crowd, he-said to-them, "Listen[b] to-me everyone and understand.[c]

TEXT—Manuscripts reading πάλιν 'again' are followed by GNT, which does not mention any variant reading. A variant reading is πάντα 'all' and it is followed by EGT, Gnd, Tay; KJV, NLT.

LEXICON—a. aorist mid. participle of προσκαλέομαι, προσκαλέω (LN 33.306) (BAGD 1.a. p. 715): 'to summon' [AB2, BAGD, WBC], 'to call to oneself' [AB1, BAGD, BNTC, Lns, NTC; ESV, KJV, NASB, NCV, NIV, TEV], 'to call together' [CEV], 'to call' [BECNT, LN; GW, NET, NLT, NRSV, REB]. This verb means to call to someone [LN].

b. aorist act. impera. of ἀκούω (LN 24.52) (BAGD 1.c. p. 32): 'to listen' [BAGD], 'to hear' [BAGD, LN]. The imperative is translated 'listen' [AB1, AB2, BECNT, WBC; all versions except CEV, ESV, KJV], 'hear' [BNTC, NTC; ESV], 'pay attention' [Lns; CEV], 'harken' [KJV]. This verb means to hear [LN]. The aorist imperative of both 'listen' and 'understand' are appropriate since they refer to a single saying [CGTC, Tay]. The aorist tense of both imperatives are normal [Gnd, Tay] and they urge the people to give their attention to the words in order to intelligently understand them [Hb].

c. aorist act. impera. of συνίημι (LN 32.5) (BAGD p. 790): 'to understand, to comprehend' [BAGD, LN], 'to perceive, to have insight into' [LN]. The imperative is translated 'understand' [AB2, BECNT, BNTC, Lns, NTC, WBC; ESV, KJV, NASB, NET, NRSV, TEV], 'understand this' [AB1; NIV, REB], 'understand what I am saying' [NCV], 'try to understand' [GW, NLT], 'try to understand what I mean' [CEV]. 'Understand' can be understood figuratively to mean 'receive it in your hearts' [TH]. This word occurs at 4:12; 6:52; 7:14; 8:17, 21.

QUESTION—What is implied by Jesus summoning the crowd *again*?

'Again' indicates that the crowd had previously gathered closely around Jesus. Perhaps the crowd had withdrawn a little when the delegation of scribes had approached Jesus in 7:1 [CBC, EBC, EGT, Hb, ICC, Lns, My, NTC]. It could be parallel to 4:1–20, 'And again he began to teach beside the lake' and mean 'again, as his custom was, he taught them'. His solemn call to be attentive recalls the summons in 4:3, 'Listen. Behold' [NICNT, WBC]. It may refer back to 6:45 where Jesus dismissed the crowd [WBC]. The word πάλιν 'again' does not have to refer back to a similar episode, and in this verse it probably serves as a simple connective particle to indicate Jesus sought to teach the crowds as he usually did [NCBC].

7:15 There-is nothing outside[a] of-the man entering[b] into him which is-able to-make- him -unclean,[c]

LEXICON—a. ἔξωθεν (LN 83.20) (BAGD 2.a. p. 279): 'outside' [BAGD, BECNT, BNTC, LN, Lns, NTC; ESV, NASB, NET, NIV, NRSV], 'from the outside' [AB1, AB2, WBC; GW, REB, TEV], 'from without' [KJV], not explicit [NCV, NLT]. The phrase 'there is nothing outside of the man'

is translated 'the food (that you put into your mouth)' [CEV]. This preposition indicates a position not contained within a particular area [LN].
b. pres. mid. (deponent = act.) participle of εἰσπορεύομαι (LN 15.93) (BAGD 1. p. 233): 'to enter' [AB1, BECNT, LN, WBC; KJV], 'to go into' [AB2, BAGD, LN, NTC; GW, NLT, REB, TEV]. The participial phrase 'entering into him' is translated 'by entering him' [BNTC], 'by going into him' [Lns; ESV, NET, NIV, NRSV], 'if it goes into him' [NASB], '(there is nothing) people put into their bodies' [NCV], '(the food that) you put into your mouth' [CEV]. This verb means to move something into a space [LN].
c. aorist act. infin. of κοινόω (LN 53.33) (BAGD 1.a. p. 438): 'to make unclean' [AB1, BECNT, BNTC, LN; GW, NCV, NIV], 'to defile' [AB2, BAGD, LN, Lns, NTC, WBC; ESV, KJV, NASB, NET, NLT, NRSV, REB], 'to make impure, to make common' [BAGD], 'to profane' [LN]. The phrase 'make him unclean' is translated 'make you ritually unclean' [TEV], 'make you unclean and unfit to worship God' [CEV]. This verb means to cause something to become unclean, profane, or ritually unacceptable [LN]. This is the verbal form of the word 'unclean' at 7:2, 5 [AB2]. This word occurs at 7:15, 18, 20, 23.

QUESTION—What are the things 'entering into' a man?

This especially refers to food eaten with unwashed hands as discussed in verse 2 [BECNT, Lns, NICNT, NIGTC, TH, TRT, WBC; CEV]. The comment in 7:18–19 makes it clear that it refers to food [WBC]. The Pharisees and scribes were saying that people who eat with unwashed hands ritually defile the food they touched. Then, by eating that food, they themselves became defiled [BECNT, Lns, WBC]. Jesus is teaching them that eating food with unwashed hands cannot cause spiritual uncleanness [WBC]. The principle is that anything external cannot defile a person's spiritual nature [Sw].

but the (things) coming-out[a] from the man are the (things) making- the man -unclean."

LEXICON—a. pres. mid./pass. (deponent = act.) participle of ἐκπορεύομαι (LN 15.40) (BAGD 2. p. 244): 'to come out of' [AB1, AB2, BAGD, BECNT, BNTC, NTC, WBC; ESV, GW, KJV, NCV, NRSV, REB], 'to proceed out of' [Lns; NASB], 'to go out of' [BAGD, LN], 'to depart out of, to leave from within' [LN]. The phrase 'the things coming out from the man' is translated 'the bad words that come out of your mouth' [CEV], 'by what comes from your heart' [NLT]. This verb means to move out of an enclosed or well defined area [LN].

QUESTION—What are the things that come out of a man that make him unclean?

These are moral and spiritual things [Lns]. The 'heart' of a man is the source of spiritual and moral conduct [NICNT, NTC, TH]. The things that make a man unclean originate in the inner moral nature of a man himself [Hb]. Originating in the heart, they are outwardly expressed by sinful deeds and words [TH]. It refers to evil thoughts of all kinds [ICC, TRT, WBC], and also words and actions [TRT, WBC]. This is referring to the sins and evil desires that are listed in 7:21–23 [NTC, TH].

7:16 (**If anyone has ears to hear, let him hear.**)

TEXT—Manuscripts omitting this verse are given an A rating by GNT to indicate the omission was regarded to be certain. Instead of omitting this verse, some manuscripts read εἴ τις ἔχει ὦτα ἀκούειν ἀκουέτω 'if anyone has ears to hear, let him hear' and they are followed by AB1, BNTC, NCBC; KJV. Another variant reading is ὁ ἔχων ὦτα ἀκούειν ἀκουέτω 'the one having ears to hear, let him hear'.

7:17 **And when he-entered into a-house from**[a] **the crowd, his disciples were-asking him (about) the parable.**[b]

LEXICON—a. ἀπό (LN 89.122): 'from, separated from' [LN]. The phrase ἀπὸ τοῦ ὄχλου 'from the crowd/multitude/people' [Lns; KJV] is also translated 'away from the crowd/people' [AB2, BECNT, BNTC, WBC]. A verb is supplied to indicate this was the purpose for entering the house: 'to get away from the crowd' [NLT]. A verb is supplied to indicate this was a separate action: '(he entered the house) and left the people' [ESV]. The event of getting away from the crowd is moved ahead of the verb 'he entered': '(when/after) he had left the people/crowd' [NTC; all versions except ESV, KJV, NLT]. This preposition indicates a dissociation from something [LN].

b. παραβολή (LN 33.15) (BAGD 2. p. 612): 'parable' [BAGD, LN; all translations except CEV, GW, NCV, TEV], 'illustration' [BAGD], 'saying' [CEV, TEV], 'story' [NCV], 'illustration' [GW], 'figure, allegory' [LN]. This noun denotes a relatively short narrative with symbolic meaning [LN]. This word occurs at 3:23; 4:2, 10, 11, 13, 30, 33, 34; 7:17; 12:1, 12; 13:28.

QUESTION—What was τὴν παραβολήν '*the* parable' the disciples asked about?

The 'parable' refers to the statement Jesus made in 7:15 [Hb]. This 'parable' [AB1, BECNT, BNTC, NTC, WBC; ESV, KJV, NASB, NET, NIV, NLT, NRSV, REB] was little more than a saying [BNTC, ICC, Lns, NICNT, NTC, Sw; CEV, TEV], an illustration [TH; GW], a riddle [AB2, Hb, NICNT], a story [NCV]. Even riddles fall within the range of meaning of the Hebrew word for 'proverb' [AB2]. By calling the straightforward statement in verse 15 a parable, Mark is stressing how blind the disciples really were [NCBC].

7:18 And he-says to-them, "Thus[a] even you are without-understanding[b]? Do-you- not -understand[c] that every thing entering into the man from-the-outside is- not -able to- make- him -unclean

LEXICON—a. οὕτως (LN 61.9) (BAGD 1.b. p. 597): 'thus, so' [BAGD, LN], 'in this way' [LN], 'in this manner' [BAGD]. The first question is translated 'Then are you also without understanding?' [AB2; ESV], 'Then do you also fail to understand?' [NRSV]. 'Are you also so lacking in understanding?' [NTC; similarly KJV, NASB], 'Are you also as lacking in understanding?' [WBC], 'So are you also without understanding?' [BECNT], 'Are you as dull as the rest?' [AB1; REB], 'Don't you know what I am talking about by now?' [CEV], 'Don't you understand?' [GW], 'Don't you understand either?' [NLT], 'Do you still not understand?' [NCV], 'Are you so foolish?' [NET], 'Are you so dull?' [BNTC; NIV]. This question is translated as a statement: 'Thus even you are without understanding!' [Lns], 'You are no more intelligent than the others' [TEV]. This adverb refers to that which precedes it [BAGD, LN].

b. ἀσύνετος (LN 32.49) (BAGD 1. p. 118): 'without understanding' [LN], 'senseless, foolish' [BAGD, LN]. See translations of this word in the preceding lexical item *a*. This adjective indicates a lack of capacity for insight and understanding [LN].

c. pres. act. indic. of νοέω (LN 32.2) (BAGD 1.b. p. 540): 'to understand' [AB1, BAGD, BNTC, LN; NASB, NET, TEV], 'to know' [AB2, BECNT, WBC; CEV, GW, NCV], 'to gain insight into' [BAGD, LN], 'to comprehend' [LN, Lns], 'to apprehend' [BAGD], 'to perceive' [LN; KJV], 'to see' [ESV, NIV, NLT, NRSV, REB]. This verb means to comprehend something on the basis of careful thought and consideration [LN]. This word occurs at 7:18; 8:17; 13:14.

QUESTION—What is the function of the question, 'Do you not understand that…'?

It is a rhetorical question that implies the disciples should have understood by now [CEV]. This rhetorical question functions as a rebuke [Hb, Lns]. It is translated as a statement; 'You surely know that…' [CEV; similarly NCV].

QUESTION—What does 'everything entering into the man' refer to?

Jesus is speaking about every kind of food [Lns]. The food goes into the man's mouth [TH]. It is 'the food you put into your mouth' [CEV].

7:19 because it-does- not -enter into his heart[a] but into the stomach, and goes-out into the latrine[b]?" making-clean[c] all foods.

TEXT—Manuscripts reading καθαρίζων 'making clean' (a masculine participle) are given an A rating by GNT to indicate it was regarded to be certain. A variant reading is καθαρίζον 'making clean' (a neuter participle) and it is followed by KJV.

LEXICON—a. καρδία (LN 26.3): 'heart' [LN; all translations except AB1; GW, NCV], 'inner self' [LN], 'mind' [AB1, LN; NCV], 'thoughts' [GW]. This noun is a figurative extension of the word 'heart'. It particularly refers to a person's thoughts and functions as the causative source of a person's psychological life [LN]. In biblical literature, the heart most commonly represents the essential personality of a person, and includes the spiritual and intellectual processes along with the will [NIGTC].

b. ἀφεδρῶν (LN 7.72) (BAGD p. 124): 'latrine' [BAGD, LN], 'toilet' [LN]. The phrase 'and goes/comes out into the latrine' [AB2, NTC, WBC] is also translated 'and passes out into the latrine' [BECNT], 'and then goes out into the sewer' [BNTC; NET, NRSV; similarly NLT], 'and then into a toilet' [GW], 'and goes out into the privy' [Lns], 'and so goes out into the drain' [REB], 'and then passes into the drain' [AB1], 'and goeth out into the draught' [KJV], 'then it goes out of the body' [NCV], 'and then goes on out of the body' [TEV], 'and then out of his body' [NIV; similarly NCV], 'and is expelled' [ESV], 'and is eliminated' [NASB]. This noun denotes a place of defecation [LN].

c. pres. act. participle of καθαρίζω (LN 79.49) (BAGD 2.a. p. 387): 'to make clean' [BAGD, LN], 'to declare clean' [BAGD], 'to cleanse' [LN]. The phrase 'making clean all foods' is translated as Jesus' words: 'making all food clean' [Lns], 'purging all meats' [KJV]. All other translations indicate that this is Mark's comment: 'By saying this, he declared all foods clean' [REB], 'In saying this, Jesus declared that all foods are fit to be eaten' [TEV], 'By saying this, Jesus meant that all foods were fit to eat' [CEV]. Most translations enclose the words within parenthesis marks: (declaring all foods clean) [AB2], (Thus he cleansed all foods) [WBC], (Thus he declared all foods clean) [BNTC; ESV, NASB, NRSV; similarly NTC], (This he said cleansing all foods) [BECNT], (In saying this, Jesus declared all foods 'clean') [NIV; similarly AB1], (By saying this, Jesus declared all foods acceptable) [GW], (This means all foods are clean) [NET], (When Jesus said this, he meant that no longer was any food unclean for people to eat) [NCV], (By saying this, he declared that every kind of food is acceptable in God's eyes) [NLT]. This verb means to cause something to become clean [LN]. This word occurs at 1:40, 41, 42; 7:19.

QUESTION—What relationship is indicated by the conjunction ὅτι 'because'?

This conjunction indicates the reason why eating food cannot make a person unclean [Hb, Lns, WBC]. Food does not enter into a man's heart (mind), and therefore it can not change his moral nature [Hb].

QUESTION—What is it that 'does not enter into the heart'?

This refers to any kind of food [TH; CEV, NLT]. When food goes into the body, it temporarily stays in the stomach (which represents the whole digestive system) and then goes out of the stomach into the latrine. So it makes no contact with the part of the body that really matters [NIGTC]. In the natural course of eating, the food enters from the outside, passes through the body, and then is expelled [Lns].

QUESTION—How is the phrase 'making clean all foods' related to the context?

1. This is a comment made by Mark to point out the significance of Jesus' words [AB1, AB2, BECNT, BNTC, CBC, CGTC, EBC, Hb, ICC, Lns,

NAC, NCBC, NICNT, NIGTC, NTC, PNTC, Sw, Tay, TH, TRT, WBC; all versions except KJV].
2. This is a continuation of what Jesus was telling his disciples [GNT, Lns; KJV].

QUESTION—What is the significance of the last clause, 'making clean all foods'?

This is a natural deduction from the principle stated by Jesus in 7:15 and then elaborated in 7:18–19 [NIGTC, WBC]. The disciples did not realize this implication until later, as demonstrated by Peter's reaction when he had the vision of the sheet with all kinds of food on it [CBC, Hb]. Since the Christian Church still vacillated in its attitude toward the Jewish food laws (Gal. 2:11–17; Rom. 14:14; Col. 2:20–22), Mark probably pointed out the implication of what Jesus said for the benefit of his readers in Rome [BNTC, NICNT, PNTC]. This is to be taken as 'declaring that all foods had *now* become pure' [AB2]. It almost seems to argue that all food laws such as found in Lev. 11:47 were *never* really binding. Yet Jesus clearly accepted Moses' authority as a teacher. So this must be understood in the light of the eschatological fact that the kingdom of God had now come and the Son of God had authority to pronounce the will of God. The period of tutelage under the Law had come to an end and the food laws of Moses had given way to the freedom pronounced by the Son of God [BECNT]. By adding 'making clean all food' Mark meant that no food was to be regarded as ritually unclean any longer [NIGTC].

7:20 And he-was-saying, "The (thing) coming out-of the man, that (is) what makes- the man -unclean.^{a}

LEXICON—a. pres. act. indic. of κοινόω (LN 53.33) (BAGD 1.a. p. 438): 'to make unclean' [LN], 'to defile' [BAGD, LN]. This verb means to cause something to become unclean, profane, or ritually unacceptable [LN]. This word occurs at 7:15, 18, 20, 23.

QUESTION—How is this verse connected with its context?

With the words 'and he was saying', Mark indicates that his short comment at the end of 7:19 is finished and he is resuming his report of what Jesus said [Hb; probably all versions]. This verse repeats in the singular what was stated in the plural in verse 15 [Tay]. Now Jesus begins to state what really makes a person unclean and starts with this summary statement [Lns].

7:21 Because from-within, out-of the heart of-the men the thoughts^a the evil (ones) come-out, fornications,^{b} thefts,^{c} murders,^{d}

TEXT—Manuscripts having the order 'fornications, thefts, murders [22]adulteries, greedinesses' are followed by GNT, which does not mention any variant orderings. A variant order is 'fornications, thefts, murders, adulteries, [22]greedinesses' and it is followed by ESV, GW, NASB, NCV, NIV. Another variant order is 'adulteries, fornications, murders, [22]thefts, greedinesses' and it is followed by KJV.

LEXICON—a. διαλογισμός (LN 30.10) (BAGD 1. p. 186): 'thought, opinion' [BAGD], 'reasoning' [BAGD, LN]. The phrase 'the thoughts, the evil ones' is translated 'the considerations, the base ones' [Lns], 'evil thoughts' [AB1, AB2, BECNT; all versions except NET, NRSV, TEV], 'evil intentions' [BNTC; NRSV], 'evil devisings' [WBC], 'evil schemes' [NTC], 'evil ideas' [NET, TEV]. This noun denotes the thoughts that result from thinking or reasoning with thoroughness and completeness [LN]. These are the thoughts that give rise to the evil behaviors and attitudes that follow [WBC].
   b. πορνεία (LN 88.271) (BAGD 1. p. 693): 'fornication, prostitution' [BAGD, LN], 'sexual immorality' [LN], 'unchastity' [BAGD]. This plural form is translated 'fornications' [BECNT, Lns; KJV, NASB], 'acts of fornications' [BNTC; REB], 'fornication' [NRSV], 'vulgar deeds' [CEV], 'sexual sins' [AB2, NTC; GW, NCV], 'immoralities' [WBC], 'sexual immorality' [AB1; ESV, NET, NIV, NLT], '(the evil ideas which lead you) to do immoral things' [TEV]. This noun denotes the result of engaging in sexual immorality of any kind, but it is often used to refer to prostitution [LN]. Fornication is a broad term that covers every kind of unlawful sexual intercourse [Hb, NICNT, NTC], but in this list it is distinguished from adulteries, which denotes unlawful sexual relations of married people [Hb]. If a married man had sexual relations with a prostitute, he would be charged with fornication, but if he had sexual relations with someone else's wife, he would be charged with adultery [TH].
   c. κλοπή (LN 57.232) (BAGD p. 436): 'theft, stealing' [BAGD, LN]. The plural form is translated 'thefts' [BECNT, BNTC, Lns, NTC, WBC; KJV, NASB], 'theft' [AB1; ESV, NET, NIV, NLT, NRSV, REB], 'stealing' [CEV, GW, NCV], 'robberies' [AB2], '(the evil ideas which lead you...) to rob' [TEV]. This noun denotes the act of secretly taking the property of someone else without permission [LN]. This is different from robbery, which is accompanied with a threat of violence [TH].
   d. φόνος (LN 20.82) (BAGD p. 864): 'murder' [BAGD, LN], 'killing' [BAGD]. The plural form is translated 'murders' [AB2, BECNT, BNTC, NTC, WBC; KJV, NASB], 'murder' [AB1; all versions except KJV, NASB, TEV], '(the evil ideas which lead you...) to kill' [TEV]. This noun denotes the intentional act of depriving a person of life [LN]. It is a general term for covering socially unsanctioned killing [TH].

QUESTION—What relationship is indicated by the conjunction γάρ 'because'? This conjunction introduces the justification for the preceding statement in verse 20 [Hb].

QUESTION—What is meant by οἱ διαλογισμοὶ οἱ κακοί 'the thoughts, the evil ones'?
   1. This is a general designation of the evil thoughts that are then specified in the list that follows [AB2, BNTC, CGTC, EBC, Gnd, Hb, ICC, Lns, My, NTC, PNTC, Sw, Tay, WBC; NRSV, TEV]. Evil thoughts bring about the

following list of evil acts [CGTC]. The wording 'the thoughts, the evil ones' stresses the nature of the thoughts as being morally bad [Hb]. Standing before the verb, the evil thoughts are presented as the root of the various evils in the list that follows [CGTC, Hb]. The commission of any sin is preceded by a deliberation in the mind of the sinner [Sw].
2. This is the first in the list of evil things that are named [AB1; all versions except NRSV, TEV].

7:22 adulteries,ᵃ greedinesses,ᵇ wickednesses,ᶜ

LEXICON—a. μοιχεία (LN 88.276) (BAGD p. 526): 'adultery' [BAGD, LN], 'adulterous acts' [BAGD]. The plural form is translated 'adulteries' [AB2, BECNT, BNTC, Lns, NTC, WBC; KJV, NASB], 'adultery' [AB1; ESV, GW, NCV, NET, NIV, NLT, NRSV, REB] 'unfaithfulness in marriage' [CEV], '(the evil ideas which lead you to...) commit adultery' [TEV]. This noun denotes sexual intercourse of a man with a married woman other than his own spouse [LN]. It is the violation of the marriage bond: a married man's sexual intercourse with someone other than his wife, or a married woman's sexual intercourse with someone other than her husband [NTC].

b. πλεονεξία (LN 25.22, 88.144) (BAGD p. 667): 'greediness, insatiableness' [BAGD], 'greed' [LN (25.22)], 'avarice, covetousness' [BAGD, LN (25.22)], 'exploitation' [LN (88.144)]. The plural form is translated 'greedy actions' [WBC], 'actions motivated by greed' [AB2], 'greed' [CEV, GW, NCV, NET, NIV, NLT, REB], 'covetings' [BECNT, Lns, NTC], 'deeds of coveting' [NASB], 'deeds of avarice' [BNTC], 'avarice' [NRSV], 'covetousness' [KJV], 'coveting' [ESV], 'lust of possession' [AB1], '(the evil ideas which lead you to...) be greedy' [TEV]. This noun denotes a strong desire to acquire more and more material possessions or to possess more things than other people have, all irrespective of need [LN (25.22)], or it means to take advantage of someone, usually being motivated by greed [LN (88.144)]. The plural form refers to the various expressions of greed [BAGD, Hb].

c. πονηρία (LN **88.109**) (BAGD p. 690): 'wickedness, baseness, maliciousness, sinfulness' [BAGD], 'wicked deeds, doing evil things' [LN]. The plural form is translated 'deeds of wickedness' [NASB], 'wickedness' [Lns; ESV, GW, KJV, NLT, NRSV], 'wicked actions' [AB2], 'evil actions' [NCV], 'evil deeds' [**LN**, WBC], 'evils' [BECNT], 'evil' [NET], 'malicious acts' [BNTC, NTC], 'malice' [AB1; NIV, REB], 'meanness' [CEV] '(the evil ideas which lead you to...) do all sorts of evil things' [TEV]. This noun always occurs in the plural and denotes deeds that are wicked and evil [TH]. This general term could be a summing up of all manifestations of wickedness [Lns, NTC]. This generic term for evil in this list probably refers to 'malice' [AB1, BNTC, ICC, NTC; NIV, REB].

MARK 7:22

deceit,[a] licentiousness,[b] an-evil[c] eye, blasphemy,[d] pride,[e] foolishness.[f]

LEXICON—a. δόλος (LN 88.154) (BAGD p. 203): 'deceit' [AB1, AB2, BAGD, BECNT, BNTC, Lns, NTC, WBC; all versions except GW, NCV, REB], 'cunning' [BAGD], 'treachery' [BAGD, LN], 'fraud' [REB], 'lying' [NCV], 'cheating' [GW]. This noun denotes deceit that is achieved by trickery and falsehood [LN]. It covers deceit, cunning, and treachery [TH].

b. ἀσέλγεια (LN 88.272) (BAGD p. 114): 'licentiousness' [BAGD, BECNT; NRSV], 'licentious behavior, extreme immorality' [LN], 'fornication' [AB1], 'debauchery' [BAGD; NET], 'sensuality' [BAGD, WBC; ESV, NASB], 'shameless lust' [GW], 'lasciviousness' [Lns; KJV], 'lustful desires' [NLT], 'lewdness' [NTC; NIV], 'indecency' [AB2, BNTC; CEV, REB, TEV], 'doing sinful things' [NCV]. This noun denotes behavior completely lacking in moral restraint and usually implies sexual licentiousness [LN]. It denotes the absence of self-restraint [ICC, NTC], an unbridled passion or cruelty [ICC]. It refers to giving free play to perverse impulses [NTC]. It is open immorality [NICNT].

c. πονηρός (LN 88.165) (BAGD 1.b.β. p. 691): 'evil, wicked, bad. worthless, vicious, degenerate' [BAGD]. The phrase 'an evil eye' [AB2; KJV] is also translated 'a wicked eye' [Lns], 'envy' [AB1, BECNT, BNTC, NTC; all versions except KJV, NCV, TEV], 'jealousy' [LN; NCV, TEV], 'selfishness' [WBC]. The phrase ὀφθαλμὸς πονηρός 'evil eye' is an idiom denoting a feeling of jealousy and resentment because of what someone else has or does [LN]. This idiom refers to envy [CGTC, NIGTC, TRT], jealousy [NICNT, Sw], envious jealousy [EBC]. Others take it to mean a lack of generosity [NIGTC], grudgingness [CGTC], stinginess [Gnd, NICNT, TRT].

d. βλασφημία (LN 33.400) (BAGD 1. p. 143) 'slander' [AB1, BAGD, BECNT, BNTC; ESV, NASB, NET, NIV, NLT, NRSV, REB, TEV], 'defamation' [BAGD], 'insults' [CEV], 'reviling' [LN], 'cursing' [GW], 'abusive speech' [AB2, NTC], 'blasphemy' [BAGD, LN, Lns, WBC; KJV], 'speaking evil of others' [NCV]. This noun denotes speech against someone that harms or injures that person's reputation [LN]. In this context, it probably refers to slander directed against people [AB2, BECNT, Gnd, ICC, NTC, Tay, TH; probably all versions except KJV]. All the other sins are social ones, so probably this sin refers to verbal abuse of other people [AB2]. It refers to scornful and insolent language directed against someone [NTC]. A few take this to be blasphemous language directed against God [CGTC, NICNT; KJV]. In the OT, this word always describes an affront to the majesty of God and should be translated blasphemy here [Lns, NICNT, WBC]. Still another view is that this is vicious language directed against either people or God [Lns, TRT]. It is speaking evil of either God or people [EBC].

e. ὑπερηφανία (LN **88.213**) (BAGD p. 841): 'haughtiness' [BAGD, **LN**], 'arrogance' [AB1, AB2, BAGD, BECNT, BNTC, LN, Lns, NTC, WBC;

GW, NIV, REB], 'pride' [BAGD, LN; all versions except GW, NIV, REB]. This noun denotes a state of ostentatious pride or arrogance bordering on insolence [LN]. It describes a person who exalts himself above all the others, and regards them with scornful contempt [NTC]. It is an arrogance that express itself in self-approval [NICNT].

f. ἀφροσύνη (LN **32.53**) (BAGD p. 127): 'foolishness' [AB2, BAGD, **LN**, Lns; CEV, ESV, GW, KJV, NASB, NLT], 'foolish living' [NCV], 'folly' [AB1, BECNT, BNTC, NTC; NET, NIV, NRSV, REB, TEV], 'lack of sense' [BAGD], 'lack of moral sense' [WBC]. This noun denotes the state of not using one's capacity for understanding [LN]. It refers to the stupidity of a person who lacks moral judgment [EBC, Hb, ICC, NAC, Tay]. It is the moral stupidity of unbelief and sin [Sw, TH]. In OT wisdom literature, it is a wrong attitude toward God that prevents the person from knowing how to behave properly [NIGTC]. This probably serves to sum up the preceding five sinful drives just as the word 'wickednesses' summed up the evil deeds [NTC].

QUESTION—Why are these last six evil things listed as singular words while all of the preceding evil things are plural words?

The first list of nouns with plural forms are evil *acts* [AB1, BNTC, CGTC, NICNT, NTC, PNTC, Tay, TH], actions that are repeated [NCBC]. The following six nouns are in the singular to indicate moral defects or vices [CGTC, NICNT, Tay], generic vices [AB1, NCBC], attitudes [PNTC], the sins themselves [TH], the evil drives and words that are related to the preceding and similar actions [NTC].

7:23 **All these evil[a] (things) come-out from-within and make- the man -unclean.[c]**

LEXICON—a. πονηρός (LN 88.110) (BAGD 2.c. p. 691): 'evil' [BAGD, LN], 'immoral, wicked' [LN]. The phrase ταῦτα τὰ πονηρὰ 'these evil things' [AB1, AB2, BECNT, BNTC, NTC, WBC; ESV, KJV, NASB, NCV, NRSV, REB, TEV] is also translated 'these wicked things' [Lns], 'these vile things' [NLT], 'these evils' [GW, NET, NIV], 'these' [CEV]. This adjective pertains to being morally corrupt and evil [LN]. Being an adjectival pronoun, it means 'wicked thoughts' and 'evil deeds' [BAGD].

b. pres. act. indic. of κοινόω (LN 53.33) (BAGD 1.a. p. 438): 'to make unclean' [LN], 'to defile' [BAGD, LN]. This verb means to cause something to become unclean, profane, or ritually unacceptable [LN]. This word occurs at 7:15, 18, 20, 23.

QUESTION—What is the function of this verse?

It is a summary statement of 7:20–22 [BECNT, Gnd, Hb, WBC] and of 7:15 [BECNT]. It repeats the key term 'make unclean' that began this subject at 7:1–2 [WBC]. The words 'come out' and 'make unclean' echo the words in the introduction of the list at 7:20 where it says 'that which comes out of the man, that is what makes the man unclean' [Gnd].

QUESTION—What is the conclusion?

All evil things in the list originate in the heart and then appear in word and deed [Lns]. Coming from the heart, they pollute the man's entire intellectual, emotional, and volitional life [NTC]. This uncleanness is moral rather than ritual [NAC]. These evil things make a person 'unfit to worship God' [CEV].

DISCOURSE UNIT—7:24–8:13 [Hb]. The topic is the third withdrawal and return.

DISCOURSE UNIT—7:24–8:10 [NIGTC]. The topic is the extension of the mission to neighboring peoples.

DISCOURSE UNIT—7:24–8:9 [PNTC]. The topic is a witness to Gentiles.

DISCOURSE UNIT—7:24–37 [NASB]. The topic is the Syrophoenician woman.

DISCOURSE UNIT—7:24–30 [CBC, EBC, Hb, NICNT; CEV, ESV, GW, NCV, NET, NIV, NLT, NRSV, TEV]. The topic is the appeal of the Syrophoenician woman [Hb], a woman's faith [CEV, TEV], the Syrophoenician woman's faith [EBC; ESV, NET, NIV, NRSV], the faith of a Gentile [NICNT], the faith of a Gentile woman [NLT], the faith of a Greek woman [GW], the Syrophoenician woman's faith leads to healing [CBC], Jesus helps a non-Jewish woman [NCV].

7:24 And from-there having-arisen/left[a] he-went-away[b] to the regions[c] of-Tyre. And having-entered into a-house he-wanted no-one to-know,[d] but he-was- not -able to-escape-notice.[e]

TEXT—Manuscripts reading Τύρου 'of Tyre' are given a B rating by GNT to indicate it was regarded to be almost certain. A variant reading is Τύρου καὶ Σιδῶνος 'of Tyre and Sidon' and it is followed by ESV, KJV.

LEXICON—a. aorist act. participle of ἀνίσταμαι, ἀνίστημι (LN 15.36, 17.6) (BAGD 2.d. p. 70): 'to arise' [Lns, NTC, WBC; ESV, KJV], 'to rise' [BAGD, BECNT], 'to get up' [AB2; NASB], 'to stand up' [LN (17.6)], 'to get ready' [BAGD], 'to leave' [AB1, BNTC, LN (15.36); CEV, GW, NCV, NET, NIV, NLT, TEV], 'to set out' [BAGD; NRSV], 'to depart, to go away from' [LN (15.36)]. The phrase 'having left he went away' is translated 'he moved on' [REB]. This verb means to assume a standing position [LN (17.6)], or to move away from a reference point, possibly implying both 'getting up' and 'leaving' [LN (15.36)]. The verb's basic meaning 'to rise up' has been weakened to indicate the beginning of an action expressed by another verb [BAGD].

b. aorist act. indic. of ἀπέρχομαι (LN 15.37) (BAGD 2. p. 84): 'to go away' [AB2; BAGD, BNTC, LN, Lns; ESV, NASB, NRSV, TEV], 'to go' [AB1, NTC, WBC; CEV, GW, KJV, NCV, NET, NIV, NLT], 'to depart' [BAGD, BECNT, LN], 'to leave' [LN]. This verb means to move away from a reference point, the emphasis bring upon the act of departure [LN].

c. ὅριον (LN **1.79**) (BAGD p. 581): 'region' [BAGD, LN], 'border, district' [BAGD], 'territory, land' [LN]. The genitive construction τὰ ὅρια Τύρου 'the regions of Tyre' [BECNT] is also translated 'the region of Tyre' [NTC; ESV, NASB, NET, NLT, NRSV], 'the region near the city of Tyre' [CEV], 'the region around Tyre' [AB2], 'the district of Tyre' [BNTC], 'the territory of Tyre' [WBC; GW, REB], 'the territory near the city of Tyre' [TEV], 'the territory near to Tyre' [AB1], 'the territory near the city of Tyre' [TEV], 'the area around Tyre' [NCV], 'the vicinity of Tyre' [NIV], 'the borders of Tyre' [Lns; KJV]. This noun always occurs in a plural form to denote a region or regions of the earth. It is usually used in relation to some ethnic group or geographical center [LN]. The noun denotes a boundary, and the plural form 'boundaries' denotes a region or district [BAGD]. The word denotes the boundaries of a territory, and may refer to the country included within those boundaries [ICC]. This word occurs at 5:17; 7:24, 31; 10:1.
d. aorist act. infin. of γινώσκω (LN 27.2) (BAGD 4.b. p. 161): 'to learn, to find out' [LN], 'to notice, to realize' [BAGD]. The clause 'he wanted no one to know' is translated 'he did not want anyone to know' [ESV, NET], 'he did not want anyone to know it' [AB2, BNTC; NIV, NTC; similarly NASB], 'would have no man know it' [KJV], 'he wanted no one to know about it' [WBC], 'he did not want anyone to know he was there' [CEV, NCV, NRSV, TEV; similarly AB1], 'he was wishing that no one would know that he was there' [BECNT], 'he didn't want anyone to know (that he was staying in a house there)' [GW], 'he didn't want anyone to know (which house he was staying in)' [NLT], 'would have liked to remain unrecognized' [REB]. This verb means to acquire information by any means [LN].
e. aorist act. infin. of λανθάνω (LN **28.83**) (BAGD p. 466): 'to escape notice' [BAGD, LN], 'to be hidden' [BAGD], 'to remain hidden' [LN]. The clause 'and he was not able to escape notice' [BECNT, **LN**] is also translated 'but he was unable to escape notice' [AB2], 'but/yet he could not escape notice' [NTC; NASB, NRSV; similarly AB1, WBC; NET], 'but he couldn't keep it a secret' [NLT], 'however, it couldn't be kept a secret' [GW], 'yet he could not keep his presence secret' [NIV], 'yet he could not be hidden' [ESV; similarly KJV], 'but he could not stay hidden' [NCV], 'but they found out anyway' [CEV], 'and he was not able to keep secret where he was', 'he was not able to remain unnoticed', 'he was not able to keep people from knowing where he was' [**LN**]. This verb means to keep oneself from being known, and implies concealment and secrecy [LN]. Jesus could not prevent people from discovering where he was [TH].

QUESTION—What location is referred to by the adverb ἐκεῖθεν 'from there'?

This could refer to leaving the house (7:17), Gennesaret (6:53), or some other place [EBC]. Jesus departed from the house mentioned in 7:17 where he had spoken with his disciples [BECNT, Gnd, WBC]. Jesus departed from the place in Galilee where the controversy with the Jewish leaders had taken place (7:1–13) [Hb, Lns]. Jesus left Galilee [NLT].

QUESTION—What is meant by the verb ἀναστὰς 'having arisen/having left'?
1. It has the basic meaning of the verb: Jesus stood up [AB2, BECNT, Gnd, Hb, ICC, Lns, NTC, WBC; ESV, KJV, NASB]. Jesus got up from the seated position he had taken to teach his disciples in the house mentioned in 7:17 [Gnd]. 'Arose' marks a preparatory action for leaving [Hb].
2. Instead of simply getting up, it has the extended meaning of leaving [AB1, BNTC, PNTC, TH; CEV, GW, NCV, NET, NIV, NLT, NRSV, REB, TEV]. It has the specialized sense of beginning an action indicated by another verb, 'he got ready' or 'he set out' [TH].

QUESTION—Where was the district of Tyre?
Tyre was a Phonecian city located on the coast of the Mediterranean Sea where modern Lebanon is located [PNTC]. The territory of Phonecia bordered on Galilee about twenty miles northwest of Capernaum [NICNT].

QUESTION—What is meant by ἀπῆλθεν εἰς τὰ ὅρια Τύρου 'he departed into/to the district of Tyre'
This does not say that Jesus visited the city of Tyre itself, but merely the district administered by Tyre [NIGTC]. Jesus crossed the border from Galilee and went into the Gentile land of Tyre [CGTC, EGT, Hb, ICC, NICNT, NTC, Sw, Tay, WBC]. Jesus went to the region near the city of Tyre [CEV, NCV]. It is impossible to know how far Jesus penetrated into Phonecia [EBC, NICNT] since the '*district* of Tyre' simply designates the district for which Tyre was the metropolitan center [NICNT, WBC]. There is no reason to think that he went far across the border [Tay].

QUESTION—What is meant by εἰσελθὼν εἰς οἰκίαν 'having entered into a house'?
It is not that Jesus entered a particular house. It means that he established residence in this location for a short time [TH]. Since he desired privacy, it is likely that this was the house of a Gentile stranger rather than the house of a friend [EGT]. Mark was not concerned about the identity of the owner of the house since the focus of this story is on the Syrophoenician woman [Hb].

QUESTION—Why didn't Jesus want anyone to know he was living in that house?
Jesus came to this region for relief from the pressure of the crowds [Hb] and wanted privacy in order to have uninterrupted time to instruct his disciples [CGTC, Hb, NIVfn], even though they are not mentioned in this section [CGTC, NIVfn]. Perhaps he went there in order to reflect upon the scope and course of his ministry [CGTC, Tay].

QUESTION—Why wasn't Jesus able to escape notice?
In 3:8 it tells about people coming from Tyre and Sidon to hear Jesus and to be healed by him, so his fame had already spread throughout the area [BECNT, EBC, Hb, WBC].

7:25 But immediately a-woman having-heard[a] about him, whose little-daughter[b] had[c] an-unclean spirit, having-come she-fell-down[d] at his feet.

TEXT—Manuscripts reading ἀλλ' εὐθὺς ἀκούσασα γυνή 'but immediately a woman having heard' are followed by GNT, which does not mention any variant reading. A variant reading is ἀκούσασα γὰρ γυνή 'because a woman heard' and it is followed by KJV.

LEXICON—a. aorist act. participle of ἀκούω (LN 33.212): 'to hear' [LN; KJV], 'to receive news' [LN]. The participial phrase 'having heard… about him' [BECNT, Lns] is also translated 'heard about him/Jesus' [AB2, BNTC, NTC; GW, NET, NIV, NLT, NRSV, TEV], 'heard of him' [AB1; ESV, KJV, REB], 'heard that he was there' [NCV], 'heard where Jesus was' [CEV], 'after hearing of him' [NASB; similarly WBC]. This verb means to receive information about something by word of mouth [LN].

b. θυγάτριον (LN 10.47) (BAGD p. 365): 'little daughter' [BAGD, BECNT, BNTC, LN, Lns, NTC; ESV, GW, NASB, NIV, NRSV], 'small daughter' [REB], 'little girl' [NLT], 'young daughter' [KJV, NET], 'daughter' [AB1, AB2, WBC; CEV, NCV, TEV], 'dear daughter' [LN]. This noun is a diminutive derivative of θυγάτηρα 'daughter', possibly used to emphasize her young age and to indicate the mother's affection for her. The only other occurrence of this word is in Mark 5:23 where the text specifically says that the 'little' daughter was twelve years of age [LN]. The little daughter was perhaps around six of seven years old [TH]. Yet, she might have been old enough to be married [Hb].

c. pres. act. indic. of ἐνέχομαι, ἔχω (LN 90.65) (BAGD 1.2.e.α. p. 332): 'to have' [BAGD, LN], 'to be possessed by' [BAGD]. The phrase 'had an unclean spirit' [AB2, BECNT, BNTC, Lns, WBC; ESV, KJV, NASB, NET, NRSV] is also translated 'had an evil spirit' [GW], 'had an evil spirit in her' [CEV, NCV, TEV], 'was possessed by an unclean spirit' [NTC; REB], 'was possessed by an evil spirit' [NIV, NLT], 'had a disorder of the mind' [AB1]. This verb means to experience some state or condition [LN]. A reference to 'having' a demon occurs at 3:22, 30; 5:15; 7:25; 9:17.

d. aorist act. indic. of προσπίπτω (LN 17.22) (BAGD 1. p. 718): 'to prostrate oneself before' [LN], 'to fall down before' [BAGD, LN], 'to fall down at the feet of' [BAGD]. The phrase 'fell down at his feet' [AB2, Lns; ESV, NASB] is also translated 'fell at his feet' [BECNT, BNTC, WBC; KJV, NCV, NET, NIV, NLT, REB, TEV], 'knelt down at his feet' [CEV], 'bowed down at his feet' [NRSV], 'bowed down' [GW], 'prostrated herself' [AB1]. The verb means to prostrate oneself in supplication before some person [LN, NCBC, PNTC]. This act indicates her profound grief and her deep respect for Jesus [AB1, NAC, NICNT]. It indicates her humility, reverence, submissiveness, and anxiety [NTC]. It demonstrated the urgency of her request [BECNT]. A translation must not give the idea that the woman accidentally tripped over something and fell down at his feet [TH]. This word occurs at 3:11; 5:33; 7:25.

QUESTION—What relationship is indicated by the conjunction ἀλλά 'but'

This contrasts Jesus desire for privacy with the coming of the woman as soon as she heard he was there [Hb].

QUESTION—What does the verb εὐθύς 'immediately' modify?
1. The adverb modifies the verb ἐλθοῦσα προσέπεσεν 'having heard' [AB1, AB2, BNTC, Gnd, ICC, TRT; ESV, NET, NRSV, REB, TEV]: she *immediately heard* about Jesus.
2. The adverb modifies the verb phrase ἐλθοῦσα 'having come' [BECNT, EGT, Hb, Lns, NTC, PNTC, TH, WBC; CEV, NASB, NCV, NLT, TEV]: when she heard about Jesus she *immediately came*.

QUESTION—What had the woman heard about Jesus?

She heard that Jesus had arrived in the vicinity [Hb, Lns, NICNT; NCV]. She heard where he was staying [CEV]. She heard about his fame or his presence, or perhaps both [Tay]. She heard 'about him' means that she heard that Jesus was in a certain house. His miracles and exorcisms had already been known in this region for some time (3:8) [Gnd].

7:26 Now the woman was a Greek,a a Syrophoenician by-race.b

LEXICON—a. Ἑλληνίς (LN **11.91**) (BAGD 2. p. 252): 'Greek' [LN; CEV, NCV], 'a Greek' [AB1, AB2, BECNT, LN, NTC, WBC; CEV, GW, KJV, NET, NIV], 'a Greek woman' [LN], 'a Gentile' [BNTC, Lns; ESV, NASB, NLT, NRSV, REB, TEV], 'a Gentile woman' [BAGD]. This noun denotes a woman of Greek culture and language [LN].

b. γένος (LN 10.1) (BAGD 3. p. 156): 'race' [AB1, AB2, BAGD, BECNT, **LN**, Lns; NASB], 'people' [BAGD], 'ethnic group' [LN], 'nation' [BAGD, LN; KJV], 'nationality' [NTC], 'by birth' [BNTC, WBC; ESV]. The phrase 'a Syrophoenician by race' is translated 'of Syrophoenician origin' [NET, NRSV], 'a Phoenician of Syria by nationality' [REB], 'born in Phoenicia in Syria' [GW, NCV], 'born in the region of Phoenicia in Syria' [TEV], 'born in Syrian Phoenecia' [NIV, NLT], 'had been born in the part of Syria known as Phoenicia' [CEV]. This noun denotes a relatively large group of people regarded to be biologically related [LN]. It defines her nationality [TH]. Her country is called 'Syrian-Phoenicia' in order to distinguish it from Libyan or Carthagenian Phoenicia in North Africa [CBC, EGT, ICC, My, NAC, NCBC, NIVfn].

QUESTION—What is the function of this sentence?

The conjunction δέ 'now' introduces a parenthetical comment about the woman's nationality [Lns], so some translations enclose the sentence with parenthesis marks [AB1, AB2; REB]. This information is necessary for understanding the remarks Jesus makes about Jewish children and Gentile dogs [Lns, WBC]. One translation even moves this sentence to the end of verse 26 to begin a new paragraph: 'Since she was a Gentile, born in Syrian Phoenicia, 27Jesus told her...' [NLT].

QUESTION—What is meant by the statement that this woman was a Ἑλληνίς 'Greek'?

Although the word Ἑλληνίς literally means 'Greek', this term was commonly used by the Jews to refer to any Gentile since there was such a wide diffusion of the Greek race and language [ICC, Lns, My, NTC, Tay, WBC]. The following clause shows that this woman was not a Greek by nationality, so this designation means that she was either a Greek-speaking woman living in a Greek culture or simply that she was a non-Jew, a Gentile [CGTC, EBC, Hb]. In the context of verses 7:27–28, the purpose of this comment is to inform us that the woman was non-Jewish rather than to identify her linguistic or cultural background [BECNT, CGTC, My, NCBC, Sw, TRT]. Many translations use the word 'Gentile' here [BNTC, Lns; ESV, NASB, NLT, NRSV, REB, TEV].

And she-was-asking[a] him that he-would-cast-out[b] the demon[c] from her daughter.

LEXICON—a. imperf. act. indic. of ἐρωτάω (LN 33.161) (BAGD 2. p. 312): 'to ask' [AB2, BAGD, BECNT, LN, NTC, WBC; GW, NASB, NET], 'to request' [BAGD, LN, Lns], 'to beseech' [BAGD, BNTC; KJV], 'to beg' [AB1; CEV, ESV, NCV, NIV, NLT, NRSV, REB, TEV]. This verb means to ask for something [LN]. The imperfect tense indicates that she continued to press her request [Hb, NTC, WBC; NASB].
  b. aorist act. subj. of ἐκβάλλω (LN 53.102) (BAGD 1. p. 237): 'to cast out, to make to go out, to exorcise' [LN], 'to drive out, to expel' [BAGD]. This verb means to cause a demon to stop possessing or controlling a person [LN]. In reference to 'casting' out demons, this verb occurs at 1:34, 39; 3:15, 22, 23; 6:13; 7:26; 9:18, 28, 38; 16:9, 17.
  c. δαιμόνιον (LN 12.37) (BAGD 2. p. 169): 'demon' [AB1, AB2, BAGD, BECNT, BNTC, LN, Lns, NTC, WBC; all versions except KJV], 'devil' [KJV], 'evil spirit' [BAGD, LN]. This noun denotes an evil supernatural being or spirit [LN]. This word occurs at 1:34, 39; 3:15, 22; 6:13; 7:26, 29, 30; 9:38; 16:9, 17.

7:27 And he-was-saying to her, "First let[a] the children be-satisfied,[b] because it-is not good[c] to-take the bread of-the children and to-throw (it) to-the dogs.[d]"

LEXICON—a. aorist act. impera. of ἀφίημι (LN 13.140) (BAGD 4. p. 126): 'to let, to allow' [BAGD, LN], 'to permit' [BAGD]. This is translated as a command addressed to the woman: 'let the children be satisfied first' [AB2; NASB, NET, REB], 'first let the children eat all they want' [NTC; GW, NCV, NIV], 'let the children be fed first' [AB1, BNTC; ESV, NRSV], 'let the children first be filled' [WBC; KJV; similarly Lns], 'permit first the children to be filled' [BECNT]. This is translated as a requirement that must be met: 'the children must first be fed' [CEV], 'let us first feed the children' [TEV], 'first I should feed the children—my

own family, the Jews' [NLT]. This verb means to leave it up to someone to do something [LN].
  b. aorist pass. infin. of χορτάζομαι, χορτάζω (LN 23.15) (BAGD 2.a. p. 884): 'to be satisfied' [AB2, BAGD; NASB, NET, REB], 'to be filled' [BECNT, Lns, WBC; KJV], 'to be fed' [AB1, BNTC; CEV, ESV, NLT, NRSV, TEV], 'to eat all one wants' [NTC; GW, NCV, NIV], 'to eat one's fill' [BAGD, LN]. This verb means to eat until reaching a state of being satisfied [LN]. This word occurs at 6:42; 7:27; 8:4, 8.
  c. καλός (LN 66.2) (BAGD 3.b. p. 400): 'good' [LN; NASB], 'right' [AB1, AB2, BECNT, BNTC, WBC; all versions except KJV, NASB, NRSV], 'proper' [NTC], 'fair' [NRSV], 'fitting' [LN], 'meet' [KJV], 'excellent' [Lns], 'morally good, pleasing to God' [BAGD]. This adjective describes something as being fitting and good [LN].
  d. κυνάριον (LN 4.34) (BAGD p. 457): 'dog' [AB1, AB2, BAGD, BECNT, BNTC, WBC; all versions], 'house dog' [LN, NTC], 'little dog' [BAGD, LN], 'little pet dog' [Lns]. This noun is the diminutive form of κύωνα 'dog'. The diminutive force may have become lost in the NT even though a component of emotive attachment or affection is no doubt retained. Probably this refers to a housedog [LN]. This diminutive form denotes a housedog or lap dog in contrast with a street dog or farm dog, but it can also be used without any diminutive force at all [BAGD].

QUESTION—Why did Jesus talk about children being filled?
  His response is given in the form of a parable [Lns, NIGTC]. In this parable the 'children' represent the Jews and the 'dogs' represent the Gentiles [AB2, BECNT, ESVfn, ICC, Lns, My, NCBC, NIGTC, NTC, PNTC, TH, TRT]. The Jews could naturally be called children in the sense that they were children in God's family [Hb, NICNT]. The bread stands for the blessings Jesus offered to the Jews [Hb, Lns, PNTC]. The bread refers to the gospel message [ESVfn, NCBC].

QUESTION—What is implied by the adverb προτον 'first'?
  This implies that first the children will eat and then the dogs will have a turn [AB2, BNTC, CGTC, EGT, ESVfn, Hb, ICC, Lns, NCBC, NIGTC, NLTfn, NTC, PNTC, Tay, WBC]. This statement gives an implicit promise to the Gentiles [NCBC]. The word 'first' has a note of hope to the Gentile woman since it implies that the time for the Gentiles is coming [Hb].

QUESTION—What relationship is indicated by the conjunction γάρ 'because'?
  This indicates why the children should be fed first [BECNT]. It gives the reason for refusing to heal the woman's daughter [Hb]. Although it appears that Jesus was harshly and insensitively refusing to help in her need, this refusal was actually intended to invite a renewed appeal [NICNT].

QUESTION—Who are referred to as κυναρίοις 'dogs', and what is the force of its diminutive form, 'little dogs'?
  The term κύων 'dog' was the conventional Jewish term for speaking disrespectfully of the Gentiles [BNTC, NICNT, NIGTC, TH].

1. The use of the diminutive form κυναρίοις 'little dogs' is significant [CGTC, EBC, Gnd, Hb, Lns, NAC, NCBC, NETfn, NICNT, PNTC, Sw, Tay, TH, TRT]. This word does not refer to the fierce dogs of the streets [TH], but to the little house dogs [EBC, Sw, Tay, TH, TRT] that were pets [CGTC, NCBC, PNTC, TRT]. The 'little dogs' refers to the household pets that had a place in the affairs of the household [Hb]. Speaking of the 'little dogs' which were admitted into the house and could be found under the table at meal time is not at all parallel to the Jewish use of 'dogs' in the pejorative sense [NICNT]. Another view is that instead of softening the offensive use of 'dog', this could mean that since the woman was a Gentile dog, her little child could be referred to as a little dog [Gnd].
2. The use of the diminutive form is not significant [BNTC, ICC; probably AB1, AB2, BAGD, BECNT, WBC; and all versions since these do not use the diminutive form]. 'Dog' was always used as a term of contempt, but Jesus was using the term in ironical conformity to the common Jewish sneer since he himself had experienced the way Jews treated people with contempt [ICC]. A Gentile would consider it just as offensive to be called a little dog as to be called a dog [BNTC].

QUESTION—What is the point of this saying?

Jesus was replying with a proverb [Hb, NIGTC, TRT]. It was meant to instruct both this woman and his disciples [Hb, Lns]. Jesus wanted his disciples to understand that this trip to Gentile territory did not mean that he was abandoning his ministry to the Jews since the Jews had first claim on his ministry. The parable was meant to test the woman to see if she would be willing to accept the lowly position Jesus assigned to her [Hb]. It tested the woman's faith [ESVfn, NAC, NCBC, NICNT, NIGTC, NLTfn, TRT]. Jesus told this parable to challenge the woman to justify her request [BNTC]. This harsh response did not encourage the woman to expect help at the present time, yet it was a challenge for her to justify her request [NIGTC]. This teaches that the Jews took precedence over Gentiles during this time of his ministry [NAC, Sw], and yet they didn't have exclusive rights to the Gospel [Sw].

7:28 **But she-answered and says to-him, "Lord,[a] even the dogs under the table eat from the children's crumbs.[b]"**

TEXT—Manuscripts reading κύριε 'Lord' are given a B rating by GNT to indicate it was regarded to be almost certain. A variant reading is ναί, κύριέ 'yes, Lord' and it is followed by Hb, ICC, NIGTC, Tay; ESV, KJV, NASB, NCV, NET, NIV, NLT, NRSV.

LEXICON—a. κύριος (LN 87.53) (BAGD 2.c.β. p. 459): 'lord' [AB2, BECNT, LN, Lns, NTC, WBC; all versions except NRSV, REB, TEV], 'sir' [AB1, BNTC, LN (87.53); NRSV, REB, TEV]. The noun is a title of respect used in addressing or speaking to a man [LN]. In this context the meaning is 'sir' [AB1, BNTC, CGTC, Hb, Tay, TH; NRSV, REB, TEV], a normal form of polite Gentile address [BNTC, NCBC], a title of respect [TH].

The woman's belief in the supernatural powers of Jesus is evident [Gnd], so this word has a higher meaning than just 'sir', so 'Lord' is more appropriate [BECNT, Gnd, NAC, WBC].
- b. ψιχίον (LN 5.5) (BAGD p. 894): 'crumb' [LN, WBC; CEV, ESV, KJV, NASB, NCV, NET, NIV, NRSV], 'scrap' [AB1, BECNT, BNTC, LN, Lns, NTC; GW, REB], 'scraps (from the children's plates)' [NLT], 'small piece of bread' [BAGD], 'leftovers' [AB2; TEV]. This noun denotes a small piece of food and is normally used in reference to bread [LN].

QUESTION—What is meant by the dogs eating ἀπὸ τῶν ψιχίων τῶν παιδίων 'from the children's crumbs'?
1. The crumbs accidentally fall off the table while the children are eating [Gnd, Lns; CEV].
2. As the children are eating, they feed crumbs from their food to the dogs under the table [AB2, EGT, Hb]. The dogs are waiting under the table for the small bits of bread the children sneak to them [Hb].
3. These are the leftover crumbs that remain after the children have finished eating [AB2, Sw; TEV]. The dogs are fed the crumbs that the children leave [Sw].

QUESTION—What is the point of the woman's reply?

The woman accepted what Jesus told her and then carried the figurative scene on to her own conclusion: "Quite so, Lord, and in that case I may have a crumb" [EBC, Tay]. She agreed with the priority of the Jews, but argued that there was more than enough food for the dogs as well [BECNT, Hb, NIGTC, NLTfn]. Instead of using the loophole provided by Jesus when he said, '*First* let the children be satisfied', she makes the point that the dogs eat the children's crumbs *during* the meal [WBC]. The dogs under the table do not have to wait until the children are first fed. They can eat at the same time the children do and don't have to wait their turn [Gnd, NICNT]. While Jesus was on earth, his ministry was not limited exclusively to the Jewish nation [NTC].

7:29 And he-said to-her, "Because-of this word[a], go.[b] The demon has-gone-out[c] of your daughter." 7:30 And having-departed to her house she-found the child having-been-put[d] on the bed and the demon having-gone-out.

LEXICON—a. λόγος (LN 33.98) (BAGD 1.a.γ. p. 477): 'word' [BAGD, LN, Lns, WBC], 'statement' [BAGD, LN, NTC; ESV], 'saying' [KJV], 'answer' [NASB, NCV, TEV], 'reply' [BNTC]. The phrase 'because of this word' is translated 'because you have said this' [AB2; GW; similarly NET], 'on account of what you said' [BECNT], 'for saying that/this' [AB1; NRSV, REB], 'for such a reply' [NIV], 'Good answer!' [NLT], 'That's true!' [CEV]. This noun denotes that which has been stated or said, and its primary focus is upon the content of that communication [LN].
- b. pres. act. impera. of ὑπάγω (LN 15.52) (BAGD 1. p. 836): 'to depart, to leave, to go away' [BAGD, LN]. The command ὕπαγε 'go' [AB2,

BECNT, BNTC, WBC; ESV, NASB, REB] is also translated 'go your way' [NTC; KJV], 'be going' [Lns], 'you may go' [NCV, NET, NIV, NRSV], 'you may go now' [CEV], 'you may go on your way' [ESV], 'go back home' [TEV], 'now go home' [NLT], 'go home' [AB1]. This verb means to depart from someone's presence [BAGD, LN].

c. perf. act. indic. of ἐξέρχομαι (LN 15.40) (BAGD 1.a.δ. p. 274): 'to go out of' [AB2, BAGD, BECNT, LN, Lns; KJV, NASB, TEV; similarly AB1], 'to come out of' [BNTC], 'to depart out of' [LN], 'to depart from' [WBC], 'to leave' [NTC; CEV, ESV, NCV, NET, NIV, NLT, NRSV, REB]. This verb means to move out of an enclosed or well defined two or three-dimensional area [LN]. The perfect tense indicates that the demon had already gone out of the child [TH]. The perfect tense indicates that the cure was complete [Hb].

d. perf. pass. participle of βάλλω (LN 85.34) (BAGD 1.b. p. 131): 'to be put' [LN], 'to be thrown' [BAGD, LN]. The phrase 'having been put on the bed' is translated 'having been laid upon the bed' [Lns], 'lying on the bed' [BNTC, WBC; CEV, GW, NASB, NET, NIV, REB, TEV; similarly BECNT; KJV], 'lying in bed' [AB1, NTC; ESV, NCV], 'lying quietly in bed' [NLT], 'cast onto her bed' [AB2]. This verb means to be put or thrown into a place [LN].

QUESTION—What relationship is indicated by the conjunction διὰ τοῦτον 'because of this'?

Jesus granted the woman's request because of her reply [CBC, CGTC, Hb, NIGTC, Tay, TH]. The woman's words gave evidence of her strong faith and confidence in Jesus [BECNT, EBC, EGT, ESVfn, Hb, Lns, My, NAC, NICNT, NTC, TRT, WBC]. Because of the woman's response and her recognition of his authority, Jesus changed his *apparent* intention. Verse 27 does not indicate whether what Jesus had said to her was deliberately designed to provoke such a response, or whether Jesus really did intend to refuse her request until her argument persuaded him to grant it [NIGTC].

QUESTION—What is meant by the child βεβλημένον 'having been put' on the bed?

This verb can mean that the child was lying on the bed in a peaceful repose that showed she was in normal health or that she was lying exhausted as a result of a final attack by the demon when he withdrew [TH].

1. The child was merely lying on the bed [EGT, Hb, Lns, My, NTC, Sw, TRT; probably all versions]. She was in a state of peaceful repose on the bed [Hb, NTC, TRT]. Having been cured by Jesus, she would not have been a bit weak and exhausted. The fact that she was resting quietly on the bed assured her mother that she was now free from the demon [Lns]. Some think that she was in bed because she was still weary and exhausted from her experience [My, Sw].

2. The child had been violently thrown onto the bed. [AB1, AB2, EBC, ICC, NICNT]. It appeared that the girl had been thrown onto the bed by the cast-out demon [AB2]. When the demon left the child he probably caused

her to have a violent convulsion in the same way as happened when other demoniacs had been cured (9:26) [EBC, ICC]. She was probably exhausted [AB1, NICNT] after having that final paroxysm [AB1].

DISCOURSE UNIT—7:31–37 [EBC, Hb, NICNT; ESV, GW, NCV, NLT, NRSV]. The topic is the healing in the Decapolis [NICNT], the cure of the deaf stammerer [Hb], Jesus heals a deaf man [CBC; CEV, ESV, NCV, NET, NIV, NLT, TEV], Jesus cures a deaf man [GW, NRSV], Jesus heals a man who was deaf and could hardly talk [CEV], healing a deaf and mute man [EBC], the healing of a deaf and mute man [NIV], Jesus heals a deaf and mute man [CBC], healing a deaf mute [NET], Jesus heals a deaf-mute [TEV].

7:31 **And again having-come-out from the region of-Tyre he-came through**[a] **Sidon to the Lake of-Galilee in the midst**[b] **of-the region of-Decapolis.**

TEXT—Manuscripts reading Τύρου ἦλθεν διὰ Σιδῶνος 'of Tyre he came through Sidon' are given an A rating by GNT to indicate it was regarded to be certain. A variant reading is Τύρου καὶ Σιδῶνος ἦλθεν 'of Tyre and Sidon he came' and it is followed by KJV.

LEXICON—a. διά (LN 84.29): 'through' [AB1, AB2, BNTC, LN, Lns, WBC; ESV, GW, NASB, NCV, NET, NIV, TEV], 'by way of' [BECNT, NTC; CEV, NRSV, REB], 'to' [NLT]. This preposition indicates extension through an area or object [LN].

b. μέσος (LN 83.10) (BAGD 2. p. 507): 'in the midst' [LN], 'in the middle' [BAGD, LN], 'through' [LN (84.29)], not explicit [ESV, NCV, NLT]. The phrase ἀνὰ μέσον 'in the midst' [Lns] is also translated 'into the middle' [WBC], 'within' [BAGD; NASB], 'well within' [REB], 'in' [ESV, NET, NRSV], 'into' [NIV], 'passing through' [AB1], 'through the middle of' [AB2, BECNT], 'through the midst' [KJV], 'through' [BAGD; CEV, GW], 'right through' [BNTC], 'by way of' [TEV], 'crossing' [NTC]. This adjective describes something as being in an area that is in the middle of a larger area [LN]. Most think this means 'through' or 'by the way of' the province of Decapolis [AB1, BAGD, BNTC, NTC; CEV, GW, TEV]. A few think it means that Jesus passed through 'the middle of' the province [AB2, WBC].

QUESTION—Which verb does the adverb πάλιν 'again' modify?
Many do not translate this adverb [AB1, Lns; CEV, ESV, GW, NCV, NIV, NLT, NRSV, REB, TEV].
1. 'Again' modifies the participle 'having come out' [AB2, BNTC, Gnd, Hb, Lns, NTC, Sw, WBC; NASB, NET]. It merely means that Jesus started out on a trip once more [Hb, Lns].
2. 'Again' modifies the main verb 'came' [BECNT; KJV]. It refers to coming back again to the Lake of Galilee where he had been teaching when he left to go to the region of Tyre [BECNT, Hb].

QUESTION—What was the route Jesus took to the Lake of Galilee?

Jesus left the place where he was staying in the neighborhood of the city of Tyre (7:24) and went further north along the coast of the Mediterranean Sea and through the city of Sidon [Hb, NICNT], which was about twenty miles north of Tyre [BNTC, Hb, NICNT, PNTC, Sw, WBC]. After passing through Tyre, he turned southward toward the southeastern shore of the Lake of Galilee within the region of Decapolis [NICNT].This would be a journey of about 120 miles [PNTC]. Since this was a roundabout way to get to the lake, perhaps Jesus kept to areas where he would not be recognized in order to give his full time to his disciples [Hb, NAC]. Lake Galilee was the end of the journey [BECNT, Gnd, Tay, TH, TRT, WBC]. The phrase 'in the midst of the region of Decapolis' means 'between the borders of Decapolis' and it does not indicate the location of the lake, but names the region Jesus traveled through in order to arrive at the lake [Gnd, TH]. Some change the order in which the locations are mentioned: 'went through Sidon into the middle of the territory of the Decapolis to the Sea of Galilee' [WBC], 'he went through Sidon and the territory of the Ten Cities to the Sea of Galilee' [GW], 'he again came to the Sea of Galilee by way of Sidon through the middle of the Decapolis' [BECNT].

7:32 And they-bring to-him (a man who was) deaf[a] and hardly-able-to-speak/mute[b] and they-beg[c] him that he-would-put-upon[d] him (his) hand.

LEXICON—a. κωφός (LN 24.68) (BAGD 2. p. 462): 'deaf' [BAGD, LN; all translations]. This adjective describes someone as being unable to hear [LN]. This word literally means 'blunt' or 'dull' and it was used in regard to hearing, speaking, or sight. In this incident it means 'deaf' [CGTC, Hb, WBC].

b. μογιλάλος (LN 33.107) (BAGD 1. or 2. p. 525): 'hardly able to speak/talk' [AB1, BECNT, LN, NAC, WBC; CEV, NIV, TEV], 'scarcely able to speak' [AB2], 'speaking with difficulty' [BAGD (1.), LN, NTC; NASB, NET], 'unable to talk plainly' [NCV], 'having a speech impediment' [BAGD (1.); ESV, KJV, NLT, NRSV, REB], 'having a speech defect' [GW], 'dumb' [BNTC, Lns]. This adjective describes someone as being almost mute [LN]. The meaning 'hardly able to speak' is supported by verse 35, while the meaning 'mute, impaired in speech' is supported by ancient versions that give that sense [BAGD].

c. pres. act. indic. of παρακαλέω (LN 33.168) (BAGD 3. p. 617): 'to beg' [AB1, BNTC, NTC; CEV, ESV, GW, NCV, NIV, NLT, NRSV, REB], 'to request' [BAGD, LN], 'to appeal to' [BAGD, LN, WBC], 'to beseech' [Lns; KJV], 'to implore' [BAGD; NASB], 'to plead' [AB2, BECNT, LN], 'to entreat' [BAGD], 'to ask' [NET]. This verb means to earnestly ask for something [LN].

d. aorist act. subj. of ἐπιτίθημι (LN 85.51) (BAGD 1.a.α. p. 303): 'to put on' [AB2, BAGD, LN; KJV, NCV], 'to place on' [BAGD, LN, NTC; NET, NIV, TEV], 'to lay on' [AB1, BAGD, BNTC, LN, Lns, WBC;

ESV, GW, NASB, NRSV, REB], 'to set on' [BECNT], 'to touch' [CEV], 'to lay on to heal' [NLT]. This verb means to place something on something [LN]. They obviously wanted Jesus to put his hand on the man in order to heal him [EBC; NLT].

QUESTION—Who brought this man to Jesus?

The third person plural verb φέρουσιν 'they brought' has the impersonal plural meaning of 'people (men) brought' [AB2, NTC, TH]. These men would be from the Decapolis region where the healing power of Jesus had already been made known by the testimony given by the Gadarene demoniac (5:20) [Gnd, Hb, NIGTC, WBC].

QUESTION—What is meant by the word μογιλάλον 'mute'?

1. The man had a speech impediment [AB1, AB2, BECNT, CGTC, EBC, Hb, ICC, NCBC, NICNT, NIGTC, NTC, PNTC, Tay, WBC; all versions]. Probably this man had had a severe disease or injury that resulted in him becoming deaf along with a spasmodic condition of his tongue that prevented him from articulating his words [NICNT]. He was unable to speak plainly because of his deafness [Hb]. This meaning is supported by 7:35 where it says 'he began speaking *normally*' [AB2, CGTC, EBC, ICC, NCBC].

2. The man was both deaf and dumb, making him unable to speak at all [BNTC, CBC, EGT, Lns, My, Sw, WBC]. In verse 37, the people proclaim the fact the Jesus has made the dumb speak [BNTC]. Any sounds he might make were unintelligible [EBC, Lns].

7:33 And having-taken- him -aside[a] from the crowd privately,[b] he-put his fingers into[c] his ears[d] and having-spit[e] he touched his tongue,

LEXICON—a. aorist mid. participle of ἀπολαμβάνω (LN 15.177) (BAGD 3. p. 94): 'to take aside' [BAGD, BECNT, LN, NTC, WBC; CEV, ESV, KJV, NASB, NET, NIV, NRSV, REB], 'to take away' [AB1, AB2, LN; GW], 'to take' [BNTC], 'to lead away' [LN; NCV, NLT], 'to take to himself' [Lns], 'to take off' [TEV], 'to lead off' [LN]. This verb means to lead or take away from a particular point [LN].

b. ἴδιος (LN 28.67) (BAGD 4. p. 371): 'by oneself' [BAGD]. The phrase κατ' ἰδίαν 'privately' [AB1, AB2, BAGD, BECNT, LN, WBC; ESV, NET] is also translated 'in private' [Lns; NRSV], 'by himself' [NTC; NASB, NCV], 'alone' [TEV], 'to be alone with him' [GW, NLT], 'on his own' [BNTC], not explicit [AB2; CEV, KJV, NIV, REB]. The phrase κατ' ἰδίαν 'according to that which is private' is an idiom pertaining to what occurs in a private setting. It has the sense of not being made known publicly [LN]. The miracle was performed away from the crowd [BECNT, TRT].

c. εἰς (LN 84.22): 'into' [LN]. The phrase 'put into' [AB1, BECNT, BNTC, NTC, WBC; ESV, GW, KJV, NASB, NIV, NLT, NRSV] is also translated 'put in' [NCV, NET, REB, TEV], 'thrust into' [AB2], 'pushed

into' [Lns], 'stuck in' [CEV]. This preposition indicates an extension toward a goal that is inside an area [LN].
d. οὖς (LN 8.24) (BAGD 1. p. 595): 'ear' [BAGD, LN; all translations].
e. aorist act. participle of πτύω (LN 23.43) (BAGD p. 727): 'to spit' [AB1, AB2, BAGD, BECNT, BNTC, LN, Lns, NTC, WBC; ESV, GW, KJV, NCV, NET, NIV, NRSV, TEV]. The clause 'having spit he touched his tongue' is translated 'after spitting he touched his tongue with the saliva' [NASB], 'touched his tongue with spittle' [REB], 'he spit and put it on the man's tongue' [CEV], 'spitting on his own fingers, he touched the man's tongue' [NLT]. This verb means to spit on or at something or someone [LN].

QUESTION—Why did Jesus put his fingers into the man's ears and how did he do this?

It would be useless to speak to the deaf man, so Jesus expressed his concern by touching him [NAC]. He did this to make the man aware that something was going to be done to his ears in reference to his deafness [Hb, ICC, Lns, NTC]. Jesus probably touched the opening to the man's ears with only one or two fingers [TRT]. Jesus put one finger of his right hand into one of the man's ears and one finger of his other hand into the man's other ear [EGT]. Sticking his fingers into the ears pictured the opening of the man's ears in order for him to hear [Gnd]. Perhaps Jesus took hold of the man's ears and stretched them open [NICNT].

QUESTION—Why did Jesus spit and touch the man's tongue and how did he do this?

This was done to call the man's attention to his need for help in regard to his mouth and tongue. It also conveyed the information that Jesus had the power to do something about his inability to speak [Hb, NICNT]. This action would have caused the man to realize that the one who stood before him was going to heal him [Hb, ICC, NICNT, NTC]. Touching the man was only a symbolic action since the miracles were wrought completely by the Lord's will [Lns]. Some think that touching him was involved in healing him. The healing of the woman in 5:25–34 and the summaries of the healings in 3:10 and 6:56 highlight Jesus' touch as being a means of healing [WBC], so probably each touch was part of the healing miracle [Gnd, WBC].

1. Jesus spat onto his own fingers and applied the spittle to the man's tongue [AB2, Gnd, ICC, NICNT, NIGTC, NTC, PNTC, Tay, TH; CEV, NASB, NLT, REB].
2. Jesus spat onto the ground and then touched the man's tongue [Hb, Lns, WBC]. Spitting on the ground was another symbolic act to call attention to the man's tongue and mouth that were in need of healing [Hb].
3. Jesus spat directly onto the man's tongue and then touched the man's tongue with his fingers [My].

7:34 and having-looked-up to heaven he-sighed[a] and says to-him, "*Ephphatha*,[b]" which means 'be-opened'.[c]

LEXICON—a. aorist act. indic. of στενάζω (LN 25.143) (BAGD p. 766): 'to sigh' [AB1, AB2, BAGD, BECNT, BNTC, LN, Lns, NTC, WBC; ESV, GW, KJV, NCV, NLT, NRSV, REB], 'to groan' [BAGD, LN; CEV], 'to give a deep groan' [TEV]. The verb 'he sighed' is translated 'with a sigh' [NET], 'with a deep sigh' [NASB, NIV]. This verb means to groan or sigh as the result of deep concern or stress [LN]. In connection with a healing, it probably is an expression of power ready to act [BAGD].

b. εφφαθα (LN 79.11) (BAGD p. 331): 'ephphatha' [AB1, AB2, BECNT, BNTC, LN, Lns, NTC, WBC; all versions except CEV], 'effatha' [CEV]. This verb is an Aramaic word meaning 'be opened' [LN]. This word is italicized to indicate it is a foreign word in the Greek text [NET, NLT, TEV].

c. aorist act. pass. of διανοίγω (LN 79.110) (BAGD 1.b. p. 187): 'to be opened' [BAGD, LN]. This command is translated 'be opened' [AB1, AB2, BECNT, BNTC, NTC, WBC; all versions except CEV, TEV], 'be completely opened' [Lns], 'open up' [CEV, TEV]. This verb means to cause something to be open [LN].

QUESTION—Why did Jesus look up toward heaven?

This was a position regularly taken in prayer [AB1, BECNT, EBC, EGT, NICNT, NTC, Tay, TH]. By looking upward, Jesus let the deaf man know the source and nature of the power needed to heal him [EBC, Hb, Lns, NAC, NTC]. This indicated Jesus' relation with God who gave him the power to feed the crowds (6:11) and heal the sick [NCBC, WBC].

QUESTION—Why did Jesus sigh?

Jesus expressed his strong emotions with a sigh or groan [CGTC, EGT, Hb, ICC, NICNT, NIGTC, NTC, Tay, TH]. This sigh has been interpreted as an expression of power, anger, grief, or compassion [BNTC]. It indicated his strong emotions as he urgently prayed for help to wage war against the power of Satan [CGTC]. As Jesus looked up to heaven, his sigh was a prayerful gesture [EBC, Lns, My, NLTfn, TRT]. The sigh showed the deep sympathy and compassion Jesus had for the man [AB1, EGT, Hb, ICC, My, NTC, PNTC, Tay]. It indicated the exhausting nature of his healing ministry [EGT].

QUESTION—Why did Mark write the actual Aramaic word '*Ephphatha*' since he was writing the book in Greek and had to explain what the word meant to his Greek readers?

Mark used Aramaic for emphasis here and in 5:41 [Gnd]. Aramaic was the normal mode of speech for Jesus and those who reported the incident [AB1, AB2]. Mark wanted his readers to have the very sounds that came from Jesus' lips as he was performing the miracle [Lns]. The use of the Aramaic word is not particularly significant since it was widely spoken in Jewish circles [NIGTC, WBC].

QUESTION—What did Jesus command to be opened?

The pronoun in the phrase λέγει αὐτῷ 'says to him' is masculine singular and so is the verb διανοίχθητι 'be opened'. So the text seems to view the whole man as being concentrated in his ears [Gnd]. This passive command 'be opened' is presumably related to the ears, yet it was addressed to the man. Jesus was saying to the man, 'Your ears will be opened', or else he was commanding the ears, 'Open up, ears' [TH].

1. Jesus commanded the man's ears to be opened [EGT, My, NIGTC]. This command was specifically addressed to the man's ears, although the loosing of the tongue was part of the result [EGT]. Even though the form is singular and was formally addressed to the man, it was the man's ears that were commanded to begin functioning again [NIGTC].
2. Jesus commanded both the man's organs of hearing and speech to be opened [Hb, Lns, My].
3. Jesus commanded the man to be opened [CGTC, ICC, NICNT, NTC]. There is no need for determining which particular part of the person was told to be opened since the whole person would be opened when released from the power of Satan who had bound him [CGTC]. This was addressed to the man who was going to be opened to both sound and speech through the opening of the involved organs [ICC, NICNT, NTC].

7:35 And immediately his ears^a were opened,^a and the bond^b of-his tongue was loosed^c and he-began-speaking normally.^d

TEXT—Manuscripts reading εὐθέως 'immediately' are given a C rating by GNT to indicate that choosing it over a variant text was difficult. A variant reading omits this word.

LEXICON—a. aorist pass. indic. of ἀνοίγω (LN 24.69, 79.110) (BAGD 1.e.γ. p. 71): 'to be opened' [BAGD, LN (79.110)]. The phrase ἠνοίγησαν αὐτοῦ αἱ ἀκοαί 'his ears were opened' [AB1, AB2, BECNT, BNTC, NTC, WBC; ESV, KJV, NASB, NET, NIV, NRSV] is also translated 'his ears were completely opened' [Lns], 'his hearing was restored' [LN (24.69); REB], 'he was again able to hear' [LN (24.69); similarly NCV, TEV], 'the man could hear' [CEV, GW], 'the man could hear perfectly' [NLT]. This verb means to cause something to be open [LN (79.110)], and the idiom ἀνοίγουσιν αἱ ἀκοαί 'the ears open' or possibly 'hearing opens' means to become able to hear [LN (24.69)]. Speaking of the ears being 'opened' is an idiom meaning that the man was now able to hear. It does not suggest that the man's ears had been pinched shut or plugged with something [TRT].

b. δεσμός (LN 23.156) (BAGD 1. p. 176): 'bond' [BAGD, BNTC, LN, Lns], 'fetter' [BAGD, WBC], 'string' [KJV], 'illness' [LN], not explicit [AB1, AB2, BECNT, NTC; all versions except KJV]. This noun is a figurative extension of meaning of δεσμός 'bond' that denotes a state of physical incapacity or illness [LN]. It denotes a bond or hindrance that prevents mutes from using their tongues [BAGD]. This does not necessarily imply that the man was tongue-tied [Hb, Sw]. This is a figurative description of the cure [Tay]. The bond or fetter refers to a chain that binds a prisoner, and breaking the fetter is a picture of Jesus liberating the man of his speech impediments [PNTC]. 'Bond' is used figuratively for whatever stood in the way of the man's speech, and in this case the bond is the deafness that prevented him from talking properly [ICC].

c. aorist pass. indic. of λύω (LN 18.18) (BAGD 1.b. p. 483): 'to be loosened, to be untied' [BAGD, LN]. The phrase 'the bond of/on his tongue was loosed' [BNTC, Lns] is also translated 'the string of his tongue was loosed' [KJV], 'his tongue's fetter was loosed' [WBC], 'the impediment of his tongue was removed' [NASB], 'his speech impediment was removed' [AB1; TEV; similarly REB], 'his tongue was loosened' [NET, NIV], 'his tongue was released' [NTC; ESV, NRSV], 'his tongue was freed' [NLT], 'his tongue was unchained' [BECNT], 'his tongue was unshackled' [AB2], 'the man was able…to use his tongue' [NCV]. The phrase 'his tongue was loosened and he began speaking' is translated 'he had no more trouble talking' [CEV], 'the man could…talk' [GW]. This verb means to reverse the result of tying by untying [LN].

d. ὀρθῶς (LN 72.13) (BAGD p. 580): 'normally' [AB2, BAGD; GW], 'properly' [WBC], 'plainly' [ESV, NASB, NET, NIV, NLT, NRSV; similarly KJV], 'correctly' [BAGD, BECNT, LN], 'rightly' [Lns], 'clearly' [BNTC; CEV, NCV, REB], 'distinctly' [NTC], 'without difficulty' [AB1], 'without any trouble' [TEV]. This adverb refers to doing something in a way that conforms closely to an accepted norm or standard [LN].

QUESTION—What is meant by the man's ἀκοαί 'ears'?

The word used in 7.33 was ὦτα 'ears' (7:33), but here the word is ἀκοαί 'ears', which literally means 'hearings' [Gnd]. The focus is now on the restoration of the *function* of the outwardly visible organs into which Jesus had put his fingers [Gnd, NIGTC]. Literally 'hearings', this word is applied by metonymy to the ears as the organs of hearing [EGT, ICC].

QUESTION—What is implied by the words 'he began speaking normally'?

Some languages must specify whether this speaking was a return to a previous state of speaking normally or if the man had never spoken normally before. There is no indication in the Greek text one way or the other. The fact that the man was now speaking *normally* seems to imply that he had not been completely deaf, so this refers to a restoration of the ability to speak rather than a miraculous ability to speak after total congenital deafness [TH]. Rather than speaking with difficulty (7:32), he now was speaking plainly [CGTC, Gnd, Hb]. This former mumbler or stammerer was now speaking distinctly and clearly [NTC]. He had only been able to utter unintelligible sounds [EGT] as a deaf mute [Lns].

MARK 7:36 393

7:36 And he-ordered[a] them that they-should-tell no-one. But as-much-as[b] he-was-ordering them, all-the-more[c] exceedingly[d] they were-proclaiming[e] (it).

LEXICON—a. aorist mid. indic. of διαστέλλομαι, διαστέλλω (LN **33.323**) (BAGD p. 188): 'to order' [BAGD, **LN**; ESV, GW, NET, NRSV, TEV], 'to give orders' [NASB], 'to command' [AB2, BECNT, LN, WBC; NCV, NIV], 'to charge' [Lns, NTC; ESV, KJV], 'to tell' [CEV, NLT], 'to give strict instructions' [BNTC]. The clause 'he ordered them that they should tell no one' is translated 'Jesus forbade them to tell anyone' [AB1; REB]. This verb means to state with force and/or authority what others must do [LN]. This verb occurs at 5:43; 7:36; 8:15; 9:9.

  b. ὅσος (LN **78.52**) (BAGD 3. p. 586): 'as much as' [BAGD, LN], 'to the degree that, to the same degree, as much as' [LN]. The phrase ὅσον δὲ αὐτοῖς διεστέλλετο 'as much as he ordered/charged them' [Lns; NET] is also translated 'as much as he commanded them (not to speak about it)' [**LN**], 'the more he told/charged/ordered/commanded/instructed them' [AB1, AB2, BECNT, BNTC, NTC, WBC; all versions except NET, NIV], 'the more he did so' [NIV]. This word refers to the degree of correlative extent [LN].

  c. μᾶλλον (LN 78.28) (BAGD 78.28) (BAGD 1. p. 489) 'even more, more than, to a greater degree' [LN]. See the following lexical item for translations of this word. This comparative adverb indicates a degree that surpasses in some manner a point on an explicit or implicit scale of extent [LN].

  d. περισσότερος (LN 78.31) (BAGD 3. p. 651): 'very great, excessive, extremely, surpassing, all the more, much greater' [LN], 'much more' [BAGD]. The phrase μᾶλλον περισσότερον 'all the more exceedingly' is translated 'all the more greatly' [AB2], 'the more beyond measure' [Lns], 'all the more' [NET], 'so much the more a great deal' [KJV], 'the more' [BNTC, WBC; CEV, GW, NCV, NIV, NLT, REB, TEV], 'the more widely' [NTC; NASB], 'the more zealously' [BECNT; ESV, NRSV], 'the more persistently' [AB1]. This refers to a degree that is considerably in excess of some point on an implied or explicit scale of extent [LN].

  e. imperf. act. indic. of κηρύσσω (LN 33.207) (BAGD 2.a. p. 431): 'to proclaim' [LN, WBC; ESV, NET, NRSV], 'to continue to proclaim' [NASB], 'to tell' [LN; TEV], 'to tell about' [NCV], 'to talk about' [CEV, NIV], 'to speak of, to mention publicly' [BAGD], 'to preach' [BECNT], 'to publish' [NTC; KJV], 'to spread around' [REB], 'to spread the news' [AB1, AB2; GW, NLT]. This verb means to announce extensively and publicly [LN]. This verb is used with the same meaning at 1:45; 5:20; 7:36.

QUESTION—Who is the referent of the pronoun αὐτοῖς 'them' whom Jesus ordered?

  Jesus was speaking to the man who was healed and to his friends who had brought him to Jesus [Hb, NIGTC]. It includes all who witnessed the change in the man [BNTC]. It refers to the whole crowd [Gnd, Lns]. 'Them' is translated 'the people' [CEV, GW, NCV, TEV], 'the crowd' [NLT].

QUESTION—What shouldn't they tell?

They shouldn't tell people anything [NET], that is, anything about what Jesus had done [CEV], anything about what had happened [NCV].

QUESTION—What is indicated by the two imperfect verbs in the clause 'as much as *he was ordering* them, all the more exceedingly they *were proclaiming* it'?

These two imperfect verbs suggest that Jesus made repeated appeals for silence and there were just as many acts of disobedience [BECNT, CBC, Lns, NIGTC, NTC, Sw, Tay, TH; NASB]. Since the initial command was not heeded, Jesus repeated it on different occasions [Hb].

7:37 And they-were- extremely[a] -amazed[b] saying, "He-has-done[c] all (things) well,[d] even/and[e] the deaf (ones) he-makes to-hear and the mute[f] (ones) to-speak.

LEXICON—a. ὑπερπερισσῶς (LN 78.34) (BAGD p. 842): 'extremely' [**LN**], 'completely' [AB1; CEV, GW, NCV, NET, NLT, TEV], 'utterly' [NASB], 'beyond (all) measure' [BAGD, BNTC, Lns, NTC; ESV, KJV, NRSV], 'exceedingly' [AB2, BECNT], 'absolutely' [WBC]. The phrase 'they were extremely amazed' is translated 'their astonishment knew no bounds' [REB], 'people were overwhelmed with amazement' [NIV]. This adjective indicates an extraordinary degree, a considerable excess over what would be expected [LN].

b. imperf. pass. indic. of ἐκπλήσσομαι, ἐκπλήσσω (LN 25.219) (BAGD 2. p. 244): 'to be amazed' [BAGD, LN, Lns; CEV, NCV, NLT, TEV; similarly GW], 'to be astonished' [AB1, AB2, BECNT, BNTC, NTC; ESV, KJV, NASB], 'to be astounded' [LN; NET, NRSV], 'to be overwhelmed' [BAGD, WBC]. See the preceding lexical item for translations of the phrase 'they extremely amazed' for NIV and REB. This verb means to be so amazed as to be practically overwhelmed [LN]. The imperfect tense denotes a continuing state of astonishment [Gnd, Hb, Lns]. This word occurs at 1:22; 6:2; 7:37; 10:26; 11:18.

c. perf. act. indic. of ποιέω (LN 42.7): 'to do' [AB1, AB2, BECNT, BNTC, LN, Lns, NTC, WBC; all versions], 'to act, to carry out, to accomplish, to perform' [LN]. This verb means to do or perform almost any type of activity [LN]. The perfect tense 'has done' with the plural 'all things' indicates that Jesus had healed more than just the deaf mute on this occasion [Hb, Lns], or it includes past healings [EGT].

d. καλῶς (LN 65.23) (BAGD 1. p. 401): This is translated as an adverb modifying the manner in which he does all things: 'well' [AB1, AB2, BAGD, BECNT, BNTC, LN, WBC; all versions except CEV, NLT], 'excellently' [Lns, NTC], 'good' [LN; CEV], 'wonderful' [NLT]. This adverb/adjective pertains to events that measure up to their intended purpose [LN]. This adverb stands emphatically forward to stress that what

Jesus had done was not only good in a moral sense, but also admirable and noble [Hb].
  e. καί (LN 89.93): 'even' [AB1, LN, NTC; all versions except GW, KJV, NASB], 'and, and also, also, in addition' [LN], not explicit [AB2, BECNT, BNTC, Lns, WBC; GW, KJV, NASB]. This conjunction indicates an additive relationship that is not coordinate [LN].
  f. ἄλαλος (LN **33.106**) (BAGD p. 35): 'mute' [BAGD, LN], 'dumb' [**LN**], 'unable to speak' [BAGD, LN], 'incapable of talking' [LN]. The adjectival plural noun is translated 'the mute' [AB2, BECNT, WBC; ESV, GW, NASB, NET, NIV, NRSV], 'the dumb' [AB1, BNTC; KJV, REB, TEV], 'the speechless' [Lns, NTC], 'people who cannot talk' [CEV; similarly NCV], 'those who cannot speak' [NLT]. This adjective pertains to not being able to speak or talk [LN]. This word occurs at 7:37; 9:17, 25.

QUESTION—What is the significance of describing the crowd as being 'extremely amazed'?

This healing was a matter of particular amazement since healing the deaf and the dumb are two elements in Isaiah 35:5 that describe the blessings that will result from God's own eschatological coming [AB1, AB2, CGTC, NICNT, NIGTC, WBC]. They were so astonished that they were wondering whether Jesus was the Messiah [ESVfn].

QUESTION—What is indicated by the use of the present tense ποιε 'he makes'?

The present tense is used in a general sense [Hb, Lns, NIGTC]. Jesus can at any time make any deaf person able to hear and make any speechless person able to speak [Lns, NIGTC]. This miracle typifies the miraculous activity of Jesus as a whole since the healing of this one deaf mute is an example of many such healings [Gnd].

DISCOURSE UNIT—8:1–26 [NASB]. The topic is the four thousand are fed.

DISCOURSE UNIT—8:1–13 [NIV]. The topic is Jesus feeds the four thousand.

DISCOURSE UNIT—8:1–10 [CBC, EBC, Hb, NICNT; CEV, ESV, GW, NCV, NET, NLT, NRSV, TEV]. The topic is the provision of bread in the Decapolis [NICNT], the feeding of the four thousand [EBC, Hb; NET, NRSV], Jesus feeds four thousand people [CBC; CEV, ESV, GW, NLT, TEV], more than four thousand people fed [NCV].

8:1 In those days again there-being[a] a-large crowd and not having anything they-might-eat, having called[b] the disciples he-says to-them,
LEXICON—a. pres. act. participle of εἰμί (LN **85.1**) (BAGD 1.6. p. 223): 'to be' [AB2, BECNT, **LN**, Lns, WBC; GW, KJV, NASB, NCV, NET, NRSV], 'to be present' [BAGD], 'to collect' [REB], 'to gather' [AB1, BNTC, NTC; ESV, NIV, NLT], 'to gather around' [CEV], 'to come together' [TEV]. This verb means to be in a place [LN].

b. aorist mid. participle of προσκαλέομαι (LN 33.308): 'to call' [AB1, AB2, BECNT, LN; GW, NASB, NCV, NET, NLT, NRSV, REB, TEV], 'to call to oneself' [Lns, NTC; ESV, KJV, NIV], 'to call together' [CEV], 'to summon' [AB2, WBC]. This verb means to call to oneself [LN].

QUESTION—What does ἐν ἐκείναις ταῖς ἡμέραις 'in those days' refer to?

This phrase is simply a general indicator of temporal sequence that means 'at that time' [TH]. 'Those days' refer to the days when Jesus was journeying through the region of Decapolis along the east side of Lake Galilee (7:31) [CGTC, EBC, Gnd, Hb, ICC, Lns, NAC, NICNT, NIGTC, NIVfn, NTC, PNTC, Sw, Tay, WBC].

QUESTION—What does πάλιν 'again' refer to?

It could simply mean a large crowd was present just like in previous days, [Lns]. Verse 2 says that these people had been receiving instruction from Jesus over a period of three days [EBC]. It could refer to the previous crowd mentioned in 7:33 [My, NTC, Tay], or in 6:31–34, 44, 55–56 [NTC]. It especially refers to the last reference of a *large* crowd in 6:34–44 when 5,000 men were fed [BECNT, Gnd, Hb, ICC, Sw, WBC; NRSV].

QUESTION—What is indicated by the use of the participles ὄντος 'there being' and μὴ ἐχόντων 'not having'?

1. Both participles indicate the *reason* Jesus called his disciples to himself [NCV, NET]: *because* a large crowd had gathered and did not have anything to eat, Jesus called the disciples to him.
2. Both participles indicate the *time* when Jesus called his disciples to himself [AB2, BECNT, BNTC, Lns; ESV, NASB, NRSV]: *when* a large crowd had gathered and the people no longer had anything to eat, Jesus called the disciples to him. This also includes the reason he felt compassion for them [BNTC].
3. Both participles indicate the *setting* for this account and are translated as a separate sentence [WBC; GW, NLT]: *a large crowd was gathered together and they did not have anything to eat. Jesus called the disciples to him.*
4. The participle ὄντος 'there being' indicates the setting for this account while the participle μὴ ἐχόντων 'not having' indicates the reason Jesus called the disciples to himself [AB1; CEV, NIV, REB]: *a large crowd was gathered together. Because they did not have anything to eat,* Jesus called the disciples to him.

8:2 "I-have-compassion[a] on the crowd, because already[b] they-have-remained-with[c] me three days and they-do- not -have anything they-can-eat.

LEXICON—a. pres. mid./pass. (deponent = act.) indic. of σπλαγχνίζομαι (LN 25.49) (BAGD p. 762): 'to have compassion' [BECNT, LN, Lns, WBC; ESV, KJV, NET, NIV, NRSV], 'to feel compassion' [LN; NASB], 'to have great affection' [LN], 'to have pity, to feel sympathy' [BAGD], 'to be full of pity' [BNTC], 'to take pity' [AB2], 'to feel sorry' [AB1; CEV,

GW, NCV, NLT, TEV]. The phrase 'I have compassion on' is translated 'my heart goes out to' [NTC; REB]. This verb means to experience great affection and compassion for someone [LN]. This word occurs at 1:41; 6:34; 8:2; 9:22.

b. ἤδη (LN 67.20) (BAGD 1.a. p. 344): 'already' [BAGD, LN, Lns, NTC; NCV, NET, NIV, NLT], 'now' [AB1, BAGD, BNTC; ESV, GW, KJV, NRSV, REB], 'by this time' [BAGD], not explicit [AB2, BECNT, WBC; CEV, TEV]. This adverb refers to a point of time preceding another point of time and implies completion [LN].

c. pres. act. indic. of προσμένω (LN 85.59) (BAGD 1.a.α. p. 717): 'to remain with' [AB2, BECNT, LN, Lns, NTC; NASB], 'to stay with' [BNTC, LN, WBC], 'to be with' [AB1; all versions except NASB]. This verb means to stay or remain in a place beyond some point of time [LN].

QUESTION—Why didn't the crowd have anything to eat?

After being with Jesus for three days, the people had eaten all of the food they had brought with them [Hb, Lns, NICNT, NTC, Sw, TH].

8:3 **And if I-send- them -away hungry[a] to their house,[b] they-will-faint[c] on the way, and some of-them have-come from far-away."**

LEXICON—a. νῆστις (LN 23.31) (BAGD p. 538): 'hungry' [BAGD, BECNT, BNTC, LN, NTC; CEV, ESV, NASB, NCV, NET, NIV, NLT, REB], 'lacking food' [LN], 'without food' [WBC], 'without eating' [AB2], 'not eating' [BAGD], 'unfed' [AB1], 'fasting' [Lns; KJV]. The phrase 'send them away hungry' is translated 'send them...before they've eaten' [GW], 'send them...without feeding them' [TEV]. This adjective refers to being very hungry, presumably for a considerable time out of necessity rather than choice [LN].

b. οἶκος (LN 7.2) (BAGD 1.a.α. p. 560): 'house' [BAGD, LN], 'home' [BAGD], The phrase 'to their house' is translated 'to their own houses' [KJV], 'to their home' [Lns], 'to their homes' [BECNT, NTC; ESV, NASB, NRSV], 'home' [AB1, AB2, BNTC, WBC; CEV, GW, NCV, NET, NIV, NLT, REB, TEV]. This noun denotes a building with one or more rooms, usually a dwelling place [LN].

c. fut. pass. indic. of ἐκλύομαι, ἐκλύω (LN 23.79) (BAGD p. 243): 'to faint' [AB1, AB2, BECNT, BNTC; all versions except GW, NIV], 'to faint from exhaustion' [LN], 'to collapse' [NTC, WBC; NIV], 'to become exhausted' [Lns; GW], 'to give out' [BAGD, LN], 'to become weary' [BAGD, LN]. This verb means to become so tired and weary that one gives out, possibly even fainting from exhaustion [LN]. They might physically collapse along the trail [EBC, Hb, TH].

8:4 And his disciples answered him, "From-where[a] will- anyone -be-able to-satisfy[b] these (people) with-loaves-of-bread here in a-desolate-place[c]?" **8:5** And he-asked them, "How many loaves-of-bread do-you-have?" And they said, "Seven."

LEXICON—a. πόθεν (LN 84.6) (BAGD 1. p. 680): 'from where' [BAGD, LN], 'from whence' [KJV], 'from what place' [BAGD], 'from what source' [WBC], 'whence' [BAGD, LN], 'where' [AB2, LN; CEV, GW, NASB, NET, NIV, TEV], 'how' [AB1; CEV, NCV, NLT, NRSV, REB]. This adverb indicates extension from a source [LN].

    b. aorist act. infin. of χορτάζω (LN 23.16) (BAGD 2.a. p. 884): 'to satisfy, to feed' [BAGD], 'to satisfy with food, to cause to eat one's fill' [LN]. The clause 'from where will anyone be able to satisfy these people with loaves of bread' is translated 'from whence can a man satisfy these men with bread' [KJV], 'where will anyone be able to get the loaves to satisfy these people' [AB2], 'where can someone get enough bread…to satisfy these people' [NET; similarly BNTC; NASB], 'from what source can anyone fill these people with bread' [WBC; similarly Lns], 'where could anyone get enough bread/food to feed these people' [GW; similarly NTC; NIV, TEV], 'how can one feed these people with bread' [NRSV], 'how will anyone be able…to provide these people with bread' [BECNT; similarly REB], 'how can we get enough bread to feed all these people' [NCV], 'where can we find enough food to feed such a crowd' [CEV], 'how can one feed these people with bread' [ESV], 'how can anyone provide food for all these people' [AB1], 'how are we supposed to find enough food to feed them' [NLT]. This verb means to eat so as to be in a satisfied state [LN]. This word occurs at 6:42; 7:27; 8:4, 8.

    c. ἐρημία (LN 1.86) (BAGD p. 309): 'desolate place' [ESV, NASB, NET], 'remote place' [NIV, REB], 'lonely place' [AB1, LN], 'wilderness' [LN, WBC; KJV, NLT], 'desert' [BAGD, LN; NRSV, TEV], 'place like a desert' [CEV], 'place where no one lives' [GW], 'uninhabited region' [BAGD], 'far away from any town' [NCV]. This noun denotes a largely uninhabited region that normally has only sparse vegetation [LN].

QUESTION—Who had the seven loaves of bread?

Seven loaves were all that the disciples had left of their own supplies [Hb].

8:6 And he-orders[a] the crowd to-recline[b] on the ground. And having-taken the seven loaves-of-bread (and) having-given-thanks[c] he broke (them) and was-giving (the pieces) to his disciples so-that they-might-distribute[d] (them) and they-distributed (them) to-the crowd.

LEXICON—a. pres. act. indic. of παραγγέλλω (LN 33.327) (BAGD p. 613): 'to order' [AB1, BAGD, LN, NTC; GW, NRSV, REB, TEV], 'to instruct' [BAGD, BNTC], 'to direct' [BAGD; ESV, NASB, NET], 'to command' [AB2, BAGD, BECNT, LN, WBC; KJV], 'to pass an order to' [Lns], 'to tell' [CEV, NCV, NIV, NLT]. This verb means to announce what must be done [LN].

b. aorist act. infin. of ἀναπίπτω (LN 17.23) (BAGD 1. p. 59): 'to recline' [BAGD, BECNT, LN, Lns, WBC], 'to sit down' [AB1, AB2, BNTC, LN; all versions except NCV], 'to sit' [NCV], 'to take their places' [NTC]. This verb means to be in a reclining position as one eats [LN]. This word occurs at 6:40; 8:6.

c. aorist act. participle of εὐχαριστέω (LN 33.349) (BAGD 2. p. 328): 'to give thanks' [AB2, BAGD, BECNT, BNTC, Lns, NTC, WBC; ESV, KJV, NASB, NET, NIV, NRSV; similarly LN], 'to give thanks to God' [AB1; GW, NCV, REB, TEV], 'to thank God (for them)' [NLT], 'to bless (them)' [CEV]. This verb means to express gratitude for benefits or blessings [LN]. It refers to pronouncing the usual prayer at a meal [Lns]. This word occurs at 8:6; 14:23.

d. pres. act. subj. of παρατίθημι (LN 57.116) (BAGD 1.a. p. 622): 'to give food to, to provide with food' [LN], 'to set before' [BAGD]. The phrase 'so that they might distribute them' [AB2, BECNT] is also translated 'to distribute to the crowd' [TEV], 'to distribute' [AB1, BNTC; NRSV, REB], 'in order to place before them' [Lns], 'to set before the people/them' [NTC; ESV, KJV, NIV], 'to serve to the people/them' [GW, NASB], 'to serve' [WBC; NET], 'to give to the people' [NCV]. The words 'was giving them to his disciples so that they might serve, and they served the crowd' is translated 'he gave them to his disciples, who distributed the bread to the crowd' [NLT], 'handed them to his disciples, who passed them out to the crowd' [CEV]. This verb means to give or to provide something, usually in connection with placing food in front of a person [LN]. This word occurs at 6:41; 8:6, 7.

QUESTION—How did Jesus give this order to the crowd?

1. Jesus directly addressed the crowd and told everybody to sit on the ground [Hb, PNTC, Sw, Tay, TH, TRT, WBC; CEV, ESV, GW, KJV, NASB, NCV, NET].
2. Jesus told his disciples to order the crowd to sit on the ground [ICC, Lns]. Jesus had the disciples pass along his order to the crowd [Lns]. The verb 'he orders' is used to denote the transmission of orders through subordinates [ICC].

QUESTION—When did the miracle of multiplying the seven loaves happen?

The miracle probably happened as Jesus broke the bread and kept handing the pieces to the disciples for distribution to the crowd [Hb, Lns, NTC]. The iterative imperfect verb ἐδίδου 'was giving' the broken pieces of bread refers to the multiplication of the food in Jesus' hands as he loaded each basket again and again [Hb, Lns, NTC].

8:7 And/also[a] they had a-few small-fish.[b] And having-blessed[c] them he-said[d] (that) these also should-be-served.

TEXT—Manuscripts reading εὐλογήσας αὐτά 'having blessed them' are given a B rating by GNT to indicate it was regarded to be almost certain. A variant reading is εὐλογήσας 'having blessed' and it is followed by KJV. Other variant readings are ταῦτα εὐλογήσας 'having blessed these things', and εὐχαριστήσας 'having given thanks'.

LEXICON—a. καί (LN 89.92, 89.93) (BAGD II.1. p. 393): 'and' [AB2, BNTC, LN (80.92), Lns; ESV, KJV], 'also' [AB1, BAGD, LN (89.93), NTC, WBC; CEV, GW, NASB, NCV, NET, NRSV, REB, TEV], 'and also' [BECNT, LN (89.93)], 'too' [NLT], 'as well' [NIV]. This conjunction indicates a coordinate relationship [LN (80.92)] or an additive relationship which is not coordinate [LN (89.93)]. It functions as an adverb and means 'also' [BAGD].

b. ἰχθύδιον (LN 4.60) (BAGD p. 384): 'small fish' [all translations except CEV], 'little fish' [BAGD, LN; CEV]. This noun is the diminutive of ἰχθύς 'fish' and denotes any kind of relatively small fish [LN].

c. aorist act. participle of εὐλογέω (LN 33.356, 33.470) (BAGD 1, or 2.b. p. 322): 'to give thanks' [BAGD (1.)], 'to praise, to speak well of' [BAGD (1.), LN (33.356)], 'to consecrate' [BAGD (2.b.)]. The participial phrase εὐλογήσας αὐτά 'having blessed them/these' [BECNT, BNTC, Lns; ESV] is also translated 'blessing these' [WBC], 'after he had blessed them' [NASB; similarly NRSV], 'after Jesus had blessed these' [CEV], 'so Jesus also blessed these' [NLT], 'which he blessed' [REB], 'he blessed them' [GW], 'he said the blessing over them' [AB2], 'after giving thanks for these' [NET], 'after he had given thanks for them' [NTC], 'he gave thanks for them' [NIV; similarly TEV], 'after Jesus gave thanks for the fish' [NCV], 'after giving thanks to God' [AB1]. This verb means to praise or speak well of someone in favorable terms [LN (33.356)], or to ask God to bestow his divine favor on something [LN (33.470)]. It means to give thanks and praise [BAGD (1.)], or to call down God's gracious power on something, thereby causing it be consecrated [BAGD (2.b.)]. This word occurs at 6:41; 8:7; 11:9, 10; 14:22.

d. aorist act. indic. of λέγω, εἶπον (LN 33.69) (BAGD 3.c. p. 226): 'to say' [BECNT, LN, Lns; ESV, GW], 'to tell' [AB2, BAGD, LN, WBC; CEV, NCV, NET, NLT, TEV], 'to order' [AB1, BAGD, BNTC, NTC; NRSV, REB], 'to command' [KJV, NASB]. This verb means to speak or talk about something [LN]. Jesus said this to his disciples [TH].

QUESTION—When were the fish served to the crowd?
The account reads as though the fish were a second course [Hb, NIGTC, WBC]. The fish were prayed for and distributed after the bread had already been distributed [AB1, EBC, Hb].

QUESTION—Who had the few fish?
In verse 5 the disciples were the ones who had the bread [TRT], so probably they also had the fish [TH, TRT; NCV].

QUESTION—What kind of fish did they have?
These were not fresh fish [Lns, NTC, TH]. They were dried fish that were commonly eaten along with bread [Hb, NTC].

QUESTION—What is the object of the verb εὐλογήσας 'having blessed' and how does the act of *blessing* in regard to the fish differ from *giving thanks* for the loaves of bread in verse 6?

It is doubtful that Mark meant to draw a distinction between εὐλογέω 'to bless' concerning the fish in this verse and εὐχαριστέω 'to give thanks' concerning the loaves in the preceding verse. The phrase probably means 'thanking God for the fish' [TH]. The act of εὐλογήσας 'blessing' the fish has the same function as εὐχαριστήσας 'having given thanks' for the bread in verse 6 [BECNT, CGTC, EBC, Hb, Lns, NAC, NIGTC, NTC, Sw, Tay, TH, WBC]. This was an act of praising God in the sense of thanking him [AB1, NAC, NTC, Sw, Tay, TH; NCV, NET, NIV, TEV].

8:8 And they-ate and were-satisfied,[a] and they-picked-up[b] an-abundance[c] of-pieces, seven baskets.[d] 8:9 And there-were about four-thousand. And he sent- them -away.[e]

TEXT—In 8:9, manuscripts reading ἦσαν δὲ 'And there were' are followed by GNT, which does not mention any variant reading. A variant reading is ἦσαν δὲ οἱ φαγντες 'And there were those who ate' and it is followed by KJV.

LEXICON—a. aorist pass. indic. of χορτάζομαι, χορτάζω (LN 23.15) (BAGD 2.a. p. 884): 'to be satisfied' [AB2, BAGD, BNTC; ESV, NASB, NCV, NET, NIV, REB], 'to have enough' [AB1], 'to be filled' [BECNT, Lns, NTC, WBC; KJV, NRSV], 'to eat one's fill' [BAGD, LN]. The phrase 'they ate and were satisfied' is translated 'the crowd...ate all they wanted' [CEV], 'the people ate as much as they wanted' [GW; similarly NLT], 'everyone ate and had enough' [AB1; TEV]. This verb means to eat so as to be in a state of being satisfied [LN]. This word occurs at 6:42; 7:27; 8:4, 8.

   b. aorist act. indic. of αἴρω (LN 15.203) (BAGD 3. p. 24): 'to pick up' [BECNT, NTC; GW, NASB, NET, NIV, NLT], 'to take up' [AB2, Lns; ESV, KJV, NRSV, TEV], 'to gather up' [BECNT], 'to lift up and carry away' [BAGD], 'to carry away, to carry off, to take away' [LN], 'to remove' [BAGD, LN]. The clause 'they picked up an abundance of pieces, seven baskets' is translated 'his followers filled seven baskets with the leftover pieces of food' [NCV], 'seven baskets were filled with what was left over' [REB], 'seven baskets were filled with the scraps left over' [AB1], 'there were seven large baskets of leftover pieces' [WBC], 'the leftovers filled seven large baskets' [CEV]. This verb means to lift up and carry away [LN].

   c. περίσσευμα (LN 59.53) (BAGD 2. p. 650): 'abundance' [LN], 'a great deal of' [LN], 'what was leftover' [AB1, BAGD, LN, Lns, NTC, WBC; all versions], 'what remains' [BAGD, BECNT, Lns], not explicit [AB2, BNTC]. This noun denotes that which exists in abundance [LN]. This excess refers to what was 'remaining' or 'left over' [TH].

   d. σπυρίς (LN 6.149) (BAGD p. 764): 'basket' [AB1, BAGD, BECNT, LN, Lns; ESV, KJV, NCV, NET, NIV, NRSV, REB, TEV], 'large basket'

[AB2, BECNT, BNTC, LN, WBC; CEV, GW, NASB, NLT], 'hamper' [BAGD, NTC]. The noun denotes a basket that is presumably somewhat larger than the κόφινος 'basket' used to gather the leftover food in 6:43 [LN]. This word occurs at 8:8, 20.

e. aorist act. indic. of ἀπολύω (LN 15.43) (BAGD 2.b. p. 96): 'to dismiss' [BAGD, LN; NET, REB], 'to send away' [AB1, AB2, BAGD, BECNT, BNTC; CEV, ESV, KJV, NASB, NIV, NRSV, TEV], 'to send on their way' [GW], 'to send home' [NCV, NLT]. This verb means to cause (or permit) someone to leave a particular location [LN]. In relation to crowds, this word occurs at 6:36, 45; 8:3, 9.

QUESTION—How many people were there?

The text says that there were about τετρακισχίλιοι 'four-thousand' and since the gender of this word is masculine it could refer specifically to men or to people of both genders. Some just translate the number [Lns, WBC; KJV, NASB, NET]. Some supply the word 'men' [NTC; NIV] and others supply the word 'people' [AB1, AB2, BECNT, BNTC, TH; CEV, ESV, GW, NCV, NLT, NRSV, REB, TEV], which could refer to just men or to men, women, and children. Some think this was the total of those present [CBC, PNTC]. The parallel account in Matthew 15:38 says 'The ones eating were four-thousand men apart from the women and children' [Hb, Lns, NETfn, NTC]. Probably the number of people was determined from the arrangement of the people in definite groups as was done on a previous occasion [Hb, Sw].

QUESTION—Who picked up the pieces of food and where was the food?

The disciples picked up the pieces of food [AB1, AB2, BECNT, Gnd, Hb, Lns, NTC, TRT; GW, NCV, NIV, NLT, TEV]. This does not mean that they picked up leftovers from off the ground. They collected the leftovers directly from the people [TRT].

QUESTION—How large were the σπυρίδας 'baskets'?

In 6:43 the baskets used to pick up the food were κοφίνων 'wicker baskets' in which Jews ordinarily carried their food when traveling [EBC, NIGTC]. The word used in this verse denotes a larger basket called a σπυρίς 'basket'. Such baskets was made in various large sizes, the largest being the kind in which Paul was lowered from the wall of Damascus [AB1, CBC, CGTC, EBC, Hb, NIGTC, NTC, Sw, Tay, TRT, WBC].

QUESTION—How is the clause 'and he sent them away' at the end of verse 9 grammatically connected with the rest of the text?

1. This clause is translated as a separate sentence [Lns, NTC; ESV, GW, NCV, NET, NLT, NRSV].
2. All of verse 9 is translated as one sentence [AB2, BECNT, WBC; KJV, NASB].
3. This clause begins a sentence that continues into verse 10 [AB1, BNTC; CEV, NIV, REB, TEV].

DISCOURSE UNIT—8:10–9:29 [PNTC]. The topic is removing the veil.

8:10 **And immediately having-gotten into the boat with his disciples he came into the region of-Dalmanutha.**
TEXT—Manuscripts reading τὰ μέρη Δαλμανουθά 'the region of Dalmanutha' are given a B rating by GNT to indicate it was regarded to be almost certain. Variant readings are τὸ ὄρος Δαλμοῦναι 'the mountain Dalmounai', τὰ μέρη Μαγδαλά 'the region of Magdala', τὸ ὄρος Μαγεδά 'the mountain Mageda', and τὰ ὅρια Μελεγαδά 'the region of Melegada'.
QUESTION—What is the function of this verse?
   1. This verse finishes the discourse unit 8:1–10 [AB1, BNTC, CBC, CGTC, EBC, Hb, My, NAC, NCBC, NICNT, NIGTC, NTC, Tay, TRT; CEV, ESV, GW, NASB, NCV, NET, NIV, NLT, NRSV, REB, TEV].
   2. This verse begins a new discourse unit [AB2, BECNT, Gnd, ICC, PNTC, Sw, WBC].
QUESTION—Where was the region of Dalmanutha?
A region called 'Dalmanutha' located along the shore of Lake Galilee is unknown [all commentaries]. Matthew 15:39 says that they went to the vicinity of 'Magadan', which is also unknown [AB2, EBC, EGT, Hb, NAC, NIGTC, Sw]. This region must have been located on the western side of the lake [AB2, BECNT, Hb, ICC, Lns, My, NICNT, NIGTC], perhaps at the southern end of the plain of Gennesaret [Hb, ICC, NTC]. This unknown name may be due to an early corruption of the text [WBC].

DISCOURSE UNIT—8:11–21 [NIGTC]. The topic is that both opponents and supporters still have a lot to learn.

DISCOURSE UNIT—8:11–13 [CBC, EBC, Hb, NICNT; CEV, ESV, NCV, NET, NLT, NRSV, TEV]. The topic is the request/demand for a sign [NICNT; NET, NRSV], Pharisees demand a sign [CBC; ESV], Pharisees demand a miraculous sign [NLT], the Pharisees ask for a miracle [TEV], the leaders ask for a miracle [NCV], the request for a sign from heaven [EBC, Hb], a sign from heaven [CEV].

DISCOURSE UNIT—8:11–13a [GW]. The topic is the Pharisees asking for a sign from heaven.

8:11 **And the Pharisees came-out[a] and they-began to-argue[b] with-him, demanding/seeking[c] from him a-sign[d] from heaven, testing/tempting[e] him.**
LEXICON—a. aorist act. indic. of ἐξέρχομαι (LN 15.40) (BAGD 1.a. p. 275): 'to come out' [AB1, AB2, BAGD, BNTC, Lns, NTC; CEV, NASB, REB], 'to come forth' [KJV], 'to go out of, to depart out of, to leave from within' [LN], 'to go out' [BAGD, BECNT], 'to come' [WBC; ESV, NET, NIV, NLT, NRSV], The verb 'came out' is translated 'came to Jesus' [NCV, TEV], 'went to Jesus' [GW]. This verb means to move out of an enclosed or well-defined two or three-dimensional area [LN].
   b. pres. act. infin. of συζητέω (LN 33.440) (BAGD 2. p. 775): 'to argue' [AB1, BAGD, BECNT, NTC; CEV, GW, NASB, NET, NLT, NRSV, REB, TEV], 'to dispute' [AB2, BAGD, BNTC, LN, Lns, WBC], 'to

debate' [BAGD], 'to ask questions' [NCV], 'to question' [KJV, NIV]. The phrase 'began to argue' is translated 'started an argument' [CEV]. This verb means to express forceful differences of opinion without necessarily having the goal of seeking a solution [LN].

c. pres. act. participle of ζητέω (LN 33.167, 57.59) (BAGD 2.c. p. 339): 'to demand' [BAGD, LN (33.167); GW, NLT], 'to seek' [AB2, BECNT, BNTC, LN (57.59), Lns, NTC, WBC; ESV, KJV, NASB], 'to ask for' [AB1, BAGD; CEV, NCV, NET, NIV, NRSV, REB, TEV], 'to ask earnestly for' [LN (33.167)], 'to request' [BAGD], 'to try to obtain, to attempt to get' [LN (57.59)]. This verb means to ask for something that is being especially sought [LN (33.167)], or to try to obtain something from someone [LN (57.59)].

d. σημεῖον (LN 33.477) (BAGD 2.a. p. 748): 'sign' [BAGD, LN; all translations except GW, NCV], 'miraculous sign' [GW], 'miracle' [BAGD; NCV]. This noun denotes an event that is believed to have some special meaning. This kind of event would have to be an unusual or even miraculous type of occurrence, so 'sign' is often translated 'miracle' [LN]. A sign is a miracle, something that is contrary to the usual course of nature [BAGD]. This would be a wonder or miracle that was clearly of divine origin [TH]. This word occurs at 8:11, 12; 13:4, 22; 16:17, 20.

e. pres. act. participle of πειράζω (LN 27.31, 27.46) (BAGD 2.c. p. 640): 'to test' [AB1, AB2, BECNT, BNTC, WBC; all versions except KJV, NCV, TEV], 'to try' [BAGD], 'to put to the test' [BAGD, LN (27.46)], 'to test, to examine' [LN (27.46)], 'to try to trap, to attempt to catch in a mistake' [LN (27.31)], 'to hope to trap' [NCV], 'to want to trap' [TEV], 'to tempt' [Lns, NTC; KJV]. This verb means to try to learn the nature or character of someone by submitting him to a thorough and extensive testing [LN (27.46)], or to obtain information to be used against a person by trying to cause him to make a mistake [LN (27.31)]. It means 'to put to the test' and is used in the sense of testing someone in order to bring out something to be used against him. It is not used in the sense of enticing someone to sin [BAGD]. This word occurs at 1:13; 8:11;10:2; 12:15.

QUESTION—What did the Pharisees 'come out' of?

The Pharisees probably came out of their homes when they heard that Jesus had arrived [Hb, Lns]. They came out of the town Dalmanutha [Sw, Tay] or some other town on the west side of Lake Galilee [Sw]. Some translations simply say that they came to Jesus [ESV, NET, NIV, NLT, NRSV].

QUESTION—In what way were they testing or tempting Jesus?

This added phrase, 'testing/tempting him' is a comment added to reveal the purpose behind the demand made by the Pharisees [BECNT, NIGTC, TH].

1. They were *testing* Jesus [AB1, AB2, BECNT, BNTC, Hb, ICC, NICNT, NLTfn, PNTC, Tay, TH, TRT, WBC]. They were asking him to prove the source of his powers [AB1, AB2, BECNT, BNTC, ICC, NICNT, NLTfn, Sw, Tay, TH, WBC]. There are provisions in Deut. 13:2–6 and 18:18–22 about testing a prophet in order to determine whether or not he really had

been sent by God [NICNT]. Some enemies of Jesus had said that his exorcisms were done by the power of Beelzebul, so these Pharisees were now asking for a sign from heaven that would leave no doubt about the source of his power [Tay]. A miraculous sign from God would conclusively show that Jesus was the Messiah [NLTfn]. The Pharisees were really seeking for an excuse for not responding to the clear evidence already apparent in Jesus' ministry and teaching [NIGTC]. If Jesus tried to perform such a miracle and failed, he would be exposed as an imposter. If he refused to attempt such a sign it would be proof that he was not really the Messiah [Hb, NTC].
  2. They were *tempting* Jesus [CGTC, Lns, NTC, Sw; KJV]. They thought if they could tempt Jesus to try to produce a sign, he would fail and be discredited [NTC]. Even if Jesus gave in to them and could produce such a sign, he would be abandoning the path of messianic veiledness ordained by God, and there would be no need for personal decisions of faith [CGTC].

QUESTION—What is meant by 'a sign from heaven'?
  1. The word 'heaven' refers to the sky, so they were asking that some sign would be visible in the sky [EGT, Hb, ICC, Lns, NTC]. The miracles performed by Jesus had been confined to healings done on earth, but now they wanted some startling audible or visible celestial phenomenon that would establish his claims of messianic authority [Hb]. They wanted a voice from heaven or something that would come visibly from above [ICC]. They wanted a sign in heaven like those that had occurred when Joshua made the sun and moon stand still and Elijah caused fire to fall from heaven [Lns, NTC].
  2. The Jews used the word 'heaven' when referring to God, so it means that they were asking for a supernatural sign from God [AB2, BAGD, BECNT, EBC, NAC, NCBC, NICNT, NIGTC, NLTfn, PNTC, Sw, TH, WBC; NCV, TEV]. Jesus' ability to work miracles on earth was already well known (1:32–34, 45; 3:7–12; 6:53–56). What they wanted was a miraculous sign directly from God that would conclusively prove that Jesus was the Messiah [BECNT, NLTfn]. This 'sign' would have to be a wonder or miracle that was clearly of divine origin [TH]. The sign would have to be some compelling display of power that would prove Jesus had divine authority for his ministry [AB2, CGTC, EBC, NIVfn, PNTC, WBC].

8:12 And having-sighed-deeply[a] in his spirit,[b] he says, "Why (does) this generation[c] seek[d] a-sign? Truly I-say to-you, if[e] a-sign will-be-given to-this generation—"

LEXICON—a. aorist act. participle of ἀναστενάζω (LN 25.44) (BAGD p. 61): 'to sigh deeply' [AB1, BECNT, LN, Lns, WBC; ESV, KJV, NASB, NCV, NET, NIV, NLT, NRSV, REB], 'to sigh' [AB2], 'with a deep sigh'

[BNTC; GW], 'to groan' [CEV], 'to groan deeply' [LN], 'to give a deep groan' [TEV]. This verb means to groan or sigh deeply [LN].

b. πνεῦμα (LN 26.9) (BAGD 3.b. p. 675): 'spirit' [BAGD, LN], 'inner being' [LN]. The phrase 'having sighed deeply in his spirit' [BECNT, Lns] is also translated 'sighing deeply in his spirit' [WBC; NASB, NET; similarly ESV, NRSV], '(When he heard this,) he sighed deeply in his spirit' [NLT], 'he sighed in his spirit' [AB2; KJV], 'he sighed deeply to himself' [AB1], 'with a deep sigh within himself' [BNTC], 'he/Jesus sighed deeply' [LN (24.44); NCV, NIV, REB], 'with a deep sigh' [GW], 'Jesus gave a deep groan' [TEV], 'Jesus groaned' [CEV]. This noun denotes the non-material, psychological faculty that is potentially sensitive and responsive to God [LN]. The spirit is the source and seat of insight, feeling, and will. It represents the inner life of man [BAGD].

c. γενεά (LN 11.4): 'those of the same time, those of the same generation' [LN]. The phrase 'this generation' [AB1, AB2, BECNT, BNTC, Lns, WBC; ESV, KJV, NASB, NET, NIV, NRSV, REB] is also translated 'the people of this day' [TEV], 'these people' [GW, NLT], 'you people' [NCV], 'you' [CEV]. This noun denotes the people living at the same time and belonging to the same reproductive age-class [LN]. This word occurs at 8:12, 38; 9:19; 13:30.

d. pres. act. indic. of ζητέω (LN **33.167**, **57.59**) (BAGD 2.c. p. 339): 'to seek' [AB2, BECNT, LN (57.59), Lns, WBC; ESV, KJV, NASB], 'to try to get' [**LN** (57.59)], 'to try to obtain' [LN (57.59)], 'to look for' [CEV, NET], 'to demand' [BNTC, **LN** (33.167); GW, NLT], 'to ask earnestly for' [LN (33.167)], 'to ask for' [AB1; NCV, NIV, NRSV, REB, TEV]. This verb means to try to obtain something from someone [LN (57.59)], or to ask for something that is being especially sought [LN (33.167)].

e. εἰ (LN 89.65) (BAGD IV. p. 219): 'if' [LN], 'certainly not' [BAGD]. The unfinished conditional clause 'if a sign will/shall be given to this generation—' [Lns] is translated as an elliptical oath formula with the apodosis supplied: 'May God's judgment fall upon me, if a sign will be given to this generation' [BECNT], 'May I be accursed, should a sign be given to this generation' [WBC]. The conditional clause is completed: 'If these people are given a sign, it will be far different than what they want!' [GW]. The conditional clause is restructured as a statement: 'a sign shall not be given to this generation' [BNTC], 'no sign will/shall be given to this generation' [AB1, NTC; ESV, NASB, NET, NRSV, REB; similarly KJV, NIV], 'no sign will be given to you' [NCV], 'I can promise you that you will not be given one' [CEV], 'I will not give this generation any such sign' [NLT], 'No such proof will be given to these people!' [TEV], 'God forbid that a sign should be given to this generation' [AB2]. This conjunction indicates a condition, whether real or hypothetical, actual or contrary to fact [LN]. The conditional particle εἰ 'if' was used in Hebrew oaths to mean '*May this or that happen to me, if...*' [BAGD]. The conditional clause 'if a sign will be given to this generation' lacks an implied main clause something like 'may God do so and so to me' [NIGTC], 'may God's judgment fall upon me' [NLTfn]. 'may God punish me' [EGT], 'may I die' [EGT, WBC], 'may I be cursed!' [WBC]. This amounts to a strong negation, 'certainly not!' [BAGD, NIGTC, Tay]. It is equivalent to saying 'No sign shall be given!' [CGTC, EGT, Hb, ICC, NICNT, Sw]. It is a formula that indicates an emphatic denial of the request [PNTC, WBC].

QUESTION—What is meant by 'sighing deeply in his spirit'?

In this context, 'spirit' is used in a sense much like 'heart' or 'inner being' [NTC]. It is the center of a person's emotions [TRT]. This groan came from the depths of his inner being and shows his distress over the moral perversity of those Jewish leaders [Hb]. He was distressed over the unresponsiveness of this generation [NIGTC]. It revealed either his grief or his anger at their hardness of heart [BNTC]. It revealed both his grief and indignation [NICNT].

QUESTION—What type of question was Jesus asking?

He asked a rhetorical question that expressed his exasperation [NICNT]. The question was addressed meditatively to himself. It implied that their persistent seeking for signs was unjustified since they had deliberately rejected the evidence already available to them [Hb].

QUESTION—What did Jesus mean by 'this generation'?

This refers to his contemporaries [Hb, TH]. It refers to Jesus' contemporaries as represented by the men who are asking for a sign from heaven [Gnd, Hb, Lns]. It refers to the people among whom he lived [NTC]. The Pharisees represented 'this generation' [BECNT]. Since he mentions 'this generation' twice, it appears that the unbelief of those who demanded a sign was not just confined to the Pharisees [NIGTC].

QUESTION—Didn't Jesus ever give a sign?

'No sign' refers to a sign of the kind they asked for [Hb]. Matthew 12:39 and Luke 11:29 have the addition 'except for the sign of Jonah' [AB1]. The verb 'will be given' is a divine passive that means that no sign will be given *by God* [AB2, BECNT]. God will not give authenticating signs on demand [AB2]. The message of Jesus was self-authenticating [AB1].

8:13 And having-left[a] them,

LEXICON—a. aorist act. participle of ἀφίημι (LN 15.48) (BAGD 3.a. p. 125): 'to leave' [AB1, AB2, BAGD, BECNT, BNTC, LN, Lns, WBC; all versions except GW], 'to take leave of' [Lns], 'to depart from' [LN]. This participial clause is translated as a statement that ends the discourse unit comprising 8:11–13a: 'Then he left them there.' [GW]. This verb means to move away from something [LN].

QUESTION—Who were the people whom Jesus left?

Jesus left the Pharisees [TH; NCV] while his disciples accompanied him in the boat [TH].

QUESTION—What is indicated by the use the participle ἀφεὶς 'having left'?
Although the verb 'having left' is often used to move a story along, here it indicates Jesus' deliberate disengagement from his discussion with the Pharisees in order to concentrate on instructing his disciples [NIGTC]. It finalizes Jesus refusal to provide a sign from heaven [Gnd]. The abrupt departure from the Pharisees expressed Jesus' indignation. Nothing good could come from further discussion with them [NICNT]. Yet, 'having left' is not a technical term for rejection. It is never used to indicate a permanent ending of a mission or rejecting a people, so it does not mean that Jesus was now ending his Galilean mission or rejecting the Jewish people in Galilee [BECNT].

DISCOURSE UNIT—8:13b–21 [GW]. The topic is the yeast of the Pharisees.

again having-gotten-into[a] (the-boat) he-departed[b] to the other-side.[c]

TEXT—Manuscripts reading πάλιν ἐμβὰς 'again having gotten into' are followed by GNT, which does not mention any variant reading. A variant reading is ἐμβὰς πάλιν εἰς τὸ πλοῖον 'having gotten again into the boat' and it is followed by KJV.

LEXICON—a. aorist act. participle of ἐμβαίνω (LN 15.95) (BAGD p. 254): 'to get into' [BAGD, LN], 'to get into a/the boat' [LN; CEV, ESV, GW, NRSV], 'to enter the boat/ship' [AB2; KJV], 'to embark' [BAGD, BNTC, LN, Lns, NTC, WBC; NASB]. The phrase 'again having gotten into the boat' is translated 'got back into the boat' [AB1; NET, NIV, NLT, TEV], 'having again boarded' [BECNT], 're-embarked' [REB]. The whole clause is translated 'and went in the boat to the other side of the lake' [NCV]. This verb means 'to go into', and in this verse he got into a boat [LN].

b. aorist act. indic. of ἀπέρχομαι (15.37) (BAGD 2. p. 84): 'to depart' [BAGD, BECNT, LN; KJV], 'to go away' [BAGD, LN, Lns, NTC; NASB], 'to go' [ESV, NCV, NET], 'to leave' [LN]. The phrase 'departed to' is translated 'started across to' [TEV], 'went to' [WBC], 'went away to' [AB2], 'went across to' [AB1, BNTC; NRSV], 'and crossed to' [GW, NIV, NLT], 'and crossed over to' [CEV], 'and made for' [REB]. This verb means to move away from a reference point with the emphasis upon the departure [LN].

c. πέραν (LN 83.43) (BAGD 1. p. 643): 'the other side' [AB2, BECNT, LN, NTC, WBC; ESV, KJV, NASB, NET, NIV, NRSV], 'the other shore' [BNTC; REB], 'the other side of the lake' [AB1; CEV, NCV, NLT, TEV], 'the other side of the Sea of Galilee' [GW]. This adjective indicates a position opposite another position, with something intervening [LN]. Used as a substantive with the article, it means 'the shore or land on the other side' [BAGD].

QUESTION—What does the adverb πάλιν 'again' modify?
This adverb goes with the following verb 'getting into a boat', not with the preceding verb 'leaving' [BECNT, CGTC, Gnd, ICC, Tay, TH, WBC; all

translations]. Jesus got into a boat in verse 10 and now he does so again [BECNT, Gnd].

QUESTION—Where was the other side?

The other side was the shore on the east side of the Lake of Galilee [BECNT, EBC, ICC, Lns, My, NICNT, TH]. It was the northeastern shore where the town of Bethsaida was located [Gnd, Hb, WBC].

DISCOURSE UNIT—8:14–9:56 [Hb]. The topic is the fourth withdrawal and return.

DISCOURSE UNIT—8:14–21 [CBC, EBC, Hb, NICNT; CEV, ESV, NCV, NET, NIV, NLT, NRSV, TEV]. The topic is the yeast of the Pharisees and Herod [EBC; CEV, NET, NIV, NLT, NRSV, TEV], the leaven of the Pharisees and Herod [ESV], the dialogue about yeast among the Pharisees and Herod [CBC], the failure to understand [NICNT], the warning concerning leaven [Hb], guard against wrong teachings [NCV].

8:14 And they-forgot to-take loaves-of-bread and except[a] (for) one loaf-of-bread they-did- not –have (any) with them in the boat.

LEXICON—a. εἰ μή (LN 89.131): This phrase is translated 'except' [AB1, AB2, BECNT, LN, Lns, WBC; NET, NIV], 'but only' [LN]. The phrase 'except for one loaf of bread they did not have any with them in the boat' is translated 'they did not have more than one loaf in the boat with them' [NASB], 'they had only one loaf with them in the boat' [BNTC; CEV, ESV, GW, NCV, NRSV, TEV; similarly NTC; NLT, REB], 'neither had they in the ship with them more than one loaf' [KJV]. This phrase indicates contrast by designating an exception [LN]. They hadn't obtained bread especially for the trip in the boat, but there happened to be one loaf already in the boat [TH].

QUESTION—What is the function of verse 14?

The mention of bread sets the stage for talking about the subject of yeast [Gnd, WBC]. Jesus wanted to warn them about the Pharisees while his encounter with the Pharisees was still fresh in their minds [Hb, NICNT]. The disciples' need for more bread also provided an opportunity for Jesus to remind them that they had seen his power at work when he fed the five thousand and the four thousand [Gnd].

8:15 And he-was-giving-orders[a] to-them saying "Take-care,[b] beware[c] of the yeast[d] of-the Pharisees and the yeast of-Herod."

TEXT—Manuscripts reading Ἡρῴδου 'of Herod' are given an A rating by GNT to indicate it was regarded to be certain. A variant reading is τῶν Ἡρῳδιανῶν 'of the Herodians'.

LEXICON—a. imperf. mid. indic. of διαστέλλομαι, διαστέλλω (LN 33.323) (BAGD p. 188): 'to give orders' [BAGD; NASB], 'to order' [BAGD, LN; NET], 'to command' [AB2, LN], 'to charge' [Lns; KJV], 'to admonish' [BECNT, WBC], 'to warn' [AB1, BNTC, NTC; CEV, GW, NCV, NIV, NLT, REB, TEV], 'to caution' [ESV, NRSV]. This verb means to state

with force and/or authority what others must do [LN]. This word occurs at 5:43; 7:36; 8:15; 9:9.
- b. pres. act. impera. of ὁράω (LN 30.45) (BAGD 2.b. p. 578): 'to take care' [BAGD, WBC; TEV], 'to watch out' [CEV, ESV, NASB, NET, NRSV], 'to look out' [BNTC, NTC], 'to be careful' [GW, NCV], 'to take heed' [KJV], 'to look' [AB2, BECNT], 'to look to it' [Lns], 'to take notice, to consider, to pay attention, to concern oneself with' [LN], 'to beware' [AB1; REB], not explicit [NIV, NLT]. This verb means to take special notice of something [LN]. It calls for mental alertness [Hb]. The idea is, 'keep your 'eye' (mind) on it so that you can avoid it' [Sw].
- c. pres. act. impera. of βλέπω (LN 27.58) (BAGD 6. p. 143): 'to beware of' [AB2, BAGD, BECNT, BNTC, LN, Lns, WBC; ESV, KJV, NASB, NCV, NET, NLT, NRSV], 'to watch out for' [LN; GW, NIV], 'to be on guard against' [AB1, Lns, NTC; TEV], 'to guard against' [CEV; similarly REB]. This verb is a figurative extension of meaning of βλέπω 'to see' and means to be ready to learn about future dangers and be prepared to respond appropriately [LN].
- d. ζύμη (LN 5.11, **88.237**) (BAGD 2. p. 340): 'yeast' [BAGD, LN (5.11), NTC; CEV, GW, NCV, NET, NIV, NLT, NRSV, TEV], 'leaven' [AB1, AB2, BECNT, BNTC, Lns, WBC; ESV, KJV, NASB, REB], 'hypocrisy' [**LN** (88.237)], 'pretense' [LN (88.237)]. This noun denotes the leaven employed in making bread rise [LN (5.11)], and the figurative extension of 'yeast' is 'hypocritical behavior', probably implying the presence of hidden attitudes and motivations [LN (88.237)]. The reference to 'leaven' in this verse refers not to yeast alone, but to unbaked dough containing the yeast culture that would be added to new dough so that it would rise [AB2, BECNT]. The word 'yeast' is used metaphorically of the attitudes of the Pharisees and of Herod [BAGD].

QUESTION—What is meant by the yeast of the Pharisees and the yeast of Herod?

Yeast symbolizes evil in 1 Corinthians 5:8, but yeast symbolizes the growth of the kingdom in Matt. 13:33. Its main metaphorical use concerns yeast's powerful growth and influence [NIGTC]. Yeast is used in the parallel passage of Matt. 16:12 to refer to the teachings of the Pharisees and Sadducees, but in the parallel passage of Luke 12:1 it is used to refer to the hypocrisy of the Pharisees. Since the warning about the yeast of the Pharisees and the yeast of Herod is not developed in Mark, the metaphoric meaning of 'yeast' is uncertain [AB2, BECNT, Gnd, NIGTC, PNTC]. The disciples misunderstood the reference to yeast, so it is best to translate yeast literally here [TRT].

1. The repetition of the article in the words '*the* yeast of the Pharisees and *the* yeast of Herod' implies that the two yeasts are distinct [CGTC, EGT, Hb, ICC, NLTfn, Sw, TRT]. *The leaven of the Pharisees* was the bad influence their false teachings had on others [Hb, NLTfn, Sw, TRT]. It refers to their blindness to spiritual things [ICC, TH], their unbelief

[NLTfn], their hardness of heart [NLTfn]. *The leaven of Herod* was the corrupting influence of Herod's evil ways [Hb, TRT], his irreligious and self-seeking conduct [Hb], his worldliness [ICC, TH], his unwillingness to accept what he knew was true [NLTfn], his unbelief springing from his love of the world with its immoralities [Sw], his inclination to impress God and man by an arrogant exercise of secular authority [NCBC].

2. Yeast is used in the same way for both the Pharisees and Herod [BECNT, BNTC, EBC, Lns, NICNT, NIVfn, PNTC, WBC]. Yeast is used in the evil sense of the corrupting power of the teaching of the Pharisees and Herod. [Lns], their evil disposition to believe only if signs are produced that will compel faith [EBC, NICNT, NIVfn, Tay], their hardness of heart that led to their hostile attitude [BNTC], their unbelief connected with miracles [NAC]. This is a warning against the misunderstanding or even disbelief that the disciples were displaying [PNTC].

8:16 **And they-were-discussing**ᵃ **among themselves that/because**ᵇ **they-do-not -have loaves-of-bread.**

TEXT—Manuscripts reading οὐκ ἔχουσιν 'they do not have' are followed by GNT, which does not mention any variant reading. A variant reading is οὐκ ἔχομεν 'we do not have' and it is followed by KJV.

LEXICON—a. imperf. mid./pass. (deponent = act.) indic. of διαλογίζομαι (LN **33.158**) (BAGD 2. p. 186): 'to discuss' [BAGD, BECNT, BNTC, **LN**, NTC, WBC; ESV, GW, NASB, NCV, NET, NIV, TEV], 'to talk (this) over' [CEV], 'to consider' [Lns], 'to reason' [AB2, NTC; KJV], 'to converse' [LN], 'to say' [AB1; NRSV, REB], 'to argue' [NLT]. This verb means to engage in some relatively detailed discussion of a matter [LN].

b. ὅτι (LN 89.3, 90.20): 'because, since, for, in view of the fact that' [LN (89.33)], 'that, the fact that' [LN (90.20)]. The phrase 'that/because they do not have loaves of bread' is translated 'that they didn't have any bread' [GW], 'the fact that they had no bread' [WBC; ESV, NASB], 'the fact that they had no loaves' [WBC], 'why they had no bread' [BNTC], 'about having no bread' [NET, REB], 'that he said it because they had no loaves' [AB2], 'because they hadn't brought any bread' [NLT]. Some translate ὅτι as a marker of direct discourse: 'saying, "Bread-cakes we have not"' [Lns], 'saying/said, "It is because we have no bread."' [KJV, NIV, NRSV; similarly NTC, TEV], "We have no bread." [AB1], 'saying, "He said this because we have no bread."' [NCV], "He must be saying this because we don't have bread." [CEV], "Did he say this because they had no bread?" [BECNT]. This conjunction indicates cause or reason [LN (89.33)], or indicates the discourse content, whether direct or indirect [LN (90.20)].

QUESTION—What were the disciples discussing?

1. They were discussing the meaning of Christ's warning given in verse 15 [Hb]. They were preoccupied with the fact that they had not brought any bread for the journey across the lake (8:14), so the reference to yeast in

this verse led them to think that Jesus was warning them against buying bread from enemies like the Pharisees and the supporters of Herod [Gnd, Hb, ICC, NTC].
2. They were simply ignoring the warning given in verse 15 because of their concern about there being no bread in the boat [CBC, WBC]. They were discussing whose fault it was that there wasn't any bread in the boat [NCBC, NICNT, Sw, Tay] and what could be done to obtain some [Sw, Tay].

8:17 **And having-known[a] he-says to-them, "Why are-you-discussing that you-do- not -have loaves-of-bread? Do-you- not-yet –perceive[b] nor understand[c]? Do you-have your heart hardened[d]?**

TEXT—Manuscripts reading πεπωρωμένην 'hardened' are followed by GNT, which does not mention any variant reading. A variant reading is ἔτι πεπωρωμένην 'yet hardened' and it is followed by KJV.

LEXICON—a. aorist act. participle of γινώσκω (LN 27.2) (BAGD 4.b. p. 161): 'to learn, to find out' [LN], 'to notice, to perceive, to realize' [BAGD]. The phrase 'having known' is translated 'aware of this' [ESV, NASB], 'aware of their discussion' [NIV], 'knowing it' [BNTC], 'knowing this' [BECNT, WBC; REB], 'knowing what they were talking about' [NCV], 'becoming aware of it/this' [AB1; NRSV], 'when Jesus knew it' [Lns; KJV; similarly AB2], 'when he learned of this' [NET], 'when he noticed this' [NTC], 'Jesus knew what they were thinking' [CEV], 'Jesus knew what they were saying' [GW, NLT, TEV]. This verb means to acquire information by some means [LN].

b. pres. act. indic. of νοέω (LN 32.2) (BAGD 1.e. p. 540): 'to perceive' [AB2, BAGD, LN; ESV, KJV, NRSV], 'to understand' [BAGD, BECNT, BNTC, LN; GW], 'to comprehend' [LN, Lns], 'to know' [AB1, WBC; NLT, TEV], 'to gain insight into' [LN], 'to apprehend' [BAGD], 'to have an inkling' [REB], 'to see' [NASB, NCV, NET, NIV]. The clause 'Do you not yet comprehend?' is translated 'Do you still lack understanding?' [NTC]. The clause 'Do you not yet perceive nor understand?' is translated 'Don't you understand?' [CEV]. This verb means to comprehend something on the basis of careful thought and consideration [LN]. This word occurs at 7:18; 8:17; 13:14.

c. pres. act. indic. of συνίημι (LN 32.5) (BAGD p. 790): 'to understand' [AB1, AB2, BAGD, BECNT, LN, Lns, WBC; all versions except GW], 'to comprehend' [BNTC, LN], 'to perceive, to have insight into' [LN], 'to grasp' [NTC], 'to gain an insight into' [BAGD], 'to catch on' [GW]. This verb means to employ one's capacity for understanding [LN]. This word occurs at 4:12; 6:52; 7:14; 8:17, 21.

d. perf. pass. participle of πωρόω (LN 27.52) (BAGD p. 732): 'to be completely unwilling to learn, to close one's mind' [LN], 'to be made dull, obtuse, or blind' [BAGD]. The question 'Do you (plural) have your heart (singular) hardened?' is translated 'Have you your hearts hardened?'

[Lns], 'Do you have hardened hearts?' [BECNT, WBC], 'Are your hearts hardened?' [BNTC, NTC; ESV, NIV, NRSV], 'Have your hearts been hardened?' [NET], 'Has your heart been hardened?' [AB2], 'have ye your heart (yet) hardened?' [KJV], 'Do you have a hardened heart?' [NASB], 'Are your hearts too hard to take it in?' [NLT], 'Are your minds closed?' [GW, NCV, REB], 'Are your minds still closed?' [CEV], 'Are your minds so dull?' [TEV]. This verb is a figurative extension of meaning of πωρόω 'to harden' and means to cause someone to be completely unwilling to learn and accept new information [LN]. It refers to the spiritual sluggishness of the disciples [NTC]. See this word in relation to hearts at 3:5, 6:52, 8:17.

QUESTION—What did Jesus know?

Jesus had noticed the discussion going on in the boat among the disciples [AB1], and he knew what they were discussing [TH].

QUESTION—What is the difference between the verbs in the question "Do you not yet *perceive* nor *understand?*"

This is saying the same thing in two similar ways in order to emphasize their lack of understanding [TRT]. It could be taken to refer to two successive steps in understanding. The first involves perception while the second involves judgment [TH]. This concerns their understanding about the significance of the feeding of the crowds, not the saying about leaven [AB1, BECNT, CBC, Tay]. They should have understood that their supply of bread was not relevant when Jesus was with them [NLTfn]. Jesus was not implying that the disciples could always expect a miraculous meal when they forget to bring along food. If they had remembered and understood Jesus' miracles, they would not have been so preoccupied with their own anxieties that they failed to recognize his authority and give him their full attention [CGTC].

QUESTION—What does the adverb οὔπω 'not yet' imply?

'Not yet' implies that after seeing the miracles of supplying the five thousand people and the four thousand people with bread, there was no reason for the disciples to be disturbed by a lack of bread in the boat [Gnd].

8:18 **Having eyes do-you- not -see[a] and having ears do-you- not -hear[b]?**

LEXICON—a. pres. act. indic. of βλέπω (LN 24.7): 'to see, to become aware of, to notice' [LN]. The question 'Having eyes do you not see?' [AB2, BECNT, Lns, NTC, WBC; ESV, NASB; similarly KJV] is also translated 'Do you have eyes but fail to see?' [NIV; similarly NRSV], 'Are your eyes blind?' [CEV], 'Are you blind?' [GW], 'You have eyes—can't you see?' [AB1, BNTC; NLT, TEV; similarly REB], 'Though you have eyes, don't you see?' [NET], 'You have eyes, but you don't really see' [NCV]. The verb 'to see' frequently has the sense of becoming aware of or taking notice of something [LN].

b. pres. act. indic. of ἀκούω (LN 24.52): 'to hear' [LN]. The question 'and having ears do you not hear?' [AB2, BECNT, Lns, NTC, WBC; ESV, NASB; similarly KJV] is also translated 'Do you have ears, and fail to hear?' [NRSV; similarly NIV], 'And though you have ears, can't you hear?' [NET], 'are your ears deaf?' [CEV], 'and are you deaf?' [GW], 'you have ears—can't you hear?' [AB1, BNTC; NLT, TEV; similarly REB], 'you have ears, but you don't really listen' [NCV]. This verb means to hear something [LN].

QUESTION—What is the function of these questions?

The rhetorical questions in verse 17 rebuke the disciples for their lack of understanding [EBC, Lns, My], and they are asked if they have become like those 'outsiders' in 4:11–12 who had eyes, but did not see, and had ears, but did not hear [BNTC, EBC, Hb, Sw, WBC]. The Twelve appear to be no better off than the 'outsiders' to whom this text had already been applied [NICNT, NIGTC]. The addition of the adverb οὔπω 'not yet' in verses 17 and 21 implies that, unlike the outsiders, the incomprehension of the disciples is only temporary [NIGTC].

And do-you- not -remember,[a]

LEXICON—a. pres. act. indic. of μνημονεύω (LN 29.7) (BAGD 1.e. p. 525): 'to remember' [BAGD, LN], 'to recall, to think about again' [LN], 'to keep in mind, to think of' [BAGD]. This clause is translated as a separate question: 'And do you not remember?' [BECNT, Lns, NTC, WBC; ESV, KJV, NRSV; similarly AB2; GW, NET, NIV], 'Don't you remember anything at all?' [NLT], 'Have you forgotten?' [AB1; REB]. Some continue this clause into the next verse: 'Do you not remember how many basketfuls of pieces you picked up when…?' [BNTC; similarly CEV, NASB], 'Don't you remember when I broke the five loaves for the five thousand people?' [TEV], 'Remember when I divided five loaves of bread for the five thousand?' [NCV]. This verb means to recall information from memory [LN].

QUESTION—How does this question relate to the following verse?

1. This begins a question that continues into the following verse [BNTC, Gnd, ICC, TRT; CEV, NASB, NCV, TEV]: *And do you not remember when I broke the five loaves of bread for the five thousand how many baskets full of pieces you picked up?* Treating the clause 'And do you not remember' as a separate question may result in a simpler syntactic arrangement, but then the question would be less meaningful. The GNT Greek text joins these words directly to verse 19 [TH].

2. This clause is translated as a separate question [NIGTC, NTC, PNTC, WBC; ESV, GW, KJV, NET, NIV, NLT, NRSV, REB]: *And do you not remember?* It functions as a further staccato question [NIGTC]. The question ties the present incident to the two other times when the disciples lacked bread and faced a great need [BECNT]. The answer as to what they did not know and understand is made clear by the following two questions concerning the times when the multitudes were miraculously fed [WBC].

QUESTION—What is the function of the adverb οὐ 'not' in this question?
The adverb οὐ 'not' with the indicative verb in a question expects an affirmative answer [Gnd, WBC], and means 'You remember, don't you, when I broke the five loaves for the five thousands how many baskets full of fragments you picked up?' The correct answers of the disciples show that they really did remember [Gnd].

8:19 when I-broke[a] the five loaves-of-bread for the five-thousand, how-many baskets[b] full of-pieces did-you-pick-up[c]?" They-say to-him, "Twelve." **8:20** "When[d] the seven for the four-thousand, how-many baskets[e] full of-pieces did-you-pick-up?" And they-say to-him, "Seven."

LEXICON—a. aorist act. indic. of κλάω (LN 19.34) (BAGD p. 433): 'to break' [BAGD, LN; all translations except CEV, NCV, NLT], 'to divide' [NCV], not explicit [CEV, NLT]. This verb means to break an object into two or more parts [LN].

b. κόφινος (LN 6.150) (BAGD p. 447): 'basket' [BAGD], 'large basket' [LN]. The phrase κοφίνους κλασμάτων πλήρεις 'baskets full of pieces' [NTC; NET] is also translated 'baskets full of broken pieces' [Lns, WBC; ESV, NASB, NRSV], 'basketfuls of pieces' [BNTC; NIV, REB], 'baskets full of fragments' [KJV], 'baskets...with leftover pieces' [GW, NCV], 'baskets full of fragments' [AB2], 'baskets full of leftover pieces' [TEV], 'baskets of leftover scraps' [AB1], 'full baskets of fragments' [BECNT], 'baskets of leftovers' [CEV, NLT]. This noun denotes a relatively large basket used primarily for food or produce [LN]. It denotes a large, heavy basket for carrying things [BAGD]. This word occurs at 6:43; 8:19.

c. aorist act. indic. of αἴρω (LN 15.203) (BAGD 3. p. 24): 'to pick up' [AB1, BNTC, NTC, WBC; CEV, NASB, NET, NIV, NLT, REB], 'to take up' [AB2, BECNT, Lns; ESV, KJV, TEV], 'to carry away' [BAGD LN], 'to carry off, to take away' [LN], 'to collect' [NRSV], 'to remove' [BAGD, LN], 'to fill' [GW, NCV]. This verb means to lift up and carry away [BAGD, LN].

d. ὅτε (LN 67.30): 'when' [LN]. The clause 'when the seven' [Lns; KJV] is also translated 'and the seven' [ESV, NRSV], 'when I broke the seven' [NASB; similarly BNTC], 'when I broke the seven loaves' [AB1, AB2, BECNT, WBC; GW, NET, NIV, REB, TEV; similarly NTC], 'when I broke seven small loaves of bread' [CEV], 'when I divided seven loaves of bread' [NCV], 'when I fed...with seven loaves' [NLT]. This conjunction indicates a point of time that is roughly simultaneous to or overlaps with another point of time [LN].

e. σπυρίς (LN 6.149) (BAGD p. 764): 'basket' [AB1, BAGD, BECNT, Lns; CEV, ESV, KJV, NCV, NET, NIV, NRSV, TEV], 'large/big basket' [AB2, BNTC, LN, WBC; GW, NASB, NLT], 'hamper' [BAGD, NTC], not explicit [REB]. The noun denotes a basket that is presumably somewhat larger than a κόφινος 'basket' (6.150) [LN]. This word occurs at 8:8, 20.

QUESTION—When the question 'And do you not remember' in verse 18 is taken to continue into verse 19, what is the direct object of the verb 'remember'?
1. The second clause of verse 19 is the direct object [BNTC, Gnd, ICC; CEV, NASB], and moving the direct object directly after the verb may be necessary to make the connection clear [TH]: 'And do you not *remember how many baskets full of pieces you picked up* when I broke the five loaves of bread for the five thousand?'
2. The first clause of verse 19 is the direct object [TRT; NCV, TEV]: 'And do you not *remember when I broke the five loaves of bread for the five thousand?* How many baskets full of pieces did you pick up?'

QUESTION—In verse 20, what is meant by the words 'When the seven for the four thousand'?
This ellipsis is a concise way of repeating the full wording of verse 19 in regard to this second occasion: 'When *I broke* the seven *loaves of bread* for the four thousand' [Gnd, TH]. Most translations fill out the ellipsis [AB1, AB2, BECNT, BNTC, NTC, WBC; CEV, GW, NASB, NCV, NET, NIV, NLT, REB, TEV].

8:21 And he-was-saying to-them, "Do-you- not-yet -understand^a?"
LEXICON—a. pres. act. indic. of συνίημι (LN 32.5) (BAGD p. 790): 'to understand, to comprehend' [BAGD, LN], 'to perceive, to have insight into' [LN]. This question is translated 'Do you not yet understand?' [AB2, BECNT, Lns, WBC; ESV, NASB, NRSV], 'Don't you understand yet?' [NCV, NLT], 'Do you still not understand?' [AB1; NET, NIV, REB], 'How is it that ye do not understand?' [KJV], 'And you still don't understand?' [TEV], 'Do you still not comprehend?' [BNTC], 'Do you still fail to grasp?' [NTC], 'Don't you catch on?' [GW], 'Don't you know what I am talking about by now?' [CEV]. This verb means to employ one's capacity for understanding [LN]. This word occurs at 4:12; 6:52; 7:14; 8:17, 21.

QUESTION—Why did Jesus repeat the question he asked in verse 17?
1. This question still has the same rebuke that the question had in verse 17 [AB1, AB2, BECNT, BNTC, CBC, EBC, Gnd, NICNT, NIGTC]. When Jesus asked, 'Do you not yet comprehend nor understand?' in verse 17, they hadn't understood. In verses 19–20 Jesus pointed out they should have remembered how abundantly he had provided for them on two different occasions. Now that he was with them in the boat, what else could they want or need? Almost pleadingly he repeated his question in this verse [EBC]. This question indicates that the disciples still did not understand that Jesus' works pointed to the fact that he was the Messiah and Lord [NICNT]. Even after being reminded of what they had seen and heard, they could not understand because their hearts were hardened [BNTC]. The question still has the critical tone it had in verse 17 [Gnd].

2. This is a different question [Hb, Lns]. Jesus had given the disciples time to think about what he has said and now when he asks the question a second time, it is no longer a rebuke. The words 'not yet understand' in this question have a different referent than it does in verse 17 where it referred to all of their previous experiences. Here it refers to the rebuke they have just heard [Lns]. After what he has just said, Jesus asks if they did not yet have a better understanding. Matthew adds that they now realized that Jesus was not talking about bread, but about the teaching of the Pharisees and Sadducees. Jesus' concern was not about material bread but the permeating effects of false teaching [Hb, Lns].

DISCOURSE UNIT—8:22–10:52 [AB2, NIGTC]. The topic is act two: on the way to Jerusalem (learning about the cross) [NIGTC], fourth major section [AB2].

DISCOURSE UNIT—8:22–26 [CBC, EBC, Hb, NICNT, NIGTC; CEV, ESV, GW, NCV, NET, NIV, NLT, NRSV, TEV]. The topic is the blind man at Bethsaida [Hb], the opening of blind eyes [NICNT], the first healing of a blind man [NIGTC], Jesus gives sight to a blind man [GW], Jesus heals a blind man [NCV, NLT], Jesus heals a blind man at Bethsaida [EBC; CEV, ESV, TEV], Jesus cures a blind man at Bethsaida [NRSV], the healing of a blind man at Bethsaida [CBC; NIV], a two-stage healing [NET], Jesus heals a blind man in two stages [AB2].

8:22 **And they-come to Bethsaida. And they-bring**[a] **a-blind (man) to-him and they-beg**[b] **him that he-might-touch**[c] **him.**
LEXICON—a. pres. act. indic. of φέρω (LN 15.166) (BAGD 4.b.β. p. 855): 'to bring' [BAGD, LN; all translations], 'to lead' [BAGD], 'to take' [LN]. This verb means to cause someone to move somewhere [LN].
  b. pres. act. indic. of παρακαλέω (LN 33.168) (BAGD 3. p. 617): 'to beg' [AB1, BNTC, NTC; all versions except KJV, NASB, NET], 'to implore' [BAGD; NASB], 'to beseech' [Lns; KJV], 'to plead' [AB2, BECNT, LN], 'to request' [BAGD, LN], 'to ask' [LN; NET], 'to appeal to' [BAGD, LN, WBC], 'to entreat' [BAGD]. This verb means to earnestly ask for something [LN].
  c. aorist mid. subj. of ἅπτομαι, ἅπτω (LN 24.73) (BAGD 2.b. p. 103): 'to touch' [BAGD, LN; all translations except NLT], 'to touch and heal' [NLT]. This verb means to touch with a relatively firm contact [LN].
QUESTION—Who came to Bethsaida?
  The pronoun 'they' refers to Jesus and his disciples [BECNT, Gnd, ICC, NICNT, PNTC, TH, TRT; CEV, NCV].
QUESTION—Who brought a blind man?
  The third person plural verb φέρουσιν 'they bring' functions as an impersonal plural [AB1, AB2, BECNT, TH]: 'some *people* brought him to Jesus' [AB1, AB2, EBC, Gnd, NCBC, Tay, TH; CEV, ESV, GW, NCV,

NIV, NLT, NRSV, REB, TEV], or 'some *men* brought him to Jesus' [TH]. They were relatives or friends of the blind man [Hb].

QUESTION—How did they bring him?

They led the blind man to Jesus [TH].

QUESTION—What did they want Jesus to do?

They wanted Jesus to touch the blind man with his finger or hand [TH] in order to heal him [Gnd, NICNT, NIGTC; NLT]. They assumed that personal contact was necessary for the man to be cured [Hb].

8:23 And taking[a] the hand of the blind (man) he-led[b] him out of-the village[c] and having-spit[d] on his eyes, (and) having-put[e] (his) hands on-him he-asked him, "Do-you-see[f] anything?"

LEXICON—a. aorist middle (deponent = pres.) participle of ἐπιλαμβάνομαι (LN 18.2) (BAGD 1. p. 295): 'to take' [**LN**; all translations except AB1, Lns], 'to take hold of, to grasp' [LN], 'to lay hold of' [Lns]. The first clause is translated 'He led the blind man away by the hand out of the village' [AB1]. This verb means to take hold of or grasp someone [LN].

    b. aorist act. indic. of ἐκφέρω (LN **15.174**) (BAGD 2. p. 246): 'to lead out' [AB1, AB2, BAGD, BNTC, **LN**; all versions except NASB, NET, NIV], 'to bring forth' [LN]. The phrase 'he led him out' is translated, 'he led him outside' [NTC; NIV], 'he brought him out/outside' [BECNT, Lns, WBC; NASB, NET]. This verb means to lead or bring someone out of something [LN].

    c. κώμη (LN **1.92**) (BAGD 1. p. 461): 'village' [BAGD, LN; all translations except KJV], 'town' [KJV], 'small town' [BAGD]. This noun denotes a relatively unimportant population center [LN]. This word occurs at 6:6, 36, 56; 8:23, 26. 27; 11:2.

    d. aorist act. participle of πτύω (LN 23.43) (BAGD p. 727): 'to spit' [BAGD, LN]. The phrase 'having spit on his eyes' [Lns] is also translated 'and he spat on his eyes' [AB2, BNTC], 'when he had spit on his/the man's eyes' [ESV, KJV, NIV], 'after spitting in his eyes' [WBC], 'then/after spitting on his/the man's eyes' [AB1, NTC; NASB, NLT, TEV], 'then he spit on his/the man's eyes' [NCV, REB], 'he spit into the man's eyes' [CEV, GW; similarly BECNT], 'when he had put saliva on his eyes' [NRSV]. This verb means to spit on or at something or someone [LN].

    e. aorist act. participle of ἐπιτίθημι (LN 85.51) (BAGD 1.a.α. p. 303): 'to put on' [BAGD, LN; KJV, NIV], 'to lay on' [AB1, AB2, BAGD, BNTC, LN, Lns, NTC, WBC; ESV, NASB, NLT, NRSV, REB], 'to place on' [LN; CEV, GW, NCV, NET, TEV], 'to set upon' [BECNT]. This verb means to place something on something [LN].

    f. pres. act. indic. of βλέπω (LN 24.7) (BAGD 1.a. p. 143): 'to see' [BAGD, LN]. The question Εἴ τι βλέπεις; 'Do you see anything?' [AB2, BECNT, Lns, NTC; ESV, NASB, NET, NIV] is also translated 'Can you see anything?' [BNTC; GW, NRSV, TEV], 'Can you see anything now?'

[NLT], 'Can you see now?' [NCV], 'What do you see?' [WBC]. Others translate this as an indirect quotation: 'asked him if he could see anything' [CEV], 'asked whether he could see anything' [REB], 'he asked him if he saw anything/ought' [AB1; KJV]. This verb means to see something [LN].

QUESTION—Why did Jesus lead the blind man out of the village?

Jesus led him out of the village so that they would not have a crowd around them [BECNT, NAC]. He wanted to be away from the clamor of a crowd [EBC]. He wanted to be in a quiet place where he could have the man's full attention [Hb].

QUESTION—Where did Jesus spit on the blind man and why did he do that?

The Greek preposition εἰς can be translated either 'on' or 'into' the man's eyes [TH]. Many merely say that Jesus spit *on* the man's eyes [AB1, AB2, BNTC, EBC, EGT, NICNT, NTC]. Others are more specific and say Jesus spit directly *into* the man's blind eyes [BECNT, Gnd, NIGTC, WBC; CEV, GW]. The man's eyes were probably open when Jesus spat into them [TRT]. When the man felt the spittle on his eyes he would realize that Jesus was going to deal with his blind eyes [Hb]. It sent the message, 'Something will be done for your eyes, and I will do it' [NTC]. Another interpretation is that Jesus spit on the man's *closed* eyelids to assure him that his eyes would receive sight. The spittle itself had no healing powers [Lns]. The man didn't open his eyes until Jesus asked what he saw [Hb].

QUESTION—Where did Jesus put his hand on the blind man and why did he do that?

Jesus placed his hands on the man's eyes [Gnd, Lns, TH]. That he touched the man's eyes is made clear in verse 25, where it says '*again* he placed his hands *on* his eyes' [AB2, TH]. A physical contact would be especially important to a blind man [NIGTC]. The touch of Jesus' hands would give the man assurance that something was to happen to his eyes [Hb, Sw]. After Jesus briefly placed a hand on each of the man's eyes, he removed them and asked him if could see anything [TRT].

QUESTION—Why did Jesus ask the man if he saw anything?

This question indicates that Jesus knew the restoration of sight would only be partial at this stage [Hb, Sw]. The question would get the man involved in his own cure [NTC]. Jesus was not doubting his own ability to heal [BNTC].

8:24 And having-looked-up/having-regained-sight[a] he said, "I see people[b] that-is/because[c] like trees I-see (them) walking-around."

LEXICON—a. aorist act. participle of ἀναβλέπω (LN 24.19, 24.42) (BAGD 1. p. 50): 'to look up' [AB1, AB2, BAGD, BNTC, LN (24.19), Lns; all versions except NET, NLT, REB], 'to look around' [NLT], 'to regain sight' [BECNT, LN (24.42), WBC; NET], 'to gain sight, to be able to see' [LN (24.42)], 'the man's sight began to come back' [REB]. This verb means to direct one's vision upward [LN (24.19)], or to be able to see either again or for the first time [LN (24.42)]. It doesn't mean that he looked straight up into the sky, he just looked up high enough to see people [TRT]. Although the word 'he looked up' refers to the recovery of sight in 10:52, it appears to simply refer to a reflex action of raising the head in this verse [NCBC]. Even though he would have to look around to see the people, this verse probably just means that he received his sight [CBC].

b. ἄνθρωπος (LN 9.1): 'person' [LN]. The plural form ἀνθρώπους is translated 'people' [AB2, LN, WBC; all versions except ESV, KJV, NASB], 'men' [AB1, BECNT, BNTC, Lns; ESV, KJV, NASB]. This noun denotes a human being [LN].

c. ὅτι (LN 89.33; 91.15): 'because, since, for, in view of the fact that' [LN (89.33)], 'that is, namely' [LN (91.15)]. The clause 'that is/because like trees I see them walking around' is translated 'they look like trees walking about' [AB1, BNTC]. 'as trees, walking' [KJV], 'they look like trees walking around' [GW, NIV], 'they look like trees, but they are walking about' [REB], 'but they look like trees, walking' [ESV, NRSV], 'but they look like trees walking around' [CEV, NCV, TEV; similarly NET], '(I see people) walking, but they are like trees' [WBC], 'but I can't see them very clearly. They look like trees walking around' [NLT], 'because I see people like walking trees' [AB2], 'for I see them walking like trees' [BECNT], 'for I see them like trees, walking around' [NASB; similarly Lns]. This conjunction introduces identificational and explanatory clauses [LN (91.15)], or it indicates the cause or reason based on some evident fact [LN (89.33)].

QUESTION—How long had the man been blind?

It is inferred that the man had not been born blind because he could recognize the objects he saw when he could see again [AB1, CBC, EGT, Hb, Lns, NICNT, NTC, Tay]. He already knew how people looked [NTC]. However, another thinks there is no reason to assume that this man hadn't been born blind [BECNT].

QUESTION—Does the conjunction ὅτι 'that is/because' indicate an explanation or a reason?

1. The conjunction is explanatory and describes the degree of success that the cure had attained so far: 'I see men walking around, but they are so indistinct they might as well be trees' [AB1, BNTC, CGTC, Gnd, NIGTC, WBC; possibly CEV, ESV, NCV, NLT, NRSV, REB, TEV which use the conjunction 'but']. When the man looked at the people walking around in the nearby village, he found it hard to distinguish them from each other, so he compared them to clumps of trees with branches and leaves moving about in the wind [Gnd].

2. The conjunction indicates the reason the man knew the indistinct objects that looked like trees were actually men: 'I see men, I know they are men because even though they look like trees, they are walking around and only men can do that' [AB2, BECNT, EGT, Hb, ICC, Lns, My, NCBC, NTC, TH; NASB]. Since his sight was still imperfect, the conjunction

'because' indicates his reason for identifying the indistinct objects he saw to be men [Hb]. The reasoning is, 'I see men, because even though the things I perceive look like trees, they are walking around' [NTC, TH].

8:25 Then again he-placed (his) hands on (his) eyes, and he-opened-(his)-eyes[a] and he-was-restored[b] and he-was-seeing everything clearly.[c]

TEXT—Manuscripts reading διέβλεψεν 'he opened his eyes' are given an A rating by GNT to indicate it was regarded to be certain. A variant reading is ἐποίησεν αὐτὸν ἀναβλέψαι 'made him look up' and it is followed by KJV.

TEXT—Manuscripts reading the neuter plural ἅπαντα 'every (thing)' are given an A rating by GNT to indicate it was regarded to be certain. A variant reading has the masculine plural ἅπαντας 'every (man)' and it is followed by KJV.

LEXICON—a. aorist act. indic. of διαβλέπω (LN 24.35) (BAGD 1. p. 181): 'to look intently, to open ones eyes wide' [BAGD], 'to see clearly, to be able to distinguish clearly' [LN]. The verb 'he opened his eyes' [ESV, NET], is also translated 'he opened them wide' [BNTC, NTC], 'the man opened his eyes widely' [NCV], 'he looked intently' [NASB, NRSV], 'this time the man looked intently' [TEV], 'this time the man stared' [CEV], 'he looked hard' [AB1; REB], 'he/the man saw clearly' [BECNT, WBC; GW], 'his eyes were opened' [NIV, NLT], 'his sight broke through' [AB2], not explicit [Lns]. This verb means to be able to see clearly or plainly [LN, Tay]. It means to look intently or to open one's eyes (wide) [BAGD]. The verb means he opened his eyelids wide [Gnd].

b. aorist act. indic. of ἀποκαθίστημι (LN 13.65) (BAGD 1. p. 92): 'to restore' [BAGD, LN]. The verb 'he was restored' [AB2, Lns, WBC; KJV, NASB] is also translated 'he was fully restored' [NTC], 'he was healed' [BECNT], 'he was cured' [AB1, BNTC], 'his sight was restored' [ESV, NET, NIV, NRSV], 'his sight was completely restored' [NLT], 'his eyesight returned' [TEV], 'his sight was normal again' [GW], 'his eyes were healed' [CEV; similarly NCV], 'now he was cured' [REB]. This verb means to change to a previous good state [LN].

c. τηλαυγῶς (LN **24.36**) (BAGD p. 814): 'clearly' [AB1, AB2, BAGD, BNTC, **LN**, NTC; all versions], 'plainly' [BAGD, BECNT, LN], 'distinctly' [LN, WBC], 'afar' [Lns]. This adverb indicates a particularly clear or plain visual image [LN]. It means the man saw things 'clearly at a distance' [EBC, EGT, Tay], which indicates that his sight was completely restored [EBC].

QUESTION—Who are the participants in this verse?

Jesus placed his hands on the man's eyes and the man opened his eyes. Since the man was the subject in verse 24, many languages must make the references to Jesus and the man clear in this verse [TH].

QUESTION—What is meant by the man being 'restored'?

The words καὶ ἀπεκατέστη 'and he was restored' means that the man was restored to full health with the proper function of the eyes [AB1, AB2,

BECNT, BNTC, Gnd, My, NIGTC, WBC; REB]. Many translations say that *his sight* was restored [ESV, GW, NET, NIV, NLT, NRSV, TEV]. Some change the singular verb to a plural subject and say that *his eyes* were healed [CEV, NCV].

QUESTION—How did Jesus place his hands on the man's eyes?

The words 'hands' and 'eyes' are both in the plural to indicate that one hand was placed on one eye and the other hand was placed on the other eye [BECNT].

QUESTION—What is implied by the imperfect voice of the verb ἐνέβλεπεν 'he was seeing'?

The imperfect voice means 'he continued to see' [AB2, CGTC, Hb, My, NTC, WBC], or 'he began to see' [AB1].

8:26 And he-sent him to his house saying, "Do- not-even -go^a into the village."

TEXT—Manuscripts reading μηδὲ εἰς τὴν κώμην εἰσέλθῃς 'do not even go into the village' are given a B rating by GNT to indicate it was regarded to be almost certain. A variant reading is μηδὲ εἰς τὴν κώμην εἰσέλθῃς μηδὲ εἴπῃς τινὶ ἐν τῇ κώμῃ 'do not even go into the village nor speak to anyone in the village' and it is followed by KJV. Another variant is μηδενὶ εἴπῃς εἰς τὴν κώμην 'speak to no one in the village' and it is followed by AB1, CGTC, Tay. Other variant readings are καὶ ἐὰν εἰς τὴν κώμην εἰσέλθῃς μηδενὶ εἴπῃς ἐν τῇ κώμῃ 'and if you go into the village, speak to no one in the village', ὕπαγε εἰς τὸν οἶκον σου καὶ μηδενὶ εἴπῃς ἐν τῇ κώμῃ 'go into your house and speak to no one in the village', and ὕπαγε εἰς οἶκον σου καὶ ἐὰν εἰς τὴν κώμην εἰσέλθῃς μηδενὶ εἴπῃς ἐν τῇ κώμῃ 'go into your house and if you go into the village speak to no one in the village'.

LEXICON—a. aorist act. subj. of εἰσέρχομαι (LN 15.95) (BAGD 1.a.β. p. 232): 'to go into' [AB2, BAGD, LN, Lns, NTC; CEV, GW, KJV, NCV, NET, NIV, NLT, NRSV, REB], 'to enter' [BAGD, BECNT, BNTC, LN, WBC; ESV, NASB], 'to go back' [TEV]. The verb means to move into a space that is either two-dimensional or three-dimensional [LN].

QUESTION—Where was the man's house located and how could a formerly blind man know how to get there?

Mark does not supply information about whether the man lived in Bethsaida or near it [BECNT]. The command to return home and not enter Bethsaida only makes sense if the man's home was somewhere else [ICC, WBC]. The blind man probably had been brought to Bethsaida when the news came that Jesus had arrived there. Jesus led him outside of Bethsaida to cure him and then instructed him to go straight back home without stopping in Bethsaida [EBC, Hb, My, NIGTC, TH]. It is possible that this blind man had come to beg in Bethsaida and while there he learned that Jesus had just arrived [TRT]. Jesus told him to go straight home without making a detour to tell everyone in Bethsaida what had happened [BNTC]. The aorist tense of the verb in the command 'do not go' indicates that this was a temporary restriction about going back to Bethsaida. Jesus gave this command because he wanted to be alone with his disciples and didn't want the news of the cure to bring out crowds of people from Bethsaida [Hb, TH]. Whether this formerly blind man had friends to show him where he lived or he had to ask for directions is not known [BECNT].

DISCOURSE UNIT—8:27–16:8 [CBC]. The topic is on to Jerusalem, passion, and vindication.

DISCOURSE UNIT—8:27–10:52 [CBC; NLT]. The topic is preparing for Jerusalem [NLT], passion predictions and discipleship teaching [CBC].

DISCOURSE UNIT—8:27–9:50 [NLT]. The topic is the ministry outside Galilee.

DISCOURSE UNIT—8:27–9:29 [REB]. The topic is the cross foreshadowed.

DISCOURSE UNIT—8:27–9:13 [NIGTC]. The topic is learning to recognize Jesus.

DISCOURSE UNIT—8:27–9:1 [NCV]. The topic is Peter says Jesus is the Christ.

DISCOURSE UNIT—8:27–38 [NASB]. The topic is Peter's confession of Christ.

DISCOURSE UNIT—8:27–33 [AB2]. Jesus is recognized as Messiah and prophesies his death.

DISCOURSE UNIT—8:27–30 [CBC, EBC, Hb, NICNT; CEV, ESV, GW, NET, NIV, NLT, NRSV, TEV]. The topic is "Who is Jesus?" [CEV], the recognition of the Messiah [NICNT], recognizing Jesus as Messiah [EBC], Peter's confession [Hb; NET], Peter's confession at Caesarea Philippi [CBC], Peter's declaration of faith [NLT], Peter's declaration about Jesus [NRSV, TEV], Peter declares his belief about Jesus [GW], Peter's confession of Christ [NIV], Peter confesses Jesus as the Christ [ESV].

8:27 **And Jesus went-out[a] and his disciples to the villages of-Caesarea Philippi. And on the way he-was-asking[b] his disciples saying to-them, "Who do- people -say I am[c]?"**

LEXICON—a. aorist act. indic. of ἐξέρχομαι (LN 15.40): 'to go out' [AB2, LN, Lns, WBC; KJV, NASB], 'to go on' [ESV, NIV, NRSV], 'to go away' [NTC; TEV], 'to go' [BECNT; CEV, GW, NCV, NET], 'to set out' [AB1; REB], 'to leave (Galilee)' [NLT], 'to go/depart out of, to leave from within' [LN], 'to leave for' [BNTC]. This verb means to move out of an enclosed or well-defined two or three-dimensional area [LN].

    b. imperf. act. indic. of ἐπερωτάω (LN 33.180): 'to ask, to ask a question' [LN]. The clause 'he was asking his disciples saying to them' [AB2, BECNT, WBC] is also translated 'he asked his disciples, saying unto

them' [KJV], 'he questioned his disciples, saying to them' [BNTC; NASB], 'he was asking his disciples' [NTC], 'he/Jesus asked his disciples/them' [AB1; all versions except KJV, NASB]. This verb means to ask for information [LN]. The words 'he was asking his disciple saying to them' is a Semitic form of redundancy [AB2].
  c. pres. act, infin. of εἰμί (LN 13.4) (BAGD II.6.e. p. 224): 'to be' [BAGD, LN]. The question 'Who do people say I am?' [BNTC; GW, NASB, NCV, NIV, NLT, REB; similarly NTC] is also translated 'Who do people/men say that I am?' [AB1, AB2, BECNT, WBC; ESV, KJV, NET, NRSV], 'What do people say about me?' [CEV], 'Tell me, who do people say I am?' [TEV], 'Whom are men saying me to be?' [Lns]. This verb means to be identical with [LN].

QUESTION—What did Jesus go out of?

Jesus went out of the village of Bethsaida [EGT, Hb]. Jesus and his disciples left Bethsaida and went northwards towards Caesarea Philippi, which was twenty-five or thirty miles away [EGT].

QUESTION—What is meant by the phrase 'the villages of Caesarea Philippi'?

The name Καισαρείας 'Caesarea' is qualified by the words τῆς Φιλίππου 'of Philip', to distinguish this city near the Lake of Galilee from the larger city of Caesarea that was built on the shore of the Mediterranean Sea by Herod the Great [NAC].

  1. The designation 'Caesarea Philippi' is *the name of the major city* in the region where the villages were located [Hb, NTC, TRT; CEV, GW, NCV, NIV, NLT, TEV]: Jesus went to the villages located around *the city of Caesarea Philippi*. It means the villages/towns *around* the city of Caesarea Philippi [Hb, NTC; GW, NCV, NIV]. It means the villages *near* the city of Caesarea Philippi [CEV, NLT, TEV].
  2. The designation 'Caesarea Philippi' is *the name of the region* in which Caesarea Philippi was the major city [AB2, CGTC, EGT, Gnd, ICC, NCBC, TH; probably AB1, BECNT, BNTC, Lns, WBC; ESV, KJV, NASB, NET, NRSV, REB which say 'the villages of Caesarea Philippi']: Jesus went to the villages located in *Caesarea Philippi*. The words Caesarea Philippi should be treated as the proper name of a unit, 'the region called Caesarea Philippi' [TH]. The mention of 'villages' is odd, and 'the district of Caesarea Philippi' would have been clearer [AB2]. This refers to the territory of the city-state of Caesarea Philippi [NCBC]. The name 'Caesarea Philippi' refers to the villages in the vicinity of the town of Caesarea, which was built by Herod Philip [Gnd].

QUESTION—Why did Jesus ask about the opinions of people in general?

The disciples had mingled with the crowds and were in a better position than Jesus to know the popular reactions to his ministry [NIGTC, Tay]. This question also prepares the way for the more personal question Jesus will ask them in verse 29 [EBC, NICNT, Tay]. Stating the views of the common masses would help his disciples see how inadequate those views were when they are asked to state their own convictions [Hb].

8:28 And they told[a] him saying, "John the Baptist; and others, Elijah; and[b] others, one of-the prophets."

TEXT—Manuscripts reading εἶπαν αὐτῷ λέγοντες ὅτι 'they told him saying' are followed by GNT, which does not mention any variant reading. A variant reading is ἀπεκρίθησαν 'they replied' and it is followed by KJV.

LEXICON—a. aorist act. indic. of λέγω (LN 33.69): 'to tell, to say, to talk, to speak' [LN]. The phrase 'they told him saying' [Lns; NASB] is also translated 'they said to him, saying' [WBC], 'they told him' [ESV], 'they said to him' [AB2, BECNT], 'they said' [NET], 'they replied' [AB1; NIV, NLT], 'they answered him' [BNTC, Lns, NTC; GW, NRSV], 'the disciples/they answered' [CEV, KJV, NCV, REB, TEV]. This verb means to speak or to talk about something [LN].

    b. δέ (LN 89.94, 89.124): 'and' [LN (89.94)], 'but, on the other hand' [LN (89.124)]. The clause ἄλλοι δὲ ὅτ εἷς τῶν προφητῶν 'and others, one of the prophets' [BNTC; ESV, KJV, REB] is also translated 'but others, one of the prophets' [WBC; NASB], 'and others that you are one of the prophets' [AB2], 'while others say that you are one of the prophets' [TEV], 'and still others, one of the prophets' [Lns, NTC; GW, NET, NIV, NRSV], 'and yet others one of the prophets' [AB2], 'and others say you are one of the prophets' [NCV; similarly BECNT; CEV], 'and others say you are one of the other prophets' [NLT]. This conjunction indicates an additive relation, and may imply there is some contrast involved [LN (89.94)], or it indicates contrast [LN (89.124)]. Some think that this passes into a direct quote [EGT, TH]: 'still others say, "He is one of the prophets."' [TH].

QUESTION—How did 'they' tell Jesus these different views?

    Probably different disciples spoke up to tell Jesus about the particular view he had heard people express [Hb, TRT].

QUESTION—Why would some think that Jesus was John the Baptist?

    Some thought that Jesus was the eschatological realization of John the Baptist [AB1, NICNT]. Others thought he was actually a reappearance of John [NIGTC, WBC], who had returned from the dead [AB2, Lns, NTC, PNTC]. This belief is puzzling since the careers of John and Jesus overlapped [BECNT]. Also see the discussion about this question in 6:14.

QUESTION—Why would some think that Jesus was Elijah?

    Some thought that Jesus was the eschatological realization of Elijah [AB1, NICNT, WBC]. Others thought he was actually a reappearance of Elijah [AB2, Lns, NIGTC, NTC, PNTC].

QUESTION—Why would some think that Jesus was one of the prophets?

    They thought he was an ordinary prophet of the kind that had appeared so many times in the history of Israel [Gnd, NICNT]. They thought he was a reappearance of a past and well-known prophet [AB1, AB2, BECNT, BNTC, Lns, NIGTC, NTC, WBC]. Some may have had Deut. 18:15–19 in mind where Moses said that God will raise up a prophet like Moses from among the people [BECNT, PNTC].

8:29 And he asked them, "But you(pl), who do-you(pl)-say I am?" Answering, Peter says to-him, "You are the Messiah.ᵃ"

LEXICON—a. Χριστός (LN 53.82) (BAGD 1. p. 887): With the article it is translated 'the Messiah' [AB1, BAGD, LN, WBC; CEV, GW, NLT, NRSV, REB, TEV], 'the Christ' [AB2, BAGD, BECNT, BNTC, Lns, NTC; ESV, KJV, NASB, NCV, NET, NIV]. This noun literally means 'the one who has been anointed'. In the NT it is a title for Jesus who is 'the Messiah, the Christ'. In other contexts, especially when it is without an article, Χριστός functions as part of the name, 'Jesus Christ' [LN]. This word occurs at 1:1; 8:29; 9:41; 12:35; 13:21; 14:61;15:32.

QUESTION—What relationship is indicated by the conjunction δέ 'but' in Jesus' question?

This contrasts the views of the other people with the views of the disciples [AB1, BECNT, BNTC, CGTC, Hb, ICC, Lns, NICNT, NTC, Sw, Tay]. A better answer was still needed [BECNT, NIGTC]. The other people were wrong [Gnd]. The pronoun 'you' stresses the contrast between the disciples who were present and people in general [AB2, BECNT, Hb, ICC, Lns, NAC, Tay]. The repetition of 'you' should be noted, 'But what about *you*? Who do *you*, my most intimate and trusted friends, say I am?' [EBC]. 'Whatever *they* may say, tell me what *you* say' [Lns].

QUESTION—Why didn't the other disciples also give answers?

Peter acted as a spokesman for all of the disciples present [BNTC, CGTC, Hb, ICC, Lns, NAC, NICNT]. The other disciples probably indicated their assent in some way [Lns].

QUESTION—What did Peter mean when he said that Jesus was the Messiah?

Peter recognized that Jesus was God's appointed agent, whose coming marked the fulfillment of God's promise and the realization of Israel's hopes [NICNT]. Jesus was the fulfillment of the age-long hopes for the restoration of the people of God [AB1]. Peter's concept of Jesus' messiahship was far from perfect as shown by verses 31–33 [CGTC, EBC, NAC, NICNT].

8:30 And he-orderedᵃ them that they-should-tell no-one aboutᵇ him.

LEXICON—a. aorist act. indic. of ἐπιτιμάω (LN 33.331) (BAGD 1. p. 303): 'to order' [AB1, BAGD; GW, TEV], 'to sternly order' [NRSV], 'to strictly order' [BECNT], 'to give strict orders' [Lns; REB], 'to vehemently order' [AB2], 'to charge' [KJV], 'to strictly charge' [WBC; ESV], 'to give strict instructions' [BNTC], 'to command' [BAGD, LN], 'to warn' [BAGD, NTC; CEV, NASB, NCV, NET, NIV, NLT]. This verb means to command someone with an implied threat [LN]. The verb indicates a prohibition that would receive a strong censure from Jesus if they violated it [Hb].

b. περί (LN 9.24): 'about' [AB1, AB2, BNTC, LN, NTC; all versions except KJV, NCV], 'concerning' [BECNT, LN, Lns, WBC], 'of' [LN; KJV]. The phrase 'about him' is translated 'who he was' [NCV]. This preposition refers to the general content of something [LN].

QUESTION—What could they not tell others about Jesus?

A translation should not imply that they must not speak to anyone about Jesus. In this context, Jesus had just asked his disciples whom they thought he was, and Peter replied, "You are the Messiah." Then Jesus immediately commanded them not to tell *this fact* about him to any one else [TH]. It was a command to refrain from disclosing the specific information that Jesus was the Messiah [AB1, BNTC, EBC, EGT, Hb, Lns, NIGTC, Tay, TH, TRT; NCV]. Even though it was true that Jesus was the Messiah, this information was not for public proclamation. It was dangerous to publicly use a title that already had certain connotations among the Jews that were very different from what Jesus considered his mission to be [NIGTC]. The popular concept of a messiah involved political and revolutionary hopes of liberation from Roman rule [BECNT, ESVfn]. The disciples still needed more instruction before they could proclaim that Jesus was the Messiah without restraint [EBC, Hb].

DISCOURSE UNIT—8:31–10:52 [EBC, NICNT]. The topic is the journey to Jerusalem.

DISCOURSE UNIT—8:31–9:1 [Hb; CEV, ESV, NIV, NRSV, TEV]. The topic is the announcement concerning the cross [Hb], Jesus predicts his death [NIV], Jesus speaks about his suffering and death [CEV, TEV], Jesus foretells his death and resurrection [ESV, NRSV].

DISCOURSE UNIT—8:31-33 [CBC, EBC, NICNT; GW, NET, NLT]. The topic is the first prediction of the Passion [EBC], Jesus first predicts his death [NLT], Jesus begins to speak about his death and resurrection [CBC], Jesus foretells that he will die and come back to life [GW], the first prediction of Jesus' death and resurrection [NET], the sufferings of the Messiah: the first major prophecy of the passion [NICNT].

DISCOURSE UNIT—8:31–32a [Hb]. The topic is the coming passion foretold.

8:31 And he-began^a to-teach them that^b it-is-necessary (for) the Son^c of-Man to-suffer^d much/many-things

LEXICON—a. aorist mid. indic. of ἄρχομαι, ἄρχω (LN 68.1) (BAGD 2.a.α. p. 113): 'to begin' [BAGD, LN], 'to commence' [LN]. The phrase 'he began to teach them' [all translations except CEV, NLT, TEV] is also translated 'Jesus began to teach his disciples' [TEV], 'Jesus began to tell them' [NLT], 'Jesus began telling his disciples what would happen to him' [CEV]. This verb means to initiate an action, process, or state of being [LN]. It introduces the beginning of a new section with a new teaching [NICNT]. This a turning point in his teaching as he begins to teach them about his imminent suffering and death [Hb, Lns].

b. ὅτι (LN 90.20): 'that' [LN; all versions except CEV, TEV], replaced by quotation marks to indicate direct speech [CEV, TEV]. This conjunction marks either direct or indirect discourse content [LN].

c. υἱὸς τοῦ ἀνθρώπου (LN 9.3) (BAGD 2.e. p. 835): This phrase is translated 'the Son of Man' [BAGD, LN; all translations except AB1], 'The Man' [AB1]. It is a title with Messianic implications that Jesus used concerning himself [LN]. Jewish teachings at the time described a heavenly being who was looked upon as a 'Son of Man' or 'Man' and who exercised Messianic functions such as judging the world [BAGD]. See 2:10 for a discussion of this title.

d. aorist act. infin. of πάσχω (LN 24.78) (BAGD 3.b. p. 634): 'to suffer' [BAGD, LN], 'to be in pain' [LN]. The phrase πολλὰ παθεῖν 'to suffer much/many-things' is translated 'suffer much' [**LN** (30.117); TEV], 'suffer a lot' [GW], 'undergo great suffering' [AB1; NRSV], 'endure great suffering' [BNTC; REB], 'suffer terribly' [CEV], 'suffer many things' [AB2, BECNT, Lns, NTC, WBC; ESV, KJV, NASB, NCV, NET, NIV], 'suffer many terrible things' [NLT]. This verb means to suffer pain [LN]. This word occurs at 5:26; 8:31; 9:12.

QUESTION—Does the conjunction ὅτι indicate an indirect or a direct quotation?

    1. It indicates indirect discourse [all translation except CEV, TEV]: he began to teach them that…

    2. It indicates direct discourse [TRT; CEV, TEV]: 'He said, "The nation's leaders, the chief priests, and the teachers of the Law of Moses will make the Son of Man suffer…but three days later he will rise to life."' [CEV]. Probably this is a direct quotation since Mark uses similar grammar in 9:31 and 10:33 where most translations use direct quotes. Jesus almost always refers to himself in the third person when he speaks of being 'the Son of Man' [TRT].

QUESTION—What made it necessary for the Son of Man to undergo all of these things?

Suffering was part of the God-appointed mission for the Son of Man, not an impersonal fate or destiny [TH]. The fact that his suffering was necessary does not rule out any freedom of choice and decision-making ability on the part of Jesus [NCBC]. It was the purpose of his ministry [BECNT]. It was necessary since it was God's will for him [CGTC, Hb, ICC, Lns, NAC, NICNT, TRT, WBC]. It was also necessary in order for Scripture to be fulfilled [Lns, NCBC, NICNT, Sw, WBC]. In verses 9:12; 14:21, 49 the necessity for his suffering is traced to the divine purpose revealed in Scripture [NIGTC]. From a human point of view, it would be the inevitable result of his rejection by the Jewish leaders [Hb], and the hostility of men [ICC].

QUESTION—Would Jesus suffer 'much' or 'many things'?

    1. Jesus would suffer much [AB1; BNTC, **LN** (30.117); CEV, GW, NRSV, REB, TEV].

2. Jesus would suffer many things [AB2, BECNT, ICC, Lns, NTC, WBC; ESV, KJV, NASB, NCV, NET, NIV, NLT].
3. Both are included [Hb, Lns].

and to-be-rejected[a] by the elders[b] and the chief-priests[c] and the scribes[d] and to-be-killed[e] and after three days to-rise.[f]

LEXICON—a. aorist pass. infin. of ἀποδοκιμάζω (LN 30.117) (BAGD 2. p. 91): 'to be rejected' [BAGD, LN; all translations], 'to be regarded as not worthy' [LN], 'to be declared useless' [BAGD]. This verb means to judge someone or something as not being worthy or genuine and thus to be rejected [LN]. This specifically refers to an official rejection by the national council after an examination of Jesus' claims [Sw].

b. πρεσβύτερος (LN 53.77) (BAGD 2.a.β. p. 700) 'elder' [AB1; AB2, BAGD, LN]. The phrase 'the elders' [BECNT, BNTC, Lns, NTC, WBC; all versions except CEV, GW, NCV] is also translated 'the leaders' [GW], 'the nation's leaders' [CEV], 'the older Jewish leaders' [NCV]. This noun denotes a person of responsibility and authority in matters of socio-religious concerns, both in Jewish and Christian societies [LN]. The elders were the lay members of the Sanhedrin [BNTC, EBC, NIGTC, Sw, TH]. These were the old, experienced men who had served as judges and risen to membership in the highest Jewish court [Lns]. This word occurs at 7:3, 5; 8:31; 11:27; 14:43, 53; 15:1.

c. ἀρχιερεύς (LN 53.88) (BAGD 1.b. p. 112): 'high priest' [BAGD, LN], 'chief priest' [LN]. The plural form is translated 'chief priests' [AB1; AB2, BECNT, BNTC, NTC; all versions except NCV, NLT], 'the leading priests' [NCV, NLT], 'the ruling priests' [WBC], 'the high priests' [Lns]. This noun denotes a principal priest who belongs to one of the high priestly families [LN]. The chief priests included the high priest Caiaphas, the emeritus high priest Annas, and the members of the high priestly families in Jerusalem [EBC, TH].

d. γραμματεύς (LN 53.94) (BAGD 2. p. 165): 'scribe' [AB2, BAGD, BECNT, BNTC, Lns, NTC, WBC; ESV, GW, KJV, NASB, NRSV, REB], 'expert in the Law' [BAGD, LN; NET], 'one who is learned in the Law' [BAGD, LN], 'teacher of the Law/law' [AB1; NCV, NIV, TEV], 'teacher of the law of Moses' [CEV], 'teacher of religious law' [NLT]. This noun denotes a recognized expert in Jewish law, including both canonical and traditional laws and regulations [LN]. This word occurs at 1:22; 2:6, 16; 3:22; 7:1, 5; 8:31; 9:11, 14; 10:33; 11:27; 12:28, 32, 38; 14:1, 43, 53; 15:1, 31.

e. aorist pass. infin. of ἀποκτείνω (LN 20.61): 'to be killed' [AB2, BECNT, LN, Lns, NTC, WBC; all versions except REB, TEV], 'to be put to death' [AB1, BNTC; REB, TEV]. This verb means to cause someone's death, usually by violent means [LN]. It implies a violent death but does not hint of a crucifixion [NICNT].

f. aorist act. infin. of ἀνίσταμαι, ἀνίστημι (LN 23.93): 'to rise up' [BNTC, WBC], 'to arise' [AB2], 'to rise again' [Lns, NTC; ESV, KJV, NASB, NET, NIV, NRSV, REB], 'to rise to life' [CEV, TEV], 'to come back to life' [LN; GW], 'to live again, to be resurrected' [LN], 'to rise from the dead' [BECNT; NCV, NLT], 'to be raised again' [AB1]. This verb means to come back to life after having died [LN].

QUESTION—What is significant about being rejected by these three groups of men?

The elders, the chief-priests, and the scribes were the three groups of men who made up the Sanhedrin, the Jewish high court [EBC, Hb, NICNT, NIGTC, PNTC, TH]. It was the most influential political and religious authority in Israel [NIGTC].

QUESTION—What did Jesus mean about rising 'after three days'?

It means 'on the third day after this one', which is 'the day after tomorrow'. It has the same meaning as 'on the third day' in Matthew and Luke [BECNT, BNTC, EBC, Hb, Lns, My, NAC, NIGTC, TH, WBC]. On this occasion it was an indefinite expression for a short time [CGTC, NICNT].

8:32 **And he was speaking the word**[a] **with-plainness.**[b]

LEXICON—a. λόγος (LN 33.98) (BAGD 1.a.ε. p. 477): 'word' [BAGD]. The phrase 'the word' [BECNT, BNTC] is also translated 'the matter' [WBC; NASB], 'this statement' [AB2, Lns], 'this fact' [NTC], 'that saying' [KJV], 'of/about this' [AB1; NET, NIV, NLT], 'all this' [NRSV], 'this' [ESV, TEV], 'about it' [REB], 'what he meant' [CEV, GW], 'what would happen' [NCV]. This noun denotes that which has been stated or said [LN]. A few think that the phrase τὸν λόγον 'the word' is used in its technical sense of the gospel message [BECNT, BNTC, PNTC]. This was the beginning of a new stage in the Gospel message that concerns Jesus' death and resurrection [BECNT]

b. παρρησία (LN 25.158) (BAGD 1. p. 630): 'outspokenness, frankness, plainness of speech' [BAGD]. The phrase 'with plainness' is translated 'with openness' [Lns], 'without any reservation' [NTC], '(he made this) very clear' [TEV]. It is translated as an adverb: 'plainly' [BECNT, BNTC, WBC; ESV, NASB, NCV, NIV, REB], 'very plainly' [AB1], 'clearly' [CEV], 'very clearly' [GW], 'frankly' [AB2], 'openly' [KJV, NET, NLT], 'quite openly' [NRSV]. This noun denotes a state of boldness and confidence [LN]. It denotes speech that conceals nothing and passes over nothing. It is to speak plainly and openly [BAGD]. The imperfect tense indicates that Jesus began to speak of his death and continued speaking about it [WBC].

QUESTION—What 'word' was Jesus speaking with plainness?

1. This is Mark's comment about the announcement Jesus had just made in verse 31 [AB2, CGTC, Gnd, Lns, My, NCBC, NICNT, NIGTC, NTC, Tay, WBC; ESV, KJV, NRSV]. Jesus was speaking clearly about his

coming death instead of just alluding to it as he had in 2:20 when he spoke of a bridegroom being 'taken away' [AB2].
2. This tells what Jesus did after he made his announcement in verse 31 [Hb; CEV, NLT; probably AB2; GW]. The imperfect tense indicates that the information he gave in verse 31 was repeated or enlarged upon in clear and unambiguous language [Hb].

DISCOURSE UNIT—8:32b–33 [Hb]. The topic is a rebuke to Peter.

8:32b And Peter having-taken- him -aside^a began to-rebuke^b him.

LEXICON—a. aorist mid. participle of προσλαμβάνομαι, προσλαμβάνω (LN 15.180) (BAGD 2.a. p. 717): 'to take aside' [AB1, AB2, BAGD, BECNT, BNTC, LN, NTC, WBC; all versions except KJV, REB], 'to take' [KJV], 'to take to himself' [Lns], 'to take hold of' [REB], 'to lead aside' [LN]. This verb means to take or lead someone aside [LN]. Peter drew Jesus aside in order to remonstrate with him for his own good [Hb].
  b. pres. act. infin. of ἐπιτιμάω (LN 33.419) (BAGD 1. p. 303): 'to rebuke' [BAGD, LN], 'to reprove' [AB1, BAGD, BNTC]. The clause 'began to rebuke him' [AB2, BECNT, Lns, NTC, WBC; ESV, KJV, NASB, NET, NIV, NRSV, REB, TEV] is also translated 'began to tell him not to talk like that' [NCV], 'began to reprimand him for saying such things' [NLT], 'told him to stop talking like that' [CEV], 'objected to this' [GW]. This verb means to express strong disapproval of someone [LN]. The purpose of the rebuke is to prevent some action or to bring it to an end [BAGD]. That he 'began' to rebuke Jesus implies that Peter was cut short by a severe response from Jesus [Hb, Lns].

QUESTION—Why did Peter take Jesus aside?
Peter drew Jesus aside so that he might not appear to be reproving his master in the presence of the other disciples [CGTC, Sw]. He took Jesus aside so that Jesus would listen more readily to a rebuke [Lns]. Peter wanted to prevent any more open discussion of such a dangerous topic [ICC].

QUESTION—What did Peter rebuke Jesus about?
Peter rebuked Jesus for thinking and planning such a course of action. A close equivalent of the Greek is 'he said to him, "Don't talk this way"' [TH]. Peter thought that such a prediction of defeat was unworthy of Jesus [ICC]. Peter felt that he must pressure Jesus to remove such gloomy thoughts from his mind [Hb]. A rejected messiah was unthinkable to Jewish convictions and hopes [NICNT]. Their idea of messiahship excluded suffering and execution [NTC]. Mark includes this information in order to underscore the surprising nature of Jesus' prediction [WBC].

8:33 And he, having-turned-around and having-looked-at^a his disciples, rebuked^b Peter and says, "Go-away^c behind me, Satan, because you-are-not -thinking^d the (things) of-God but the (things) of-men."

LEXICON—a. aorist act. participle of ὁράω, εἶδον (LN 24.1) (BAGD 1.a. p. 220): 'to look at' [AB1, AB2, BAGD; GW, NCV, NET, NIV, NLT,

NRSV, REB, TEV], 'to look on' [KJV], 'to see' [BAGD, BECNT, BNTC, LN, Lns, NTC, WBC; CEV, ESV, NASB]. This verb means to see [LN].

b. aorist act. indic. of ἐπιτιμάω (LN 33.419) (BAGD 1. p. 303): 'to rebuke' [AB2, BAGD, BECNT, LN, Lns, NTC, WBC; ESV, KJV, NASB, NET, NIV, NRSV, REB, TEV], 'to reprove' [AB1, BAGD, BNTC]. The phrase 'rebuked Peter' is translated 'then reprimanded Peter' [NLT], 'he corrected Peter' [CEV], 'and objected to what Peter said' [GW], 'he told Peter not to talk that way' [NCV]. This verb means to express strong disapproval of someone [LN]. This is the same verb used in verse 32 where Peter 'began to rebuke' Jesus. In this verse, it means that Jesus 'scolded' Peter [TH].

c. pres. act. impera. of ὑπάγω (LN 15.52) (BAGD 1. p. 836): 'to go away, to go' [BAGD], 'to depart, to leave' [LN]. The clause 'go away behind me' is translated 'get behind me' [AB2, BECNT, BNTC, Lns, WBC; ESV, NASB, NET, NIV, NRSV; similarly KJV], 'get away from me' [CEV, NLT, TEV], 'go away from me' [NCV], 'away with you' [AB1], 'get out of my way' [GW], 'get out of my sight' [NTC], 'out of my sight' [REB]. This verb means to depart from someone's presence [LN].

d. pres. act. indic. of φρονέω (LN 31.1) (BAGD 2. p. 866): 'to set one's mind on, to be intent on following' [BAGD], 'to hold a view, to have an opinion, to consider, to regard' [LN]. The phrase 'you are not thinking the things of God' [WBC] is also translated 'you do not have in mind the things of God' [Lns; NIV], 'you are fixing your thoughts not on the things of God' [AB2], 'you are not setting your mind on the things of God' [ESV], 'you are setting your mind not on the things that come from God' [BECNT], 'you are setting your mind not on divine things' [NRSV], 'you are not setting your mind on God's interests' [NASB, NET], 'you are looking at things not from God's point of view' [NTC], 'you are not thinking the way God thinks' [GW], 'your thoughts don't come from God' [TEV], 'you don't care about the things of God' [NCV], 'thou savourest not the things of God' [KJV], 'your interests are…not those of God' [AB1], 'you think (as men think), not as God thinks' [REB], 'you are thinking (in men's way), not God's' [BNTC], '(you are thinking like everyone else) and not like God' [CEV], '(you are seeing things merely from a human point of view,) not from God's' [NLT]. This verb means to hold a view or to have an opinion with regard to something [LN].

QUESTION—What is meant by the two participial phrases, 'having turned around and having looked at his disciples'?

1. Jesus was facing Peter while Peter was rebuking him and afterwards Jesus turned around to look at the other disciples [AB2, EBC; probably BECNT, BNTC, Gnd, NCBC, NTC, WBC; GW, NET, NRSV, REB]. This may indicate that Peter was acting as the spokesman for the other disciples or that Peter's rebuke of Jesus was seen by the other disciples, making it necessary for Jesus to respond publicly [BECNT]. The rest of

the disciples probably thought the same as Peter and needed the rebuke as well [AB2, BNTC]. Yet there is no reason to think that the others heard what Peter said in his private conversation with Jesus. This comment merely differentiates Peter from the other disciples [Gnd].
2. When Jesus turned around to face Peter, he saw the other disciples in the background [AB1, Hb, ICC, Lns, My, Sw, Tay]. Peter had come up to the side of Jesus to rebuke him, so Jesus turned to face Peter and as he turned he also saw the other disciples. [ICC, Lns]. Seeing the rest of the disciples gives the reason for his stern rebuke [My]. When Jesus turned around to face Peter, he saw that the other disciples knew and approved of what Peter was saying [Hb]. Seeing the effect of Peter's action on the disciples, Jesus wanted them all to hear the rebuke [ICC]. Jesus intended that all should hear the rebuke since it might also apply to their own thoughts [Lns]. Since the other disciples probably shared Peter's views, a public reproof would be necessary [Sw].

QUESTION—What did Jesus mean when he told Peter to go away behind him?
1. Jesus told Peter to leave and get out of his sight [BECNT, BNTC, CGTC, Lns, NAC, NCBC, NIGTC, NTC, Sw, TRT]. This was a dismissal [NIGTC]. The reference to Satan makes it likely Jesus meant for Peter to get out of sight and stop tempting him [NAC]. If Peter was going to act Satan's part, then he must be banished from the sight of Jesus [Sw].
2. Peter should take his place among the other disciples who were following along behind Jesus [AB2, Gnd, NICNT, WBC]. Jesus told Peter to go back to his position among the disciples where he belonged. He should not have taken Jesus aside by walking ahead of him or at least beside him [Gnd]. It was an order for Peter to resume the path of discipleship instead of trying to lead Jesus [AB2].
3. Peter was to get out of Jesus' way because he was 'a stumbling block' to Jesus (Matt. 16:23) [Hb].

QUESTION—Why did Jesus address Peter as 'Satan'?
Jesus called Peter 'Satan' in order to indicate the role Peter was playing. Peter was acting like Satan by putting temptation in Jesus' way [AB1, BECNT, CGTC, Gnd, ICC, Sw]. It does not mean that Peter was indwelt by Satan or was used by Satan to tempt Jesus away from God's plan [BECNT]. Peter may have had the best of intentions, but he was making himself a tool of Satan [Hb, Lns]. Peter had unwittingly spoken for Satan by repeating Satan's temptation recorded in Matt. 4:8–10 [NLTfn]. Peter's attempt to persuade Jesus not to go to the cross was the same kind of temptation that Satan had used at the beginning of Jesus' ministry when he offered Jesus the option of using the world's means of accomplishing his mission [EBC, NLTfn, Tay]. Peter had temporarily become 'a Satan' because he was opposing the revealed will of God [AB2]. Peter was acting as a spokesman for Satan by opposing God's plans for the Messiah [NIGTC]. It was only Peter's thoughts, not Peter personally, that Jesus rejected as being satanic [ESVfn]. The use of the word 'Satan' might have been adjectival rather than

identifying Peter with the person of Satan. He was saying 'Get behind me, you who oppose me!' [WBC].

QUESTION—What were 'the things of God' that Peter was not thinking about? This refers to God's purposes [Hb, Lns]. It refers to the things mentioned in verse 31 [Gnd, NIGTC, WBC]. These things were what God had planned for the Son of Man to experience: his suffering, rejection, death, and resurrection [Gnd].

QUESTION—What were 'the things of men' that Peter was thinking about? These are the blind, erring, sinful purposes and ways of men [Lns]. God's purpose for the Messiah described in verse 31 made no sense to Peter [NIGTC]. Peter was motivated by the concerns of fallible human beings [Hb]. The things of humans, whether Jewish or Roman, were oriented towards conquest and assertion of power [WBC]. Although one would have expected the text to read 'the things that come from Satan', it reads 'the things that come from men' since Satan is the 'god of this world' and the fallen world's values reflect satanic values [BECNT].

DISCOURSE UNIT—8:34–9:1 [AB2, CBC, EBC, Hb; GW, NET, NLT]. The topic is the requirements of discipleship [EBC], the requirements for following Jesus [NICNT], Jesus proclaims the gains and loses in following him [AB2], what it means to follow Jesus [GW], following Jesus [CBC; NET], teachings about discipleship [NLT], teaching about cross-bearing [Hb].

8:34 **And having-summoned**[a] **the crowd along-with his disciples he said to-them, "If someone wants to-follow**[b] **after me, let-him-deny**[c] **himself and let-him-take-up**[d] **his cross**[e] **and let-him-follow me.**

TEXT—Manuscripts reading ἀκολουθεῖν 'to follow' are followed by GNT, which does not mention any variant reading. A variant reading is ἐλθεῖν 'to come'. and it is followed by CBC, EGT, Lns, NTC, Sw, Tay; ESV, KJV, NASB, NIV, TEV.

LEXICON—a. aorist mid. participle of προσκαλέομαι (LN 33.308): 'to call' [BECNT, LN; NET, NLT, NRSV], 'to call to oneself' [AB1, BNTC, Lns, NTC; ESV, GW, KJV, NCV, NIV, REB, TEV], 'to summon' [AB2, WBC; NASB], 'to tell to come closer' [CEV]. This verb means to call people to oneself [LN]. It means 'to summon' or 'to call to oneself' [TH].

b. pres. act. infin. of ἀκολουθέω (LN 36.31) (BAGD 3. p. 31): 'to follow' [AB2, BAGD, BECNT, BNTC, LN, WBC; GW, NCV], 'to come' [Lns, NTC; ESV, KJV, NASB, NIV, TEV]. The phrase 'to follow after me' is translated 'to be a follower of mine' [AB1, LN; REB], 'to be my follower' [CEV, NLT], 'to become my follower' [NET, NRSV]. This verb means to be a follower or disciple of a leader by following his teachings and instructions and also promoting his cause [LN]. 'Following' Jesus refers to discipleship [ICC, TRT]. It refers to that common commitment to Jesus that all Christians must have [NICNT]. It means to attach oneself to Jesus as his disciple. 'Follow' is a figure of speech based on the fact that Jesus'

followers often accompanied Jesus by literally walking along behind him [NTC].
  c. aorist mid. (deponent = act.) impera. of ἀπαρνέομαι (LN 30.52) (BAGD p. 81): 'to deny' [BAGD], 'to disregard, to pay no attention to, to say "No" to' [LN]. The statement 'let him deny himself' [BECNT, Lns, NTC, WBC; ESV, KJV; similarly NRSV] is also translated 'he must deny himself' [NASB, NET, NIV], 'he must renounce himself' [BNTC; similarly AB2; REB], 'he must disown self' [AB1], 'he must say "No" to himself' [**LN**] 'they must say no to the things they want' [GW], 'they must give up the things they want' [NCV], 'you must turn from your selfish ways' [NLT], 'you must forget yourself' [TEV], 'you must forget about yourself' [CEV]. This verb means to refuse to give thought to or express concern about something. It means to refuse to pay attention to what one's own desires are saying or to refuse to think about what one wants for oneself [LN]. One denies oneself by giving up all claims upon himself [TH]. The aorist imperative form indicates that a definite decision has to be made [CGTC].
  d. aorist act. impera. of αἴρω (LN 15.203, 24.83) (BAGD 2. p. 24): 'to take up' [AB1, AB2, BECNT, BNTC, Lns, NTC, WBC; CEV, ESV, KJV, NASB, NET, NIV, NLT, NRSV, REB], 'to pick up' [GW], 'to carry (away)' [LN (15.203)], 'to lift up and take or carry along' [BAGD]. The clause 'let him take up his cross' is translated 'they must be willing even to give up their lives' [NCV]. This verb means to lift up and carry away [LN (15.203)], and the idiom αἴρω τὸν σταυρόν 'to take one's cross' or 'to carry one's cross' means to be prepared to endure severe suffering, even to the point of death [LN (24.83)]. It means to lift up and carry away (on one's shoulder) [TH].
  e. σταυρός (LN 6:27) (BAGD 2. p. 765): 'cross' [BAGD, LN; all translations]. This noun denotes a pole stuck into the ground in an upright position with a crosspiece attached to its upper part so that it is shaped like a † or a T [BAGD, LN].
QUESTION—How did Jesus summon the crowd?
  The people were near enough to be called [Lns]. The presence of the crowd emphasizes Jesus' magnetism and there was no need for Mark to indicate where the crowd came from [Gnd]. Probably the residents of the town of Caesarea Philippi had learned of his presence [Hb] and were already waiting nearby [Hb, TRT].
QUESTION—Who are the ones to whom the warnings in verses 34–38 apply?
  1. Jesus was addressing these words to the whole crowd that included his disciples [BECNT, EBC, Hb, Lns, NICNT, NIGTC, NTC, Sw, WBC]. This invitation to the unconverted appears to be also given to those who were already his followers [BECNT]. These verses apply to everyone who might wish to join the movement and also to the Twelve. Disciples will have to answer for their loyalty or cowardice [NIGTC]. All must understand just what it means to follow Jesus [NICNT]. He talked about

situations in which Christians would face the alternatives of confessing Christ or denying him. It is a warning to the disciples who might be tempted to defect under trial [EBC].
2. Jesus was addressing these words to those in the crowd who were not his disciples. He is addressing the non-disciples how to start following him [Gnd].

QUESTION—What is meant by 'denying' oneself?

It means to cease making self the object of one's life and actions [EBC, ICC, NIVfn]. It means to renounce all claims of self and no longer make one's own interests and desires the supreme concern in life [BNTC, Hb]. It is to replace one's self-determination with complete obedience to the Messiah [ESVfn]. It does not refer to asceticism, self-rejection, self-hatred, or even disowning particular sins. It means to place God's will before self-will [NAC]. One must let Jesus determine the goals and purposes in life [NLTfn].

QUESTION—What is meant by taking up one's cross?

This is a metaphor [NLTfn, Tay]. The comparison is made with someone being crucified and experiencing a painful and shameful death [TH]. This metaphor pictures a condemned man being required to carry the cross-beam of his cross to the place of execution [ESV, Gnd, NICNT, NIVfn].
1. It means a disciple must be prepared to suffer and even be willing to die for following Jesus [AB1, AB2, BECNT, CBC, CGTC, EBC, ICC, LN, NAC, NCBC, NICNT, NIGTC, NIVfn, NLTfn, Tay, TH, TRT, WBC; NCV]. Since commitment to Jesus permits no turning back, a disciple must be prepared to die if necessary [NICNT]. Let that person deny himself and carry out his self-denial even to the point of death [ICC]. This is to be taken in terms of the loss of life and not just discomforts. Even though it may include other aspects of suffering, the focus is on the possibility of literal death [NIGTC].
2. It means to be ready to endure suffering for being a follower of Jesus [BNTC, Gnd, Hb, Lns, NTC, Sw]. The metaphor is not about being nailed to a cross, but about taking up the horizontal beam of a cross for the journey to the place of execution. Since only criminals were condemned to take up crosses and carry them through the streets of the city, this requirement focuses upon exposing oneself to shame and ridicule for following Jesus. The aspect of losing one's life does not come up until verses 35–37 [Gnd]. The requirement to take up one's cross daily does not mean that a new cross must literally be taken up daily. It means that a disciple must be willing to suffer every day of his life [Hb]. It refers to being prepared to face the shame and disgrace that discipleship might encounter [BNTC, Sw]. A disciple accepts the pain, shame, and persecution that comes because of his loyalty to Christ and his cause [NTC].

QUESTION—How is the final clause 'and let him follow me' connected?
1. This is a third requirement for discipleship [AB1, AB2, BECNT, BNTC, CBC, Gnd, Lns, NTC, Tay]. This closing command is not redundant since actual following goes beyond just wanting to follow [Gnd]. The three

conditions of disciples consist of two acts of committal and a third act of continuing one's relationship with Jesus [AB1, Tay].
2. This is a repetition of the initial conditional part of the sentence, 'if someone wants to follow after me' [CGTC, EBC, ICC, NICNT]. The way to follow Jesus is to be found in the two actions of self-denial and cross-bearing [ICC]. The idea is 'And so let him follow me', describing a continuous relationship that results from the two decisive acts [CGTC].

8:35 Because whoever wants to-save[a] his life[b] will-lose[c] it,
LEXICON—a. aorist act. infin. of σῴζω (LN 21.8) (BAGD 1.a. p. 798): 'to save' [BAGD; all translations except AB1; NLT], 'to hang onto' [NLT], 'to preserve' [AB1], 'to deliver, to rescue, to make safe' [LN]. This verb means to rescue from danger and to restore to a former state of safety and well-being [LN]. It means to be saved from death [BAGD].
b. ψυχή (LN 23.88) (BAGD 1.d. p. 893): 'life' [BAGD, LN; all translations except AB1], 'soul' [BAGD], 'self' [AB1]. This noun denotes a person's life [LN]. It denotes the 'life' or 'soul', and since the soul is the center of both the earthly life and the supernatural life, a man can find himself facing the decision of which of the two he wishes to preserve [BAGD].
c. fut. act. indic. of ἀπόλλυμι (LN 57.68) (BAGD 1.b. p. 95): 'to lose' [LN; all translations except AB2; CEV, NCV], 'to destroy' [AB2; CEV]. The phrase 'will lose it' is translated 'will give up true life' [NCV]. This verb means to lose something that one already possesses [LN].
QUESTION—What relationship is indicated by the conjunction γάρ 'because'?
It indicates why one should accept the invitation to discipleship given in verse 34 [BECNT, PNTC]. It indicates the reason why a person should be ready to die for following Jesus [CGTC, ICC, Lns]. It justifies the stringent conditions laid down in the preceding verse by stating the consequences of rejecting those conditions, and also the consequences of accepting them [Hb]. It is a combined warning and promise [Lns].
QUESTION—What is the 'life' that this person wants to save?
1. This 'life' refers to the physical life of the body [CBC, CGTC, EBC, Gnd, ICC, NAC, NCBC, NICNT, NIGTC, NIVfn, PNTC, Tay, TH]. It is one's present life [Gnd]. It is one's natural life, the life in the body [ICC, TH]. Clinging to life itself is set in contrast with the acceptance of death by martyrdom [NIGTC]. It pictures a man appearing before a court and denying any association with Jesus in order to escape execution [NICNT]. He wants to keep from being killed [NTC].
2. This 'life' is the kind of life one wants to live on earth [BECNT, ESVfn, Hb, Lns, NLTfn, NTC, Sw]. It is the outward, earthly life with its pleasures and goals [Hb, NTC]. It is human existence with personal goals and desires [BECNT]. It is a self-centered life focused on this present world [ESVfn]. This refers to trying to hang on to one's life by keeping it from Jesus [NLTfn]. It means to try to keep one's life-style by keeping away from Christ and his self-sacrificing demands [Hb]. One's personal

safety and success is his goal [Sw]. He does not want to deny himself [BECNT].

QUESTION—What is the 'life' that one would lose?

This is the eternal life of the soul [BECNT, EBC, ESVfn, Gnd, Hb, ICC, Lns, NICNT, NIVfn, PNTC, Sw, Tay, TH, TRT]. Even though he enjoys every earthly delight, his soul is doomed [Lns]. He will not have eternal life with God [ESVfn]. This life is an inward spiritual life that begins while one is physically alive and continues on into eternity [Hb]. If he denies Christ in an attempt to save his physical life, he will lose eternal life and salvation [EBC].

but whoever will-lose[a] his life for-the-sake[b] of-me and the gospel will save[c] it.

TEXT—Manuscripts reading ἐμοῦ καὶ 'of me and' are followed by GNT, which does not mention any variant reading. A variant reading omits these words and it is followed by WBC.

LEXICON—a. fut. act. indic. of ἀπόλλυμι (LN 23.114, 57.68) (BAGD 1.b. p. 95): 'to lose' [BAGD, BECNT, BNTC, LN (57.68), Lns, NTC, WBC; ESV, GW, KJV, NASB, NET, NIV, NRSV], 'to give up' [CEV, NCV, NLT, REB, TEV], 'to destroy' [AB2]. The phrase 'will lose his life' is translated 'will let himself be lost' [AB1]. This verb means to lose something that one already possesses [LN (57.68)]. The idiom ἀπόλλυμι τὴν ψυχήν 'to lose one's life' means 'to die' [LN (23.114)].

b. ἕνεκεν, ἕνεκα (LN 89.3) (BAGD p. 264): 'for the sake of' [AB1, BAGD, BNTC, NTC, WBC; ESV, KJV, NASB, NET, NLT, NRSV, REB], 'for' [AB2, BECNT; CEV, GW, NCV, NIV, TEV], 'on account of' [BAGD, LN, Lns], 'because of' [BAGD, LN]. This preposition indicates purpose in the sense of 'for the sake of' [LN].

c. fut. act. indic. of σῴζω (LN 21.27) (BAGD 2.a.β. p. 798): 'to save' [LN; all translations except NCV]. The phrase 'will save it' is translated 'will have true life' [NCV], 'that man is safe' [AB1]. This verb means to cause someone to experience divine salvation [LN]. It means to save or preserve from eternal death [BAGD].

QUESTION—What is the 'life' that one will lose for the sake of Jesus and the gospel?

1. This 'life' refers to the physical life of the body [CBC, CGTC, EBC, Gnd, NCBC, NICNT, NIGTC, NIVfn, PNTC, Tay]. It refers to being put to death for one's allegiance to Christ and for remaining true to him and confessing him under duress [EBC]. It is literal martyrdom because of being a disciple of Christ [NIGTC]. This is not a command to die for the sake of Jesus and the gospel. The command is to deny themselves, take up their crosses, and follow Jesus. Even if some happen to lose their physical lives because of that, they need not worry since they will save their spiritual lives for the world to come [Gnd].

2. This 'life' refers to the outward, earthly life [BECNT, ESVfn, Hb, NLTfn, NTC, Sw]. It is a life concerned about preserving one's personal interests in the present life by avoiding Christ's self-sacrificing demands [Hb]. Losing such a life means to give up one's self-centered life of rebellion against God [ESVfn]. A person loses his life by devoting himself completely to Christ [NTC]. This refers to denying oneself by taking up one's cross and following Jesus [BECNT].

QUESTION—What is the 'life' that one will save?
The word 'it' refers to eternal spiritual life [CGTC, EBC, ESVfn, Gnd, Hb, Lns, NICNT, NIGTC, NIVfn, PNTC, TRT]. It is eternal existence [NICNT]. This is eternal life and salvation [EBC]. It is the true or eternal life [NIGTC]. It is a person's eternal being [PNTC]. It is everlasting communion with God [ESVfn].

8:36 Because what does it profit[a] a-man to-gain[b] the whole world and to-forfeit[c] his life[d]?

LEXICON—a. pres. act. indic. of ὠφελέω (LN 35.2) (BAGD 1.a. p. 900): 'to benefit' [BAGD], 'to help' [BAGD, LN]. The question 'what does it profit a man/person' [BECNT, WBC; ESV, NASB; similarly KJV, NRSV] is also translated 'what profit is it' [BNTC], 'what does it benefit a man' [Lns], 'what benefit is it for a person' [NET], 'what do you benefit' [NLT], 'what good is it for a man' [NIV], 'what good does it do a man' [NTC], 'what good does it do for people' [GW], 'what does a man gain' [AB1], 'what does anyone gain' [REB], 'what will you gain if you (own)' [CEV], 'Do you gain anything' [TEV], 'it is worth nothing for them' [NCV], 'what use would it be for a human being' [AB2]. This verb means to provide assistance that is beneficial to someone [LN].

b. aorist act. infin. of κερδαίνω (LN 57.189) (BAGD 1.a. p. 429): 'to gain' [AB2, BAGD, BECNT, BNTC, LN, Lns, NTC, WBC; ESV, KJV, NASB, NET, NIV, NLT, NRSV], 'to win' [AB1; GW, REB, TEV], 'to own' [CEV], 'to have' [NCV]. This verb means to gain something by means of one's activity or investment [LN].

c. aorist pass. infin. of ζημιόομαι, ζημιόω (LN 57.69) (BAGD 1. p. 338): 'to forfeit' [AB2, BAGD, LN, Lns, NTC; ESV, NASB, NET, NIV, NRSV], 'to lose' [AB1, BNTC, WBC; GW, KJV, NCV, NLT, TEV], 'to suffer loss' [BAGD, BECNT, LN], 'to destroy' [CEV], 'at the cost of' [REB]. This verb means to suffer the loss of something that one has previously possessed, and it is implied that this loss involves considerable hardship or suffering [LN].

d. ψυχή (LN 23.88, 26.4) (BAGD 1.d. p. 893): 'life' [AB2, BAGD, BECNT, BNTC, LN, Lns, NTC, WBC; GW, NET, NRSV, REB, TEV], 'soul' [BAGD; ESV, KJV, NASB, NCV, NIV, NLT], 'his true self' [AB1], 'yourself' [CEV]. This noun denotes life [LN].

QUESTION—What relationship is indicated by the conjunction γάρ 'because'?
It indicates the reason why one should be willing to lose one's life in order to gain eternal life [BECNT, CGTC, ICC]. The whole world does not come close to the value to one's soul [EBC].

QUESTION—What kind of question is this?
This is a rhetorical question that implies the answer, 'Nothing at all!' [BECNT]. It profits him in no way because there is nothing more valuable to a person than his life [Gnd].

QUESTION—What is meant by 'gaining' the whole world?
This is a metaphor making a comparison with a commercial transaction [BECNT, BNTC, Hb, NICNT, Tay, TH, WBC; ESV, KJV, NASB, NRSV]. There would be no profit in gaining the whole world if that transaction required the person's death [Hb]. Gaining 'the whole world' focuses on acquiring the total amount of earthly wealth [TH]. The 'whole world' refers to the total sum of things [Hb, ICC, Lns]. Even though it is impossible for any human being to gain the whole world, it is treated as a possibility for the sake of argument [Hb, Lns]. No conceivable price can be placed upon one's true self [AB1].

QUESTION—What is meant by 'forfeiting' one's life?
It means more than just dying. It is to suffer the loss of one's true or real life [TH]. The profit and loss metaphor is not limited to just life on earth [AB2]. This speaks of the eschatological life of one's soul [EBC]. To lose one's life means to fail to acquire eternal life [BECNT, NICNT, NIVfn, NLTfn].

8:37 Because what can- a-man -give in-exchange[a] (for) his life?

LEXICON—a. ἀντάλλαγμα (LN 57,143) (BAGD p. 72): 'something given in exchange' [BAGD, LN]. This question is translated 'what can a person give in exchange for his life?' [NET; similarly AB2, BECNT, BNTC, EBC, NTC], 'what should a person give in exchange for life?' [GW], 'what can they give in return for their life?' [NRSV], 'what can he give to buy his life back?' [REB], 'what can he give to buy back that self?' [AB1], 'what can a man give in exchange for his soul?' [NIV], 'what will a man give in exchange for his soul?' [NASB], 'what should a man give in exchange for his soul?' [KJV], 'what would a man give as exchange for his life?' [Lns], 'what can a man give in return for his soul?' [ESV], 'what could you give to get back your soul?' [CEV], 'is anything worth more than your soul?' [NLT]. This rhetorical question is translated as a statement: 'There is nothing you can give to regain your life.' [TEV], 'They could never pay enough to buy back their souls.' [NCV]. This noun is a derivative of ἀνταλλάσσω 'to exchange' and denotes 'that which is exchanged' or 'that which is given in exchange'. This verse means 'what would a person give as a means of exchange for his life?' or 'what would a person give in payment for his life?' [LN].

QUESTION—What relationship is indicated by γάρ 'because'?
This is another link in the chain of reasoning [Sw]. The reason is the finality of an unprofitable transaction [Hb]. It refers to the man who has forfeited his own soul [Lns].

QUESTION—What kind of question is this?
It is a rhetorical question that obviously implies the answer, 'He would give everything he could, even the whole world if he had it' [Gnd]. Nothing at all can compensate for the loss of one's life [BECNT, NIGTC]. The implied answer is that there is nothing that a man can give to compensate for the loss of his (real) life, the loss of his very self. [TH]. No exchange is possible [Hb]. Even if he had the whole world, it could not buy back eternal life for a man. Once a man forfeits his share in eternal life, there is no way to get it back [EBC]. No sane person would forfeit his life for any amount of wealth [WBC].

8:38 **Because whoever is-ashamed-of**[a] **me and my words**[b] **in**[c] **this adulterous**[d] **and sinful**[e] **generation/age,**[f]

TEXT—Manuscripts reading τοὺς ἐμοὺς λόγους 'my words' are given a B rating by GNT to indicate it was regarded to be almost certain. A variant reading is τοὺς ἐμούς 'my (people)' and it is followed by AB1.

LEXICON—a. aorist pass. (deponent = act.) subj. of ἐπαισχύνομαι (LN 25.193) (BAGD 1. p. 282): 'to be ashamed of' [AB1, AB2, BAGD, BECNT, BNTC, LN, Lns, NTC, WBC; all versions]. This verb means to experience or feel shame or disgrace because of some particular event or activity [LN].

b. λόγος (LN 33.98) (BAGD 1.b.β. p. 478): 'word' [BAGD, LN], 'message, saying, statement' [LN]. The phrase 'my words' [AB2, BECNT, BNTC, NTC, WBC; ESV, KJV, NASB, NET, NIV, NRSV, REB] is also translated 'my message' [CEV, NLT], 'my teaching' [NCV, TEV], 'my statements' [Lns], 'what I say' [GW]. This noun denotes the content of what has been stated or said [LN]. It refers to the divine revelation through Christ [BAGD]. It is the substance of what Jesus says [Lns].

c. ἐν (LN 83.9) (BAGD 1.4.a. p. 258): 'in' [AB1, AB2, BECNT, BNTC, Lns, NTC, WBC; all versions except CEV, NCV], 'among (these people)' [CEV]. The clause 'in this adulterous and sinful generation' is translated 'The people who live now are living in a sinful and evil time. If people (are ashamed...)' [NCV]. This preposition indicates a position within an area determined by other objects and distributed among such objects [LN]. It denotes a rather close relationship with others [BAGD].

d. μοιχαλίς (LN 31.101) (BAGD 2.a. p. 526): 'adulterous' [AB2, BAGD, BECNT, LN, Lns, NTC, WBC; ESV, KJV, NASB, NET, NIV, NLT, NRSV], 'unfaithful' [LN; CEV, GW], 'godless' [AB1, BNTC; REB, TEV], 'evil' [NCV]. This adjective pertains to being unfaithful to one's earlier beliefs [LN]. This adjective is used figuratively in Hosea where

God's relationship with his people is depicted as a marriage and any beclouding of it becomes adultery [BAGD].

e. ἁμαρτωλός (LN 88.294) (BAGD 1. p. 44): 'sinful' [AB1, AB2, BAGD, BECNT, LN, Lns, NTC, WBC; all versions except REB, TEV], 'wicked' [BNTC; REB, TEV]. This adjective pertains to sinful behavior [LN].

f. γενεά (LN 11.4, 67.144) (BAGD 2. p. 154): 'generation, contemporaries' [BAGD], 'those of the same generation, those of the same time' [LN (11.4)], 'age, epoch' [LN (67.144)]. The interpretation 'this generation' [AB2, BECNT, Lns, NTC, WBC; ESV, GW, KJV, NASB, NET, NIV, NRSV] is also translated 'these people' [CEV], 'the people who live now' [NCV]. The alternative interpretation 'this age' [AB1, BNTC; REB] is also translated 'this (godless and wicked) day' [TEV], 'these (adulterous and sinful) days' [NLT]. This noun denotes the people living at the same time and belonging to the same reproductive age-class [LN (11.4)], or it denotes an indefinite period of time that is closely related to human existence [LN (67.144)]. This word occurs at 8:12, 38; 9:19; 13:30.

QUESTION—What relationship is indicated by γάρ 'because'?

The thought explained by the γάρ 'because' clause is not expressed and must be supplied from the context. The thought is, '*Let no disciple fail to testify*, because if he is ashamed to testify..., the Son of Man will also be ashamed of him' [BAGD (1.e. p. 152)]. '*Let no one reject this appeal*, because...' [NTC]. This conjunction gives the reason for all that Jesus has said in verses 34–38 [ICC, NICNT]. It indicates the reason for the demands made on discipleship by relating them to the eschatological victory of the Son of Man [Hb]. This verse gives another reason for accepting Jesus' invitation to follow him, but it is now directed at those who are already his disciples [BECNT].

QUESTION—What is meant by 'being ashamed of' Christ?

It means to be ashamed to confess allegiance to Christ publicly, to be ashamed to acknowledge one's relation to Christ [TH]. The person who will not accept the demands of discipleship shows that he is ashamed of Christ [Hb]. This refers mostly to one's actions and not one's internal emotions and it specifically refers to denying Jesus in times of persecution instead of confessing him [BECNT]. It refers to denying Jesus, preferring the world, and turning from Jesus [Lns].

QUESTION—What were Jesus' 'words'?

These 'words' refer to the substance of whatever Jesus says [Lns], his teachings [BECNT], the gospel [BECNT, NICNT]. This matches the words in verse 35, 'will lose his life for the sake of *me and the gospel*' [Lns]. Another says that these 'words' probably refer to the authoritative demands that Jesus has just made [BNTC].

QUESTION—Does the phrase γενεᾷ ταύτῃ mean 'this generation' or 'this age'?

1. It refers to the people of 'this generation' [AB2, BECNT, CBC, Gnd, Hb, Lns, NAC, NCBC, NICNT, NIGTC, NTC, PNTC, Sw, Tay, TH, WBC;

all versions except NLT, REB, TEV]. This is the same word that occurs in 8:12 where it refers to people [TH].
2. It refers to the period of time covered in 'this age' [AB1, BNTC, CGTC; NLT, REB, TEV].

QUESTION—What is meant by an 'adulterous' generation?

The adjective 'adulterous' is used in a religious sense of being unfaithful to God. This concept is based on the OT references to God's people being 'betrothed' to God like a wife is betrothed to a husband [TH]. There are frequent charges in OT prophecy that Israel was committing adultery against God, her true husband [NIGTC]. It was spiritual unfaithfulness to their covenant relationship with God [Hb]. It describes the people who are unfaithful to God [LN, NAC, TH; CEV, GW]. They are faithless to their covenant obligations and vows [EGT, ICC, Lns, NICNT, WBC], and they live lives that are wicked [REB, TEV], evil [NCV], irreligious, godless, and irreverent [TH]. 'This generation' refers to the people of Jesus' own generation, and their apostasy was shown by their attitude toward Jesus [Sw].

QUESTION—What is meant by a 'sinful' generation?

The word 'sinful' is broader than being unfaithful and helps define what kind of people comprised this generation [Lns]. It refers to their moral state [Hb].

of-him the Son^a of-Man also will-be-ashamed when he-comes in^b the glory^c of his Father with the holy^d angels.

TEXT—Manuscripts reading μετὰ τῶν ἀγγέλων τῶν ἁγίων 'with the holy angels' are given an A rating by GNT to indicate it was regarded to be certain. A variant reading is καὶ τῶν ἀγγέλων τῶν ἁγίων 'and the holy angels'.

LEXICON—a. υἱὸς τοῦ ἀνθρώπου (LN 9.3) (BAGD 2.e. p. 835): This title is translated 'the Son of Man' [BAGD, LN; all translations except AB1], 'The Man' [AB1]. See 2:10 for a discussion of this title.
  b. ἐν (LN 13.8) (BAGD 1.4.b. p. 259): 'in' [AB2, BAGD, BECNT, BNTC, LN, Lns, NTC, WBC; all versions except NCV], 'with' [BAGD, LN; NCV]. This preposition indicates being in some state or condition [LN]. This preposition is used in reference to being clothed in something other than clothes, such as 'clothed in flesh', 'clothed in all his glory', and in this verse, 'clothed in his Father's glory' [BAGD].
  c. δόξα (LN 14.49): 'glory' [LN; all translations], 'brightness, shining, radiance' [LN]. This noun denotes the state of brightness or shining [LN]. It can refer to God's power, authority, presence, or brightness [TRT].
  d. ἅγιος (LN 88.24) (BAGD 1.b.β. p. 9): 'holy' [BAGD, LN; all translations], 'pure' [BAGD, LN], 'perfect, worthy of God' [BAGD]. This adjective pertains to being holy in the sense of having superior moral qualities and possessing certain essentially divine qualities in contrast with what is human [LN]. The angels are called holy because they belong in the glory of the Father [Lns].

MARK 8:38

QUESTION—What is meant by the Son of Man coming 'in the glory of his Father'?

There is a question about the location of where the Son of Man is coming to. In Daniel 7, the 'one like the son of man' comes to 'the Ancient of Days' and is given dominion, glory, and a kingdom. Yet the mention of the holy angels seems to point to his coming to earth as in 2 Thess. 1:7 where he comes to earth in blazing fire with his powerful angels to punish those who do not know God and do not obey his gospel [BNTC].

1. This describes the final judgment of the world that has been committed to the Son of Man [AB2, BECNT, CBC, CGTC, EBC, Gnd, Hb, ICC, Lns, My, NAC, NCBC, NICNT, NLTfn, NTC, Sw, Tay, TRT, WBC]. This passage has transformed the Daniel imagery so that the Son of Man comes from heaven rather than to it [AB2]. The mention of his Father's glory and being accompanied by the holy angels suggests that this is the final judgment [EBC]. Ironically, when a person denies Jesus, he has denied the final Judge who possesses the glory of his Father. The 'glory of the Father' is all of his divine attributes that shine forth for his creatures to see. Jesus will be seen as also possessing that glory equally with the Father [Lns].

2. This description comes from Daniel's vision in which the Son of Man is presented before the throne of God to be given eternal sovereignty over all nations. Here Jesus appears before God, who is seated on his throne and surrounded by the angelic court. Jesus will be given authority to rule over all the earth, and the disciples will have to answer to him for their loyalty or their cowardice [NIGTC].

QUESTION—What is meant by the Son of Man being ashamed of those who are ashamed of him?

This is a judgment scene in which the Son of Man either has the role of a judge or an advocate [BNTC]. It means that Jesus will deny that such a person is one of his disciples, and will disown and reject that person forever [Lns]. Christ will find it morally impossible to have such a one as his disciple [Hb]. In regard to those in the crowd who were not yet his disciples, this warns them that if they allow shame over Jesus and his words to keep them from becoming disciples, then Jesus will disown them [Gnd].

QUESTION—What is meant by Jesus coming in the glory of his Father?

Jesus will come *with* the glory of his Father [TH]. The Son of Man shares his Father's divine attribute of glory [AB2]. This glory is the sum of the divine attributes as they shine forth for his creatures to see. [Lns].

QUESTION—Why will he be accompanied by the holy angels?

The angels will appear as an army of warriors escorting the Son of Man [Gnd]. The presence of the accompanying angels emphasizes the dignity and power of the returning Lord [Hb]. These angels will be his servants in the great judgment and are called holy because they are accompanying the Son of Man as he comes in the glory of his Father [Lns].

www.ingramcontent.com/pod-product-compliance
Lightning Source LLC
Chambersburg PA
CBHW071235300426
44116CB00008B/1040